JAVA™ PROGRAMMING

W9-ATO-004

EIGHTH EDITION

JAVA™ PROGRAMMING

JOYCE FARRELL

CENGAGE
Learning®

Australia • Brazil • Japan • Korea • Mexico • Singapore • Spain • United Kingdom • United States

Java Programming,
Eighth Edition
Joyce Farrell

Product Director:
Kathleen McMahon

Senior Content Developer:
Alyssa Pratt

Development Editor: Dan Seiter

Marketing Manager: Eric LaScola

Manufacturing Planner:
Julio Esperas

Art Director: Jack Pendleton

**Production Management,
Copyediting, Composition,
Proofreading, and Indexing:**
Integra Software Services Pvt. Ltd.

Cover Photo:
©Maram/Shutterstock.com

© 2016, 2014, 2012 Cengage Learning
WCN: 01-100-101

ALL RIGHTS RESERVED. No part of this work covered by the copyright herein may be reproduced, transmitted, stored, or used in any form or by any means graphic, electronic, or mechanical, including but not limited to photocopying, recording, scanning, digitizing, taping, Web distribution, information networks, or information storage and retrieval systems, except as permitted under Section 107 or 108 of the 1976 United States Copyright Act, without the prior written permission of the publisher.

For product information and technology assistance, contact us at
Cengage Learning Customer & Sales Support, 1-800-354-9706

For permission to use material from this text or product, submit all requests online at **www.cengage.com/permissions.**
Further permissions questions can be emailed to
permissionrequest@cengage.com.

Library of Congress Control Number: 2014956152

ISBN: 978-1-285-85691-9

Cengage Learning
20 Channel Center Street
Boston, MA 02210
USA

Cengage Learning is a leading provider of customized learning solutions with office locations around the globe, including Singapore, the United Kingdom, Australia, Mexico, Brazil, and Japan. Locate your local office at **www.cengage.com/global.**

Cengage Learning products are represented in Canada by Nelson Education, Ltd.

All images © 2016 Cengage Learning®. All rights reserved.

To learn more about Cengage Learning Solutions, visit **www.cengage.com.**

Purchase any of our products at your local college store or at our preferred online store **www.cengagebrain.com.**

Printed in the United States of America
Print Number: 02   Print Year: 2015

Brief Contents

Contents

viii

Preface

Java Programming, Eighth Edition, provides the beginning programmer with a guide to developing applications using the Java programming language. Java is popular among professional programmers because it can be used to build visually interesting graphical user interface (GUI) and Web-based applications. Java also provides an excellent environment for the beginning programmer—a student can quickly build useful programs while learning the basics of structured and object-oriented programming techniques.

This textbook assumes that you have little or no programming experience. It provides a solid background in good object-oriented programming techniques and introduces terminology using clear, familiar language. The programming examples are business examples; they do not assume a mathematical background beyond high-school business math. In addition, the examples illustrate only one or two major points; they do not contain so many features that you become lost following irrelevant and extraneous details. Complete, working programs appear frequently in each chapter; these examples help students make the transition from the theoretical to the practical. The code presented in each chapter can also be downloaded from the publisher's Web site, so students can easily run the programs and experiment with changes to them.

The student using *Java Programming, Eighth Edition,* builds applications from the bottom up rather than starting with existing objects. This facilitates a deeper understanding of the concepts used in object-oriented programming and engenders appreciation for the existing objects students use as their knowledge of the language advances. When students complete this book, they will know how to modify and create simple Java programs, and they will have the tools to create more complex examples. They also will have a fundamental knowledge of object-oriented programming, which will serve them well in advanced Java courses or in studying other object-oriented languages such as C++, C#, and Visual Basic.

Organization and Coverage

Java Programming, Eighth Edition, presents Java programming concepts, enforcing good style, logical thinking, and the object-oriented paradigm. Objects are covered right from the beginning, earlier than in many other textbooks. You create your first Java program in Chapter 1. Chapters 2, 3, and 4 increase your understanding of how data, classes, objects, and methods interact in an object-oriented environment.

Chapters 5 and 6 explore input and repetition structures, which are the backbone of programming logic and essential to creating useful programs in any language. You learn the special considerations of string and array manipulation in Chapters 7, 8, and 9.

Chapters 10, 11, and 12 thoroughly cover inheritance and exception handling. Inheritance is the object-oriented concept that allows you to develop new objects quickly by adapting the features of existing objects; exception handling is the object-oriented approach to handling errors. Both are important concepts in object-oriented design. Chapter 13 provides information on handling files so you can permanently store and retrieve program output.

Chapters 14, 15, and 16 introduce GUI Swing components (Java's visually pleasing, user-friendly widgets), their layout managers, and graphics.

Features

The following features are new for the Eighth Edition:

- **JAVA 8E:** All programs have been tested using Java 8e, the newest edition of Java.

- **WINDOWS 8.1:** All programs have been tested in Windows 8.1, and all screen shots have been taken in this new environment.

- **DATE AND TIME CLASSES:** This edition provides thorough coverage of the java.time package, which is new in Java 8e.

- **ON-SCREEN KEYBOARD:** This edition provides instructions for displaying and using an on-screen keyboard with either a touch screen or a standard screen.

- **MODERNIZED GRAPHICS OUTPUT:** The chapter on graphics (Chapter 16) has been completely rewritten to focus on Swing component graphics production using the paintComponent() method.

- **MODERNIZED OVERRIDING:** The @Override tag is introduced.

- **EXPANDED COVERAGE OF THE EQUALS() METHOD:** The book provides a thorough explanation of the difference between overloading and overriding the equals() method.

- **PROGRAMMING EXERCISES:** Each chapter contains several new programming exercises not seen in previous editions. All exercises and their solutions from the previous edition that were replaced in this edition are still available in the Instructor's Resource Kit.

Additionally, *Java Programming, Eighth Edition*, includes the following features:

- **OBJECTIVES:** Each chapter begins with a list of objectives so you know the topics that will be presented in the chapter. In addition to providing a quick reference to topics covered, this feature provides a useful study aid.

- **YOU DO IT:** In each chapter, step-by-step exercises help students create multiple working programs that emphasize the logic a programmer uses in choosing statements to include. These sections provide a means for students to achieve success on their own—even those in online or distance learning classes.

- **NOTES:** These highlighted tips provide additional information—for example, an alternative method of performing a procedure, another term for a concept, background information on a technique, or a common error to avoid.

- **EMPHASIS ON STUDENT RESEARCH:** The student frequently is directed to the Java Web site to investigate classes and methods. Computer languages evolve, and programming professionals must understand how to find the latest language improvements. This book encourages independent research.

- **FIGURES:** Each chapter contains many figures. Code figures are most frequently 25 lines or fewer, illustrating one concept at a time. Frequent screen shots show exactly how program output appears. Callouts appear where needed to emphasize a point.

- **COLOR:** The code figures in each chapter contain all Java keywords in blue. This helps students identify keywords more easily, distinguishing them from programmer-selected names.

- **FILES:** More than 200 student files can be downloaded from the publisher's Web site. Most files contain the code presented in the figures in each chapter; students can run the code for themselves, view the output, and make changes to the code to observe the effects. Other files include debugging exercises that help students improve their programming skills.

- **TWO TRUTHS & A LIE:** A short quiz reviews each chapter section, with answers provided. This quiz contains three statements based on the preceding section of text—two statements are true and one is false. Over the years, students have requested answers to problems, but we have hesitated to distribute them in case instructors want to use problems as assignments or test questions. These true–false quizzes provide students with immediate feedback as they read, without "giving away" answers to the multiple-choice questions and programming exercises.

- **DON'T DO IT:** This section at the end of each chapter summarizes common mistakes and pitfalls that plague new programmers while learning the current topic.

- **KEY TERMS:** Each chapter includes a list of newly introduced vocabulary, shown in the order of appearance in the text. The list of key terms provides a short review of the major concepts in the chapter.

- **SUMMARIES:** Following each chapter is a summary that recaps the programming concepts and techniques covered in the chapter. This feature provides a concise means for students to check their understanding of the main points in each chapter.

- **REVIEW QUESTIONS:** Each chapter includes 20 multiple-choice questions that serve as a review of chapter topics.

- **GAME ZONE:** Each chapter provides one or more exercises in which students can create interactive games using the programming techniques learned up to that point; 70 game programs are suggested in the book. The games are fun to create and play; writing them motivates students to master the necessary programming techniques. Students might exchange completed game programs with each other, suggesting improvements and discovering alternate ways to accomplish tasks.

- **CASES:** Each chapter contains two running case problems. These cases represent projects that continue to grow throughout a semester using concepts learned in each new chapter. Two cases allow instructors to assign different cases in alternate semesters or to divide students in a class into two case teams.

- **GLOSSARY:** This edition contains an alphabetized list of all key terms identified in the book, along with their definitions.

- **APPENDICES:** This edition includes useful appendices on working with the Java platform, data representation, formatting output, generating random numbers, and creating Javadoc comments.

- **QUALITY:** Every program example, exercise, and game solution was tested by the author and then tested again by a quality assurance team using Java Standard Edition (SE) 8, the most recent version available.

CourseMate

The more you study, the better the results. Make the most of your study time by accessing everything you need to succeed in one place. Read your textbook, take notes, review flashcards, watch videos, and take practice quizzes online. CourseMate goes beyond the book to deliver what you need! Learn more at *www.cengage.com/coursemate*.

The *Java Programming* CourseMate includes:

- **Debugging Exercises:** Four error-filled programs accompany each chapter. By debugging these programs, students can gain expertise in program logic in general and the Java programming language in particular.

- **Video Lessons:** Each chapter is accompanied by at least three video lessons that help to explain important chapter concepts. These videos were created and narrated by the author.

- **Interactive Study Aids:** An interactive eBook, quizzes, flashcards, and more!

Instructors may add CourseMate to the textbook package, or students may purchase CourseMate directly at *www.CengageBrain.com*.

Instructor Resources

The following teaching tools are available for download at our Instructor Companion Site. Simply search for this text at *sso.cengage.com*. An instructor login is required.

- **Electronic Instructor's Manual:** The Instructor's Manual that accompanies this textbook contains additional instructional material to assist in class preparation, including items such as Overviews, Chapter Objectives, Teaching Tips, Quick Quizzes, Class Discussion Topics, Additional Projects, Additional Resources, and Key Terms. A sample syllabus is also available. Additional exercises in the Instructor's Manual include:

  ○ **Tough Questions:** Two or more fairly difficult questions that an applicant might encounter in a technical job interview accompany each chapter. These questions are often open-ended; some involve coding and others might involve research.

○ **Up for Discussion:** A few thought-provoking questions concerning programming in general or Java in particular supplement each chapter. The questions can be used to start classroom or online discussions, or to develop and encourage research, writing, and language skills.

○ **Programming Exercises and Solutions:** Each chapter is accompanied by several programming exercises to supplement those offered in the text. Instructors can use these exercises as additional or alternate assignments, or as the basis for lectures.

● **Test Bank:** Cengage Learning Testing Powered by Cognero is a flexible, online system that allows you to:

○ Author, edit, and manage test bank content from multiple Cengage Learning solutions.

○ Create multiple test versions in an instant.

○ Deliver tests from your LMS, your classroom, or anywhere you want.

● **PowerPoint Presentations:** This text provides PowerPoint slides to accompany each chapter. Slides may be used to guide classroom presentations, to make available to students for chapter review, or to print as classroom handouts. Files are provided for every figure in the text. Instructors may use the files to customize PowerPoint slides, illustrate quizzes, or create handouts.

● **Solutions:** Solutions to "You Do It" exercises and all end-of-chapter exercises are available. Annotated solutions are provided for some of the multiple-choice Review Questions. For example, if students are likely to debate answer choices or not understand the choice deemed to be the correct one, a rationale is provided.

Acknowledgments

I would like to thank all of the people who helped to make this book a reality, including Dan Seiter, Development Editor; Alyssa Pratt, Senior Content Developer; Carmel Isaac, Content Project Manager; and Chris Scriver and Danielle Shaw, quality assurance testers. I am lucky to work with these professionals who are dedicated to producing high-quality instructional materials.

I am also grateful to the reviewers who provided comments and encouragement during this book's development, including Bernice Cunningham, Wayne County Community College District; Bev Eckel, Iowa Western Community College; John Russo, Wentworth Institute of Technology; Leslie Spivey, Edison Community College; and Angeline Surber, Mesa Community College.

Thanks, too, to my husband, Geoff, for his constant support and encouragement. Finally, this book is dedicated to the newest Farrell, coming March 2015. As this book goes to production, I don't know your name or even your gender, but I do know that I love you.

Joyce Farrell

Read This Before You Begin

The following information will help you as you prepare to use this textbook.

To the User of the Data Files

To complete the steps and projects in this book, you need data files that have been created specifically for this book. Your instructor will provide the data files to you. You also can obtain the files electronically from *www.CengageBrain.com.* Find the ISBN of your title on the back cover of your book, then enter the ISBN in the search box at the top of the Cengage Brain home page. You can find the data files on the product page that opens. Note that you can use a computer in your school lab or your own computer to complete the exercises in this book.

Using Your Own Computer

To use your own computer to complete the steps and exercises, you need the following:

- **Software:** Java SE 8, available from *www.oracle.com/technetwork/java/index.html.* Although almost all of the examples in this book will work with earlier versions of Java, this book was created using Java 8. The book clearly points out the few cases when an example is based on Java 7 and will not work with earlier versions of Java. You also need a text editor, such as Notepad. A few exercises ask you to use a browser for research.

- **Hardware:** If you are using Windows 8, the Java Web site suggests at least 128 MB of memory and at least 181 MB of disk space. For other operating system requirements, see *http://java.com/en/download/help.*

Features

This text focuses on helping students become better programmers and understand Java program development through a variety of key features. In addition to Chapter Objectives, Summaries, and Key Terms, these useful features will help students regardless of their learning styles.

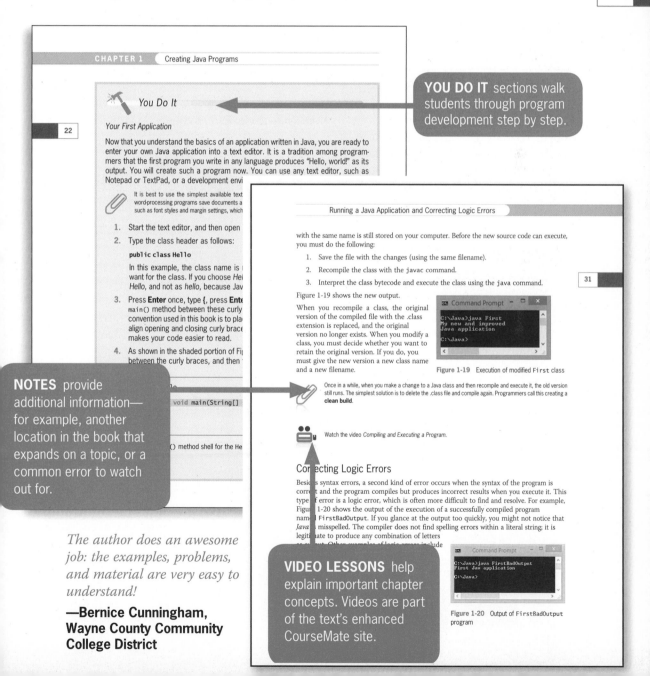

YOU DO IT sections walk students through program development step by step.

22

You Do It

Your First Application

Now that you understand the basics of an application written in Java, you are ready to enter your own Java application into a text editor. It is a tradition among programmers that the first program you write in any language produces "Hello, world!" as its output. You will create such a program now. You can use any text editor, such as Notepad or TextPad, or a development envi

> It is best to use the simplest available text
> word-processing programs save documents a
> such as font styles and margin settings, which

1. Start the text editor, and then open

2. Type the class header as follows:

   `public class Hello`

   In this example, the class name is
   want for the class. If you choose *Hel*
   Hello, and not as *hello*, because Jav

3. Press **Enter** once, type **{**, press **Ente**
   main() method between these curly
   convention used in this book is to plac
   align opening and closing curly brace
   makes your code easier to read.

4. As shown in the shaded portion of Fig
   between the curly braces, and then

`void main(String[]`

() method shell for the He

NOTES provide additional information— for example, another location in the book that expands on a topic, or a common error to watch out for.

with the same name is still stored on your computer. Before the new source code can execute, you must do the following:

1. Save the file with the changes (using the same filename).
2. Recompile the class with the javac command.
3. Interpret the class bytecode and execute the class using the java command.

31

Figure 1-19 shows the new output.

When you recompile a class, the original version of the compiled file with the .class extension is replaced, and the original version no longer exists. When you modify a class, you must decide whether you want to retain the original version. If you do, you must give the new version a new class name and a new filename.

Figure 1-19 Execution of modified First class

> Once in a while, when you make a change to a Java class and then recompile and execute it, the old version still runs. The simplest solution is to delete the .class file and compile again. Programmers call this creating a **clean build**.

Watch the video *Compiling and Executing a Program.*

Correcting Logic Errors

Besides syntax errors, a second kind of error occurs when the syntax of the program is correct and the program compiles but produces incorrect results when you execute it. This type of error is a logic error, which is often more difficult to find and resolve. For example, Figure 1-20 shows the output of the execution of a successfully compiled program named FirstBadOutput. If you glance at the output too quickly, you might not notice that *Java* is misspelled. The compiler does not find spelling errors within a literal string; it is legitimate to produce any combination of letters

VIDEO LESSONS help explain important chapter concepts. Videos are part of the text's enhanced CourseMate site.

Figure 1-20 Output of FirstBadOutput program

The author does an awesome job: the examples, problems, and material are very easy to understand!

—Bernice Cunningham, Wayne County Community College District

xxviii

Analyzing a Java Application that Produces Console Output

```
public class AnyClassName
{
    public static void main(String[] args)
    {
        /******/
    }
}
```

Figure 1-8 Shell code

Saving a Java Class

When you write a Java class, you must save it using a writable storage medium, such as a disk, DVD, or USB device. In Java, if a class is public (that is, if you use the public access specifier before the class name), you must save the class in a file with exactly the same name and a .java extension. For example, the First class must be stored in a file named First.java. The class name and filename must match exactly, including the use of uppercase and lowercase characters. If the extension is not .java, the Java compiler does not recognize the file as containing a Java class. Appendix A contains additional information on saving a Java application.

TWO TRUTHS & A LIE

Analyzing a Java Application that Produces Console Output

1. In the method header public static void main(String[] args), the word public is an access specifier.

2. In the method header public static void main(String[] args), the word static means that a method is accessible and usable, even though no objects of the class exist.

3. In the method header public static void main(String[] args), the word void means that the main() method is an empty method.

The false statement is #3. In the method header public static void main(String[] args), the word void means that the main() method does not return any value when it is called.

TWO TRUTHS & A LIE quizzes appear after each chapter section, with answers provided. The quiz contains three statements based on the preceding section of text—two statements are true and one is false. Answers give immediate feedback without "giving away" answers to the multiple-choice questions and programming problems later in the chapter. Students also have the option to take these quizzes electronically through the enhanced CourseMate site.

106

(continued)

7. Save, compile, and execute the program. Now, the fractional portion of the result is omitted again. That's because the result of sum / 2 is calculated first, and the result is an integer. Then, the whole-number result is cast to a double and assigned to a double—but the fractional part of the answer was already lost and casting is too late. Remove the newly added parentheses, save the program, compile it, and execute it again to confirm that the fractional part of the answer is reinstated.

8. As an alternative to the explicit cast in the division statement in the ArithmeticDemo program, you could write the average calculation as follows:

   `average = sum / 2.0;`

   In this calculation, when the integer sum is divided by the double constant 2.0, the result is a double. The result then does not require any cast to be assigned to the double average without loss of data. Try this in your program.

9. Go to the Java Web site (**www.oracle.com/technetwork/java/index.html**), select **Java APIs**, and then select **Java SE 8**. Scroll through the list of **All Classes**, and select **PrintStream**, which is the data type for the out object used with the println() method. Scroll down to view the list of methods in the Method Summary. As you did in a previous exercise, notice the many versions of the print() and println() methods, including ones that accept a String, an int, and a long. Notice, however, that no versions accept a byte or a short. That's because when a byte or short is sent to the print() or println() method, it is automatically promoted to an int, so that version of the method is used.

DON'T DO IT sections at the end of each chapter list advice for avoiding common programming errors.

Don't Do It

- Don't mispronounce "integer." People who are unfamiliar with the term often say "interger," inserting an extra r.

- Don't attempt to assign a literal constant floating-point number, such as 2.5, to a float without following the constant with an uppercase or lowercase F. By default, constant floating-point values are doubles.

- Don't try to use a Java keyword as an identifier for a variable or constant. Table 1-1 in Chapter 1 contains a list of Java keywords.

- Don't attempt to assign a constant value under −2,147,483,648 or over +2,147,483,647 to a long variable without following the constant with an uppercase or lowercase L. By default, constant integers are ints, and a value under −2,147,483,648 or over +2,147,483,647 is too large to be an int.

Using the Scanner Class to Accept Keyboard Input

It is legal to write a single prompt that requests multiple input values—for example, "Please enter your age, area code, and zip code >>". The user could then enter the three values separated with spaces, tabs, or Enter key presses. The values would be interpreted as separate tokens and could be retrieved with three separate nextInt() method calls. However, asking a user to enter multiple values often leads to mistakes. This book will follow the practice of using a separate prompt for each input value required.

81

Pitfall: Using nextLine() Following One of the Other Scanner Input Methods

You can encounter a problem when you use one of the numeric Scanner class retrieval methods or the next() method before you use the nextLine() method. Consider the program in Figure 2-19. It is identical to the one in Figure 2-17, except that the user is asked for an age before being asked for a name. (See shading.) Figure 2-20 shows a typical execution.

```
import java.util.Scanner;
public class GetUserInfo2
{
    public static void main(String[] args)
    {
        String name;
        int age;
        Scanner inputDevice = new Scanner(System.in);
        System.out.print("Please enter your age >> ");
        age = inputDevice.nextInt();
        System.out.print("Please enter your name >> ");
        name = inputDevice.nextLine();
        System.out.println("Your name is " + name +
            " and you are " + age + " years old.");
    }
}
```

Don't Do It
If you accept numeric input prior to string input, the string input is ignored unless you take special action.

Figure 2-19 The GetUserInfo2 class

Figure 2-20 Typical execution of the GetUserInfo2 program

THE DON'T DO IT ICON illustrates how NOT to do something—for example, having a dead code path in a program. This icon provides a visual jolt to the student, emphasizing that particular figures are NOT to be emulated and making students more careful to recognize problems in existing code.

Assessment

I found the author's explanation of difficult topics to be very clear and thorough.

**—Leslie Spivey,
Edison Community College**

xxix

PROGRAMMING EXERCISES provide opportunities to practice concepts. These exercises increase in difficulty and allow students to explore each major programming concept presented in the chapter. Additional programming exercises are available in the Instructor's Resource Kit.

Review Questions

Review Questions

A sequence of characters enclosed within double quotation marks is a _____.

a. symbolic string   c. prompt
b. literal string   d. command

383

To create a String object, you can use the keyword _____ before the constructor call, but you are not required to use this format.

a. object   c. char
b. create   d. new

A String variable name is a _____.

a. reference   c. constant
b. value   d. literal

The term that programmers use to describe objects that c _____ is _____.

a. irrevocable   c. immutable
b. nonvolatile   d. stable

Suppose that you declare two String objects as:

```
String word1 = new String("happy");
String word2;
```

174

When you ask a user to enter a value for word2, if the user word1 == word2 is _____.

a. true   c. illegal
b. false   d. unknown

If you declare two String objects as:

```
String word1 = new String("happy");
String word2 = new String("happy");
```

the value of word1.equals(word2) is _____.

a. true   c. illegal
b. false   d. unknown

The method that determines whether two String objects of case, is _____.

a. equalsNoCase()   c. equalsIgn
b. toUpperCase()   d. equals()

---

20. If you use the automatically supplied default constructor when you create an object, _____.

   a. numeric fields are set to 0 (zero)   c. Boolean fields are set to true
   b. character fields are set to blank   d. All of these are true.

Exercises

Programming Exercises

1. Suppose that you have created a program with only the following variables.

   ```
   int a = 5;
   int b = 6;
   ```

   Suppose that you also have a method with the following header:

   ```
   public static void mathMethod(int a)
   ```

   Which of the following method calls are legal?

   a. mathMethod(a);   f. mathMethod(12.78);
   b. mathMethod(b);   g. mathMethod(29987L);
   c. mathMethod(a + b);   h. mathMethod();
   d. mathMethod(a, b);   i. mathMethod(x);
   e. mathMethod(2361);   j. mathMethod(a / b);

2. Suppose that you have created a program with only the following variables.

   ```
   int age = 34;
   int weight = 180;
   double height = 5.9;
   ```

   Suppose that you also have a method with the following header:

   ```
   public static void calculate(int age, double size)
   ```

   Which of the following method calls are legal?

   a. calculate(age, weight);   f. calculate(12, 120.2);
   b. calculate(age, height);   g. calculate(age, size);
   c. calculate(weight, height);   h. calculate(2, 3);
   d. calculate(height, age);   i. calculate(age);
   e. calculate(45.5, 120);   j. calculate(weight, weight);

REVIEW QUESTIONS test udent comprehension of the ajor ideas and techniques resented. Twenty questions llow each chapter.

xxx

118

 Case Problems

1. Carly's Catering provides meals for parties and special events. Write a program that prompts the user for the number of guests attending an event and then computes the total price, which is $35 per person. Display the company motto with the border that you created in the CarlysMotto2 class in Chapter 1, and then display the number of guests, price per guest, and total price. Also display a message that indicates true or false depending on whether the job is classified as a large event—an event with 50 or more guests. Save the file as **CarlysEventPrice.java**.

2. Sammy's Seashore Supplies rents beach equipment such as kayaks, canoes, beach chairs, and umbrellas to tourists. Write a program that prompts the user for the number of minutes he rented a piece of sports equipment. Compute the rental cost as $40 per hour plus $1 per additional minute. (You might have surmised already that this rate has a logical flaw, but for now, calculate rates as described here. You can fix the problem after you read the chapter on decision making.) Display Sammy's motto with the border that you created in the SammysMotto2 class in Chapter 1. Then display the hours, minutes, and total price. Save the file as **SammysRentalPrice.java**.

DEBUGGING EXERCISES are included with each chapter because examining programs critically and closely is a crucial programming skill. Students can download these exercises at *www.CengageBrain.com* and through the CourseMate available for this text. These files are also available to instructors through *sso.cengage.com*.

Exercises

 Debugging Exercises

1. Each of the following files in the Chapter05 folder of your downloadable student files has syntax and/or logic errors. In each case, determine the problem and fix the program. After you correct the errors, save each file using the same filename preceded with *Fix*. For example, save DebugFive1.java as **FixDebugFive1.java**.

   a. DebugFive1.java
   b. DebugFive2.java
   c. DebugFive3.java
   d. DebugFive4.java

297

Game Zone

1. In Chapter 1, you created a class called RandomGuess. In this game, players guess a number, the application generates a random number, and players determine whether they were correct. Now that you can make decisions, modify the application so it allows a player to enter a guess before the random number is displayed, and then displays a message indicating whether the player's guess was correct, too high, or too low. Save the file as **RandomGuess2.java**. (After you finish the next chapter, you will be able to modify the application so that the user can continue to guess until the correct answer is entered.)

2. Create a lottery game application. Generate three random numbers (see Appendix D for help in doing so), each between 0 and 9. Allow the user to guess three numbers. Compare each of the user's guesses to the three random numbers and display a message that includes the user's guess, the randomly determined three-digit number, and the amount of money the user has won as follows:

Matching Numbers	Award ($)
Any one matching	10
Two matching	100
Three matching, not in order	1,000
Three matching in exact order	1,000,000
No matches	0

Make certain that your application accommodates repeating digits. For example, if a user guesses 1, 2, and 3, and the randomly generated digits are 1, 1, and 1, do not give the user credit for three correct guesses—just one. Save the file as **Lottery.java**.

CASE PROBLEMS provide opportunities to build more detailed programs that continue to incorporate increasing functionality throughout the book.

GAME ZONE EXERCISES are included at the end of each chapter. Students can create games as an additional entertaining way to understand key programming concepts.

CHAPTER 1

Creating Java Programs

In this chapter, you will:

- ◎ Define basic programming terminology
- ◎ Compare procedural and object-oriented programming
- ◎ Describe the features of the Java programming language
- ◎ Analyze a Java application that produces console output
- ◎ Compile a Java class and correct syntax errors
- ◎ Run a Java application and correct logic errors
- ◎ Add comments to a Java class
- ◎ Create a Java application that produces GUI output
- ◎ Find help

Learning Programming Terminology

A **computer program** is a set of instructions that you write to tell a computer what to do. Computer equipment, such as a monitor or keyboard, is **hardware**, and programs are **software**. A program that performs a task for a user (such as calculating and producing paychecks, word processing, or playing a game) is **application software**; a program that manages the computer itself (such as Windows or Linux) is **system software**. The **logic** behind any computer program, whether it is an application or system program, determines the exact order of instructions needed to produce desired results. Much of this book describes how to develop the logic to create application software.

All computer programs ultimately are converted to machine language. **Machine language**, or **machine code**, is the most basic set of instructions that a computer can execute. Each type of processor (the internal hardware that handles computer instructions) has its own set of machine language instructions. Programmers often describe machine language using 1s and 0s to represent the on-and-off circuitry of computer systems.

The system that uses only 1s and 0s is the *binary numbering system*. Appendix B describes the binary system in detail. Later in this chapter, you will learn that *bytecode* is the name for the binary code created when Java programs are converted to machine language.

Machine language is a **low-level programming language**, or one that corresponds closely to a computer processor's circuitry. Low-level languages require you to use memory addresses for specific machines when you create commands. This means that low-level languages are difficult to use and must be customized for every type of machine on which a program runs.

Fortunately, programming has evolved into an easier task because of the development of high-level programming languages. A **high-level programming language** allows you to use a vocabulary of reasonable terms, such as *read, write,* or *add,* instead of the sequences of 1s and 0s that perform these tasks. High-level languages also allow you to assign single-word, intuitive names to areas of computer memory where you store data. This means you can use identifiers such as hoursWorked or rateOfPay, rather than having to remember their memory locations. Currently, over 2,000 high-level programming languages are available to developers; Java is one of them.

Each high-level language has its own **syntax**, or rules about how language elements are combined correctly to produce usable statements. For example, depending on the specific high-level language, you might use the verb *print* or *write* to produce output. All languages have a specific, limited vocabulary (the language's **keywords**) and a specific set of rules for using that vocabulary. When you are learning a computer programming language, such as Java, C++, or Visual Basic, you really are learning the vocabulary and syntax for that language.

Using a programming language, programmers write a series of **program statements**, similar to English sentences, to carry out the tasks they want the program to perform. Program statements are also known as **commands** because they are orders to the computer, such as "output this word" or "add these two numbers."

After the program statements are written, high-level language programmers use a computer program called a **compiler** or **interpreter** to translate their language statements into machine language. A compiler translates an entire program before carrying out any statements, or **executing** them, whereas an interpreter translates one program statement at a time, executing a statement as soon as it is translated.

 Whether you use a compiler or interpreter often depends on the programming language you use. For example, C++ is a compiled language, and Visual Basic is an interpreted language. Each type of translator has its supporters; programs written in compiled languages execute more quickly, whereas programs written in interpreted languages can be easier to develop and debug. Java uses the best of both technologies: a compiler to translate your programming statements and an interpreter to read the compiled code line by line when the program executes (also called **at run time**).

Compilers and interpreters issue one or more error messages each time they encounter an invalid program statement—that is, a statement containing a **syntax error**, or misuse of the language. Examples of syntax errors include misspelling a keyword or omitting a word that a statement requires. When a syntax error is detected, the programmer can correct the error and attempt another translation. Repairing all syntax errors is the first part of the process of **debugging** a program—freeing the program of all flaws or errors, also known as **bugs**. Figure 1-1 illustrates the steps a programmer takes while developing an executable program. You will learn more about debugging Java programs later in this chapter.

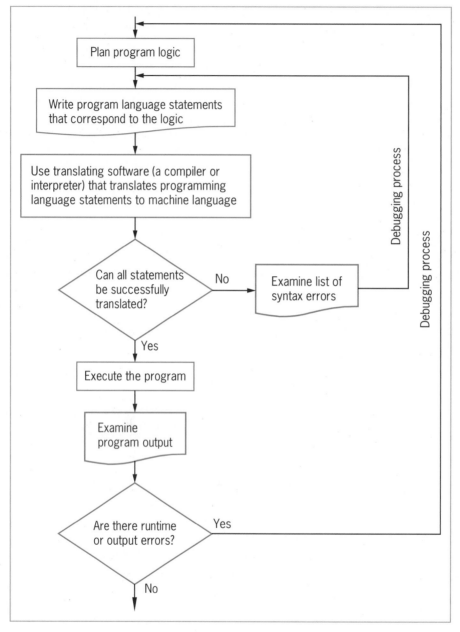

Figure 1-1 The program development process

As Figure 1-1 shows, you might write a program with correct syntax that still contains logic errors. A **logic error** is a bug that allows a program to run, but that causes it to operate incorrectly. Correct logic requires that all the right commands be issued in the appropriate order. Examples of logic errors include multiplying two values when you meant to divide

5

them or producing output prior to obtaining the appropriate input. When you develop a program of any significant size, you should plan its logic before you write any program statements.

Correcting logic errors is much more difficult than correcting syntax errors. Syntax errors are discovered by the language translator when you compile a program, but a program can be free of syntax errors and execute while still retaining logic errors. Often you can identify logic errors only when you examine a program's output. For example, if you know an employee's paycheck should contain the value $4,000, but when you examine a payroll program's output you see that it holds $40, then a logic error has occurred. Perhaps an incorrect calculation was performed, or maybe the hours worked value was output by mistake instead of the net pay value. When output is incorrect, the programmer must carefully examine all the statements within the program, revise or move the offending statements, and translate and test the program again.

Just because a program produces correct output does not mean it is free from logic errors. For example, suppose that a program should multiply two values entered by the user, that the user enters two 2s, and the output is 4. The program might actually be adding the values by mistake. The programmer would discover the logic error only by entering different values, such as 5 and 7, and examining the result.

Programmers call some logic errors **semantic errors**. For example, if you misspell a programming language word, you commit a syntax error, but if you use a correct word in the wrong context, you commit a semantic error.

TWO TRUTHS & A LIE

Learning Programming Terminology

In each "Two Truths & a Lie" section, two of the numbered statements are true, and one is false. Identify the false statement and explain why it is false.

1. Unlike a low-level programming language, a high-level programming language allows you to use a vocabulary of reasonable terms instead of the sequences of on-and-off switches that perform the corresponding tasks.

2. A syntax error occurs when you misuse a language; locating and repairing all syntax errors is part of the process of debugging a program.

3. Logic errors are fairly easy to find because the software that translates a program finds all the logic errors for you.

The false statement is #3. A language translator finds syntax errors, but logic errors can usually be discovered only by examining a program's output.

Comparing Procedural and Object-Oriented Programming Concepts

Two popular approaches to writing computer programs are procedural programming and object-oriented programming.

Procedural Programming

Procedural programming is a style of programming in which operations are executed one after another in sequence. In procedural applications, you create names for computer memory locations that can hold values—for example, numbers and text—in electronic form. The named computer memory locations are called **variables** because they hold values that might vary. For example, a payroll program might contain a variable named `rateOfPay`. The memory location referenced by the name `rateOfPay` might contain different values (a different value for every employee of the company) at different times. During the execution of the payroll program, each value stored under the name `rateOfPay` might have many operations performed on it—for example, the value might be read from an input device, be multiplied by another variable representing hours worked, and be printed on paper.

For convenience, the individual operations used in a computer program are often grouped into logical units called **procedures**. For example, a series of four or five comparisons and calculations that together determine a person's federal withholding tax value might be grouped as a procedure named `calculateFederalWithholding`. A procedural program defines the variable memory locations and then calls a series of procedures to input, manipulate, and output the values stored in those locations. When a program **calls a procedure**, the current logic is temporarily abandoned so that the procedure's commands can execute. A single procedural program often contains hundreds of variables and procedure calls. Procedures are also called *modules, methods, functions,* and *subroutines*. Users of different programming languages tend to use different terms. As you will learn later in this chapter, Java programmers most frequently use the term *method*.

Object-Oriented Programming

Object-oriented programming is an extension of procedural programming in which you take a slightly different approach to writing computer programs. Writing **object-oriented programs** involves:

- Creating classes, which are blueprints for objects
- Creating objects, which are specific instances of those classes
- Creating applications that manipulate or use those objects

Programmers use *OO* as an abbreviation for *object-oriented*; it is pronounced "oh oh." Object-oriented programming is abbreviated *OOP*, and pronounced to rhyme with *soup*.

Originally, object-oriented programming was used most frequently for two major types of applications:

- **Computer simulations**, which attempt to mimic real-world activities so that their processes can be improved or so that users can better understand how the real-world processes operate

- **Graphical user interfaces**, or **GUIs** (pronounced "gooeys"), which allow users to interact with a program in a graphical environment

Thinking about objects in these two types of applications makes sense. For example, a city might want to develop a program that simulates traffic patterns to help prevent traffic tie-ups. Programmers would create classes for objects such as cars and pedestrians that contain their own data and rules for behavior. For example, each car has a speed and a method for changing that speed. The specific instances of cars could be set in motion to create a simulation of a real city at rush hour.

Creating a GUI environment for users is also a natural use for object orientation. It is easy to think of the components a user manipulates on a computer screen, such as buttons and scroll bars, as similar to real-world objects. Each GUI object contains data—for example, a button on a screen has a specific size and color. Each object also contains behaviors—for example, each button can be clicked and reacts in a specific way when clicked. Some people consider the term *object-oriented programming* to be synonymous with GUI programming, but object-oriented programming means more. Although many GUI programs are object oriented, not all object-oriented programs use GUI objects. Modern businesses use object-oriented design techniques when developing all sorts of business applications, whether they are GUI applications or not. In the first 13 chapters of this book, you will learn object-oriented techniques that are appropriate for any program type; in the last chapters, you will apply what you have learned about those techniques specifically to GUI applications.

Understanding object-oriented programming requires grasping three basic concepts:

- Encapsulation as it applies to classes as objects

- Inheritance

- Polymorphism

Understanding Classes, Objects, and Encapsulation

In object-oriented terminology, a **class** is a term that describes a group or collection of objects with common properties. In the same way that a blueprint exists before any houses are built from it, and a recipe exists before any cookies are baked from it, a class definition exists before any objects are created from it. A **class definition** describes what attributes its objects will have and what those objects will be able to do. **Attributes** are the characteristics that define an object; they are **properties** of the object. When you learn a programming language such as Java, you learn to work with two types of classes: those that have already been developed by the language's creators and your own new, customized classes.

8

An **object** is a specific, concrete **instance** of a class. Creating an instance is called **instantiation**. You can create objects from classes that you write and from classes written by other programmers, including Java's creators. The values contained in an object's properties often differentiate instances of the same class from one another. For example, the class `Automobile` describes what `Automobile` objects are like. Some properties of the `Automobile` class are make, model, year, and color. Each `Automobile` object possesses the same attributes, but not necessarily the same values for those attributes. One `Automobile` might be a 2010 white Ford Taurus and another might be a 2015 red Chevrolet Camaro. Similarly, your dog has the properties of all `Dogs`, including a breed, name, age, and whether its shots are current. The values of the properties of an object are referred to as the object's **state**. In other words, you can think of objects as roughly equivalent to nouns, and of their attributes as similar to adjectives that describe the nouns.

When you understand an object's class, you understand the characteristics of the object. If your friend purchases an `Automobile`, you know it has a model name, and if your friend gets a `Dog`, you know the dog has a breed. Knowing what attributes exist for classes allows you to ask appropriate questions about the states or values of those attributes. For example, you might ask how many miles the car gets per gallon, but you would not ask whether the car has had shots. Similarly, in a GUI operating environment, you expect each component to have specific, consistent attributes and methods, such as a window having a title bar and a close button, because each component gains these properties as a member of the general class of GUI components. Figure 1-2 shows the relationship of some `Dog` objects to the `Dog` class.

By convention, programmers using Java begin their class names with an uppercase letter. Thus, the class that defines the attributes and methods of an automobile would probably be named `Automobile`, and the class for dogs would probably be named `Dog`. However, following this convention is not required to produce a workable program.

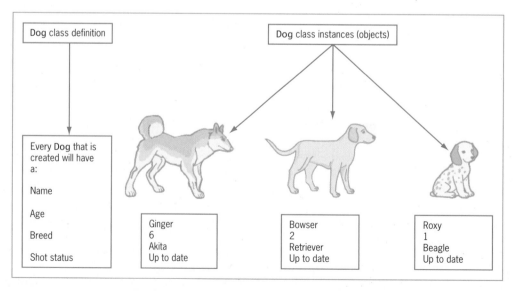

Figure 1-2 Dog class definition and some objects created from it

Besides defining properties, classes define methods their objects can use. A **method** is a self-contained block of program code that carries out some action, similar to a procedure in a procedural program. An `Automobile`, for example, might have methods for moving forward, moving backward, and determining the status of its gas tank. Similarly, a `Dog` might have methods for walking, eating, and determining its name, and a program's GUI components might have methods for maximizing and minimizing them as well as determining their size. In other words, if objects are similar to nouns, then methods are similar to verbs.

In object-oriented classes, attributes and methods are encapsulated into objects. **Encapsulation** refers to two closely related object-oriented notions:

- Encapsulation is the enclosure of data and methods within an object. Encapsulation allows you to treat all of an object's methods and data as a single entity. Just as an actual dog contains all of its attributes and abilities, so would a program's `Dog` object.

- Encapsulation also refers to the concealment of an object's data and methods from outside sources. Concealing data is sometimes called *information hiding*, and concealing how methods work is *implementation hiding*; you will learn more about both terms in the chapter "Using Methods, Classes, and Objects." Encapsulation lets you hide specific object attributes and methods from outside sources and provides the security that keeps data and methods safe from inadvertent changes.

If an object's methods are well written, the user can be unaware of the low-level details of how the methods are executed, and the user must simply understand the interface or interaction between the method and the object. For example, if you can fill your `Automobile` with gasoline, it is because you understand the interface between the gas pump nozzle and the vehicle's gas tank opening. You don't need to understand how the pump works mechanically or where the gas tank is located inside your vehicle. If you can read your speedometer, it does not matter how the displayed figure is calculated. As a matter of fact, if someone produces a superior, more accurate speed-determining device and inserts it in your `Automobile`, you don't have to know or care how it operates, as long as your interface remains the same. The same principles apply to well-constructed classes used in object-oriented programs— programs that use classes only need to work with interfaces.

Understanding Inheritance and Polymorphism

An important feature of object-oriented program design is **inheritance**—the ability to create classes that share the attributes and methods of existing classes, but with more specific features. For example, `Automobile` is a class, and all `Automobile` objects share many traits and abilities. `Convertible` is a class that inherits from the `Automobile` class; a `Convertible` is a type of `Automobile` that has and can do everything a "plain" `Automobile` does—but with an added ability to lower its top. (In turn, `Automobile` inherits from the `Vehicle` class.) `Convertible` is not an object—it is a class. A specific `Convertible` is an object—for example, `my1967BlueMustangConvertible`.

Inheritance helps you understand real-world objects. For example, the first time you encounter a convertible, you already understand how the ignition, brakes, door locks, and other systems work because you realize that a convertible is a type of automobile, so you need to be concerned only with the attributes and methods that are "new" with a convertible. The advantages in programming are the same—you can build new classes based on existing classes and concentrate on the specialized features you are adding.

A final important concept in object-oriented terminology is **polymorphism**. Literally, polymorphism means "many forms"—it describes the feature of languages that allows the same word or symbol to be interpreted correctly in different situations based on the context. For example, although the classes Automobile, Sailboat, and Airplane all inherit from Vehicle, turn and stop methods work differently for instances of those classes. The advantages of polymorphism will become more apparent when you begin to create GUI applications containing features such as windows, buttons, and menu bars. In a GUI application, it is convenient to remember one method name, such as setColor or setHeight, and have it work correctly no matter what type of object you are modifying.

When you see a plus sign (+) between two numbers, you understand they are being added. When you see it carved in a tree between two names, you understand that the names are linked romantically. Because the symbol has diverse meanings based on context, it is polymorphic. Chapters 10 and 11 provide more information about inheritance and polymorphism and how they are implemented in Java.

 Watch the video *Object-Oriented Programming*.

TWO TRUTHS & A LIE

Comparing Procedural and Object-Oriented Programming Concepts

1. An instance of a class is a created object that possesses the attributes and methods described in the class definition.

2. Encapsulation protects data by hiding it within an object.

3. Polymorphism is the ability to create classes that share the attributes and methods of existing classes, but with more specific features.

The false statement is #3. Inheritance is the ability to create classes that share the attributes and methods of existing classes, but with more specific features; polymorphism describes the ability to use one term to cause multiple actions.

Features of the Java Programming Language

Java was developed by Sun Microsystems as an object-oriented language for general-purpose business applications and for interactive, World Wide Web-based Internet applications. (Sun was later acquired by Oracle Corporation.) Some of the advantages that make Java a popular language are its security features and the fact that it is **architecturally neutral**: Unlike other languages, you can use Java to write a program that runs on any operating system (such as Windows, Mac OS, or Linux) or device (such as PCs, phones, and tablet computers).

Java can be run on a wide variety of computers and devices because it does not execute instructions on a computer directly. Instead, Java runs on a hypothetical computer known as the **Java Virtual Machine (JVM)**. When programmers call the JVM *hypothetical*, they mean it is not a physical entity created from hardware, but is composed only of software.

Figure 1-3 shows the Java environment. Programming statements written in a high-level programming language are **source code**. When you write a Java program, you first construct the source code using a text editor such as Notepad or a development environment and source code editor such as **jGRASP**, which you can download from the Web for free. A **development environment** is a set of tools that help you write programs by providing such features as displaying a language's keywords in color. The statements are saved in a file; then, the Java compiler converts the source code into a binary program of **bytecode**. A program called the **Java interpreter** then checks the bytecode and communicates with the operating system, executing the bytecode instructions line by line within the Java Virtual Machine. Because the Java program is isolated from the operating system, it is also insulated from the particular hardware on which it is run. Because of this insulation, the JVM provides security against intruders accessing your computer's hardware through the operating system. Therefore, Java is more secure than other languages. Another advantage provided by the JVM means less work for programmers—when using other programming languages, software vendors usually have to produce multiple versions of the same product (a Windows version, Macintosh version, UNIX version, Linux version, and so on) so all users can run the program. With Java, one program version runs on all these platforms. **"Write once, run anywhere" (WORA)** is the slogan developed by Sun Microsystems to describe the ability of one Java program version to work correctly on multiple platforms.

Java also is simpler to use than many other object-oriented languages. Java is modeled after C++. Although neither language is easy to read or understand on first exposure, Java does eliminate some of the most difficult-to-understand features in C++, such as pointers and multiple inheritance.

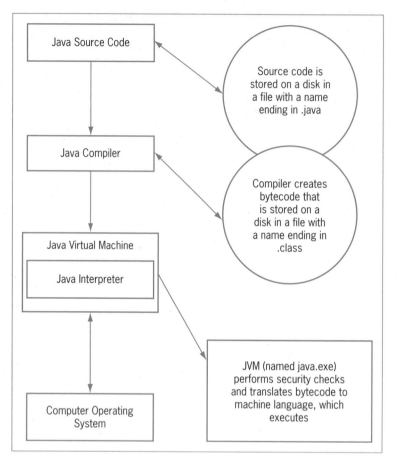

Figure 1-3   The Java environment

Java Program Types

You can write two kinds of programs using Java:

- **Applets** are programs that are embedded in a Web page. You can read about applets in a special section at the end of this chapter.

- **Java applications** are stand-alone programs. Java applications can be further subdivided into **console applications**, which support character or text output to a computer screen, and **windowed applications**, which create a GUI with elements such as menus, toolbars, and dialog boxes. Console applications are the easier applications to create; you start using them in the next section.

TWO TRUTHS & A LIE

Features of the Java Programming Language

1. Java was developed to be architecturally neutral, which means that anyone can build an application without extensive study.

2. After you write a Java program, the compiler converts the source code into a binary program of bytecode.

3. Java programs that are embedded in a Web page are called applets, while stand-alone programs are called Java applications.

The false statement is #1. Java was developed to be architecturally neutral, which means that you can use Java to write a program that will run on any platform.

Analyzing a Java Application that Produces Console Output

At first glance, even the simplest Java application involves a fair amount of confusing syntax. Consider the application in Figure 1-4. This program is written on seven lines, and its only task is to display "First Java application" on the screen.

```java
public class First
{
    public static void main(String[] args)
    {
        System.out.println("First Java application");
    }
}
```

Figure 1-4   The First class

In program code in figures in this book, Java keywords as well as true, false, and null are blue, and all other program elements are black. A complete list of Java keywords is shown later in this chapter.

The code for every complete program shown in this book is available in a set of student files you can download so that you can execute the programs on your own computer.

Understanding the Statement that Produces the Output

Although the program in Figure 1-4 occupies several lines, it contains only one Java programming statement. The statement `System.out.println("First Java application");` does the actual work in this program. Like all Java statements, this one ends with a semicolon. Most Java programming statements can be spread across as many lines as you choose, as long as you place line breaks in appropriate places. For example, in the program in Figure 1-4, you could place a line break before or after the opening parenthesis, or before or after the closing parenthesis. However, you usually want to place a short statement on a single line.

The text "First Java application" is a **literal string** of characters—a series of characters that will appear in output exactly as entered. Any literal string in Java is written between double quotation marks. In Java, a literal string cannot be broken and placed on multiple lines. Figure 1-5 labels this string and the other parts of the statement.

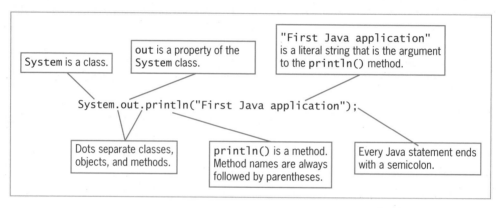

Figure 1-5 Anatomy of a Java statement

The string "First Java application" appears within parentheses because the string is an argument to a method, and arguments to methods always appear within parentheses. **Arguments** are pieces of information that are sent into a method. The act of sending arguments to a method is called **passing arguments** to the method. As an analogy, consider placing a catalog order with a company that sells sporting goods. Processing a catalog order is a method that consists of a set of standard procedures—recording the order, checking the availability of the item, pulling the item from the warehouse, and so on. Each catalog order also requires a set of data items, such as which item number you are ordering and the quantity of the item desired; these data items can be considered the arguments to the order-processing method. If you order two of item 5432 from a catalog, you expect different results than if you order 1,000 of item 9008. Likewise, if you pass the argument "Happy Holidays" to a Java display method, you expect different results than if you pass the argument "First Java application".

Within the statement `System.out.println("First Java application");`, the method to which you are passing `"First Java application"` is named `println()`. The Java methods `println()` and `print()` both produce output. With `println()`, after the output is displayed, the insertion point moves to the following line so that subsequent output appears on a new line. With `print()`, however, the insertion point does not advance to a new line, so subsequent output appears at the end of the current line.

When you call a method, you always use parentheses following the method name. In this book, you will learn about many methods that require arguments between their parentheses, and many others for which you leave the parentheses empty. The `println()` method can be used with no arguments when you want to output a blank line. Later in this chapter, you will learn about a method named `showMessageDialog()` that requires two arguments. Other methods require more.

Within the statement `System.out.println("First Java application");`, `out` is an object that is a property of the `System` class that refers to the **standard output device** for a system, normally the monitor. The `out` object itself is an instance of the `PrintStream` class, which contains several methods, including `println()`. Technically, you could create the `out` object and write the instructions within the `println()`method yourself, but it would be time consuming, and the creators of Java assumed you frequently would want to display output on a screen. Therefore, the `System` and `PrintStream` classes, the `out` object, and the `println()` method were created as a convenience to the programmer.

Within the statement `System.out.println("First Java application");`, `System` is a class. Therefore, `System` defines attributes for `System` objects, just as the `Dog` class defines the attributes for `Dog` objects. One of the `System` attributes is `out`. (You can probably guess that another attribute is `in` and that it represents an input device.)

The dots (periods) in `System.out.println()` are used to separate the names of the components in the statement. You will use this format repeatedly in your Java programs.

Java is case sensitive; the class named `System` is a completely different class from one named `system`, `SYSTEM`, or even `sYsTeM`, and `out` is a different object from one named `Out` or `OUT`. You must pay close attention to using correct uppercase and lowercase values when you write Java programs.

So, the statement that displays the string "First Java application" contains a class, an object reference, a method call, a method argument, and a statement-ending semicolon, but the statement cannot stand alone; it is embedded within a class, as shown in Figure 1-4.

Understanding the `First` Class

Everything that you use within a Java program must be part of a class. When you write `public class First`, you are defining a class named `First`. You can define a Java class using any name or **identifier** you need, as long as it meets the following requirements:

- A Java identifier must begin with a letter of the English alphabet, a non-English letter (such as α or π), an underscore, or a dollar sign. A class name cannot begin with a digit.

- A Java identifier can contain only letters, digits, underscores, or dollar signs.

- A Java identifier cannot be a reserved keyword, such as public or class. (See Table 1-1 for a list of reserved keywords.)

- A Java identifier cannot be one of the following values: true, false, or null. These are not keywords (they are primitive values), but they are reserved and cannot be used.

Java is based on **Unicode**, which is an international system of character representation. The term *letter* indicates English-language letters as well as characters from Arabic, Greek, and other alphabets. You can learn more about Unicode in Appendix B.

abstract	continue	for	new	switch
assert	default	goto	package	synchronized
boolean	do	if	private	this
break	double	implements	protected	throw
byte	else	import	public	throws
case	enum	instanceof	return	transient
catch	extends	int	short	try
char	final	interface	static	void
class	finally	long	strictfp	volatile
const	float	native	super	while

Table 1-1   Java reserved keywords

Although const and goto are reserved as keywords, they are not used in Java programs, and they have no function. Both words are used in other languages and were reserved in case developers of future versions of Java wanted to implement them.

It is a Java standard, although not a requirement, to begin class identifiers with an uppercase letter and employ other uppercase letters as needed to improve readability. (By contrast, method identifiers, like println(), conventionally begin with a lowercase letter.) The style that joins words in which each word begins with an uppercase letter is called **Pascal casing**, or sometimes **upper camel casing**. You should follow established conventions for Java so your programs will be easy for other programmers to interpret and follow. This book uses established Java programming conventions.

Table 1-2 lists some valid and conventional class names that you could use when writing programs in Java. Table 1-3 provides some examples of class names that *could* be used in Java (if you use these class names, the class will compile) but that are unconventional and not recommended. Table 1-4 provides some class name examples that are illegal.

Class Name	Description
Employee	Begins with an uppercase letter
UnderGradStudent	Begins with an uppercase letter, contains no spaces, and emphasizes each new word with an initial uppercase letter
InventoryItem	Begins with an uppercase letter, contains no spaces, and emphasizes the second word with an initial uppercase letter
Budget2016	Begins with an uppercase letter and contains no spaces

Table 1-2 Some valid class names in Java

Class Name	Description
Undergradstudent	New words are not indicated with initial uppercase letters, making this identifier difficult to read
Inventory_Item	Underscore is not commonly used to indicate new words
BUDGET2016	Using all uppercase letters for class identifiers is not conventional
budget2016	Conventionally, class names do not begin with a lowercase letter

Table 1-3 Legal but unconventional and nonrecommended class names in Java

Class Name	Description
Inventory Item	Space character is illegal in an identifier
class	class is a reserved word
2016Budget	Class names cannot begin with a digit
phone#	The number symbol (#) is illegal in an identifier

Table 1-4 Some illegal class names in Java

In Figure 1-4 (and again in Figure 1-6), the line public class First is the class header; it contains the keyword class, which identifies First as a class. The reserved word public is an access specifier. An **access specifier** defines the circumstances under which a class can be accessed and the other classes that have the right to use a class. Public access is the most liberal type of access; you will learn about public access and other types of access in the chapter "Using Methods, Classes, and Objects."

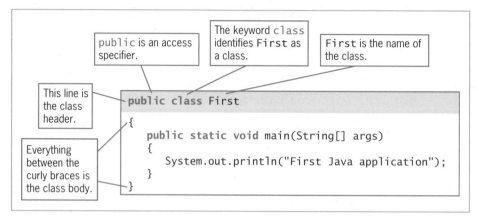

Figure 1-6   The parts of a typical class

After the class header, you enclose the contents of a class within curly braces ({ and }); any data items and methods between the curly braces make up the **class body**. A class body can be composed of any number of data items and methods. In Figure 1-4 (and again in Figure 1-6), the class First contains only one method within its curly braces. The name of the method is main(), and the main() method, like the println() method, includes its own set of parentheses. The main() method in the First class contains only one statement—the statement that uses the println() method. The main() method does not *contain* any other methods, but it *calls* the println() method.

Indent Style

In general, whitespace is optional in Java. **Whitespace** is any combination of nonprinting characters. You use whitespace to organize your program code and make it easier to read. You can insert whitespace between words or lines in your program code by typing spaces, tabs, or blank lines because the compiler ignores these extra spaces. However, you cannot use whitespace within an identifier or keyword, or surrounding the dots in any class-object-method combination.

For every opening curly brace ({) in a Java program, there must be a corresponding closing curly brace (}), but the placement of the opening and closing curly braces is not important to the compiler. For example, the following class executes in exactly the same way as the one shown in Figure 1-4. The only difference is the layout of the braces—the line breaks occur in different locations.

```java
public class First{
    public static void main(String[] args){
        System.out.println("First Java application");
    }
}
```

The indent style shown in the preceding example, in which opening braces do not stand alone on separate lines, is known as the **K & R style** and is named for Kernighan and Ritchie, who wrote the first book on the C programming language. The indent style shown in Figure 1-4 and used throughout this book, in which curly braces are aligned and each occupies its own line, is called the **Allman style** and is named for Eric Allman, a programmer who popularized the style. Java programmers use a variety of indent styles, and all can produce workable Java programs. When you write your own code, you should develop a consistent style. In school, your instructor might have a preferred style, and when you get a job as a Java programmer, your organization most likely will have a preferred style. With many development environments, indentations are made for you automatically as you type.

Most programmers indent a method's statements a few spaces more than its curly braces. Some programmers indent two spaces, some three, and some four. Some programmers use the Tab key to create indentations, but others are opposed to this practice because the Tab key can indicate different indentation sizes on different systems. Some programmers don't care whether tabs or spaces are used, as long as you don't mix them in the same program. The Java compiler does not care how you indent. Again, the most important rule is to develop a consistent style of which your organization approves.

Understanding the `main()` Method

The method header for the `main()` method is quite complex. Figure 1-7 shows the parts of the `main()` method.

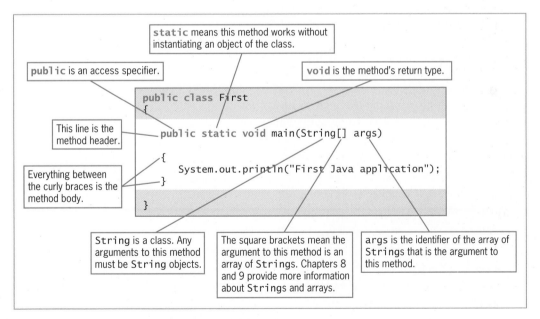

Figure 1-7 The parts of a typical `main()` method

The meaning and purpose of each of the terms used in the method header will become clearer as you complete this textbook; a brief explanation will suffice for now.

- In the method header `public static void main(String[] args)`, the word `public` is an access specifier, just as it is when you use it to define the `First` class.

- In Java, the reserved keyword **static** means that a method is accessible and usable even though no objects of the class exist.

- The keyword **void** used in the `main()` method header indicates that the `main()` method does not return any value when it is called. This doesn't mean that `main()` doesn't produce output—in fact, the method in Figure 1-4 (and in Figure 1-7) does. It only means that the `main()` method does not send any value back to any other method that might use it. You will learn more about return values in the chapter "Methods, Classes, and Objects."

- The name of the method is `main()`. As is the convention with Java methods, its identifier begins with a lowercase letter. Not all classes have a `main()` method; in fact, many do not. All Java *applications*, however, must include a class containing a public method named `main()`, and most Java applications have additional classes and methods. When you execute a Java application, the JVM always executes the `main()` method first.

- In the method header `public static void main(String[] args)`, the contents between the parentheses, `String[] args`, represent the type of argument that can be passed to the `main()` method, just as the string `"First Java application"` is an argument passed to the `println()` method. `String` is a Java class that can be used to hold character strings (according to Java convention, it begins with an uppercase letter, like other classes). The identifier `args` is used to hold any `String` objects that might be sent to the `main()` method. The `main()` method could do something with those arguments, such as display them, but in Figure 1-4, the `main()` method does not actually use the `args` identifier. Nevertheless, you must place an identifier within the `main()` method's parentheses. The identifier does not need to be named `args`—it could be any legal Java identifier—but the name `args` is traditional.

In this book, you won't pass any arguments to the `main()` method, but when you run a program, you could. Even though you pass no arguments, the `main()` method must contain `String[]` and a legal identifier (such as `args`) within its parentheses. When you refer to the `String` class in the `main()` method header, the square brackets indicate an array of `String` objects. You will learn more about the `String` class and arrays in Chapters 7, 8, and 9.

The simple application shown in Figure 1-4 has many pieces to remember. However, for now you can use the Java code shown in Figure 1-8 as a shell, in which you replace `AnyClassName` with a class name you choose and the line `/******/` with any statements that you want to execute.

Watch the video *A Java Program*.

```
public class AnyClassName
{
    public static void main(String[] args)
    {
        /******/
    }
}
```

Figure 1-8   Shell code

Saving a Java Class

When you write a Java class, you must save it using a writable storage medium such as a disk, DVD, or USB device. In Java, if a class is public (that is, if you use the public access specifier before the class name), you must save the class in a file with exactly the same name and a .java extension. For example, the First class must be stored in a file named First.java. The class name and filename must match exactly, including the use of uppercase and lowercase characters. If the extension is not .java, the Java compiler does not recognize the file as containing a Java class. Appendix A contains additional information on saving a Java application.

TWO TRUTHS & A LIE

Analyzing a Java Application that Produces Console Output

1. In the method header public static void main(String[] args), the word public is an access specifier.

2. In the method header public static void main(String[] args), the word static means that a method is accessible and usable, even though no objects of the class exist.

3. In the method header public static void main(String[] args), the word void means that the main() method is an empty method.

The false statement is #3. In the method header public static void main(String[] args), the word void means that the main() method does not return any value when it is called.

You Do It

22

Your First Application

Now that you understand the basics of an application written in Java, you are ready to enter your own Java application into a text editor. It is a tradition among programmers that the first program you write in any language produces "Hello, world!" as its output. You will create such a program now. You can use any text editor, such as Notepad or TextPad, or a development environment, such as jGRASP.

 It is best to use the simplest available text editor when writing Java programs. Multifeatured word-processing programs save documents as much larger files because of all the built-in features, such as font styles and margin settings, which the Java compiler cannot interpret.

1. Start the text editor, and then open a new document.

2. Type the class header as follows:

   ```
   public class Hello
   ```

   In this example, the class name is `Hello`. You can use any valid name you want for the class. If you choose *Hello*, you always must refer to the class as *Hello*, and not as *hello*, because Java is case sensitive.

3. Press **Enter** once, type **{**, press **Enter** again, and then type **}**. You will add the `main()` method between these curly braces. Although it is not required, the convention used in this book is to place each curly brace on its own line and to align opening and closing curly brace pairs with each other. Using this format makes your code easier to read.

4. As shown in the shaded portion of Figure 1-9, add the `main()` method header between the curly braces, and then type a set of curly braces for `main()`.

```
public class Hello
{
    public static void main(String[] args)
    {
    }
}
```

Figure 1-9   The `main()` method shell for the `Hello` class

(continues)

(continued)

5. Next, add the statement within the `main()` method that will produce the output "Hello, world!". Use Figure 1-10 as a guide for adding the shaded `println()` statement to the `main()` method.

```
public class Hello
{
    public static void main(String[] args)
    {
        System.out.println("Hello, world!");
    }
}
```

Figure 1-10 Complete `Hello` class

6. Save the application as **Hello.java**. The class name and filename must match exactly, and you must use the .java extension.

Compiling a Java Class and Correcting Syntax Errors

After you write and save an application, two steps must occur before you can view the application's output.

1. You must compile the class you wrote (called the *source code*) into bytecode.

2. You must use the Java interpreter to translate the bytecode into executable statements.

Compiling a Java Class

If you are using a development environment such as jGRASP, you can compile your program by clicking the Compile button, or by clicking the Build menu and selecting Compile. If you are using a text editor such as Notepad, you can compile your source code file from the command line. Your prompt should show the folder or directory where your program file is stored. Then, you type `javac` followed by the name of the file that contains the source code. For example, to compile a file named First.java, you type the following and then press Enter:

```
javac First.java
```

Compiling the program will produce one of three outcomes:

- You receive a message such as `'javac' is not recognized as an internal or external command, operable program or batch file.`

- You receive one or more programming language error messages.

- You receive no messages, which means that the application compiled successfully.

When compiling, if the source code file is not in the current path, you can type a full path with the filename. For example:

`javac c:\java\MyClasses\Chapter.01\First.java`

In a DOS environment, you can change directories using the **cd** command. For example, to change from the current directory to a subdirectory named `MyClasses`, you type **cd** `MyClasses` and press Enter. Within any directory, you can back up to the root directory by typing **cd** and pressing Enter.

If you receive an error message that the command is not recognized, it might mean one of the following:

- You misspelled the command `javac`.
- You misspelled the filename.
- You are not within the correct subfolder or subdirectory on your command line.
- Java was not installed properly. (See Appendix A for information on installation.)

If you receive a programming language error message, there are one or more syntax errors in the source code. Recall that a syntax error is a programming error that occurs when you introduce typing errors into your program or use the programming language incorrectly. For example, if your class name is `first` (with a lowercase *f*) in the source code but you saved the file as First.java (with an uppercase *F*), you will receive an error message when you compile the application. The error message will be similar to `class first is public, should be declared in a file named first.java` because *first* and *First* are not the same in a case-sensitive language. If this error occurs, you must reopen the text file that contains the source code and make the necessary corrections, and then save the file and attempt to compile it again.

Appendix A contains information on troubleshooting, including how to change filenames in a Windows environment.

If you receive no error messages after compiling the code in a file named First.java, the application compiled successfully. In that case, a file named First.class is created and saved in the same folder as the text file that holds the source code. After a successful compile, you can execute the program (run the class file) on any computer that has a Java language interpreter.

Correcting Syntax Errors

Frequently, you might make typing errors as you enter Java statements into your text editor. When you issue the command to compile a class containing errors, the Java compiler produces one or more error messages. The exact error message that appears varies depending on the compiler you are using.

The `FirstWithMissingSemicolon` class shown in Figure 1-11 contains an error—the semicolon is missing from the end of the `println()` statement. (Of course, this class has been helpfully named to alert you to the error.) When you compile this class, an error message similar to the one shown in Figure 1-12 is displayed.

```
public class FirstWithMissingSemicolon
{

  public static void main(String[] args)

    {
        System.out.println("First Java application")
    }

}
```

The statement-ending semicolon has been omitted.

Figure 1-11   The FirstWithMissingSemicolon class

```
Command Prompt                                      _  □  X

C:\Java>javac FirstWithMissingSemicolon.java
FirstWithMissingSemicolon.java:5: error: ';' expected
        System.out.println("First Java application")
                                                    ^
1 error

C:\Java>_
```

Figure 1-12   Error message generated when the FirstWithMissingSemicolon class is compiled

The first line of the error message in Figure 1-12 displays the name of the file in which the error was found (FirstWithMissingSemicolon.java), the line number in which it was found (5), and the nature of the error (';' expected). The next line of the error message displays the statement that contains the error, including a caret that points to the exact location where the error was first discovered. As you will see when you write and compile Java programs, the place where an error is discovered is not necessarily where the error was made. Sometimes, it takes a little detective work to interpret an error message and determine its cause.

Finally, the message generated in Figure 1-12 includes a count of the number of errors found—in this case, there is just one error. This is an example of a **compile-time error**, or one in which the compiler detects a violation of language syntax rules and is unable to translate the source code to machine code.

When you compile a class, the compiler reports as many errors as it can find so that you can fix as many errors as possible. Sometimes, one error in syntax causes multiple error messages that normally would not be errors if the first syntax error did not exist, so fixing one error might eliminate multiple error messages. Sometimes, when you fix a compile-time error and recompile a program, new error messages are generated. That's because when you fix the first error, the compiler can proceed beyond that point and possibly discover new errors. Of course, no programmer intends to type a program containing syntax errors, but when you do, the compiler finds them all for you.

26

TWO TRUTHS & A LIE

Compiling a Java Class and Correcting Syntax Errors

1. After you write and save an application, you can compile the bytecode to create source code.

2. When you compile a class, you create a new file with the same name as the original file but with a .class extension.

3. Syntax errors are compile-time errors.

The false statement is #1. After you write and save an application, you can compile the source code to create bytecode.

 You Do It

Compiling a Java Class

You are ready to compile the `Hello` class that you created in the previous "You Do It" section.

1. If it is not still open on your screen, open the **Hello.java** file that you saved in the previous "You Do It" section.

2. If you are using jGRASP or another similar development environment, you can compile a program by clicking the **Compile** button. Otherwise, you can compile a program from the command prompt. Go to the command-line prompt for the drive and folder or subdirectory in which you saved Hello.java. At the command line, type:

   `javac Hello.java`

After a few moments, you should return to the command prompt. If you see error messages instead, reread the previous section to discover whether you can determine the source of the error.

If the error message indicates that the command was not recognized, make sure that you spelled the `javac` command correctly, including using the correct case. Also, make sure you are using the correct directory or folder where the Hello.java file is stored.

If the error message indicates a language error, check your file against Figure 1-10, making sure it matches exactly. Fix any errors, and compile the application again. If errors persist, read through the next section to see if you can discover the solution.

(continues)

(continued)

Correcting Syntax Errors

In this section, you examine error messages and gain firsthand experience with syntax errors.

1. If your version of the `Hello` class did not compile successfully, examine the syntax error messages. Now that you know the messages contain line numbers and carets to pinpoint mistakes, it might be easier for you to fix problems. After you determine the nature of any errors, resave the file and recompile it.

2. Even if your `Hello` class compiled successfully, you need to gain experience with error messages. Your student files contain a file named **HelloErrors.java**. Find this file and open it in your text editor. If you do not have access to the student files that accompany this book, you can type the file yourself, as shown in Figure 1-13.

```
public class HelloErrors
{
   public static void main(String[] args)
   {
      System.out.println("Hello");
      System.out.println("This is a test");
   }
}
```

Figure 1-13 The `HelloErrors` class

3. Save the file as **HelloErrors.java** in the folder in which you want to work. Then compile the class using the following command to confirm that it compiles without error:

   `javac HelloErrors.java`

4. In the first line of the file, remove the **c** from `class`, making the first line read **public lass HelloErrors**. Save the file and compile the program. Error messages are generated similar to those shown in Figure 1-14. Even though you changed only one keystroke in the file, four error messages appear. The first indicates that `class`, `enum`, or `interface` is expected in line 1. You haven't learned about the Java keywords `enum` or `interface` yet, but you know that you caused the error by altering the word `class`. The next three errors in lines 3, 6, and 7 show that the compile is continuing to look for one of the three keywords, but fails to find them.

(continues)

28

(continued)

```
C:\Java>javac HelloErrors.java
HelloErrors.java:1: error: class, interface, or enum expected
public lass HelloErrors
       ^
HelloErrors.java:3: error: class, interface, or enum expected
    public static void main(String[] args)
                  ^
HelloErrors.java:6: error: class, interface, or enum expected
        System.out.println("This is a test");
        ^
HelloErrors.java:7: error: class, interface, or enum expected
    }
    ^
4 errors

C:\Java>
```

Figure 1-14 Error messages generated when `class` is misspelled in the `HelloErrors` program

5. Repair the program by reinserting the **c** in `class`. Save the file and compile it again. The program should compile successfully. In this case, when you fix one error, four error messages are removed.

6. Next, remove the word **void** from the third line of the program. Save the file and compile it. Figure 1-15 shows the error message, which indicates that a return type is required. The message does not indicate that `void` is missing because Java supports many return types for methods. In this case, however, `void` is the correct return type, so reinsert it into the correct place in the program, and then save and recompile the file.

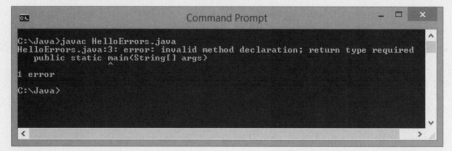

```
C:\Java>javac HelloErrors.java
HelloErrors.java:3: error: invalid method declaration; return type required
    public static main(String[] args)
                  ^
1 error

C:\Java>
```

Figure 1-15 Error message generated when `void` is omitted from the `main()` method header in the `HelloErrors` program

7. Remove the final closing curly brace from the `HelloErrors` program. Save the file and recompile it. Figure 1-16 shows the generated message "reached end of file while parsing." **Parsing** is the process the compiler uses to divide your source code into meaningful portions; the message means that the compiler

(continues)

(continued)

was in the process of analyzing the code when the end of the file was encountered prematurely. If you repair the error by reinserting the closing curly brace, saving the file, and recompiling it, you remove the error message.

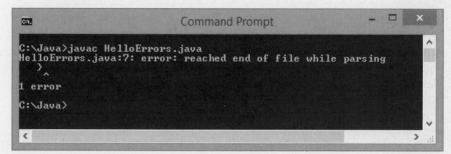

Figure 1-16 Error message generated when the closing curly brace is omitted from the HelloErrors program

8. Continue to introduce errors in the program by misspelling words, omitting punctuation, and adding extraneous keystrokes. Remember to save each program version before you recompile it; otherwise, you will recompile the previous version. When error messages are generated, read them carefully and try to understand their meaning in the context of the error you purposely caused. Occasionally, even though you inserted an error into the program, no error messages will be generated. That does not mean your program is correct. It only means that the program contains no syntax errors. A program can be free of syntax errors but still not be correct, as you will learn in the next section.

Running a Java Application and Correcting Logic Errors

After a program compiles with no syntax errors, you can execute it. However, just because a program compiles and executes, that does not mean the program is error free.

Running a Java Application

To run an application from jGRASP, you can click the Run button or click the Build menu and then click Run. To run the First application in Figure 1-4 from the command line, you type the following:

`java First`

Figure 1-17 shows the application's output in the command window. In this example, you can see that the First class is stored in a

Figure 1-17 Output of the First application

folder named Java on the C drive. After you type the `java` command to execute the program, the literal string in the call to the `println()` method is output, so `First Java application` appears on the screen. Control then returns to the command prompt.

> The procedure to confirm the storage location of your First.java class varies depending on your operating system. In a Windows operating system, for example, you can open Windows Explorer, locate the icon representing the storage device you are using, find the folder in which you have saved the file, and expand the folder. You should see the First.java file.

When you run a Java application using the `java` command, do not add the .class extension to the filename. If you type `java First`, the interpreter looks for a file named *First.class*. If you type `java First.class`, the interpreter looks for a file named *First.class.class*.

Modifying a Compiled Java Class

After viewing the application output, you might decide to modify the class to get a different result. For example, you might decide to change the `First` application's output from `First Java application` to the following:

```
My new and improved
Java application
```

To produce the new output, first you must modify the text file that contains the existing class. You need to change the existing literal string, and then add an output statement for another text string. Figure 1-18 shows the class that changes the output.

```java
public class First
{
    public static void main(String[] args)
    {
        System.out.println("My new and improved");
        System.out.println("Java application");
    }
}
```

Figure 1-18   `First` class containing output modified from the original version

The changes to the `First` class include the addition of the statement `System.out.println ("My new and improved");` and the removal of the word *First* from the string in the other `println()` statement.

If you make changes to the file, as shown in Figure 1-18, and save the file without recompiling it, then when you execute the program by typing `java First` at the command line, you will not see the new output—you will see the old output without the added line. Even though you save a text file that contains the modified source code for a class, the class in the already-compiled class file executes. After you save the file named First.java, the old compiled version of the class with the same name is still stored on your computer. Before the new source code can execute, you must do the following:

1. Save the file with the changes (using the same filename).

2. Recompile the class with the `javac` command.

3. Interpret the class bytecode and execute the class using the `java` command.

Figure 1-19 shows the new output.

When you recompile a class, the original version of the compiled file with the .class extension is replaced, and the original version no longer exists. When you modify a class, you must decide whether you want to retain the original version. If you do, you must give the new version a new class name and a new filename.

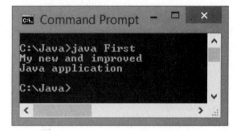

Figure 1-19 Execution of modified `First` class

 Once in a while, when you make a change to a Java class and then recompile and execute it, the old version still runs. The simplest solution is to delete the .class file and compile again. Programmers call this creating a **clean build**.

 Watch the video *Compiling and Executing a Program*.

Correcting Logic Errors

Besides syntax errors, a second kind of error occurs when the syntax of the program is correct and the program compiles but produces incorrect results when you execute it. This type of error is a logic error, which is often more difficult to find and resolve. For example, Figure 1-20 shows the output of the execution of a successfully compiled program named `FirstBadOutput`. If you glance at the output too quickly, you might not notice that *Java* is misspelled. The compiler does not find spelling errors within a literal string; it is legitimate to produce any combination of letters as output. Other examples of logic errors include multiplying two values when you meant to add, printing one copy of a report when you meant to print five, or forgetting to produce a total at the end of a business report when a user has requested one. Errors of this type must be detected by carefully examining the program output. It is the responsibility of the program author to test programs and find any logic errors.

Figure 1-20 Output of `FirstBadOutput` program

You have already learned that syntax errors are compile-time errors. A logic error is a type of **run-time error**—an error not detected until the program asks the computer to do something wrong, or even illegal, while executing. Not all run-time errors are the fault of the programmer. For example, a computer's hardware might fail while a program is executing. However, good programming practices can help to minimize errors.

 The process of fixing computer errors has been known as *debugging* since a large moth was found wedged into the circuitry of a mainframe computer at Harvard University in 1947. See these Web sites for interesting details and pictures: *www.jamesshuggins.com/h/tek1/first_computer_bug.htm* and *www.history.navy.mil/photos/images/h96000/h96566kc.htm*.

TWO TRUTHS & A LIE

Running a Java Application and Correcting Logic Errors

1. In Java, if a class is `public`, you must save the class in a file with exactly the same name and a .java extension.

2. To compile a file named MyProgram.java, you type `java MyProgram`, but to execute the program you type `java MyProgram.java`.

3. When you compile a program, sometimes one error in syntax causes multiple error messages.

The false statement is #2. To compile a file named MyProgram.java, you type `javac MyProgram.java`, but to execute the program you type the following:
`java MyProgram`

Adding Comments to a Java Class

As you can see, even the simplest Java class requires several lines of code and contains somewhat perplexing syntax. Large applications that perform many tasks include much more code, and as you write larger applications it becomes increasingly difficult to remember why you included steps or how you intended to use particular variables. Documenting your program code helps you remember why you wrote lines of code the way you did. **Program comments** are nonexecuting statements that you add to a program for the purpose of documentation. In other words, comments are designed for people reading the source code and not for the computer executing the program.

Programmers use comments to leave notes for themselves and for others who might read their programs in the future. At the very least, your Java class files should include comments indicating the author, the date, and the class name or function. The best practice dictates that you also include a brief comment to describe the purpose of each method you create within a class.

As you work through this book, add comments as the first lines of every file. The comments should contain the class name and purpose, your name, and the date. Your instructor might ask you to include additional comments.

Turning some program statements into comments can sometimes be useful when you are developing an application. If a program is not performing as expected, you can "comment out" various statements and subsequently run the program to observe the effect. When you **comment out** a statement, you turn it into a comment so the compiler does not translate it, and the JVM does not execute its command. This can help you pinpoint the location of errant statements in malfunctioning programs.

There are three types of comments in Java:

- **Line comments** start with two forward slashes (//) and continue to the end of the current line. A line comment can appear on a line by itself or at the end (and to the right) of a line following executable code. Line comments do not require an ending symbol.

- **Block comments** start with a forward slash and an asterisk (/*) and end with an asterisk and a forward slash (*/). A block comment can appear on a line by itself, on a line before executable code, or on a line after executable code. Block comments also can extend across as many lines as needed.

- **Javadoc** comments are a special case of block comments called **documentation comments** because they are used to automatically generate nicely formatted program documentation with a program named javadoc. Javadoc comments begin with a forward slash and two asterisks (/**) and end with an asterisk and a forward slash (*/). Appendix E teaches you how to create javadoc comments.

The forward slash (/) and the backslash (\ ) characters often are confused, but they are two distinct characters. You cannot use them interchangeably.

The Java Development Kit (JDK) includes the javadoc tool, which you can use when writing programs in Java. The tool produces HTML pages that describe classes and their contents.

Figure 1-21 shows how comments are used in code. In this example, the only statement that executes is the System.out.println("Hello"); statement; everything else (all the shaded parts) is a comment.

```
// Demonstrating comments
/* This shows
   that these comments
   don't matter */
System.out.println("Hello"); // This line executes
   // up to where the comment started
/* Everything but the println()
     is a comment */
```

Figure 1-21 A program segment containing several comments

You might want to create comments simply for aesthetics. For example, you might want to use a comment that is simply a row of dashes or asterisks to use as a visual dividing line between parts of a program.

When a program is used in a business setting, the program frequently is modified over time because of changing business needs. If a programmer changes code but does not change the comments that go with it, it's very possible that people who read the program in the future will be confused or misled. When you modify a program, it's important to change any relevant comments.

TWO TRUTHS & A LIE

Adding Comments to a Java Class

1. Line comments start with two forward slashes (//) and end with two backslashes (\\ ); they can extend across as many lines as needed.

2. Block comments start with a forward slash and an asterisk (/*) and end with an asterisk and a forward slash (*/); they can extend across as many lines as needed.

3. Javadoc comments begin with a forward slash and two asterisks (/**) and end with an asterisk and a forward slash (*/); they are used to generate documentation with a program named javadoc.

The false statement is #1. Line comments start with two forward slashes (//) and continue to the end of the current line; they do not require an ending symbol.

You Do It

Adding Comments to a Class

In this exercise, you add comments to your Hello.java application and save it as a new class named Hello2 so that you can retain copies of both the original and modified classes.

1. Open the **Hello.java** file you created earlier in this chapter. Enter the following comments at the top of the file, inserting your name and today's date where indicated.

   ```
   // Filename Hello2.java
   // Written by <your name>
   // Written on <today's date>
   ```

(continues)

(continued)

2.   Change the class name to **Hello2**, and then type the following block comment after the class header:

     /* This class demonstrates the use of the println()
     method to print the message Hello, world! */

3.   Save the file as **Hello2.java**. The file must be named Hello2.java because the class name is Hello2.

4.   Go to the command-line prompt for the drive and folder or subdirectory in which you saved Hello2.java, and type the following command to compile the program:

     javac Hello2.java

5.   When the compile is successful, execute your application by typing **java Hello2** at the command line. The comments have no effect on program execution; the output should appear on the next line.

   After the application compiles successfully, a file named Hello2.class is created and stored in the same folder as the Hello2.java file. If your application compiled without error but you receive an error message, such as "Exception in thread 'main' java.lang.NoClassDefFoundError," when you try to execute the application, you probably do not have your class path set correctly. See Appendix A for details.

Creating a Java Application that Produces GUI Output

Besides allowing you to use the System class to produce command window output, Java provides built-in classes that produce GUI output. For example, Java contains a class named JOptionPane that allows you to produce dialog boxes. A **dialog box** is a GUI object resembling a window in which you can place messages you want to display. Figure 1-22 shows a class named FirstDialog. The FirstDialog class contains many elements that are familiar to you; only the two shaded lines are new.

```
import javax.swing.JOptionPane;
public class FirstDialog
{
    public static void main(String[] args)
    {
        JOptionPane.showMessageDialog(null, "First Java dialog");
    }
}
```

Figure 1-22   The FirstDialog class

In older versions of Java, any application that used a `JOptionPane` dialog was required to end with a `System.exit(0);` statement or the application would not terminate. You can add this statement to your programs, and they will work correctly, but it is not necessary. However, you might see this line when examining programs written by others.

In Figure 1-22, the first shaded line is an `import` statement. You use an **import statement** when you want to access a built-in Java class that is contained in a group of classes called a **package**. To use the `JOptionPane` class, you must import the package named `javax.swing.JOptionPane`. Any `import` statement you use must be placed outside of any class you write in a file. You will learn more about `import` statements in general, and the javax.swing packages in particular, as you continue to study Java.

You do not need to use an `import` statement when you use the `System` class (as with the `System.out.println()` method) because the `System` class is contained in the package `java.lang`, which is automatically imported in every Java program. You *could* include the statement `import java.lang;` at the top of any file in which you use the `System` class, but you are not required to do so.

The second shaded statement in the `FirstDialog` class in Figure 1-22 uses the `showMessageDialog()` method that is part of the `JOptionPane` class. Like the `println()` method that is used for console output, the `showMessageDialog()` method starts with a lowercase letter and is followed by a set of parentheses. However, whereas the `println()` method requires only one argument between its parentheses to produce an output string, the `showMessageDialog()` method requires two arguments. Whenever a method requires multiple arguments, they are separated by commas. When the first argument to `showMessageDialog()` is `null`, as it is in the class in Figure 1-22, it means the output message box should be placed in the center of the screen. (You will learn more about dialog boxes, including how to position them in different locations and how to add more options to them, in Chapter 2.) The second argument, after the comma, is the literal string that is displayed.

Earlier in this chapter, you learned that `true`, `false`, and `null` are all reserved words that represent values.

When a user executes the `FirstDialog` class, the dialog box in Figure 1-23 is displayed. The user must click the OK button or the Close button to dismiss the dialog box. If the user has a touch screen, the user can touch the OK button or the Close button.

Figure 1-23　Output of the `FirstDialog` application

TWO TRUTHS & A LIE

Creating a Java Application that Produces GUI Output

1. A dialog box is a GUI object resembling a window, in which you can place messages you want to display.

2. You use an append statement when you want to access a built-in Java class that is contained in a group of classes called a package.

3. Different methods can require different numbers of arguments.

The false statement is #2. You use an import statement when you want to access a built-in Java class that is contained in a group of classes called a package.

 You Do It

Creating a Dialog Box

Next, you write a Java application that produces output in a dialog box.

1. Open a new file in your text editor. Type comments similar to the following, inserting your own name and today's date where indicated.

```
// Filename HelloDialog.java
// Written by <your name>
// Written on <today's date>
```

2. Enter the import statement that allows you to use the JOptionPane class:

```
import javax.swing.JOptionPane;
```

3. Enter the HelloDialog class:

```
public class HelloDialog
{
    public static void main(String[] args)
    {
        JOptionPane.showMessageDialog(null, "Hello, world!");
    }
}
```

(continues)

(continued)

4. Save the file as **HelloDialog.java**. Compile the class using the following command:

    `javac HelloDialog.java`

    If necessary, eliminate any syntax errors, resave the file, and recompile. Then execute the program using the following command:

    `java HelloDialog`

    The output appears as shown in Figure 1-24.

Figure 1-24   Output of `HelloDialog` application

5. Click **OK** to dismiss the dialog box.

Finding Help

As you write Java programs, you can frequently consult this book as well as other Java documentation. A great wealth of helpful material exists at the Java Web site, *www.oracle .com/technetwork/java/index.html*. Of particular value is the Java application programming interface, more commonly referred to as the **Java API**. The Java API is also called the Java class library; it contains information about how to use every prewritten Java class, including lists of all the methods you can use with the classes.

Also of interest at the Java Web site are frequently asked questions (**FAQs**) that provide brief answers to many common questions about Java software and products. You can also find several versions of the Java Development Kit (**JDK**) that you can download for free. The JDK is an **SDK**—a software development kit that includes tools used by programmers. Versions are available for Windows, Linux, and Solaris operating systems. You can search and browse documentation online or you can download the documentation file for the JDK and install it on your computer. After it is installed, you can search and browse documentation locally.

A downloadable set of lessons titled "The Java Tutorial" with hundreds of complete working examples is available from *http://docs.oracle.com/javase/tutorial/*. The tutorial is organized into trails—groups of lessons on a particular subject. You can start the tutorial at the beginning and navigate sequentially to the end, or you can jump from one trail to another. As you study each chapter in this book, you are encouraged to make good use of these support materials.

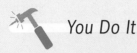 *You Do It*

Exploring the Java Web Site

In this section, you explore some of the material at the Java Web site.

1. Open an Internet browser and navigate to **www.oracle.com/technetwork/ java/index.html**.

2. Oracle could change the layout of its Web site after this book is published. However, you should be able to find and click a link for **Java APIs** and then another for **Java SE 8**. (If you are using an older version of Java, you can select that version instead.)

3. All the Java classes are listed in a panel labeled **All Classes**. Scroll until you can select the System class. The largest panel on the page should display details about the System class.

4. You can see that the System class contains three fields. You are already familiar with the out field, and you can see that it is an object of type PrintStream. Click the hypertext for the **PrintStream** type to be taken to a new page with details about that class.

5. Scroll through the methods of the PrintStream class. Notice that the class contains several versions of the print() and println() methods. Find the version of the println() method that accepts a String argument. Click the link to the method to read details about it, such as that it "prints a String and then terminates the line."

6. Many parts of the Java documentation won't mean much to you until you study data types and methods in more detail in the next few chapters of this book. For now, you can explore the Java Web site to get an idea of the wealth of classes that have been created for you.

Don't Do It

At the end of each chapter, a Don't Do It list will alert you to common mistakes made by beginning programmers.

- Don't forget that in Java, a public file's name must match the name of the class it contains. For example, if a file is named Program1.java, you can't simply rename it Program1BackUp.java and expect it to compile unless you change the class name within the file.

- Don't confuse the terms *parentheses, braces, brackets, curly braces, square brackets,* and *angle brackets.* When you are writing a program or performing some other computerized task and someone tells you, "Now, type some braces," you might want to clarify which term is meant. Table 1-5 summarizes these punctuation marks.

Punctuation	Name	Typical use in Java	Alternate names
( )	Parentheses	Follows method names as in `println()`	Parentheses can be called *round brackets,* but such usage is unusual
{ }	Curly braces	A pair surrounds a class body, a method body, and a block of code; when you learn about arrays in Chapter 8, you will find that curly braces also surround lists of array values	Curly braces might also be called *curly brackets*
[ ]	Square brackets	A pair signifies an array; arrays are covered in Chapter 8	Square brackets might be called *box brackets* or *square braces*
< >	Angle brackets	Angle brackets are used with generic arguments in parameterized classes; you won't use them in this book	When angle brackets appear with nothing between them, they are called a *chevron*

Table 1-5   Braces and brackets used in Java

- Don't forget to end a block comment. Every /* must have a corresponding */, even if it is several lines later. It's harder to make a mistake with line comments (those that start with //), but remember that nothing on the line after the // will execute.

- Don't forget that Java is case sensitive.

- Don't forget to end every statement with a semicolon, but *not* to end class or method headers with a semicolon.

- Don't forget to recompile a program to which you have made changes. It can be very frustrating to fix an error, run a program, and not understand why you don't see evidence of your changes. The reason might be that the .class file does not contain your changes because you forgot to recompile.

- Don't panic when you see a lot of compiler error messages. Often, fixing one will fix several.

- Don't think your program is perfect when all compiler errors are eliminated. Only by running the program multiple times and carefully examining the output can you be assured that your program is logically correct.

Key Terms

A **computer program** is a set of instructions that you write to tell a computer what to do.

Hardware is the general term for computer equipment.

Software is the general term for computer programs.

Application software performs tasks for users.

System software manages the computer.

The **logic** behind any program involves executing the various statements and procedures in the correct order to produce the desired results.

Machine language is a circuitry-level language that represents a series of on and off switches.

Machine code is another term for machine language.

A **low-level programming language** is written to correspond closely to a computer processor's circuitry.

A **high-level programming language** allows you to use an English-like vocabulary to write programs.

Syntax refers to the rules that define the ways language elements are used together correctly to create usable statements.

Keywords are the words that are part of a programming language.

Program statements are similar to English sentences; they carry out the tasks that programs perform.

Commands are program statements.

A **compiler** is a program that translates language statements into machine code; it translates an entire program at once before any part of the program can execute.

An **interpreter** is a program that translates language statements into machine code; it translates one statement at a time, allowing a program to execute partially.

Executing a statement or program means to carry it out.

At run time is a phrase that describes the period of time during which a program executes.

A **syntax error** is a programming error that occurs when you introduce typing errors into your program or use the programming language incorrectly; a program containing syntax errors cannot be translated into an executable program.

Debugging a program is the process that frees it of all errors.

A **bug** is a flaw or mistake in a computer program.

A **logic error** is a programming bug that allows a source program to be translated to an executable program successfully, but that produces incorrect results.

Semantic errors occur when you use a correct word in the wrong context in program code.

Procedural programming is a style of programming in which sets of operations are executed one after another in sequence.

Variables are named computer memory locations that hold values that might vary.

Procedures are sets of operations performed by a computer program.

To **call a procedure** is to temporarily abandon the current logic so that the procedure's commands can execute.

Writing **object-oriented programs** involves creating classes, creating objects from those classes, and creating applications that use those objects.

Computer simulations are programs that attempt to mimic real-world activities so that their processes can be improved or so that users can better understand how the real-world processes operate.

Graphical user interfaces, or **GUIs** (pronounced "gooeys"), allow users to interact with a program in a graphical environment.

A **class** is a group or collection of objects with common properties.

A **class definition** describes what attributes its objects will have and what those objects will be able to do.

Attributes are the characteristics that define an object as part of a class.

Properties are attributes of a class.

An **object** is an instance of a class.

An **instance** of a class is an object.

Instantiation is the process of creating an object.

The **state** of an object is the set of values for its attributes.

A **method** is a self-contained block of program code, similar to a procedure.

Encapsulation refers to the enclosure of data and methods within an object.

Inheritance is the ability to create classes that share the attributes and methods of existing classes, but with more specific features.

Polymorphism describes the feature of languages that allows the same word to be interpreted correctly in different situations based on the context.

Java is an object-oriented language used both for general-purpose business applications and for interactive, World Wide Web-based Internet applications.

Architecturally neutral describes the feature of Java that allows you to write programs that run on any platform (operating system).

The **Java Virtual Machine (JVM)** is a hypothetical (software-based) computer on which Java runs.

Source code consists of programming statements written in a high-level programming language.

jGRASP is a development environment and source code editor.

A **development environment** is a set of tools that help you write programs by providing such features as displaying a language's keywords in color.

Bytecode consists of programming statements that have been compiled into binary format.

The **Java interpreter** is a program that checks bytecode and communicates with the operating system, executing the bytecode instructions line by line within the Java Virtual Machine.

"Write once, run anywhere" (WORA) is the slogan developed by Sun Microsystems to describe the ability of one Java program version to work correctly on multiple platforms.

Applets are Java programs that are embedded in a Web page.

Java applications are stand-alone Java programs.

Console applications support character or text output to a computer screen.

Windowed applications create a graphical user interface (GUI) with elements such as menus, toolbars, and dialog boxes.

A **literal string** is a series of characters that appear exactly as entered. Any literal string in Java appears between double quotation marks.

Arguments are information passed to a method so it can perform its task.

Passing arguments is the act of sending them to a method.

The **standard output device** is normally the monitor.

An **identifier** is a name of a program component such as a class, object, or variable.

Unicode is an international system of character representation.

Pascal casing is a naming convention in which identifiers start with an uppercase letter and use an uppercase letter to start each new word.

Upper camel casing is Pascal casing.

An **access specifier** defines the circumstances under which a class can be accessed and the other classes that have the right to use a class.

The **class body** is the set of data items and methods between the curly braces that follow the class header.

Whitespace is any combination of nonprinting characters, such as spaces, tabs, and carriage returns (blank lines).

The **K & R style** is the indent style in which the opening brace follows the header on the same line; it is named for Kernighan and Ritchie, who wrote the first book on the C programming language.

The **Allman style** is the indent style in which curly braces are aligned and each occupies its own line; it is named for Eric Allman, a programmer who popularized the style.

The keyword **static** means that a method is accessible and usable even though no objects of the class exist.

The keyword **void**, when used in a method header, indicates that the method does not return any value when it is called.

A **compile-time error** is one in which the compiler detects a violation of language syntax and is unable to translate the source code to machine code.

Parsing is the process the compiler uses to divide source code into meaningful portions for analysis.

A **clean build** is created when you delete all previously compiled versions of a class before compiling again.

A **run-time error** occurs when a program compiles successfully but does not execute.

Program comments are nonexecuting statements that you add to a Java file for the purpose of documentation.

To **comment out** a statement is to turn it into a comment so the compiler will not execute its command.

Line comments start with two forward slashes (//) and continue to the end of the current line. Line comments can appear on a line by themselves or at the end of a line following executable code.

Block comments start with a forward slash and an asterisk (/*) and end with an asterisk and a forward slash (*/). Block comments can appear on a line by themselves, on a line before executable code, or on a line after executable code. Block comments also can extend across as many lines as needed.

Javadoc comments are block comments that generate documentation. They begin with a forward slash and two asterisks (/**) and end with an asterisk and a forward slash (*/).

Documentation comments are comments that automatically generate nicely formatted program documentation.

A **dialog box** is a GUI object resembling a window in which you can place messages you want to display.

An `import statement` accesses a built-in Java class that is contained in a package.

A **package** contains a group of built-in Java classes.

The **Java API** is the application programming interface, a collection of information about how to use every prewritten Java class.

FAQs are frequently asked questions.

The **JDK** is the Java Development Kit.

An **SDK** is a software development kit, or a set of tools useful to programmers.

Chapter Summary

- A computer program is a set of instructions that tells a computer what to do. You can write a program using a high-level programming language, which has its own syntax, or rules of the language. After you write a program, you use a compiler or interpreter to translate the language statements into machine code.

- Writing object-oriented programs involves creating classes, creating objects from those classes, and creating applications—stand-alone executable programs that use those objects. Object-oriented programming languages support encapsulation, inheritance, and polymorphism.

- A program written in Java is run on a standardized hypothetical computer called the Java Virtual Machine (JVM). When your class is compiled into bytecode, an interpreter within the JVM subsequently interprets the bytecode and communicates with your operating system to produce the program results.

- Everything within a Java program must be part of a class and contained within opening and closing curly braces. Methods within classes hold statements, and every statement ends with a semicolon. Dots are used to separate classes, objects, and methods in program code. All Java applications must have a method named `main()`, and most Java applications contain additional methods.

- To compile your source code from the command line, type `javac` followed by the name of the file that contains the source code. The compiler might issue syntax error messages that you must correct. When you successfully compile your source code, the compiler creates a file with a .class extension.

- You can run a compiled .class file on any computer that has a Java language interpreter by entering the `java` command followed by the name of the class file. When you modify a class, you must recompile it for the changes to take effect. After a program executes, you must examine the output for logic errors.

- Program comments are nonexecuting statements that you add to a file for the purpose of documentation. Java provides you with three types of comments: line comments, block comments, and javadoc comments.

- Java provides you with built-in classes that produce GUI output. For example, Java contains a class named JOptionPane that allows you to produce dialog boxes.

- A great wealth of helpful material exists online at the Java Web site.

Review Questions

1. The most basic circuitry-level computer language is ——————.

     a.   C++   c.   high-level language

     b.   Java   d.   machine language

2. Languages that let you use an easily understood vocabulary of descriptive terms, such as *read, write,* or *add,* are known as —————— languages.

     a.   procedural   c.   high-level

     b.   machine   d.   object-oriented

3. The rules of a programming language constitute its ——————.

     a.   syntax   c.   format

     b.   logic   d.   objects

4. A —————— translates high-level language statements into machine code.

     a.   programmer   c.   compiler

     b.   syntax detector   d.   decipherer

5. Named computer memory locations are called ——————.

     a.   compilers   c.   addresses

     b.   variables   d.   appellations

6. The individual operations used in a computer program are often grouped into logical units called ——————.

     a.   procedures   c.   constants

     b.   variables   d.   logistics

7. Envisioning program components as objects that are similar to concrete objects in the real world is the hallmark of ——————.

     a.   command-line operating systems   c.   object-oriented programming

     b.   procedural programming   d.   machine languages

8. The values of an object's attributes are known as its ——————.

     a.   state   c.   methods

     b.   orientation   d.   condition

9. An instance of a class is a(n) _____ .

    a. method   c. object
    b. procedure   d. case

10. Java is architecturally _____ .

    a. specific   c. neutral
    b. oriented   d. abstract

11. You must compile classes written in Java into _____ .

    a. bytecode   c. javadoc statements
    b. source code   d. object code

12. All Java programming statements must end with a _____ .

    a. period   c. semicolon
    b. comma   d. closing parenthesis

13. Arguments to methods always appear within _____ .

    a. parentheses   c. single quotation marks
    b. double quotation marks   d. curly braces

14. In a Java program, you must use _____ to separate classes, objects, and methods.

    a. commas   c. dots
    b. semicolons   d. forward slashes

15. All Java applications must have a method named _____ .

    a. method()   c. java()
    b. main()   d. Hello()

16. Nonexecuting program statements that provide documentation are called _____ .

    a. classes   c. comments
    b. notes   d. commands

17. Java supports three types of comments: _____ , _____ , and javadoc.

    a. line, block   c. constant, variable
    b. string, literal   d. single, multiple

18. After you write and save a Java application file, you _____ it.

    a. interpret and then compile   c. compile and then resave
    b. interpret and then execute   d. compile and then interpret

19. The command to execute a compiled Java application is _____ .

   a. run   c. javac

   b. execute   d. java

20. You save text files containing Java source code using the file extension _____ .

   a. .java   c. .txt

   b. .class   d. .src

Exercises

 Programming Exercises

1. Is each of the following class identifiers (a) legal and conventional, (b) legal but unconventional, or (c) illegal?

   a. associationRules   f. Apartment

   b. void   g. Phone#

   c. Golden Retriever   h. 8888

   d. Invoice   i. displayTotal()

   e. 36542ZipCode   j. Accounts_Receivable

2. Is each of the following method identifiers (a) legal and conventional, (b) legal but unconventional, or (c) illegal?

   a. associationRules()   f. Apartment()

   b. void()   g. Phone#()

   c. Golden Retriever()   h. 8888()

   d. Invoice()   i. displayTotal()

   e. 36542ZipCode()   j. Accounts_Receivable()

3. Name at least three attributes that might be appropriate for each of the following classes:

   a. Classroom

   b. InsurancePolicy

   c. CreditCardBill

4. Name at least three real-life objects that are instances of each of the following classes:

   a. Movie

   b. Team

   c. Musician

5. Name at least three classes to which each of these objects might belong:
    a. mySchoolPlayground
    b. shrimpAlfredo
    c. grandmasRockingChair

6. Write, compile, and test a class that displays your favorite movie quote on the screen. Save the class as **MovieQuote.java**.

 As you work through the programming exercises in this book, you will create many files. To organize them, you might want to create a separate folder in which to store the files for each chapter.

7. Write, compile, and test a class that displays your favorite movie quote, the movie it comes from, the character who said it, and the year of the movie. Save the class as **MovieQuoteInfo.java**.

8. Write, compile, and test a class that displays the following pattern on the screen:

```
X                        X
X                        X
X        XXXXXXXXX        X
XXXXX    X          X    XXXXX
X    X    X          X    X    X
X    X    X          X    X    X
```

    Save the class as **TableAndChairs.java**.

9. Write, compile, and test a class that displays at least four lines of your favorite song. Save the class as **FavoriteSong.java**.

10. Write, compile, and test a class that uses the command window to display the following statement about comments:

    "Program comments are nonexecuting statements you add to a file for the purpose of documentation."

    Also include the same statement in three different comments in the class; each comment should use one of the three different methods of including comments in a Java class. Save the class as **Comments.java**.

11. Modify the Comments.java program in Exercise 10 so that the statement about comments is displayed in a dialog box. Save the class as **CommentsDialog.java**.

12. From 1925 through 1963, Burma Shave advertising signs appeared next to highways all across the United States. There were always four or five signs in a row containing pieces of a rhyme, followed by a final sign that read "Burma Shave." For example, one set of signs that has been preserved by the Smithsonian Institution reads as follows:

```
Shaving brushes
You'll soon see 'em
On a shelf
In some museum
Burma Shave
```

Find a classic Burma Shave rhyme on the Web. Write, compile, and test a class that produces a series of four dialog boxes so that each displays one line of a Burma Shave slogan in turn. Save the class as **BurmaShave.java**.

Debugging Exercises

1. Each of the following files in the Chapter01 folder in your downloadable student files has syntax and/or logic errors. In each case, determine the problem and fix the errors. After you correct the errors, save each file using the same filename preceded with *Fix*. For example, DebugOne1.java will become **FixDebugOne1.java**.

   a. DebugOne1.java   c. DebugOne3.java

   b. DebugOne2.java   d. DebugOne4.java

When you change a filename, remember to change every instance of the class name within the file so that it matches the new filename. In Java, the filename and class name must always match.

Game Zone

1. In 1952, A. S. Douglas wrote his University of Cambridge Ph.D. dissertation on human-computer interaction, and created the first graphical computer game—a version of Tic-Tac-Toe. The game was programmed on an EDSAC vacuum-tube mainframe computer. The first computer game is generally assumed to be "Spacewar!", developed in 1962 at MIT; the first commercially available video game was "Pong," introduced by Atari in 1973. In 1980, Atari's "Asteroids" and "Lunar Lander" became the first video games to be registered in the U. S. Copyright Office. Throughout the 1980s, players spent hours with games that now seem very simple and unglamorous; do you recall playing "Adventure," "Oregon Trail," "Where in the World Is Carmen Sandiego?," or "Myst"?

   Today, commercial computer games are much more complex; they require many programmers, graphic artists, and testers to develop them, and large management and marketing staffs are needed to promote them. A game might cost many millions of dollars to develop and market, but a successful game might earn hundreds of millions of dollars. Obviously, with the brief introduction to programming you have had in this chapter, you cannot create a very sophisticated game. However, you can get started.

For games to hold your interest, they almost always include some random, unpredictable behavior. For example, a game in which you shoot asteroids loses some of its fun if the asteroids follow the same, predictable path each time you play the game. Therefore, generating random values is a key component in creating most interesting computer games.

Appendix D contains information on generating random numbers. To fully understand the process, you must learn more about Java classes and methods. However, for now, you can copy the following statement to generate and use a dialog box that displays a random number between 1 and 10:

```
JOptionPane.showMessageDialog(null,"The  number  is  "+
  (1  +  (int)(Math.random()  *  10)));
```

Write a Java application that displays two dialog boxes in sequence. The first asks you to think of a number between 1 and 10. The second displays a randomly generated number; the user can see whether his or her guess was accurate. (In future chapters, you will improve this game so that the user can enter a guess and the program can determine whether the user was correct. If you wish, you also can tell the user how far off the guess was, whether the guess was high or low, and provide a specific number of repeat attempts.) Save the file as **RandomGuess.java**.

Case Problems

The case problems in this section introduce two fictional businesses. Throughout this book, you will create increasingly complex classes for these businesses that use the newest concepts you have mastered in each chapter.

1. Carly's Catering provides meals for parties and special events. Write a program that displays Carly's motto, which is "Carly's makes the food that makes it a party." Save the file as **CarlysMotto.java**. Create a second program that displays the motto surrounded by a border composed of asterisks. Save the file as **CarlysMotto2.java**.

2. Sammy's Seashore Supplies rents beach equipment such as kayaks, canoes, beach chairs, and umbrellas to tourists. Write a program that displays Sammy's motto, which is "Sammy's makes it fun in the sun." Save the file as **SammysMotto.java**. Create a second program that displays the motto surrounded by a border composed of repeated *S*s. Save the file as **SammysMotto2.java**.

A NOTE ON JAVA APPLETS

An applet is a Java program that is called within another application—often a Web browser. The name *applet* means "little application." In other words, an applet is not a full-blown program; it relies on other programs to execute it.

 Many of an applet's behaviors come from methods that reside in a Java class named JApplet. You will see a couple of references to this class in this book.

Applets were introduced with the first version of Java released in 1995, and became very popular immediately because they were considered easier to write than Java programs. However, applets have caused multiple security problems in recent years, so most browsers no longer run applets unless they have a signed certificate from an authority who has verified the sender. A certificate of authority vouches for the applet's creator, providing a degree of confidence that the applet can be trusted not to contain malicious code that can harm the local computer or steal data. Unsigned applets are no longer accepted by most browsers, so professional applet developers are required to purchase certificates from authorities and renew them annually.

Because of the difficulties imposed by certificate requirements, applet writing is not covered in this book. However, after you have learned to write Java applications, learning to write applets is relatively easy because they use the same syntax, contain many of the same elements, are saved using the same .java file extension, and are compiled in the same way. If you encounter an applet on the job, you can recognize it because of the following features in the code:

- The phrase extends JApplet appears after the class name.

- Unlike the applications introduced in this chapter, applets do not contain a main() method. Instead, they contain one or more of the following method identifiers: init(), start(), paint(), stop(), and destroy().

CHAPTER 2

Using Data

In this chapter, you will:

◎ Declare and use constants and variables

◎ Use integer data types

◎ Use the `boolean` data type

◎ Use floating-point data types

◎ Use the `char` data type

◎ Use the `Scanner` class to accept keyboard input

◎ Use the `JOptionPane` class to accept GUI input

◎ Perform arithmetic

◎ Understand type conversion

Declaring and Using Constants and Variables

A data item is **constant** when its value cannot be changed while a program is running. For example, when you include the following statement in a Java class, the number 459 is a constant:

```
System.out.println(459);
```

Every time an application containing the constant 459 is executed, the value 459 is displayed. Programmers refer to a number like 459 in several ways:

- It is a **literal constant** because its value is taken literally at each use.

- It is a **numeric constant** as opposed to a character or string constant.

- It is an **unnamed constant** as opposed to a named one, because no identifier is associated with it.

Instead of using constant data, you can set up a data item to be variable. A **variable** is a named memory location that can store a value. A variable can hold only one value at a time, but the value it holds can change. For example, if you create a variable named ovenTemperature, it might hold 0 when the application starts, later be altered to hold 350, and still later be altered to hold 400.

Whether a data item is variable or constant, in Java it always has a data type. An item's **data type** describes the type of data that can be stored there, how much memory the item occupies, and what types of operations can be performed on the data. Java provides for eight primitive types of data. A **primitive type** is a simple data type. Java's eight data types are described in Table 2-1. Later in this chapter, you will learn more specific information about several of these data types.

Keyword	Description
byte	Byte-length integer
short	Short integer
int	Integer
long	Long integer
float	Single-precision floating point
double	Double-precision floating point
char	A single character
boolean	A Boolean value (true or false)

Table 2-1   Java primitive data types

The eight data types in Table 2-1 are called *primitive* because they are simple and uncomplicated. Primitive types also serve as the building blocks for more complex data types, called **reference types**, which hold memory addresses. The classes you will begin creating in Chapter 3 are examples of reference types, as are the System class you used in Chapter 1 and the Scanner class you will use later in this chapter.

Declaring Variables

A **variable declaration** is a statement that reserves a named memory location and includes the following:

- A data type that identifies the type of data that the variable will store

- An identifier that is the variable's name

- An optional assignment operator and assigned value, if you want a variable to contain an initial value

- An ending semicolon

Variable names must be legal Java identifiers. (You learned the requirements for legal identifiers in Chapter 1.) Basically, a variable name must start with a letter and cannot be a reserved keyword. You must declare a variable before you can use it. You can declare a variable at any point before you use it, but it is common practice to declare variables first in a method and to place executable statements after the declarations. Java is a **strongly typed language**, or one in which each variable has a well-defined data type that limits the operations you can perform with it; strong typing implies that all variables must be declared before they can be used.

Variable names conventionally begin with lowercase letters to distinguish them from class names. However, as with class names, a program can compile without error even if names are constructed unconventionally. Beginning an identifier with a lowercase letter and capitalizing subsequent words within the identifier is a style known as **camel casing**. An identifier such as lastName resembles a camel because of the uppercase "hump" in the middle.

For example, the following declaration creates a conventionally named int variable, myAge, and assigns it an initial value of 25:

```
int myAge = 25;
```

This declaration is a complete, executable statement, so it ends with a semicolon. The equal sign (=) is the **assignment operator**. Any value to the right of the assignment operator is assigned to the memory location named on the left. An assignment made when you declare a variable is an **initialization**; an assignment made later is simply an **assignment**. Thus, the first statement that follows is an initialization, and the second is an assignment:

```
int myAge = 25;
myAge = 42;
```

You declare a variable just once in a method, but you might assign new values to it any number of times.

Note that an expression with a literal to the left of the assignment operator (such as 25 = myAge) is illegal. The assignment operator has right-to-left associativity. **Associativity** refers to the order in which values are used with operators. The associativity of every operator is either right-to-left or left-to-right. An identifier that can appear on the left side of an assignment operator sometimes is referred to as an **lvalue**, and an item that can appear only on the right side of an assignment operator is an **rvalue**. A variable can be used as an lvalue or an rvalue, but a literal constant can only be an rvalue.

When you declare a variable within a method but do not assign a value to it, it is an **uninitialized variable**. For example, the following variable declaration declares a variable of type int named myAge, but no value is assigned at the time of creation:

```
int myAge;
```

An uninitialized variable contains an unknown value called a **garbage value**. Java protects you from inadvertently using the garbage value that is stored in an uninitialized variable. For example, if you attempt to display garbage or use it as part of a calculation, you receive an error message stating that the variable might not have been initialized, and the program will not compile.

When you learn about creating classes in the chapter "Using Methods, Classes, and Objects," you will discover that variables declared in a class, but outside any method, are automatically initialized for you.

You can declare multiple variables of the same type in separate statements. You also can declare two or more variables of the same type in a single statement by separating the variable declarations with a comma, as shown in the following statement:

```
int height = 70, weight = 190;
```

By convention, many programmers declare each variable in its own separate statement, but some follow the convention of declaring multiple variables in the same statement if their purposes are closely related. Remember that even if a statement occupies multiple lines, the statement is not complete until the semicolon is reached.

You can declare as many variables in a statement as you want, as long as the variables are the same data type. However, if you want to declare variables of different types, you must use a separate statement for each type.

Declaring Named Constants

A variable is a named memory location for which the contents can change. If a named location's value should not change during the execution of a program, you can create it to be a **named constant**. A named constant is also known as a **symbolic constant**. A named constant is similar to a variable in that it has a data type, a name, and a value. A named constant differs from a variable in several ways:

- In its declaration statement, the data type of a named constant is preceded by the keyword **final**.

- A named constant can be assigned a value only once, and then it cannot be changed later in the program. Usually you initialize a named constant when you declare it; if you do not initialize the constant at declaration, it is known as a **blank final**, and you can assign a value later. Either way, you must assign a value to a constant before it is used.

- Although it is not a requirement, named constants conventionally are given identifiers using all uppercase letters, using underscores as needed to separate words.

For example, each of the following defines a conventionally named constant:

```
final int NUMBER_OF_DEPTS = 20;
final double PI = 3.14159;
final double TAX_RATE = 0.015;
final string COMPANY = "ABC Manufacturing";
```

You can use each of these named constants anywhere you use a variable of the same type, except on the left side of an assignment statement after the first value has been assigned. In other words, when it receives a value, a named constant is an lvalue, but after the assignment, a named constant is an rvalue.

A constant always has the same value within a program, so you might wonder why you should not use the actual, literal value. For example, why not use the unnamed constant *20* when you need the number of departments in a company rather than going to the trouble of creating the NUMBER_OF_DEPTS named constant? There are several good reasons to use the named constant rather than the literal one:

- The number 20 is more easily recognized as the number of departments if it is associated with an identifier. Using named constants makes your programs easier to read and understand. Some programmers refer to the use of a literal numeric constant, such as 20, as using a **magic number**—a value that does not have immediate, intuitive meaning or a number that cannot be explained without additional knowledge. For example, you might write a program that uses the value 7 for several purposes, so you might use constants such as DAYS_IN_WEEK and NUM_RETAIL_OUTLETS that both hold the value 7 but more clearly describe the purposes. Avoiding magic numbers helps provide internal documentation for your programs.

- If the number of departments in your organization changes, you would change the value of NUMBER_OF_DEPTS at one location within your program—where the constant is defined— rather than searching for every use of 20 to change it to a different number. Being able to make the change at one location saves you time, and prevents you from missing a reference to the number of departments.

- Even if you are willing to search for every instance of 20 in a program to change it to the new department number value, you might inadvertently change the value of one instance of 20 that is being used for something else, such as a payroll deduction value.

- Using named constants reduces typographical errors. For example, if you must include 20 at several places within a program, you might inadvertently type 10 or 200 for one of the instances, and the compiler will not recognize the mistake. However, if you use the identifier NUMBER_OF_DEPTS, the compiler will ensure that you spell it correctly.

- When you use a named constant in an expression, it stands out as different from a variable. For example, in the following arithmetic statement, it is easy to see which elements are variable and which are constant because the constants have been named conventionally using all uppercase letters and underscores to separate words:

```
double payAmount = hoursWorked * STD_PAY_RATE -
    numDependents * DEDUCTION;
```

Although many programmers use named constants to stand for most of the constant values in their programs, many make an exception when using 0 or 1.

The Scope of Variables and Constants

A data item's **scope** is the area in which it is visible to a program and in which you can refer to it using its simple identifier. A variable or constant is in scope from the point it is declared until the end of the block of code in which the declaration lies. A **block of code** is the code contained between a set of curly braces. So, if you declare a variable or constant within a method, it can be used from its declaration until the end of the method unless the method contains multiple sets of curly braces. Then, a data item is usable only until the end of the block that holds the declaration.

 In the chapter "Using Methods, Classes, and Objects," you will start to create classes that contain multiple sets of curly braces. In the chapter "More Object Concepts," you will learn some techniques for using variables that are not currently in scope.

Concatenating Strings to Variables and Constants

As you learned in Chapter 1, you can use a print() or println() statement for console output. The only difference between them is that the println() statement starts a new line after output. You can display a variable or a constant in a print() or println() statement alone or in combination with a string. For example, the NumbersPrintln class shown in Figure 2-1 declares an integer billingDate, which is initialized to 5. In the first shaded statement, the value of billingDate is sent alone to the print() method; in the second shaded statement, billingDate is combined with, or **concatenated** to, a String. In Java, when a numeric variable is concatenated to a String using the plus sign, the entire expression becomes a String. In Figure 2-1, print() and println() method calls are used to display different data types, including simple Strings, an int, and a concatenated String. The output of the application shown in Figure 2-1 appears in Figure 2-2.

```
public class NumbersPrintln
{
    public static void main(String[] args)
    {
        int billingDate = 5;
        System.out.print("Bills are sent on day ");
        System.out.print(billingDate);
        System.out.println(" of the month");
        System.out.println("Next bill: October " +
            billingDate);
    }
}
```

Figure 2-1   NumbersPrintln class

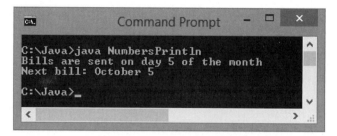

Figure 2-2   Output of NumbersPrintln application

The last output statement in Figure 2-1 is spread across two lines because it is relatively long. The statement could be written on a single line, or it could break to a new line before or after either parenthesis or before or after the plus sign. When a line is long and contains a plus sign, this book will follow the convention of breaking the line following the sign. When you are reading a line, seeing a plus sign at the end makes it easier for you to recognize that the statement continues on the following line.

Later in this chapter, you will learn that a plus sign (+) between two numeric values indicates an addition operation. However, when you place a string on one or both sides of a plus sign, concatenation occurs. In Chapter 1, you learned that *polymorphism* describes the feature of languages that allows the same word or symbol to be interpreted correctly in different situations based on the context. The plus sign is polymorphic in that it indicates concatenation when used with strings but addition when used with numbers.

When you concatenate Strings with numbers, the entire expression is a String. Therefore, the expression "A" + 3 + 4 results in the String "A34". If your intention is to create the String "A7", then you could add parentheses to write "A" + (3 + 4) so that the numeric expression is evaluated first.

The program in Figure 2-1 uses the command line to display output, but you also can use a dialog box. Recall from Chapter 1 that you can use the showMessageDialog() method with two arguments: null, which indicates the box should appear in the center of the screen, and the String to be displayed in the box. Figure 2-3 shows a NumbersDialog class that uses the showMessageDialog() method twice to display an integer declared as creditDays and initialized to 30. In each shaded statement in the class, the numeric variable is concatenated to a String, making the entire second argument a String. In the first shaded statement, the concatenated String is an empty String (or **null** String), created by typing a set of quotes with nothing between them. The application produces the two dialog boxes shown in Figures 2-4 and 2-5. The first dialog box shows just the value 30; after it is dismissed by clicking OK, the second dialog box appears.

```
import javax.swing.JOptionPane;
public class NumbersDialog
{
   public static void main(String[] args)
   {
      int creditDays = 30;
      JOptionPane.showMessageDialog(null, "" + creditDays);
      JOptionPane.showMessageDialog
         (null, "Every bill is due in " + creditDays + " days");
   }
}
```

Figure 2-3   NumbersDialog class

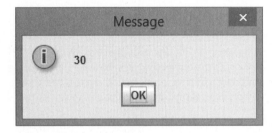

Figure 2-4   First dialog box created by NumbersDialog application

Figure 2-5   Second dialog box created by NumbersDialog application

Pitfall: Forgetting that a Variable Holds One Value at a Time

Each variable can hold just one value at a time. Suppose you have two variables, x and y, and x
holds 2 and y holds 10. Suppose further that you want to switch their values so that x holds 10
and y holds 2. You cannot simply make an assignment such as x = y because then both

variables will hold 10, and the 2 will be lost. Similarly, if you make the assignment y = x, then both variables will hold 2, and the 10 will be lost. The solution is to declare and use a third variable, as in the following sequence of events:

```
int x = 2, y = 10, z;
z = x;
x = y;
y = z;
```

In this example, the third variable, z, is used as a temporary holding spot for one of the original values. The variable z is assigned the value of x, so z becomes 2. Then the value of y, 10, is assigned to x. Finally, the 2 held in z is assigned to y. The extra variable is used because as soon as you assign a value to a variable, any value that was previously in the memory location is gone.

 Watch the video *Declaring Variables and Constants*.

TWO TRUTHS & A LIE

Declaring and Using Constants and Variables

1. A variable is a named memory location that you can use to store a value; it can hold only one value at a time, but the value it holds can change.

2. An item's data type determines what legal identifiers can be used to describe variables and whether the variables can occupy memory.

3. A variable declaration is a statement that reserves a named memory location and includes a data type, an identifier, an optional assignment operator and assigned value, and an ending semicolon.

The false statement is #2. An item's data type describes the type of data that can be stored, how much memory the item occupies, and what types of operations can be performed on the data. The data type does not alter the rules for a legal identifier, and the data type does not determine whether variables can occupy memory—all variables occupy memory.

You Do It

Declaring and Using a Variable

In this section, you write an application to work with a variable and a constant.

1. Open a new document in your text editor. Create a class header and an opening and closing curly brace for a new class named `DataDemo` by typing the following:

```
public class DataDemo
{
}
```

2. Between the curly braces, indent a few spaces and type the following `main()` method header and its curly braces:

```
public static void main(String[] args)
{
}
```

3. Between the `main()` method's curly braces, type the following variable declaration:

```
int aWholeNumber = 315;
```

4. Type the following output statements. The first uses the `print()` method to display a string that includes a space before the closing quotation mark and leaves the insertion point for the next output on the same line. The second statement uses `println()` to display the value of `aWholeNumber` and then advance to a new line.

```
System.out.print("The number is ");
System.out.println(aWholeNumber);
```

5. Save the file as **DataDemo.java**.

6. Up to this point in the book, every `print()` and `println()` statement you have seen has used a `String` as an argument. When you added the last two statements to the `DataDemo` class, you wrote a `println()` statement that uses an `int` as an argument. As a matter of fact, there are many different versions of `print()` and `println()` that use different data types. Go to the Java Web site (***www.oracle.com/technetwork/java/index.html***), select **Java APIs**, and then select **Java SE 8**. Scroll through the list of **All Classes**, and select **PrintStream**; you will recall from Chapter 1 that `PrintStream` is the data type for the `out` object used with the `println()` method. Scroll down to view the list of methods in the **Method Summary**, and notice the many versions of the `print()` and `println()` methods, including ones that accept a `String`, an `int`, a `long`, and so on. In the last two statements you added to this program, one used a method version that accepts a `String` and the other used a method version that

(continues)

(continued)

accepts an `int`. Recall that the ability of a method to work appropriately depending on the context is *polymorphism*.

7. Compile the file from the command line by typing **javac DataDemo.java**. If necessary, correct any errors, save the file, and then compile again.

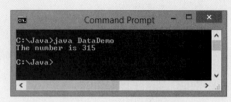

8. Execute the application from the command line by typing **java DataDemo**. The command window output is shown in Figure 2-6.

Figure 2-6 Output of the `DataDemo` application

Trying to Use an Uninitialized Variable

In this section, you see what happens when a variable is uninitialized.

1. In the `DataDemo` class, remove the assignment operator and the initialization value of the `aWholeNumber` variable so the declaration becomes:

   ```
   int aWholeNumber;
   ```

2. Save the class and recompile it. An error message appears as shown in Figure 2-7. Notice that the declaration statement does not generate an error because you can declare a variable without initializing it. However, the `println()` statement generates the error message because in Java, you cannot display an uninitialized variable.

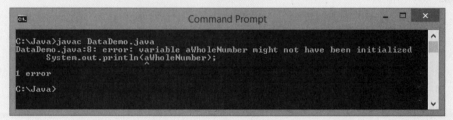

Figure 2-7 Error message generated when a variable is not initialized

3. Modify the `aWholeNumber` declaration so that the variable is again initialized to 315. Compile the class, and execute it again.

Adding a Named Constant to a Program

In this section, you add a named constant to the `DataDemo` program.

1. After the declaration of the `aWholeNumber` variable in the `DataDemo` class, insert a new line in your program and type the following constant declaration:

   ```
   final int STATES_IN_US = 50;
   ```

(continues)

(continued)

2. Following the last println() statement in the existing program, add a new statement to display a concatenated string and numeric constant. The println() method call uses the version that accepts a String argument.

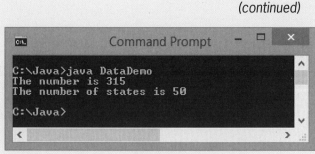

Figure 2-8   Output of DataDemo program after recent changes

```
System.out.println("The number of states is " +
    STATES_IN_US);
```

3. Save the program, and then compile and execute it. The output appears in Figure 2-8.

Learning About Integer Data Types

In Java, you can use variables of data types byte, short, int, and long to store (or hold) integers; an **integer** is a whole number without decimal places.

The int data type is the most commonly used integer type. A variable of type int can hold any whole number value from –2,147,483,648 to +2,147,483,647. When you assign a value to an int variable, you do not type any commas or periods. The newest versions of Java allow underscores in numbers; these typically are used to make long numbers easier to read, as in the following statement:

```
corporateBudget = 8_435_000;
```

However, when you type a number, you usually type only digits and an optional plus or minus sign to indicate a positive or negative integer.

The data types **byte**, **short**, and **long** are all variations of the integer type. The byte and short types occupy less memory and can hold only smaller values; the long type occupies more memory and can hold larger values. Table 2-2 shows the upper and lower value limits for each of these types. In other programming languages, the format and size of primitive data types might depend on the platform on which a program is running. By contrast, Java consistently specifies the size and format of its primitive data types.

Type	Minimum Value	Maximum Value	Size in Bytes
byte	−128	127	1
short	−32,768	32,767	2
int	−2,147,483,648	2,147,483,647	4
long	−9,223,372,036,854,775,808	9,223,372,036,854,775,807	8

Table 2-2   Limits on integer values by type

It is important to choose appropriate types for the variables you will use in an application. If you attempt to assign a value that is too large for the data type of the variable, the compiler issues an error message, and the application does not execute. If you choose a data type that is larger than you need, you waste memory. For example, a personnel application might use a byte variable for number of dependents (because a limit of 127 is more than enough), a short for hours worked in a month (because 127 isn't enough), and an int for an annual salary (because even though a limit of 32,000 might be large enough for your salary, it isn't enough for the CEO's).

 Some famous glitches have occurred because programmers did not pay attention to the limits of various data types. For example, a hospital computer system in Washington, D.C., used the equivalent of a short to count days elapsed since January 1, 1900. The system collapsed on the 32,768th day (which was in 1989), requiring manual operations for a lengthy period.

If an application uses a literal constant integer, such as 932, the number is an int by default. If you need to use a constant higher than 2,147,483,647, the letter L must follow the number to indicate long. For example, the following statement stores a number that is greater than the maximum limit for the int type.

```
long mosquitosInTheNorthWoods = 2444555888L;
```

You can type either an uppercase or a lowercase L after the digits to indicate the long type, but the uppercase L is preferred to avoid confusion with the number 1. You don't need any special notation to store a numeric constant in an int, byte, or a short.

Because integer constants, such as 18, are type int by default, the examples in this book almost always declare a variable as type int when the variable's purpose is to hold a whole number. That is, even if the expected value is less than 128, such as hoursWorkedToday, this book will declare the variable to be an int. If you are writing an application in which saving memory is important, you might choose to declare the same variable as a byte. Saving memory is seldom an issue for an application that runs on a PC. However, when you write applications for small devices with limited memory, like phones, conserving memory becomes more important.

TWO TRUTHS & A LIE

Learning About Integer Data Types

1. A variable of type `int` can hold any whole number value from approximately negative two billion to positive two billion.

2. When you assign a value to an `int` variable, you do not type any commas; you type only digits and an optional plus or minus sign to indicate a positive or negative integer.

3. You can use the data types `byte` or `short` to hold larger values than can be accommodated by an `int`.

The false statement is #3. You use a long if you know you will be working with very large values; you use a byte or a short if you know a variable will need to hold only small values.

You Do It

Working with Integers

In this section, you work more with integer values.

1. Open a new file in your text editor, and create a shell for an `IntegerDemo` class as follows:

```
public class IntegerDemo
{
}
```

2. Between the curly braces, indent a few spaces and write the shell for a `main()` method as follows:

```
public static void main(String[] args)
{
}
```

3. Within the `main()` method, create four declarations, one each for the four integer data types.

```
int anInt = 12;
byte aByte = 12;
short aShort = 12;
long aLong = 12;
```

(continues)

(continued)

4. Next, add four output statements that describe and display each of the values. The spaces are included at the ends of the string literals so that the values will be aligned vertically when they are displayed.

```
System.out.println("The int is   " + anInt);
System.out.println("The byte is  " + aByte);
System.out.println("The short is " + aShort);
System.out.println("The long is  " + aLong);
```

5. Save the file as **IntegerDemo.java**. Then compile and execute it. Figure 2-9 shows the output. All the values are legal sizes for each data type, so the program compiles and executes without error.

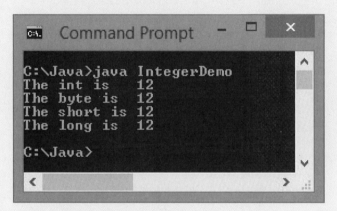

Figure 2-9 Output of the IntegerDemo program

6. Change each assigned value in the application from 12 to **1234**, and then save and recompile the program. Figure 2-10 shows the error message generated because 1234 is too large to be placed in a byte variable. The message "possible lossy conversion from int to byte" means that if the large number had been inserted into the small space, the accuracy of the number would have been compromised. A **lossy conversion** is one in which some data is lost. The opposite of a lossy conversion is a **lossless conversion**—one in which no data is lost. (The error message differs in other development environments and in some earlier versions of Java.)

(continues)

68

(continued)

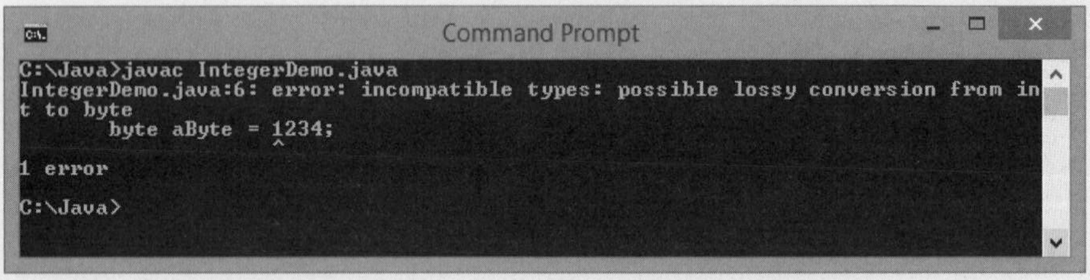

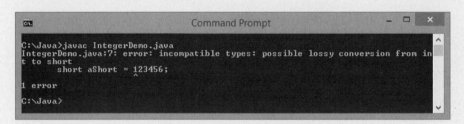

Figure 2-10   Error message generated when a value that is too large is assigned to a byte variable

7.   Change the value of aByte back to **12**. Change the value of aShort to **123456**. Save and recompile the program. Figure 2-11 shows the result. The error message "possible lossy conversion" is the same as when the byte value was invalid, but the error indicates that the problem is now with the short variable.

Figure 2-11   Error message generated when a value that is too large is assigned to a short variable

8.   Change the value of the short variable to **12345**, and then save and compile the program. Now, the program compiles without error. Execute the program, and confirm that it runs as expected.

9.   At the Java Web site (*www.oracle.com/technetwork/java/index.html*), examine the list of println() methods in the PrintStream class. Although you can find versions that accept String, int, and long arguments, you cannot find ones that accept byte or short values. Yet, the println() statements in the latest version of the program work correctly. The reason has to do with *type conversion*, which you will learn about later in this chapter.

10.   Replace the value of aLong with **1234567890987654321**. Save the program and compile it. Figure 2-12 shows the error message that indicates that the integer number is too large. The message does not say that the value is too big for a long type variable. Instead, it means that the literal constant was evaluated and found to be too large to be a default int before any attempt was made to store it in the long variable.

(continues)

```
C:\Java>javac IntegerDemo.java
IntegerDemo.java:8: error: integer number too large: 1234567890987654321
        long aLong = 1234567890987654321;
                     ^
1 error

C:\Java>
```

Figure 2-12 Error message generated when a value that is too large is assigned to a `long` variable

11. Remedy the problem by adding an **L** to the end of the `long` numeric value. Now, the constant is the correct data type that can be assigned to the `long` variable. Save, compile, and execute the program; it executes successfully.

12. Watch out for errors that occur when data values are acceptable for a data type when used alone, but together might produce arithmetic results that are out of range. To demonstrate, add the following declaration at the end of the current list of variable declarations in the `IntegerDemo` program:

```
int anotherInt = anInt * 10000000;
```

13. At the end of the current list of output statements, add another output statement so that you can see the result of the arithmetic:

```
System.out.println("Another int is " + anotherInt);
```

Save, compile, and execute the program. The output appears in Figure 2-13. Although 1234 and 10000000 are both acceptable `int` values, their product is out of range for an `int`, and the resulting `int` does not appear to have been calculated correctly. Because the arithmetic result was too large, some information about the value has been lost, including the result's sign. If you see such unreasonable results in your programs, you need to consider using different data types for your values.

```
C:\Java>javac IntegerDemo.java

C:\Java>java IntegerDemo
The int is    1234
The byte is   12
The short is 12345
The long is   1234567890987654321
Another int is -544901888

C:\Java>
```

Figure 2-13 Output of the modified `IntegerDemo` program with an out-of-range integer

Using the `boolean` Data Type

Boolean logic is based on true or false comparisons. Whereas an `int` variable can hold millions of different values (at different times), a **boolean variable** can hold only one of two values—`true` or `false`. The following statements declare and assign appropriate values to Boolean variables:

```
boolean isItPayday = false;
boolean areYouBroke = true;
```

Although you can use any legal identifier for Boolean variables, they are easily identified as Boolean if you use a form of *to be* (such as *is* or *are*) as part of the variable name, as in `isItPayday`.

Besides assigning `true` and `false`, you also can assign a value to a Boolean variable based on the result of a comparison. Java supports six relational operators that are used to make comparisons. A **relational operator** compares two items; it is sometimes called a **comparison operator**. The value of an expression that contains a relational operator is always `true` or `false`. Table 2-3 describes the relational operators.

 When you use *Boolean* as an adjective, as in *Boolean operators*, you usually begin with an uppercase *B* because the data type is named for Sir George Boole, the founder of symbolic logic, who lived from 1815 to 1864. The Java data type `boolean`, however, begins with a lowercase *b*.

Operator	Description	True Example	False Example
<	Less than	3 < 8	8 < 3
>	Greater than	4 > 2	2 > 4
==	Equal to	7 == 7	3 == 9
<=	Less than or equal to	5 <= 5	8 <= 6
>=	Greater than or equal to	7 >= 3	1 >= 2
!=	Not equal to	5 != 6	3 != 3

Table 2-3   Relational operators

When you use any of the operators that have two symbols (`==`, `<=`, `>=`, or `!=`), you cannot place any whitespace between the two symbols. You also cannot reverse the order of the symbols. That is, `=<`, `=>`, and `=!` are all invalid operators.

Legal declaration statements might include the following statements, which compare two values directly:

```
boolean isSixBigger = (6 > 5);
 // Value stored would be true
boolean isSevenSmallerOrEqual = (7 <= 4);
 // Value stored would be false
```

Boolean expressions are more meaningful when a variable is used for one or both of the operands in a comparison, as in the following three examples, in which a variable is compared to a literal constant (40), a variable is compared to a named constant (HIGH_CUTOFF), and two variables are compared.

```
boolean isOvertimePay = (hours > 40);
boolean isTaxBracketHigh = (income > HIGH_CUTOFF);
boolean isFirstScoreHigher = (score1 > score2);
```

Boolean expressions will become far more useful to you when you learn about decision making and looping in Chapters 5 and 6.

TWO TRUTHS & A LIE

Using the boolean Data Type

1. A Boolean variable can hold only one of two values—true or false.

2. Java supports six relational operators that are used to make comparisons: =, <, >, =<, =>, and =!.

3. An expression that contains a relational operator has a Boolean value.

The false statement is #2. The six relational operators used to make comparisons are == (two equal signs), <, >, <= (the less-than sign precedes the equal sign), >= (the greater-than sign precedes the equal sign), and != (the exclamation point precedes the equal sign).

Learning About Floating-Point Data Types

A **floating-point** number contains decimal positions. Java supports two floating-point data types: float and double. A **float** data type can hold floating-point values of up to six or seven significant digits of accuracy. A **double** data type requires more memory than a float, and can hold 14 or 15 significant digits of accuracy. The term **significant digits** refers to the mathematical accuracy of a value. For example, a float given the value 0.324616777 is displayed as 0.324617 because the value is accurate only to the sixth decimal position. Table 2-4 shows the minimum and maximum values for each floating-point data type. Notice that the maximum value for a double is $3.4 * 10$ to the 38th power, which means 3.4 times 10 with 38 trailing zeros—a very large number.

Depending on the environment in which you run your program, a float given the value 324616777 is displayed using a decimal point after the 3 and only six or seven digits followed by e+008 or E8. This format is called **scientific notation**, and means that the value is approximately 3.24617 times 10 to the 8th power, or 324617000. The e in the displayed value stands for *exponent*; the 8 means the true decimal point is eight positions to the right of where it is displayed, indicating a very large number. (A negative number following the e would mean that the true decimal point belongs to the left, indicating a very small number.)

A programmer might choose to store a value as a float instead of a double to save memory. However, if high levels of accuracy are needed, such as in graphics-intensive software, the programmer might choose to use a double, opting for high accuracy over saved memory.

Type	Minimum	Maximum	Size in Bytes
float	$-3.4 * 10^{38}$	$3.4 * 10^{38}$	4
double	$-1.7 * 10^{308}$	$1.7 * 10^{308}$	8

Table 2-4   Limits on floating-point values

A value stored in a double is a **double-precision floating-point number**; a value in a float is a **single-precision floating-point number**.

Just as an integer constant, such as 18, is a value of type int by default, a floating-point constant, such as 18.23, is a double by default. To indicate that a floating-point numeric constant is a float, you can type the letter *F* after the number, as in the following:

```
float pocketChange = 4.87F;
```

You can type either a lowercase or an uppercase *F*. You also can type *D* (or *d*) after a floating-point constant to indicate it is a double, but even without the *D*, the value will be stored as a double by default. Floating-point numbers can be imprecise, as you will see later in this chapter.

TWO TRUTHS & A LIE

Learning About Floating-Point Data Types

1. Java supports two floating-point data types: float and double. The double data type requires more memory and can hold more significant digits.

2. A floating-point constant, such as 5.6, is a float by default.

3. As with integers, you can perform the mathematical operations of addition, subtraction, multiplication, and division with floating-point numbers.

The false statement is #2. A floating-point constant, such as 5.6, is a double by default.

Using the char Data Type

You use the **char** data type to hold any single character. You place constant character values within single quotation marks because the computer stores characters and integers differently. For example, the following are typical character declarations:

```
char middleInitial = 'M';
char gradeInChemistry = 'A';
char aStar = '*';
```

Some programmers prefer to pronounce *char* as *care* because it represents the first syllable in the word *character*. Others prefer to pronounce the word as *char* to rhyme with *car*. You should use the preferred pronunciation in your organization.

A character can be any letter—uppercase or lowercase. It might also be a punctuation mark or digit. A character that is a digit is represented in computer memory differently than a numeric value represented by the same digit. For example, the following two statements are legal:

```
char aCharValue = '9';
int aNumValue = 9;
```

If you display each of these values using a println() statement, you see a 9. However, only the numeric value, aNumValue, can be used to represent the value 9 in arithmetic statements.

A numeric constant can be stored in a character variable and a character that represents a number can be stored in a numeric variable. For example, the following two statements are legal, but unless you understand their meanings, they might produce undesirable results:

```
char aCharValue = 9;
int aNumValue = '9';
```

If these variables are displayed using println() statements, then the resulting output is a blank for aCharValue and the number 57 for aNumValue. The unexpected values are Unicode values. Every computer stores every character it uses as a number; every character is assigned a unique numeric code using Unicode. Table 2-5 shows some Unicode decimal values and their character equivalents. For example, the character *A* is stored using the value 65, and the character *B* is stored using the value 66. Appendix B contains more information on Unicode.

Dec	Char	Dec	Char	Dec	Char	Dec	Char
0	nul	32		64	@	96	`
1	soh^A	33	!	65	A	97	a
2	stx^B	34	"	66	B	98	b
3	etx^C	35	#	67	C	99	c
4	eot^D	36	$	68	D	100	d
5	enq^E	37	%	69	E	101	e
6	ask^F	38	&	70	F	102	f
7	bel^G	39	'	71	G	103	g
8	bs^H	40	(	72	H	104	h
9	ht^I	41	)	73	I	105	i
10	lf^J	42	*	74	J	106	j

Table 2-5   Unicode values 0 through 127 and their character equivalents (*continues*)

(continued)

Dec	Char	Dec	Char	Dec	Char	Dec	Char
11	vt^K	43	+	75	K	107	k
12	ff^L	44	,	76	L	108	l
13	cr^M	45	-	77	M	109	m
14	so^N	46	.	78	N	110	n
15	si^O	47	/	79	O	111	o
16	dle^P	48	0	80	P	112	p
17	dc1^Q	49	1	81	Q	113	q
18	dc2^R	50	2	82	R	114	r
19	dc3^S	51	3	83	S	115	s
20	dc4^T	52	4	84	T	116	t
21	nak^U	53	5	85	U	117	u
22	syn^V	54	6	86	V	118	v
23	etb^W	55	7	87	W	119	w
24	can^X	56	8	88	X	120	x
25	em^Y	57	9	89	Y	121	y
26	sub^Z	58	:	90	Z	122	z
27	esc	59	;	91	[	123	{
28	fs	60	<	92	\	124		
29	gs	61	=	93	]	125	}
30	rs	62	>	94	^	126	~
31	us	63	?	95	_	127	del

Table 2-5   Unicode values 0 through 127 and their character equivalents

A variable of type char can hold only one character. To store a string of characters, such as a person's name, you must use a data structure called a String. In Java, **String** is a built-in class that provides you with the means for storing and manipulating character strings. Unlike single characters, which use single quotation marks, string constants are written between double quotation marks. For example, the expression that stores the name *Audrey* as a string in a variable named firstName is:

```
String firstName = "Audrey";
```

You will learn more about strings and the String class in the chapter "Characters, Strings, and the StringBuilder."

You can store any character—including nonprinting characters such as a backspace or a tab—in a char variable. To store these characters, you can use an **escape sequence**, which always begins with a backslash followed by a character—the pair represents a single character. For example, the following code stores a newline character and a tab character in the char variables aNewLine and aTabChar:

```
char aNewLine = '\n';
char aTabChar = '\t';
```

In the declarations of aNewLine and aTabChar, the backslash and character pair acts as a single character; the escape sequence serves to give a new meaning to the character. That is, the literal characters in the preceding code have different values from the "plain" characters 'n' or 't'. Table 2-6 describes some common escape sequences that you can use with command window output in Java.

Escape Sequence	Description
\b	Backspace; moves the cursor one space to the left
\t	Tab; moves the cursor to the next tab stop
\n	Newline or linefeed; moves the cursor to the beginning of the next line
\r	Carriage return; moves the cursor to the beginning of the current line
\"	Double quotation mark; displays a double quotation mark
\'	Single quotation mark; displays a single quotation mark
\\	Backslash; displays a backslash character

Table 2-6   Common escape sequences

When you display values within JOptionPane dialog boxes rather than in a command window, the escape sequences '\n' (newline), '\"' (double quote), and '\\' (backslash) operate as expected within a JOptionPane object, but '\t', '\b', and '\r' do not work in the GUI environment.

When you want to produce console output on multiple lines in the command window, you have two options: You can use the newline escape sequence, or you can use the println() method multiple times. For example, Figures 2-14 and 2-15 both show classes that produce the same output: "Hello" on one line and "there" on another. The version you choose to use is up to you. The example in Figure 2-14 is more efficient—from a typist's point of view because the text System.out.println appears only once, and from the compiler's point of view because the println() method is called only once. The example in Figure 2-15, however, might be easier to read and understand. When programming in Java, you will find occasions when each of these approaches makes sense.

76

```
public class HelloThereNewLine
{
    public static void main(String[] args)
    {
        System.out.println("Hello\nthere");
    }
}
```

Figure 2-14 HelloThereNewLine class

```
public class HelloTherePrintlnTwice
{
    public static void main(String[] args)
    {
        System.out.println("Hello");
        System.out.println("there");
    }
}
```

Figure 2-15 HelloTherePrintlnTwice class

The println() method uses the local platform's line terminator character, which might or might not be the newline character '\n'.

TWO TRUTHS & A LIE

Using the char Data Type

1. You use the char data type to hold any single character; you place constant character values within single quotation marks.

2. To store a string of characters, you use a data structure called a Text; string constants are written between parentheses.

3. An escape sequence always begins with a backslash followed by a character; the pair represents a single character.

The false statement is #2. To store a string of characters, you use a data structure called a String; string constants are written between double quotation marks.

You Do It

Working with the char Data Type

In the steps in this section, you create an application that demonstrates some features of the char data type.

1. Create the shells for a class named CharDemo and its main() method as follows:

```
public class CharDemo
{
   public static void main(String[] args)
   {
   }
}
```

2. Between the curly braces for the main() method, declare a char variable, and provide an initialization value:

```
char initial = 'A';
```

3. Add two statements. The first displays the variable, and the second demonstrates some escape sequence characters.

```
System.out.println(initial);
System.out.print("\t\"abc\\def\bghi\n\njkl");
```

4. Save the file as **CharDemo.java**, and then compile and execute it. Figure 2-16 shows the output. The first line of output contains the value of the char variable. The next line starts with a tab created by the escape sequence \t. The tab is followed by a quotation mark produced by the escape sequence \". Then abc is displayed, followed by the next escape sequence that produces a slash. The next series of characters to display is def, but because those letters are followed by a backspace escape sequence, the f is overridden by ghi. After ghi, two newline escape sequences provide a double-spaced effect. Finally, the last three characters jkl are displayed.

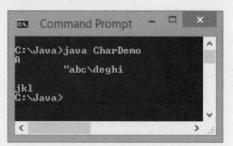

Figure 2-16   Output of the CharDemo program

5. Modify, recompile, and execute the CharDemo program as many times as you like until you can accurately predict what will be displayed when you use various combinations of characters and escape sequences.

Using the Scanner Class to Accept Keyboard Input

Although you can assign values to variables you declare, programs typically become more useful when a user can supply different values for variables each time a program executes. In Chapter 1, you learned how to display output on the monitor using the System.out property. System.out refers to the standard output device, which usually is the monitor. To create interactive programs that accept input from a user, you can use System.in, which refers to the **standard input device** (normally the keyboard).

You have learned that you can use the print() and println() methods to display many data types; for example, you can use them to display a double, int, or String. The System.in object is not as flexible; it is designed to read only bytes. That's a problem, because you often want to accept data of other types. Fortunately, the designers of Java have created a class named Scanner that makes System.in more flexible.

To create a Scanner object and connect it to the System.in object, you write a statement similar to the following:

```
Scanner inputDevice = new Scanner(System.in);
```

The portion of the statement to the left of the assignment operator, Scanner inputDevice, declares an object of type Scanner with the programmer-chosen name inputDevice, in exactly the same way that int x; declares an integer with the programmer-chosen name x.

The portion of the statement to the right of the assignment operator, new Scanner(System.in), creates a Scanner object that is connected to the System.in property. In other words, the created Scanner object is connected to the default input device. The keyword new is required by Java; you will use it whenever you create objects that are more complex than the primitive data types.

In the chapter "More Object Concepts," you will learn that the second part of the Scanner declaration calls a special method called a constructor that is part of the prewritten Scanner class. You also will learn more about the Java keyword new in the next two chapters.

The assignment operator in the Scanner declaration statement assigns the value of the new object—that is, its memory address—to the inputDevice object in the program.

The Scanner class contains methods that retrieve values from an input device. Each retrieved value is a **token**, which is a set of characters that is separated from the next set by whitespace. Most often, this means that data is accepted when a user presses the Enter key, but it could also mean that a token is accepted after a space or tab. Table 2-7 summarizes some of the most useful methods that read different data types from the default input device. Each retrieves a value from the keyboard and returns it if the next token is the correct data type.

Method	Description
nextDouble()	Retrieves input as a double
nextInt()	Retrieves input as an int
nextLine()	Retrieves the next line of data and returns it as a String
next()	Retrieves the next complete token as a String
nextShort()	Retrieves input as a short
nextByte()	Retrieves input as a byte
nextFloat()	Retrieves input as a float. Note that when you enter an input value that will be stored as a float, you do not type an F. The F is used only with constants coded within a program.
nextLong()	Retrieves input as a long. Note that when you enter an input value that will be stored as a long, you do not type an L. The L is used only with constants coded within a program.

Table 2-7   Selected Scanner class methods

The Scanner class does not contain a nextChar() method. To retrieve a single character from the keyboard, you can use the nextLine() method and then use the charAt() method. The chapter "Characters, Strings, and the StringBuilder" provides more details about the charAt() method.

Figure 2-17 contains a program that uses two of the Scanner class methods, and Figure 2-18 shows a typical execution. The program reads a string and an integer from the keyboard and displays them. The Scanner class is used in the four shaded statements in the figure.

- The first shaded statement imports the package necessary to use the Scanner class.

- The second shaded statement declares a Scanner object named inputDevice.

- The third shaded statement uses the nextLine() method to retrieve a line of text from the keyboard and store it in the name variable.

- The last shaded statement uses the nextInt() method to retrieve an integer from the keyboard and store it in the age variable.

Java programmers would say that the Scanner methods *return* the appropriate value. That also means that the value of the method is the appropriate value, and that you can assign the returned value to a variable, display it, or use it in other legal statements. In the chapter "Using Methods, Classes, and Objects," you will learn how to write your own methods that return values.

```
import java.util.Scanner;
public class GetUserInfo
{
    public static void main(String[] args)
    {
        String name;
        int age;
        Scanner inputDevice = new Scanner(System.in);
        System.out.print("Please enter your name >> ");
        name = inputDevice.nextLine();
        System.out.print("Please enter your age >> ");
        age = inputDevice.nextInt();
        System.out.println("Your name is " + name +
            " and you are " + age + " years old.");
    }
}
```

> Repeating as output what a user has entered as input is called **echoing the input**. Echoing input is a good programming practice; it helps eliminate misunderstandings when the user can visually confirm what was entered.

Figure 2-17   The GetUserInfo class

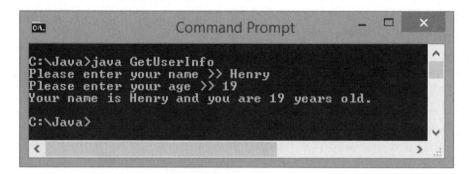

Figure 2-18   Typical execution of the GetUserInfo program

If you use any of the Scanner methods and the next token cannot be converted to the right data type, you receive an error message. For example, the program in Figure 2-17 uses nextInt() to retrieve age, so if the user entered a noninteger value for age, such as the double 19.5 or the String "nineteen", an error would occur. You will learn how to recover from this type of error in the chapter "Exception Handling," but for now, you will have to trust the user to enter the correct data type.

The literal Strings contained in the print() statements that appear before each input statement in Figure 2-17 are examples of prompts. A **prompt** is a message displayed for the user that requests and describes input. Interactive programs would work without prompts, but they would not be as user-friendly. Each prompt in the GetUserInfo class ends with two greater-than signs and a space. This punctuation is not required; it just separates the words in the prompt from the user's input value on the screen, improving readability. You might prefer to use a series of periods, several dashes, or just a few spaces.

It is legal to write a single prompt that requests multiple input values—for example, "Please enter your age, area code, and zip code >>". The user could then enter the three values separated with spaces, tabs, or Enter key presses. The values would be interpreted as separate tokens and could be retrieved with three separate `nextInt()` method calls. However, asking a user to enter multiple values often leads to mistakes. This book will follow the practice of using a separate prompt for each input value required.

Pitfall: Using `nextLine()` Following One of the Other **Scanner** Input Methods

You can encounter a problem when you use one of the numeric **Scanner** class retrieval methods or the `next()` method before you use the `nextLine()` method. Consider the program in Figure 2-19. It is identical to the one in Figure 2-17, except that the user is asked for an age before being asked for a name. (See shading.) Figure 2-20 shows a typical execution.

```java
import java.util.Scanner;
public class GetUserInfo2
{
    public static void main(String[] args)
    {
        String name;
        int age;
        Scanner inputDevice = new Scanner(System.in);
        System.out.print("Please enter your age >> ");
        age = inputDevice.nextInt();
        System.out.print("Please enter your name >> ");
        name = inputDevice.nextLine();
        System.out.println("Your name is " + name +
            " and you are " + age + " years old.");
    }
}
```

Don't Do It
If you accept numeric input prior to string input, the string input is ignored unless you take special action.

Figure 2-19 The `GetUserInfo2` class

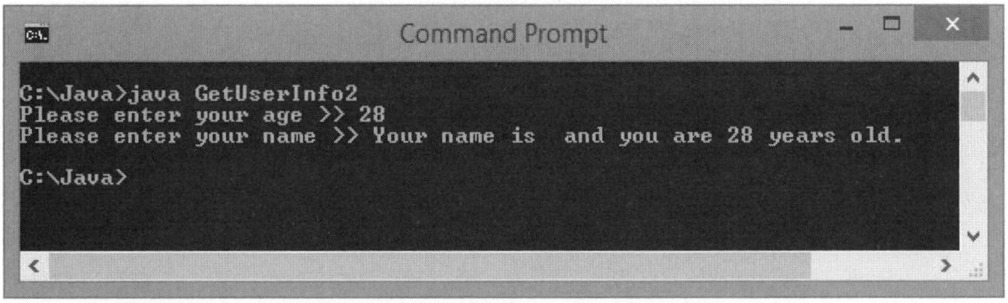

```
C:\.                        Command Prompt                    - □ ×

C:\Java>java GetUserInfo2
Please enter your age >> 28
Please enter your name >> Your name is  and you are 28 years old.

C:\Java>
```

Figure 2-20 Typical execution of the `GetUserInfo2` program

In Figure 2-20, the user is prompted correctly for an age. However, after the user enters an age and the prompt for the name is displayed, the program does not pause to let the user enter a name. Instead, the program proceeds directly to the output statement, which does not contain a valid name.

When you type characters using the keyboard, they are stored temporarily in a location in memory called the **keyboard buffer** or the **type-ahead buffer**. All keystrokes are stored in the keyboard buffer, including the Enter key. The problem occurs because of a difference in the way the nextLine() method and the other Scanner retrieval methods work:

- The Scanner methods next(), nextInt(), and nextDouble() retrieve the next token in the buffer up to the next whitespace, which might be a space, tab, or Enter key.

- The nextLine() method reads all data up to the Enter key character.

So, in the execution of the program in Figure 2-20, the user is prompted for an age, types *28*, and presses Enter. The call to the nextInt() method retrieves the 28 and leaves the Enter key press in the input buffer. Then, the name prompt is displayed and the call to nextLine() retrieves the waiting Enter key before the user has time to type a name.

The solution to the problem is simple. After any next(), nextInt(), or nextDouble() call, you can add an extra nextLine() method call that will retrieve the abandoned Enter key character. Then, no matter what type of input follows, the program will execute smoothly. Figure 2-21 shows a program that contains just one change from Figure 2-19—the addition of the shaded statement that retrieves the abandoned Enter key character from the input buffer. Although you could assign the Enter key value to a character variable, there is no need to do so. When you accept an entry and discard it without using it, programmers say that the entry is **consumed**. Figure 2-21 shows that the call to nextInt() accepts the integer, the first call to nextLine() consumes the Enter key that follows the integer entry, and the second nextLine() call accepts both the entered name and the Enter key that follows it. Figure 2-22 shows that the revised program executes correctly.

```
import java.util.Scanner;
public class GetUserInfo3
{
    public static void main(String[] args)
    {
        String name;
        int age;
        Scanner inputDevice = new Scanner(System.in);
        System.out.print("Please enter your age >> ");
        age = inputDevice.nextInt();
        inputDevice.nextLine();
        System.out.print("Please enter your name >> ");
        name = inputDevice.nextLine();
        System.out.println("Your name is " + name +
            " and you are " + age + " years old.");
    }
}
```

This statement gets the integer.

This statement consumes the Enter key that follows the integer.

This statement gets the name and discards the Enter key that follows the name.

Figure 2-21 The GetUserInfo3 class

Figure 2-22 Typical execution of the GetUserInfo3 program

 When you write programs that accept user input, there is a risk that the user will enter the wrong type of data. For example, if you include a `nextInt()` method call in your program, but the user types an alphabetic character, an error will occur, and your program will stop running. You will learn to handle this type of error later in this book.

TWO TRUTHS & A LIE

Using the Scanner Class to Accept Keyboard Input

1. `System.in` refers to the standard input device, which normally is the keyboard.

2. `System.in` is more flexible than `System.out` because it can read all the basic Java data types.

3. When a user types data followed by the Enter key, the Enter key character is left in the keyboard buffer after `Scanner` class methods retrieve the other keystrokes.

The false statement is #2. `System.in` is not as flexible as `System.out`. `System.out` can display various data types, but `System.in` is designed to read only bytes.

 You Do It

Accepting User Input

In the next steps you create a program that accepts user input.

1. Open the **IntegerDemo.java** file you created in a "You Do It" section earlier in this chapter. Change the class name to `IntegerDemoInteractive`, and save the file as **IntegerDemoInteractive.java**.

2. As the first line in the file, insert an `import` statement that will allow you to use the `Scanner` class:

   ```
   import java.util.Scanner;
   ```

3. Remove the assignment operator and the assigned values from each of the four numeric variable declarations.

4. Following the numeric variable declarations, insert a `Scanner` object declaration:

   ```
   Scanner input = new Scanner(System.in);
   ```

5. Following the variable declarations, insert a prompt for the integer value, and an input statement that accepts the value, as follows:

   ```
   System.out.print("Please enter an integer >> ");
   anInt = input.nextInt();
   ```

(continues)

(continued)

6. Then add similar statements for the other three variables:

```
System.out.print("Please enter a byte integer >> ");
aByte = input.nextByte();
System.out.print("Please enter a short integer >> ");
aShort = input.nextShort();
System.out.print("Please enter a long integer >> ");
aLong = input.nextLong();
```

7. Save the file, and then compile and execute it. Figure 2-23 shows a typical execution. Execute the program a few more times, using different values each time and confirming that the correct values have been accepted from the keyboard.

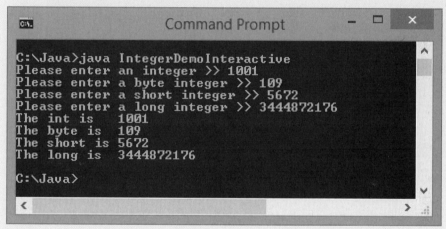

Figure 2-23 Typical execution of the IntegerDemoInteractive program

Adding String Input

Next, you add String input to the IntegerDemoInteractive program.

1. Change the class name of the IntegerDemoInteractive program to **IntegerDemoInteractiveWithName**, and immediately save the file as **IntegerDemoInteractiveWithName.java**.

2. Add a new variable with the other variable declarations as follows:

```
String name;
```

3. After the last input statement (that gets the value for aLong), add three statements that prompt the user for a name, accept the name, and use the name as follows:

```
System.out.print("Please enter your name >> ");
name = input.nextLine();
System.out.println("Thank you, " + name);
```

(continues)

(continued)

86

4. Save the file, and compile and execute it. Figure 2-24 shows a typical execution. You can enter the numbers, but when the prompt for the name appears, you are not given the opportunity to respond. Instead, the string "Thank you, ", including the ending comma and space, is output immediately, and the program ends. This output is incorrect because the input statement that should retrieve the name from the keyboard instead retrieves the Enter key that was still in the keyboard buffer after the last numeric entry.

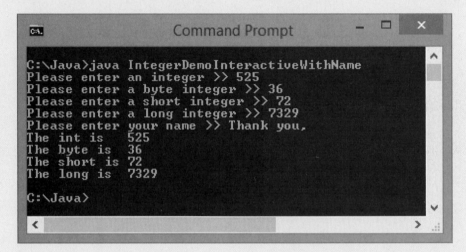

Figure 2-24   Typical execution of incomplete IntegerDemoInteractiveWithName application that does not accept a name

5. To fix the problem, insert an extra call to the nextLine() method just before the statement that accepts the name. This call will consume the Enter key. You do not need an assignment operator with this statement, because there is no need to store the Enter key character.

```
input.nextLine();
```

(continues)

(continued)

6. Save, compile, and execute the program. Figure 2-25 shows a typical successful execution.

```
C:\Java>java IntegerDemoInteractiveWithName
Please enter an integer >> 814
Please enter a byte integer >> 52
Please enter a short integer >> 190
Please enter a long integer >> 129654
Please enter your name >> Sarah
Thank you, Sarah
The int is    814
The byte is   52
The short is  190
The long is   129654

C:\Java>
```

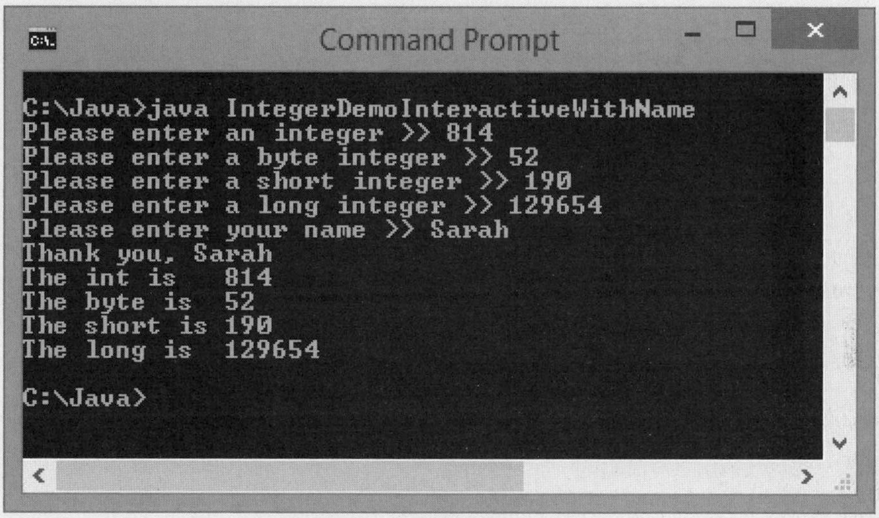

Figure 2-25   Typical successful execution of `IntegerDemoInteractiveWithName` application

Using the `JOptionPane` Class to Accept GUI Input

In Chapter 1, you learned how to display output at the command line and how to create GUI message boxes to display `String` objects. Earlier in this chapter, you learned to accept input from the keyboard at the command line. You also can accept input in a GUI dialog box using the `JOptionPane` class.

Two dialog boxes that can be used to accept user input are:

- `InputDialog`—Prompts the user for text input
- `ConfirmDialog`—Asks the user a question, providing buttons that the user can click for Yes, No, and Cancel responses

Using Input Dialog Boxes

An **input dialog box** asks a question and provides a text field in which the user can enter a response. You can create an input dialog box using the `showInputDialog()` method. Six versions of this method are available, but the simplest version uses a single argument that is the prompt you want to display within the dialog box. The `showInputDialog()` method returns a `String` that represents a user's response; this means that you can assign the `showInputDialog()` method to a `String` variable and the variable will hold the value that the user enters.

For example, Figure 2-26 shows an application that creates an input dialog box containing a prompt for a first name. When the user executes the application, types *William*, then clicks the OK button or presses Enter on the keyboard, the result String will contain "William". In the application in Figure 2-26, the response is concatenated with a welcoming message and displayed in a message dialog box. Figure 2-27 shows the dialog box containing a user's response, and Figure 2-28 shows the resulting output message box.

```java
import javax.swing.JOptionPane;
public class HelloNameDialog
{
    public static void main(String[] args)
    {
        String result;
        result = JOptionPane.showInputDialog(null, "What is your name?");
        JOptionPane.showMessageDialog(null, "Hello, " + result + "!");
    }
}
```

Figure 2-26   The HelloNameDialog class

Figure 2-27   Input dialog box of the HelloNameDialog application

Figure 2-28   Output of the HelloNameDialog application

 When a computer has a touch screen, you might want the user to be able to use the operating system's virtual keyboard to enter data. You will learn how to display the virtual keyboard after you learn about exception handling in Chapter 12.

A different version of the showInputDialog() method requires four arguments that allow the programmer flexibility in controlling the appearance of the input dialog box. The four arguments to showInputDialog() include:

- The parent component, which is the screen component, such as a frame, in front of which the dialog box will appear. If this argument is null, the dialog box is centered on the screen.

- The message the user will see before entering a value. Usually this message is a String, but it actually can be any type of object.

- The title to be displayed in the title bar of the input dialog box.

- A class field describing the type of dialog box; it can be one of the following: ERROR_MESSAGE, INFORMATION_MESSAGE, PLAIN_MESSAGE, QUESTION_MESSAGE, or WARNING_MESSAGE.

For example, when the following statement executes, it displays the input dialog box shown in Figure 2-29.

```
JOptionPane.showInputDialog(null,
    "What is your area code?",
    "Area code information",
    JOptionPane.QUESTION_MESSAGE);
```

Note that the title bar displays "Area code information," and the dialog box shows a question mark icon.

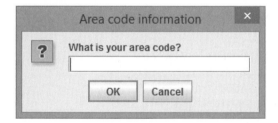

Figure 2-29 An input dialog box with a String in the title bar and a question mark icon

The showInputDialog() method returns a String object that holds the combination of keystrokes a user types into the dialog box. If the value that the user enters is intended to be used as a number, as in an arithmetic statement, the returned String must be converted to the correct numeric type. Later in this chapter, you will learn how to change primitive data from one data type to another. However, the techniques you will learn only work with primitive data types—double, int, char, and so on—not with class objects (that are reference types) such as a String. To convert a String to an integer or double, you must use methods from the built-in Java classes Integer and Double. Each primitive type in Java has a corresponding class contained in the java.lang package; like most classes, the names of these classes begin with uppercase letters. These classes are called **type-wrapper classes**. They include methods that can process primitive type values.

Figure 2-30 shows a `SalaryDialog` application that contains two `String` objects—
`wageString` and `dependentsString`. Two `showInputDialog()` methods are called, and the
answers are stored in the declared `Strings`. The shaded statements in Figure 2-30 show how
the `Strings` are converted to numeric values using methods from the type-wrapper classes
`Integer` and `Double`. The `double` value is converted using the `Double.parseDouble()`
method, and the integer is converted using the `Integer.parseInt()` method. Figure 2-31
shows a typical execution of the application.

Remember that in Java, the reserved keyword `static` means that a method is accessible and usable even
though no objects of the class exist. You can tell that the method `Double.parseDouble()` is a
`static` method, because the method name is used with the class name `Double`—no object is needed.
Similarly, you can tell that `Integer.parseInt()` is also a `static` method.

The term **parse** means to break into component parts. Grammarians talk about "parsing a sentence"—
deconstructing it so as to describe its grammatical components. Parsing a `String` converts it to its
numeric equivalent.

```java
import javax.swing.JOptionPane;
public class SalaryDialog
{
   public static void main(String[] args)
   {
       String wageString, dependentsString;
       double wage, weeklyPay;
       int dependents;
       final double HOURS_IN_WEEK = 37.5;
       wageString = JOptionPane.showInputDialog(null,
           "Enter employee's hourly wage", "Salary dialog 1",
           JOptionPane.INFORMATION_MESSAGE);
       weeklyPay = Double.parseDouble(wageString) *
           HOURS_IN_WEEK;
       dependentsString = JOptionPane.showInputDialog(null,
           "How many dependents?", "Salary dialog 2",
           JOptionPane.QUESTION_MESSAGE);
       dependents = Integer.parseInt(dependentsString);
       JOptionPane.showMessageDialog(null, "Weekly salary is $" +
           weeklyPay + "\nDeductions will be made for " +
           dependents + " dependents");
   }
}
```

Figure 2-30   The `SalaryDialog` class

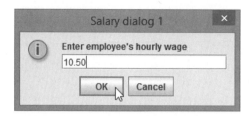

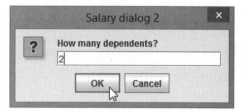

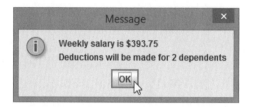

Figure 2-31   Sample execution of the SalaryDialog application

Using Confirm Dialog Boxes

Sometimes, the input you want from a user does not have to be typed from the keyboard. When
you present simple options to a user, you can offer buttons that the user can click to confirm a
choice. A **confirm dialog box** that displays the options *Yes, No,* and *Cancel* can be created
using the showConfirmDialog() method in the JOptionPane class. Four versions of the method
are available; the simplest requires a parent component (which can be null) and the String
prompt that is displayed in the box. The showConfirmDialog() method returns an integer
containing one of three possible values: JOptionPane.YES_OPTION, JOptionPane.NO_OPTION, or
JOptionPane.CANCEL_OPTION. Figure 2-32 shows an application that asks a user a question. The
shaded statement displays the dialog box shown in Figure 2-33 and stores the user's response in
the integer variable named selection.

```
import javax.swing.JOptionPane;
public class AirlineDialog
{
   public static void main(String[] args)
   {
      int selection;
      boolean isYes;
      selection = JOptionPane.showConfirmDialog(null,
         "Do you want to upgrade to first class?");
      isYes = (selection == JOptionPane.YES_OPTION);
      JOptionPane.showMessageDialog(null,
         "You responded " + isYes);
   }
}
```

Figure 2-32   The AirlineDialog class

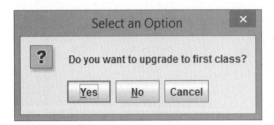

Figure 2-33   The confirm dialog box displayed by the `AirlineDialog` application

After a value is stored in `selection`, a Boolean variable named `isYes` is set to the result when `selection` and `JOptionPane.YES_OPTION` are compared. If the user has selected the Yes button in the dialog box, this variable is set to `true`; otherwise, the variable is set to `false`. Finally, the true or false result is displayed; Figure 2-34 shows the result when a user clicks the Yes button in the dialog box.

Figure 2-34   Output of `AirlineDialog` application when user clicks Yes

You can also create a confirm dialog box with five arguments, as follows:

- The parent component, which can be `null`

- The prompt message

- The title to be displayed in the title bar

- An integer that indicates which option button will be shown (It should be one of the constants YES_NO_CANCEL_OPTION or YES_NO_OPTION.)

- An integer that describes the kind of dialog box (It should be one of the constants ERROR_MESSAGE, INFORMATION_MESSAGE, PLAIN_MESSAGE, QUESTION_MESSAGE, or WARNING_MESSAGE.)

For example, when the following statement is executed, it displays a confirm dialog box, as shown in Figure 2-35:

```
JOptionPane.showConfirmDialog(null,
      "A data input error has occurred. Continue?",
      "Data input error", JOptionPane.YES_NO_OPTION,
      JOptionPane.ERROR_MESSAGE);
```

Figure 2-35   Confirm dialog box with title, Yes and No buttons, and error icon

   Confirm dialog boxes provide more practical uses when your applications can make decisions based on the users' responses. In the chapter "Making Decisions," you will learn how to make decisions within programs.

93

TWO TRUTHS & A LIE

Using the JOptionPane Class to Accept GUI Input

1. You can create an input dialog box using the showInputDialog() method; the method returns a String that represents a user's response.

2. You can use methods from the Java classes Integer and Double when you want to convert a dialog box's returned values to numbers.

3. A confirm dialog box can be created using the showConfirmDialog() method in the JOptionPane class; a confirm dialog box displays the options Accept, Reject, and Escape.

The false statement is #3. A confirm dialog box displays the options Yes, No, and Cancel.

   Watch the video *Getting Input*.

Performing Arithmetic

Table 2-8 describes the five **standard arithmetic operators** that you use to perform calculations with values in your programs. A value used on either side of an operator is an **operand**. For example, in the expression 45 + 2, the numbers 45 and 2 are operands. The arithmetic operators are examples of **binary operators**, so named because they require two operands.

   You will learn about the Java shortcut arithmetic operators in the chapter "Looping."

Operator	Description	Example
+	Addition	45 + 2, the result is 47
−	Subtraction	45 − 2, the result is 43
*	Multiplication	45 * 2, the result is 90
/	Division	45.0 / 2, the result is 22.5 45 / 2, the result is 22 (not 22.5)
%	Remainder (modulus)	45 % 2, the result is 1 (that is, 45 / 2 = 22 with a remainder of 1)

Table 2-8 Arithmetic operators

The operators / and % deserve special consideration. Java supports two types of division:

- **Floating-point division** occurs when either or both of the operands are floating-point values. For example, 45.0 / 2 is 22.5.

- **Integer division** occurs when both of the operands are integers. The result is an integer, and any fractional part of the result is lost. For example, the result of 45 / 2 is 22. As another example, 39 / 5 is 7 because 5 goes into 39 seven whole times; 38 / 5, 37 / 5, 36 / 5, and 35 / 5 all evaluate to 7.

The percent sign is the **remainder operator**. The remainder operator is most often used with two integers, and the result is an integer with the value of the remainder after division takes place. For example, the result of 45 % 2 is 1 because 2 "goes into" 45 twenty-two times with a remainder of 1. Other examples of remainder operations include the following:

- 39 % 5 is 4 because 5 goes into 39 seven times with a remainder of 4.

- 20 % 3 is 2 because when 20 is divided by 3, the remainder is 2.

- 36 % 4 is 0 because there is no remainder when 4 is divided into 36.

Note that when you perform paper-and-pencil division, you divide first to determine a remainder. In Java, you do not need to perform a division operation before you can perform a remainder operation. A remainder operation can stand alone.

Although the remainder operator is most often used with integers, it is legal but less often useful to use the operator with floating-point values. In Java, when you use the % operator with floating-point values, the result is the remainder from a rounded division.

The remainder operator is also called the **modulus operator**, or sometimes just **mod**. Mathematicians would argue that *remainder* is the better term because in Java, the result of using the remainder operator can be negative, but in mathematics, the result of a modulus operation can never be negative.

Associativity and Precedence

When you combine mathematical operations in a single statement, you must understand both associativity and precedence. The associativity of arithmetic operators with the same precedence is left to right. In a statement such as answer = x + y + z;, the x and y are added first, producing a temporary result, and then z is added to the temporary sum. After the sum is computed, the result is assigned to answer.

Operator precedence refers to the rules for the order in which parts of a mathematical expression are evaluated. The multiplication, division, and remainder operators have the same precedence, and it is higher than the precedence of the addition and subtraction operators. In other words, an arithmetic expression is evaluated from left to right, and any multiplication, division, and remainder operations take place. Then, the expression is evaluated from left to right again, and any addition and subtraction operations execute. Table 2-9 summarizes the precedence of the arithmetic operators.

Operators	Descriptions	Relative Precedence
* / %	Multiplication, division, remainder	Higher
+ –	Addition, subtraction	Lower

Table 2-9 Relative precedence of arithmetic operators

For example, the following statement assigns 14 to result:

```
int result = 2 + 3 * 4;
```

The multiplication operation (3 * 4) occurs before adding 2. You can override normal operator precedence by putting the operation to perform first in parentheses. The following statement assigns 20 to result:

```
int result = (2 + 3) * 4;
```

The addition within the parentheses takes place first, and then the intermediate result (5) is multiplied by 4. When multiple pairs of parentheses are used in a statement, the innermost expression surrounded by parentheses is evaluated first. For example, the value of the following expression is 46:

```
2 * (3 + (4 * 5))
```

First, 4 * 5 evaluates to 20, and then 3 is added, giving 23. Finally, the value is multiplied by 2, giving 46.

Remembering that *, /, and % have the same precedence is important in arithmetic calculations. These operations are performed from left to right, regardless of the order in which they appear. For example, the value of the following expression is 9:

```
25 / 8 * 3
```

First, 25 is divided by 8. The result is 3 because with integer division, you lose any remainder. Then 3 is multiplied by 3, giving 9. If you assumed that multiplication was performed before division, you would calculate an incorrect answer.

You will learn more about operator precedence in the chapter "Making Decisions."

Writing Arithmetic Statements Efficiently

You can make your programs operate more efficiently if you avoid unnecessary repetition of arithmetic statements. For example, suppose you know the values for an employee's hourly pay and pay rate and you want to compute state and federal withholding tax based on known rates. You could write two statements as follows:

```
stateWithholding = hours * rate * STATE_RATE;
federalWithholding = hours * rate * FED_RATE;
```

With this approach, you perform the multiplication of hours * rate twice. It is more efficient to perform the calculation once, as follows:

```
grossPay = hours * rate;
stateWithholding = grossPay * STATE_RATE;
federalWithholding = grossPay * FED_RATE;
```

The time saved is very small, but these savings would be more important if the calculation was more complicated or if it was repeated many times in a program. As you think about the programs you write, remain on the lookout for ways to improve efficiency by avoiding duplication of operations.

Pitfall: Not Understanding Imprecision in Floating-Point Numbers

Integer values are exact, but floating-point numbers frequently are only approximations. For example, when you divide 1.0 by 3.0, the mathematical result is 0.3333333…, with the 3s continuing infinitely. No matter how many decimal places you can store, the result is only an approximation. Even values that don't repeat indefinitely in our usual numbering system, such as 0.1, cannot be represented precisely in the binary format used by computers. Imprecision leads to several problems:

- When you produce floating-point output, it might not look like what you expect or want.

- When you make comparisons with floating-point numbers, the comparisons might not be what you expect or want.

Appendix B provides a more thorough explanation of numbering systems and why fractional values cannot be represented accurately.

For example, Figure 2-36 shows a class in which an answer is computed as 2.20 − 2.00. Mathematically, the result should be 0.20. But, as the output in Figure 2-37 shows, the result is calculated as a value that is slightly more than 0.20, and when answer is compared to 0.20, the result is false.

```java
public class ImprecisionDemo
{
    public static void main(String[] args)
    {
        double answer = 2.20 - 2.00;
        boolean isEqual = answer == 0.20;
        System.out.println("answer is " + answer);
        System.out.println("isEqual is " + isEqual);
    }
}
```

Figure 2-36 The ImprecisionDemo program

Figure 2-37 Execution of the ImprecisionDemo program

For now, you might choose to accept the slight imprecisions generated when you use floating-point numbers. However, if you want to eliminate the imprecisions, you can use one of several techniques to round values. Appendix C contains directions on how to round numbers and how to format a floating-point number so it displays the desired number of decimal positions.

 Several movies have used the fact that floating-point numbers are not precise as a plot element. For example, in the movies *Superman III* and *Office Space*, thieves round currency values and divert the remaining fractions of cents to their own accounts.

 Watch the video *Arithmetic*.

TWO TRUTHS & A LIE

Performing Arithmetic

1. The arithmetic operators are examples of unary operators, which are so named because they perform one operation at a time.

2. In Java, operator precedence dictates that multiplication, division, and remainder always take place prior to addition or subtraction in an expression.

3. Floating-point arithmetic might produce imprecise results.

The false statement is #1. The arithmetic operators are examples of binary operators, which are so named because they require two operands.

You Do It

Using Arithmetic Operators

In these steps, you create a program that uses arithmetic operators.

1. Open a new file in your text editor, and type the `import` statement needed for interactive input with the `Scanner` class:

   ```
   import java.util.Scanner;
   ```

2. Type the class header and its curly braces for a class named `ArithmeticDemo`. Within the class's curly braces, enter the `main()` method header and its braces.

   ```
   public class ArithmeticDemo
   {
       public static void main(String[] args)
       {
       }
   }
   ```

3. Within the `main()` method, declare five `int` variables that will be used to hold two input values and their sum, difference, and average:

   ```
   int firstNumber;
   int secondNumber;
   int sum;
   int difference;
   int average;
   ```

(continues)

(continued)

4. Also declare a `Scanner` object so that keyboard input can be accepted.

   ```
   Scanner input = new Scanner(System.in);
   ```

5. Prompt the user for and accept two integers:

   ```
   System.out.print("Please enter an integer >> ");
   firstNumber = input.nextInt();
   System.out.print("Please enter another integer >> ");
   secondNumber = input.nextInt();
   ```

6. Add statements to perform the necessary arithmetic operations:

   ```
   sum = firstNumber + secondNumber;
   difference = firstNumber - secondNumber;
   average = sum / 2;
   ```

7. Display the three calculated values:

   ```
   System.out.println(firstNumber + " + " +
       secondNumber + " is " + sum);
   System.out.println(firstNumber + " - " +
       secondNumber + " is " + difference);
   System.out.println("The average of " + firstNumber +
       " and " + secondNumber + " is " + average);
   ```

8. Save the file as **ArithmeticDemo.java**, and then compile and execute it. Enter values of your choice. Figure 2-38 shows a typical execution. Notice that because integer division was used to compute the average, the answer is an integer.

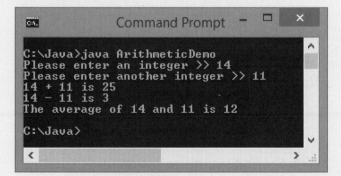

Figure 2-38 Typical execution of `ArithmeticDemo` application

9. Execute the program multiple times using various integer values, and confirm that the results are accurate.

(continues)

Performing Floating-Point Arithmetic   *(continued)*

Next, you will modify the `ArithmeticDemo` application to work with floating-point values instead of integers.

1. Within the `ArithmeticDemo` application, change the class name to **ArithmeticDemo2**, and immediately save the file as **ArithmeticDemo2.java**. Change all the variables' data types to `double`. Change the two prompts to request `double` values, and change the two calls to the `nextInt()` method to `nextDouble()`. Save, compile, and execute the program again. Figure 2-39 shows a typical execution. Notice that the average calculation now includes decimal places.

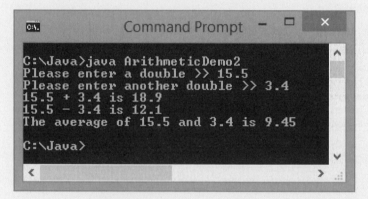

Figure 2-39   Typical execution of the `ArithmeticDemo2` application

2. Rerun the program, experimenting with various input values. Some of your output might appear with imprecisions similar to those shown in Figure 2-40. If you are not satisfied with the slight imprecisions created when using floating-point arithmetic, you can round or change the display of the values, as discussed in Appendix C.

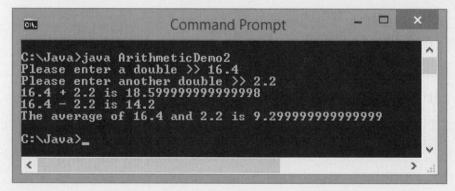

Figure 2-40   Another typical execution of the `ArithmeticDemo2` application

Understanding Type Conversion

When you perform arithmetic with variables or constants of the same type, the result of the operation retains the same type. For example, when you divide two ints, the result is an int, and when you subtract two doubles, the result is a double. Often, however, you might want to perform mathematical operations on operands with unlike types. The process of converting one data type to another is **type conversion**. Java performs some conversions for you automatically or implicitly, but other conversions must be requested explicitly by the programmer.

Automatic Type Conversion

When you perform arithmetic operations with operands of unlike types, Java chooses a unifying type for the result. The **unifying type** is the type to which all operands in an expression are converted so that they are compatible with each other. Java performs an **implicit conversion**; that is, it automatically converts nonconforming operands to the unifying type. Implicit conversions also are called **promotions**. Figure 2-41 shows the order for establishing unifying types between values.

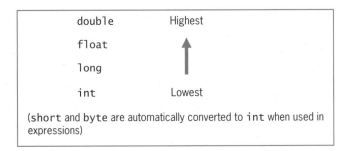

```
    double          Highest
    float             ↑
    long
    int             Lowest
```
(short and byte are automatically converted to int when used in expressions)

Figure 2-41   Order for establishing unifying data types

When two unlike types are used in an expression, the unifying type is the one that is higher in the list in Figure 2-41. In other words, when an operand that is a type lower on the list is combined with a type that is higher, the lower-type operand is converted to the higher one. For example, the addition of a double and an int results in a double, and the subtraction of a long from a float results in a float.

Boolean values cannot be converted to another type. In some languages, such as C++, Boolean values are actually numbers. However, this is not the case in Java.

For example, assume that an int, hoursWorked, and a double, payRate, are defined and then multiplied as follows:

```
int hoursWorked = 37;
double payRate = 16.73;
double grossPay = hoursWorked * payRate;
```

The result of the multiplication is a double because when a double and an int are multiplied, the int is promoted to the higher-ranking unifying type double—the type that is higher in the list in Figure 2-41. Therefore, assigning the result to grossPay is legal.

The following code will not compile because hoursWorked times payRate is a double, and Java does not allow the loss of precision that occurs if you try to store the calculated double result in an int.

```
int hoursWorked = 37;
double payRate = 16.73;
int grossPay = hoursWorked * payRate;
```

The data types char, short, and byte all are promoted to int when used in statements with unlike types. If you perform a calculation with any combination of char, short, and byte values, the result is an int by default. For example, if you add two bytes, the result is an int, not a byte.

Explicit Type Conversions

You can purposely override the unifying type imposed by Java by performing a type cast. **Type casting** forces a value of one data type to be used as a value of another type. To perform a type cast, you use a **cast operator**, which is created by placing the desired result type in parentheses. Using a cast operator is an **explicit conversion**. The cast operator is followed by the variable or constant to be cast. For example, a type cast is performed in the following code:

```
double bankBalance = 189.66;
float weeklyBudget = (float) (bankBalance / 4);
   // weeklyBudget is 47.415, one-fourth of bankBalance
```

The cast operator is more completely called the **unary cast operator**. Unlike a binary operator that requires two operands, a **unary operator** uses only one operand. The unary cast operator is followed by its operand.

In this example, the double value bankBalance is divided by the integer 4, and the result is a double. Then, the double result is converted to a float before it is stored in weeklyBudget.

Without the conversion, the statement that assigns the result to weeklyBudget would not compile. Similarly, a cast from a float to an int occurs in this code segment:

```
float myMoney = 47.82f;
int dollars = (int) myMoney;
  // dollars is 47, the integer part of myMoney
```

In this example, the float value myMoney is converted to an int before it is stored in the integer variable named dollars. When the float value is converted to an int, the decimal place values are lost. The cast operator does not permanently alter any variable's data type; the alteration is only for the duration of the current operation. In other words, if myMoney was used again in the previous example, it would still be a float and its value would still be 47.82.

 The word *cast* is used in a similar fashion when referring to molding metal, as in *cast iron*. In a Java arithmetic cast, a value is "molded" into a different type.

 It is easy to lose data when performing a cast. For example, the largest byte value is 127 and the largest int value is 2,147,483,647, so the following statements produce distorted results:

```
int anOkayInt = 200;
byte aBadByte = (byte)anOkayInt;
```

A byte is constructed from eight 1s and 0s, or binary digits. The first binary digit, or bit, holds a 0 or 1 to represent positive or negative. The remaining seven bits store the actual value. When the integer value 200 is stored in the byte variable, its large value consumes the eighth bit, turning it to a 1, and forcing the aBadByte variable to appear to hold the value −72, which is inaccurate and misleading.

You do not need to perform a cast when assigning a value to a higher unifying type. For example, when you write a statement such as the following, Java automatically promotes the integer constant 10 to be a double so that it can be stored in the payRate variable:

```
double payRate = 10;
```

However, for clarity, if you want to assign 10 to payRate, you might prefer to write the following:

```
double payRate = 10.0;
```

The result is identical whether you assign the literal double 10.0 or the literal int 10 to the double variable.

104

TWO TRUTHS & A LIE

Understanding Type Conversion

1. When you perform arithmetic operations with operands of unlike types, you must make an explicit conversion to a unifying type.

2. Summing a double, int, and float results in a double.

3. You can explicitly override the unifying type imposed by Java by performing a type cast; type casting forces a value of one data type to be used as a value of another type.

The false statement is #1. When you perform arithmetic operations with operands of unlike types, Java performs an implicit conversion to a unifying type.

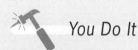 *You Do It*

Implicit and Explicit Casting

In this section, you explore the concepts of the unifying types and casting.

1. Open the **ArithmeticDemo.java** file that uses integer values to calculate a sum, difference, and average. Change the class name to `ArithmeticDemo3`, and immediately save the file as **ArithmeticDemo3.java**.

2. In the previous version of the program, the average was calculated without decimal places because when two integers are divided, the result is an integer. To compute a more accurate average, change the data type for the average variable from int to `double`.

3. Save, compile, and execute the program. As the sample execution in Figure 2-42 shows, the program compiles and executes, but the average is still not accurate. The average of 20 and 19 is calculated to be just 19.0 because when two integers are divided, the decimal portion of the arithmetic result is lost.

(continues)

(continued)

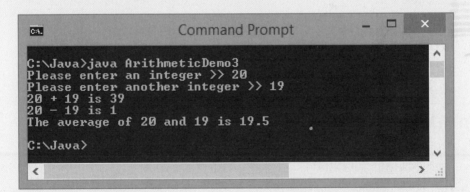

Figure 2-42 Typical execution of `ArithmeticDemo3` application

4. Change the statement that computes the average to include a cast as follows:

```
average = (double) sum / 2;
```

5. Save, compile, and execute the program. As shown in Figure 2-43, now the program displays a more accurate average. The integer `sum` has been cast to a `double`, and when the `double` is divided by the integer, the result is a `double`, which is then assigned to `average`.

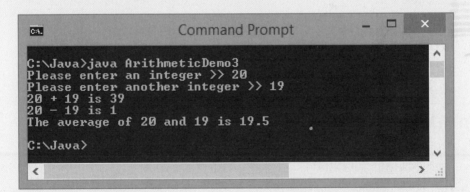

Figure 2-43 Typical execution of `ArithmeticDemo3` application after addition of a cast operation for the average

6. Change the statement that computes the average to include a second set of parentheses, as follows:

```
average = (double) (sum / 2);
```

(continues)

(continued)

7. Save, compile, and execute the program. Now, the fractional portion of the result is omitted again. That's because the result of sum / 2 is calculated first, and the result is an integer. Then, the whole-number result is cast to a double and assigned to a double—but the fractional part of the answer was already lost and casting is too late. Remove the newly added parentheses, save the program, compile it, and execute it again to confirm that the fractional part of the answer is reinstated.

8. As an alternative to the explicit cast in the division statement in the ArithmeticDemo program, you could write the average calculation as follows:

   ```
   average = sum / 2.0;
   ```

   In this calculation, when the integer sum is divided by the double constant 2.0, the result is a double. The result then does not require any cast to be assigned to the double average without loss of data. Try this in your program.

9. Go to the Java Web site (**www.oracle.com/technetwork/java/index.html**), select **Java APIs**, and then select **Java SE 8**. Scroll through the list of **All Classes**, and select **PrintStream**, which is the data type for the out object used with the println() method. Scroll down to view the list of methods in the Method Summary. As you did in a previous exercise, notice the many versions of the print() and println() methods, including ones that accept a String, an int, and a long. Notice, however, that no versions accept a byte or a short. That's because when a byte or short is sent to the print() or println() method, it is automatically promoted to an int, so that version of the method is used.

Don't Do It

- Don't mispronounce "integer." People who are unfamiliar with the term often say "interger," inserting an extra *r*.

- Don't attempt to assign a literal constant floating-point number, such as 2.5, to a float without following the constant with an uppercase or lowercase *F*. By default, constant floating-point values are doubles.

- Don't try to use a Java keyword as an identifier for a variable or constant. Table 1-1 in Chapter 1 contains a list of Java keywords.

- Don't attempt to assign a constant value under −2,147,483,648 or over +2,147,483,647 to a long variable without following the constant with an uppercase or lowercase *L*. By default, constant integers are ints, and a value under −2,147,483,648 or over 2,147,483,647 is too large to be an int.

- Don't assume that you must divide numbers as a step to determining a remainder; the remainder operator (%) is all that's needed.

- Don't try to use a variable or named constant that has not yet been assigned a value.

- Don't forget to consume the Enter key after numeric input using the Scanner class when a nextLine() method call follows.

- Don't forget to use the appropriate import statement when using the Scanner or JOptionPane class.

- Don't forget precedence rules when you write statements that contain multiple arithmetic operations. For example, score1 + score2 / 2 does not compute the average of two scores. Instead, it adds half of score2 to score1. To compute the average, you would write (score1 + score2) / 2.

- Don't forget that integer division results in an integer, dropping any fractional part. For example, 1/2 is not equal to 0.5; it is equal to 0.

- Don't forget that extra parentheses can change the result of an operation that includes casting.

- Don't forget that floating-point numbers are imprecise.

- Don't attempt to assign a constant decimal value to an integer using a leading 0. For example, if you declare int num = 021; and then display num, you will see 17. The leading 0 indicates that the value is in base 8 (octal), so its value is two 8s plus one *1*. In the decimal system, 21 and 021 mean the same thing, but not in Java.

- Don't use a single equal sign (=) in a Boolean comparison for equality. The operator used for equivalency is composed of two equal signs (==).

- Don't try to store a string of characters, such as a name, in a char variable. A char variable can hold only a single character.

- Don't forget that when a String and a numeric value are concatenated, the resulting expression is a string. For example, "X" + 2 + 4 results in "X24", *not* "X6". If you want the result to be "X6", you can use the expression "X" + (2 + 4).

Key Terms

Constant describes values that cannot be changed during the execution of an application.

A **literal constant** is a value that is taken literally at each use.

A **numeric constant** is a number whose value is taken literally at each use.

An **unnamed constant** has no identifier associated with it.

A **variable** is a named memory location that you can use to store a value.

An item's **data type** describes the type of data that can be stored there, how much memory the item occupies, and what types of operations can be performed on the data.

108

A **primitive type** is a simple data type. Java's primitive types are byte, short, int, long, float, double, char, and boolean.

Reference types are complex data types that are constructed from primitive types.

A **variable declaration** is a statement that reserves a named memory location.

A **strongly typed language** is one in which each variable has a well-defined type that limits the operations you can perform with it; strong typing implies that variables must be declared before they can be used.

Camel casing is a style in which an identifier begins with a lowercase letter and subsequent words within the identifier are capitalized.

The **assignment operator** is the equal sign (=); any value to the right of the equal sign is assigned to the variable on the left of the equal sign.

An **initialization** is an assignment made when you declare a variable.

An **assignment** is the act of providing a value for a variable.

Associativity refers to the order in which operands are used with operators.

An **lvalue** is an expression that can appear on the left side of an assignment statement.

An **rvalue** is an expression that can appear only on the right side of an assignment statement.

An **uninitialized variable** is one that has not been assigned a value.

A **garbage value** is the unknown value stored in an uninitialized variable.

A **named constant** is a named memory location whose assigned value cannot change during program execution.

A **symbolic constant** is a named constant.

The keyword **final** precedes named constant declarations.

A **blank final** is a final variable that has not yet been assigned a value.

A **magic number** is a value that does not have immediate, intuitive meaning or a number that cannot be explained without additional knowledge. Unnamed constants are magic numbers.

The **scope** of a data item is the area in which it is visible to a program and in which you can refer to it using its simple identifier.

A **block of code** is the code contained between a set of curly braces.

Concatenated describes values that are attached end to end.

A **null** String is an empty String created by typing a set of quotes with nothing between them.

An **integer** is a whole number without decimal places.

The **int** data type is used to declare variables and constants that store integers in the range of −2,147,483,648 to +2,147,483,647.

The **byte** data type holds very small integers, from −128 to 127.

The **short** data type holds small integers, from −32,768 to 32,767.

The **long** data type holds very large integers, from −9,223,372,036,854,775,808 to 9,223,372,036,854,775,807.

A **lossy conversion** is one in which some data is lost.

A **lossless conversion** is one in which no data is lost.

A **boolean variable** can hold only one of two values—`true` or `false`.

A **relational operator** compares two items; an expression that contains a relational operator has a Boolean value.

A **comparison operator** is another name for a relational operator.

A **floating-point** number contains decimal positions.

A **float** data type can hold a floating-point value of up to six or seven significant digits of accuracy.

A **double** data type can hold a floating-point value of up to 14 or 15 significant digits of accuracy.

The term **significant digits** refers to the mathematical accuracy of a value.

Scientific notation is a display format that more conveniently expresses large or small numeric values; a multidigit number is converted to a single-digit number and multiplied by 10 to a power.

A **double-precision floating-point number** is stored in a `double`.

A **single-precision floating-point number** is stored in a `float`.

The **char** data type is used to hold any single character.

String is a built-in Java class that provides you with the means for storing and manipulating character strings.

An **escape sequence** begins with a backslash followed by a character; the pair represents a single character.

The **standard input device** normally is the keyboard.

A **token** is a unit of data separated with whitespace.

A **prompt** is a message that requests and describes user input.

Echoing the input means to repeat the user's entry as output so the user can visually confirm the entry's accuracy.

The **keyboard buffer** is a small area of memory where keystrokes are stored before they are retrieved into a program.

The **type-ahead buffer** is the keyboard buffer.

To **consume** an entry is to retrieve and discard it without using it.

An **input dialog box** asks a question and provides a text field in which the user can enter a response.

Type-wrapper classes, contained in the `java.lang` package, include methods that can process primitive type values.

To **parse** means to break into component parts.

A **confirm dialog box** displays the options Yes, No, and Cancel.

Standard arithmetic operators are used to perform calculations with values.

An **operand** is a value used in an arithmetic statement.

Binary operators require two operands.

Floating-point division is the operation in which two values are divided and either or both are floating-point values.

Integer division is the operation in which two values are divided and both are integers; the result contains no fractional part.

The **remainder operator** is the percent sign; when it is used with two integers, the result is an integer with the value of the remainder after division takes place.

The **modulus operator**, sometimes abbreviated as **mod**, is an alternate name for the remainder operator.

Operator precedence is the rules for the order in which parts of a mathematical expression are evaluated.

Type conversion is the process of converting one data type to another.

A **unifying type** is a single data type to which all operands in an expression are converted.

An **implicit conversion** is the automatic transformation of one data type to another.

Promotion is an implicit conversion.

Type casting forces a value of one data type to be used as a value of another type.

A **cast operator** performs an explicit type conversion; it is created by placing the desired result type in parentheses before the expression to be converted.

An **explicit conversion** is the data type transformation caused using a cast operator.

The **unary cast operator** is a more complete name for the cast operator that performs explicit conversions.

A **unary operator** uses only one operand.

Chapter Summary

- Variables are named memory locations in which programs store values; the value of a variable can change. You must declare all variables you want to use in a program by providing a data type and a name. Java provides for eight primitive types of data: `boolean`, `byte`, `char`, `double`, `float`, `int`, `long`, and `short`. A named constant is a memory location that holds a value that cannot be changed after it is assigned; it is preceded by the keyword `final`.

111

- A variable of type `int` can hold any whole number value from −2,147,483,648 to +2,147,483,647. The types `byte`, `short`, and `long` are all variations of the integer type.

- A `boolean` type variable can hold a `true` or `false` value. Java supports six relational operators: >, <, ==, >=, <=, and !=.

- A floating-point number contains decimal positions. Java supports two floating-point data types: `float` and `double`.

- You use the `char` data type to hold any single character. You type constant character values between single quotation marks and `String` constants between double quotation marks. You can store some characters using an escape sequence, which always begins with a backslash.

- You can use the `Scanner` class and the `System.in` object to accept user input from the keyboard. Several methods are available to convert input to usable data, including `nextDouble()`, `nextInt()`, and `nextLine()`.

- You can accept input using the `JOptionPane` class. The `showInputDialog()` method returns a `String`, which must be converted to a number using a type-wrapper class before you can use it as a numeric value.

- There are five standard arithmetic operators: +, −, *, /, and %. Operator precedence is the order in which parts of a mathematical expression are evaluated. Multiplication, division, and remainder always take place prior to addition or subtraction in an expression. Parentheses can be added to an expression to change precedence. When multiple pairs of parentheses are included in an expression, the expression in the innermost parentheses is evaluated first.

- When you perform mathematical operations on unlike types, Java implicitly converts the variables to a unifying type. You can explicitly override the unifying type imposed by Java by performing a type cast.

Review Questions

1. When data cannot be changed after a class is compiled, the data is _____.

   a. constant   c. volatile

   b. variable   d. mutable

2. Which of the following is not a primitive data type in Java?

   a. `boolean`

   c. `int`

   b. `byte`

   d. `sector`

3. Which of the following elements is not required in a variable declaration?

   a. a type

   c. an assigned value

   b. an identifier

   d. a semicolon

4. The assignment operator in Java is _____.

   a. `=`

   c. `:=`

   b. `==`

   d. `::`

5. Assuming you have declared `shoeSize` to be a variable of type `int`, which of the following is a valid assignment statement in Java?

   a. `shoeSize = 9;`

   c. `shoeSize = '9';`

   b. `shoeSize = 9.5;`

   d. `shoeSize = "nine";`

6. Which of the following data types can store a value in the least amount of memory?

   a. `short`

   c. `int`

   b. `long`

   d. `byte`

7. A `boolean` variable can hold _____.

   a. any character

   c. any decimal number

   b. any whole number

   d. the value `true` or `false`

8. The value 137.68 can be held by a variable of type _____.

   a. `int`

   b. `float`

   c. `double`

   d. Two of the preceding answers are correct.

9. An escape sequence always begins with a(n) _____.

   a. e

   c. backslash

   b. forward slash

   d. equal sign

10. Which Java statement produces the following output?
    ```
    w
    xyz
    ```

    a. `System.out.println("wxyz");`

    b. `System.out.println("w" + "xyz");`

    c. `System.out.println("w\nxyz");`

    d. `System.out.println("w\nx\ny\nz");`

11. The remainder operator _____.

    a. is represented by a forward slash

    b. must follow a division operation

    c. provides the quotient of integer division

    d. is none of the above

12. According to the rules of operator precedence, when division occurs in the same arithmetic statement as _____, the division operation always takes place first.

    a. multiplication

    b. remainder

    c. subtraction

    d. Answers a and b are correct.

13. The "equal to" relational operator is _____.

    a. =   c. !=

    b. ==   d. !!

14. When you perform arithmetic with values of diverse types, Java _____.

    a. issues an error message

    b. implicitly converts the values to a unifying type

    c. requires you to explicitly convert the values to a unifying type

    d. implicitly converts the values to the type of the first operand

15. If you attempt to add a `float`, an `int`, and a `byte`, the result will be a(n) _____.

    a. `float`   c. `byte`

    b. `int`   d. error message

16. You use a _____ to explicitly override an implicit type.

    a. mistake   c. format

    b. type cast   d. type set

17. In Java, what is the value of 3 + 7 * 4 + 2?

    a. 21   c. 42

    b. 33   d. 48

18. Which assignment is correct in Java?

    a. `int value = (float) 4.5;`   c. `double value = 2.12;`

    b. `float value = 4 (double);`   d. `char value = 5c;`

19. Which assignment is correct in Java?

    a. `double money = 12;`   c. `double money = 12.0d;`

    b. `double money = 12.0;`   d. All of the above are correct.

20. Which assignment is correct in Java?

    a. `char aChar = 5.5;`

    b. `char aChar = "W";`

    c. `char aChar = '*';`

    d. Two of the preceding answers are correct.

Exercises

 Programming Exercises

1. What is the numeric value of each of the following expressions as evaluated by Java?

    a. 4 + 6 * 2   f. 39 / 10

    b. 10 / 5 + 8   g. 19 % (2 + 3)

    c. 12 / 4 + 16 / 2   h. 3 + 4 * 20 / 3

    d. 17 / 2   i. 36 % (6 + 2)

    e. 22 / 5   j. 8 % 2 * 0

2. What is the value of each of the following Boolean expressions?

    a. 15 > 13   f. 5 < 8 − 3

    b. 8 <= (2 + 6)   g. 7 != 7

    c. 5 == 15   h. 8 != (2 + 5)

    d. 3 >= 3   i. 10 − 20 == -10

    e. 3 * 3 == 2 * 4   j. 3 + 2 * 6 == 15

3. Choose the best data type for each of the following so that any reasonable value is accommodated but no memory storage is wasted. Give an example of a typical value that would be held by the variable, and explain why you chose the type you did.

    a. the number of siblings you have   f. one player's score in a Scrabble game

    b. your final grade in this class   g. one team's score in a Major League Baseball game

    c. the population of Earth

    d. the population of a U.S. county   h. the year an historical event occurred

    e. the number of passengers on a bus   i. the number of legs on an animal

                                     j. the price of an automobile

4. a. Write a Java class that declares a named constant to hold the number of quarts in a gallon (4). Also declare a variable to represent the number of quarts needed for a painting job, and assign an appropriate value—for example, 18. Compute and display the number of gallons and quarts needed for the job. Display explanatory text with the values—for example, A job that needs 18 quarts requires 4 gallons plus 2 quarts. Save the class as **QuartsToGallons. java**.

   b. Convert the QuartsToGallons class to an interactive application. Instead of assigning a value to the number of quarts, accept the value from the user as input. Save the revised class as **QuartsToGallonsInteractive.java**.

5. a. Write a Java class that declares named constants to represent the number of kilometers (1.852) and the number of miles (1.150779) in a nautical mile. Also declare a variable to represent a number of nautical miles and assign a value to it. Compute and display, with explanatory text, the value in kilometers and in miles. Save the class as **NauticalMiles.java**.

   b. Convert the NauticalMiles class to an interactive application. Instead of assigning a value to the nautical miles variable, accept it from the user as input. Save the revised class as **NauticalMilesInteractive.java**.

6. a. Write a class that declares a variable named inches, which holds a length in inches, and assign a value. Display the value in feet and inches; for example, 86 inches becomes 7 feet and 2 inches. Be sure to use a named constant where appropriate. Save the class as **InchesToFeet.java**.

   b. Write an interactive version of the InchesToFeet class that accepts the inches value from a user. Save the class as **InchesToFeetInteractive.java**.

7. Write a class that declares variables to hold your three initials. Display the three initials with a period following each one, as in J.M.F. Save the class as **Initials.java**.

8. Meadowdale Dairy Farm sells organic brown eggs to local customers. They charge $3.25 for a dozen eggs, or 45 cents for individual eggs that are not part of a dozen. Write a class that prompts a user for the number of eggs in the order and then display the amount owed with a full explanation. For example, typical output might be, "You ordered 27 eggs. That's 2 dozen at $3.25 per dozen and 3 loose eggs at 45 cents each for a total of $7.85." Save the class as **Eggs.java**.

9. a. The Huntington Boys and Girls Club is conducting a fundraiser by selling chili dinners to go. The price is $7 for an adult meal and $4 for a child's meal. Write a class that accepts the number of each type of meal ordered and display the total money collected for adult meals, children's meals, and all meals. Save the class as **ChiliToGo.java**.

   b. In the previous example, the costs to produce an adult meal and a child's meal are $4.35 and $3.10, respectively. Modify the ChiliToGo program to display the total profit for each type of meal as well as the grand total profit. Save the class as **ChiliToGoProfit.java**.

10. Write a class that calculates and displays the conversion of an entered number of dollars into currency denominations—*20s*, *10s*, *5s*, and *1s*. Save the class as **Dollars.java**.

11. Write a program that accepts a number of minutes and converts it both to hours and days. For example, 6000 minutes equals 100 hours and equals 4.167 days. Save the class as **MinutesConversion.java**.

12. Travel Tickets Company sells tickets for airlines, tours, and other travel-related services. Because ticket agents frequently mistype long ticket numbers, Travel Tickets has asked you to write an application that indicates invalid ticket number entries. The class prompts a ticket agent to enter a six-digit ticket number. Ticket numbers are designed so that if you drop the last digit of the number, then divide the number by 7, the remainder of the division will be identical to the last dropped digit. This process is illustrated in the following example:

Step 1	Enter the ticket number; for example, 123454.
Step 2	Remove the last digit, leaving 12345.
Step 3	Determine the remainder when the ticket number is divided by 7. In this case, 12345 divided by 7 leaves a remainder of 4.
Step 4	Assign the Boolean value of the comparison between the remainder and the digit dropped from the ticket number.
Step 5	Display the result—`true` or `false`—in a message box.

Accept the ticket number from the agent and verify whether it is a valid number. Test the application with the following ticket numbers:

- 123454; the comparison should evaluate to `true`.

- 147103; the comparison should evaluate to `true`.

- 154123; the comparison should evaluate to `false`.

Save the program as **TicketNumber.java**.

 Debugging Exercises

1. Each of the following files in the Chapter02 folder of your downloadable student files has syntax and/or logic errors. In each case, determine the problem and fix the application. After you correct the errors, save each file using the same filename preceded with *Fix*. For example, DebugTwo1.java will become **FixDebugTwo1.java**.

a. DebugTwo1.java

b. DebugTwo2.java

c. DebugTwo3.java

d. DebugTwo4.java

When you change a filename, remember to change every instance of the class name within the file so that it matches the new filename. In Java, the filename and class name must always match.

 Game Zone

1. *Mad Libs* is a children's game in which they provide a few words that are then incorporated into a silly story. The game helps children understand different parts of speech because they are asked to provide specific types of words. For example, you might ask a child for a noun, another noun, an adjective, and a past-tense verb. The child might reply with such answers as *table, book, silly,* and *studied.* The newly created Mad Lib might be:

    Mary had a little *table*

    Its *book* was *silly* as snow

    And everywhere that Mary *studied*

    The *table* was sure to go.

    Create a Mad Libs program that asks the user to provide at least four or five words, and then create and display a short story or nursery rhyme that uses them. Save the file as **MadLib.java**.

2. In the "Game Zone" section in Chapter 1, you learned how to obtain a random number. For example, the following statement generates a random number between the constants MIN and MAX inclusive and assigns it to a variable named random:

    ```
    random = 1 + (int)(Math.random() * MAX);
    ```

    Write a program that selects a random number between 1 and 5 and asks the user to guess the number. Display a message that indicates the difference between the random number and the user's guess. Display another message that displays the random number and the Boolean value true or false depending on whether the user's guess equals the random number. Save the file as **RandomGuessMatch.java**.

Case Problems

1. Carly's Catering provides meals for parties and special events. Write a program that prompts the user for the number of guests attending an event and then computes the total price, which is $35 per person. Display the company motto with the border that you created in the CarlysMotto2 class in Chapter 1, and then display the number of guests, price per guest, and total price. Also display a message that indicates true or false depending on whether the job is classified as a large event—an event with 50 or more guests. Save the file as **CarlysEventPrice.java**.

2. Sammy's Seashore Supplies rents beach equipment such as kayaks, canoes, beach chairs, and umbrellas to tourists. Write a program that prompts the user for the number of minutes he rented a piece of sports equipment. Compute the rental cost as $40 per hour plus $1 per additional minute. (You might have surmised already that this rate has a logical flaw, but for now, calculate rates as described here. You can fix the problem after you read the chapter on decision making.) Display Sammy's motto with the border that you created in the SammysMotto2 class in Chapter 1. Then display the hours, minutes, and total price. Save the file as **SammysRentalPrice.java**.

CHAPTER 3

Using Methods, Classes, and Objects

In this chapter, you will:

◎ Learn about method calls and placement

◎ Identify the parts of a method

◎ Add parameters to methods

◎ Create methods that return values

◎ Learn about classes and objects

◎ Create a class

◎ Create instance methods in a class

◎ Declare objects and use their methods

◎ Create constructors

◎ Appreciate classes as data types

Understanding Method Calls and Placement

A **method** is a program module that contains a series of statements that carry out a task. You have already seen Java classes that contain a main() method, which executes automatically when you run a program. A program's main() method can execute additional methods, and those methods can execute others. Any class can contain an unlimited number of methods, and each method can be called an unlimited number of times.

To execute a method, you **invoke** or **call** it. In other words, a **calling method** makes a **method call**, and the method call invokes a **called method**. The calling method is also known as a **client method** because a called method provides a service for its client.

Consider the simple First class that you saw in Chapter 1; it displayed a single line of output, "First Java application." Suppose that you want to add three lines of output to this application to display your company's name and address. One approach would be to simply add three new println() statements, as shown in the shaded statements in Figure 3-1.

```java
public class First
{
    public static void main(String[] args)
    {
        System.out.println("XYZ Company");
        System.out.println("8900 U.S. Hwy 14");
        System.out.println("Crystal Lake, IL 60014");
        System.out.println("First Java application");
    }
}
```

Figure 3-1   The First class

Instead of adding the three println() statements to the application in Figure 3-1, you might prefer to call a method that executes the three statements. Then the program would look like the one in Figure 3-2. The shaded line contains the call to the displayAddress() method.

```java
public class First
{
    public static void main(String[] args)
    {
        displayAddress();
        System.out.println("First Java application");
    }
}
```

Figure 3-2   The First class with a call to the displayAddress() method

There are two major advantages to creating a separate method to display the three address lines. First, the main() method remains short and easy to follow because main() contains just one statement to call the method, rather than three separate println() statements to perform the work of the method. What is more important is that a method is easily reusable. After you create the displayAddress() method, you can use it in any application that needs the company's name and address. In other words, you do the work once, and then you can use the method many times. In the following examples, a method is called from another method in its own class; later in this chapter, you learn how to call a method from a different class.

Besides adding a call to the method in the First class, you must actually write the method. You place a method within a class, but it must be outside of any other methods. In other words, you cannot place a method within another method. Figure 3-3 shows the two locations where you can place additional methods within the First class—within the curly braces of the class, but outside of (either before or after) any other methods. Methods can never overlap.

```
public class First
{
    // You can place additional methods here, before main()
    public static void main(String[] args)
    {
        displayAddress();
        System.out.println("First Java application");
    }
    // You can place additional methods here, after main()
}
```

Figure 3-3   Placement of methods within a class

The order in which methods appear in a class has no bearing on the order in which the methods are called or execute. No matter where you place it, the main() method is always executed first in any Java application, and it might call any other methods in any order and any number of times. The order in which you call methods, not their physical placement, is what makes a difference in how an application executes.

A main() method executes automatically when you run a program, but other methods do not execute simply because you place them within a class—they must be called. A class might contain methods that are never called from a particular application, just as some electronic devices might contain features you never use. For example, you might use a DVR to play movies but never to record TV programs, or you might use your microwave oven for popcorn but never to defrost.

Figure 3-4 shows the First class with two methods: the main() method and the displayAddress() method placed after main(). Figure 3-5 shows the output from the execution of the First class in Figure 3-4. When the program executes, the main() method first calls the displayAddress() method, which displays three lines of output. Then main() displays the phrase "First Java application".

 Using a method name to contain or encapsulate a series of statements is an example of the feature that programmers call **abstraction**. Consider abstract art, in which the artist tries to capture the essence of an object without focusing on the details. Similarly, when programmers employ abstraction, they use a general method name in a module rather than list all the detailed activities that will be carried out by the method.

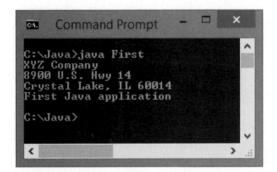

Figure 3-4   First class with main() calling displayAddress()

Figure 3-5   Output of the First application, including the displayAddress() method

 Watch the video *Methods*.

TWO TRUTHS & A LIE

Understanding Method Calls and Placement

1. Any class can contain an unlimited number of methods.

2. During one program execution, a method might be called any number of times.

3. A method is usually written within another method.

The false statement is #3. A method is written within a class, but not within any other methods.

Understanding Method Construction

Every method must include the two parts featured in Figure 3-6:

- A **method header**—A method's header provides information about how other methods can interact with it. A method header is also called a **declaration**.

- A **method body** between a pair of curly braces—The method body contains the statements that carry out the work of the method. A method's body is called its **implementation**. Technically, a method is not required to contain any statements in its body, but you usually would have no reason to create an empty method in a class. Sometimes, while developing a program, the programmer creates an empty method as a placeholder and fills in the implementation later. An empty method is called a **stub**.

```
          public class First
          {
Method      public static void main(String[] args)
headers     {
                displayAddress();                               Method
                System.out.println("First Java application");   bodies
            }
            public static void displayAddress()
            {
                System.out.println("XYZ Company");
                System.out.println("8900 U.S. Hwy 14");
                System.out.println("Crystal Lake, IL 60014");
            }
          }
```

Figure 3-6 The headers and bodies of the methods in the First class

The method header is the first line of a method. It contains the following:

- Optional access specifiers
- A return type
- An identifier
- Parentheses

The next few figures compare these parts of a method header for the main() method and the displayAddress() method in the First class.

Access Specifiers

Figure 3-7 highlights the optional access specifiers for the two methods in the First class. The access specifier for a Java method can be any of the following modifiers: public, private, protected, or, if left unspecified, package by default. Most often, methods are given public access; this book will cover the other modifiers later. Endowing a method with public access means that any other class can use it, not just the class in which the method resides.

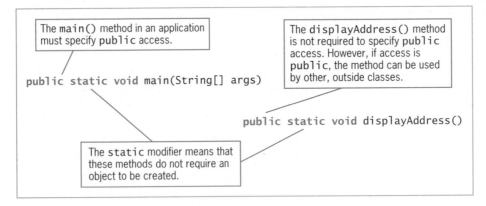

Figure 3-7   Access specifiers for two methods

You first learned the term *access specifier* in Chapter 1. Access specifiers are sometimes called **access modifiers**.

In addition, any method that can be used without instantiating an object requires the keyword modifier `static`. The `main()` method in an application must use the keyword `static`, but other methods, like `displayAddress()`, can use it too. You will learn about nonstatic methods later in this chapter.

Return Type

Figure 3-8 features the return types for the `main()` and `displayAddress()` methods in the `First` class. A **return type** describes the type of data the method sends back to its calling method. Not all methods **return a value** to their calling methods; a method that returns no data has a return type of `void`. The `main()` method in an application must have a return type of `void`; in this example, `displayAddress()` also has a `void` return type. Other methods that you will see later in this chapter have different return types. The phrases *void method* and *method of type void* both refer to a method that has a `void` return type.

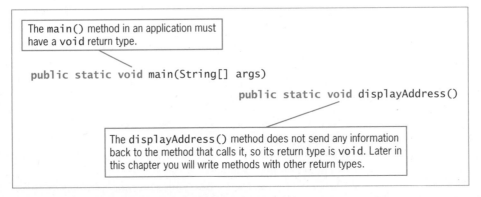

Figure 3-8   Return types for two methods

Method Name

Figure 3-9 highlights the names of the two methods in the `First` class. A method's name can be any legal identifier. That is, like identifiers for classes and variables, a method's identifier must be one word with no embedded spaces, and cannot be a Java keyword. The method that executes first when you run an application must be named `main()`, but you have a lot of leeway in naming other methods that you create. Technically, you could even name another method `main()` as long as you did not include `String[]` within the parentheses, but doing so would be confusing and is not recommended. Because methods "do" something—that is, perform an action—their names frequently contain a verb, such as `print` or `display`.

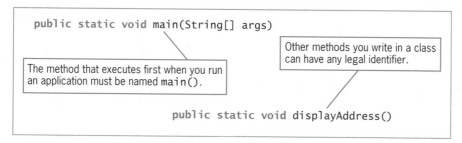

Figure 3-9   Identifiers for two methods

Parentheses

As Figure 3-10 shows, every method header contains a set of parentheses that follow the identifier. The parentheses might contain data to be sent to the method. For example, when you write a `main()` method in a class, the parentheses in its header surround `String[] args`. The `displayAddress()` method in the `First` class requires no outside data, so its parentheses are empty. Later in this chapter, you will see several methods that accept data.

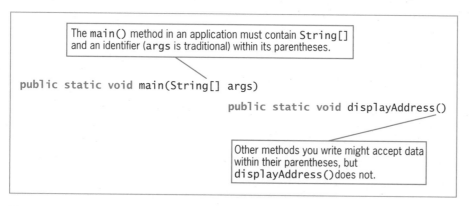

Figure 3-10   Parentheses and their contents for two methods

The full name of the `displayAddress()` method is `First.displayAddress()`, which includes the class name (`First`), a dot, and the method name, which is `displayAddress()`. (The name does not include an object because `displayAddress()` is a `static` method.) A complete name that includes the class is a **fully qualified identifier**. When you use a method within its own class, you do not need to use the fully qualified name (although you can); the simple method name alone is enough. However, if you want to use a method in another class, the compiler does not recognize the method unless you use the full name. You have used similar syntax (including a class name, dot, and method name) when calling the JOptionPane.showMessageDialog() method.

Each of two different classes can have its own method named displayAddress(). Such a method in the second class would be entirely distinct from the identically named method in the first class. You could use both methods in a third class by using their fully qualified identifiers. Two classes in an application cannot have the same name.

Think of the class name as the family name. Within your own family, you might refer to an activity as "the family reunion," but outside the family people need to use a surname as well, as in "the Anderson family reunion." Similarly, within a class a method name alone is sufficient, but outside the class you need to use the fully qualified name.

TWO TRUTHS & A LIE

Understanding Method Construction

1. A method header is also called an implementation.

2. When a method is declared with public access, methods in other classes can call it.

3. Not all methods return a value, but every method requires a return type.

The false statement is #1. A method header is a declaration; a method body is its implementation.

You Do It

Creating a static Method that Requires No Arguments and Returns No Values

Paradise Day Spa provides many personal services such as haircuts, manicures, and facials. In this section, you create a new class named ParadiseInfo, which contains a main() method that calls a displayInfo() method.

1. Open a new document in your text editor, and type the following shell for the class:

```
public class ParadiseInfo
{
}
```

(continues)

(continued)

2. Between the curly braces of the class, indent a few spaces and create the shell for the main() method:

```
public static void main(String[] args)
{
}
```

3. Between the braces of the main() method, insert a call to the displayInfo() method:
```
displayInfo();
```

4. Place the displayInfo() method outside the main() method, just before the closing curly brace for the ParadiseInfo class:

```
public static void displayInfo()
{
    System.out.println("Paradise Day Spa wants to pamper you.");
    System.out.println("We will make you look good.");
}
```

5. Save the file as **ParadiseInfo.java**.

6. Compile the class, and then execute it. The output should look like Figure 3-11.

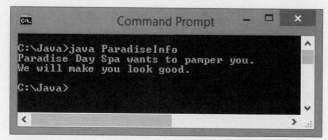

```
C:\Java>java ParadiseInfo
Paradise Day Spa wants to pamper you.
We will make you look good.

C:\Java>
```

Figure 3-11 Output of the ParadiseInfo application

Calling a `static` Method from Another Class

Next, you see how to call the displayInfo() method from a method within another class.

1. Open a new document in your text editor, and then enter the following class in which the main() method calls the displayInfo() method that resides in the ParadiseInfo class:

```
public class TestInfo
{
    public static void main(String[] args)
    {
        System.out.println("Calling method from another class:");
        ParadiseInfo.displayInfo();
    }
}
```

(continues)

(continued)

2. Save the file as **TestInfo.java** in the same folder as the ParadiseInfo class. If the files are not saved in the same folder and you try to compile the calling class, your compiler issues the error message "cannot find symbol"; the symbol named is the missing class you tried to call.

3. Compile the application and execute it. Your output should look like Figure 3-12. The TestInfo class does not contain the displayInfo() method; it uses the method from the ParadiseInfo class. It's important that the displayInfo() method is public. If you had omitted the keyword public from the definition of the displayInfo() method in the ParadiseInfo class, then the TestInfo class would not have been able to use it.

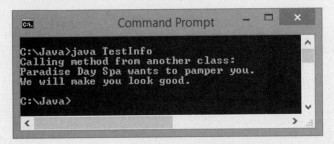

Figure 3-12   Output of the TestInfo application

Examining the Details of a Prewritten static *Method*

Recall that in Chapter 2, you used the JOptionPane class to create statements like the following:

```
JOptionPane.showMessageDialog
   (null, "Every bill is due in " + creditDays + " days");
```

In the next steps, you examine the Java API documentation for the showMessageDialog() method so that you can better understand how prewritten methods are similar to ones that you write.

1. Using a Web browser, go to the Java Web site and select **Java APIs** and **Java SE 8**.

2. In the alphabetical list of classes, find the JOptionPane class and select it.

3. Scroll through the class documentation until you find the **Method Summary**. Then, find the first listed version of the **showMessageDialog()** method. To the left, notice that the method is defined as a static void method, just like the main() and displayInfo() methods discussed earlier in this "You Do It" section. You can use the static showMessageDialog() method in your classes by using its class name, a dot, and the method name, in the same way that you used the ParadiseInfo.displayInfo() method in the outside class named TestInfo.

Adding Parameters to Methods

Some methods require that data be sent to them when they are called. Data items you use in a call to a method are called **arguments**. When the method receives the data items, they are called **parameters**. Methods that receive data are flexible because they can produce different results depending on what data they receive.

As a real-life example, when you make a restaurant reservation, you do not need to employ a different method for every date of the year at every possible time of day. Rather, you can supply the date and time as information to the person who carries out the method. The method, recording the reservation, is then carried out in the same manner, no matter what date and time are supplied.

In a program, if you design a method to square numeric values, it makes sense to design a square() method that you can supply with an argument that represents the value to be squared, rather than having to develop a square1() method (that squares the value 1), a square2() method (that squares the value 2), and so on. To call a square() method that takes an argument, you might write a statement like square(17); or square(86);. Similarly, any time it is called, the println() method can receive any one of an infinite number of arguments—for example, "Hello", "Goodbye", or any other String. No matter what message is sent to println(), the message is displayed correctly. If the println() method could not accept arguments, it would not be practical to use.

In everyday life, you use many methods without understanding how they work. For example, when you make a real-life restaurant reservation, you do not need to know how the reservation is actually recorded at the restaurant—perhaps it is written in a book, marked on a large chalkboard, or entered into a computerized database. The implementation details don't concern you as a client, and if the restaurant changes its methods from one year to the next, the change does not affect your use of the reservation method—you still call and provide your name, a date, and a time.

Similarly, object-oriented programs use **implementation hiding**, which describes the encapsulation of method details. It means that a client does not have to know how a method works internally, but only needs to know the name of the called method and what type of information to send. (Usually, you also want to know about any data returned by the method; you will learn about returned data later in this chapter.) In other words, the calling method needs to understand only the **interface** to the called method. The interface is the only part of a method that the method's client sees or with which it interacts. In addition, if you substitute a new or revised method implementation, as long as the interface to the method does not change, you won't need to make any changes in any methods that call the altered method.

Hidden implementation methods are often referred to as existing in a **black box**. Many everyday devices are black boxes—that is, you can use them without understanding how they work. For example, most of us use telephones, television sets, and automobiles without understanding much about their internal mechanisms.

Creating a Method that Receives a Single Parameter

When a method can receive a parameter, its declaration contains the same elements as one that does not accept a parameter—optional access specifiers, the return type for the method, the method name, and a set of parentheses that include two items:

- The parameter type
- A local name for the parameter

For example, the declaration for a public method named `predictRaise()` that accepts a person's annual salary and computes the value of a 10 percent raise could be written as follows:

`public static void predictRaise(double salary)`

You can think of the parentheses in a method declaration as a funnel into the method—parameters listed there contain data that is "dropped into" the method. A parameter accepted by a method can be any data type, including the primitive types, such as `int`, `double`, and `char`; it also can be a built-in class type such as `String` or `PrintStream`, or a class type you create.

In the method header for `predictRaise()`, the parameter `double salary` within the parentheses indicates that the method will receive a value of type `double`, and that within the method, the passed value will be known as `salary`. Figure 3-13 shows a complete method.

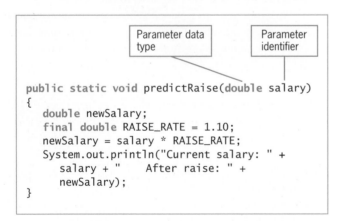

```
                 Parameter data          Parameter
                 type                     identifier

public static void predictRaise(double salary)
{
    double newSalary;
    final double RAISE_RATE = 1.10;
    newSalary = salary * RAISE_RATE;
    System.out.println("Current salary: " +
        salary + "    After raise: " +
        newSalary);
}
```

Figure 3-13   The `predictRaise()` method

The `predictRaise()` method is a `void` method because it does not need to return a value to any other method that calls it—its only function is to receive the `salary` value, multiply it by the `RAISE_RATE` constant (1.10, which results in a 10 percent salary increase), and then display the result.

The predictRaise() method's parameter is a double, so you call it using any argument that can be promoted to a double. In other words, because predictRaise() accepts a double, it can also accept a float, long, int, short, or byte. (See Figure 2-41 in Chapter 2 to review the order for establishing unifying data types.) The argument can be a constant, variable, or more complicated expression.

For example, all of the following method calls are valid:

- predictRaise(1000);—This call uses an unnamed int constant that is promoted to a double.

- predictRaise(472.25);—This call uses an unnamed double constant.

- predictRaise(16.55 * 40);—This call uses an arithmetic expression.

- predictRaise(STANDARD_SALARY);—This call uses a named constant that might be a double, float, long, int, short, or byte.

- predictRaise(mySalary);—This call uses a variable that might be a double, float, long, int, short, or byte.

- predictRaise(getCurrentSalary());—This call assumes that the getCurrentSalary() method used as an argument returns a double, float, long, int, short, or byte. You learn about methods that return data later in this chapter.

You can call the predictRaise() method any number of times, with a different argument each time. Each of these arguments becomes known as salary within the method. The identifier salary represents a variable that holds a copy of the value of any double value passed into the method.

It is interesting to note that if the value used as an argument in the method call to predictRaise() is a variable, it might possess the same identifier as salary or a different one, such as startingWage. For example, the code in Figure 3-14 shows three calls to the predictRaise() method, and Figure 3-15 shows the output. One call uses a constant, 400.00. The other two use variables—one with the same name as salary and the other with a different name, startingWage. The identifier salary in the main() method refers to a different memory location than the one in the predictRaise() method. The parameter salary is simply a placeholder while it is being used within the predictRaise() method, no matter what name its value "goes by" in the calling method. The parameter salary is a **local variable** to the predictRaise() method; that is, it is known only within the boundaries of the method. The variable and constant declared within the method are also local to the method.

132

```java
public class DemoRaise
{
   public static void main(String[] args)
   {
      double salary = 200.00;
      double startingWage = 800.00;
      System.out.println("Demonstrating some raises");
      predictRaise(400.00);
      predictRaise(salary);
      predictRaise(startingWage);
   }

   public static void predictRaise(double salary)
   {
      double newSalary;
      final double RAISE_RATE = 1.10;
      newSalary = salary * RAISE_RATE;
      System.out.println("Current salary: " +
         salary + "    After raise: " +
         newSalary);
   }
}
```

> The predictRaise() method is called three times using three different arguments.

> The parameter salary receives a copy of the value in each argument that is passed.

Figure 3-14 The DemoRaise class with a main() method that uses the predictRaise() method three times

Recall that the final modifier makes RAISE_RATE constant. Because salary is not altered within the predictRaise() method in Figure 3-14, you could also make the method's parameter constant by declaring the method header as public static void predictRaise(final double SALARY). There would be no difference in the program's execution, but declaring a parameter as final means it cannot be altered within the method. Someone reading your program would be able to see that the parameter is not intended to change.

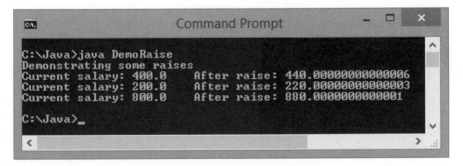

```
C:\Java>java DemoRaise
Demonstrating some raises
Current salary: 400.0    After raise: 440.00000000000006
Current salary: 200.0    After raise: 220.00000000000003
Current salary: 800.0    After raise: 880.0000000000001

C:\Java>
```

Figure 3-15 Output of the DemoRaise application

Each time the predictRaise() method in Figure 3-14 executes, a salary variable is redeclared—that is, a new memory location large enough to hold a double is set up and named salary. Within the predictRaise() method, salary holds a copy of whatever value is passed into the method by the `main()` method. When the `predictRaise()` method ends at the closing curly brace, the local `salary` variable ceases to exist. That is, if you change the value of `salary` after you have used it in the calculation within `predictRaise()`, it affects nothing else. The memory location that holds `salary` is released at the end of the method, and any changes to its value within the method do not affect any value in the calling method. In particular, don't think there would be any change in the variable named `salary` in the `main()` method; that variable, even though it has the same name as the locally declared parameter in the `predictRaise()` method, is a different variable with its own memory address.

 When a variable ceases to exist at the end of a method, programmers say the variable "goes out of scope." A variable's *scope* is the part of a program in which a variable exists and can be accessed using its unqualified name. Chapter 4 discusses scope in greater detail.

Creating a Method that Requires Multiple Parameters

A method can require more than one parameter. For example, rather than creating a `predictRaise()` method that adds a 10 percent raise to every person's salary, you might prefer to create a method to which you can pass two values—the salary to be raised as well as a percentage figure by which to raise it. Figure 3-16 shows a method that uses two such parameters.

```
public static void predictRaiseUsingRate(double salary, double rate)
{
    double newAmount;
    newAmount = salary * (1 + rate);
    System.out.println("With raise, new salary is " + newAmount);
}
```

Figure 3-16 The `predictRaiseUsingRate()` method that accepts two parameters

In Figure 3-16, two parameters (`double salary` and `double rate`) appear within the parentheses in the method header. A comma separates each parameter, and each parameter requires its own declared type (in this case, both are `double`) as well as its own identifier. Note that a declaration for a method that receives two or more parameters must list the type for each parameter separately, even if the parameters have the same type.

You can pass multiple arguments to a method by listing the arguments within the call to the method and separating them with commas. When values are passed to the method in a statement such as the following, the first value passed is referenced as `salary` within the method, and the second value passed is referenced as `rate`:

`predictRaiseUsingRate(mySalary, promisedRate);`

Arguments to a method must be passed in the correct order. The call `predictRaiseUsingRate(200.00, 0.10);` results in output representing a 10 percent raise based on a $200.00 salary amount (or $220.00), but predictRaiseUsingRate(0.10, 200.00); results in output representing a 20,000 percent raise based on a salary of 10 cents (or $20.10).

If arguments to a method are passed in the wrong order, the result is one of the following:

- If the method can still accept both arguments, the result is a logical error; that is, the program compiles and executes, but it probably produces incorrect results.

- If the method cannot accept the arguments, passing arguments in the wrong order constitutes a syntax error, and the program does not compile.

You can write a method so that it takes any number of parameters in any order. However, when you call a method, the arguments you send to a method must match in order—both in number and in type—the parameters listed in the method declaration. A method's **signature** is the combination of the method name and the number, types, and order of arguments. A method call must match the called method's signature.

Thus, a method to compute an automobile salesperson's commission amount might require arguments such as an integer dollar value of a car sold, a double percentage commission rate, and a character code for the vehicle type. The correct method executes only when three arguments of the correct types are sent in the correct order. Figure 3-17 shows a class containing a three-parameter method and a main() method that calls it twice, once using variable arguments and again using constant arguments. Figure 3-18 shows the output of the application.

```
public class ComputeCommission
{
    public static void main(String[] args)
    {
        char vType = 'S';
        int value = 23000;
        double commRate = 0.08;
        computeCommission(value, commRate, vType);
        computeCommission(40000, 0.10, 'L');
    }
    public static void computeCommission(int value,
        double rate, char vehicle)
    {
        double commission;
        commission = value * rate;
        System.out.println("\nThe " + vehicle +
            " type vehicle is worth $" + value);
        System.out.println("With " + (rate * 100) +
            "% commission rate, the commission is $" +
            commission);
    }
}
```

Figure 3-17   The ComputeCommission class

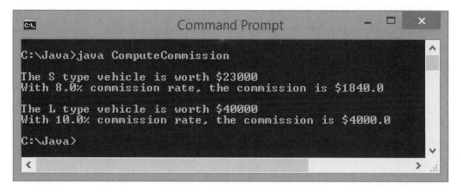

Figure 3-18   Output of the ComputeCommission application

The arguments in a method call are often referred to as **actual parameters**. The variables in the method declaration that accept the values from the actual parameters are **formal parameters**.

When you look at Java applications, you might see methods that appear to be callable in multiple ways. For example, you can use System.out.println() with no arguments to display a blank line, or with a String argument to display the String. You can use the method with different argument lists only because multiple versions of the method have been written, each taking a specific set of arguments. The ability to execute different method implementations by altering the argument used with the method name is known as method overloading, a concept you will learn about in the next chapter.

TWO TRUTHS & A LIE

Adding Parameters to Methods

1. A class can contain any number of methods, and each method can be called any number of times.

2. Arguments are used in method calls; they are passed to parameters in method headers.

3. A method header always contains a return type, an identifier, and a parameter list within parentheses.

The false statement is #3. A method header always contains a return type, an identifier, and parentheses, but the parameter list might be empty.

Creating Methods that Return Values

A method ends when any of the following events takes place:

- The method completes all of its statements. You have seen methods like this in the last section.

- The method throws an exception. Exceptions are errors; you will learn about them in the chapter "Exception Handling."

- The method reaches a `return` statement. A **return statement** causes a method to end and the program's logic to return to the calling method. Also, a `return` statement frequently sends a value back to the calling method.

The return type for a method can be any type used in Java, which includes the primitive types `int`, `double`, `char`, and so on, as well as class types (including class types you create). Of course, a method can also return nothing, in which case the return type is `void`.

A method's return type is known more succinctly as a **method's type**. For example, the declaration for the `displayAddress()` method shown earlier in Figure 3-4 is written as follows:

```
public static void displayAddress()
```

This method returns no value, so it is type `void`.

A method that prompts a user for an age and returns the age to the calling method might be declared as:

```
public static int getAge()
```

The method returns an `int`, so it is type `int`.

As another example, a method that returns `true` or `false` depending on whether an employee worked overtime hours might be declared as:

```
public static boolean workedOvertime()
```

This method returns a Boolean value, so it is type `boolean`.

The `predictRaise()` method shown earlier produces output, but does not return any value, so its return type is `void`. If you want to create a method to return the new, calculated salary value rather than display it, the header would be written as follows:

```
public static double predictRaise(double salary)
```

Figure 3-19 shows this method.

```
public static double predictRaise(double salary)
{
    double newAmount;
    final double RAISE = 1.10;
    newAmount = salary * RAISE;
    return newAmount;
}
```

Figure 3-19   The `predictRaise()` method returning a `double`

Notice the shaded return type `double` that precedes the method name in the `predictRaise()` method header in Figure 3-19. Also notice the shaded declaration of `newAmount`. This `double` variable's value is returned in the last shaded statement in the method. The `return` statement causes a value to be sent from a called method back to the calling method. A method's declared return type must match the type of the value used in the `return` statement; if it does not, the class does not compile.

A method can return one value at most. The returned value can be a variable, a named or unnamed constant, or another method call, and the returned type must match or be promotable to the return type declared in the method header. For example, a method with a `double` return type might have a `return` statement that looks like any of the following:

```
return 1;
return 1.0;
return mySalary;
return getMySalary();
```

All methods except `void` methods require a `return` statement that returns a value of the appropriate type. You can place a `return` statement in a `void` method that is simply the word `return` followed by a semicolon. However, most Java programmers do not include a `return` statement in a method when nothing is returned.

You cannot place any statements after a method's `return` statement. Such statements are **unreachable statements** because the logical flow leaves the method at the `return` statement. An unreachable statement can never execute, and it causes a compiler error. Unreachable statements are also called **dead code**.

A method can contain multiple `return` clauses if they are embedded in a decision, although this practice is not recommended because it can lead to errors that are difficult to detect. However, no other statements can be placed after the last `return` clause in a method. You will learn about decision making in the chapter "Making Decisions."

If a method returns a value, then when you call the method, you normally use the returned value, although you are not required to do so. For example, when you invoke the `predictRaise()` method, you might want to assign the returned value (also called the method's value) to a `double` variable named `myNewSalary`, as in the following statement:

```
myNewSalary = predictRaise(mySalary);
```

The `predictRaise()` method returns a `double`, so it is appropriate to assign the method's returned value to a `double` variable.

Alternatively, you can choose to use a method's returned value directly, without storing it in any variable. When you use a method's value, you use it in the same way you would use any variable of the same type. For example, you can display a return value in a statement such as the following:

```
System.out.println("New salary is " + predictRaise(mySalary));
```

In the preceding statement, the call to the predictRaise() method is made from within the println() method call. Because predictRaise() returns a double, you can use the method call in the same way that you would use any simple double value. As another example, you can perform arithmetic with a method's return value, as in the following statement:

```
double spendingMoney = predictRaise(mySalary) - expenses;
```

In this statement, the value of mySalary is not altered; the only changed variable is spendingMoney.

If you want mySalary to hold the value of the new salary with the raise, then you could use the following statement:

```
mySalary = predictRaise(mySalary);
```

Chaining Method Calls

Any method might call any number of other methods. For example, a main() method might call a predictRaise() method, and the predictRaise()method might call a calculateBonus() method, as shown in the shaded statement in Figure 3-20.

```
public static double predictRaise(double salary)
{
   double newAmount;
   double bonusAmount;
   final double RAISE = 1.10;
   newAmount = salary * RAISE;
   bonusAmount = calculateBonus(newAmount);
   newAmount = newAmount + bonusAmount;
   return newAmount;
}
```

Figure 3-20   The predictRaise() method calling the calculateBonus() method

Looking at the call to the calculateBonus() method from the predictRaise() method, you do not know how calculateBonus()works. You only know that the calculateBonus() method accepts a double as a parameter (because newAmount is passed into it) and that it must return either a double or a type that can automatically be promoted to a double (because the result is stored in bonusAmount). In other words, the method acts as a black box.

As examples, the calculateBonus() method might look like either of the versions shown in Figure 3-21. The first version simply adds a $50.00 bonus to a salary parameter. The second version calls another method named trickyCalculation() that returns a value added to salary. When you read the calculateBonus() method, you don't know what happens in the trickyCalculation() method, and when you read the predictRaise() method that calls calculateBonus(), you don't even necessarily know that trickyCalculation() is called.

```
public static double calculateBonus(double salary)
{
    final double BONUS_AMT = 50.00;
    salary = salary + BONUS_AMT;
    return salary;
}

public static double calculateBonus(double salary)
{
    salary = salary + trickyCalculation();
    return salary;
}
```

Figure 3-21 Two possible versions of the `calculateBonus()` method

You also can chain method calls in a single statement. If `calculateBonus()` accepts and returns a `double`, and `predictRaise()` also accepts and returns a `double`, then the following statement is legal:

`double salaryGoingForward = calculateBonus(predictRaise(300.00));`

In this statement, the constant 300.00 is passed to `predictRaise()`, and the value returned from that call is passed to `calculateBonus()`. Finally, the value returned from `calculateBonus()` is assigned to `salaryGoingForward`.

 Watch the video *Methods and Parameters*.

TWO TRUTHS & A LIE

Creating Methods that Return Values

1. The return type for a method can be any type used in Java, including `int`, `double`, and `void`.

2. A method's declared return type must match the type of the value used in the parameter list.

3. You cannot place a method within another method, but you can call a method from within another method.

The false statement is #2. A method's declared return type must match the type of the value used in the return statement.

You Do It

Creating `static` Methods that Accept Arguments and Return a Value

In this section, you add a method to the `ParadiseInfo` class you started in the last "You Do It" section. The new method receives two parameters and returns a value. The purpose of the method is to accept a minimum price for the current week's featured discount and the percentage discount, and to return the minimum amount the customer will save.

1. Open the **ParadiseInfo.java** file in your text editor, and then change the class name to `ParadiseInfo2`. Immediately save the file as **ParadiseInfo2.java**.

2. As the first line of the file, add the `import` statement that allows user input:

    ```
    import java.util.Scanner;
    ```

3. Add four declarations as the first statements following the opening curly brace of the `main()` method. One holds the minimum price for which a discount will be allowed, and another holds the discount rate. The third variable is the minimum savings, which is calculated by multiplying the minimum price for a discount and the discount rate. The fourth variable is a `Scanner` object to use for keyboard input.

    ```
    double price;
    double discount;
    double savings;
    Scanner keyboard = new Scanner(System.in);
    ```

 Instead of importing the `Scanner` class to provide console input, you could substitute `JOptionPane` and include program statements that provide GUI input. The input process can use other techniques too, such as getting data from a storage device—you will learn about file input in the chapter "File Input and Output." The concept of input (getting data into memory from the outside) is the same, no matter what specific technique or type of hardware device you use.

4. Following the declarations, prompt the user for the minimum discount price, and accept a value from the keyboard:

    ```
    System.out.print("Enter cutoff price for discount >> ");
    price = keyboard.nextDouble();
    ```

5. Prompt the user for the discount rate, and accept it.

    ```
    System.out.print("Enter discount rate as a whole number >> ");
    discount = keyboard.nextDouble();
    ```

(continues)

(continued)

6. After the call to `displayInfo()`, insert a call to `computeDiscountInfo()`. You will pass the `price` and `discount` values to the method, and the method returns the minimum that a consumer will save, which is stored in `savings`:

   ```
   savings = computeDiscountInfo(price, discount);
   ```

7. Just before the closing curly brace for the `main()` method, display the savings information:

   ```
   System.out.println("Special this week on any service over " +
       price);
   System.out.println("Discount of " + discount + " percent");
   System.out.println("That's a savings of at least $" + savings);
   ```

8. After the `displayInfo()` method implementation, but before the closing curly brace for the class, add the `computeDiscountInfo()` method. It accepts two `double`s and returns a `double`.

   ```java
   public static double computeDiscountInfo(double pr, double dscnt)
   {
      double savings;
      savings = pr * dscnt / 100;
      return savings;
   }
   ```

9. Save the file, and then compile and execute it. Figure 3-22 shows a typical execution. After the user is prompted for the cutoff price for the week's sale and the discount to be applied, the program executes the `displayInfo()` method. Then the program executes the `computeDiscountInfo()` method, which returns a value to store in the `savings` variable. Finally, the discount information is displayed.

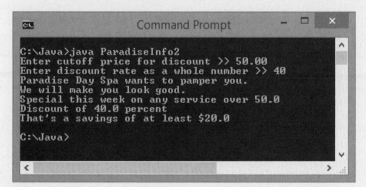

Figure 3-22 Typical execution of the `ParadiseInfo2` program

(continues)

(continued)

Understanding that Methods Can Be Used as Black Boxes

In this chapter, you have learned that methods can be used without knowing the details of their implementation. As an example of how professional programmers use implementation hiding, you can visit the Java Web site to see the interfaces for thousands of prewritten methods that reside in the Java prewritten classes. You are not allowed to see the code inside these methods; you see only their interfaces, which is all you need to be able to use the methods.

1. Open your Web browser, go to the Java Web site, and navigate to the Java APIs for Java SE 8.

2. From the alphabetical list of classes, select `PrintStream`.

3. At the `PrintStream` page, read the descriptions of several methods for the class. Note that for each method, you can see the return type, method name, and parameter list, but you do not see the implementation for any of the existing methods.

4. Examine other classes. Again, note that the Java documentation provides you with method interfaces but not implementations. When you develop your own classes in the future, you might choose to provide your users with similar documentation and compiled classes so that they cannot see, modify, or steal the code you have worked hard to develop.

Learning About Classes and Objects

When you think in an object-oriented manner, everything is an object, and every object is a member of a class. You can think of any inanimate physical item as an object—your desk, your computer, and the building in which you live are all called objects in everyday conversation. You can also think of living things as objects—your houseplant, your pet fish, and your sister are objects. Events are also objects—the stock purchase you made, the mortgage closing you attended, and a graduation party that was held in your honor are all objects.

Everything is an object, and every object is a member of a more general class. Your desk is a member of the class that includes all desks, and your pet fish is a member of the class that contains all fish. An object-oriented programmer would say that your desk is an instance of the Desk class and your fish is an instance of the Fish class. These statements represent **is-a relationships**—that is, relationships in which the object "is a" concrete example of the class. Expressing an is-a relationship is correct only when you refer to the object and the class in the proper order. You can say, "My oak desk with the scratch on top *is a* Desk, and my goldfish named Moby *is a* Fish." You don't define a Desk by saying, "A Desk *is an* oak desk with a scratch on top," or explain what a Fish is by saying, "A Fish *is a* goldfish named Moby," because both a `Desk` and a Fish are much more general. The difference between a class and an object parallels the difference between abstract and concrete. An object is an **instantiation** of a class, or one tangible example of a class. Your goldfish, my guppy, and the zoo's shark each constitute one instantiation of the `Fish` class.

 Programmers also use the phrase "is-a" when talking about inheritance relationships. You will learn more about inheritance in the chapters "Introduction to Inheritance" and "Advanced Inheritance Concepts."

The concept of a class is useful because of its reusability. Objects gain their attributes from their classes, and all objects have predictable attributes because they are members of certain classes. For example, if you are invited to a graduation party, you automatically know many things about it. You assume there will be a starting time, a certain number of guests, and some quantity of food. You understand what a party object entails because of your previous knowledge of the `Party` class. You don't know the number of guests or what food will be served at this particular party, but you understand that because all parties have guests and refreshments, this one must too. Because you understand the general characteristics of a `Party`, you anticipate different attributes than if you plan to attend a `TheaterPerformance` object or a `DentalAppointment` object.

In addition to their attributes, objects have methods associated with them, and every object that is an instance of a class is assumed to possess the same methods. For example, for all `Party` objects, a date and time are set at some point. In a program, you might name these methods `setDate()` and `setTime()`. Party guests need to know the date and time and might use methods named `getDate()` and `getTime()` to find out the date and time of any `Party` object. Method names that begin with *get* and *set* are very typical. You will learn more about get and set methods in the next section.

Your graduation party, then, might have the identifier `myGraduationParty`. As a member of the `Party` class, `myGraduationParty`, like all `Party` objects, might have data methods `setDate()` and `setTime()`. When you use them, the `setDate()` and `setTime()` methods require arguments, or information passed to them. For example, statements such as `myGraduationParty.setDate("May 12")` and `myGraduationParty.setTime("6 P.M.")` invoke methods that are available for the `myGraduationParty` object. When you use an object and its methods, think of being able to send a message to the object to direct it to accomplish some task—you can tell the `Party` object named `myGraduationParty` to set the date and time you request. Even though `yourAnniversaryParty` is also a member of the `Party` class, and even though it also has access to `setDate()` and `setTime()` methods, the arguments you send to `yourAnniversaryParty` methods will be different from those you send to `myGraduationParty` methods. Within any object-oriented program, you are continuously making requests to objects' methods and often including arguments as part of those requests.

In addition, some methods used in an application must return a message or value. If one of your party guests uses the `getDate()` method, the guest hopes that the method will respond with the desired information. Similarly, within object-oriented programs, methods are often called upon to return a piece of information to the source of the request. For example, a method within a `Payroll` class that calculates federal withholding tax might return a tax

144

amount in dollars and cents, and a method within an `Inventory` class might return `true` or `false`, depending on the method's determination of whether an item is at the reorder point.

With object-oriented programming, sometimes you create classes so that you can instantiate objects from them, and other times you create classes to run as applications. Application classes frequently instantiate objects that use the objects of other classes (and their data and methods). Sometimes you write classes that do both. The same programmer does not need to write every class he or she uses. Often, you will write programs that use classes created by others. For example, many programs you have seen so far in this book have used the `System` class. You did not have to create it or its `println()` method; both were provided for you by Java's creators. Similarly, you might create a class that others will use to instantiate objects within their own applications. You can call an application or class that instantiates objects of another class a **class client** or **class user**.

You can identify a class that is an application because it contains a `public static void main()` method. The `main()` method is the starting point for any application. You will write and use many classes that do not contain a `main()` method—these classes can be used by other classes that are applications or applets. (You will learn about applets in the chapter "Applets, Images, and Sound.")

A Java application can contain only one method with the header `public static void main(String[] args)`. If you write a class that imports another class, and both classes have a `public main()` method, your application will not compile.

So far, you've learned that object-oriented programming involves objects that send messages to other objects requesting they perform tasks, and that every object belongs to a class. Understanding classes and how objects are instantiated from them is the heart of object-oriented thinking.

TWO TRUTHS & A LIE

Learning About Classes and Objects

1. A class is an instantiation of many objects.

2. Objects gain their attributes and methods from their classes.

3. An application or class that instantiates objects of another prewritten class is a class client.

The false statement is #1. An object is one instantiation of a class.

Creating a Class

When you create a class, you must assign a name to the class, and you must determine what data and methods will be part of the class. Suppose you decide to create a class named `Employee`. One instance variable of `Employee` might be an employee number, and two necessary methods might be a method to set (or provide a value for) the employee number and another method to get (or retrieve) that employee number. To begin, you create a class header with three parts:

- An optional access specifier
- The keyword `class`
- Any legal identifier you choose for the name of your class—starting with an uppercase letter is conventional

For example, a header for a class that represents an employee might be:

```
public class Employee
```

The most liberal form of access is `public`. The keyword `public` is a class modifier. Classes that are `public` are accessible by all objects. Public classes also can be **extended**, or used as a basis for any other class. Making access `public` means that if you develop a good `Employee` class, and someday you want to develop two classes that are more specific, `SalariedEmployee` and `HourlyEmployee`, then you do not have to start from scratch. Each new class can become an extension of the original `Employee` class, inheriting its data and methods. Although other specifiers exist, you will use the `public` specifier for most of your classes.

 You will learn about extended classes in the chapter "Introduction to Inheritance."

After writing the class header `public class Employee`, you write the body of the `Employee` class between a set of curly braces. The body contains the data and methods for the class. The data components of a class are often referred to as **data fields** to help distinguish them from other variables you might use. Figure 3-23 shows an `Employee` class that contains one data field named `empNum`. Data fields are variables you declare within a class but outside of any method.

In Figure 3-23, the data field `empNum` is not preceded by the keyword `static`. If the keyword `static` had been inserted there, only one `empNum` value would be shared by all `Employee` objects that are eventually instantiated. Because the `empNum` field in Figure 3-23 is not preceded by `static`,

```
public class Employee
{
    private int empNum;
}
```

Figure 3-23   The `Employee` class with one field

when you eventually create, or instantiate, objects from the class, each Employee can have its own unique empNum. Each object gets its own copy of each nonstatic data field. A nonstatic field like empNum is an **instance variable** for the class.

146

You have already learned that the access specifier for most Java methods is public. However, most fields, like empNum in the Employee class, are private, which provides the highest level of security. Assigning **private access** to a field means that no other classes can access the field's values, and only methods of the same class are allowed to set, get, or otherwise use private variables. The principle used in creating private access is sometimes called **information hiding** and is an important component of object-oriented programs. A class's private data can be changed or manipulated only by a class's own methods and not by methods that belong to other classes. In contrast to fields, which are usually private, most class methods are public. The resulting private data/public method arrangement provides a means for you to control outside access to your data—only a class's nonprivate methods can be used to access a class's private data. The situation is similar to hiring a public receptionist to sit in front of your private office and control which messages you receive (perhaps deflecting trivial or hostile ones) and which messages you send (perhaps checking your spelling, grammar, and any legal implications). The way in which the nonprivate methods are written controls how you use the private data.

The first release of Java (1.0) supported five access levels—the four listed previously plus private protected. The private protected access level is not supported in versions of Java higher than 1.0; you should not use it in your Java programs.

In summary, a class's data fields are most often private and not static. The exception occurs when you want to use a nonchanging value without being required to create an object—in that case you make the field both static and final. For example, the Java Math class contains a final, public, static field named PI that you can use without instantiating a Math object. You will learn about the Math class in the next chapter.

TWO TRUTHS & A LIE

Creating a Class

1. A class header contains an optional access specifier, the keyword class, and an identifier.

2. When you instantiate objects, each has its own copy of each static data field in the class.

3. Most fields in a class are private, and most methods are public.

The false statement is #2. When you instantiate objects, each has its own copy of each nonstatic data field in the class.

Creating Instance Methods in a Class

Besides data, classes contain methods. For example, one method you need for an `Employee` class that contains an `empNum` is the method to retrieve (or return) any `Employee`'s `empNum` for use by another class. A reasonable name for this method is `getEmpNum()`, and its declaration is `public int getEmpNum()` because it will have `public` access, return an integer (the employee number), and possess the identifier `getEmpNum()`.

Similarly, you need a method with which to set the `empNum` field. A reasonable name for this method is `setEmpNum()`, and its declaration is `public void setEmpNum(int emp)` because it will have `public` access, return nothing, possess the identifier `setEmpNum()`, and require a parameter that represents the employee's ID number, which is type `int`.

Methods that set or change field values are called **mutator methods**; methods that retrieve values are called **accessor methods**. In Java, mutator methods conventionally start with the prefix set, and accessor methods conventionally start with the prefix get. Using these three-letter prefixes with your method names is not required, but it is conventional. Figure 3-24 shows the get and set methods for the `empNum` field for the `Employee` class.

```
public void setEmpNum(int emp)
{
    empNum = emp;
}

public int getEmpNum()
{
    return empNum;
}
```

Figure 3-24   The `setEmpNum()` and `getEmpNum()` methods

Notice that, unlike the methods you created earlier in this chapter, the `getEmpNum()` and `setEmpNum()` methods do not employ the `static` modifier. The keyword `static` is used for classwide methods, but not for methods that "belong" to objects. If you are creating a program with a `main()` method that you will execute to perform some task, many of your methods will be static so you can call them from within `main()` without creating objects. However, if you are creating a class from which objects will be instantiated, most methods will probably be nonstatic because you will associate the methods with individual objects. For example, the `getEmpNum()` method must be nonstatic because it returns a different `empNum` value for every `Employee` object you ever create. **Nonstatic methods**, those methods used with object instantiations, are called **instance methods**. You *can* use either a `static` or nonstatic method with an object, but only nonstatic methods behave uniquely for each object. You cannot use a nonstatic method without an object.

Understanding when to declare fields and methods as static and nonstatic is a challenge for new programmers. To help you determine whether a data field should be `static` or not, you can ask yourself how many times it occurs. If it occurs once per class, it is `static`, but if it occurs once per object, it is not `static`. Table 3-1 provides a summary.

Static	Nonstatic
In Java, `static` is a keyword. It also can be used as an adjective.	There is no keyword for nonstatic items. When you do not explicitly declare a field or method to be static, it is nonstatic by default.
Static fields in a class are called class fields.	Nonstatic fields in a class are called instance variables.
Static methods in a class are called class methods.	Nonstatic methods in a class are called instance methods.
When you use a static field or method, you do not need to use an object; for example: `JOptionPane.showDialog();`	When you use a nonstatic field or method, you must use an object; for example: `System.out.println();`
When you create a class with a static field and instantiate 100 objects, only one copy of that field exists in memory.	When you create a class with a nonstatic field and instantiate 100 objects, then 100 copies of that field exist in memory.
When you create a static method in a class and instantiate 100 objects, only one copy of the method exists in memory and the method does not receive a `this` reference.	When you create a nonstatic method in a class and instantiate 100 objects, only one copy of the method exists in memory, but the method receives a `this` reference that contains the address of the object currently using it.
Static class variables are not instance variables. The system allocates memory to hold class variables once per class, no matter how many instances of the class you instantiate. The system allocates memory for class variables the first time it encounters a class, and every instance of a class shares the same copy of any static class variables.	Instance fields and methods are nonstatic. The system allocates a separate memory location for each nonstatic field in each instance.

Table 3-1   Comparison of static and nonstatic

Table 3-1 mentions the `this` reference. You will learn about the `this` reference in the next chapter.

Figure 3-25 also provides a summary of how `public`, `private`, `static`, and nonstatic class members can be used by another class. The figure shows a class named `MyClass` that contains four methods that are `public static`, `private static`, `public` nonstatic, and `private` nonstatic. The figure also shows a `TestClass` that instantiates a `MyClass` object. The `TestClass` contains eight method calls. The three valid calls are all to `public` methods. The call to the nonstatic method uses an object, and the two calls to the static method can use an object or not. The rest of the TestClass code after the comment is invalid. Private methods cannot be called from outside the class, and nonstatic methods require an object.

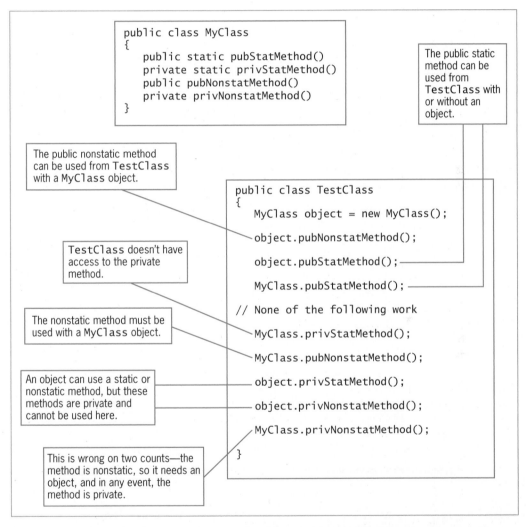

Figure 3-25   Summary of legal and illegal method calls based on combinations of method modifiers

Figure 3-26 shows the complete Employee class containing one private data field and two public methods, all of which are nonstatic. This class becomes the model for a new data type named Employee; when Employee objects eventually are created, each will have its own empNum field, and each will have access to two methods—one that provides a value for its empNum field and another that retrieves the value stored there.

```
public class Employee
{
    private int empNum;
    public int getEmpNum()
    {
        return empNum;
    }
    public void setEmpNum(int emp)
    {
        empNum = emp;
    }
}
```

Figure 3-26   The `Employee` class with one field and two methods

When you create a class like `Employee`, you can compile it, which will identify typographical errors. However, you cannot execute the class because it does not contain a `main()` method. A class like `Employee` is intended to be used as a data type for objects within other applications, as you will see in the next section.

Organizing Classes

Most classes that you create have multiple data fields and methods. For example, in addition to requiring an employee number, an `Employee` needs a last name, a first name, and a salary, as well as methods to set and get those fields. Figure 3-27 shows how you could code the data fields for the `Employee` class.

```
public class Employee
{
    private int empNum;
    private String empLastName;
    private String empFirstName;
    private double empSalary;
    // Methods will go here
}
```

Figure 3-27   An `Employee` class with several data fields

Although there is no requirement to do so, most programmers place data fields in some logical order at the beginning of a class. For example, `empNum` is most likely used as a unique identifier for each employee (what database users often call a **primary key**), so it makes sense to list the employee number first in the class. An employee's last name and first name "go together," so it makes sense to store these two `Employee` components adjacently. Despite these commonsense rules, you have a lot of flexibility in how you position your data fields within any class.

A unique identifier is one that should have no duplicates within an application. For example, an organization might have many employees with the last name Johnson or a weekly salary of $400.00, but there is only one employee with employee number 128.

Because there are two `String` components in the current `Employee` class, they might be declared within the same statement, such as the following:

```
private String empLastName, empFirstName;
```

However, it is usually easier to identify each `Employee` field at a glance if the fields are listed vertically.

You can place a class's data fields and methods in any order within a class. For example, you could place all the methods first, followed by all the data fields, or you could organize the class so that several data fields are followed by methods that use them, and then several more data fields are followed by the methods that use them. This book follows the convention of placing all data fields first so that you can see their names and data types before reading the methods that use them.

The `Employee` class started in Figure 3-27 contains only four fields. Even if only one `set` method and one `get` method are needed for each, eight methods are required. Consider an employee record for most organizations, and you will realize that many more fields are often required (such as address, phone number, hire date, number of dependents, and so on), as well as many more methods. Finding your way through the list can become a formidable task. For ease in locating class methods, many programmers store them in alphabetical order. Other programmers arrange values in pairs of get and set methods, an order that also results in functional groupings. Figure 3-28 shows how the complete class definition for an `Employee` might appear.

```
public class Employee
{
    private int empNum;
    private String empLastName;
    private String empFirstName;
    private double empSalary;
    public int getEmpNum()
    {
        return empNum;
    }
    public void setEmpNum(int emp)
    {
        empNum = emp;
    }
    public String getEmpLastName()
    {
        return empLastName;
    }
}
```

Figure 3-28 The `Employee` class with several data fields and corresponding methods *(continues)*

(continued)

```java
    public void setEmpLastName(String name)
    {
        empLastName = name;
    }
    public String getEmpFirstName()
    {
        return empFirstName;
    }
    public void setEmpFirstName(String name)
    {
        empFirstName = name;
    }
    public double getEmpSalary()
    {
        return empSalary;
    }
    public void setEmpSalary(double sal)
    {
        empSalary = sal;
    }
}
```

Figure 3-28   The `Employee` class with several data fields and corresponding methods

The `Employee` class is still not a particularly large class, and each of its methods is very short, but it is already becoming quite difficult to manage. It certainly can support some well-placed comments. For example, the purpose of the class and the programmer's name might appear in comments at the top of the file, and comments might be used to separate the data and method sections of the class. Your organization might have specific recommendations or requirements for placing comments within a class.

TWO TRUTHS & A LIE

Creating Instance Methods in a Class

1. The keyword `static` is used with classwide methods, but not for methods that "belong" to objects.

2. When you create a class from which objects will be instantiated, most methods are nonstatic because they are associated with individual objects.

3. Static methods are instance methods.

The false statement is #3. Nonstatic methods are instance methods; static methods are class methods.

You Do It

Creating a Class that Contains Instance Fields and Methods

Next, you create a class to store information about event services offered at Paradise Day Spa.

1. Open a new document in your text editor, and type the following class header and the curly braces to surround the class body:

```
public class SpaService
{
}
```

2. Between the curly braces for the class, insert two private data fields that will hold data about a spa service:

```
private String serviceDescription;
private double price;
```

3. Within the class's curly braces and after the field declarations, enter the following two methods that set the field values. The setServiceDescription() method accepts a String parameter and assigns it to the serviceDescription field for each object that eventually will be instantiated. Similarly, the setPrice() method accepts a double parameter and assigns it to the price field. Note that neither of these methods is static.

```
public void setServiceDescription(String service)
{
    serviceDescription = service;
}
public void setPrice(double pr)
{
    price = pr;
}
```

4. Next, add two methods that retrieve the field values as follows:

```
public String getServiceDescription()
{
    return serviceDescription;
}
public double getPrice()
{
    return price;
}
```

5. Save the file as **SpaService.java**, compile it, and then correct any syntax errors. Remember, you cannot run this file as a program because it does not contain a public static main() method. After you read the next section, you will use this class to create objects.

Declaring Objects and Using their Methods

Declaring a class does not create any actual objects. A class is just an abstract description of what an object will be like if any objects are ever actually instantiated. Just as you might understand all the characteristics of an item you intend to manufacture long before the first item rolls off the assembly line, you can create a class with fields and methods long before you instantiate any objects that are members of that class.

A two-step process creates an object that is an instance of a class. First, you supply a type and an identifier—just as when you declare any variable—and then you allocate computer memory for that object. For example, you might declare an integer as `int someValue;` and you might declare an `Employee` as follows:

```
Employee someEmployee;
```

In this statement, `someEmployee` can be any legal identifier, but objects conventionally start with a lowercase letter.

When you declare an integer as `int someValue;`, you notify the compiler that an integer named `someValue` will exist, and you reserve computer memory for it at the same time. When you declare the `someEmployee` instance of the `Employee` class, you are notifying the compiler that you will use the identifier `someEmployee`. However, you are not yet setting aside computer memory in which the `Employee` named `someEmployee` might be stored—that is done automatically only for primitive type variables. To allocate the needed memory for an object, you must use the **new operator**. Two statements that actually set aside enough memory to hold an `Employee` are as follows:

```
Employee someEmployee;
someEmployee = new Employee();
```

You first learned about the **new** operator when you created a `Scanner` object in Chapter 2.

Instead of using two statements, you can declare and reserve memory for `someEmployee` in one statement, as in the following:

```
Employee someEmployee = new Employee();
```

In this statement, `Employee` is the object's type (as well as its class), and `someEmployee` is the name of the object. Also, `someEmployee` becomes a **reference to the object**—the name for a memory address where the object is held. Every object name is also a reference—that is, a computer memory location. In Chapter 2, you learned that a class like `Employee` is a *reference type*.

The equal sign is the assignment operator, so a value is being assigned to `someEmployee` in the declaration. The `new` operator is allocating a new, unused portion of computer memory for `someEmployee`. The value that the statement is assigning to `someEmployee` is a memory address at which `someEmployee` is to be located. You do not need to be concerned with what the actual memory address is—when you refer to `someEmployee`, the compiler locates it at the appropriate address for you.

The final portion of the statement after the new operator, Employee(), with its parentheses, looks suspiciously like a method name. In fact, it is the name of a method that constructs an Employee object. The Employee() method is a **constructor**, a special type of method that creates and initializes objects. You can write your own constructor for a class, and you will learn how later in this chapter. However, when you don't write a constructor for a class, Java writes one for you. Whether you write your own constructor or use the one automatically created by Java, the name of the constructor is always the same as the name of the class whose objects it constructs.

155

After an object has been instantiated, its methods can be accessed using the object's identifier, a dot, and a method call. For example, Figure 3-29 shows an application that instantiates two Employee objects. The two objects, clerk and driver, each use the setEmpNum() and getEmpNum() method one time. The DeclareTwoEmployees application can use these methods because they are public, and it must use each of them with an Employee object because the methods are not static. Figure 3-30 shows the output of the application.

```java
public class DeclareTwoEmployees
{
    public static void main(String[] args)
    {
        Employee clerk = new Employee();
        Employee driver = new Employee();
        clerk.setEmpNum(345);
        driver.setEmpNum(567);
        System.out.println("The clerk's number is " +
            clerk.getEmpNum() + " and the driver's number is " +
            driver.getEmpNum());
    }
}
```

Figure 3-29   The DeclareTwoEmployees class

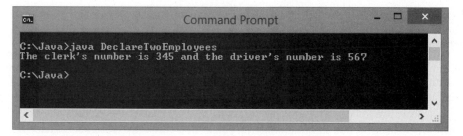

Figure 3-30   Output of the DeclareTwoEmployees application

The program in Figure 3-29 assumes that the Employee.java file is stored in the same folder as the application. If the Employee.java file was stored in a different folder, you would need an import statement at the top of the file, similar to the ones you use for the Scanner and JOptionPane classes.

Understanding Data Hiding

Within the `DeclareTwoEmployees` class, you must use the public methods `setEmpNum()` and `getEmpNum()` to be able to set and retrieve the value of the `empNum` field for each `Employee` because you cannot access the private `empNum` field directly. For example, the following statement would not be allowed:

```
clerk.empNum = 789;
```

This statement generates the error message "empNum has private access in Employee", meaning you cannot access `empNum` from the `DeclareTwoEmployees` class. If you made `empNum` **public** instead of **private**, a direct assignment statement would work, but you would violate an important principle of object-oriented programming—that of data hiding using encapsulation. Data fields should usually be private, and a client application should be able to access them only through the public interfaces—that is, through the class's public methods. However, you might reasonably ask, "When I write an application, if I *can't* set an object's data field directly, but I *can* set it using a public method, what's the difference? The field value is set either way!" Actually, the `setEmpNum()` method in the `Employee` class in Figure 3-26 *does* accept any integer value you send into it. However, you could rewrite the `setEmpNum()` method to prevent invalid data from being assigned to an object's data fields. For example, perhaps your organization has rules for valid employee ID numbers—they must be no fewer than five digits, or they must start with a 9, for instance—or perhaps you calculate a check-digit that is appended to every employee ID number. The statements that enforce these requirements would be part of the `setEmpNum()` method. Checking a value for validity requires decision making. You will learn more in the chapter "Making Decisions."

A check-digit is a number appended to a field, typically an ID number or account number. The check-digit ensures that the number is valid. For example, an organization might use five-digit employee ID numbers in which the fifth digit is calculated by dividing the first four by 7 and taking the remainder. As an example, if the first four digits of your ID number are 7235, then the fifth digit is 4, the remainder when you divide the first four digits by 7. So the five-digit ID becomes 72354. Later, if you make a mistake and enter your ID into a company application as 82354, the application would divide the first four digits, 8235, by 7. The remainder is not 4, and the ID would be found invalid.

Similarly, a `get` method might control how a value is retrieved. Perhaps you do not want clients to have access to part of an employee's ID number, or perhaps you always want to add a company code to every ID before it is returned to the client. Even when a field has no data value requirements or restrictions, making data private and providing public `set` and `get` methods establishes a framework that makes such modifications easier in the future. You will not necessarily write `set` and `get` methods for every field in a class; there are some fields that clients will not be allowed to alter. Some fields will simply be assigned values, and some field values might be calculated from the values of others.

Watch the video *Classes and Objects*.

TWO TRUTHS & A LIE

Declaring Objects and Using Their Methods

1. When you declare an object, you give it a name and set aside enough memory for the object to be stored.

2. An object name is a reference; it holds a memory address.

3. When you don't write a constructor for a class, Java creates one for you; the name of the constructor is always the same as the name of its class.

The false statement is #1. When you declare an object, you are not yet setting aside computer memory in which the object is stored; to allocate the needed memory for an object, you must use the new operator.

You Do It

Declaring and Using Objects

In the last "You Do It" section, you created a class named SpaService. Now you create an application that instantiates and uses SpaService objects.

1. Open a new file in your text editor, and type the import statement needed for an interactive program that accepts user keyboard input:

   ```
   import java.util.Scanner;
   ```

2. Create the shell for a class named CreateSpaServices:

   ```
   public class CreateSpaServices
   {
   }
   ```

3. Between the curly braces of the CreateSpaServices class, create the shell for a main() method for the application:

   ```
   public static void main(String[] args)
   {
   }
   ```

(continues)

(continued)

4. Within the `main()` method, declare variables to hold a service description and price that a user can enter from the keyboard:

```
String service;
double price;
```

5. Next, declare three objects. Two are `SpaService` objects that use the class you created in the last set of "You Do It" steps. The third object uses the built-in Java `Scanner` class. Both classes use the `new` operator to allocate memory for their objects, and both call a constructor that has the same name as the class. The difference is that the `Scanner` constructor requires an argument (`System.in`), but the `SpaService` class does not.

```
SpaService firstService = new SpaService();
SpaService secondService = new SpaService();
Scanner keyboard = new Scanner(System.in);
```

6. In the next statements, you prompt the user for a service, accept it from the keyboard, prompt the user for a price, and accept it from the keyboard.

```
System.out.print("Enter service >> ");
service = keyboard.nextLine();
System.out.print("Enter price >> ");
price = keyboard.nextDouble();
```

7. Recall that the `setServiceDescription()` method in the `SpaService` class is nonstatic, meaning it is used with an object, and that it requires a `String` argument. Write the statement that sends the service the user entered to the `setServiceDescription()` method for the `firstService` object:

```
firstService.setServiceDescription(service);
```

8. Similarly, send the price the user entered to the `setPrice()` method for the `firstService` object. Recall that this method is nonstatic and requires a `double` argument.

```
firstService.setPrice(price);
```

9. Make a call to the `nextLine()` method to remove the Enter key that remains in the input buffer after the last numeric entry. Then repeat the prompts, and accept data for the second `SpaService` object.

```
keyboard.nextLine();
System.out.print("Enter service >> ");
service = keyboard.nextLine();
System.out.print("Enter price >> ");
price = keyboard.nextDouble();
secondService.setServiceDescription(service);
secondService.setPrice(price);
```

(continues)

(continued)

10. Display the details for the firstService object.

```
System.out.println("First service details:");
    System.out.println(firstService.getServiceDescription() +
    " $" + firstService.getPrice());
```

11. Display the details for the secondService object.

```
System.out.println("Second service details:");
    System.out.println(secondService.getServiceDescription() +
    " $" + secondService.getPrice());
```

12. Save the file as **CreateSpaServices.java**. Compile and execute the program. Figure 3-31 shows a typical execution. Make sure you understand how the user's entered values are assigned to and retrieved from the two SpaService objects.

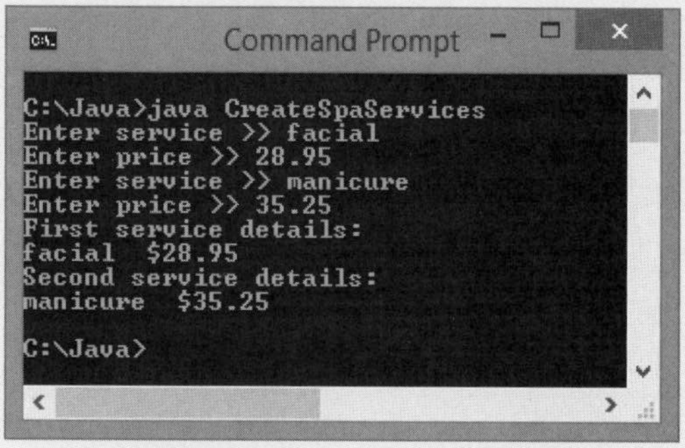

```
C:\Java>java CreateSpaServices
Enter service >> facial
Enter price >> 28.95
Enter service >> manicure
Enter price >> 35.25
First service details:
facial  $28.95
Second service details:
manicure  $35.25

C:\Java>
```

Figure 3-31   Typical execution of the CreateSpaServices program

An Introduction to Using Constructors

When you create a class, such as Employee, and instantiate an object with a statement such as the following, you are actually calling the Employee class constructor that is provided by default by the Java compiler:

```
Employee chauffeur = new Employee();
```

A constructor establishes an object; a **default constructor** is one that requires no arguments. A default constructor is created automatically by the Java compiler for any class you create whenever you do not write your own constructor.

When the prewritten, default constructor for the Employee class is called, it establishes one Employee object with the identifier provided. The automatically supplied default constructor provides the following specific initial values to an object's data fields:

- Numeric fields are set to 0 (zero).

- Character fields are set to Unicode '\u0000'.

- Boolean fields are set to `false`.

- Fields that are object references (for example, `String` fields) are set to `null` (or empty).

If you do not want each field in an object to hold these default values, or if you want to perform additional tasks when you create an instance of a class, you can write your own constructor. Any constructor you write must have the same name as the class it constructs, and constructors cannot have a return type—not even `void`. Normally, you declare constructors to be public so that other classes can instantiate objects that belong to the class. When you write a constructor for a class, you no longer have access to the automatically created version.

For example, if you want every `Employee` object to have a default starting salary of $300.00 per week, you could write the constructor for the `Employee` class that appears in Figure 3-32. Any `Employee` object instantiated will have an `empSalary` field value equal to 300.00, and the other `Employee` data fields will contain the automatically supplied default values. Even though you might want a field to hold the default value, you still might prefer to explicitly initialize the field for clarity.

```
public Employee()
{
    empSalary = 300.00;
}
```

Figure 3-32　The `Employee` class constructor that assigns a salary

The `Employee` class constructor in Figure 3-32 takes no parameters. Therefore, it is a default constructor. You will learn about nondefault constructors that take parameters in the next chapter.

You can write any Java statement in a constructor. Although you usually have no reason to do so, you could display a message from within a constructor or perform any other task.

You can place the constructor anywhere inside the class, outside of any other method. Typically, a constructor is placed with the other methods. Often, programmers list the constructor first because it is the first method used when an object is created.

You never are required to write a constructor for a class; Java provides you with a default version if the class contains no explicit constructor.

A class can contain multiple constructors. You will learn how to overload constructors in the next chapter.

Watch the video *Constructors*.

TWO TRUTHS & A LIE

An Introduction to Using Constructors

1. In Java, you cannot write a default constructor; it must be supplied for you automatically.

2. The automatically supplied default constructor sets all numeric fields to 0, character fields to Unicode '\u0000', Boolean fields to `false`, and fields that are object references to `null`.

3. When you write a constructor, it must have the same name as the class it constructs, and it cannot have a return type.

The false statement is #1. A default constructor is one that takes no parameters. If you do not create a constructor for a class, Java creates a default constructor for you. However, you can create a default constructor that replaces the automatically supplied one.

You Do It

Adding a Constructor to a Class

1. Open the **SpaService.java** file that you created in a "You Do It" section earlier in this chapter.

2. After the field declarations, and before the method declarations, insert an explicit default constructor that sets `serviceDescription` to "XXX" and `price` to 0. Because numeric fields in objects are set to 0 by default, the last assignment is not really necessary. However, programmers sometimes code a statement like the one that sets `price` to 0 so that their intentions are clear to people reading their programs.

(continues)

(continued)

```
public SpaService()
{
    serviceDescription = "XXX";
    price = 0;
}
```

3. Save the class and compile it.

4. Open the **CreateSpaServices.java** file. Comment out the seven statements that prompt for, receive, and set the values for the secondService object by placing double slashes at the start of their lines, as shown below. By commenting out these lines, you change the program so that the user does not enter values for the secondService object. Instead, the values assigned by the constructor are the final values for the object.

```
//      keyboard.nextLine();
//      System.out.print("Enter service >> ");
//      service = keyboard.nextLine();
//      System.out.print("Enter price >> ");
//      price = keyboard.nextDouble();
//      secondService.setServiceDescription(service);
//      secondService.setPrice(price);
```

5. Save the file, and then compile and execute it. Figure 3-33 shows a typical execution. The firstService object contains values supplied by the user, but the secondService object shows the values assigned during the object's construction.

Figure 3-33 Typical execution of CreateSpaServices program that uses constructor values for the second object

Understanding that Classes Are Data Types

The classes that you create become data types. Programmers sometimes refer to classes as **abstract data types**, or **ADTs**. An abstract data type is a type whose implementation is hidden and accessed through its public methods. A class that you create can also be called a **programmer-defined data type**; in other words, it is a type that is not built into the language. A class is a composite type—that is, a class is composed from smaller parts.

Java's primitive types are not composite. Java has eight built-in primitive data types such as `int` and `double`. Primitive types can also be called *scalar* types. You do not have to define these simple types; the creators of Java have already done so. For example, when the `int` type was first created, the programmers who designed it had to think of the following:

Q: What shall we call it?

A: `int`.

Q: What are its attributes?

A: An `int` is stored in four bytes; it holds whole-number values.

Q: What methods are needed by `int`?

A: A method to assign a value to a variable (for example, `num = 32;`).

Q: Any other methods?

A: Some operators to perform arithmetic with variables (for example, `num + 6`).

Q: Any other methods?

A: Of course, there are even more attributes and methods of an int, but these are a good start.

Your job in constructing a new data type is similar. If you need a class for employees, you should ask:

Q: What shall we call it?

A: `Employee`.

Q: What are its attributes?

A: It has an integer ID number, a `String` last name, and a `double` salary.

Q: What methods are needed by `Employee`?

A: A method to assign values to a member of this class (for example, one `Employee`'s ID number is 3232, her last name is "Walters", and her salary is 30,000).

Q: Any other methods?

A: A method to display data in a member of this class (for example, display one `Employee`'s data).

Q: Any other methods?

A: Probably, but this is enough to get started.

When you declare a primitive type object, you provide its type and an identifier. When you declare an object from one of your classes, you do the same. After each exists, you can use them in very similar ways. For example, suppose you declare an int named myInt and an Employee named myEmployee. Then each can be passed into a method, returned from a method, or assigned to another object of the same data type.

For example, Figure 3-34 shows a program in which the main() method uses two other methods. One method accepts an Employee as a parameter, and the other returns an Employee. (The Employee class is defined in Figure 3-28.) Figure 3-35 shows a typical execution. You can see in this sample program that an Employee is passed into and out of methods just like a primitive object would be. Classes are not mysterious; they are just new data types that you invent.

```java
import java.util.Scanner;
class MethodsThatUseAnEmployee
{
    public static void main (String args[])
    {
        Employee myEmployee;
        myEmployee = getEmployeeData();
        displayEmployee(myEmployee);
    }
    public static Employee getEmployeeData()
    {
        Employee tempEmp = new Employee();
        int id;
        double sal;
        Scanner input = new Scanner(System.in);
        System.out.print("Enter employee ID >> ");
        id = input.nextInt();
        tempEmp.setEmpNum(id);
        System.out.print("Enter employee salary >> ");
        sal = input.nextDouble();
        tempEmp.setEmpSalary(sal);
        return tempEmp;
    }
    public static void displayEmployee(Employee anEmp)
    {
        System.out.println("\nEmployee #" + anEmp.getEmpNum() +
            " Salary is " + anEmp.getEmpSalary());
    }
}
```

Figure 3-34   The MethodsThatUseAnEmployee application

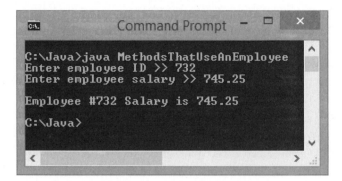

```
C:\Java>java MethodsThatUseAnEmployee
Enter employee ID >> 732
Enter employee salary >> 745.25

Employee #732 Salary is 745.25

C:\Java>
```

Figure 3-35 Typical execution of the MethodsThatUseAnEmployee application

Notice in the application in Figure 3-34 that the Employee declared in the main() method is not constructed there. An Employee is constructed in the getEmployeeData() method and passed back to the main() method, where it is assigned to the myEmployee reference. The Employee constructor could have been called in main(), but the values assigned would have been overwritten after the call to getEmployeeData().

TWO TRUTHS & A LIE

Understanding that Classes Are Data Types

1. When you declare a primitive variable or instantiate an object from a class, you provide both a type and an identifier.

2. Unlike a primitive variable, an instantiated object cannot be passed into or returned from a method.

3. The address of an instantiated object can be assigned to a declared reference of the same type.

The false statement is #2. An instantiated object can be passed into or returned from a method.

165

You Do It

Understanding that Classes Are Data Types

In this section, you modify the CreateSpaServices class to include a method for data entry. This change makes the main() method shorter, gives you the ability to reuse code, and shows that an object of the SpaService class data type can be returned from a method as easily as a primitive data type.

1. Open the **CreateSpaServices.java** file if it is not still open in your text editor.

2. Delete the declarations for service, price, and keyboard. Declarations for these variables will now be part of the data entry method that you will create.

3. Delete the six statements that prompt the user and get values for the firstService objects. Also delete the seven statements that prompt the user and retrieve data for the secondService object. You commented out these statements in the previous "You Do It" section.

4. In place of the statements you just deleted, insert two new statements. The first sends a copy of the firstService object to a method named getData(). The method returns a SpaService object that will be filled with appropriate data, and this object is assigned to firstService. The second statement does the same thing for secondService.

   ```
   firstService = getData(firstService);
   secondService = getData(secondService);
   ```

5. After the closing curly brace for the main() method, but before the closing curly brace for the class, start the following public static getData() method. The header indicates that the method both accepts and returns a SpaService object. Include the opening curly brace for the method, and make declarations for service, price, and keyboard.

   ```
   public static SpaService getData(SpaService s)
   {
       String service;
       double price;
       Scanner keyboard = new Scanner(System.in);
   ```

   (continues)

(continued)

6. Continue the method by prompting the user for and accepting a service and its price. Include a final call to `nextLine()` so that the input buffer is cleared after the last numeric entry.

```
System.out.print("Enter service >> ");
service = keyboard.nextLine();
System.out.print("Enter price >> ");
price = keyboard.nextDouble();
keyboard.nextLine();
```

7. Finish the method by assigning the entered service and price to the `SpaService` object parameter using the `SpaService` class's `setServiceDescription()` and `setPrice()` methods. Then return the full object to the `main()` method, where it is assigned to the object used in the method call. Add a closing curly brace for the method.

```
    s.setServiceDescription(service);
    s.setPrice(price);
    return s;
}
```

8. Save the file, compile it, and execute it. Figure 3-36 shows a typical execution. The execution is no different from the original version of the program, but by creating a method that accepts an unfilled `SpaService` object and returns one filled with data, you have made the `main()` method shorter and reused the data entry code.

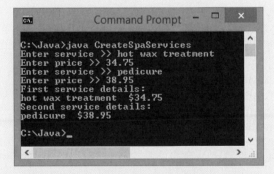

Figure 3-36 Typical execution of the `CreateSpaServices` program that uses a data entry method

Don't Do It

- Don't place a semicolon at the end of a method header. After you get used to putting semicolons at the end of every statement, it's easy to start putting them in too many places. Method headers never end in a semicolon.

- Don't think "default constructor" means only the automatically supplied constructor. Although a class's automatically supplied constructor is a default constructor, so is any constructor you create that accepts no parameters.

- Don't think that a class's methods must accept its own fields' values as parameters or return values to its own fields. When a class contains both fields and methods, each method has direct access to every field within the class.

- Don't create a class method that has a parameter with the same identifier as a class field—yet. If you do, you will only be allowed to access the local variable within the method, and you will not be able to access the field. You will be able to use the same identifier and still access both values after you read the next chapter. For now, make sure that the parameter in any method has a different identifier from any field.

Key Terms

A **method** is a program module that contains a series of statements that carry out a task.

When you **invoke** or **call** a method, you execute it.

The **calling method** makes a **method call** that invokes the **called method**.

A **client method** is a method that calls another.

Abstraction is the programming feature that allows you to use a method name to encapsulate a series of statements.

The **method header** is the first line of the method and contains information about how other methods can interact with it.

A **declaration** is another name for a method header.

A **method body** is the set of statements between curly braces that follow the header and that carry out the method's actions.

Implementation describes the actions that execute within a method—the method body.

A **stub** is a method that contains no statements; programmers create stubs as temporary placeholders during the program development process.

Access modifier is sometimes used as another term for *access specifier*.

A **return type** indicates the type of data that, upon completion of the method, is sent back to its calling method.

To **return a value** is to send the value from a called method back to the calling method.

A **fully qualified identifier** includes a class name and a dot before the identifier.

Arguments are data items sent to methods in a method call.

Parameters are the data items received by a method.

Implementation hiding is a principle of object-oriented programming that describes the encapsulation of method details within a class.

The **interface** to a method includes the method's return type, name, and arguments. It is the part that a client sees and uses.

A **black box** is a device you can use without understanding how it works.

A **local variable** is known only within the boundaries of a method.

A method's **signature** is the combination of the method name and the number, types, and order of arguments.

Actual parameters are the arguments in a method call.

Formal parameters are the variables in a method declaration that accept the values from actual parameters.

A **return statement** ends a method and frequently sends a value from a called method back to the calling method.

A **method's type** is its return type.

Unreachable statements are those that cannot be executed because the logical path can never encounter them; an unreachable statement causes a compiler error.

Dead code is a set of statements that are logically unreachable.

An **is-a relationship** is the relationship between an object and the class of which it is a member.

An **instantiation** of a class is an object; in other words, it is one tangible example of a class.

A **class client** or **class user** is an application or class that instantiates objects of another prewritten class.

Classes can be **extended**, or used as a basis for any other class.

Data fields are data variables declared in a class outside of any method.

The **instance variables** of a class are its data components.

Assigning **private access** to a field means that no other classes can access the field's values, and only methods of the same class are allowed to set, get, or otherwise use private variables.

Information hiding is the object-oriented programming principle used when creating private access for data fields; a class's private data can be changed or manipulated only by a class's own methods and not by methods that belong to other classes.

Mutator methods set values.

Accessor methods retrieve values.

Nonstatic methods, those methods used with object instantiations, are called **instance methods**.

A **primary key** is a unique identifier for data within a database.

The **new operator** allocates the memory needed to hold an object.

A **reference to an object** is the name for a memory address where the object is held.

A **constructor** is a method that establishes an object.

A **default constructor** is one that requires no parameters; if you do not write one, a default constructor is created for a class automatically by the Java compiler.

An **abstract data type (ADT)** is a type whose implementation is hidden and accessed through its public methods.

A **programmer-defined data type** is one that is created by a programmer and not built into the language.

Chapter Summary

- A method is a series of statements that carry out a task. Any method can call, or invoke, another. You place a method within a class outside of any other methods.

- Methods must include a declaration (or header or definition) and a pair of curly braces that enclose the method body. A method declaration contains optional access specifiers, the return type for the method, the method name, and a pair of parentheses that might contain a list of parameters.

- When a method can receive a parameter, its declaration must contain the parameter type and an identifier within parentheses. A method can accept multiple parameters separated with commas. The arguments sent to a method must match (both in number and in type) the parameters listed in the method declaration.

- The return type for a method (the method's type) can be any Java type, including `void`. A `return` statement sends a value back to a calling method.

- Objects are concrete instances of classes. Objects gain their attributes from their classes, and all objects have predictable attributes because they are members of certain classes. In addition to their attributes, objects have methods associated with them, and every object that is an instance of a class is assumed to possess the same methods.

- A class header contains an optional access specifier, the keyword `class`, and any legal identifier you choose for the name of your class. A class contains fields, which are frequently private, and methods, which are frequently public.

- Nonstatic instance methods operate uniquely for every object. Within a class, fields can be placed before or after methods, and methods can be placed in any logical order.

- To create an object that is an instance of a class, you supply a type and an identifier, and then you allocate computer memory for that object using the new operator and the class constructor. With well-written object-oriented programming methods, using implementation hiding—or the encapsulation of method details within a class—means that the calling method needs to understand only the interface to the called method.

- A constructor establishes an object and provides specific initial values for the object's data fields. A constructor always has the same name as the class of which it is a member. By default, numeric fields are set to 0 (zero), character fields are set to Unicode '\u0000', Boolean fields are set to false, and object type fields are set to null.

- A class is an abstract, programmer-defined data type, similar to Java's built-in, primitive data types.

Review Questions

1. In Java, methods must include all of the following except _____.

   a. a declaration

   b. a call to another method

   c. curly braces

   d. a body

2. All method declarations contain _____.

   a. the keyword static

   b. one or more explicitly named access specifiers

   c. arguments

   d. parentheses

3. A public static method named computeSum() is located in classA. To call the method from within classB, use the statement _____.

   a. computeSum(classB);

   b. classB(computeSum());

   c. classA.computeSum();

   d. You cannot call computeSum() from within classB.

4. Which of the following method declarations is correct for a static method named displayFacts() if the method receives an int argument?

   a. public static int displayFacts()

   b. public void displayFacts(int data)

   c. public static void displayFacts(int data)

   d. Two of these are correct.

5. The method with the declaration `public static int aMethod(double d)` has a method type of _____.

    a. `static`

    b. `int`

    c. `double`

    d. You cannot determine the method type.

6. Which of the following is a correct call to a method declared as `public static void aMethod(char code)`?

    a. `void aMethod();`   c. `aMethod(char 'M');`

    b. `void aMethod('V');`   d. `aMethod('Q');`

7. A method is declared as `public static void showResults(double d, int i)`. Which of the following is a correct method call?

    a. `showResults(double d, int i);`   c. `showResults(4, 99.7);`

    b. `showResults(12.2, 67);`   d. Two of these are correct.

8. The method with the declaration `public static char procedure(double d)` has a method type of _____.

    a. `public`   c. `char`

    b. `static`   d. `double`

9. The method `public static boolean testValue(int response)` returns _____.

    a. a `boolean` value

    b. an `int` value

    c. no value

    d. You cannot determine what is returned.

10. Which of the following could be the last legally coded line of a method declared as `public static int getVal(double sum)`?

    a. `return;`

    b. `return 77;`

    c. `return 2.3;`

    d. Any of these could be the last coded line of the method.

11. The nonstatic data components of a class often are referred to as the _____ of that class.

    a. access types   c. methods

    b. instance variables   d. objects

12. Objects contain methods and data items, which are also known as ――――――.

    a. fields   c. themes
    b. functions   d. instances

13. You send messages or information to an object through its ――――――.

    a. fields   c. classes
    b. methods   d. type

14. A program or class that instantiates objects of another prewritten class is a(n) ――――――.

    a. class client   c. object
    b. superclass   d. patron

15. The body of a class is always written ――――――.

    a. in a single line, as the first statement in a class
    b. within parentheses
    c. between curly braces
    d. as a method call

16. Most class data fields are ――――――.

    a. `private`   c. `static`
    b. `public`   d. `final`

17. The concept of allowing a class's private data to be changed only by a class's own methods is known as ――――――.

    a. structured logic   c. information hiding
    b. object orientation   d. data masking

18. Suppose you declare an object as `Book thisBook;`. Before you store data in `thisBook`, you ――――――.

    a. also must explicitly allocate memory for it
    b. need not explicitly allocate memory for it
    c. must explicitly allocate memory for it only if it has a constructor
    d. can declare it to use no memory

19. If a class is named `Student`, the class constructor name is ――――――.

    a. any legal Java identifier
    b. any legal Java identifier that begins with *S*
    c. `StudentConstructor`
    d. `Student`

20. If you use the automatically supplied default constructor when you create an object, ─────── .

    a. numeric fields are set to 0 (zero)   c. Boolean fields are set to true
    b. character fields are set to blank   d. All of these are true.

Exercises

 Programming Exercises

1. Suppose that you have created a program with only the following variables.

    ```
    int a = 5;
    int b = 6;
    ```

    Suppose that you also have a method with the following header:

    ```
    public static void mathMethod(int a)
    ```

    Which of the following method calls are legal?

    a. `mathMethod(a);`   f. `mathMethod(12.78);`
    b. `mathMethod(b);`   g. `mathMethod(29987L);`
    c. `mathMethod(a + b);`   h. `mathMethod();`
    d. `mathMethod(a, b);`   i. `mathMethod(x);`
    e. `mathMethod(2361);`   j. `mathMethod(a / b);`

2. Suppose that you have created a program with only the following variables.

    ```
    int age = 34;
    int weight = 180;
    double height = 5.9;
    ```

    Suppose that you also have a method with the following header:

    ```
    public static void calculate(int age, double size)
    ```

    Which of the following method calls are legal?

    a. `calculate(age, weight);`   f. `calculate(12, 120.2);`
    b. `calculate(age, height);`   g. `calculate(age, size);`
    c. `calculate(weight, height);`   h. `calculate(2, 3);`
    d. `calculate(height, age);`   i. `calculate(age);`
    e. `calculate(45.5, 120);`   j. `calculate(weight, weight);`

3. Suppose that a class named `Bicycle` contains a private nonstatic integer named `height`, a public nonstatic `String` named `model`, and a public static integer named `wheels`. Which of the following are legal statements in a class named `BicycleDemo` that has instantiated an object as `Bicycle myBike = new Bicycle();?`

a. `myBike.height = 26;`

b. `myBike.model = "Cyclone";`

c. `myBike.wheels = 3;`

d. `myBike.model = 108;`

e. `Bicycle.height = 24;`

f. `Bicycle.model = "Hurricane";`

g. `Bicycle.int = 3;`

h. `Bicycle.model = 108;`

i. `Bicycle.wheels = 2;`

j. `Bicycle yourBike = myBike;`

4. a. Create an application named `NumbersDemo` whose `main()` method holds two integer variables. Assign values to the variables. In turn, pass each value to methods named `displayTwiceTheNumber()`, `displayNumberPlusFive()`, and `displayNumberSquared()`. Create each method to perform the task its name implies. Save the application as **NumbersDemo.java**.

   b. Modify the `NumbersDemo` class to accept the values of the two integers from a user at the keyboard. Save the file as **NumbersDemo2.java**.

5. a. Create an application named `Percentages` whose `main()` method holds two `double` variables. Assign values to the variables. Pass both variables to a method named `computePercent()` that displays the two values and the value of the first number as a percentage of the second one. For example, if the numbers are 2.0 and 5.0, the method should display a statement similar to "2.0 is 40 percent of 5.0." Then call the method a second time, passing the values in reverse order. Save the application as **Percentages.java**.

   b. Modify the `Percentages` class to accept the values of the two `doubles` from a user at the keyboard. Save the file as **Percentages2.java**.

6. To encourage good grades, Hermosa High School has decided to award each student a bookstore credit that is 10 times the student's grade point average. In other words, a student with a 3.2 grade point average receives a $32 credit. Create a class that prompts a student for a name and grade point average, and then passes the values to a method that displays a descriptive message. The message uses the student's name, echoes the grade point average, and computes and displays the credit. Save the application as **BookstoreCredit.java**.

7. There are 2.54 centimeters in an inch, and there are 3.7854 liters in a U.S. gallon. Create a class named `MetricConversion`. Its `main()` method accepts an integer value from a user at the keyboard, and in turn passes the entered value to two methods. One converts the value from inches to centimeters and the other converts the same value from gallons to liters. Each method displays the results with appropriate explanation. Save the application as **MetricConversion.java**.

8. Assume that a gallon of paint covers about 350 square feet of wall space. Create an application with a main() method that prompts the user for the length, width, and height of a rectangular room. Pass these three values to a method that does the following:

- Calculates the wall area for a room

- Passes the calculated wall area to another method that calculates and returns the number of gallons of paint needed

- Displays the number of gallons needed

- Computes the price based on a paint price of $32 per gallon, assuming that the painter can buy any fraction of a gallon of paint at the same price as a whole gallon

- Returns the price to the main() method

The main() method displays the final price. For example, the cost to paint a 15-by-20-foot room with 10-foot ceilings is $64. Save the application as **PaintCalculator.java**.

9. The Harrison Group Life Insurance company computes annual policy premiums based on the age the customer turns in the current calendar year. The premium is computed by taking the decade of the customer's age, adding 15 to it, and multiplying by 20. For example, a 34 year old would pay $360, which is calculated by adding the decades (3) to 15, and then multiplying by 20. Write an application that prompts a user for the current year and a birth year. Pass both to a method that calculates and returns the premium amount, and then display the returned amount. Save the application as **Insurance.java**.

10. Caitlyn's Crafty Creations computes a retail price for each product as the cost of materials plus $12 multiplied by the number of hours of work required to create the product, plus $7 shipping and handling. Create a class that contains a main() method that prompts the user for the name of a product (for example, "woven purse"), the cost of materials, and the number of hours of work required. Pass the numeric data to a method that computes the retail price of the product and returns the computed value to the main() method where the product name and price are displayed. Save the program as **CraftPricing.java**.

11. a. Create a class named Sandwich. Data fields include a String for the main ingredient (such as "tuna"), a String for bread type (such as "wheat"), and a double for price (such as 4.99). Include methods to get and set values for each of these fields. Save the class as **Sandwich.java**.

    b. Create an application named TestSandwich that instantiates one Sandwich object and demonstrates the use of the set and get methods. Save this application as **TestSandwich.java**.

12. a. Create a class named Student. A Student has fields for an ID number, number of credit hours earned, and number of points earned. (For example, many schools compute grade point averages based on a scale of 4, so a three-credit-hour class in which a student earns an A is worth 12 points.) Include methods to assign values to all fields. A Student also has a field for grade point average. Include a method to

compute the grade point average field by dividing points by credit hours earned. Write methods to display the values in each Student field. Save this class as **Student.java**.

b. Write a class named ShowStudent that instantiates a Student object from the class you created and assign values to its fields. Compute the Student grade point average, and then display all the values associated with the Student. Save the application as **ShowStudent.java**.

c. Create a constructor for the Student class you created. The constructor should initialize each Student's ID number to 9999, his or her points earned to 12, and credit hours to 3 (resulting in a grade point average of 4.0). Write a program that demonstrates that the constructor works by instantiating an object and displaying the initial values. Save the application as **ShowStudent2.java**.

13. a. Create a class named Lease with fields that hold an apartment tenant's name, apartment number, monthly rent amount, and term of the lease in months. Include a constructor that initializes the name to "XXX", the apartment number to 0, the rent to 1000, and the term to 12. Also include methods to get and set each of the fields. Include a nonstatic method named addPetFee() that adds $10 to the monthly rent value and calls a static method named explainPetPolicy() that explains the pet fee. Save the class as **Lease.java**.

b. Create a class named TestLease whose main() method declares four Lease objects. Call a getData() method three times. Within the method, prompt a user for values for each field for a Lease, and return a Lease object to the main() method where it is assigned to one of main()'s Lease objects. Do not prompt the user for values for the fourth Lease object, but let it continue to hold the default values. Then, in main(), pass one of the Lease objects to a showValues() method that displays the data. Then call the addPetFee() method using the passed Lease object and confirm that the fee explanation statement is displayed. Next, call the showValues() method for the Lease object again and confirm that the pet fee has been added to the rent. Finally, call the showValues() method with each of the other three objects; confirm that two hold the values you supplied as input and one holds the constructor default values. Save the application as **TestLease.java**.

 Debugging Exercises

1. Each of the following files saved in the Chapter03 folder in your downloadable student files has syntax and/or logic errors. In each case, determine and fix the problem. After you correct the errors, save each file using the same filename preceded with *Fix*. For example, DebugThree1.java will become **FixDebugThree1.java**.

   a. DebugThree1.java
   b. DebugThree2.java
   c. DebugThree3.java
   d. DebugThree4.java

When you change a filename, remember to change every instance of the class name within the file so that it matches the new filename. In Java, the filename and class name must always match.

Game Zone

1. Playing cards are used in many computer games, including versions of such classics as solitaire, hearts, and poker. Design a `Card` class that contains a character data field to hold a suit (*s* for spades, *h* for hearts, *d* for diamonds, or *c* for clubs) and an integer data field for a value from 1 to 13. (When you learn more about string handling in the chapter "Characters, Strings, and the `StringBuilder`," you can modify the class to hold words for the suits, such as *spades* or *hearts*, as well as words for some of the values—for example, *ace* or *king*.) Include get and set methods for each field. Save the class as **Card.java**.

   Write an application that randomly selects two playing cards and displays their values. Simply assign a suit to each of the cards, but generate a random number for each card's value. Appendix D contains information on generating random numbers. To fully understand the process, you must learn more about Java classes and methods. However, for now, you can copy the following statements to generate a random number between 1 and 13 and assign it to a variable:

   ```
   final int CARDS_IN_SUIT = 13;
   myValue = ((int)(Math.random() * 100) % CARDS_IN_SUIT + 1);
   ```

   After reading the chapter "Making Decisions," you will be able to have the game determine the higher card. For now, just observe how the card values change as you execute the program multiple times. Save the application as **PickTwoCards.java**.

   You use the `Math.random()` function to generate a random number. The function call uses only a class and method name—no object—so you know the `random()` method must be a static method.

2. Computer games often contain different characters or creatures. For example, you might design a game in which alien beings possess specific characteristics such as color, number of eyes, or number of lives. Design a character for a game, creating a class to hold at least three attributes for the character. Include methods to get and set each of the character's attributes. Save the file as **MyCharacter.java**. Then write an application in which you create at least two characters. In turn, pass each character to a display method that displays the character's attributes. Save the application as **TwoCharacters.java**.

Case Problems

1. a. Carly's Cate.ring provides meals for parties and special events. In Chapter 2, you wrote an application that prompts the user for the number of guests attending an event, displays the company motto with a border, and then displays the price of the event and whether the event is a large one. Now modify the program so that the main() method contains only three executable statements that each call a method as follows:

    • The first executable statement calls a public static int method that prompts the user for the number of guests and returns the value to the main() method.

    • The second executable statement calls a public static void method that displays the company motto with the border.

    • The last executable statement passes the number of guests to a public static void method that computes the price of the event, displays the price, and displays whether the event is a large event.

    Save the file as **CarlysEventPriceWithMethods.java**.

    b. Create a class to hold Event data for Carly's Catering. The class contains:

    • Two public final static fields that hold the price per guest ($35) and the cutoff value for a large event (50 guests)

    • Three private fields that hold an event number, number of guests for the event, and the price. The event number is stored as a String because Carly plans to assign event numbers such as *M312*.

    • Two public set methods that set the event number (setEventNumber()) and the number of guests (setGuests()). The price does not have a set method because the setGuests() method will calculate the price as the number of guests multiplied by the price per guest every time the number of guests is set.

    • Three public get methods that return the values in the three nonstatic fields

    Save the file as **Event.java**.

    c. Use the CarlysEventPriceWithMethods class you created in Step 1a as a starting point for a program that demonstrates the Event class you created in Step 1b, but make the following changes:

    • You already have a method that gets a number of guests from a user; now add a method that gets an event number. The main() method should declare an Event object, call the two data entry methods, and use their returned values to set the fields in the Event object.

- Call the method from the `CarlysEventPriceWithMethods` class that displays the company motto with the border. The method is accessible because it is public, but you must fully qualify the name because it is in another class.

- Revise the method that displays the event details so that it accepts the newly created `Event` object. The method should display the event number, and it should still display the number of guests, the price per guest, the total price, and whether the event is a large event.

Save the program as **EventDemo.java**.

2. a. Sammy's Seashore Supplies rents beach equipment such as kayaks, canoes, beach chairs, and umbrellas to tourists. In Chapter 2, you wrote an application that prompts the user for the number of minutes a piece of sports equipment was rented, displays the company motto with a border, and displays the price for the rental. Now modify the program so that the `main()` method contains only three executable statements that each call a method as follows:

- The first executable statement calls a method that prompts the user for the rental time in minutes and returns the value to the `main()` method.

- The second executable statement calls a method that displays the company motto with the border.

- The last executable statement passes the number of minutes to a method that computes the hours, extra minutes, and price for the rental, and then displays all the details.

Save the file as **SammysRentalPriceWithMethods.java**.

    b. Create a class to hold `Rental` data for Sammy's Seashore Supplies. The class contains:

- Two `public final static` fields that hold the number of minutes in an hour and the hourly rental rate ($40)

- Four `private` fields that hold a contract number, number of hours for the rental, number of minutes over an hour, and the price. The contract number is stored as a `String` because Sammy plans to assign contract numbers such as *K681*.

- Two `public` set methods. One sets the contract number (`setContractNumber()`). The other is named `setHoursAndMinutes()`, and it accepts the number of minutes for the rental and then sets the hours, extra minutes over an hour, and the total price. Recall from Chapter 2 that the price is $40 per hour plus $1 for every extra minute.

- Four `public` get methods that return the values in the four nonstatic fields

Save the file as **Rental.java**.

c. Use the SammysRentalPriceWithMethods class you created in Step 2a as a starting point for a program that demonstrates the Rental class you created in Step 2b, but make the following changes:

- You already have a method that gets a number of minutes from a user; now add a method that gets a contract number. The main() method should declare a Rental object, call the two data entry methods, and use their returned values to set the fields in the Rental object.

- From the SammysRentalPriceWithMethods class, call the RentalDemo method that displays the company motto with the border. The method is accessible because it is public, but you must fully qualify the name because it is in another class.

- Revise the method that displays the rental details so that it accepts the newly created Rental object. The method should display the contract number, and it should still display the hours and minutes, the hourly rate, and the total price.

Save the program as **RentalDemo.java**.

CHAPTER 4

More Object Concepts

In this chapter, you will:

- ◎ Understand blocks and scope
- ◎ Overload a method
- ◎ Avoid ambiguity
- ◎ Create and call constructors with parameters
- ◎ Use the `this` reference
- ◎ Use static fields
- ◎ Use automatically imported, prewritten constants and methods
- ◎ Use composition and nest classes

Understanding Blocks and Scope

Within any class or method, the code between a pair of curly braces is called a **block**. For example, the method shown in Figure 4-1 contains two blocks. An **outer block** begins at the first opening curly brace and ends at the last closing curly brace, at the end of the method. The **inner block** starts with the second opening curly brace and ends with the first closing curly brace. It contains two executable statements: the declaration of anotherNumber and a println() statement. The inner block is **nested**, or contained entirely, within the outer block.

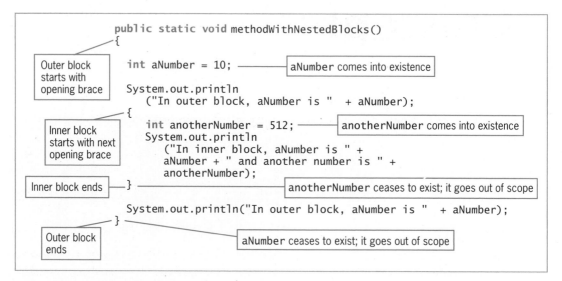

Figure 4-1   A method with nested blocks

A block can exist entirely within another block or entirely outside and separate from another block, but blocks can never overlap. For example, if a method contains two opening curly braces, indicating the start of two blocks, the first opening brace and last closing brace are a pair that define the outer block, and the second opening brace and first closing brace are a pair that define the inner block.

You cannot refer to a variable outside the block in which it is declared. As you learned in Chapter 3, the portion of a program within which you can refer to a variable is the variable's **scope**; in this part of the program, the variable exists and can be accessed using its unqualified name. In Java, a variable comes into existence, or **comes into scope**, when you declare it, and a variable ceases to exist, or **goes out of scope**, at the end of the block in which it is declared. Programmers say that a Java variable's **scope level** is its block.

Although you can create as many variables and blocks as you need within any program, it is not wise to do so without a reason. The use of unnecessary variables and blocks increases the likelihood of improper use of variable names and scope.

In the `methodWithNestedBlocks()` method shown in Figure 4-1, the variable `aNumber` exists from the point of its declaration until the end of the method. This means `aNumber` exists both in the outer block and in the inner block and can be used anywhere in the method. The variable `anotherNumber` comes into existence within the inner block; `anotherNumber` goes out of scope when the inner block ends and cannot be used beyond its block. Figure 4-2 shows the output when the method in Figure 4-1 executes.

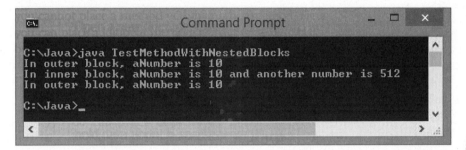

Figure 4-2   Output produced by application that uses `methodWithNestedBlocks()`

 The program that produces the output shown in Figure 4-2 is available in your downloadable student files.

You cannot use a data item that is not in scope. For example, Figure 4-3 shows a method that contains two blocks and some shaded, invalid statements. The opening and closing braces for each block are vertically aligned. You are not required to vertically align the opening and closing braces for a block, but your programs are much easier to read if you do.

```
public static void methodWithInvalidStatements()
{
    aNumber = 75;                Illegal statement; this variable has not been declared yet
    int aNumber = 22;
    aNumber = 6;
    anotherNumber = 489;         Illegal statement; this variable has not been declared yet
    {
        anotherNumber = 165;       Illegal statement; this variable still has not been declared
        int anotherNumber = 99;
        anotherNumber = 2;
    }                            Illegal statement; this variable was declared in the inner block
    aNumber = 50;                and has gone out of scope here
    anotherNumber = 34;
}
aNumber = 29;                    Illegal statement; this variable has gone out of scope
```

Figure 4-3   The `methodWithInvalidStatements()` method

The first assignment statement in the first, outer block in Figure 4-3, aNumber = 75;, is invalid because aNumber has not been declared yet. Similarly, the statements that attempt to assign 489 and 165 to anotherNumber are invalid because anotherNumber has not been declared yet. After anotherNumber is declared, it can be used for the remainder of the inner block, but the statement that attempts to assign 34 to it is outside the block in which anotherNumber was declared. The last shaded statement in Figure 4-3, aNumber = 29;, does not work because it falls outside the block in which aNumber was declared; it actually falls outside the entire methodWithInvalidStatements() method.

Within a method, you can declare a variable with the same name multiple times, as long as each declaration is in its own nonoverlapping block. For example, the two declarations of variables named someVar in Figure 4-4 are valid because each variable is contained within its own block. The first instance of someVar has gone out of scope before the second instance comes into scope.

```
                  public static void twoDeclarations()
Don't declare    {
blocks for no        {
reason. A                int someVar = 7;
new block                System.out.println(someVar);
starts here          }
only to              {
demonstrate              int someVar = 845;
scope.                   System.out.println(someVar);
                     }
                  }
```

This variable will go out of scope at the next closing curly brace.

This variable is totally different from the one in the previous block even though their identifiers are the same.

Figure 4-4 The twoDeclarations() method

You cannot declare the same variable name more than once within a block, even if a block contains other blocks. When you declare a variable more than once in a block, you are attempting to **redeclare the variable**, which is an illegal action. For example, in Figure 4-5, the second declaration of aValue causes an error because you cannot declare the same variable twice within the outer block of the method. By the same reasoning, the third declaration of aValue is also invalid, even though it appears within a new block. The block that contains the third declaration is entirely within the outer block, so the first declaration of aValue has not gone out of scope.

```
public static void invalidRedeclarationMethod()
{
    int aValue = 35;
    int aValue = 44;
    {
        int anotherValue = 0;
        int aValue = 10;
    }
}
```

Invalid redeclaration of aValue because it is in the same block as the first declaration

Invalid redeclaration of aValue; even though this is a new block, this block is inside the first block

Figure 4-5 The invalidRedeclarationMethod()

Although you cannot declare a variable twice within the same block, you can declare a variable within one method of a class and use the same variable name within another method of the class. In this case, the variable declared inside each method resides in its own location in computer memory. When you use the variable's name within the method in which it is declared, it takes precedence over, or **overrides**, any other variable with the same name in another method. In other words, a locally declared variable always masks or hides another variable with the same name elsewhere in the class.

For example, consider the class in Figure 4-6. In the `main()` method of the `OverridingVariable` class, aNumber is declared and assigned the value 10. When the program calls `firstMethod()`, a new variable is declared with the same name but with a different memory address and a new value. The new variable exists only within `firstMethod()`, where it is displayed holding the value 77. After `firstMethod()` executes and the logic returns to the `main()` method, the original aNumber is displayed, containing 10. When aNumber is passed to `secondMethod()`, a copy is made within the method. This copy has the same identifier as the original aNumber, but a different memory address. So, within `secondMethod()`, when the value is changed to 862 and displayed, it has no effect on the original variable in `main()`. When the logic returns to `main()` after `secondMethod()`, the original value is displayed again. Examine the output in Figure 4-7 to understand the sequence of events.

```
public class OverridingVariable
{
    public static void main(String[] args)          aNumber is declared in
    {                                                main().
        int aNumber = 10;
        System.out.println("In main(), aNumber is " + aNumber);      Whenever aNumber
        firstMethod();                                               is used in main(), it
        System.out.println("Back in main(), aNumber is " + aNumber); retains its value of 10.
        secondMethod(aNumber);
        System.out.println("Back in main() again, aNumber is " + aNumber);
    }
    public static void firstMethod()
    {                                            This aNumber resides at a different
        int aNumber = 77;                        memory address from the one in main().
        System.out.println("In firstMethod(), aNumber is "  It is declared locally in this method.
            + aNumber);
    }                                            This aNumber also resides at a different
    public static void secondMethod(int aNumber) memory address from the one in main().
    {                                            It is declared locally in this method.
        System.out.println("In secondMethod(), at first " +
            "aNumber is " + aNumber);
        aNumber = 862;
        System.out.println("In secondMethod(), after an assignment " +
            "aNumber is " + aNumber);
    }
}
```

Figure 4-6 The `OverridingVariable` class

188

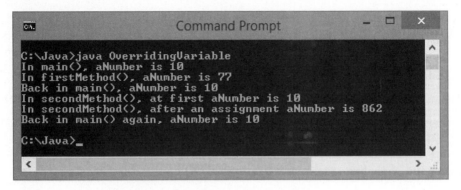

Figure 4-7   Output of the OverridingVariable application

 Object-oriented programmers also use the term *override* when a child class contains a field or method that has the same name as one in the parent class. You will learn more about inheritance in the chapters "Introduction to Inheritance" and "Advanced Inheritance Concepts."

 You are familiar with local names overriding names defined elsewhere. If someone in your household is named Eric, and someone in the house next door is named Eric, members of your household who talk about Eric are referring to the local version. They would add a qualifier such as *Eric Johnson or Eric next door* to refer to the nonlocal version.

When they have the same name, variables within methods of a class override or hide the class's fields. Java calls this phenomenon **shadowing**; a variable that hides another shadows it. For example, Figure 4-8 shows an Employee class that contains two instance variables and three void methods. The setValues() method provides values for the two class instance fields. Whenever the method named methodThatUsesInstanceAttributes() is used with an Employee object, the instance values for empNum and empPayRate are used. However, when the other method, methodThatUsesLocalVariables(), is used with an Employee object, the local variable values within the method, 33333 and 555.55, shadow the class's instance variables. Figure 4-9 shows a short application that declares an Employee object and uses each method; Figure 4-10 shows the output.

```java
public class Employee
{
    private int empNum;
    private double empPayRate;
    public void setValues()        ┌─────────────────────────────┐
    {                              │ This method uses the class fields. │
        empNum = 111;              └─────────────────────────────┘
        empPayRate = 22.22;
    }                                        ┌─────────────────────┐
    public void methodThatUsesInstanceAttributes()  │ This method also uses │
    {                                        │ the class fields.    │
        System.out.println("Employee number is " + empNum);  └─────────────────────┘
        System.out.println("Pay rate is " + empPayRate);
    }
    public void methodThatUsesLocalVariables()
    {
        int empNum = 33333;
        double empPayRate = 555.55;
        System.out.println("Employee number is " + empNum);
        System.out.println("Pay rate is " + empPayRate);
    }                        ┌───────────────────────────────────┐
}                            │ This method uses the locally declared │
                             │ variables that happen to have the     │
                             │ same names as the class fields.       │
                             └───────────────────────────────────┘
```

Figure 4-8 The Employee class

```java
public class TestEmployeeMethods
{
    public static void main(String[] args)
    {
        Employee aWorker = new Employee();
        aWorker.setValues();
        aWorker.methodThatUsesInstanceAttributes();
        aWorker.methodThatUsesLocalVariables();
    }
}
```

Figure 4-9 The TestEmployeeMethods application

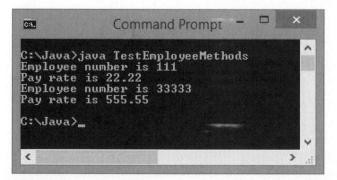

Figure 4-10 Output of the TestEmployeeMethods application

In the `methodThatUsesLocalVariables()` method in Figure 4-8, the locally declared `empNum` and `empPayRate` are assigned 33333 and 555.55, respectively. These local variables are said to be **closer in scope** than the variables with the same name at the top of the class that are shadowed. When you write programs, you might choose to avoid confusing situations that arise when you give the same name to a class's instance field and to a local method variable. But, if you do use the same name, be aware that within the method, the method's local variable overrides the instance variable.

Programmers frequently use the same name for an instance field and a parameter to a method in the same class simply because it is the "best name" to use; in these cases, the programmer must use the `this` reference, which you will learn about later in this chapter.

It is important to understand the impact that blocks and methods have on your variables. Variables and fields with the same names represent different memory locations when they are declared within different scopes. After you understand the scope of variables, you can avoid many potential errors in your programs.

TWO TRUTHS & A LIE

Understanding Blocks and Scope

1. A variable ceases to exist, or goes out of scope, at the end of the block in which it is declared.

2. You cannot declare the same variable name more than once within a block, even if a block contains other blocks.

3. A class's instance variables override locally declared variables with the same names that are declared within the class's methods.

The false statement is #3. When they have the same name, variables within methods of a class override a class's instance variables.

You Do It

Demonstrating Scope

In this section, you create a method with several blocks to demonstrate block scope.

1. Start your text editor, and then open a new document, if necessary.

2. Type the first few lines for a class named `DemoBlock`:

(continues)

```
public class DemoBlock
{
   public static void main(String[] args)
   {
```

3. Add a statement that displays the purpose of the program:

```
System.out.println("Demonstrating block scope");
```

4. On a new line, declare an integer named x, assign the value 1111 to it, and display its value:

```
int x = 1111;
System.out.println("In first block x is " + x);
```

5. Begin a new block by typing an opening curly brace on the next line. Within the new block, declare another integer named y, and display x and y. The value of x is 1111, and the value of y is 2222:

```
{
   int y = 2222;
   System.out.println("In second block x is " + x);
   System.out.println("In second block y is " + y);
}
```

6. On the next line, begin another new block. Within this new block, declare a new integer with the same name as the integer declared in the previous block; then display x and y. The value of y is 3333. Call a method named demoMethod(), and display x and y again. Even though you will include statements within demoMethod() that assign different values to x and y, the x and y displayed here are still 1111 and 3333:

```
{
   int y = 3333;
   System.out.println("In third block x is " + x);
   System.out.println("In third block y is " + y);
   demoMethod();
   System.out.println("After method x is " + x);
   System.out.println("After method block y is " + y);
}
```

7. On a new line after the end of the block, type the following:

```
System.out.println("At the end x is " + x);
```

This last statement in the main() method displays the value of x, which is still 1111. Type a closing curly brace.

(continued)

8. Finally, enter the following `demoMethod()` that creates its own x and y variables, assigns different values, and then displays them:

    ```
    public static void demoMethod()
    {
        int x = 8888, y = 9999;
        System.out.println("In demoMethod x is " + x);
        System.out.println("In demoMethod block y is " + y);
    }
    ```

9. Type the final closing curly brace, and then save the file as **DemoBlock.java**. At the command prompt, compile the file by typing the command **javac DemoBlock.java**. If necessary, correct any errors, and compile the program again.

10. Run the program by typing the command **java DemoBlock**. Your output should look like Figure 4-11. Make certain you understand how the values of x and y are determined in each line of output.

11. To gain a more complete understanding of blocks and scope levels, change the values of x and y in several locations throughout the program, and try to predict the exact output before resaving, recompiling, and rerunning the program.

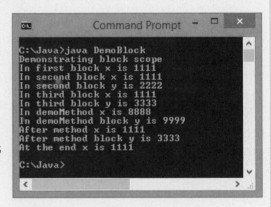

Figure 4-11 Output of the DemoBlock application

Overloading a Method

Overloading a method allows you to use one identifier to execute diverse tasks. In Java, it more specifically means writing multiple methods in the same scope that have the same name but different parameter lists. In overloaded methods, the parameter identifiers do not have to be different, but the parameter lists must satisfy one or both of these conditions:

*   The lists must have different numbers of parameters. For example, one list could have one `double`, another list could have two `doubles`, and a third list could have 10 `doubles`.

*   The lists must have parameter data types in different orders. For example, one list could have two `doubles`, another could have an `int` and a `double`, and a third could have a `double` and an `int`.

When you use the English language, you overload words all the time. When you say "open the door," "open your eyes," and "open a computer file," you are talking about three very different actions using very different methods and producing very different results. However, anyone who speaks English fluently has no trouble understanding your meaning because the verb *open* is understood in the context of the noun that follows it.

When you overload a Java method, multiple methods share a name, and the compiler understands which one to use based on the arguments in the method call. For example, suppose you create a class method to apply a simple interest rate to a bank balance. The method is named `calculateInterest()`; it receives two `double` parameters—the balance and the interest rate—and displays the multiplied result. Figure 4-12 shows the method.

```
public static void calculateInterest(double bal, double rate)
{
    double interest;
    interest = bal * rate;
    System.out.println("Simple interest on $" + bal +
        " at " + rate + "% rate is " + interest);
}
```

Figure 4-12 The `calculateInterest()` method with two `double` parameters

When an application calls the `calculateInterest()` method and passes two `double` values, as in `calculateInterest(1000.00, 0.04)`, the interest is calculated correctly as 4% of $1000.00.

Assume, however, that different users want to calculate interest using different argument types. Some users who want to indicate an interest rate of 4% might use 0.04; others might use 4 and assume that it means 4%. When the `calculateInterest()` method is called with the arguments 1000.00 and 0.04, the interest is calculated correctly as 40.00. When the method is called using 1000.00 and 4, the method works because the integer argument is promoted to a `double`, but the interest is calculated incorrectly as 4000.00, which is 100 times too high.

A solution for the conflicting use of numbers to represent parameter values is to overload the `calculateInterest()` method. For example, in addition to the `calculateInterest()` method shown in Figure 4-12, you could add the method shown in Figure 4-13.

```
                                      ┌─────────────────────┐
                                      │ Notice the data type │
                                      │ for rate.            │
                                      └──────────┬──────────┘
                                                 │
public static void calculateInterest(double bal, int rate)
{
    double interest, rateAsPercent;
    rateAsPercent = rate / 100.0; ──── ┌────────────────────────────┐
    interest = bal * rateAsPercent;    │ Dividing by 100.0 converts rate │
    System.out.println("Simple interest on $" + │ to its percent equivalent. │
        bal + " at  " + rate + "% rate is " + └────────────────────────────┘
        interest);
}
```

Figure 4-13 The `calculateInterest()` method with a `double` parameter and an `int` parameter

In Figure 4-13, note that `rateAsPercent` is calculated by dividing by 100.0 and not by 100. If two integers are divided, the result is a truncated integer; dividing by a `double` 100.0 causes the result to be a `double`. Alternatively, you could use an explicit cast such as `rateAsPercent = (double)rate / 100`.

If an application calls the method `calculateInterest()` using two `double` arguments—for example, `calculateInterest(1000.00, 0.04)`—the first version of the method, the one shown in Figure 4-12, executes. However, if an integer is used as the second argument in a call to `calculateInterest()`—as in `calculateInterest(1000.00, 4)`—the second version of the method, the one shown in Figure 4-13, executes. In this second example, the whole number rate figure is correctly divided by 100.0 before it is used to determine the interest earned.

Of course, you could use methods with different names to solve the dilemma of producing an accurate interest figure—for example, `calculateInterestUsingDouble()` and `calculateInterestUsingInt()`. However, it is easier and more convenient for programmers who use your methods to remember just one method name they can use in the form that is most appropriate for their programs. It is convenient to be able to use one reasonable name for tasks that are functionally identical except for the argument types that can be passed to them. The compiler knows which method version to call based on the passed arguments.

In Chapter 3, you learned that the `print()` and `println()` methods have been created to accept different argument types (including no argument) and that this feature is called *method overloading*.

Automatic Type Promotion in Method Calls

In Chapter 2, you learned that Java casts variables to a unifying type when you perform arithmetic with unlike types. For example, when you multiply an `int` and a `double`, the result is a `double`. In a similar way, Java can promote one data type to another when you pass a parameter to a method. For example, if a method has a `double` parameter and you pass in an integer, the integer is promoted to a `double`. Recall that the order of promotion is `double`, `float`, `long`, and `int`. Any type in this list can be promoted to any type that precedes it.

When an application contains just one version of a method, you can call the method using a parameter of the correct data type or one that can be promoted to the correct data type. For example, consider the simple method shown in Figure 4-14.

```
public static void simpleMethod(double d)
{
    System.out.println("Method receives double parameter");
}
```

Figure 4-14   The `simpleMethod()` method with a `double` parameter

If you write an application in which you declare `doubleValue` as a `double` variable and `intValue` as an `int` variable (as shown in Figure 4-15), either of the two method calls `simpleMethod(doubleValue);` or `simpleMethod(intValue);` results in the output "Method receives double parameter". The call that uses the integer works because the integer is cast as (or promoted to) a `double`. The output of the program in Figure 4-15 is shown in Figure 4-16.

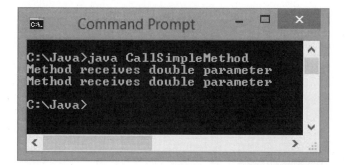

```
public class CallSimpleMethod
{
    public static void main(String[] args)
    {
        double doubleValue = 45.67;
        int intValue = 17;
        simpleMethod(doubleValue);
        simpleMethod(intValue);
    }
    public static void simpleMethod(double d)
    {
        System.out.println("Method receives double parameter");
    }
}
```

Either a `double` or an `int` can be sent to a method that accepts a `double`.

Figure 4-15 The `CallSimpleMethod` application that calls `simpleMethod()` with a `double` and an `int`

```
Command Prompt                        -  □  ×

C:\Java>java CallSimpleMethod
Method receives double parameter
Method receives double parameter

C:\Java>
```

Figure 4-16 Output of the `CallSimpleMethod` application

Note that if the method with the declaration `void simpleMethod(double d)` did not exist, but the declaration `void simpleMethod(int i)` did exist, then the method call `simpleMethod(doubleValue);` would fail. Although an `int` can be promoted to a `double`, a `double` is not automatically reduced to an `int`. This makes sense if you consider the potential loss of information when a `double` value is reduced to an integer.

Suppose that you add an overloaded version of `simpleMethod()` to the program in Figure 4-15. This version accepts an integer parameter, as shown in Figure 4-17. When you properly overload a method, you can call it providing different argument lists, and the appropriate version of the method executes. Now, the output changes when you call `simpleMethod(intValue);`. Instead of promoting an integer argument to a `double`, the compiler recognizes a more exact match for the method call that uses the integer argument, so it calls the version of the method that produces the output "Method receives integer parameter". Figure 4-18 shows the output.

```java
public class CallSimpleMethodAgain
{
    public static void main(String[] args)
    {                                                    The call with an int
        double doubleValue = 45.67;                      argument uses the
        int intValue = 17;                               method that is a better
        simpleMethod(doubleValue);                       match when it is
        simpleMethod(intValue);                          available.
    }
    public static void simpleMethod(double d)
    {
        System.out.println("Method receives double parameter");
    }
    public static void simpleMethod(int d)
    {
        System.out.println("Method receives integer parameter");
    }
}
```

Figure 4-17   The `CallSimpleMethodAgain` application that calls `simpleMethod()` with a `double` and an `int`

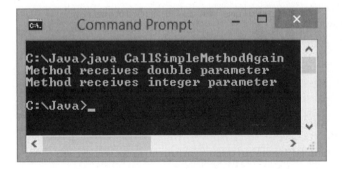

Figure 4-18   Output of the `CallSimpleMethodAgain` application

TWO TRUTHS & A LIE

Overloading a Method

1. When you overload Java methods, you write multiple methods with a shared name.

2. When you overload Java methods, the methods are called using different arguments.

3. Instead of overloading methods, it is preferable to write methods with unique identifiers.

The false statement is #3. Overloading methods is preferable to using unique identifiers because it is convenient for programmers to use one reasonable name for tasks that are functionally identical, except for the argument types that can be passed to them.

 You Do It

Overloading Methods

In this section, you overload methods to display dates. The date-displaying methods might be used by many different applications in an organization, such as those that schedule jobs, appointments, and employee reviews. The methods take one, two, or three integer arguments. If there is one argument, it is the month, and the date becomes the first day of the given month in the year 2016. If there are two arguments, they are the month and the day in the year 2016. Three arguments represent the month, day, and year.

 Instead of creating your own class to store dates, you can use the built-in Java class `LocalDate` to handle dates. You work with the class later in this chapter. This exercise provides you with some insight into considerations taken by the creators of Java's built-in `LocalDate` class.

1. Open a new file in your text editor.

2. Begin the following `DemoOverload` class with three integer variables to test the method and three calls to a `displayDate()` method:

```
public class DemoOverload
{
    public static void main(String[] args)
```

(continues)

198

(continued)

```
{
    int month = 6, day = 24, year = 2017;
    displayDate(month);
    displayDate(month, day);
    displayDate(month, day, year);
}
```

3. Create the following `displayDate()` method that requires one parameter to represent the month and uses default values for the day and year:

```
public static void displayDate(int mm)
{
    System.out.println("Event date " + mm + "/1/2016");
}
```

4. Create the following `displayDate()` method that requires two parameters to represent the month and day and uses a default value for the year:

```
public static void displayDate(int mm, int dd)
{
    System.out.println("Event date " + mm + "/" + dd + "/2016");
}
```

5. Create the following `displayDate()` method that requires three parameters used as the month, day, and year:

```
public static void displayDate(int mm, int dd, int yy)
{
    System.out.println("Event date " + mm + "/" + dd + "/" + yy);
}
```

6. Type the closing curly brace for the DemoOverload class.

7. Save the file as **DemoOverload.java**.

8. Compile the program, correct any errors, recompile if necessary, and then execute the program. Figure 4-19 shows the output. Notice that whether you call the displayDate() method using one, two, or three arguments, the date is displayed correctly because you have successfully overloaded the displayDate() method.

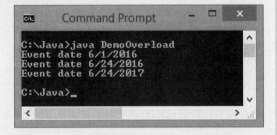

Figure 4-19   Output of the DemoOverload application

Learning About Ambiguity

Overloading methods is useful because you can use a single identifier to execute different instructions depending on the arguments you send to the method. However, when you overload methods, you risk creating an **ambiguous** situation—one in which the compiler cannot determine which method to use. For example, consider the following overloaded computeBalance() method declarations:

```
public static void computeBalance(double deposit)
public static void computeBalance(double withdrawal)
```

If you declare a double variable named myDeposit and make a method call such as computeBalance(myDeposit);, you will have created an ambiguous situation. Both methods are exact matches for your call. You might argue that a call using a variable named myDeposit "seems" like it should go to the version of the method with the parameter named deposit, but Java makes no assumptions based on variable names. Each version of computeBalance() could accept a double, and Java does not presume which one you intended to use.

Sometimes, it is hard to recognize potentially ambiguous situations. For example, consider the following two method declarations:

```
public static void calculateInterest(int bal, double rate)
public static void calculateInterest(double bal, int rate)
```

These calculateInterest() methods have different types in their parameter lists. A call to calculateInterest() with an int and a double argument (in that order) executes the first version of the method, and a call to calculateInterest() with a double and an int argument executes the second version of the method. With each of these calls, the compiler can find an exact match for the arguments you send. However, if you call calculateInterest() using two integer arguments, as in calculateInterest(300, 6);, an ambiguous situation arises because there is no exact match for the method call. Because either of the two integers in the method call can be promoted to a double, the call matches both versions of the method. The compiler can't determine which version of the calculateInterest() method to use, and the program does not compile.

The two versions of calculateInterest() could coexist if no ambiguous calls were ever made. An overloaded method is not ambiguous on its own—it only becomes ambiguous if you create an ambiguous situation. A program containing a potentially ambiguous situation will run problem-free if you do not make any ambiguous method calls.

It is important to note that you can overload methods correctly by providing different parameter lists for methods with the same name. Methods with identical names that have identical parameter lists but different return types are not overloaded—they are illegal.

For example, the following two methods are illegal in the same class:

```
int aMethod(int x)
void aMethod(int x)
```

The compiler determines which of several versions of a method to call based on the arguments in the method call, and does not consider the return type.

The compiler determines which version of a method to call by the method's signature. In Chapter 3, you learned that a method's signature is the combination of the method name and the number, types, and order of parameters.

If the keyword `final` appears in a method's parameter list, it is ignored when determining ambiguity. In other words, two methods with the headers `void aMethod(int x)` and `void aMethod(final int x)` are ambiguous.

Watch the video *Overloading Methods*.

TWO TRUTHS & A LIE

Learning About Ambiguity

1. When it is part of the same program as `void myMethod(int age, String name)`, the following method would be ambiguous:

   `void myMethod(String name, int age)`

2. When it is part of the same program as `void myMethod(int age, String name)`, the following method would be ambiguous:

   `String myMethod(int zipCode, String address)`

3. When it is part of the same program as `void myMethod(int age, String name)`, the following method would be ambiguous:

   `void myMethod(int x, String y)`

The false statement is #1. A method that accepts an `int` parameter followed by a `String` is not ambiguous with one that accepts the parameters in the reverse order.

Creating and Calling Constructors with Parameters

In Chapter 3, you learned that Java automatically provides a constructor when you create a class. You also learned that you can write your own constructor, and that you often do so when you want to ensure that fields within classes are initialized to some appropriate default value. You learned that the automatically provided constructor is a default constructor (one that does not require arguments), and that you can write a custom default constructor. However, when you write your own constructors, you can also write versions that receive parameters. Such parameters are often used to initialize data fields for an object.

For example, consider the `Employee` class with just one data field, shown in Figure 4-20. Its constructor assigns 999 to the `empNum` of each potentially instantiated `Employee` object. Anytime an `Employee` object is created using a statement such as `Employee partTimeWorker = new Employee();`, even if no other data-assigning methods are ever used, you ensure that the `partTimeWorker Employee`, like all `Employee` objects, will have an initial `empNum` of 999.

```
public class Employee
{
    private int empNum;
    Employee()
    {
        empNum = 999;
    }
}
```

Figure 4-20   The `Employee` class with a default constructor that initializes the `empNum` field

Alternatively, you might choose to create `Employee` objects with initial `empNum` values that differ for each `Employee`. To accomplish this when the object is instantiated, you can pass an employee number to the constructor. Figure 4-21 shows an `Employee` class that contains a constructor that receives a parameter. With this constructor, an argument is passed using a statement such as the following:

```
Employee partTimeWorker = new Employee(881);
```

When the constructor executes, the integer within the constructor call is passed to `Employee()` as the parameter `num`, which is assigned to the `empNum` field.

When you create an `Employee` class with a constructor such as the one shown in Figure 4-21, every `Employee` object you create must have an integer argument in its constructor call. In other words, with this new version of the class, the following statement no longer works:

```
public class Employee
{
    private int empNum;
    Employee(int num)
    {
        empNum = num;
    }
}
```

Figure 4-21   The `Employee` class with a constructor that accepts a value

```
Employee partTimeWorker = new Employee();
```

After you write a constructor for a class, you no longer receive the automatically provided default constructor. If a class's only constructor requires an argument, you must provide an argument for every object of the class that you create. If you want to create a constructor with parameters and provide a default constructor, you can overload the constructors.

Overloading Constructors

As with any other method, you can overload constructors. Overloading constructors provides you with a way to create objects with different initializing arguments, or none, as needed. For example, in addition to using the provided constructor shown in Figure 4-21, you can create a second constructor for the `Employee` class; Figure 4-22 shows an `Employee`

202

class that contains two constructors. When you use this class to create an Employee object, you have the option of creating the object either with or without an initial empNum value. When you create an Employee object with the statement Employee aWorker = new Employee();, the constructor with no parameters is called, and the Employee object receives an initial empNum value of 999. When you create an Employee object with Employee anotherWorker = new Employee(7677);, the constructor version that requires an integer is used, and the anotherWorker Employee receives an initial empNum of 7677.

```
public class Employee
{
    private int empNum;
    Employee(int num)
    {
        empNum = num;
    }
    Employee()
    {
        empNum = 999;
    }
}
```

Figure 4-22   The Employee class that contains two constructors

You can use constructor arguments to initialize field values, but you can also use them for any other purpose. For example, you could use the presence or absence of an argument simply to determine which of two possible constructors to call, yet not make use of the argument within the constructor. As long as the constructor parameter lists differ, the constructors are not ambiguous.

 Watch the video *Overloading Constructors*.

TWO TRUTHS & A LIE

Creating and Calling Constructors with Parameters

1. A default constructor is one that is automatically created.

2. When you write a constructor, it can be written to receive parameters or not.

3. If a class's only constructor requires an argument, you must provide an argument for every object of the class that you create.

The false statement is #1. A default constructor is one that takes no arguments. The constructor that is automatically created when you do not write your own version is a default constructor, but so is one that you write to take no arguments.

You Do It

Creating Overloaded Constructors

In this section, you create a class with overloaded constructors and demonstrate how they work.

1. Open a new file in your text editor, and start the `CarInsurancePolicy` class as follows. The class contains three fields that hold a policy number, the number of payments the policyholder will make annually, and the policyholder's city of residence.

```
public class CarInsurancePolicy
{
    private int policyNumber;
    private int numPayments;
    private String residentCity;
```

2. Create a constructor that requires parameters for all three data fields.

```
public CarInsurancePolicy(int num, int payments, String city)
{
    policyNumber = num;
    numPayments = payments;
    residentCity = city;
}
```

3. Suppose the agency that sells car insurance policies is in the city of Mayfield. Create a two-parameter constructor that requires only a policy number and the number of payments. This constructor assigns *Mayfield* to `residentCity`.

```
public CarInsurancePolicy(int num, int payments)
{
    policyNumber = num;
    numPayments = payments;
    residentCity = "Mayfield";
}
```

4. Add a third constructor that requires only a policy number parameter. This constructor uses the default values of two annual payments and Mayfield as the resident city. (Later in this chapter, you will learn how to eliminate the duplicated assignments in these constructors.)

```
public CarInsurancePolicy(int num)
{
    policyNumber = num;
    numPayments = 2;
    residentCity = "Mayfield";
}
```

(continues)

(continued)

5. Add a `display()` method that outputs all the insurance policy data:

```java
public void display()
{
    System.out.println("Policy #" + policyNumber + ". " +
        numPayments + " payments annually. Driver resides in " +
        residentCity + ".");
}
```

6. Add a closing curly brace for the class. Save the file as
   CarInsurancePolicy.java.

7. Open a new text file to create a short application that demonstrates the
   constructors at work. The application declares three `CarInsurancePolicy`
   objects using a different constructor version each time. Type the following code:

```java
public class CreatePolicies
{
    public static void main(String[] args)
    {
        CarInsurancePolicy first = new CarInsurancePolicy(123);
        CarInsurancePolicy second = new CarInsurancePolicy(456, 4);
        CarInsurancePolicy third = new CarInsurancePolicy
            (789, 12, "Newcastle");
```

8. Display each object, and add closing curly braces for the method and the class:

```java
        first.display();
        second.display();
        third.display();
    }
}
```

9. Save the file as **CreatePolicies.java**, and then compile and test the program.
   The output appears in Figure 4-23.

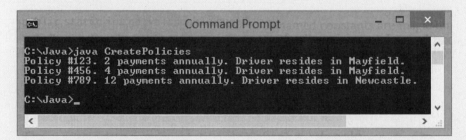

Figure 4-23 Output of the `CreatePolicies` program

(continues)

(continued)

10. Add a fourth declaration to the `CreatePolicies` class that attempts to create a `CarInsurancePolicy` object using a default constructor:

    `CarInsurancePolicy fourth = new CarInsurancePolicy();`

11. Save and compile the revised `CreatePolicies` program. The class does not compile because the `CarInsurancePolicy` class does not contain a default constructor. Change the newly added declaration to a comment, compile the class again, and observe that the class now compiles correctly.

Examining Prewritten Overloaded Methods

In this section, you examine some built-in classes and recognize their correctly overloaded methods.

1. Using a Web browser, go to the Java Web site at ***www.oracle.com/technetwork/java/index.html***, and select **Java APIs** and **Java SE 8**.

2. Using the alphabetical list of classes, find the **`PrintStream`** class, and select it.

3. Examine the list of constructors for the class, and notice that each version has a unique parameter list.

4. Examine the list of methods named **`print()`** and **`println()`**. Notice that each overloaded version has a unique parameter list.

5. Using the alphabetical list of classes, find the **`JOptionPane`** class, and select it.

6. Examine the list of constructors for the class, and notice that each version has a unique parameter list.

7. Examine the list of methods named **`showConfirmDialog()`** and **`showInputDialog()`**. Notice that each overloaded version has a unique parameter list.

Learning About the `this` Reference

When you start creating classes, they can become large very quickly. Besides data fields, each class can have many methods, including several overloaded versions. On paper, a single class might require several pages of coded statements.

When you instantiate an object from a class, memory is reserved for each instance field in the class. For example, if a class contains 20 data fields, when you create one object from that class, enough memory is reserved to hold the 20 field values for that object. When you create 200 objects of the same class, the computer reserves enough memory for 4,000 data fields—20 fields for each of the 200 objects. In many applications, the computer memory requirements can become substantial. Fortunately, objects can share some variables and methods.

In Chapter 3, you learned that if a field or method name is preceded by the keyword static when it is declared, only one field or method exists, no matter how many objects are instantiated. In other words, if a field is static, then only one copy of the field exists, and all objects created have the same value for that field. However, you frequently want each instantiation of a class to have its own copy of each data field so that each object can hold unique values. For example, if an Employee class contains fields for employee number, name, and salary, every individual Employee object needs a unique number, name, and salary value. Fields that hold unique values for each object are not defined as static.

When you create a method that uses a nonstatic field value for a class—for example, to get or set the field value—the method must be nonstatic. That means it performs in a different way for each object. However, it would take an enormous amount of memory to store a separate copy of each method for every object created from a class, and it would be wasteful, especially because each method's code would be identical. Luckily, in Java just one copy of each nonstatic method in a class is stored, and all instantiated objects can use that copy. The secret behind a single method copy's ability to work with multiple object fields is that each nonstatic method in a class automatically receives the memory address of the object it references.

When you use a nonstatic method, you use the object name, a dot, and the method name—for example, aWorker.getEmpNum() or anotherWorker.getEmpNum(). When you execute the getEmpNum() method, you are running the only copy of the method. However, within the getEmpNum() method, when you access the empNum *field*, you access a different field depending on the object. The compiler accesses the correct object's field because every time you call a nonstatic method, a **reference**—an object's memory address—is implicitly understood. The reference to an object that is passed to any object's nonstatic method is called the **this reference**; this is a reserved word in Java. Only nonstatic, instance methods have a this reference. For example, the two getEmpNum() methods for the Employee class shown in Figure 4-24 perform identically. The first method simply uses the this reference without your being aware of it; the second method uses the this reference explicitly. Both methods return the empNum of the object used to call the method.

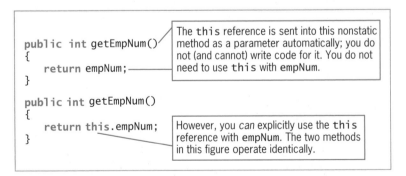

```
public int getEmpNum()
{
    return empNum;
}
```
The this reference is sent into this nonstatic method as a parameter automatically; you do not (and cannot) write code for it. You do not need to use this with empNum.

```
public int getEmpNum()
{
    return this.empNum;
}
```
However, you *can* explicitly use the this reference with empNum. The two methods in this figure operate identically.

Figure 4-24   Two versions of the getEmpNum() method, with and without an explicit this reference

Frequently, you neither want nor need to refer to the this reference within the instance methods that you write, but the this reference is always there, working behind the scenes, so that the data field for the correct object can be accessed.

On a few occasions, you must use the this reference to make your classes work correctly; one example is shown in the Student class in Figure 4-25. Within the constructor for this class, the parameter names stuNum and gpa are identical to the class field names. Within the constructor, stuNum and gpa refer to the locally declared names, not the class field names. The statement stuNum = stuNum accomplishes nothing—it assigns the local variable value to itself. The client application in Figure 4-26 attempts to create a Student object with an ID number of 111 and a grade point average of 3.5, but Figure 4-27 shows the incorrect output. The values are not assigned to the fields; instead, they are just zeroes.

```java
public class Student
{
   private int stuNum;
   private double gpa;
   public Student (int stuNum, double gpa)
   {
      stuNum = stuNum;
      gpa = gpa;
   }
   public void showStudent()
   {
      System.out.println("Student #" + stuNum +
         " gpa is " + gpa);
   }
}
```

Don't Do It
All four variables used in these two statements are the local versions declared in the method's parameter list. The fields are never accessed because the local variables shadow the fields. These two assignment statements accomplish nothing.

Figure 4-25   A Student class whose constructor does not work

```java
public class TestStudent
{
   public static void main(String[] args)
   {
      Student aPsychMajor = new Student(111, 3.5);
      aPsychMajor.showStudent();
   }
}
```

Figure 4-26   The TestStudent class that instantiates a Student object

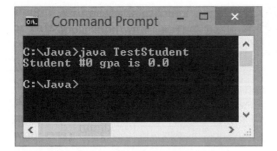

Figure 4-27   Output of the TestStudent application using the incorrect Student class in Figure 4-25

One way to fix the problem with the Student class is to use different identifiers for the class's fields and the parameters to the constructor. However, sometimes the identifiers you have chosen are the best and simplest identifiers for a value. If you choose to use the same identifiers, you can use the this reference explicitly to identify the fields. Figure 4-28 shows a modified Student class. The only difference between this class and the one in Figure 4-25 is the explicit use of the this reference within the constructor. When the this reference is used with a field name in a method, the reference is to the class's data field instead of to the local variable declared within the method. When the TestStudent application uses this new version of the Student class, the output appears as expected, as shown in Figure 4-29.

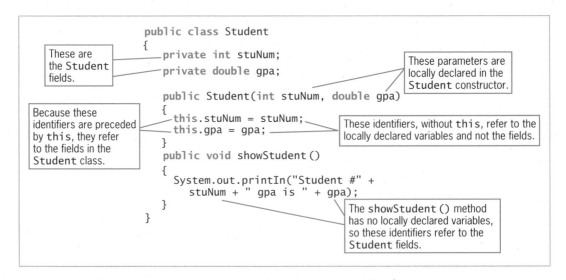

Figure 4-28   The Student class using the explicit this reference within the constructor

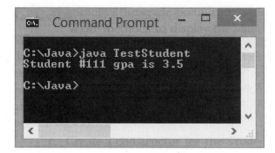

Figure 4-29 Output of the TestStudent application using the new version of the Student class

Using the this Reference to Make Overloaded Constructors More Efficient

Suppose you create a Student class with data fields for a student number and a grade point average. Further suppose you want four overloaded constructors as follows:

- A constructor that accepts an int and a double and assigns them the student number and grade point average, respectively

- A constructor that accepts a double and assigns it to the grade point average, but initializes every student number to 999

- A constructor that accepts an int and assigns it to the student number, but initializes every grade point average to 0.0

- A default constructor that assigns 999 to every student number and 0.0 to every grade point average

Figure 4-30 shows the class. Although this class works, and allows Students to be constructed in four different ways, there is a lot of repetition within the constructors.

```
public class Student
{
    private int stuNum;
    private double gpa;
    Student (int num, double avg)
    {
        stuNum = num;
        gpa = avg;
    }
    Student (double avg)
    {
        stuNum = 999;
        gpa = avg;
    }
    Student (int num)
    {
        stuNum = num;
        gpa = 0.0;
    }
    Student ()
    {
        stuNum = 999;
        gpa = 0.0;
    }
}
```

Each constructor contains similar statements.

Figure 4-30   Student class with four constructors

You can reduce the amount of repeated code in Figure 4-30 and make the code less error-prone by calling one constructor version from the others. To do so, you use the this reference from one constructor version to call another version. Figure 4-31 shows how the Student class can be rewritten.

```
public class Student
{
    private int stuNum;
    private double gpa;
    Student(int num, double avg)
    {
        stuNum = num;
        gpa = avg;
    }
    Student(double avg)
    {
        this(999, avg);
    }
    Student(int num)
    {
        this(num, 0.0);
    }
    Student()
    {
        this(999, 0.0);
    }
}
```

Each of these calls to this() calls the two-parameter version of the constructor.

Figure 4-31   The Student class using this in three of four constructors

By writing each constructor to call one master constructor, you save coding and reduce the chance for errors. For example, if code is added later to ensure that all student ID numbers are three digits, or that no grade point average is greater than 4.0, the new code will be written only in the two-parameter version of the constructor, and all the other versions will use it. (Testing a variable to ensure it falls within the proper range of values requires decision making. The next chapter covers this topic.)

Although you can use the this reference with field names in any method within a class, you cannot call this() from other methods in a class; you can only call it from constructors. Additionally, if you call this() from a constructor, it must be the first statement within the constructor.

 Watch the video *The this Reference*.

TWO TRUTHS & A LIE

Learning About the this Reference

1. Usually, you want each instantiation of a class to have its own nonstatic data fields, but each object does not need its own copy of most methods.

2. When you use a nonstatic method, the compiler accesses the correct object's field because you implicitly pass an object reference to the method.

3. The this reference is supplied automatically in classes; you cannot use it explicitly.

The false statement is #3. Usually, you neither want nor need to refer to the this reference within the methods you write, but you can use it—for example, when there are conflicts between identifiers for fields and local variables.

 You Do It

Using the this Reference to Make Constructors More Efficient

In this section, you modify the CarInsurancePolicy class so that its constructors are more efficient.

1. Open the **CarInsurancePolicy.java** file. Change the class name to **CarInsurancePolicy2**, and immediately save the file as **CarInsurancePolicy2.java**.

2. Change the name of the three-parameter constructor from CarInsurancePolicy() to **CarInsurancePolicy2()**.

3. Replace the constructor that accepts a single parameter for the policy number with the following constructor. The name of the constructor is changed from the earlier version, and this one passes the policy number and two constant values to the three-parameter constructor:

```
public CarInsurancePolicy2(int num)
{
    this(num, 2, "Mayfield");
}
```

(continues)

(continued)

4. Replace the constructor that accepts two parameters (for the policy number and number of payments) with the following constructor. This constructor has a new name and passes the two parameters and one constant value to the three-parameter constructor:

```
public CarInsurancePolicy2(int num, int payments)
{
    this(num, payments, "Mayfield");
}
```

5. Save the file, and compile it.

6. Open the **CreatePolicies.java** file that demonstrates the use of the different constructor versions. Change the class name to `CreatePolicies2`, and save the file as **CreatePolicies2.java**.

7. Add the digit **2** in six places—three times to change the class name `CarInsurancePolicy` to `CarInsurancePolicy2` when the name is used as a data type, and in the three constructor calls.

8. Save the file, and then compile and execute it. The output is identical to that shown in Figure 4-23 in the previous "You Do It" section, but the repetitious constructor code has been eliminated.

9. You can further reduce the code in the `CarInsurancePolicy` class by changing the single-parameter constructor to the following, which removes the constant `"Mayfield"` from the constructor call:

```
public CarInsurancePolicy2(int num)
{
    this(num, 2);
}
```

Now, the single-parameter version calls the two-parameter version and passes the policy number and the constant 2. In turn, the two-parameter version calls the three-parameter version, adding `"Mayfield"` as the city.

10. Save this version of the `CarInsurancePolicy2` class, and compile it. Then recompile the **CreatePolicies2.java** file, and execute it. The output remains the same.

Using `static` Fields

In Chapter 3, you learned that methods you create to use without objects are static. For example, the `main()` method in a program and the methods that `main()` calls without an object reference are static. You also learned that most methods you create within a class from which objects will be instantiated are nonstatic. Static methods do not have a `this` reference because they have no object associated with them; therefore, they are called **class methods**.

You can also create **class variables**, which are variables that are shared by every instantiation of a class. Whereas instance variables in a class exist separately for every object you create, there is only one copy of each static class variable per class. For example, consider the BaseballPlayer class in Figure 4-32. The BaseballPlayer class contains a shaded static field named count, and two nonstatic fields named number and battingAverage. The BaseballPlayer constructor sets values for number and battingAverage and increases the count by one. In other words, every time a BaseballPlayer object is constructed, it contains individual values for number and battingAverage, and the count field contains a count of the number of existing objects and is shared by all BaseballPlayer objects.

```
public class BaseballPlayer
{
    private static int count = 0;
    private int number;
    private double battingAverage;
    public BaseballPlayer(int id, double avg)
    {
        number = id;
        battingAverage = avg;
        count = count + 1;
    }
    public void showPlayer()
    {
        System.out.println("Player #" + number +
            " batting average is " + battingAverage +
            " There are " + count + " players");
    }
}
```

Figure 4-32   The BaseballPlayer class

The showPlayer() method in the BaseballPlayer class displays a BaseballPlayer's number, batting average, and a count of all current players. The showPlayer() method is not static—it accesses an individual object's data. Methods declared as static cannot access instance variables, but nonstatic instance methods like showPlayer() can access both static and instance variables.

The TestPlayer class in Figure 4-33 is an application that declares two BaseballPlayer objects, displays them, and then creates a third BaseballPlayer object and displays it. When you examine the output in Figure 4-34, you can see that by the time the first two objects are declared, the count value that they share is 2. Whether count is accessed using the aCatcher object or the aShortstop object, the count is the same. After the third object is declared, its count value is 3, as is the value of count associated with both of the previously declared objects. In other words, the count variable is incremented within the constructor, so its value changes with each new instantiation, and because the field is static, each object has access to the single memory location that holds the count value. No matter how many BaseballPlayer objects are eventually instantiated, each refers to the single count field.

```
public class TestPlayer
{
    public static void main(String[] args)
    {
        BaseballPlayer aCatcher = new BaseballPlayer(12, .218);
        BaseballPlayer aShortstop = new BaseballPlayer(31, .385);
        aCatcher.showPlayer();
        aShortstop.showPlayer();
        BaseballPlayer anOutfielder = new BaseballPlayer(44, .505);
        anOutfielder.showPlayer();
        aCatcher.showPlayer();
    }
}
```

Figure 4-33   The TestPlayer class

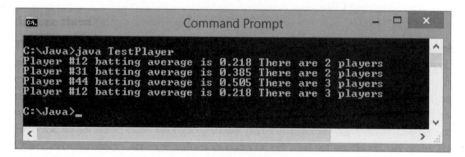

Figure 4-34   Output of the TestPlayer application

Using Constant Fields

In Chapter 2, you learned to create named constants by using the keyword final. Sometimes a data field in a class should be constant. For example, you might want to store a school ID value that is the same for every Student object you create, so you declare it to be static. In addition, if you want the value for the school ID to be fixed so that all Student objects use the same ID value—for example, when applying to scholarship-granting organizations or when registering for standardized tests—you might want to make the school ID unalterable. As with ordinary variables, you use the keyword final with a field to make its value unalterable after construction. For example, the class in Figure 4-35 contains the symbolic constant SCHOOL_ID. Because it is static, all objects share a single memory location for the field, and because it is final, it cannot change during program execution.

```
public class Student
{
    private static final int SCHOOL_ID = 12345;
    private int stuNum;
    private double gpa;
    public Student(int stuNum, double gpa)
    {
        this.stuNum = stuNum;
        this.gpa = gpa;
    }
    public void showStudent()
    {
        System.out.println("Student #" + stuNum +
            " gpa is " + gpa);
    }
}
```

Figure 4-35   The Student class containing a symbolic constant

A *nonstatic* final field's value can be assigned a value in a constructor. For example, you can set it using a constant, or you can set it using a parameter passed into the constructor. However, a static final field's value must be set at declaration, as in the Student class example in Figure 4-35. This makes sense because only one static field is stored for every object instantiated, so it would be redundant to continually reset the field's value during object construction.

You can use the keyword final with methods or classes as well as with fields. When used in this manner, final indicates limitations placed on inheritance. You will learn more about inheritance in the chapters "Introduction to Inheritance" and "Advanced Inheritance Concepts."

Fields that are final can also be initialized in a static initialization block. For more details about this technique, see the Java Web site.

Fields declared to be static are not always final. Conversely, final fields are not always static. In summary:

- If you want to create a field that all instantiations of the class can access, but the field value can change, then it is static but not final. For example, in the last section you saw a nonfinal static field in the BaseballPlayer class that held a changing count of all instantiated objects.

- If you want each object created from a class to contain its own final value, you would declare the field to be final but not static. For example, you might want each BaseballPlayer object to have its own, nonchanging date of joining the team.

- If you want all objects to share a single nonchanging value, then the field is static and final.

TWO TRUTHS & A LIE

Using static Fields

1. Methods declared as static receive a this reference that contains a reference to the object associated with them.

2. Methods declared as static are called class methods.

3. A final static field's value is shared by every object of a class.

The false statement is #1. Static methods do not have a this reference because they have no object associated with them.

You Do It

Using Static and Nonstatic final Fields

In this section, you create a class for the Riverdale Kennel Club to demonstrate the use of static and nonstatic final fields. The club enters its dogs in an annual triathlon event in which each dog receives three scores in agility, conformation, and obedience.

1. Open a new file in your text editor, and enter the first few lines for a DogTriathlonParticipant class. The class contains a final field that holds the number of events in which the dog participated. Once a final field is set, it should never change. The field is not static because it is different for each dog. The class also contains a static field that holds the total cumulative score for all the participating dogs. The field is not final because its value increases as each dog participates in the triathlon, but it is static because at any moment in time, it is the same for all participants.

```
public class DogTriathlonParticipant
{
    private final int NUM_EVENTS;
    private static int totalCumulativeScore = 0;
```

2. Add six private fields that hold the participating dog's name, the dog's score in three events, the total score, and the average score:

```
private String name;
private int obedienceScore;
private int conformationScore;
private int agilityScore;
private int total;
private double avg;
```

(continues)

(continued)

3. The constructor for the class requires five parameters—the dog's name, the number of events in which the dog participated, and the dog's scores in the three events. (After you read the chapter on decision making, you will be able to ensure that the number of nonzero scores entered matches the number of events, but for now no such checks will be made.) The constructor assigns each value to the appropriate field.

```java
public DogTriathlonParticipant(String name,
    int numEvents, int score1, int score2, int score3)
{
    this.name = name;
    NUM_EVENTS = numEvents;
    obedienceScore = score1;
    conformationScore = score2;
    agilityScore = score3;
```

4. After the assignments, the constructor calculates the total score for the participant and the participant's average score. Notice the result of the division is cast to a `double` so that any fractional part of the calculated average is not lost. Also, add the participant's total score to the cumulative score for all participants. Recall that this field is `static` because it should be the same for all participants at any point in time. After these statements, add a closing curly brace for the constructor.

```java
    total = obedienceScore +
        conformationScore + agilityScore;
    avg = (double) total / NUM_EVENTS;
    totalCumulativeScore = totalCumulativeScore +
        total;
}
```

5. Start a method that displays the data for each triathlon participant.

```java
public void display()
{
    System.out.println(name + " participated in " +
        NUM_EVENTS +
        " events and has an average score of " + avg);
    System.out.println(" " + name +
        " has a total score of " + total +
        " bringing the total cumulative score to " +
        totalCumulativeScore);
}
```

6. Add a closing curly brace for the class. Then, save the file as **DogTriathlonParticipant.java**. Compile the class, and correct any errors.

(continues)

(continued)

7. Open a new file in your text editor, and then enter the header and opening and closing curly braces for a class you can use to test the DogTriathlonParticipant class. Also include a main() method header and its opening and closing braces.

```
public class TestDogs
{
   public static void main(String[] args)
   {
   }
}
```

8. Between the braces of the main() method, declare a DogTriathlonParticipant object. Provide values for the participant's name, number of events, and three scores, and then display the object.

```
DogTriathlonParticipant dog1 =
   new DogTriathlonParticipant("Bowser", 2, 85, 89, 0);
dog1.display();
```

9. Create and display two more objects within the main() method.

```
DogTriathlonParticipant dog2 =
   new DogTriathlonParticipant("Rush", 3, 78, 72, 80);
dog2.display();
DogTriathlonParticipant dog3 =
   new DogTriathlonParticipant("Ginger", 3, 90, 86, 72);
dog3.display();
```

10. Save the file as **TestDogs.java**. Compile and execute the program. The output looks like Figure 4-36. Visually confirm that each total, average, and cumulative total is correct.

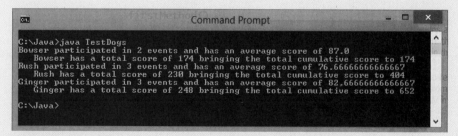

Figure 4-36   Output of the TestDogs program

(continues)

(continued)

11. Experiment with the DogTriathlonParticipant class and its test class. For example, try the following:

- Add a new statement at the end of the TestDogs class that again displays the data for any one of the participants. Note that as long as no new objects are created, the cumulative score for all participants remains the same no matter which participant uses it.

- Try to assign a value to the NUM_EVENTS constant from the display() method, and then compile the class and read the error message generated.

- Remove the keyword static from the definition of totalCumulativeScore in the DogTriathlonParticipant class, and then recompile the classes and run the program. Notice in the output that the nonstatic cumulative score no longer reflects the cumulative score for all objects, but only the score for the current object using the display() method.

- Use 0 as the number of events for an object. When the participant's average is calculated, the result is not numeric, and *NaN* is displayed. **NaN** is an acronym for *Not a Number*. In the next chapter, you will learn to make decisions, and then you can prevent the *NaN* output.

Using Automatically Imported, Prewritten Constants and Methods

If you write Java programs for an organization, you will most likely create dozens or hundreds of custom-made classes eventually. For example, you might create an Employee class with fields appropriate for describing employees in your organization, and an Inventory class with fields appropriate for whatever type of item you sell or manufacture. However, many classes do not require customization for specific businesses. Instead, they are commonly used by a wide variety of programmers. Rather than have each Java programmer "reinvent the wheel," the creators of Java have produced hundreds of classes for you to use in your programs.

You have already used several of these prewritten classes; for example, you have used the System and JOptionPane classes to produce output. Each of these classes is stored in a **package**, or a **library of classes**, which is simply a folder that provides a convenient grouping for classes. Java has two categories of packages:

- The **java.lang** package is implicitly imported into every program you write. The classes it contains are **fundamental classes** that provide the basis of the Java programming language. The System class, which you have used to access print() and println(), is an automatically imported class in the java.lang package. Others include the Object class, which you will learn about in Chapter 11; wrapper classes such as Integer, Float, and Double, which you will learn about in Chapter 7; and the Math class, which is discussed in the next section. Some references list a few other Java classes as also being "fundamental," but the java.lang package is the only automatically imported, named package.

- All other Java packages are available only if you explicitly name them within your program. These packages contain the **optional classes**. For example, when you use JOptionPane, you must import the javax.swing package into your program, and when you use the LocalDate class, you must import the java.time package, as you learn later in this chapter.

The Math Class

The class java.lang.Math contains constants and methods that you can use to perform common mathematical functions. All of the constants and methods in the Math class are static—they are class variables and class methods. In other words, you do not create any Math objects when you use the class.

For example, PI is a commonly used Math class constant. In geometry, *pi* is an approximation of a circle's radius based on the ratio of the circumference of the circle to its diameter. Within the Math class, the declaration for PI is as follows:

```
public final static double PI = 3.14159265358979323846;
```

Notice that PI is:

- public, so any program can access it directly

- final, so it cannot be changed

- static, so only one copy exists and you can access it without declaring a Math object

- double, so it holds a floating-point value

You can use the value of PI within any program you write by referencing the full package path in which PI is defined; for example, you can calculate the area of a circle using the following statement:

```
areaOfCircle = java.lang.Math.PI * radius * radius;
```

However, the java.lang package is imported automatically into your programs, so if you simply reference Math.PI, Java recognizes this code as a shortcut to the full package path. Therefore, the preferred (and simpler) statement is the following:

```
areaOfCircle = Math.PI * radius * radius;
```

In addition to constants, many useful methods are available within the Math class. For example, the Math.max() method returns the larger of two values, and the method Math.abs() returns the absolute value of a number. Table 4-1 lists some common Math class methods.

222

Method	Value that the Method Returns
abs(x)	Absolute value of x
acos(x)	Arc cosine of x
asin(x)	Arc sine of x
atan(x)	Arc tangent of x
atan2(x, y)	Theta component of the polar coordinate (r, theta) that corresponds to the Cartesian coordinate x, y
ceil(x)	Smallest integral value not less than x (ceiling)
cos(x)	Cosine of x
exp(x)	Exponent, where x is the base of the natural logarithms
floor(x)	Largest integral value not greater than x
log(x)	Natural logarithm of x
max(x, y)	Larger of x and y
min(x, y)	Smaller of x and y
pow(x, y)	x raised to the y power
random()	Random double number between 0.0 and 1.0
rint(x)	Closest integer to x (x is a double, and the return value is expressed as a double)
round(x)	Closest integer to x (where x is a float or double, and the return value is an int or long)
sin(x)	Sine of x
sqrt(x)	Square root of x
tan(x)	Tangent of x

Table 4-1   Common Math class methods

Because all constants and methods in the Math class are classwide (that is, static), there is no need to create an instance of the Math class. You cannot instantiate objects of type Math because the constructor for the Math class is private, and your programs cannot access the constructor.

 Unless you are a mathematician, you won't use many of these Math class methods, and it is unwise to do so unless you understand their purposes. For example, because the square root of a negative number is undefined, if you display the result after the method call imaginaryNumber = Math.sqrt(-12);, you see *NaN*.

Importing Classes that Are Not Imported Automatically

Java contains hundreds of classes, only a few of which—those in the java.lang package—are included automatically in the programs you write. To use any of the other prewritten classes, you must use one of three methods:

- Use the entire path with the class name.
- Import the class.
- Import the package that contains the class you are using.

For example, in its java.time package, Java includes several classes that are useful when working with dates and time. One of the classes, LocalDate, holds data about a date, including a month, day, and year, and contains methods that allow you to easily work with dates. You can declare a LocalDate reference by using the full class path, as in the following:

java.time.LocalDate myAnniversary;

The java.time package is new in Java 8. Several other classes such as Calendar and GregorianCalendar were used for working with time in earlier Java versions. The classes defined in java.time base their calendar system on the ISO calendar, which is an international standard for expressing dates and times.

However, you probably prefer to use a shorter statement. You have seen examples in this book in which the Scanner and JOptionPane classes were imported using the following statements:

import java.util.Scanner;
import javax.swing.JOptionPane;

These import statements allow you to create Scanner and JOptionPane references without typing the complete paths.

Similarly, you can import the LocalDate class using the following statement:

import java.time.LocalDate;

Then you can declare a LocalDate reference with a shortened statement such as the following:

LocalDate myAnniversary;

An alternative to importing a class is to import an entire package of classes. You can use the asterisk (*) as a **wildcard symbol**, which indicates that it can be replaced by any set of characters. In a Java import statement, you use a wildcard symbol to represent all the classes in a package. Therefore, the following statement imports the LocalDate class and any other java.time classes as well:

import java.time.*;

The import statement does not move the entire imported class or package into your program, as its name implies. Rather, it simply notifies the program that you will use the data and method names that are part of the imported class or package.

There is no performance disadvantage to importing an entire package instead of just the classes you need, and you will commonly see the wildcard method in professionally written Java programs. However, you have the alternative of importing each class you need individually. Importing all of a package's classes at once saves typing, but importing each class by name, without wildcards, can be a form of documentation, specifically to show which parts of the package are being used. Additionally, if two or more packages contain classes with the same identifiers, then using the wildcard can result in conflicts.

You cannot use the `import` statement wildcard exactly like a DOS or UNIX wildcard because you cannot import all the Java classes with `import java.*;`. The Java wildcard works only with specific packages such as `import java.util.*;` or `import java.time.*;`. Also, note that the asterisk in an `import` statement imports all of the classes in a package, but not other packages that are within the imported package.

Your own classes are included in applications without `import` statements because of your `classpath` settings. See Appendix A for more information on `classpath`.

Java also uses the question mark character (?) as a wildcard when instantiating generic data types. You will learn about this topic as you continue to study Java.

Using the LocalDate Class

Several ways exist to create a `LocalDate` object. For example, you can create two `LocalDate` objects with the current date and May 29, 2018, using the following statements:

```
LocalDate today = LocalDate.now();
LocalDate graduationDate = LocalDate.of(2018, 5, 29);
```

The `LocalDate` class is so named to distinguish it from other Java classes that include time zone information in their dates—in other words, dates that are not "local."

These statements use the static methods `now()` and `of()`, respectively. You can tell the methods are static because they are used with the class name and without an object. The `now()` method accepts no arguments, and the `of()` method accepts three integers that represent a year, month, and day. You can tell from these two statements that both the `now()` and `of()` methods have a return type of `LocalDate` because their returned values are assigned to `LocalDate` objects.

Unlike the other classes you have seen, you do not use the `new` operator and call a constructor when creating `LocalDate` objects; instead you use `of()` or `now()`. The class's constructors are not usable because they are not `public`.

A `LocalDate` object can be displayed as a `String` with dashes separating the year, month, and day. For example, Figure 4-37 shows a program that creates two `LocalDate` objects on October 15, 2015, and then displays them. Figure 4-38 shows the output.

```
import java.time.*;
public class LocalDateDemo
{
   public static void main(String[] args)
   {
      LocalDate today = LocalDate.now();
      LocalDate graduationDate = LocalDate.of(2018, 5, 29);
      System.out.println("Today is " + today);
      System.out.println("Graduation is " + graduationDate);
   }
}
```

Figure 4-37   The LocalDateDemo application

Figure 4-38   Execution of the LocalDateDemo application

Specific data field values can be retrieved from a LocalDate object by using the getYear(), getMonthValue(), and getDayOfMonth() methods that each return an integer. For example, assuming that graduationDate has been created with arguments 2018, 5, and 29, as in the program in Figure 4-37, the following statement produces the output "Graduation will be on day 29 in month 5":

```
System.out.println("Graduation will be on day " +
   graduationDate.getDayOfMonth() + " in month " +
   graduationDay.getMonthValue());
```

Other useful LocalDate methods include getMonth() and getDayOfWeek(). Each of these methods returns an **enumeration**, which is a data type that consists of a list of values. You will learn to create your own enumerations in Chapter 9, but for now, you can use Java's Month and DayOfWeek enumerations returned by these methods. The enumerations are constants with names such as JANUARY, FEBRUARY, and MARCH and SUNDAY, MONDAY, and TUESDAY. For example, assuming that graduationDate has been set as in Figure 4-37, the following statement displays "Graduation is on TUESDAY".

```
System.out.println("Graduation is on " +
graduationDate.getDayOfWeek());
```

You might choose to create a LocalDate object using one of the Month enumerations, as in the following declaration:

```
LocalDate annualMeeting = LocalDate.of(2017, Month.OCTOBER, 1);
```

Another set of methods adds and subtracts time from an existing date. Some of the most useful method names are plusDays(), plusWeeks(), plusMonths(), plusYears(), minusDays(), minusWeeks(), minusMonths(), and minusYears(). Each of these methods accepts a long argument; of course, you can pass any of the methods an int to promote it to a long. For example, Figure 4-39 shows an application that prompts a user for a furniture order date and displays details about the delivery date, which is two weeks later. Figure 4-40 shows a typical execution.

```java
import java.time.*;
import java.util.Scanner;
public class DeliveryDate
{
    public static void main(String[] args)
    {
        Scanner input = new Scanner(System.in);
        LocalDate orderDate;
        int mo;
        int day;
        int year;
        final int WEEKS_FOR_DELIVERY = 2;
        System.out.print("Enter order month ");
        mo = input.nextInt();
        System.out.print("Enter order day ");
        day = input.nextInt();
        System.out.print("Enter order year ");
        year = input.nextInt();
        orderDate = LocalDate.of(year, mo, day);
        System.out.println("Order date is " + orderDate);
        System.out.println("Delivery date is " +
            orderDate.plusWeeks(WEEKS_FOR_DELIVERY));
    }
}
```

Figure 4-39   The DeliveryDate application

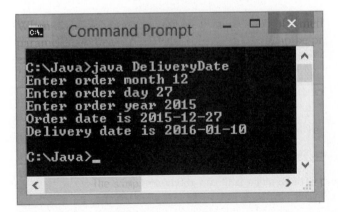

Figure 4-40   Typical execution of the DeliveryDate application

Notice in Figure 4-40 that the two-week delivery date is displayed correctly, even though it falls both in the next month and the next year. Without the built-in methods of the LocalDate class, this output would require some fairly complicated calculations and decisions, but because the creators of Java have provided the class and its methods for you, your task is greatly simplified. Many programmers need the methods in LocalDate, including those who manage personnel, inventory, and billing systems and programmers who write games that keep track of player records. Their jobs are easier because Java's creators implemented so many useful LocalDate methods. Additionally, when programmers advance to writing different types of applications or change employers, they do not have to learn how to use obscure date-handling methods that might have been written by previous programmers. Once programmers have learned about LocalDate's built-in methods and constants, they know how to work with dates in many situations.

227

TWO TRUTHS & A LIE

Using Automatically Imported, Prewritten Constants and Methods

1. The creators of Java have produced hundreds of classes for you to use in your programs.

2. Java packages are available only if you explicitly name them within your program.

3. The implicitly imported java.lang package contains fundamental Java classes.

The false statement is #2. Many Java packages are available only if you explicitly name them within your program, but others are automatically imported.

You Do It

Using the Java Web Site

In this section, you learn more about using the LocalDate class and are introduced to the LocalDateTime class.

1. Using a Web browser, go to the Java Web site, and select **Java APIs** and **Java SE 8**. Using the alphabetical list of classes, find the LocalDate class and select it.

2. Notice that java.time is cited at the top of the description, indicating that it is the containing package.

(continues)

(continued)

3. Read the history and background of the `LocalDate` class to get an idea of how many issues are involved in determining values like the first day of the week and a week's number in a year. Then read the rest of the documentation to get a feel for the fields and methods that are available with the class.

4. Find the documentation for the `LocalDateTime` class. It is similar to the `LocalDate` class, except it includes information about the time of day. Read descriptions of the methods `getHour()`, `getMinute()`, `getSecond()`, and `getNano()`. (A **nanosecond** is one-billionth of a second.)

Using an Explicitly Imported, Prewritten Class

Next, you use the `LocalDateTime` class to create an application that outputs a user's response time to a question.

1. Open a new file in your text editor, and type the following two `import` statements. You need the `JOptionPane` class to use the `showConfirmDialog()` method, and you need the `java.time` package to use the `LocalDateTime` class:

```
import javax.swing.JOptionPane;
import java.time.*;
```

2. Begin the `TimedResponse` application as follows. Declare two `LocalDateTime` objects named `time1` and `time2`. These objects will hold the exact time before a user is prompted and the exact time after the user responds. Also declare integers to hold the value of the seconds for both times. The difference between these two values is the elapsed time between the creations of the two `LocalDateTime` values.

```
public class TimedResponse
{
    public static void main(String[] args)
    {
        LocalDateTime time1, time2;
        int seconds1, seconds2, difference;
```

3. Assign the current time to the `time1` object, and then extract the value of the current `seconds` field.

```
time1 = LocalDateTime.now();
seconds1 = time1.getSecond();
```

4. Display a dialog box that asks the user to make a difficult choice.

```
JOptionPane.showConfirmDialog
(null, "Is stealing ever justified? ");
```

(continues)

(continued)

5. Next, get the system time immediately after the user responds to the dialog box, and extract its `seconds` component.

```
time2 = LocalDateTime.now();
seconds2 = time2.getSecond();
```

6. Compute the difference between the times, and display the result in a dialog box.

```
difference = seconds2 - seconds1;
    JOptionPane.showMessageDialog(null, "End seconds: " + seconds2 +
        "\nStart seconds: " + seconds1 +
        "\nIt took " + difference + " seconds for you to answer");
```

7. Add two closing curly braces—one for the method and the other for the class—and then save the file as **TimedResponse.java**.

8. Compile and execute the program. When the question appears, ponder it for a few seconds, and then choose a response. Figure 4-41 shows a typical execution.

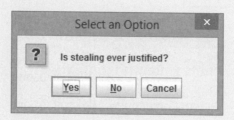

Figure 4-41   Typical execution of the `TimedResponse` application

9. The output in the `TimedResponse` application is accurate only when the first and second `LocalDateTime` objects are created during the same minute, as in the output in Figure 4-41, when the question was asked at 27 seconds after the minute and then answered 47 seconds after the same minute. If the first object is created 58 seconds after a minute starts and the user doesn't respond to the question until 2 seconds after the next minute starts, the difference between the second values will be calculated incorrectly as –56 instead of 4 seconds. On your own, modify the `TimedResponse` application to rectify this problem. Save the file as **TimedResponse2.java**.

Understanding Composition and Nested Classes

Two of the ways that you can group classes are by using composition and by nesting classes. This section takes a brief look at both concepts.

Composition

The fields in a class can be simple data types like int and double, but they can also be class types. **Composition** describes the relationship between classes when an object of one class is a data field within another class. You have already studied many classes that contain String object fields. These classes employ composition.

When you use an object as a data member of another object, you must remember to supply values for the contained object if it has no default constructor. For example, you might create a class named NameAndAddress that stores name and address information. Such a class could be used for employees, customers, students, or anyone else who has a name and address. Figure 4-42 shows a NameAndAddress class. The class contains three fields, all of which are set by the constructor. A display() method displays the name and address information on three lines.

```java
public class NameAndAddress
{
    private String name;
    private String address;
    private int zipCode;
    public NameAndAddress(String nm, String add, int zip)
    {
        name = nm;
        address = add;
        zipCode = zip;
    }
    public void display()
    {
        System.out.println(name);
        System.out.println(address);
        System.out.println(zipCode);
    }
}
```

Figure 4-42   The NameAndAddress class

Suppose you want to create a School class that holds information about a school. Instead of declaring fields for the School's name and address, you could use the NameAndAddress class. The relationship created is sometimes called a **has-a relationship** because one class "has an" instance of another. Figure 4-43 shows a School class that declares and uses a NameAndAddress object.

This statement declares a NameAndAddress object.

This statement calls the constructor in the NameAndAddress class.

This statement calls the display() method in the NameAndAddress class.

```
public class School
{
    private NameAndAddress nameAdd;
    private int enrollment;
    public School(String name, String add; int zip, int enrolled)
    {
        nameAdd = new NameAndAddress(name, add, zip);
        enrollment = enrolled;
    }
    public void display()
    {
        System.out.printIn("The school information:");
        nameAdd.display();
        System.out.printIn("Enrollment is " + enrollment);
    }
}
```

Figure 4-43 The School class

As Figure 4-43 shows, the School constructor requires four parameters. Within the constructor, three of the items—the name, address, and zip code—are passed to the NameAndAddress constructor to provide values for the appropriate fields. The fourth constructor parameter (the school's enrollment) is assigned to the School class enrollment field.

In the School class display method, the NameAndAddress object's display() method is called to display the school's name and address. The enrollment value is displayed afterward. Figure 4-44 shows a simple program that instantiates one School object. Figure 4-45 shows the execution.

```
public class SchoolDemo
{
    public static void main(String[] args)
    {
        School mySchool = new School
            ("Audubon Elementary",
            "3500 Hoyne", 60618, 350);
        mySchool.display();
    }
}
```

Figure 4-44 The SchoolDemo program

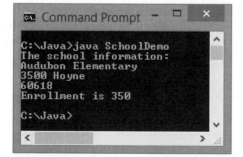

Figure 4-45 Output of the SchoolDemo program

Nested Classes

Every class you have studied so far has been stored in its own file, and the filename has always matched the class name. In Java, you can create a class within another class and store them together; such classes are **nested classes**. The containing class is the **top-level class**. There are four types of nested classes:

- **static member classes**: A static member class has access to all static methods of the top-level class.

- **Nonstatic member classes**, also known as **inner classes**: This type of class requires an instance; it has access to all data and methods of the top-level class.

- **Local classes**: These are local to a block of code.

- **Anonymous classes**: These are local classes that have no identifier.

The most common reason to nest a class inside another is because the inner class is used only by the top-level class; in other words, it is a "helper class" to the top-level class. Being able to package the classes together makes their connection easier to understand and their code easier to maintain.

For example, consider a RealEstateListing class used by a real estate company to describe houses that are available for sale. The class might contain separate fields for a listing number, the price, the street address, and the house's living area. As an alternative, you might decide that although the listing number and price "go with" the real estate listing, the street address and living area really "go with" the house. So you might create an inner class like the one shaded in Figure 4-46.

```java
public class RealEstateListing
{
    private int listingNumber;
    private double price;
    private HouseData houseData;
    public RealEstateListing(int num, double price, String address,
        int sqFt)
    {
        listingNumber = num;
        this.price = price;
        houseData = new HouseData(address, sqFt);
    }
    public void display()
    {
        System.out.println("Listing number #" + listingNumber +
            " Selling for $" + price);
        System.out.println("Address: " + houseData.streetAddress);
        System.out.println(houseData.squareFeet + " square feet");
    }
}
```

Figure 4-46   The RealEstateListing class (continues)

(continued)

```
private class HouseData
{
    private String streetAddress;
    private int squareFeet;
    public HouseData(String address, int sqFt)
    {
        streetAddress = address;
        squareFeet = sqFt;
    }
}
}
```

Figure 4-46   The RealEstateListing class

Notice that the inner HouseData class in Figure 4-46 is a private class. You don't have to make an inner class private, but doing so keeps its members hidden from outside classes. If you wanted a class's members to be accessible, you would not make it an inner class. An inner class can access its top-level class's fields and methods, even if they are private, and an outer class can access its inner class's members.

You usually will not want to create inner classes. For example, if you made the HouseData class a regular class (as opposed to an inner class) and stored it in its own file, you could use it with composition in other classes—perhaps a MortgageLoan class or an Appraisal class. As it stands, it is usable only in the class in which it now resides. You probably will not create nested classes frequently, but you will see them implemented in some built-in Java classes.

TWO TRUTHS & A LIE

Understanding Composition and Nested Classes

1. Exposition describes the relationship between classes when an object of one class is a data field within another class.

2. When you use an object as a data member of another object, you must remember to supply values for the contained object if it has no default constructor.

3. A nested class resides within another class.

The false statement is #1. Composition describes the relationship between classes when an object of one class is a data field within another class.

Don't Do It

- Don't try to use a variable that is out of scope.

- Don't assume that a constant is still a constant when passed to a method's parameter. If you want a parameter to be constant within a method, you must use `final` in the parameter list.

- Don't try to overload methods by giving them different return types. If their identifiers and parameter lists are the same, then two methods are ambiguous no matter what their return types are.

- Don't think that *default constructor* means only the automatically supplied version. A constructor with no parameters is a default constructor, whether it is the one that is automatically supplied or one you write.

- Don't forget to write a default constructor for a class that has other constructors if you want to be able to instantiate objects without using arguments.

- Don't assume that a wildcard in an `import` statement works like a DOS or UNIX wildcard. The wildcard works only with specific packages and does not import embedded packages.

Key Terms

A **block** is the code between a pair of curly braces.

An **outer block** contains another block.

An **inner block** is contained within another block.

Nested describes the state of an inner block.

Scope is the part of a program in which a variable exists and can be accessed using its unqualified name.

Comes into scope describes what happens to a variable when it becomes usable.

Goes out of scope describes what happens to a variable when it ceases to exist at the end of the block in which it is declared.

Scope level is the part of a program in which a variable exists and can be accessed using its unqualified name; in Java, this is the variable's block.

To **redeclare a variable** is to attempt to declare it twice, which is an illegal action.

A variable **overrides** another with the same name when it takes precedence over the other variable.

Shadowing is the action that occurs when a local variable hides a variable with the same name that is further away in scope.

Closer in scope describes the status of a local variable over others that it shadows.

Overloading involves using one term to indicate diverse meanings, or writing multiple methods with the same name but with different arguments.

An **ambiguous** situation is one in which the compiler cannot determine which method to use.

A **reference** is an object's memory address.

The **this reference** is a reference to an object that is passed to any object's nonstatic class method.

Class methods are static methods that do not have a this reference (because they have no object associated with them).

Class variables are static variables that are shared by every instantiation of a class.

NaN is an acronym for *Not a Number*.

A **package** is a library of classes.

A **library of classes** is a folder that provides a convenient grouping for classes.

The **java.lang** package provides classes that are fundamental to the design of the Java programming language; it is implicitly imported into every Java program.

The **fundamental classes** are basic classes contained in the java.lang package that are automatically imported into every program you write.

The **optional classes** reside in packages that must be explicitly imported into your programs.

A **wildcard symbol** is a symbol used to indicate that it can be replaced by any set of characters. In a Java import statement, the wildcard symbol is an asterisk.

An **enumeration** is a data type that consists of a list of values.

A **nanosecond** is one-billionth of a second.

Composition describes the relationship between classes when an object of one class is a data field within another class.

A **has-a relationship** is a relationship based on composition.

Nested classes are classes contained in other classes.

The **top-level class** is the containing class in nested classes.

A **static member class** is a type of nested class that has access to all static methods of its top-level class.

Nonstatic member classes, also known as **inner classes**, are nested classes that require an instance.

Local classes are a type of nested class that are local to a block of code.

Anonymous classes are nested, local classes that have no identifier.

Chapter Summary

- A variable's scope is the portion of a program within which it can be referenced. A block is the code between a pair of curly braces. Within a method, you can declare a variable with the same name multiple times, as long as each declaration is in its own nonoverlapping block. If you declare a variable within a class and use the same variable name within a method of the class, the variable used inside the method takes precedence over (or overrides, or masks) the first variable.

- Overloading involves writing multiple methods with the same name but different parameter lists. Methods that have identical parameter lists but different return types are not overloaded; they are illegal.

- When you overload methods, you risk creating an ambiguous situation—one in which the compiler cannot determine which method to use.

- When you write your own constructors, they can receive parameters. Such parameters are often used to initialize data fields for an object. After you write a constructor for a class, you no longer receive the automatically provided default constructor. If a class's only constructor requires an argument, you must provide an argument for every object of the class that you create. You can overload constructors just as you can other methods.

- Within nonstatic methods, data fields for the correct object are accessed because a `this` reference is implicitly passed to nonstatic methods. Static methods do not have a `this` reference because they have no object associated with them; static methods are also called class methods.

- Static class fields and methods are shared by every instantiation of a class. When a field in a class is `final`, it cannot change after it is assigned its initial value.

- Java contains hundreds of prewritten classes that are stored in packages, which are folders that provide convenient groupings for classes. The package that is implicitly imported into every Java program is named `java.lang`. The classes it contains are the fundamental classes, as opposed to the optional classes, which must be explicitly named. The class `java.lang.Math` contains constants and methods that can be used to perform common mathematical functions. The `LocalDate` and `LocalDateTime` classes allow you to define and manipulate dates and time.

- Composition describes the relationship between classes when an object of one class is a data field within another class. You can create nested classes that are stored in the same file. The most common reason to nest a class inside another is because the inner class is used only by the outer or top-level class; in other words, it is a "helper class" to the top-level class.

Review Questions

1. The code between a pair of curly braces in a method is a _____.

   a. function   c. brick
   b. block   d. sector

2. When a block exists within another block, the blocks are _____.

   a. structured   c. sheltered

   b. nested   d. illegal

3. The portion of a program within which you can reference a variable is the variable's _____.

   a. range   c. domain

   b. space   d. scope

4. You can declare variables with the same name multiple times _____.

   a. within a statement

   b. within a block

   c. within a method

   d. You never can declare multiple variables with the same name.

5. If you declare a variable as an instance variable within a class, and you declare and use the same variable name within a method of the class, then within the method, _____.

   a. the variable used inside the method takes precedence

   b. the class instance variable takes precedence

   c. the two variables refer to a single memory address

   d. an error will occur

6. A method variable _____ a class variable with the same name.

   a. acquiesces to   c. overrides

   b. destroys   d. alters

7. Nonambiguous, overloaded methods must have the same _____.

   a. name   c. parameter names

   b. number of parameters   d. types of parameters

8. If a method is written to receive a `double` parameter, and you pass an integer to the method, then the method will _____.

   a. work correctly; the integer will be promoted to a `double`

   b. work correctly; the integer will remain an integer

   c. execute, but any output will be incorrect

   d. not work; an error message will be issued

9. A constructor _____ parameters.

   a. can receive   c. must receive

   b. cannot receive   d. can receive a maximum of 10

10. A constructor ——————— overloaded.

    a. can be   c. must be
    b. cannot be   d. is always automatically

11. Usually, you want each instantiation of a class to have its own copy of ——————— .

    a. the data fields   c. both of the above
    b. the class methods   d. none of the above

12. If you create a class that contains one method, and instantiate two objects, you usually store ——————— for use with the objects.

    a. one copy of the method
    b. two copies of the method
    c. two different methods containing two different `this` references
    d. data only (the methods are not stored)

13. The `this` reference ——————— .

    a. can be used implicitly   c. must not be used implicitly
    b. must be used implicitly   d. must not be used

14. Methods that you reference with individual objects are ——————— .

    a. `private`   c. `static`
    b. `public`   d. `nonstatic`

15. Variables that are shared by every instantiation of a class are ——————— .

    a. class variables   c. `public` variables
    b. `private` variables   d. illegal

16. The keyword `final` used with a variable declaration indicates ——————— .

    a. the end of the program
    b. a `static` field
    c. a symbolic constant
    d. that no more variables will be declared in the program

17. Java classes are stored in a folder or ——————— .

    a. packet   c. bundle
    b. package   d. gaggle

18. Which of the following statements determines the square root of a number and assigns it to the variable s?

    a. `s = sqrt(number);`   c. `number = sqrt(s);`
    b. `s = Math.sqrt(number);`   d. `number = Math.sqrt(s);`

19. A `LocalDate` object _____.

    a. can be displayed as a `String`

    b. contains static fields with data such as the current year

    c. is created using a public default constructor

    d. all of the above

20. Which of the following expressions correctly returns an integer that represents the month of a `LocalDate` object named `hireDate`?

    a. `getMonth(hireDate)`   c. `hireDate.getMonthValue()`

    b. `getMonthValue(hireDate)`   d. all of the above

Exercises

 Programming Exercises

1. Create a class named `FormLetterWriter` that includes two overloaded methods named `displaySalutation()`. The first method takes one `String` parameter that represents a customer's last name, and it displays the salutation "Dear Mr. or Ms." followed by the last name. The second method accepts two `String` parameters that represent a first and last name, and it displays the greeting "Dear" followed by the first name, a space, and the last name. After each salutation, display the rest of a short business letter: "Thank you for your recent order." Write a `main()` method that tests each overloaded method. Save the file as **FormLetterWriter.java**.

2. Create a class named `Billing` that includes three overloaded `computeBill()` methods for a photo book store.

    ● When `computeBill()` receives a single parameter, it represents the price of one photo book ordered. Add 8% tax, and return the total due.

    ● When `computeBill()` receives two parameters, they represent the price of a photo book and the quantity ordered. Multiply the two values, add 8% tax, and return the total due.

    ● When `computeBill()` receives three parameters, they represent the price of a photo book, the quantity ordered, and a coupon value. Multiply the quantity and price, reduce the result by the coupon value, and then add 8% tax and return the total due.

    Write a `main()` method that tests all three overloaded methods. Save the application as **Billing.java**.

3. a. Create a `FitnessTracker` class that includes data fields for a fitness activity, the number of minutes spent participating, and the date. The class includes methods to get each field. In addition, create a default constructor that automatically sets the activity to "running," the minutes to 0, and the date to January 1 of the

current year. Save the file as **FitnessTracker.java**. Create an application that demonstrates each method works correctly, and save it as **TestFitnessTracker.java**.

b. Create an additional overloaded constructor for the FitnessTracker class you created in Exercise 3a. This constructor receives parameters for each of the data fields and assigns them appropriately. Add any needed statements to the TestFitnessTracker application to ensure that the overloaded constructor works correctly, save it, and then test it.

c. Modify the FitnessTracker class so that the default constructor calls the three-parameter constructor. Save the class as **FitnessTracker2.java**. Create an application to test the new version of the class, and name it **TestFitnessTracker2.java**.

4. a. Create a class named BloodData that includes fields that hold a blood type (the four blood types are *O*, *A*, *B*, and *AB*) and an Rh factor (the factors are + and –). Create a default constructor that sets the fields to "O" and "+", and an overloaded constructor that requires values for both fields. Include get and set methods for each field. Save this file as **BloodData.java**. Create an application named TestBloodData that demonstrates each method works correctly. Save the application as **TestBloodData.java**.

b. Create a class named Patient that includes an ID number, age, and BloodData. Provide a default constructor that sets the ID number to "0", the age to 0, and the BloodData to "O" and "+". Create an overloaded constructor that provides values for each field. Also provide get methods for each field. Save the file as **Patient.java**. Create an application that demonstrates that each method works correctly, and save it as **TestPatient.java**.

5. a. Create a class for the Tip Top Bakery named Bread with data fields for bread type (such as "rye") and calories per slice. Include a constructor that takes parameters for each field, and include get methods that return the values of the fields. Also include a public final static String named MOTTO and initialize it to *The staff of life*. Write an application named TestBread to instantiate three Bread objects with different values, and then display all the data, including the motto, for each object. Save both the **Bread.java** and **TestBread.java** files.

b. Create a class named SandwichFilling. Include a field for the filling type (such as "egg salad") and another for the calories in a serving. Include a constructor that takes parameters for each field, and include get methods that return the values of the fields. Write an application named TestSandwichFilling to instantiate three SandwichFilling objects with different values, and then display all the data for each object. Save both the **SandwichFilling.java** and **TestSandwichFilling.java** files.

c. Create a class named Sandwich. Include a Bread field and a SandwichFilling field. Include a constructor that takes parameters for each field needed in the two objects and assigns them to each object's constructor. Write an application named TestSandwich to instantiate three Sandwich objects with different values, and then display all the data for each object, including the total calories in a Sandwich, assuming that each Sandwich is made using two slices of Bread. Save both the **Sandwich.java** and **TestSandwich.java** files.

6. a. Create a class named `Circle` with fields named `radius`, `diameter`, and `area`. Include a constructor that sets the radius to 1 and calculates the other two values. Also include methods named `setRadius()` and `getRadius()`. The `setRadius()` method not only sets the radius, it also calculates the other two values. (The diameter of a circle is twice the radius, and the area of a circle is *pi* multiplied by the square of the radius. Use the `Math` class `PI` constant for this calculation.) Save the class as **Circle.java**.

   b. Create a class named `TestCircle` whose `main()` method declares several `Circle` objects. Using the `setRadius()` method, assign one `Circle` a small radius value, and assign another a larger radius value. Do not assign a value to the radius of the third circle; instead, retain the value assigned at construction. Display all the values for all the `Circle` objects. Save the application as **TestCircle.java**.

7. Write a Java application that uses the `Math` class to determine the answers for each of the following:

   a. The square root of 37

   b. The sine and cosine of 300

   c. The value of the floor, ceiling, and round of 22.8

   d. The larger and the smaller of the character 'D' and the integer 71

   e. A random number between 0 and 20 (*Hint*: The `random()` method returns a value between 0 and 1; you want a number that is 20 times larger.)

   Save the application as **MathTest.java**.

8. Write a program that declares two `LocalDate` objects and assign values that represent January 31 and December 31 in the current year. Display output that demonstrates the dates displayed when one, two, and three months are added to each of the objects. Save the application as **TestMonthHandling.java**.

9. Write an application that computes and displays the day on which you become (or became) 10,000 days old. Save the application as **TenThousandDaysOld.java**.

10. The `LocalDate` class includes an instance method named `lengthOfMonth()` that returns the number of days in the month. Write an application that uses methods in the `LocalDate` class to calculate how many days are left until the first day of next month. Display the result, including the name of the next month. Save the file as **DaysTilNextMonth.java**.

11. a. Create a `CertOfDeposit` class. The class contains data fields that hold a certificate number, account holder's last name, balance, issue date, and maturity date, using `LocalDate` objects for each date. Provide get and set methods for each field. Also provide a constructor that requires parameters used to set the first four fields, and sets the maturity date to exactly one year after the issue date. Save the class as **CertOfDeposit.java**.

   b. Create an interactive application that prompts the user for data for two `CertOfDeposit` objects. Prompt the user for certificate number, name, balance, and issue date for each `CertOfDeposit`, and then instantiate the objects. Display all the values, including the maturity dates. Save the application as **TestCertOfDeposit.java**.

12. Create a class named `Person` that holds the following fields: two `String` objects for the person's first and last name and a `LocalDate` object for the person's birthdate. Create a class named `Couple` that contains two `Person` objects. Create a class named `Wedding` for a wedding planner that includes the date of the wedding, the names of the `Couple` being married, and a `String` for the location. Provide constructors for each class that accept parameters for each field, and provide get methods for each field. Then write a program that creates two `Wedding` objects and in turn passes each to a method that displays all the details. Save the files as **Person.java, Couple.java, Wedding.java**, and **TestWedding.java**.

Debugging Exercises

1. Each of the following files in the Chapter04 folder of your downloadable student files has syntax and/or logic errors. In each case, determine the problem and fix the program. After you correct the errors, save each file using the same filename preceded with *Fix*. For example, save DebugFour1.java as **FixDebugFour1.java**.

   a. DebugFour1.java
   b. DebugFour2.java
   c. DebugFour3.java and DebugBox.java
   d. DebugFour4.java

When you change a filename, remember to change every instance of the class name within the file so that it matches the new filename. In Java, the filename and class name must always match.

Game Zone

1. Dice are used in many games. One die can be thrown to randomly show a value from 1 through 6. Design a `Die` class that can hold an integer data field for a value (from 1 to 6). Include a constructor that randomly assigns a value to a die object. Appendix D contains information on generating random numbers. To fully understand the process, you must learn more about Java classes and methods. However, for now, you can copy the following statement to generate a random number between 1 and 6 and assign it to a variable. Using this statement assumes you have assigned appropriate values to the static constants.

```
randomValue = ((int)(Math.random() * 100) % HIGHEST_DIE_VALUE +
    LOWEST_DIE_VALUE);
```

Also include a method in the class to return a die's value. Save the class as **Die.java**.

Write an application that randomly "throws" two dice and displays their values. After you read the chapter "Making Decisions," you will be able to have the game determine the higher die. For now, just observe how the values change as you execute the program multiple times. Save the application as **TwoDice.java**.

2. Using the `Die` class, write an application that randomly "throws" five dice for the computer and five dice for the player. Display the values and then, by observing the results, decide who wins based on the following hierarchy of `Die` values. (The computer will not decide the winner; the player will determine the winner based on observation.) Any higher combination beats a lower one; for example, five of a kind beats four of a kind.

- Five of a kind

- Four of a kind

- Three of a kind

- A pair

After you learn about decision making in the next chapter, you will be able to make the program determine whether you or the computer had the better roll, and after you read the chapter "Introduction to Arrays," you will be able to make the determination more efficient. For now, just observe how the values change as you execute the program multiple times. Save the application as **FiveDice.java**.

 ## Case Problems

These projects build on the ones you created in Chapter 3, so they have the same filenames. If you want to retain both versions of the files, save them in different folders.

1. a. Carly's Catering provides meals for parties and special events. In Chapter 3, you created an `Event` class for the company. The `Event` class contains two `public final static` fields that hold the price per guest ($35) and the cutoff value for a large event (50 guests), and three `private` fields that hold an event number, number of guests for the event, and the price. It also contains two `public` set methods and three `public` get methods.

   Now, modify the `Event` class to contain two overloaded constructors.

   - One constructor accepts an event number and number of guests as parameters. Pass these values to the `setEventNumber()` and `setGuests()` methods, respectively. The `setGuests()` method will automatically calculate the event price.

   - The other constructor is a default constructor that passes "A000" and 0 to the two-parameter constructor.

   Save the file as **Event.java**.

   b. In Chapter 3, you also created an `EventDemo` class to demonstrate using two `Event` objects. Now, modify that class to instantiate two `Event` objects, and include the following new methods in the class:

   - Instantiate one object to retain the constructor default values.

- Accept user data for the event number and guests fields, and use this data set to instantiate the second object. Display all the details for both objects.

Save the file as **EventDemo.java**.

2. a. Sammy's Seashore Supplies rents beach equipment such as kayaks, canoes, beach chairs, and umbrellas to tourists. In Chapter 3, you created a `Rental` class for the company. The `Rental` class contains two `public final static` fields that hold the number of minutes in an hour and the hourly rental rate ($40), and four `private` fields that hold a contract number, number of hours for the rental, number of minutes over an hour, and the price. It also contains two `public` set methods and four `public` get methods.

Now, modify the `Rental` class to contain two overloaded constructors.

- One constructor accepts a contract number and number of minutes as parameters. Pass these values to the `setContractNumber()` and `setHoursAndMinutes()` methods, respectively. The `setHoursAndMinutes()` method will automatically calculate the hours, extra minutes, and price.

- The other constructor is a default constructor that passes "A000" and 0 to the two-parameter constructor.

Save the file as **Rental.java**.

b. In Chapter 3, you also created a `RentalDemo` class to demonstrate a `Rental` object. Now, modify that class to instantiate two `Rental` objects.

- Instantiate one object to retain the constructor default values.

- Accept user data for the contract number and minutes fields and use this data set to instantiate the second object. Display all the details for both objects.

Save the file as **RentalDemo.java**.

Making Decisions

In this chapter, you will:

- ◎ Plan decision-making logic
- ◎ Make decisions with the `if` and `if...else` statements
- ◎ Use multiple statements in `if` and `if...else` clauses
- ◎ Nest `if` and `if...else` statements
- ◎ Use AND and OR operators
- ◎ Make accurate and efficient decisions
- ◎ Use the `switch` statement
- ◎ Use the conditional and NOT operators
- ◎ Assess operator precedence
- ◎ Add decisions and constructors to instance methods

Planning Decision-Making Logic

When computer programmers write programs, they rarely just sit down at a keyboard and begin typing. Programmers must plan the complex portions of programs using paper and pencil. Programmers often use **pseudocode**, a tool that helps them plan a program's logic by writing down in plain English the steps needed to accomplish a given task. You write pseudocode in everyday language, not the syntax used in a programming language. In fact, a task you write in pseudocode does not have to be computer-related. If you have ever written a list of directions to your house—for example, (1) go west on Algonquin Road, (2) turn left on Roselle Road, (3) enter expressway heading east, and so on—you have written pseudocode. A **flowchart** is similar to pseudocode, but you write the steps in diagram form, as a series of shapes connected by arrows.

Some programmers use a variety of shapes to represent different tasks in their flowcharts, but you can draw simple flowcharts that express very complex situations using just rectangles, diamonds, and arrows. You use a rectangle to represent any unconditional step and a diamond to represent any decision. For example, Figure 5-1 shows a flowchart describing driving directions to a friend's house. The logic in Figure 5-1 is an example of a **sequence structure**—a logical structure in which one step follows another unconditionally. A sequence structure might contain any number of steps in which one task follows another with no chance to branch away or skip a step.

Sometimes, logical steps do not follow in an unconditional sequence—some tasks might or might not occur based on decisions you make. To represent a decision, flowchart creators use a diamond shape to hold a question, and they draw paths to alternative courses of action emerging from the sides of the diamonds. Figure 5-2 includes a **decision structure**—one that involves choosing between alternative courses of action based on some value within a program. Making decisions is what makes computer programs seem "smart."

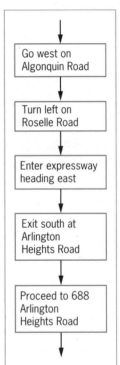

Figure 5-1　Flowchart of a series of sequential steps

When reduced to their most basic form, all computer decisions are yes-or-no decisions. That is, the answer to every computer question is yes or no (or true or false, or on or off). This is because computer circuitry consists of millions of tiny switches that are either on or off, and the result of every decision sets one of these switches in memory. As you learned in Chapter 2, the values `true` and `false` are **Boolean values**; every computer decision results in a Boolean value. Thus, internally, a program never asks, for example, "What number did the user enter?" Instead, the decisions might be "Did the user enter a *1*?" "If not, did the user enter a *2*?" "If not, did the user enter a *3*?"

Sir George Boole lived from 1815 to 1864. He developed a type of linguistic algebra, based on *0*s and *1*s, the three most basic operations of which were (and still are) AND, OR, and NOT. Programming logic is based on his discoveries.

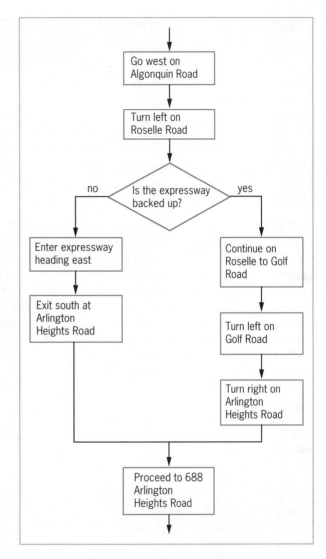

Figure 5-2 Flowchart including a decision

TWO TRUTHS & A LIE

Planning Decision-Making Logic

1. Pseudocode and flowcharts are both tools that are used to check the syntax of computer programs.

2. In a sequence structure, one step follows another unconditionally.

3. In a decision structure, alternative courses of action are chosen based on a Boolean value.

The false statement is #1. Pseudocode and flowcharts are both tools that help programmers plan a program's logic.

The if and if...else Statements

In Java, when you want to take an action if a Boolean expression is true, you use an if statement. If you want to take an action when a Boolean expression is true but take a different action when the expression is false, you use an if...else statement.

The if Statement

The simplest statement you can use to make a decision is the **if statement**. An if statement is sometimes called a **single-alternative selection** because there is only one alternative—the true alternative.

For example, suppose you have declared an integer variable named quizScore, and you want to display a message when the value of quizScore is 10. The if statement in Figure 5-3 makes the decision whether to produce output. Note that the double equal sign (==) is used to determine equality; it is Java's **equivalency operator**.

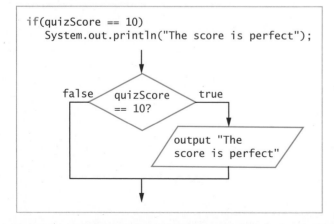

```
if(quizScore == 10)
    System.out.println("The score is perfect");
```

Figure 5-3   A Java if statement and its logic

In Figure 5-3, if `quizScore` holds the value 10, the Boolean value of the expression `quizScore == 10` is `true`, and the subsequent output statement executes. If the value of the expression `quizScore == 10` is `false`, the output statement does not execute. As the flowchart segment shows, whether the tested expression is true or false, the program continues and executes any statements that follow the `if` statement.

A Java `if` statement always includes parentheses. Within the parentheses, you can place any Boolean expression. Most often you use a comparison that includes one of the relational operators you learned about in Chapter 2 (==, <, >, <=, >=, or !=). However, you can use any expression that evaluates as true or false, such as a simple `boolean` variable or a call to a method that returns a `boolean` value.

Pitfall: Misplacing a Semicolon in an `if` Statement

In Figure 5-3, there is no semicolon at the end of the first line of the `if` statement following the parentheses because the statement does not end there. The statement ends after the `println()` call, so that is where you type the semicolon. You could type the entire `if` statement on one line and it would execute correctly; however, the two-line format for the `if` statement is more conventional and easier to read, so you usually type `if` and the Boolean expression on one line, press the Enter key, and then indent a few spaces before coding the action that occurs if the Boolean expression evaluates as `true`. Be careful—if you use the two-line format and type a semicolon at the end of the first line, as in the example shown in Figure 5-4, the results might not be what you intended.

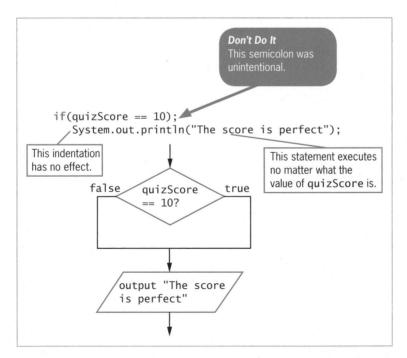

Figure 5-4   Logic that executes when an extra semicolon is inserted in an `if` statement

When the Boolean expression in Figure 5-4 is `true`, an **empty statement** that contains only a semicolon executes. Whether the tested expression evaluates as `true` or `false`, the decision is over immediately, and execution continues with the next independent statement that displays a message. In this case, because of the incorrect semicolon, the `if` statement accomplishes nothing.

Pitfall: Using the Assignment Operator Instead of the Equivalency Operator

Another common programming error occurs when a programmer uses a single equal sign rather than the double equal sign when attempting to determine equivalency. The expression `quizScore = 10` does not compare `quizScore` to 10; instead, it attempts to assign the value 10 to `quizScore`. When the expression `quizScore = 10` is used in the `if` statement, the assignment is illegal because only Boolean expressions are allowed. The confusion arises in part because the single equal sign is used within Boolean expressions in `if` statements in several older programming languages, such as COBOL, Pascal, and BASIC. Adding to the confusion, Java programmers use the word *equals* when speaking of equivalencies. For example, you might say, "If `quizScore` *equals* 10...".

The expression `if(x = true)` will compile only if x is a `boolean` variable, because it would be legal to assign `true` to x. After the assignment, the values of the variable x and the expression `(x = true)` are both `true`, so the `if` clause of the statement executes.

An alternative to using a Boolean expression in an `if` statement, such as `quizScore == 10`, is to store the Boolean expression's value in a Boolean variable. For example, if `isPerfectScore` is a Boolean variable, then the following statement compares `quizScore` to 10 and stores `true` or `false` in `isPerfectScore`:

```
isPerfectScore = (quizScore == 10);
```

Then, you can write the `if` statement as:

```
if(isPerfectScore)
   System.out.println("The score is perfect");
```

This adds an extra step to the program, but makes the `if` statement more similar to an English-language statement.

When comparing a variable to a constant, some programmers prefer to place the constant to the left of the comparison operator, as in `10 == quizScore`. This practice is a holdover from other programming languages, such as C++, in which an accidental assignment might be made when the programmer types the assignment operator (a single equal sign) instead of the comparison operator (the double equal sign). In other words, `if(quizScore = 10)` would assign 10 to `quizScore` in some languages instead of making a comparison. In Java, the compiler does not allow you to make a mistaken assignment in a Boolean expression, so Java programmers typically place the constant to the right in a Boolean expression because the statement reads more naturally.

Pitfall: Attempting to Compare Objects Using the Relational Operators

You can use the standard relational operators (==, <, >, <=, >=, and !=) to compare the values of primitive data types such as int and double. However, you cannot use <, >, <=, or >= to compare objects; a program containing such comparisons does not compile. You can use the equals and not equals comparisons (== and !=) with objects, but when you use them, you compare the objects' memory addresses instead of their values. Recall that every object name is a reference; the equivalency operators compare objects' references. In other words, == only yields true for two objects when they refer to the same object in memory, not when they are different objects with the same value. To compare the values of objects, you should write specialized methods. Remember, Strings are objects, so do not use == to compare Strings. You will learn how to compare strings in the chapter "Characters, Strings, and the StringBuilder."

Object names are references, but values that are simple data types are not. For example, suppose you have created a class named Student with a double grade point average field and a nonstatic public method named getGpa(). After instantiating two objects named student1 and student2, you can write a statement such as the following:

```
if(student1.getGpa() > student2.getGpa())
    System.out.println("The first student has a higher gpa");
```

The values represented by student1.getGpa() and student2.getGpa() are both doubles, so they can be compared using any of the relational operators.

The if...else Statement

In Java, the **if...else statement** provides the mechanism to perform one action when a Boolean expression evaluates as true and a different action when a Boolean expression evaluates as false. In other words, you use an if...else statement for a **dual-alternative selection**. For example, you would use an if...else statement if you wanted to display one message when the value of quizScore is 10 and a different message when it is not.

The code in Figure 5-5 displays one of two messages. In this example, when the value of quizScore is 10, the **if clause** of the statement executes, displaying the message "The score is perfect". When quizScore is any other value, the **else clause** of the statement executes and the program displays the message "No, it's not". You can code an if without an else, but it is illegal to code an else without an if that precedes it.

252

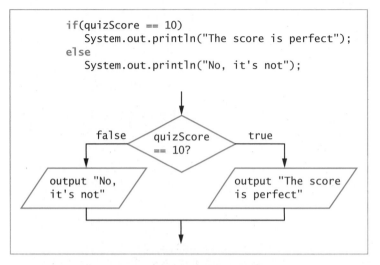

```java
if(quizScore == 10)
    System.out.println("The score is perfect");
else
    System.out.println("No, it's not");
```

Figure 5-5   An if...else statement and its logic

The indentation shown in the example code in Figure 5-5 is not required but is standard usage. You vertically align the keyword if with the keyword else, and then indent the action statements that depend on the evaluation.

When you execute an if...else statement, only one of the resulting actions takes place depending on the evaluation of the Boolean expression. Each statement, the one dependent on the if and the one dependent on the else, is a complete statement, so each ends with a semicolon.

 Watch the video *Making Decisions*.

TWO TRUTHS & A LIE

The if and if...else Statements

1. In a Java if statement, the keyword if is followed by a Boolean expression within parentheses.

2. In a Java if statement, a semicolon follows the Boolean expression.

3. When determining equivalency in Java, you use a double equal sign.

The false statement is #2. In a Java if statement, a semicolon ends the statement. It is used following the action that should occur if the Boolean expression is true. If a semicolon follows the Boolean expression, then the body of the if statement is empty.

You Do It

Using an `if...else` *Statement*

In this section, you start writing a program for Sacks Fifth Avenue, a nonprofit thrift shop. The program determines which volunteer to assign to price a donated item. To begin, you prompt the user to answer a question about whether a donation is clothing or some other type, and then the program displays the name of the volunteer who handles such donations. Clothing donations are handled by Regina, and other dona- tions are handled by Marco.

1. Start a new application by entering the following lines of code to create a class named `AssignVolunteer`. You import the `Scanner` class so that you can use keyboard input. The class contains a `main()` method that performs all the work of the class:

```
import java.util.Scanner;
public class AssignVolunteer
{
    public static void main(String[] args)
    {
```

2. On new lines, declare the variables and constants this application uses. The user will be prompted to enter one of the values stored in the two constants. That value will then be assigned to the integer `donationType` and compared to the `CLOTHING_CODE` constant. Then, based on the results of that comparison, the program will assign the value of one of the `PRICER` constants to the `String` variable `volunteer`.

```
int donationType;
String volunteer;
final int CLOTHING_CODE = 1;
final int OTHER_CODE = 2;
final String CLOTHING_PRICER = "Regina";
final String OTHER_PRICER = "Marco";
```

3. Define the input device, and then add the code that prompts the user to enter a *1* or *2* for the donation type. Accept the response, and assign it to `donationType`:

```
Scanner input = new Scanner(System.in);
System.out.println("What type of donation is this?");
System.out.print("Enter " + CLOTHING_CODE + " for clothing, " +
    OTHER_CODE + " for anything else… ");
donationType = input.nextInt();
```

(continues)

(continued)

4. Use an if...else statement to choose the name of the volunteer to be assigned to the volunteer String, as follows:

```
if(donationType == CLOTHING_CODE)
    volunteer = CLOTHING_PRICER;
else
    volunteer = OTHER_PRICER;
```

5. Display the chosen code and corresponding volunteer's name:

```
System.out.println("You entered " + donationType);
System.out.println("The volunteer who will price this item is " +
    volunteer);
```

6. Type the two closing curly braces to end the main() method and the AssignVolunteer class.

7. Save the program as **AssignVolunteer.java**, and then compile and run the program. Confirm that the program selects the correct volunteer when you choose *1* for a clothing donation or *2* for any other donation type. For example, Figure 5-6 shows a typical execution of the program when the user enters *1* for a clothing donation.

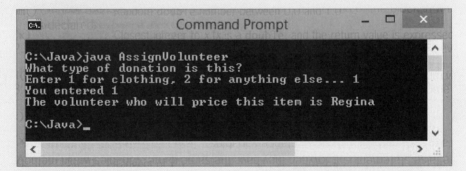

Figure 5-6 Typical execution of the AssignVolunteer application

Using Multiple Statements in if and if...else Clauses

Often, you want to take more than one action following the evaluation of a Boolean expression within an if statement. For example, you might want to display several separate lines of output or perform several mathematical calculations. To execute more than one statement that depends on the evaluation of a Boolean expression, you use a pair of curly braces to place the dependent statements within a block. For example, the program segment shown in Figure 5-7 determines whether an employee has worked more than the value of a FULL_WEEK constant; if so, the program computes regular and overtime pay.

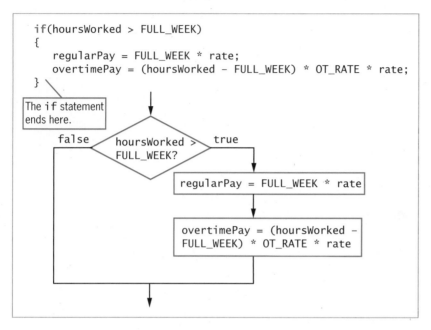

```
if(hoursWorked > FULL_WEEK)
{
    regularPay = FULL_WEEK * rate;
    overtimePay = (hoursWorked - FULL_WEEK) * OT_RATE * rate;
}
```

The `if` statement ends here.

false ◁ hoursWorked > FULL_WEEK? ▷ true

regularPay = FULL_WEEK * rate

overtimePay = (hoursWorked - FULL_WEEK) * OT_RATE * rate

Figure 5-7 An `if` statement that determines pay and its logic

When you place a block within an `if` statement, it is crucial to place the curly braces correctly. For example, in Figure 5-8, the curly braces have been omitted. Within the code segment in Figure 5-8, when hoursWorked > FULL_WEEK is true, regularPay is calculated and the `if` expression ends. The next statement that computes overtimePay executes every time the program runs, no matter what value is stored in hoursWorked. This last statement does not depend on the `if` statement; it is an independent, stand-alone statement. The indentation might be deceiving; it looks as though two statements depend on the `if` statement, but indentation does not cause statements following an `if` statement to be dependent. Rather, curly braces are required if multiple statements must be treated as a block.

When you create a block, you do not have to place multiple statements within it. It is perfectly legal to place curly braces around a single statement. For clarity, some programmers always use curly braces to surround the actions in an `if` statement, even when there is only one statement in the block.

256

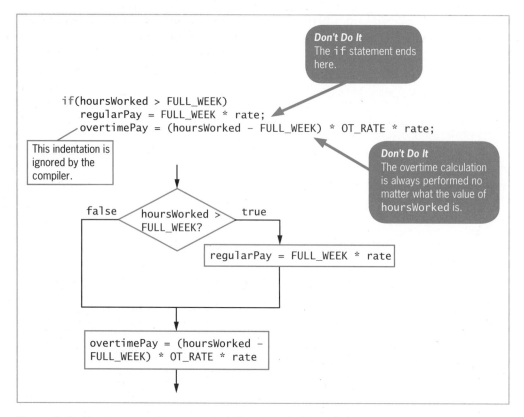

Figure 5-8 Erroneous overtime pay calculation with missing curly braces

Because the curly braces are missing, regardless of whether hoursWorked is more than FULL_WEEK, the last statement in Figure 5-8 is a new stand-alone statement that is not part of the if, and so it always executes. If hoursWorked is 30, for example, and FULL_WEEK is 40, then the program calculates the value of overtimePay as a negative number (because 30 minus 40 results in −10). Therefore, the output is incorrect. Correct blocking is crucial to achieving valid output.

When you fail to block statements that should depend on an if, and you also use an else clause, the program will not compile. For example, consider the following code:

```
if(hoursWorked > FULL_WEEK)
    regularPay = FULL_WEEK * rate;
    overtimePay = (hoursWorked - FULL_WEEK) * OT_RATE * rate;
else
    regularPay = FULL_WEEK * rate;
```

> **Don't Do It**
> These statements should be blocked.

In this case, the if statement ends after the first regularPay calculation, and the second complete stand-alone statement performs the overtimePay calculation. The third statement in this code starts with else, which is illegal. An error message will indicate that the program contains "else without if". The error message means that the else does not have a matching if.

Just as you can block statements to depend on an `if`, you can also block statements to depend on an `else`. Figure 5-9 shows an application that contains an `if` with two dependent statements and an `else` with two dependent statements. The program executes the final `println()` statement without regard to the `hoursWorked` variable's value; it is not part of the decision structure. Figure 5-10 shows the output from two executions of the program. In the first execution, the user entered 39 for the `hoursWorked` value and 20.00 for `rate`; in the second execution, the user entered 42 for `hoursWorked` and 20.00 for `rate`.

```java
import java.util.Scanner;
public class Payroll
{
    public static void main(String[] args)
    {
        double rate;
        double hoursWorked;
        double regularPay;
        double overtimePay;
        final int FULL_WEEK = 40;
        final double OT_RATE = 1.5;
        Scanner keyboard = new Scanner(System.in);
        System.out.print("How many hours did you work this week? ");
        hoursWorked = keyboard.nextDouble();
        System.out.print("What is your regular pay rate? ");
        rate = keyboard.nextDouble();
        if(hoursWorked > FULL_WEEK)
        {
            regularPay = FULL_WEEK * rate;
            overtimePay = (hoursWorked - FULL_WEEK) * OT_RATE * rate;
        }
        else
        {
            regularPay = hoursWorked * rate;
            overtimePay = 0.0;
        }
        System.out.println("Regular pay is " +
            regularPay + "\nOvertime pay is " + overtimePay);
    }
}
```

Figure 5-9 Payroll application containing an `if` and `else` clause with blocks

258

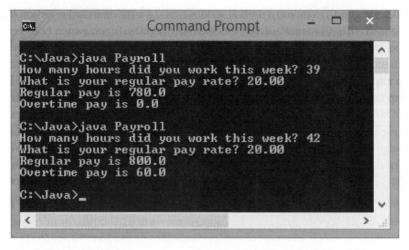

Figure 5-10   Two typical executions of the `Payroll` application

When you block statements, you must remember that any variable you declare within a block is local to that block. For example, the following code segment contains a variable named `sum` that is local to the block following the `if`. The last `println()` statement causes an error because the `sum` variable is not recognized:

```
if(a == b)
{
    int sum = a + b;
    System.out.println
        ("The two variables are equal");
}
System.out.println("The sum is " + sum);
```

The `sum` variable is declared in this block...

...so it is not recognized here.

TWO TRUTHS & A LIE

Using Multiple Statements in `if` and `if…else` Clauses

1. To execute more than one statement that depends on the evaluation of a Boolean expression, you use a pair of curly braces to place the dependent statements within a block.

2. Indentation can be used to cause statements following an `if` statement to depend on the evaluation of the Boolean expression.

3. When you declare a variable within a block, it is local to that block.

The false statement is #2. Indentation does not cause statements following an `if` statement to be dependent; curly braces are required if multiple statements must be treated as a block.

You Do It

Using Multiple Statements in `if` and `else` Clauses

In this section, you use a block of code to add multiple actions to an `if...else` statement.

1. Open the `AssignVolunteer` application from the previous "You Do It" section. Change the class name to `AssignVolunteer2`, and immediately save the file as **AssignVolunteer2.java**. Don't forget that an application's class name and its filename must match.

2. Add a `String` to the variables. This `String` will be assigned a message that displays the donation type:

   ```
   String message;
   ```

3. In place of the existing `if...else` statement in the program, insert the following statement that takes two blocked actions for each donation type. It assigns a volunteer and a value to the `message String`.

   ```
   if(donationType == CLOTHING_CODE)
   {
      volunteer = CLOTHING_PRICER;
      message = "a clothing donation";
   }
   else
   {
      volunteer = OTHER_PRICER;
      message = "a non-clothing donation";
   }
   ```

4. Following the output statement that displays the donation type, add the following statement that displays the assigned message:

   ```
   System.out.println("This is " + message);
   ```

(continues)

(continued)

5. Save the file, and compile and execute the program. Figure 5-11 shows two executions.

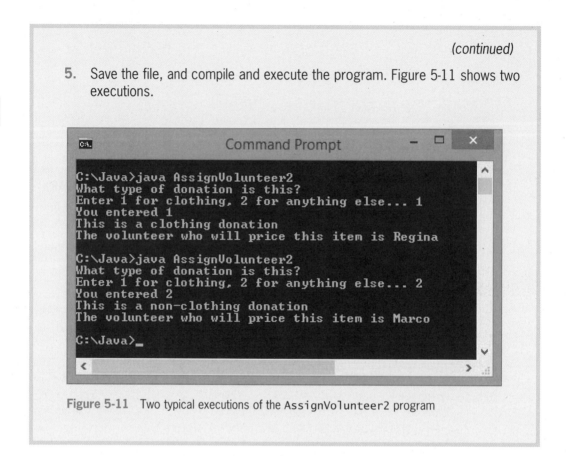

Figure 5-11   Two typical executions of the `AssignVolunteer2` program

Nesting `if` and `if...else` Statements

Within an `if` or an `else` clause, you can code as many dependent statements as you need, including other `if` and `else` statements. Statements in which a decision is contained inside either the `if` or `else` clause of another decision are **nested `if` statements**. Nested `if` statements are particularly useful when two or more conditions must be met before some action is taken.

For example, suppose you want to pay a $50 bonus to a salesperson only if the salesperson sells at least three items with a total value of $1,000 or more. Figure 5-12 shows the logic and the code to solve the problem.

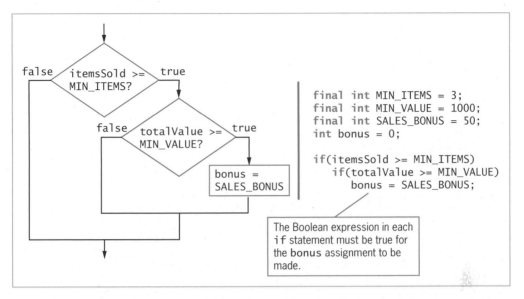

Figure 5-12 Determining whether to assign a bonus using nested `if` statements

Notice there are no semicolons in the `if` statement code shown in Figure 5-12 until after the `bonus = SALES_BONUS;` statement. The expression `itemsSold >= MIN_ITEMS` is evaluated first. Only if this expression is `true` does the program evaluate the second Boolean expression, `totalValue >= MIN_VALUE`. If that expression is also `true`, the bonus assignment statement executes, and the nested `if` statement ends.

When you use nested `if` statements, you must pay careful attention to placement of any `else` clauses. For example, suppose you want to distribute bonuses on a revised schedule as follows:

- $10 bonus for selling fewer than three items

- $25 bonus for selling three or more items whose combined value is under $1,000

- $50 bonus for selling at least three items whose combined value is at least $1,000

Figure 5-13 shows the logic.

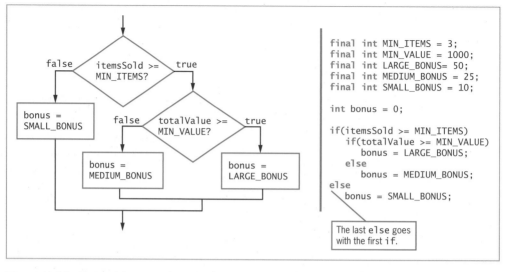

```
final int MIN_ITEMS = 3;
final int MIN_VALUE = 1000;
final int LARGE_BONUS= 50;
final int MEDIUM_BONUS = 25;
final int SMALL_BONUS = 10;

int bonus = 0;

if(itemsSold >= MIN_ITEMS)
   if(totalValue >= MIN_VALUE)
      bonus = LARGE_BONUS;
   else
      bonus = MEDIUM_BONUS;
else
   bonus = SMALL_BONUS;
```

The last else goes with the first if.

Figure 5-13   Determining one of three bonuses using nested if statements

As Figure 5-13 shows, when one if statement follows another, the first else clause encountered is paired with the most recent if encountered. In this figure, the complete nested if...else statement fits entirely within the if portion of the outer if...else statement. No matter how many levels of if...else statements are needed to produce a solution, the else statements are always associated with their ifs on a "first in-last out" basis. In Figure 5-13, the indentation of the lines of code helps to show which else statement is paired with which if statement. Remember, the compiler does not take indentation into account, but consistent indentation can help readers understand a program's logic.

TWO TRUTHS & A LIE

Nesting if and if...else Statements

1. Statements in which an if statement is contained inside another if statement commonly are called nested if statements.

2. When one if statement follows another, the first else clause encountered is paired with the first if that occurred before it.

3. A complete nested if...else statement always fits entirely within either the if portion or the else portion of its outer if...else statement.

The false statement is #2. When one if statement follows another, the first else clause encountered is paired with the most recent if encountered.

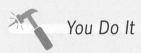 *You Do It*

Using a Nested `if` *Statement*

In this section, you add a nested `if` statement to the `AssignVolunteer2` application.

1. Rerun the `AssignVolunteer2` program, and enter an invalid code, such as *3*. The selected volunteer is Marco because the program tests only for an entered value of *1* or not *1*. Modify the program to display the entered code, volunteer, and donation type message only when the entered value is *1* or *2*, and to display the entered code and an error message otherwise. Rename the class **AssignVolunteer3**, and save the file as **AssignVolunteer3.java**. Figure 5-14 shows two typical executions of the program.

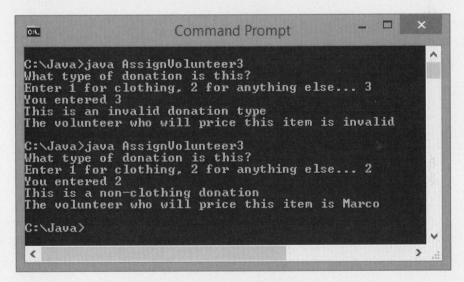

Figure 5-14 Two typical executions of the `AssignVolunteer3` program

Using Logical AND and OR Operators

In Java, you can combine Boolean tests into a single expression using the logical AND and OR operators. Such an expression is a **compound Boolean expression** or a **compound condition**.

The AND Operator

For an alternative to some nested `if` statements, you can use the **logical AND operator** between two Boolean expressions to create a compound Boolean expression that is `true` when both of its operands are true. In Java, the AND operator is written as two ampersands (&&). For example, the two statements shown in Figure 5-15 work exactly the same way. In each case, both the itemsSold variable must be at least the minimum number of items required for a bonus and the totalValue variable must be at least the minimum required value for the bonus to be set to SALES_BONUS.

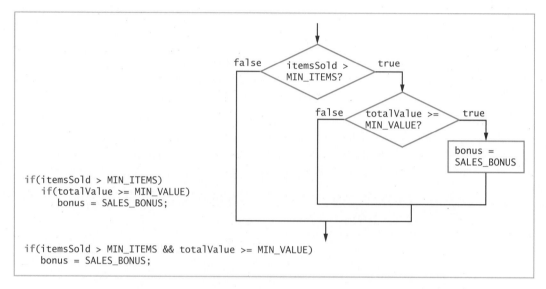

```
if(itemsSold > MIN_ITEMS)
   if(totalValue >= MIN_VALUE)
      bonus = SALES_BONUS;



if(itemsSold > MIN_ITEMS && totalValue >= MIN_VALUE)
   bonus = SALES_BONUS;
```

Figure 5-15   Code and logic for bonus-determining decision using nested ifs and the && operator

It is important to note that when you use the && operator, you must include a complete Boolean expression on each side. In other words, like many arithmetic operators, the && operator is a binary operator, meaning it requires an operand on each side. If you want to set a bonus to $400 when a saleAmount is both over $1,000 and under $5,000, the correct statement is:

```
if(saleAmount > 1000 && saleAmount < 5000)
   bonus = 400;
```

Even though the saleAmount variable is intended to be used in both parts of the AND expression, the following statement is incorrect and does not compile because there is not a complete expression on both sides of the binary && operator:

```
if(saleAmount > 1000 && < 5000)
   bonus = 400;
```

Don't Do It
This statement will not compile because it does not have a Boolean expression on each side of the && operator.

For clarity, many programmers prefer to surround each Boolean expression that is part of a compound Boolean expression with its own set of parentheses, as in the following example:

```
if((saleAmount > 1000) && (saleAmount < 5000))
    bonus = 400;
```

Use the extra parentheses if doing so makes the compound expression clearer to you.

You are never required to use the **&&** operator because using nested if statements always achieves the same result, but using the **&&** operator often makes your code more concise, less error-prone, and easier to understand.

The OR Operator

When you want some action to occur even if only one of two conditions is **true**, you can use nested if statements, or you can use the **logical OR operator**, which is written as ||. The logical OR operator is used to create a compound Boolean expression that is true when at least one of its operands is true.

For example, if you want to give a discount to any customer who satisfies at least one of two conditions—buying a minimum number of items or buying any number of items that total a minimum value—you can write the code using either of the ways shown in Figure 5-16.

 The two vertical lines used in the OR operator are sometimes called "pipes." The pipe appears on the same key as the backslash on your keyboard.

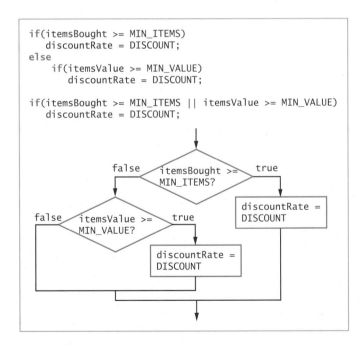

Figure 5-16 Determining customer discount when customer needs to meet only one of two criteria

As with the **&&** operator, you are never required to use the **||** operator because using nested if statements always achieves the same result. However, using the **||** operator often makes your code more concise, less error-prone, and easier to understand.

Short-Circuit Evaluation

The expressions on each side of the **&&** and **||** operators are evaluated only as far as necessary to determine whether the entire expression is `true` or `false`. This feature is called **short-circuit evaluation**. With the **&&** operator, both Boolean expression operands must be `true` before the action in the result statement can occur. (The same is true for nested ifs, as you can see in Figure 5-15.) When you use the **&&** operator, if the first tested expression is `false`, the second expression is never evaluated because its value does not matter.

The **||** operator also uses short-circuit evaluation. In other words, because only one of the Boolean expressions in an **||** expression must be true to cause the dependent statements to execute, if the expression to the left of the **||** is true, then there is no need to evaluate the expression to the right of the **||**. (The same is true for nested ifs, as you can see in Figure 5-16.) When you use the **||** operator, if the first tested expression is `true`, the second expression is never evaluated because its value does not matter.

If you are using simple comparisons as the operands for the **&&** or **||** operators, as in the examples in Figures 5-15 and 5-16, you won't notice that short-circuit evaluation is occurring. However, suppose that you have created two methods that return Boolean values and you use calls to those methods in an if statement, as in the following:

```
if(method1() && method2())
   System.out.println("OK");
```

Depending on the actions performed within the methods, it might be important to understand that in this case, if method1() is false, then method2() will not execute. If method2() contains statements that you want to execute no matter what the value of method1() is, then you should not use method2() as part of a compound condition, but should execute it on its own, as in the following example:

```
boolean isMethod2True = method2();
if(method1() && isMethod2True)
   System.out.println("OK");
```

Similarly, in the following statement, if method1() returns `true`, then method2() will not execute because only one operand in an OR expression needs to be `true` in order for the entire expression to be `true`.

```
if(method1() || method2())
   System.out.println("OK");
```

 Anything a method does besides altering local variables or returning a value is a **side effect**. Because of short-circuit evaluation, you have to be aware of the possible side effects from an unexecuted method. In some languages, any method without side effects is called a **function**, but Java programmers tend not to use that term.

Watch the video *Using && and | |.*

TWO TRUTHS & A LIE

Using Logical AND and OR Operators

1. The AND operator is written as two ampersands (&&), and the OR operator is written as two pipes (| |).

2. When you use the && and | | operators, you must include a complete Boolean expression on each side.

3. Whether you use an && or | | operator, both Boolean expressions are tested in order from left to right.

The false statement is #3. The expressions in each part of an AND or OR expression are evaluated only as much as necessary to determine whether the entire expression is true or false.

 You Do It

Using the && Operator

This section helps you create a program that demonstrates how short-circuiting works with the && operator.

1. Open a new file in your text editor, and type the header and curly braces for a class named ShortCircuitTestAnd:

```
public class ShortCircuitTestAnd
{
}
```

2. Between the curly braces for the class, type the header and braces for a main() method:

```
public static void main(String[] args)
{
}
```

(continues)

(continued)

3. Within the `main()` method, insert an `if...else` statement that tests the return values of two method calls. If both methods are `true`, then "Both are true" is displayed. Otherwise, "Both are not true" is displayed.

```
if(trueMethod() && falseMethod())
    System.out.println("Both are true");
else
    System.out.println("Both are not true");
```

4. Following the closing curly brace for the `main()` method, but before the closing curly brace for the class, insert a method named `trueMethod()`. The method displays the message "True method" and returns a `true` value.

```
public static boolean trueMethod()
{
    System.out.println("True method");
    return true;
}
```

5. Following the closing curly brace of `trueMethod()`, insert a method named `falseMethod()` that displays the message "False method" and returns a `false` value.

```
public static boolean falseMethod()
{
    System.out.println("False method");
    return false;
}
```

6. Save the file as **ShortCircuitTestAnd.java**, and then compile and execute it. Figure 5-17 shows the output. First, "True method" is displayed because `trueMethod()` was executed as the first half of the Boolean expression in the program's `if` statement. Then, the second half of the Boolean expression calls `falseMethod()`. Finally, "Both are not true" is displayed because both halves of the tested expression were not true.

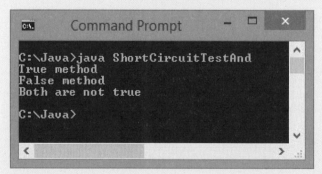

Figure 5-17 Execution of ShortCircuitTestAnd program

(continues)

(continued)

7. Change the position of the method calls in the `if` statement so that the statement becomes the following:

```
if(falseMethod() && trueMethod())
    System.out.println("Both are true");
else
    System.out.println("Both are not true");
```

8. Save the file, compile it, and execute it. Now the output looks like Figure 5-18. The `if` statement makes a call to `falseMethod()`, and its output is displayed. Because the first half of the Boolean expression is false, there is no need to test the second half, so `trueMethod()` never executes, and the program proceeds directly to the statement that displays "Both are not true".

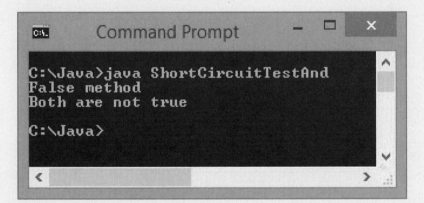

Figure 5-18 Execution of `ShortCircuitTestAnd` after reversing Boolean expressions

9. Change the class name to **ShortCircuitTestOr**, and immediately save the file as **ShortCircuitTestOr.java**. Replace the `&&` operator with the `||` operator. Compile and execute the program with `trueMethod()` to the right of the `||` operator and `falseMethod()` to its left. Then, reverse the positions of the methods, and compile and execute the program again. Make sure that you understand the output each way.

Making Accurate and Efficient Decisions

When new programmers must make a range check, they often introduce incorrect or inefficient code into their programs. In this section, you learn how to make accurate and efficient range checks, and you also learn how to use the `&&` and `||` operators appropriately.

Making Accurate Range Checks

A **range check** is a series of statements that determine to which of several consecutive series of values another value falls. Consider a situation in which salespeople can receive one of three possible commission rates based on their sales:

- 8% commission on a sale of $1,000 or more

- 6% commission on a sale of $500 to $999

- 5% commission on a sale of less than $500

Using three separate `if` statements to test single Boolean expressions might result in some incorrect commission assignments. For example, examine the code shown in Figure 5-19.

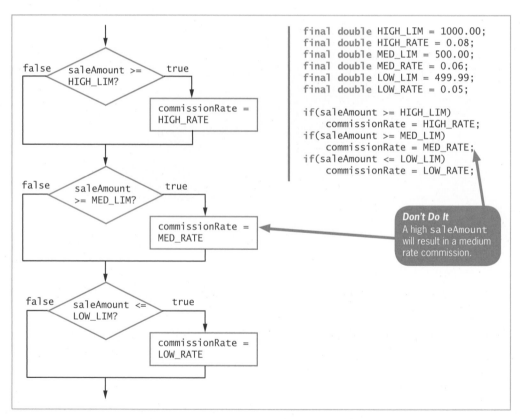

Figure 5-19 Incorrect commission-determining code and its logic

Using the code shown in Figure 5-19, when a `saleAmount` is $5,000, for example, the first `if` statement executes, and the Boolean expression (`saleAmount >= HIGH_LIM`) evaluates as `true`, so `HIGH_RATE` is correctly assigned to `commissionRate`. However, the next `if` expression, (`saleAmount >= MED_LIM`), also evaluates as `true`, so the `commissionRate`, which was just set to `HIGH_RATE`, is incorrectly reset to `MED_RATE`.

A partial solution to this problem is to use an `else` statement following the first evaluation, as shown in Figure 5-20.

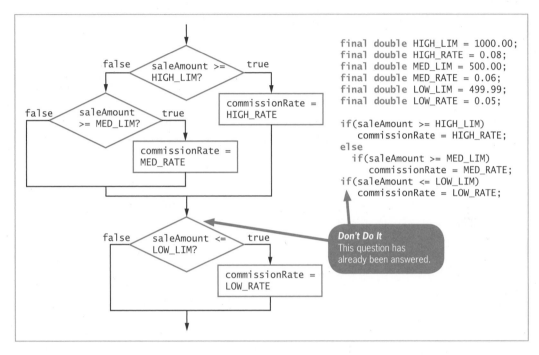

```
final double HIGH_LIM = 1000.00;
final double HIGH_RATE = 0.08;
final double MED_LIM = 500.00;
final double MED_RATE = 0.06;
final double LOW_LIM = 499.99;
final double LOW_RATE = 0.05;

if(saleAmount >= HIGH_LIM)
    commissionRate = HIGH_RATE;
else
    if(saleAmount >= MED_LIM)
        commissionRate = MED_RATE;
if(saleAmount <= LOW_LIM)
    commissionRate = LOW_RATE;
```

Don't Do It
This question has already been answered.

Figure 5-20   Improved, but inefficient, commission-determining code and its logic

With the new code in Figure 5-20, when the `saleAmount` is $5,000, the expression `(saleAmount >= HIGH_LIM)` is `true` and the `commissionRate` becomes `HIGH_RATE`; then the entire `if` statement ends. When the `saleAmount` is not greater than or equal to $1,000 (for example, $800), the first `if` expression is `false`, and the `else` statement executes and correctly sets the `commissionRate` to `MED_RATE`.

The code shown in Figure 5-20 works, but it is somewhat inefficient. When the `saleAmount` is any amount over `LOW_RATE`, either the first `if` sets `commissionRate` to `HIGH_RATE` for amounts that are at least $1,000, or its `else` sets `commissionRate` to `MED_RATE` for amounts that are at least $500. In either of these two cases, the Boolean value tested in the next statement, `if(saleAmount <= LOW_LIM)`, is always `false`, so `commissionRate` retains its correct value. However, it was unnecessary to make the `LOW_LIM` comparison.

After you know that `saleAmount` is not at least `MED_LIM`, rather than asking `if(saleAmount <= LOW_LIM)`, it's easier, more efficient, and less error-prone to use an `else`. If the `saleAmount` is not at least `HIGH_LIM` and is also not at least `MED_LIM`, it must by default be less than or equal to `LOW_LIM`. Figure 5-21 shows this improved logic. Notice that the `LOW_LIM` constant is no longer declared because it is not needed anymore—if a `saleAmount` is not greater than or equal to `MED_LIMIT`, the `commissionRate` must receive the `LOW_RATE`.

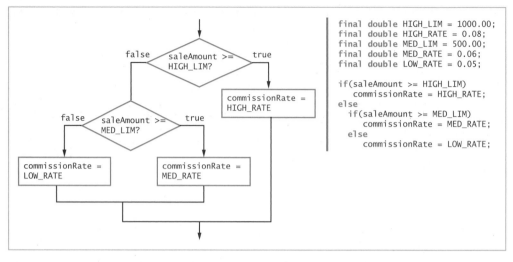

Figure 5-21 Improved and efficient commission-determining code and its logic

Making Efficient Range Checks

Within a nested if...else, like the one shown in Figure 5-21, it is most efficient to ask the question that is most likely to be true first. In other words, if you know that most saleAmount values are high, compare saleAmount to HIGH_LIM first. That way, you most frequently avoid asking multiple questions. If, however, you know that most saleAmounts are small, you should ask if(saleAmount < LOW_LIM) first. The code shown in Figure 5-22 results in the same commission value for any given saleAmount, but this sequence of decisions is more efficient when most saleAmount values are small.

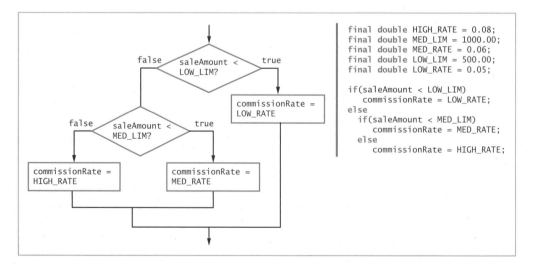

Figure 5-22 Commission-determining code and logic that evaluates smallest saleAmount first

In Figure 5-22, notice that the comparisons use the < operator instead of <=. That's because a saleAmount of $1,000.00 should result in a HIGH_RATE, and a saleAmount of $500.00 should result in a MED_RATE. If you wanted to use <= comparisons, then you could change the MED_LIM and LOW_LIM cutoff values to 999.99 and 499.99, respectively, assuming sales occur only in whole-cent increments.

Testing for a range over 500 or less than or equal to 499.99 might not always yield the same outcome if half-cents are involved. As examples, organizations might offer mileage allowances such as 42.5 cents per mile, and sales taxes are often based on values such as 8.5 percent. When you make calculations based on such values, you need to learn the business rules that govern the desired outcomes.

Using && and || Appropriately

Beginning programmers often use the && operator when they mean to use ||, and often use || when they should use &&. Part of the problem lies in the way we use the English language. For example, your boss might request, "Display an error message when an employee's hourly pay rate is under $5.85 and when an employee's hourly pay rate is over $60." You define $5.85 as a named constant LOW and $60 as HIGH. However, because your boss used the word *and* in the request, you might be tempted to write a program statement like the following:

```
if(payRate < LOW && payRate > HIGH)
    System.out.println("Error in pay rate");
```

> This message can never be output because the Boolean expression can never be true.

However, as a single variable, no payRate value can ever be both below 5.85 *and* over 60 at the same time, so the output statement can never execute, no matter what value the payRate has. In this case, you must write the following code that uses the || operator to display the error message under the correct circumstances:

```
if(payRate < LOW || payRate > HIGH)
    System.out.println("Error in pay rate");
```

Similarly, your boss might request, "Display the names of those employees in departments 1 and 2." Because the boss used the word *and* in the request, you might be tempted to write the following:

```
if(department == 1 && department == 2)
    System.out.println("Name is: " + name);
```

However, the variable department can never contain both a *1* and a *2* at the same time, so no employee name will ever be output, no matter what the value of department is. The correct statement chooses employees whose department is 1 or 2, as follows:

```
if(department == 1 || department == 2)
    System.out.println("Name is: " + name);
```

Another type of mistake occurs if you use a single ampersand or pipe when you try to indicate a logical AND or OR. Both & and | are valid Java operators, but a single & or | with integer operands operates on individual bits. You will learn more about & and | as you continue to study Java.

TWO TRUTHS & A LIE

Making Accurate and Efficient Decisions

1. A range check is a series of statements that determine within which of a set of ranges a value falls.

2. When you must make a series of decisions in a program, it is most efficient to first ask the question that is most likely to be true.

3. The statement if(payRate < 6.00 && payRate > 50.00) can be used to select payRate values that are higher or lower than the specified limits.

The false statement is #3. The statement if(payRate < 6.00 && payRate > 50.00) cannot be used to make a selection because no value for payRate can be both below 6.00 *and* above 50.00 at the same time.

Using the switch Statement

By nesting a series of if and else statements, you can choose from any number of alternatives. For example, suppose you want to display a student's class year based on a stored number. Figure 5-23 shows one possible implementation of the logic.

```
if(year == 1)
    System.out.println("Freshman");
else
    if(year == 2)
        System.out.println("Sophomore");
    else
        if(year == 3)
            System.out.println("Junior");
        else
            if(year == 4)
                System.out.println("Senior");
            else
                System.out.println("Invalid year");
```

Figure 5-23   Determining class status using nested if statements

In program segments like the one in Figure 5-23, many programmers (particularly those familiar with the Visual Basic programming language) would code each else and the if clause that follows it on the same line, and refer to the format as an **else...if clause**. Because Java ignores whitespace, the logic is the same whether each else and the subsequent if are on the same line or different lines.

An alternative to using the series of nested `if` statements shown in Figure 5-23 is to use the `switch` statement. The **switch statement** is useful when you need to test a single variable against a series of exact integer (including `int`, `byte`, and `short` types), character, or string values.

 The ability to use strings as the tested values in a `switch` statement was a new feature in Java 7; only numbers or characters could be used prior to that release.

The `switch` statement uses four keywords:

- `switch` starts the statement and is followed immediately by a test expression enclosed in parentheses.

- `case` is followed by one of the possible values for the test expression and a colon.

- `break` optionally terminates a `switch` statement at the end of each case.

- `default` optionally is used prior to any action that should occur if the test variable does not match any case.

Figure 5-24 shows the `switch` statement used to display the four school years based on an integer named `year`.

```
switch(year)
{
   case 1:
      System.out.println("Freshman");
      break;
   case 2:
      System.out.println("Sophomore");
      break;
   case 3:
      System.out.println("Junior");
      break;
   case 4:
      System.out.println("Senior");
      break;
   default:
      System.out.println("Invalid year");
}
```

Figure 5-24 Determining class status using a `switch` statement

You are not required to list the `case` values in ascending order, as shown in Figure 5-24, although doing so often makes a statement easier to understand.

The switch statement shown in Figure 5-24 begins by evaluating the year variable shown in the first line. For example, if year is equal to 3, the statement that displays "Junior" executes. The break statement bypasses the rest of the switch statement, and execution continues with any statement after the closing curly brace of the switch statement. If the year variable does not contain the same value as any of the case statements, the default statement or statements execute.

You can leave out the break statements in a switch statement. However, if you omit the break and the program finds a match for the test variable, all the statements within the switch statement execute from that point forward. For example, if you omit each break statement in the code shown in Figure 5-24, when the year is 3, the first two cases are bypassed, but *Junior, Senior,* and *Invalid year* all are output. You should intentionally omit the break statements if you want all subsequent cases to execute after the test variable is matched. For example, the switch statement in Figure 5-25 displays all the tasks that remain for the week on any particular day. When day is "Wednesday", *Send out meeting reminders, Order snacks for delivery*, and *Meeting 10 am* are all displayed.

```
switch(day)
{
   case "Monday":
      System.out.println("Reserve room for Friday meeting");
   case "Tuesday":
      System.out.println("Prepare PowerPoint slides");
   case "Wednesday":
      System.out.println("Send out meeting reminders");
   case "Thursday":
      System.out.println("Order snacks for delivery");
   case "Friday":
      System.out.println("Meeting 10 am");
   default:
      System.out.println("Invalid day");
}
```

Figure 5-25   Determining all the tasks left for the week using a switch statement

You do not need to write code for each case in a switch statement. For example, suppose that the supervisor for departments 1, 2, and 3 is *Jones,* but other departments have different supervisors. In that case, you might use the code in Figure 5-26.

```
int department;
String supervisor;
// Statements to get department go here
switch(department)
{
   case 1:
   case 2:
   case 3:
      supervisor = "Jones";
      break;
   case 4:
      supervisor = "Staples";
      break;
   case 5:
      supervisor = "Tejano";
      break;
   default:
      System.out.println("Invalid department code");
}
```

Figure 5-26 Using empty `case` statements so the same result occurs in multiple cases

On the other hand, you might use strings in a `switch` statement to determine whether a supervisor name is valid, as shown in the method in Figure 5-27.

```
public static boolean isValidSupervisor(String name)
{
   boolean isValid;
   switch(name)
   {
      case "Jones":
      case "Staples":
      case "Tejano":
         isValid = true;
         break;
      default:
         isValid = false;
   }
   return isValid;
}
```

Figure 5-27 A method that uses a `switch` statement with string values

When several `char` variables must be checked and you want to ignore whether they are uppercase or lowercase, one frequently used technique employs empty `case` statements, as in Figure 5-28.

278

```
switch(departmentCode)
{
   case 'a':
   case 'A':
      departmentName = "Accounting";
      break;
   case 'm':
   case 'M':
      departmentName = "Marketing";
      break;
   // and so on
}
```

Figure 5-28   Using a switch statement to ignore character case

You are never required to use a switch statement; you can always achieve the same results with nested if statements. The switch statement is simply convenient to use when there are several alternative courses of action that depend on a single integer, character, or string value. In addition, it makes sense to use switch only when a reasonable number of specific matching values need to be tested.

 Watch the video *Using the switch Statement*.

TWO TRUTHS & A LIE

Using the switch Statement

1. When you must make more decisions than Java can support, you use a switch statement instead of nested if…else statements.

2. The switch statement is useful when you need to test a single variable against a series of exact integer or character values.

3. A break statement bypasses the rest of its switch statement, and execution continues with any statement after the closing curly brace of the switch statement.

The false statement is #1. By nesting a series of if and else statements, you can choose from any number of alternatives. The switch statement is just a convenient alternative.

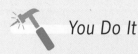 *You Do It*

Using the switch *Statement*

In this section, you alter the AssignVolunteer3 program to add more options for donation types, and then use a switch statement to assign the appropriate volunteer.

1. Open the **AssignVolunteer3.java** file that you created in a "You Do It" section earlier in this chapter. Change the class name to AssignVolunteer4, and immediately save the file as **AssignVolunteer4.java**.

2. Keep the declaration CLOTHING_CODE, but replace the OTHER_CODE declaration with three new ones:

```
final int FURNITURE_CODE = 2;
final int ELECTRONICS_CODE = 3;
final int OTHER_CODE = 4;
```

3. Retain the two pricing volunteer declarations, but add two new ones:

```
final String FURNITURE_PRICER = "Walter";
final String ELECTRONICS_PRICER = "Lydia";
```

4. Replace the output statement that asks the user to enter 1 or 2 with the following simpler statement:

```
System.out.print("Enter an integer… ");
```

In a professional program, you might want to present the user with details about all the options, but this example keeps the prompt simple to save you from excessive typing.

5. Replace the existing if…else statement with the following switch statement:

```
switch(donationType)
{
   case(CLOTHING_CODE):
      volunteer = CLOTHING_PRICER;
      message = "a clothing donation";
      break;
   case(FURNITURE_CODE):
      volunteer = FURNITURE_PRICER;
      message = "a furniture donation";
      break;
   case(ELECTRONICS_CODE):
      volunteer = ELECTRONICS_PRICER;
      message = "an electronics donation";
      break;
```

279

(continues)

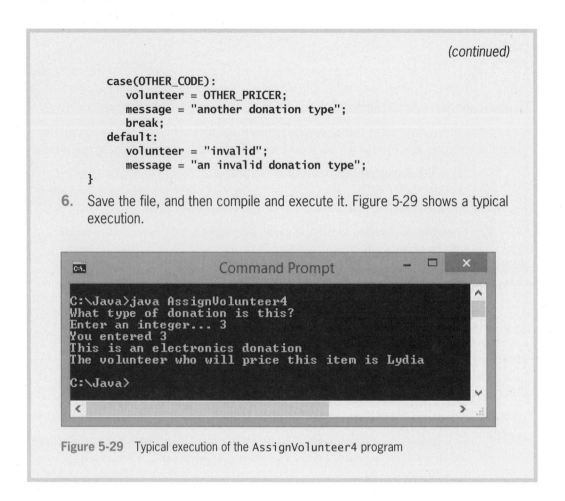

(continued)

```
        case(OTHER_CODE):
            volunteer = OTHER_PRICER;
            message = "another donation type";
            break;
        default:
            volunteer = "invalid";
            message = "an invalid donation type";
    }
```

6. Save the file, and then compile and execute it. Figure 5-29 shows a typical execution.

Figure 5-29   Typical execution of the `AssignVolunteer4` program

Using the Conditional and NOT Operators

Besides using `if` statements and `switch` statements, Java provides one more way to make decisions. The **conditional operator** requires three expressions separated with a question mark and a colon and is used as an abbreviated version of the `if...else` statement. As with the `switch` statement, you are never required to use the conditional operator; it is simply a convenient shortcut. The syntax of the conditional operator is:

`testExpression ? trueResult : falseResult;`

The first expression, `testExpression`, is a Boolean expression that is evaluated as `true` or `false`. If it is `true`, the entire conditional expression takes on the value of the expression following the question mark (`trueResult`). If the value of the `testExpression` is `false`, the entire expression takes on the value of `falseResult`.

You have seen many examples of binary operators such as == and &&. The conditional operator is a **ternary operator**—one that needs three operands. Through Java 6, the conditional operator is the only ternary operator in Java, so it is sometimes referred to as "the" ternary operator. Java 7 introduces a collapsed version of the ternary operator that checks for null values assigned to objects. The new operator is called *the Elvis operator* because it uses a question mark and colon together (?:); if you view it sideways, it reminds you of Elvis Presley.

For example, suppose you want to assign the smallest price to a sale item. Let the variable a be the advertised price and the variable b be the discounted price on the sale tag. The expression for assigning the smallest cost is:

```
smallerNum = (a < b) ? a : b;
```

When evaluating the expression a < b, where a is less than b, the entire conditional expression takes the value to the left of the colon, a, which then is assigned to smallerNum. If a is not less than b, the expression assumes the value to the right of the colon, b, and b is assigned to smallerNum.

You could achieve the same results with the following if...else statement:

```
if(a < b)
    smallerNum = a;
else
    smallerNum = b;
```

The advantage of using the conditional operator is the conciseness of the statement.

Using the NOT Operator

You use the **NOT operator**, which is written as the exclamation point (!), to negate the result of any Boolean expression. Any expression that evaluates as true becomes false when preceded by the NOT operator, and accordingly, any false expression preceded by the NOT operator becomes true.

For example, suppose a monthly car insurance premium is $200 if the driver is age 25 or younger and $125 if the driver is age 26 or older. Each of the if...else statements in Figure 5-30 correctly assigns the premium values.

```
if(age <= 25)                    if(!(age <= 25))
    premium = 200;                   premium = 125;
else                             else
    premium = 125;                   premium = 200;


if(age >= 26)                    if(!(age >= 26))
    premium = 125;                   premium = 200;
else                             else
    premium = 200;                   premium = 125;
```

Figure 5-30   Four if...else statements that all do the same thing

In Figure 5-30, the statements with the ! operator are somewhat harder to read, particularly because they require the double set of parentheses, but the result of the decision-making process is the same in each case. Using the ! operator is clearer when the value of a Boolean variable is tested. For example, a variable initialized as boolean oldEnough = (age >= 25); can become part of the relatively easy-to-read expression if(!oldEnough)....

TWO TRUTHS & A LIE

Using the Conditional and NOT Operators

1. The conditional operator is used as an abbreviated version of the if...else statement and requires two expressions separated with an exclamation point.

2. The NOT operator is written as the exclamation point (!).

3. The value of any false expression becomes true when preceded by the NOT operator.

The false statement is #1. The conditional operator requires three expressions separated with a question mark and a colon.

Understanding Operator Precedence

You can combine as many && or || operators as you need to make a decision. For example, if you want to award bonus points (defined as BONUS) to any student who receives a perfect score on any of four quizzes, you might write a statement like the following:

```
if(score1 == PERFECT || score2 == PERFECT ||
   score3 == PERFECT || score4 == PERFECT)
      bonus = BONUS;
else
   bonus = 0;
```

In this case, if at least one of the score variables is equal to the PERFECT constant, the student receives the bonus points.

Although you can combine any number of && or || operations in an expression, special care must be taken when you mix them. You learned in Chapter 2 that arithmetic operations have higher and lower precedences, and an operator's precedence makes a difference in how an expression is evaluated. For example, within an arithmetic expression, multiplication and division are always performed prior to addition or subtraction. In the same way, && has higher precedence than ||. Table 5-1 shows the precedence of the operators you have used so far.

Precedence	Operator(s)	Symbol(s)
Highest	Logical NOT	!
Intermediate	Multiplication, division, modulus	* / %
	Addition, subtraction	+ -
	Relational	> < >= <=
	Equality	== !=
	Logical AND	&&
	Logical OR	||
	Conditional	?:
Lowest	Assignment	=

Table 5-1   Operator precedence for operators used so far

For example, consider the program segments shown in Figure 5-31. These code segments are intended to be part of an insurance company program that determines whether an additional premium should be charged to a driver who meets both of the following criteria:

- Has more than two traffic tickets or is under 25 years old
- Is male

```
// Assigns extra premiums incorrectly
if(trafficTickets > 2 || age < 25 && gender == 'M')
    extraPremium = 200;
```
The expression that uses the && operator is evaluated first.

```
// Assigns extra premiums correctly
if((trafficTickets > 2 || age < 25) && gender == 'M')
    extraPremium = 200;
```
The expression within the inner parentheses is evaluated first.

Figure 5-31   Two comparisons using && and ||

One way to remember the precedence of the AND and OR operators is to remember that they are evaluated in alphabetical order.

283

Consider a 30-year-old female driver with three traffic tickets; according to the stated criteria, she should not be assigned the extra premium because she is not male. With the first `if` statement in Figure 5-31, the `&&` operator takes precedence, so `age < 25 && gender == 'M'` is evaluated first. The value is `false` because `age` is not less than 25, so the expression is reduced to `trafficTickets > 2` or `false`. Because the value of the tickets variable is greater than 2, the entire expression is `true`, and $200 is assigned to `extraPremium`, even though it should not be.

In the second `if` statement shown in Figure 5-31, parentheses have been added so the `||` operator is evaluated first. The expression `trafficTickets > 2 || age < 25` is `true` because the value of `trafficTickets` is 3. So the expression evolves to `true && gender== 'M'`. Because gender is not 'M', the value of the entire expression is `false`, and the `extraPremium` value is not assigned 200, which is the correct outcome. Even when an expression would be evaluated as you intend without adding extra parentheses, you can always add them to help others more easily understand your programs.

The following two conventions are important to keep in mind:

- The order in which you use operators makes a difference.

- You can always use parentheses to change precedence or make your intentions clearer.

TWO TRUTHS & A LIE

Understanding Operator Precedence

1. Assume p, q, and r are all Boolean variables that have been assigned the value true. After the following statement executes, the value of p is still true.

   `p = !q || r;`

2. Assume p, q, and r are all Boolean variables that have been assigned the value true. After the following statement executes, the value of p is still true.

   `p = !(!q && !r);`

3. Assume p, q, and r are all Boolean variables that have been assigned the value true. After the following statement executes, the value of p is still true.

   `p = !(q || !r);`

The false statement is #3. If p, q, and r are all Boolean variables that have been assigned the value true, then after `p = !(q || !r);` executes, the value of p is false. First q is evaluated as true, so the entire expression within the parentheses is true. The leading NOT operator reverses that result to false and assigns it to p.

Adding Decisions and Constructors to Instance Methods

You frequently will want to use what you have learned about decision making to control the allowed values in objects' fields. Whether values are assigned to objects by constructors or by mutator methods, you often will need to use decisions to restrict the values assigned to fields.

For example, suppose that you create an `Employee` class as shown in Figure 5-32. The class contains two fields that hold an employee number and pay rate. The constructor accepts values for these fields as parameters, but instead of simply assigning the parameters to the fields, the code determines whether each value is within the allowed limits for the field.

```
public class Employee
{
    private int empNum;
    private double payRate;
    public int MAX_EMP_NUM = 9999;
    public double MAX_RATE = 60.00;
    Employee(int num, double rate)
    {
        if(num <= MAX_EMP_NUM)
            empNum = num;
        else
            empNum = MAX_EMP_NUM;
        if(payRate <= MAX_RATE)
            payRate = rate;
        else
            payRate = 0;
    }
    public int getEmpNum()
    {
        return empNum;
    }
    public double getPayRate()
    {
        return payRate;
    }
}
```

Figure 5-32   The `Employee` class that contains a constructor that makes decisions

If the `Employee` class in Figure 5-32 also contained set methods for `empNum` and `payRate`, and the rules governing appropriate values were the same as the rules used in the constructor, then it would make sense for the decisions to be made in the set methods and to code the constructor to call the set methods. That way, the decisions would appear only once in the class, saving time and space. Additionally, if a change to the rules was needed in the future—for example, if different default values were desired for either of the fields—then the code would be changed in just one place, reducing the likelihood of error or inconsistency.

You Do It

Adding Decisions to Constructors and Instance Methods

In this section, you modify the `DogTriathlonParticipant` class you created in Chapter 4. Because some points are awarded for participation in each event, a score of 0 is not possible unless a dog did not participate. In the existing class, the constructor accepts the number of events in which a dog participated and the participant's score in each event. Currently, there is no way to check whether these values are in agreement. Now, you can modify the class so that the number of events matches the number of valid scores supplied to the constructor.

1. Open the **DogTriathlonParticipant.java** file that you created in Chapter 4. Change the class name to `DogTriathlonParticipant2`, and immediately save the file as **DogTriathlonParticipant2.java**.

2. Change the constructor name to `DogTriathlonParticipant2`.

3. If 0 is assigned to the number of events in the existing program, computing the average score produces a nonnumeric result. Now that you know how to use decisions, you can fix this problem. In place of the arithmetic statement that produces the average score using division, use the following `if...else` statement:

```
if(NUM_EVENTS == 0)
    avg = 0;
else
    avg = (double) total / NUM_EVENTS;
```

4. Add a Boolean field to the list of class fields. This field holds `true` if the number of events reported matches the number of nonzero scores. Otherwise, the field holds `false`:

```
private boolean scoresAgree;
```

5. There are several ways to ensure that the number of events passed to the constructor matches the number of nonzero scores passed. One way is to add 1 to a total for each nonzero score and then determine whether that total equals the passed number of events. To accomplish this, first add the following code to the constructor immediately after the statements that assign values to the name and number of events. These statements declare a variable that holds the number of nonzero scores passed to the constructor, and then add 1 to the variable for each nonzero event score:

(continues)

(continued)

```
int totalNot0 = 0;
if(score1 != 0)
   totalNot0 = totalNot0 + 1;
if(score2 != 0)
   totalNot0 = totalNot0 + 1;
if(score3 != 0)
   totalNot0 = totalNot0 + 1;
```

6. Compare the number of events to the total of nonzero scores, and set the Boolean variable scoresAgree:

```
if(numEvents == totalNot0)
   scoresAgree = true;
else
   scoresAgree = false;
```

7. Replace the statements that unconditionally assigned values to obedienceScore, conformationScore, and agilityScore with the following if...else statement, which assigns the constructor's parameters to the three scores only when scoresAgree is true.

```
if(scoresAgree)
{
   obedienceScore = score1;
   conformationScore = score2;
   agilityScore = score3;
}
else
{
   obedienceScore = 0;
   conformationScore = 0;
   agilityScore = 0;
}
```

8. In the display() method for the DogTriathlonParticipant2 class, add the following statement that displays a special notice if an error occurred in the number of events value.

```
if(!scoresAgree)
   System.out.println("\nNotice! Number of events for " +
      name + " does not agree with scores reported.");
```

9. Save the file and compile it.

10. Open the **TestDogs.java** file that you created in a "You Do It" section in Chapter 4. Rename the class **TestDogs2**, and immediately save the file as **TestDogs2.java**.

(continues)

(continued)

288

11. Change `DogTriathlonParticipant` to **DogTriathlonParticipant2** in the six places it occurs in the three object declarations.

12. Change the object declarations so that the number of events and the number of nonzero scores used as constructor arguments agree for some objects but not for others.

13. Save the file, and then compile and execute it. Figure 5-33 shows a typical execution in which one participant's entries are valid but the other two contain errors.

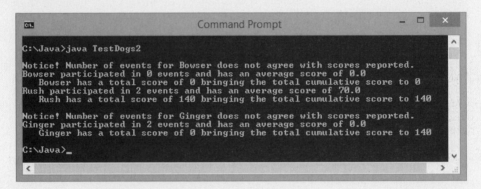

```
C:\Java>java TestDogs2
Notice! Number of events for Bowser does not agree with scores reported.
Bowser participated in 0 events and has an average score of 0.0
    Bowser has a total score of 0 bringing the total cumulative score to 0
Rush participated in 2 events and has an average score of 70.0
    Rush has a total score of 140 bringing the total cumulative score to 140

Notice! Number of events for Ginger does not agree with scores reported.
Ginger participated in 2 events and has an average score of 0.0
    Ginger has a total score of 0 bringing the total cumulative score to 140

C:\Java>_
```

Figure 5-33 Output of `TestDogs2` program

14. Change the values in the `TestDogs2` program. Recompile and reexecute the program several times to ensure that using various combinations of number of events and event scores produces appropriate results.

15. On your own, modify the `DogTriathlonParticipant2` class and rename it **DogTriathlonParticipant3**. In this version, do not use a count of the nonzero score parameters to determine whether the number of events matches the number of valid scores used as arguments. Instead, use only decisions to ensure that the parameters are in agreement. Save the file as **DogTriathlonParticipant3.java**, and create a file named **TestDogs3.java** that you can use to test the class. Be sure to test every possible combination of constructor parameters in the `TestDogs3` class—for example, when the events parameter is 2, it is correct whether the nonzero scores are the first and second, the first and third, or the second and third.

Don't Do It

- Don't ignore subtleties in boundaries used in decision making. For example, selecting employees who make less than $20 an hour is different from selecting employees who make $20 an hour or less.

- Don't use the assignment operator instead of the comparison operator when testing for equality.

- Don't insert a semicolon after the Boolean expression in an `if` statement; insert the semicolon after the entire statement is completed.

- Don't forget to block a set of statements with curly braces when several statements depend on the `if` or the `else` clause.

- Don't forget to include a complete Boolean expression on each side of an `&&` or `||` operator.

- Don't try to use a `switch` statement to test anything other than an integer, character, or string value.

- Don't forget a `break` statement if one is required by the logic of your `switch` statement.

- Don't use the standard relational operators to compare objects; use them only with the built-in Java types. In the chapter "Characters, Strings, and the `StringBuilder`," you will learn how to compare `Strings` correctly, and in the chapter "Advanced Inheritance Concepts" you will learn to compare other objects.

289

Key Terms

Pseudocode is a tool that helps programmers plan a program's logic by writing plain English statements.

A **flowchart** is a tool that helps programmers plan a program's logic by writing the steps in diagram form, as a series of shapes connected by arrows.

A **sequence structure** is a logical structure in which one step follows another unconditionally.

A **decision structure** is a logical structure that involves choosing between alternative courses of action based on some value within a program.

Boolean values are values that are `true` or `false`; every computer decision results in a Boolean value.

The **if statement** is used to write a single-alternative selection.

A **single-alternative selection** is a decision structure that performs an action, or not, based on one alternative.

The **equivalency operator** (==) compares values and returns `true` if they are equal.

An **empty statement** contains only a semicolon.

The **if...else statement** provides the mechanism to perform one action when a Boolean expression evaluates as `true` and a different action when a Boolean expression evaluates as `false`.

A **dual-alternative selection** takes one of two possible courses of action.

The **if clause** of an `if...else` statement is the part that executes when the evaluated Boolean expression is true.

The **else clause** of an `if...else` statement is the part that executes when the evaluated Boolean expression is false.

A **nested if statement** contains an `if` statement within another `if` statement.

A **compound Boolean expression** is one that contains an AND or OR operator.

A **compound condition** is tested in a compound Boolean expression.

The **logical AND operator** uses two Boolean expressions as operands, and evaluates to `true` if both operands are `true`. The AND operator is written as two ampersands (`&&`).

The **logical OR operator** uses two Boolean expressions as operands, and evaluates to `true` if either operand is `true`. The OR operator is written as two pipes (`||`).

Short-circuit evaluation describes the feature of the AND and OR operators in which evaluation is performed only as far as necessary to make a final decision.

A **side effect** is any action in a method other than returning a value.

A **function** is a method with no side effects in some programming languages.

A **range check** is a series of statements that determine within which of a set of ranges a value falls.

An **else...if clause** is a format used in nested `if` statements in which each instance of `else` and its subsequent `if` are placed on the same line.

The **switch statement** uses up to four keywords to test a single variable against a series of exact integer or character values. The keywords are `switch`, `case`, `break`, and `default`.

The **conditional operator** requires three expressions separated with a question mark and a colon, and is used as an abbreviated version of the `if...else` statement.

A **ternary operator** is one that needs three operands.

The **NOT operator** (`!`) negates or reverses the result of any Boolean expression.

Chapter Summary

- Making a decision involves choosing between two alternative courses of action based on some value within a program.

- The `if` statement is used to make a decision based on a Boolean expression. A single-alternative selection performs an action based on one alternative; a dual-alternative selection, or `if...else`, provides the mechanism for performing one action when a Boolean expression is `true` and a different action when the expression is `false`.

- Any number of statements can be blocked to be dependent on an `if` or an `else` clause.

- Nested `if` statements are particularly useful when two or more conditions must be met before some action occurs.

- The AND operator (`&&`) is used to create a compound Boolean expression that is `true` when all of its operands are `true`. The OR operator (`||`) is used to create a compound Boolean expression that is `true` when at least one of its operands is `true`.

- New programmers frequently cause errors in their `if` statements when they perform a range check incorrectly or inefficiently, or when they use the wrong operator while trying to make an AND or OR decision.

- The `switch` statement tests a single variable against a series of exact integer, character, or string values.

- The conditional operator requires three expressions, a question mark, and a colon, and is used as an abbreviated version of the `if...else` statement. The NOT operator (`!`) negates the result of any Boolean expression.

- Operator precedence controls how expressions are evaluated. You can use parentheses to change precedence or make your intentions clearer.

- Decisions are frequently used to control field values.

Review Questions

1. The logical structure in which one instruction occurs after another with no branching is a ─────────── .

   a. sequence   c. loop

   b. selection   d. case

2. Which of the following is typically used in a flowchart to indicate a decision?

   a. square   c. diamond

   b. rectangle   d. oval

3. Which of the following is not a type of `if` statement?

   a. single-alternative   c. reverse

   b. dual-alternative   d. nested

4. A decision is based on a(n) —————————— value.

    a. convoluted   c. definitive

    b. absolute   d. Boolean

5. In Java, the value of (14 > 7) is —————————— .

    a. `true`   c. 4

    b. `false`   d. 7

6. Assuming the variable `score` has been assigned the value 13, which of the following statements displays XXX?

    a. `if(score > 0) System.out.println("XXX");`

    b. `if(score > 17); System.out.println("XXX");`

    c. `if(score < 7); System.out.println("XXX");`

    d. All of the above display XXX.

7. What is the output of the following code segment?

```
t = 10;
if(t > 7)
{
    System.out.print("AAA");
    System.out.print("BBB");
}
```

    a. AAA   c. AAABBB

    b. BBB   d. nothing

8. What is the output of the following code segment?

```
t = 0;
if(t > 7)
    System.out.print("AAA");
    System.out.print("BBB");
```

    a. AAA   c. AAABBB

    b. BBB   d. nothing

9. What is the output of the following code segment?

```
t = 7;
if(t > 7)
{
    System.out.print("AAA");
    System.out.print("BBB");
}
```

    a. AAA   c. AAABBB

    b. BBB   d. nothing

10. When you code an `if` statement within another `if` statement, the statements are ——————————— .

    a. notched
    b. nestled

    c. nested
    d. sheltered

11. The operator that combines two conditions into a single Boolean value that is `true` only when both of the conditions are `true` is ——————————— .

    a. `$$`
    b. `!!`

    c. `||`
    d. `&&`

12. The operator that combines two conditions into a single Boolean value that is `true` when at least one of the conditions is `true` is ——————————— .

    a. `$$`
    b. `!!`

    c. `||`
    d. `&&`

13. Assuming a variable f has been initialized to 5, which of the following statements sets g to 0?

    a. `if(f > 6 || f == 5) g = 0;`
    b. `if(f < 3 || f > 4) g = 0;`

    c. `if(f >= 0 || f < 2) g = 0;`
    d. All of the above statements set g to 0.

14. Which of the following has the lowest precedence?

    a. `<`
    b. `==`

    c. `&&`
    d. `||`

15. Which of the following statements correctly outputs the names of voters who live in district 6 and all voters who live in district 7?

    a. `if(district == 6 || 7)`
        `System.out.println("Name is " + name);`

    b. `if(district == 6 || district == 7)`
        `System.out.println("Name is " + name);`

    c. `if(district = 6 && district == 7)`
        `System.out.println("Name is " + name);`

    d. two of these

16. Which of the following displays "Error" when a student ID is less than 1000 or more than 9999?

    a. `if(stuId < 1000) if(stuId > 9999)`
        `System.out.println("Error");`

    b. `if(stuId < 1000 && stuId > 9999)`
        `System.out.println("Error");`

```
c.  if(stuId < 1000)
        System.out.println("Error");
    else
        if(stuId > 9999)
            System.out.println("Error");
```

d. Two of these are correct.

17. You can use the ——————————— statement to terminate a `switch` statement.

    a. `switch`   c. `case`

    b. `end`   d. `break`

18. Which of the following cannot be the argument tested in a `switch` statement?

    a. `int`   c. `double`

    b. `char`   d. `String`

19. Assuming a variable w has been assigned the value 15, what does the following statement do?

```
w == 15 ? x = 2 : x = 0;
```

    a. assigns 15 to w   c. assigns 0 to x

    b. assigns 2 to x   d. nothing

20. Assuming a variable y has been assigned the value 6, the value of `!(y < 7)` is ———————————.

    a. 6   c. `true`

    b. 7   d. `false`

Exercises

Programming Exercises

1. Write an application that asks a user to enter an integer. Display a statement that indicates whether the integer is even or odd. Save the file as **EvenOdd.java**.

2. Write an application that asks a user to enter three integers. Display them in ascending and descending order. Save the file as **AscendingAndDescending.java**.

3. a. Write an application for the Summerdale Condo Sales office; the program determines the price of a condominium. Ask the user to choose *1* for park view, *2* for golf course view, or *3* for lake view. The output is the name of the chosen view as well as the price of the condo. Park view condos are $150,000, condos with golf course views are $170,000, and condos with lake views are $210,000. If the user enters an invalid code, set the price to 0. Save the file as **CondoSales.java**.

b. Add a prompt to the CondoSales application to ask the user to specify a (1) garage or a (2) parking space, but only if the view selection is valid. Add $5,000 to the price of any condo with a garage. If the parking value is invalid, display an appropriate message and assume that the price is for a condo with no garage. Save the file as **CondoSales2.java**.

4. Write a program for Horizon Phones, a provider of cellular phone service. Prompt a user for maximum monthly values for talk minutes used, text messages sent, and gigabytes of data used, and then recommend the best plan for the customer's needs. A customer who needs fewer than 500 minutes of talk and no text or data should accept Plan A at $49 per month. A customer who needs fewer than 500 minutes of talk and any text messages should accept Plan B at $55 per month. A customer who needs 500 or more minutes of talk and no data should accept either Plan C for up to 100 text messages at $61 per month or Plan D for 100 text messages or more at $70 per month. A customer who needs any data should accept Plan E for up to 2 gigabytes at $79 or Plan F for 2 gigabytes or more at $87. Save the file as **CellPhoneService.java**.

5. a. Write an application that prompts a user for a month, day, and year. Display a message that specifies whether the entered date is (1) not this year, (2) in an earlier month this year, (3) in a later month this year, or (4) this month. Save the file as **PastPresentFuture.java**.

b. Use the Web to learn how to use the LocalDate Boolean methods isBefore(), isAfter(), and equals(). Use your knowledge to write a program that prompts a user for a month, day, and year, and then displays a message specifying whether the entered day is in the past, the current date, or in the future. Save the file as **PastPresentFuture2.java**.

6. Barnhill Fastener Company runs a small factory. The company employs workers who are paid one of three hourly rates depending on skill level:

Skill Level	Hourly Pay Rate ($)
1	17.00
2	20.00
3	22.00

Each factory worker might work any number of hours per week; any hours over 40 are paid at one and one-half times the usual rate.

In addition, workers in skill levels 2 and 3 can elect the following insurance options:

Option	Explanation	Weekly Cost to Employee ($)
1	Medical insurance	32.50
2	Dental insurance	20.00
3	Long-term disability insurance	10.00

Also, workers in skill level 3 can elect to participate in the retirement plan at 3% of their gross pay.

Write an interactive Java payroll application that calculates the net pay for a factory worker. The program prompts the user for skill level and hours worked, as well as appropriate insurance and retirement options for the employee's skill level category. The application displays: (1) the hours worked, (2) the hourly pay rate, (3) the regular pay for 40 hours, (4) the overtime pay, (5) the total of regular and overtime pay, and (6) the total itemized deductions. If the deductions exceed the gross pay, display an error message; otherwise, calculate and display (7) the net pay after all the deductions have been subtracted from the gross. Save the file as **Pay.java**.

7. Create a class that holds data about a job applicant. Include a name, a phone number, and four Boolean fields that represent whether the applicant is skilled in each of the following areas: word processing, spreadsheets, databases, and graphics. Include a constructor that accepts values for each of the fields. Also include a get method for each field. Create an application that instantiates several job applicant objects and pass each in turn to a Boolean method that determines whether each applicant is qualified for an interview. Then, in the `main()` method, display an appropriate method for each applicant. A qualified applicant has at least three of the four skills. Save the files as **JobApplicant.java** and **TestJobApplicants.java**.

8. Create an `Automobile` class for a dealership. Include fields for an ID number, make, model, color, year, and miles per gallon. Include get and set methods for each field. Do not allow the ID to be negative or more than 9999; if it is, set the ID to 0. Do not allow the year to be earlier than 2000 or later than 2017; if it is, set the year to 0. Do not allow the miles per gallon to be less than 10 or more than 60; if it is, set the miles per gallon to 0. Include a constructor that accepts arguments for each field value and uses the set methods to assign the values. Write an application that declares several `Automobile` objects and demonstrates that all the methods work correctly. Save the files as **Automobile.java** and **TestAutomobiles.java**.

9. Create a class named `Apartment` that holds an apartment number, number of bedrooms, number of baths, and rent amount. Create a constructor that accepts values for each data field. Also create a get method for each field. Write an application that creates at least five `Apartment` objects. Then prompt a user to enter a minimum number of bedrooms required, a minimum number of baths required, and a maximum rent the user is willing to pay. Display data for all the `Apartment` objects that meet the user's criteria or an appropriate message if no such apartments are available. Save the files as **Apartment.java** and **TestApartments.java**.

10. Use the Web to locate the lyrics to the traditional song "The Twelve Days of Christmas." The song contains a list of gifts received for the holiday. The list is cumulative so that as each "day" passes, a new verse contains all the words of the previous verse, plus a new item. Write an application that displays the words to the song starting with any day the user enters. (*Hint*: Use a `switch` statement with `cases` in descending day order and without any `break` statements so that the lyrics for any day repeat all the lyrics for previous days.) Save the file as **TwelveDays.java**.

Debugging Exercises

1. Each of the following files in the Chapter05 folder of your downloadable student files has syntax and/or logic errors. In each case, determine the problem and fix the program. After you correct the errors, save each file using the same filename preceded with *Fix*. For example, save DebugFive1.java as **FixDebugFive1.java**.

   a. DebugFive1.java   c. DebugFive3.java

   b. DebugFive2.java   d. DebugFive4.java

Game Zone

1. In Chapter 1, you created a class called RandomGuess. In this game, players guess a number, the application generates a random number, and players determine whether they were correct. Now that you can make decisions, modify the application so it allows a player to enter a guess before the random number is displayed, and then displays a message indicating whether the player's guess was correct, too high, or too low. Save the file as **RandomGuess2.java**. (After you finish the next chapter, you will be able to modify the application so that the user can continue to guess until the correct answer is entered.)

2. Create a lottery game application. Generate three random numbers (see Appendix D for help in doing so), each between 0 and 9. Allow the user to guess three numbers. Compare each of the user's guesses to the three random numbers and display a message that includes the user's guess, the randomly determined three-digit number, and the amount of money the user has won as follows:

Matching Numbers	Award ($)
Any one matching	10
Two matching	100
Three matching, not in order	1,000
Three matching in exact order	1,000,000
No matches	0

Make certain that your application accommodates repeating digits. For example, if a user guesses 1, 2, and 3, and the randomly generated digits are 1, 1, and 1, do not give the user credit for three correct guesses—just one. Save the file as **Lottery.java**.

3. In Chapter 3, you created a Card class. Modify the Card class so the setValue() method does not allow a Card's value to be less than 1 or higher than 13. If the argument to setValue() is out of range, assign 1 to the Card's value.

   In Chapter 3, you also created a PickTwoCards application that randomly selects two playing cards and displays their values. In that application, all Card objects arbitrarily were assigned a suit represented by a single character, but they could have different values, and the player observed which of two Card objects had the higher value. Now, modify the application so the suit and the value both are chosen randomly. Using two Card objects, play a very simple version of the card game War. Deal two Cards—one for the computer and one for the player—and determine the higher card, then display a message indicating whether the cards are equal, the computer won, or the player won. (Playing cards are considered equal when they have the same value, no matter what their suit is.) For this game, assume the Ace (value 1) is low. Make sure that the two Cards dealt are not the same Card. For example, a deck cannot contain more than one Card representing the 2 of Spades. If two cards are chosen to have the same value, change the suit for one of them. Save the application as **War.java**. (After you study the chapter "Arrays," you will be able to create a more sophisticated War game in which you use an entire deck without repeating cards.)

4. In Chapter 4, you created a Die class from which you could instantiate an object containing a random value from 1 through 6. You also wrote an application that randomly "throws" two dice and displays their values. Modify the application so it determines whether the two dice are the same, the first has a higher value, or the second has a higher value. Save the application as **TwoDice2.java**.

5. In the game Rock Paper Scissors, two players simultaneously choose one of three options: rock, paper, or scissors. If both players choose the same option, then the result is a tie. However, if they choose differently, the winner is determined as follows:

   - Rock beats scissors, because a rock can break a pair of scissors.

   - Scissors beats paper, because scissors can cut paper.

   - Paper beats rock, because a piece of paper can cover a rock.

   Create a game in which the computer randomly chooses rock, paper, or scissors. Let the user enter a number 1, 2, or 3, each representing one of the three choices. Then, determine the winner. Save the application as **RockPaperScissors.java**. (In the chapter "Characters, Strings, and the StringBuilder," you will modify the game so that the user enters a string for *rock, paper,* and *scissors*, rather than just entering a number.)

Case Problems

1. a. Carly's Catering provides meals for parties and special events. In Chapters 3 and 4, you created an Event class for the company. Now, make the following changes to the class:

    - Currently, the class contains a field that holds the price for an Event. Now add another field that holds the price per guest, and add a public method to return its value.

    - Currently, the class contains a constant for the price per guest. Replace that field with two fields—a lower price per guest that is $32, and a higher price per guest that is $35.

    - Add a new method named isLargeEvent() that returns true if the number of guests is 50 or greater and otherwise returns false.

    - Modify the method that sets the number of guests so that a large Event (over 50 guests) uses the lower price per guest to set the new pricePerGuest field and calculate the total Event price. A small Event uses the higher price.

    Save the file as **Event.java**.

    b. In Chapter 4, you modified the EventDemo class to demonstrate two Event objects. Now, modify that class again as follows:

    - Instantiate three Event objects, and prompt the user for values for each object.

    - Change the method that displays Event details to use the new isLargeEvent() method and the new price per guest value. Use the display method with all three objects.

    - Create a method that accepts two Event objects and returns the larger one based on number of guests. (If the Events have the same number of guests, you can return either object.) Call this method three times—once with each pair of instantiated Events—and display the event number and number of guests for each argument as well as the event number and number of guests for the larger Event.

    Save the file as **EventDemo.java**.

2. a. Sammy's Seashore Supplies rents beach equipment such as kayaks, canoes, beach chairs, and umbrellas to tourists. In Chapters 3 and 4, you created a Rental class for the company.

Now, make the following change to the class:

- Currently, a rental price is calculated as $40 per hour plus $1 for each minute over a full hour. This means that a customer who rents equipment for 41 or more minutes past an hour pays more than a customer who waits until the next hour to return the equipment. Change the price calculation so that a customer pays $40 for each full hour and $1 for each extra minute up to and including 40 minutes.

Save the file as **Rental.java**.

b. In Chapter 4, you modified the RentalDemo class to demonstrate a Rental object. Now, modify that class again as follows:

- Instantiate three Rental objects, and prompt the user for values for each object. Display the details for each object to verify that the new price calculation works correctly.

- Create a method that accepts two Rental objects and returns the one with the longer rental time. (If the Rentals have the same time, you can return either object.) Call this method three times—once with each pair of instantiated Rentals—and display the contract number and time in hours and minutes for each argument as well as the contract number of the longer Rental.

Save the file as **RentalDemo.java**.

Looping

In this chapter, you will:

- ◎ Learn about the loop structure
- ◎ Create `while` loops
- ◎ Use shortcut arithmetic operators
- ◎ Create `for` loops
- ◎ Create `do...while` loops
- ◎ Nest loops
- ◎ Improve loop performance

Learning About the Loop Structure

If making decisions is what makes programs seem smart, looping is what makes programs seem powerful. A **loop** is a structure that allows repeated execution of a block of statements. Within a looping structure, a Boolean expression is evaluated. If it is true, a block of statements called the **loop body** executes and the Boolean expression is evaluated again. The loop body can be a single statement, or a block of statements between curly braces. As long as the expression is true, the statements in the loop body continue to execute. When the Boolean evaluation is false, the loop ends. One execution of any loop is called an **iteration**. Figure 6-1 shows a diagram of the logic of a loop.

In Java, you can use several mechanisms to create loops. In this chapter, you learn to use three types of loops:

- A while loop, in which the loop-controlling Boolean expression is the first statement in the loop

- A for loop, which is usually used as a concise format in which to execute loops

- A do...while loop, in which the loop-controlling Boolean expression is the last statement in the loop

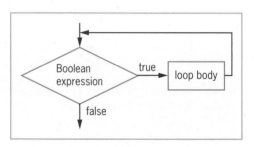

Figure 6-1 Flowchart of a loop structure

TWO TRUTHS & A LIE

Learning About the Loop Structure

1. A loop is a structure that allows repeated execution of a block of statements as long as a tested expression is true.

2. If a loop's tested Boolean expression is true, a block of statements called the loop body executes before the Boolean expression is evaluated again.

3. When the Boolean evaluation tested in a loop becomes false, the loop body executes one last time.

The false statement is #3. When the Boolean evaluation tested in a loop is false, the loop ends.

Creating while Loops

You can use a **while loop** to execute a body of statements continually as long as the Boolean expression that controls entry into the loop continues to be `true`. In Java, a while loop consists of the keyword while followed by a Boolean expression within parentheses, followed by the body of the loop.

You can use a while loop when you need to perform a task either a predetermined or unpredictable number of times. A loop that executes a specific number of times is a **definite loop** or a **counted loop**. On the other hand, the number of times the loop executes might not be determined until the program is running. Such a loop is an **indefinite loop** because you don't know how many times it will eventually loop.

Writing a Definite while Loop

To write a definite loop, you initialize a **loop control variable**, a variable whose value determines whether loop execution continues. While the Boolean value that results from comparing the loop control variable and another value is `true`, the body of the while loop continues to execute. In the body of the loop, you must include a statement that alters the loop control variable; otherwise, the loop will never end. For example, the program segment shown in Figure 6-2 displays the series of integers 1 through 10. The variable lcv is the loop control variable—it starts the loop holding a value of 1, and while the value remains under 11, lcv continues to be output and increased.

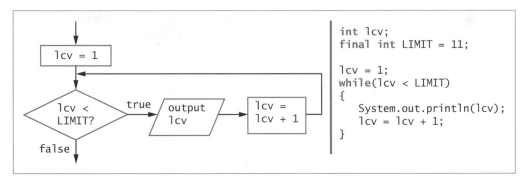

Figure 6-2 A while loop that displays the integers 1 through 10

When you write applications containing loops, it is easy to make mistakes. For example, executing the code shown in Figure 6-3 causes the message "Hello" to be displayed forever (theoretically) because there is no code to end the loop. A loop that never ends is called an **infinite loop**.

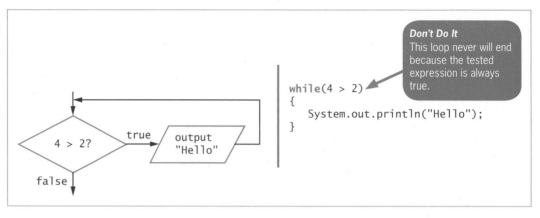

Figure 6-3   A loop that displays "Hello" infinitely

 An infinite loop might not actually execute infinitely. Depending on the tasks the loop performs, eventually the computer memory might be exhausted (literally and figuratively) and execution might stop. Also, it's possible that the processor has a time-out feature that forces the loop to end. Either way, and depending on your system, quite a bit of time could pass before the loop stops running.

 As an inside joke to programmers, the address of Apple Inc. is 1 Infinite Loop, Cupertino, California. It is the default start location in Apple's "Find My Friends" application.

In Figure 6-3, the expression 4 > 2 evaluates to true. You obviously never need to make such an evaluation, but if you do so in this while loop, the body of the loop is entered and "Hello" is displayed. Next, the expression is evaluated again. The expression 4 > 2 is still true, so the body is entered again. "Hello" is displayed repeatedly; the loop never finishes because 4 > 2 is never false.

It is a bad idea to write an infinite loop intentionally. However, even experienced programmers write them by accident. So, before you start writing loops, it is good to know how to exit from an infinite loop. You might suspect an infinite loop if the same output is displayed repeatedly, or if the screen simply remains idle for an extended period of time without displaying expected output. If you think your application is in an infinite loop, you can press and hold the Ctrl key, and then press C or the Break key; the looping program should terminate. (On many keyboards, the Break key is also the Pause key.)

To prevent a while loop from executing infinitely, three separate actions must occur:

- A loop control variable is initialized to a starting value.

- The loop control variable is tested in the while statement.

- The loop control variable is altered within the body of the loop. The variable must be altered so that the test expression can eventually evaluate to false and the loop can end.

All of these conditions are met by the example in Figure 6-4. First, a loop control variable loopCount is named and set to a value of 1. Second, loopCount is compared to 3. Third, loopCount is altered in the loop body when 1 is added to it. Note that the loop body shown in Figure 6-4 consists of two statements made into a block by their surrounding curly braces. When loopCount is 1, it is compared to 3, and because it is less than 3, the loop body executes, displaying "Hello" and increasing loopCount. The next time loopCount is evaluated, it is 2. It is still less than 3, so the loop body executes again. "Hello" is displayed a second time, and loopCount becomes 3. Finally, because the expression loopCount < 3 now evaluates to false, the loop ends. Program execution then continues with any subsequent statements.

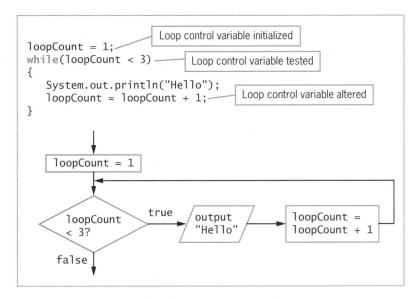

Figure 6-4 A while loop that displays "Hello" twice

Pitfall: Failing to Alter the Loop Control Variable Within the Loop Body

It is important that the loop control variable be altered within the body of the loop. Figure 6-5 shows the same code as in Figure 6-4, but the curly braces have been eliminated. In this case, the while loop body ends at the semicolon that appears at the end of the "Hello" statement. Adding 1 to the loopCount is no longer part of a block that contains the loop, so the value of loopCount never changes, and an infinite loop is created.

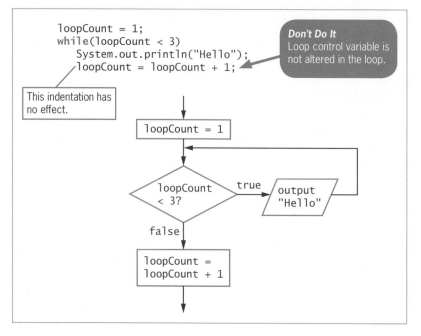

Figure 6-5 A `while` loop that displays "Hello" infinitely because `loopCount` is not altered in the loop body

Pitfall: Unintentionally Creating a Loop with an Empty Body

As with the decision-making `if` statement that you learned about in Chapter 5, placement of the statement-ending semicolon is important when you work with the `while` statement. If a semicolon is mistakenly placed at the end of the partial statement `while(loopCount < 3);`, as shown in Figure 6-6, the loop is also infinite. This loop has an **empty body**, or a body with no statements in it. So, the Boolean expression is evaluated, and because it is `true`, the loop body is entered. Because the loop body is empty, no action is taken, and the Boolean expression is evaluated again. Nothing has changed, so it is still `true`, the empty body is entered, and the infinite loop continues.

Don't Do It
This semicolon causes the loop to have an empty body.

```
loopCount = 1;
while(loopCount < 3);
{
   System.out.println("Hello");
   loopCount = loopCount + 1;
}
```

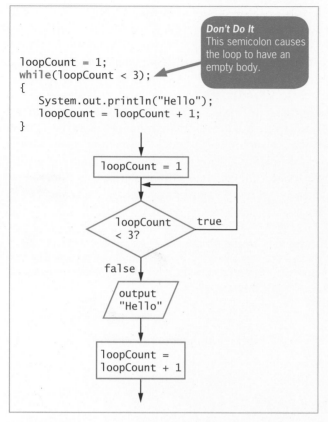

Figure 6-6 A `while` loop that loops infinitely with no output because the loop body is empty

Altering a Definite Loop's Control Variable

A definite loop is a **counter-controlled loop** because the loop control variable is changed by counting. It is very common to alter the value of a loop control variable by adding 1 to it, or **incrementing** the variable. However, not all loops are controlled by adding 1. The loop shown in Figure 6-7 displays "Hello" twice, just as the loop in Figure 6-4 does, but its loop is controlled by subtracting 1 from a loop control variable, or **decrementing** it.

```
loopCount = 3;
while(loopCount > 1)
{
   System.out.println("Hello");
   loopCount = loopCount - 1;
}
```

Figure 6-7 A `while` loop that displays "Hello" twice, decrementing the `loopCount` variable in the loop body

In the program segment shown in Figure 6-7, the variable loopCount begins with a value of 3. The loopCount is greater than 1, so the loop body displays "Hello" and decrements loopCount to 2. The Boolean expression in the while loop is tested again. Because 2 is more than 1, "Hello" is displayed again, and loopCount becomes 1. Now loopCount is not greater than 1, so the loop ends. There are many ways to execute a loop two times. For example, you can initialize a loop control variable to 10 and continue while the value is greater than 8, decreasing the value by 1 each time you pass through the loop. Similarly, you can initialize the loop control variable to 12, continue while it is greater than 2, and decrease the value by 5 each time. In general, you should not use such unusual methods to count repetitions because they simply make a program confusing. To execute a loop a specific number of times, the clearest and best method is to start the loop control variable at 0 or 1, increment by 1 each time through the loop, and stop when the loop control variable reaches the appropriate limit.

When you first start programming, it seems reasonable to initialize counter values to 1, and that is a workable approach. However, many seasoned programmers start counter values at 0 because they are used to doing so when working with arrays. When you study arrays in the chapter "Introduction to Arrays," you will learn that their elements are numbered beginning with 0.

Watch the video *Looping*.

Writing an Indefinite while Loop

You are not required to alter a loop control variable by adding to it or subtracting from it. Often, the value of a loop control variable is not altered by arithmetic, but instead is altered by user input. Instead of being a counter-controlled loop, an indefinite loop is an **event-controlled loop**. That is, an event occurs that determines whether the loop continues. An event-controlled loop is a type of indefinite loop because you don't know how many times it will eventually repeat. For example, perhaps you want to continue asking a user questions as long as the response is correct. In this case, while you are writing the program, you do not know whether the loop eventually will be executed two times or 200 times.

Consider an application in which you ask the user for a bank balance and then ask whether the user wants to see the balance after interest has accumulated. Each time the user chooses to continue, an increased balance appears, reflecting one more year of accumulated interest. When the user finally chooses to exit, the program ends. The program appears in Figure 6-8.

```
import java.util.Scanner;
public class BankBalance
{
    public static void main(String[] args)
    {
        double balance;
        int response;
        int year = 1;
        final double INT_RATE = 0.03;
        Scanner keyboard = new Scanner(System.in);
        System.out.print("Enter initial bank balance > ");
        balance = keyboard.nextDouble();
        System.out.println("Do you want to see next year's balance?");
        System.out.print("Enter 1 for yes");
        System.out.print(" or any other number for no >> ");
        response = keyboard.nextInt();
        while(response == 1)
        {
            balance = balance + balance * INT_RATE;
            System.out.println("After year " + year + " at " + INT_RATE +
                " interest rate, balance is $" + balance);
            year = year + 1;
            System.out.println("\nDo you want to see the balance " +
                "at the end of another year?");
            System.out.print("Enter 1 for yes");
            System.out.print(" or any other number for no >> ");
            response = keyboard.nextInt();
        }
    }
}
```

Figure 6-8   The BankBalance application

In the **BankBalance** program, as in any interactive program, the user must enter data that has the expected data types. If not, an error occurs and the program terminates. You will learn to manage user entry errors in the chapter "Exception Handling."

The program shown in Figure 6-8 declares needed variables and a constant for a 3 percent interest rate, and then asks the user for a balance. The application then asks the user to enter *1* if the user wants see the next year's balance. As long as the user wants to continue, the application continues to display increasing bank balances.

The loop in the application in Figure 6-8 begins with the line that contains:

```
while(response == 1)
```

If the user enters any integer value other than *1*, the loop body never executes; instead, the program ends. However, if the user enters *1*, all the statements within the loop body execute. The application increases the balance by the interest rate value, displays the new balance, adds 1 to year, and asks whether the user wants another balance. The last statement in the loop body accepts the user's response. After the loop body executes, control returns to the top of the loop, where the Boolean expression in the while loop is tested again. If the user's response is *1*, the loop is entered and the process begins again. Figure 6-9 shows the output of the BankBalance application after the user enters a starting balance and responds with *1* five times to the prompt for increased interest payments before responding *2*.

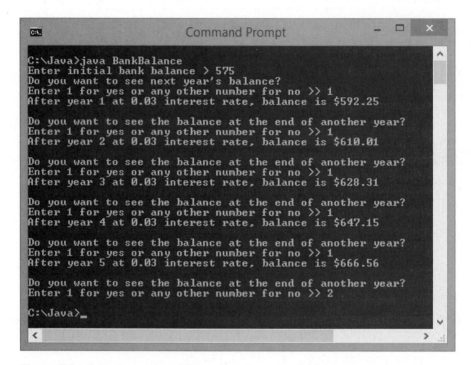

```
C:\Java>java BankBalance
Enter initial bank balance > 575
Do you want to see next year's balance?
Enter 1 for yes or any other number for no >> 1
After year 1 at 0.03 interest rate, balance is $592.25

Do you want to see the balance at the end of another year?
Enter 1 for yes or any other number for no >> 1
After year 2 at 0.03 interest rate, balance is $610.01

Do you want to see the balance at the end of another year?
Enter 1 for yes or any other number for no >> 1
After year 3 at 0.03 interest rate, balance is $628.31

Do you want to see the balance at the end of another year?
Enter 1 for yes or any other number for no >> 1
After year 4 at 0.03 interest rate, balance is $647.15

Do you want to see the balance at the end of another year?
Enter 1 for yes or any other number for no >> 1
After year 5 at 0.03 interest rate, balance is $666.56

Do you want to see the balance at the end of another year?
Enter 1 for yes or any other number for no >> 2

C:\Java>_
```

Figure 6-9 Typical execution of the BankBalance application

Many indefinite loops are written to continue while an ending value is *not* entered. A value that stops a loop is a **sentinel**. In the exercises at the end of this chapter, you will write several programs that use sentinels.

Validating Data

Programmers commonly use indefinite loops when validating input data. **Validating data** is the process of ensuring that a value falls within a specified range. For example, suppose you require a user to enter a value no greater than 3. Figure 6-10 shows an application that does not progress past the data entry loop until the user enters a correct value. If the user enters *3* or less at the first prompt, the shaded loop never executes. However, if the user enters a number greater than 3, the shaded loop executes, providing the user with another chance to enter a correct value. While the user continues to enter incorrect data, the loop repeats. Figure 6-11 shows a typical execution.

```java
import java.util.Scanner;
public class EnterSmallValue
{
    public static void main(String[] args)
    {
        int userEntry;
        final int LIMIT = 3;
        Scanner input = new Scanner(System.in);
        System.out.print("Please enter an integer no higher than " +
            LIMIT + " > ");
        userEntry = input.nextInt();
        while(userEntry > LIMIT)
        {
            System.out.println("The number you entered was too high");
            System.out.print("Please enter an integer no higher than " +
                LIMIT + " > ");
            userEntry = input.nextInt();
        }
        System.out.println("You correctly entered " + userEntry);
    }
}
```

Figure 6-10   The EnterSmallValue application

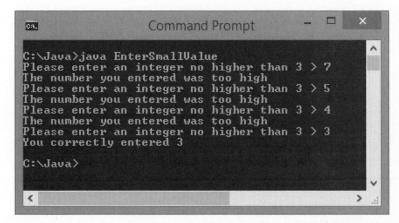

Figure 6-11   Typical execution of the EnterSmallValue program

Figure 6-10 illustrates an excellent method for validating input. Before the loop is entered, the first input is retrieved. This first input might be a value that prevents any executions of the loop. This first input statement prior to the loop is called a **priming read** or **priming input**. Within the loop, the last statement retrieves subsequent input values for the same variable that will be checked at the entrance to the loop.

Novice programmers often make the mistake of checking for invalid data using a decision instead of a loop. That is, they ask whether the data is invalid using an `if` statement; if the data is invalid, they reprompt the user. However, they forget that a user might enter incorrect data multiple times. Usually, a loop is the best structure to use when validating input data.

TWO TRUTHS & A LIE

Creating while Loops

1. A finite loop executes a specific number of times; an indefinite loop is one that never ends.

2. A well-written `while` loop contains an initialized loop control variable that is tested in the `while` expression and then altered in the loop body.

3. In an indefinite loop, you don't know how many times the loop will occur.

The false statement is #1. A loop that executes a specific number of times is a definite loop or a counted loop; a loop that never ends is an infinite loop.

 You Do It

Writing a Loop to Validate Data Entries

In Chapter 5, you created an `AssignVolunteer4` application for Sacks Fifth Avenue, a nonprofit thrift shop. The application accepts a donation code and assigns the appropriate volunteer to price the item for sale. Now, you add a loop to ensure that a valid code always is entered.

1. Open the AssignVolunteer4.java file that you created in Chapter 5. Change the class name to **AssignVolunteer5**, and immediately save the file as **AssignVolunteer5.java.**

2. After the input statement that gets a code from the user, but before the `switch` structure that assigns a volunteer, insert the following loop. The loop continues while the input `donationType` is less than the lowest valid code or higher than the highest valid code. (Recall that the values of CLOTHING_CODE, FURNITURE_CODE, ELECTRONICS_CODE, and OTHER_CODE are 1 through 4,

(continues)

(continued)

respectively.) Within the loop body, statements explain the error to the user and then get a new value for donationType.

```
while(donationType < CLOTHING_CODE || donationType > OTHER_CODE)
{
    System.out.println("You entered " + donationType +
        " which is not a valid donation type");
    System.out.print("Please enter a value between " +
        CLOTHING_CODE + " and " + OTHER_CODE + "... ");
    System.out.print("Enter an integer... ");
    donationType = input.nextInt();
}
```

3. Save the file, and compile and execute it. Figure 6-12 shows a typical execution in which a user enters an invalid code three times before entering a valid one.

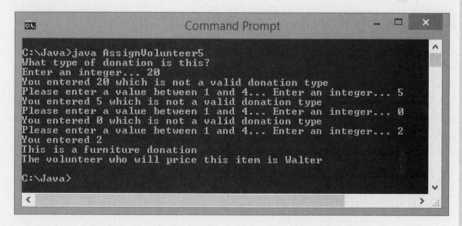

Figure 6-12 Typical execution of the AssignVolunteer5 application

4. In the current program, the default case assigns "invalid" to the volunteer. At this point, some professionals would advise that you remove the default case from the case structure because it is no longer possible for the user to enter an invalid code. Others would argue that leaving the default case in place serves two purposes. First, it provides documentation that clarifies the course of action if the entered code does not match any of the listed cases. Second, the program requirements might change in the future. For example, perhaps one of the categories will be eliminated. Then, if you remove the case instructions for that category, a default block will already be in place to handle the new error.

Using Shortcut Arithmetic Operators

Programmers commonly need to increase the value of a variable in a program. As you saw in the previous section, many loops are controlled by continually adding 1 to some variable, as in count = count + 1;. Incrementing a variable in a loop to keep track of the number of occurrences of some event is also known as **counting**. Similarly, in the looping bank balance program shown in Figure 6-8, the program not only incremented the year variable by adding 1, it also increased the bank balance by an interest amount with the statement balance = balance + balance * INT_RATE;. In other words, the bank balance became its old value *plus* a new interest amount; the process of repeatedly increasing a value by some amount is known as **accumulating**.

Because increasing a variable is so common, Java provides you with several shortcuts for incrementing and accumulating. The statement count += 1; is identical in meaning to count = count + 1. The += is the **add and assign operator**; it adds and assigns in one operation. Similarly, balance += balance * INT_RATE; increases a balance by the INT_RATE percentage. Besides using the shortcut operator +=, you can use the **subtract and assign operator** (-=), the **multiply and assign operator** (*=), the **divide and assign operator** (/=), and the **remainder and assign operator** (%=). Each of these operators is used to perform the operation and assign the result in one step. For example, balanceDue -= payment subtracts payment from balanceDue and assigns the result to balanceDue.

When you want to increase a variable's value by exactly 1, you can use two other shortcut operators—the **prefix ++**, also known as the **prefix increment operator**, and the **postfix ++**, also known as the **postfix increment operator**. To use a prefix ++, you type two plus signs before the variable name. The statement someValue = 6; followed by ++someValue; results in someValue holding 7—one more than it held before you applied the ++. To use a postfix ++, you type two plus signs just after a variable name. The statements anotherValue = 56; anotherValue++; result in anotherValue containing 57. Figure 6-13 shows four ways you can increase a value by 1; each method produces the same result. You are never required to use shortcut operators; they are merely a convenience.

```
int value;
value = 24;
++value; // Result: value is 25
value = 24;
value++; // Result: value is 25
value = 24;
value = value + 1; // Result: value is 25
value = 24;
value += 1; // Result: value is 25
```

Figure 6-13　Four ways to add 1 to a value

You cannot use the prefix ++ and postfix ++ operators with constants. An expression such as ++84; is illegal because an 84 must always remain an 84. However, you can create a variable named val, assign 84 to it, and then write ++val; or val++; to increase the variable's value.

The prefix and postfix increment operators are unary operators because you use them with one value. As you learned in Chapter 2, most arithmetic operators, such as those used for addition and multiplication, are binary operators—they operate on two values. Other examples of unary operators include the cast operator, as well as (+) and (−) when used to indicate positive and negative values.

When you simply want to increase a variable's value by 1, there is no difference in the outcome, whether you use the prefix or postfix increment operator. For example, when value is set to 24 in Figure 6-13, both ++value and value++ result in value becoming 25. However, when a prefix or postfix operator is used as part of a larger expression, it does make a difference which operator you use because they function differently in terms of what they *return*. When a prefix operator is used in an expression, the value *after* the calculation is used, but when a postfix operator is used in an expression, the value *before* the calculation is used.

When you use the prefix ++, the result is calculated, and then its value is used. For example, consider the following statements:

```
b = 4;
c = ++b;
```

The result is that both b and c hold the value 5 because b is increased to 5 and then the value of the expression is assigned to c.

When you use the postfix ++, the value of the expression before the increase is stored. For example, consider these statements:

```
b = 4;
c = b++;
```

The result is still that b is 5, but c is only 4. The value of b is assigned to c and then b is incremented. In other words, if b = 4, the value of b++ is also 4, but after the statement is completed, the value of b is 5.

Figure 6-14 shows an application that illustrates the difference between how the prefix and postfix increment operators work. Notice from the output in Figure 6-15 that when the prefix increment operator is used on myNumber, the value of myNumber increases from 17 to 18, and the result is stored in answer, which also becomes 18. After the value is reset to 17, the postfix increment operator is used; 17 is assigned to answer, and myNumber is incremented to 18.

```
public class PrefixPostfixDemo
{
    public static void main(String[] args)
    {
        int myNumber, answer;
        myNumber = 17;
        System.out.println("Before incrementing, myNumber is " +
            myNumber);
        answer = ++myNumber;
        System.out.println("After prefix increment, myNumber is " +
            myNumber);
        System.out.println(" and answer is " + answer);
        myNumber = 17;
        System.out.println("Before incrementing, myNumber is " +
            myNumber);
        answer = myNumber++;
        System.out.println("After postfix increment, myNumber is " +
            myNumber);
        System.out.println(" and answer is " + answer);
    }
}
```

Figure 6-14　The `PrefixPostfixDemo` application

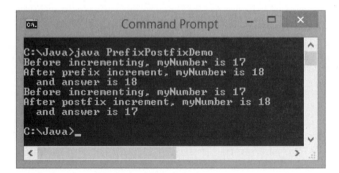

Figure 6-15　Output of the `PrefixPostfixDemo` application

Choosing whether to use a prefix or postfix operator is important when one is part of a larger expression. For example, if d is 5, then 2 * ++d is 12, but 2 * d++ is 10.

Similar logic can be applied when you use the **prefix and postfix decrement operators**. For example, if b = 4 and c = b--, 4 is assigned to c, but b is decreased and takes the value 3. If b = 4 and c = --b, b is decreased to 3 and 3 is assigned to c.

 Watch the video *Using Shortcut Arithmetic Operators*.

TWO TRUTHS & A LIE

Using Shortcut Arithmetic Operators

1. Assume that x = 4 and y = 5. The value of ++y + ++x is 11.

2. Assume that x = 4 and y = 5. The value of y == x++ is true.

3. Assume that x = 4 and y = 5. The value of y += x is 9.

The false statement is #2. If x is 4 and y is 5, then the value of x++ is 4, and so y is not equal to 4.

 You Do It

Working with Prefix and Postfix Increment Operators

Next, you write an application that demonstrates how prefix and postfix operators are used to increment variables and how incrementing affects the expressions that contain these operators.

1. Start a new application named DemoIncrement by typing:

    ```
    public class DemoIncrement
    {
        public static void main(String[] args)
        {
    ```

2. On a new line, add a variable v, and assign it a value of 4. Then declare a variable named plusPlusV, and assign it a value of ++v by typing:

    ```
    int v = 4;
    int plusPlusV = ++v;
    ```

3. The last statement, int plusPlusV = ++v;, increases v to 5, so before declaring a vPlusPlus variable to which you assign v++, reset v to 4 by typing:

    ```
    v = 4;
    int vPlusPlus = v++;
    ```

(continues)

(continued)

4. Add the following statements to display the three values:

```
System.out.println("v is " + v);
System.out.println("++v is " + plusPlusV);
System.out.println("v++ is " + vPlusPlus);
```

5. Add the closing curly brace for the `main()` method and the closing curly brace for the `DemoIncrement` class. Save the file as **DemoIncrement.java**, then compile and execute the program. Your output should look like Figure 6-16.

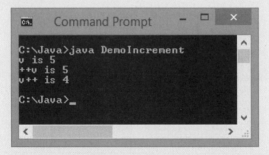

Figure 6-16 Output of the `DemoIncrement` class

6. To illustrate how comparisons are made, add a few more variables to the `DemoIncrement` program. Change the class name to **DemoIncrement2**, and immediately save the file as **DemoIncrement2.java**.

7. After the last `println()` statement, add three new integer variables and two new Boolean variables. The first Boolean variable compares `++w` to `y`; the second Boolean variable compares `x++` to `y`:

```
int w = 17, x = 17, y = 18;
boolean compare1 = (++w == y);
boolean compare2 = (x++ == y);
```

8. Add the following statements to display the values stored in the `compare` variables:

```
System.out.println("First compare is " + compare1);
System.out.println("Second compare is " + compare2);
```

9. Save, compile, and run the program. The output appears in Figure 6-17. Make certain you understand why each statement displays the values it does.

(continues)

(continued)

Experiment by changing the values of the variables, and see if you can predict the output before recompiling and rerunning the program.

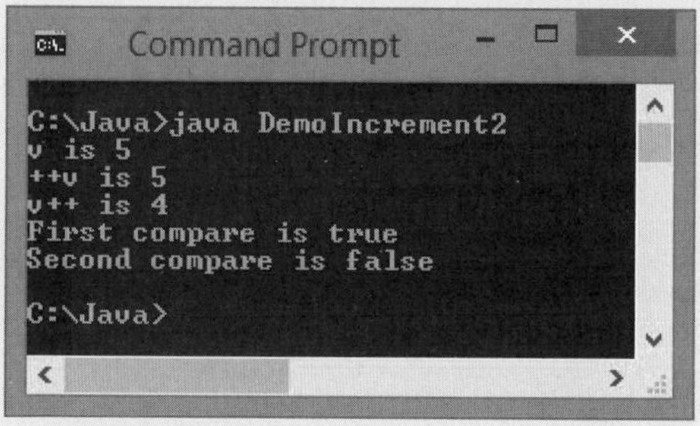

Figure 6-17 Output of the DemoIncrement2 application

Creating a for Loop

A **for loop** is a special loop that is used when a definite number of loop iterations is required; it provides a convenient way to create a counter-controlled loop. Although a while loop can also be used to meet this requirement, the for loop provides you with a shorthand notation for this type of loop. When you use a for loop, you can indicate the starting value for the loop control variable, the test condition that controls loop entry, and the expression that alters the loop control variable—all in one convenient place.

You begin a for loop with the keyword for followed by a set of parentheses. Within the parentheses are three sections separated by exactly two semicolons. The three sections are usually used for the following:

• Initializing the loop control variable

• Testing the loop control variable

• Updating the loop control variable

The body of the for statement follows the parentheses. As with an if statement or a while loop, you can use a single statement as the body of a for loop, or you can use a block of statements enclosed in curly braces. Many programmers recommend that you always use a set of curly braces to surround the body of a for loop for clarity, even when the body contains only a single statement. You should use the conventions recommended by your organization.

Assuming that a variable named val has been declared as an integer, the for statement shown in Figure 6-18 produces the same output as the while statement shown below it—both display the integers 1 through 10.

```
for(val = 1; val < 11; ++val)
{
    System.out.println(val);
}

val = 1;
while(val < 11)
{
    System.out.println(val);
    ++val;
}
```

Figure 6-18 A for loop and a while loop that display the integers 1 through 10

Within the parentheses of the for statement shown in Figure 6-18, the first section prior to the first semicolon initializes val to 1. The program executes this statement once, no matter how many times the body of the for loop executes.

After initialization, program control passes to the middle, or test section, of the for statement that lies between the two semicolons. If the Boolean expression found there evaluates to true, the body of the for loop is entered. In the program segment shown in Figure 6-18, val initially is set to 1, so when val < 11 is tested, it evaluates to true. The loop body displays val. In this example, the loop body is a single statement, so no curly braces are needed (although they could be added).

After the loop body executes, the final one-third of the for loop that follows the second semicolon executes, and val is increased to 2. Following the third section in the for statement, program control returns to the second section, where val is compared to 11 a second time. Because val is still less than 11, the body executes: val (now 2) is displayed, and then the third, altering portion of the for loop executes again. The variable val increases to 3, and the for loop continues. Eventually, when val is not less than 11 (after 1 through 10 have been displayed), the for loop ends, and the program continues with any statements that follow the for loop.

Unconventional for Loops

Although the three sections of the for loop are most commonly used to hold single expressions for initializing, testing, and incrementing, you can also perform the following tasks:

● Initialization of more than one variable in the first section of the for statement by placing commas between the separate statements, as in the following:

```
for(g = 0, h = 1; g < 6; ++g)
```

- You can declare a variable within a `for` statement, as in the following:

  ```
  for(int val = 1; val < 11; ++val)
  ```

  Programmers often use this technique when the loop control variable is not needed in any other part of the program. If you declare a variable within a `for` statement, the variable can only be used in the block that depends on the `for` statement; when the block ends, the variable goes out of scope.

- Performance of more than one test using compound conditions in the second section, as in the following:

  ```
  for(g = 0; g < 3 && h > 1; ++g)
  ```

- Decrementation or performance of some other task in the third section, as in the following:

  ```
  for(g = 5; g >= 1; --g)
  ```

- Performing multiple actions in the third section, separated by commas, as in the following:

  ```
  for(g = 0; g < 10; ++g, ++h, sum += g)
  ```

- You might use method calls in any section of the `for` statement, as in the following example. Here, the `isFinished()` method would be required to return a Boolean value and the `alter()` method would be required to return a data type accepted by x.

  ```
  for(x = initMethod(); isFinished(); x = alter(x))
  ```

- You can leave one or more portions of a `for` loop empty, although the two semicolons are still required as placeholders. For example, if x has been initialized in a previous program statement, you might write the following:

  ```
  for(; x < 10; ++x)
  ```

You might encounter `for` loops in which all three sections of the `for` statement are left empty. For example, consider the `Clock` class in Figure 6-19. The program contains a `for` loop that is meant to execute infinitely and display a clock with an updated time every second. Within the loop, the current time is retrieved using the `LocalDateTime` class. If the `getSecond()` value has changed since the last loop execution, the hour, minute, and second are displayed and the `prevSec` variable is updated. Figure 6-20 shows a typical execution; the user stopped the program after several seconds by holding down the Ctrl key and pressing C.

```
import java.time.*;
public class Clock
{
    public static void main(String[] args)
    {
        LocalDateTime now;
        int nowSec;
        int prevSec = 0;
        for (;;)
        {
            now = LocalDateTime.now();
            nowSec = now.getSecond();
            if(nowSec != prevSec)
            {
                System.out.println(now.getHour() + " : " +
                    now.getMinute() + " : " + nowSec);
                prevSec = nowSec;
            }
        }
    }
}
```

Figure 6-19   The Clock application

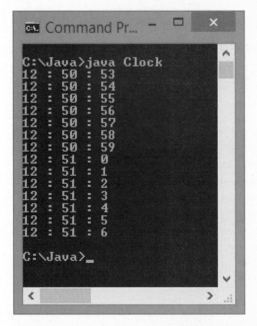

Figure 6-20   Typical execution of the Clock application

 You first learned about the LocalDateTime class in Chapter 4. This class is new in Java 8.

In general, you should use the same loop control variable in all three parts of a for statement, although you might see some programs written by others in which this is not the case. You should also avoid altering the loop control variable in the body of the loop. If a variable is altered both within a for statement and within the block it controls, it can be very difficult to follow the program's logic. This technique can also produce program bugs that are hard to find. Usually, you should use the for loop for its intended purpose—as a shorthand way of programming a definite loop.

Occasionally, you will encounter a for loop that contains no body, but was purposely written that way, such as the following:

```
for(x = 0; x < 100000; ++x);
```

Notice the final semicolon in this statement. This loop is a **do-nothing loop** that performs no actions in its body. It simply uses time—that is, it occupies the central processing unit for thousands of processing cycles because a brief pause is desired during program execution. As with if and while statements, usually you do not want to place a semicolon at the end of the for statement before the body of the loop. Java also contains a built-in method to pause program execution. The sleep() method is part of the Thread class in the java.lang package, and the time for which it pauses is more accurate than using a for loop. You will learn how to use the method as you continue to study Java.

Java also supports an enhanced for loop. You will learn about this loop in the chapter "Introduction to Arrays."

Watch the video *Using the for Loop*.

TWO TRUTHS & A LIE

Creating a for Loop

1. A for loop always must contain two semicolons within its parentheses.

2. The body of a for loop might never execute.

3. Within the parentheses of a for loop, the last section must alter the loop control variable.

The false statement is #3. Frequently, the third section of a for loop is used to alter the loop control variable, but it is not required.

You Do It

Working with Definite Loops

Suppose you want to find all the numbers that divide evenly into 100. You want to write a definite loop—one that executes exactly 100 times. In this section, you write a for loop that sets a variable to 1 and increments it to 100. Each of the 100 times through the loop, if 100 is evenly divisible by the variable, the application displays the number.

1. Start a new application named DivideEvenly by typing the following code. Use a named constant for the 100 value and a variable named var that will hold, in turn, every value from 1 through 100:

```
public class DivideEvenly
{
    public static void main(String[] args)
    {
        final int LIMIT = 100;
        int var;
```

2. Type a statement that explains the purpose of the program:

```
System.out.print(LIMIT + " is evenly divisible by ");
```

3. Write the for loop that varies var from 1 through 100. With each iteration of the loop, test whether 100 % var is 0. If you divide 100 by a number and there is no remainder, the number goes into 100 evenly.

```
for(var = 1; var <= LIMIT; ++var)
    if(LIMIT % var == 0)
        System.out.print(var + " ");
```

4. Add an empty println() statement to advance the insertion point to the next line by typing the following:

```
System.out.println();
```

5. Type the closing curly braces for the main() method and the DivideEvenly class.

6. Save the program as **DivideEvenly**. Compile and run the program. Figure 6-21 shows the output.

(continues)

(continued)

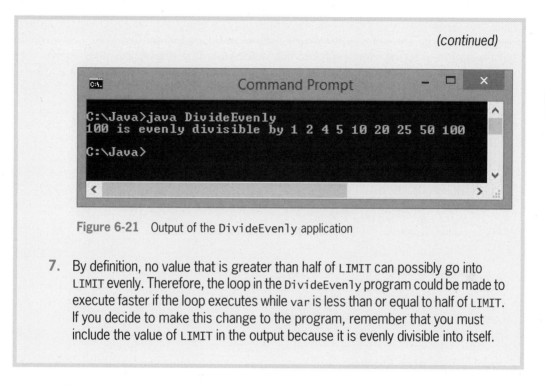

Figure 6-21   Output of the DivideEvenly application

7. By definition, no value that is greater than half of LIMIT can possibly go into LIMIT evenly. Therefore, the loop in the DivideEvenly program could be made to execute faster if the loop executes while var is less than or equal to half of LIMIT. If you decide to make this change to the program, remember that you must include the value of LIMIT in the output because it is evenly divisible into itself.

Learning How and When to Use a do...while Loop

With all the loops you have written so far, the loop body might execute many times, but it is also possible that the loop will not execute at all. For example, recall the bank balance program that displays compound interest, which was shown in Figure 6-8. The program begins by asking whether the user wants to see next year's balance. If the user doesn't enter a *1* for *yes*, the loop body never executes.

Similarly, recall the EnterSmallValue application in Figure 6-10. The user is prompted to enter a value, and if the user enters a value that is 3 or less, the error-reporting loop body never executes.

In each of these cases, the loop control variable is evaluated at the "top" of the loop before the body has a chance to execute. Both while loops and for loops are **pretest loops**—ones in which the loop control variable is tested before the loop body executes.

Sometimes, you might need to ensure that a loop body executes at least one time. If so, you want to write a loop that checks at the "bottom" of the loop after the first iteration. The **do...while loop** is such a loop; it is a **posttest loop**—one in which the loop control variable is tested after the loop body executes.

Figure 6-22 shows the general structure of a do...while loop. Notice that the loop body executes before the loop-controlling question is asked even one time. In other words, the decision is at the end of the loop body, making this a posttest loop. Figure 6-23 shows a BankBalance2 application that contains a do...while loop. The loop starts with the shaded keyword do. The body of the loop follows and is contained within curly braces. The first year's balance is output before the user has any option of responding. At the bottom of the loop, the user is prompted, "Do you want to see the balance at the end of another year?" Now the user has the option of seeing more balances, but viewing the first display was unavoidable. The user's response is checked in the shaded evaluation at the bottom of the loop; if it is *1* for *yes*, the loop repeats. Figure 6-24 shows a typical execution.

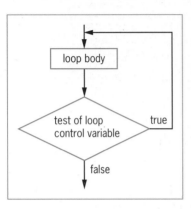

Figure 6-22 General structure of a do…while loop

```
import java.util.Scanner;
public class BankBalance2
{
    public static void main(String[] args)
    {
        double balance;
        int response;
        int year = 1;
        final double INT_RATE = 0.03;
        Scanner keyboard = new Scanner(System.in);
        System.out.print("Enter initial bank balance > ");
        balance = keyboard.nextDouble();
        keyboard.nextLine();
        do
        {
            balance = balance + balance * INT_RATE;
            System.out.println("After year " + year + " at " + INT_RATE +
                " interest rate, balance is $" + balance);
            year = year + 1;
            System.out.println("\nDo you want to see the balance " +
                "at the end of another year?");
            System.out.println("Enter 1 for yes");
            System.out.print("   or any other number for no >> ");
            response = keyboard.nextInt();
        } while(response == 1);
    }
}
```

Figure 6-23 A do…while loop for the BankBalance2 application

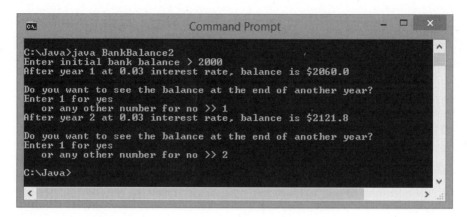

Figure 6-24 Typical execution of the BankBalance2 program

When the body of a do...while loop contains a single statement, you do not need to use curly braces to block the statement. For example, the following loop correctly adds numberValue to total while total remains less than 200:

```
do
    total += numberValue;
while(total < 200);
```

Even though curly braces are not required in this case, many programmers recommend using them. Doing so prevents the third line of code from looking like it should begin a new while loop instead of ending the previous do...while loop. Therefore, even though the result is the same, the following example that includes curly braces is less likely to be misunderstood by a reader:

```
do
{
    total += numberValue;
} while(total < 200);
```

You are never required to use a do...while loop. In the bank balance example, you could achieve the same results as the logic shown in Figure 6-23 by unconditionally displaying the first year's bank balance once before starting the loop, prompting the user, and then starting a while loop that might not be entered. However, when you know you want to perform some task at least one time, the do...while loop is convenient.

327

TWO TRUTHS & A LIE

Learning How and When to Use a do...while Loop

1. The do...while loop checks the value of the loop control variable at the top of the loop prior to loop execution.

2. When the statements in a loop body must execute at least one time, it is convenient to use a do...while loop.

3. When the body of a do...while loop contains a single statement, you do not need to use curly braces to block the statement.

The false statement is #1. The do...while loop checks the value of the loop control variable at the bottom of the loop after one repetition has occurred.

Learning About Nested Loops

Just as if statements can be nested, so can loops. You can place a while loop within a while loop, a for loop within a for loop, a while loop within a for loop, or any other combination. When loops are nested, each pair contains an **inner loop** and an **outer loop**. The inner loop must be entirely contained within the outer loop; loops can never overlap. Figure 6-25 shows a diagram in which the shaded inner loop is nested within an outer loop. You can nest virtually any number of loops; however, at some point, your machine will no longer be able to store all the necessary looping information.

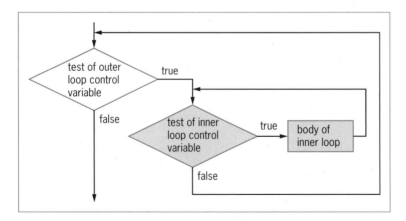

Figure 6-25   Nested loops

In Chapter 5, you learned that decisions can be nested but can never overlap. The same is true for loops.

Suppose you want to display future bank balances while varying both years and interest rates. Figure 6-26 shows an application that contains an outer loop that varies interest rates between specified limits. At the start of the outer loop, the working balance is reset to its initial value so that calculations are correct for each revised interest rate value. The shaded inner loop varies the number of years and displays each calculated balance. Figure 6-27 shows a typical execution.

```java
import java.util.Scanner;
public class BankBalanceByRateAndYear
{
    public static void main(String[] args)
    {
        double initialBalance;
        double balance;
        int year;
        double interest;
        final double LOW = 0.02;
        final double HIGH = 0.05;
        final double INCREMENT = 0.01;
        final int MAX_YEAR = 4;
        Scanner keyboard = new Scanner(System.in);
        System.out.print("Enter initial bank balance > ");
        initialBalance = keyboard.nextDouble();
        keyboard.nextLine();
        for(interest = LOW; interest <= HIGH; interest += INCREMENT)
        {
            balance = initialBalance;
            System.out.println("\nWith an initial balance of $" +
                balance + " at an interest rate of " + interest);
            for(year = 1; year <= MAX_YEAR; ++ year)
            {
                balance = balance + balance * interest;
                System.out.println("After year " + year +
                    " balance is $" + balance);
            }
        }
    }
}
```

Figure 6-26   The BankBalanceByRateAndYear class containing nested loops

```
C:\Java>java BankBalanceByRateAndYear
Enter initial bank balance > 1000.00

With an initial balance of $1000.0 at an interest rate of 0.02
After year 1 balance is $1020.0
After year 2 balance is $1040.4
After year 3 balance is $1061.208
After year 4 balance is $1082.43216

With an initial balance of $1000.0 at an interest rate of 0.03
After year 1 balance is $1030.0
After year 2 balance is $1060.9
After year 3 balance is $1092.727
After year 4 balance is $1125.50881

With an initial balance of $1000.0 at an interest rate of 0.04
After year 1 balance is $1040.0
After year 2 balance is $1081.6
After year 3 balance is $1124.8639999999998
After year 4 balance is $1169.85856

With an initial balance of $1000.0 at an interest rate of 0.05
After year 1 balance is $1050.0
After year 2 balance is $1102.5
After year 3 balance is $1157.625
After year 4 balance is $1215.50625

C:\Java>
```

Figure 6-27 Typical execution of the `BankBalanceByRateAndYear` program

In Figure 6-27, the floating-point calculations result in balances that contain fractions of pennies. If you wrote this program for a bank, you would have to ask whether interest should be compounded on fractions of a cent as it is here, or whether the amounts should be either rounded or truncated.

When you nest loops, sometimes it doesn't make any difference which variable controls the outer loop and which variable controls the inner one, but frequently it does make a difference. When you use a loop within a loop, you should always think of the outer loop as the all-encompassing loop. The variable in the outer loop changes more infrequently. For example, suppose a method named `outputLabel()` creates customer mailing labels in three different colors to use in successive promotional mailings, and that the `color` value is stored as an integer. The following nested loop calls the `outputLabel()` method 60 times and produces three labels for the first customer, three labels for the second customer, and so on:

```
for(customer = 1; customer <= 20; ++customer)
   for(color = 1; color <= 3; ++color)
      outputLabel();
```

The following nested loop also calls `outputLabel()` 60 times, and it ultimately produces the same 60 labels, but it creates 20 labels in the first color, 20 labels in the second color, and then 20 labels in the third color.

```
for(color = 1; color <= 3; ++color)
   for(customer = 1; customer <= 20; ++customer)
      outputLabel();
```

If changing the ink color is a time-consuming process that occurs in the `outputLabel()` method, the second nested loop might execute much faster than the first one.

Watch the video *Nested Loops*.

TWO TRUTHS & A LIE

Learning About Nested Loops

1. You can place a `while` loop within a `while` loop or a `for` loop within a `for` loop, but you cannot mix loop types.

2. An inner nested loop must be entirely contained within its outer loop.

3. The body of the following loop executes 20 times:

```
for(int x = 0; x < 4; ++x)
    for(int y = 0; y < 5; ++y)
        System.out.println("Hi");
```

The false statement is #1. You can place a `while` loop within a `while` loop, a `for` loop within a `for` loop, a `while` loop within a `for` loop, or any other combination.

 You Do It

Working with Nested Loops

Suppose you want to know not just what numbers go evenly into 100, but also what numbers go evenly into every positive number, up to and including 100. You can write 99 more loops—one that shows the numbers that divide evenly into 1, another that shows the numbers that divide evenly into 2, and so on—or you can place the current loop inside a different, outer loop, as you do next.

1. If necessary, open the file **DivideEvenly.java**, change the class name to `DivideEvenly2`, and then save the class as **DivideEvenly2.java**.

2. Add a new variable declaration at the beginning of the file with the other variable declarations:

   `int number;`

   (continues)

(continued)

3. Replace the existing `for` loop with the following nested loop. The outer loop varies `number` from 1 to 100. For each number in the outer loop, the inner loop uses each positive integer from 1 up to the number, and tests whether it divides evenly into the number:

```
for(number = 1; number <= LIMIT; ++number)
{
    System.out.print(number + " is evenly divisible by ");
    for(var = 1; var <= number; ++var)
        if(number % var == 0)
            System.out.print(var + " ");
    System.out.println();
}
```

4. Make certain the file ends with three curly braces—one for the `for` outer loop that varies `number`, one for the `main()` method, and one for the class. The inner loop does not need curly braces because it contains a single output statement, although you could add a set of braces for the loop.

5. Save the file as **DivideEvenly2.java**, and then compile and execute the application. When the output stops scrolling, it should look similar to Figure 6-28.

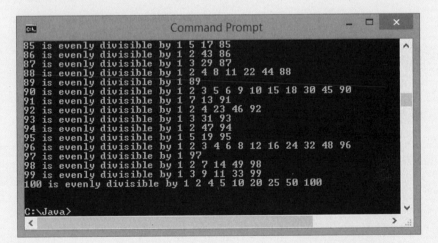

Figure 6-28   Output of the `DivideEvenly2` application when scrolling stops

Improving Loop Performance

Whether you decide to use a `while`, `for`, or `do…while` loop in an application, you can improve loop performance by doing the following:

- Making sure the loop does not include unnecessary operations or statements
- Considering the order of evaluation for short-circuit operators
- Making a comparison to 0
- Employing loop fusion to combine loops
- Using prefix incrementing rather than postfix incrementing

If a loop only executes a few times, implementing the suggestions presented in this section won't change program performance very much, but for a large-scale application in which speed is important, some of these suggestions can make a difference. Thinking about these suggestions also improves your understanding of how loops work.

Avoiding Unnecessary Operations

You can make loops more efficient by not using unnecessary operations or statements, either within a loop's tested expression or within the loop body. For example, suppose a loop should execute while x is less than the sum of two integers, a and b. The loop could be written as:

```
while(x < a + b)
    // loop body
```

Don't Do It
It might be inefficient to recalculate a + b for every loop iteration.

If this loop executes 1,000 times, then the expression a + b is calculated 1,000 times. Instead, if you use the following code, the results are the same, but the arithmetic is performed only once:

```
int sum = a + b;
while(x < sum)
    // loop body
```

Of course, if a or b is altered in the loop body, then a new sum must be calculated with every loop iteration. However, if the sum of a and b is fixed prior to the start of the loop, then writing the code the second way is far more efficient.

Similarly, if the method `getNumberOfEmployees()` always returns the same value during a program's execution, then a loop that begins as follows might unnecessarily call the method many times:

```
while(count < getNumberOfEmployees())…
```

It is more efficient to call the method once, store the result in a variable, and use the variable in the repeated evaluations, as in this example:

```
numEmployees = getNumberOfEmployees();
while(count < numEmployees)…
```

Considering the Order of Evaluation of Short-Circuit Operators

In Chapter 5, you learned that the operands in each part of an AND or an OR expression use short-circuit evaluation; that is, they are evaluated only as much as necessary to determine whether the entire expression is true or false. When a loop might execute many times, it becomes increasingly important to consider the number of evaluations that take place.

For example, suppose a user can request any number of printed copies of a report from 0 to 15, and you want to validate the user's input before proceeding. If you believe that users are far more likely to enter a value that is too high than to enter a negative one, then you want to start a loop that reprompts the user with the following expression:

```
while(requestedNum > LIMIT || requestedNum < 0)…
```

Because you believe that the first Boolean expression is more likely to be true than the second one, you can eliminate testing the second one on more occasions. The order of the expressions might not be very important in a single loop, but if this loop is nested within another loop, the difference in the number of comparisons increases. Similarly, when compound if statements are contained in a loop that might execute thousands of times, the order of the evaluations in if statements is more important than when the evaluation is made only once.

Comparing to Zero

Making a comparison to 0 is faster than making a comparison to any other value. Therefore, if your application makes comparison to 0 feasible, you can improve loop performance by structuring your loops to compare the loop control variable to 0 instead of some other value. For example, a loop that performs based on a variable that varies from 0 up to 100,000 executes the same number of times as a loop based on a variable that varies from 100,000 down to 0. However, the second loop performs slightly faster. Comparing a value to 0 instead of other values is faster because in a compiled language, condition flags for the comparison are set once, no matter how many times the loop executes. Comparing a value to 0 is faster than comparing to other values, no matter which comparison operator you use—greater than, less than, equal to, and so on.

Figure 6-29 contains a program that tests the execution times of two nested do-nothing loops, which are shaded in the figure. The program declares variables to hold a startTime before each nested loop begins and an endTime after each nested loop is complete. Before each nested loop execution, the current time is retrieved from the LocalDateTime class and the value of the nanoseconds (billionths of a second) is retrieved using the getNano() method. After each nested loop repeats 100,000 times, the current time is retrieved again. Subtracting one time from the other computes the interval, and dividing by 1 million converts nanoseconds to more readable milliseconds. As the execution in Figure 6-30 shows, there is a small difference in execution time between the two loops—about 1/20 of a second. The amount of time will vary on different machines, and varies for subsequent executions on the same machine depending on events occurring elsewhere on the machine during the same time period, but the loop that uses the 0 comparison will never be slower than the other one. The difference would become more pronounced with additional repetitions or further nesting levels. For example, if the value of the loop control variable was needed within the loops to display a count to the user, then you might be required to vary the loop starting with 0. However, if the purposes of the loops are just to count iterations, you might consider making the loop comparison use 0.

```java
import java.time.*;
public class CompareLoopTimes
{
    public static void main(String[] args)
    {
        int startTime, endTime;
        final int REPEAT = 100_000;
        final int FACTOR = 1_000_000;
        LocalDateTime now;
        now = LocalDateTime.now();
        startTime = now.getNano();
        for(int x = 0; x <= REPEAT; ++x)
            for(int y = 0; y <= REPEAT; ++y);
        now = LocalDateTime.now();
        endTime = now.getNano();
        System.out.println("Time for loops starting from 0: " +
            ((endTime - startTime) / FACTOR) + " milliseconds");
        now = LocalDateTime.now();
        startTime = now.getNano();
        for(int x = REPEAT; x >= 0; --x)
            for(int y = REPEAT; y >= 0; --y);
        now = LocalDateTime.now();
        endTime = now.getNano();
        System.out.println("Time for loops ending with 0: " +
            ((endTime - startTime) / FACTOR) + " milliseconds");
    }
}
```

Figure 6-29 The CompareLoopTimes application

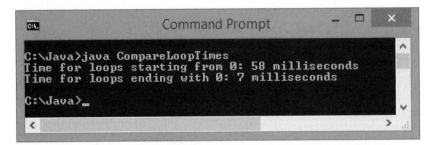

Figure 6-30　Typical execution of the CompareLoopTimes application

 Note the use of the underscores in the large numbers in the CompareLoopTimes application. In Chapter 2, you learned that the underscores are not required, but they make the numbers easier to read.

 If you execute the program in Figure 6-29, you probably will see different results. With a fast operating system, you might not see the differences shown in Figure 6-30. If so, experiment with the program by increasing the value of REPEAT or by adding more nested levels to the loops.

 When you execute the CompareLoopTimes program, you will occasionally see a negative number output. Such output occurs when the nanoseconds values retrieved fall in different seconds so that the start time is a very high nanosecond number in one second and the end time is a very low number in the next second. An exercise at the end of this chapter asks you to rectify this problem.

Employing Loop Fusion

Loop fusion is the technique of combining two loops into one. For example, suppose you want to call two methods 100 times each. You can set a constant named TIMES to 100 and use the following code:

```java
for(int x = 0; x < TIMES; ++x)
    method1();
for(int x = 0; x < TIMES; ++x)
    method2();
```

However, you can also use the following code:

```java
for(int x = 0; x < TIMES; ++x)
{
    method1();
    method2();
}
```

Fusing loops will not work in every situation; sometimes all the activities for all the executions of method1() must be finished before those in method2() can begin. However, if the two methods do not depend on each other, fusing the loops can improve performance.

Using Prefix Incrementing Rather than Postfix Incrementing

Probably the most common action after the second semicolon in a `for` statement is to increment the loop control variable. In most textbooks and in many professional programs, the postfix increment operator is used for this purpose, as in the following:

```
for(int x = 0; x < LIMIT; x++)
```

Because incrementing x is a stand-alone statement in the `for` loop, the result is identical whether you use x++ or ++x. However, using the prefix increment operator produces a faster loop. Consider the program in Figure 6-31. It is similar to the `CompareLoopTimes` application in Figure 6-29, but instead of comparing loops that count up and down, it compares loops that use prefix and postfix incrementing. The two timed, do-nothing loops that repeat 50,000 times each are shaded in the figure.

```
import java.time.*;
public class CompareLoopTimes2
{
    public static void main(String[] args)
    {
        int startTime, endTime;
        final int REPEAT = 50_000;
        final int FACTOR = 1_000_000;
        LocalDateTime now;
        now = LocalDateTime.now();
        startTime = now.getNano();
        for(int x = 0; x <= REPEAT; ++x);
        now = LocalDateTime.now();
        endTime = now.getNano();
        System.out.println("Time with prefix increment: " +
            ((endTime - startTime) / FACTOR) + " milliseconds");
        now = LocalDateTime.now();
        startTime = now.getNano();
        for(int x = 0; x <= REPEAT; x++);
        now = LocalDateTime.now();
        endTime = now.getNano();
        System.out.println("Time with postfix increment: " +
            ((endTime - startTime) / FACTOR) + " milliseconds");
    }
}
```

Figure 6-31   The `CompareLoopTimes2` program

Figure 6-32 shows a typical execution of the program. The program that uses prefix incrementing runs slightly faster than the one that uses postfix incrementing because when the compiler uses postfix incrementing, it first makes a copy of the variable it uses as the expression's value, and then it increments the variable. In other words, the operators are methods that behave as follows:

- When you use the prefix incrementing method, as in ++x, the method receives a reference to x, increases it, and returns the increased value.

- When you use the postfix incrementing method, as in x++, the method receives a reference to x, makes a copy of the value and stores it, increments the value indicated by the reference, and returns the copy. The extra time required to make the copy is what causes postfix incrementing to take longer.

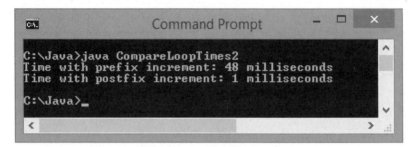

Figure 6-32   Typical execution of the `CompareLoopTimes2` application

As you can see in Figure 6-32, the difference in duration for 50,000 loops is very small—only 47/1000 of a second. If you run the program multiple times, you will get different results. However, using the prefix operator typically saves a small amount of time. As a professional, you will encounter programmers who insist on using either postfix or prefix increments in their loops. You should follow the conventions established by your organization, but now you have the tools to prove that prefix incrementing is faster.

A Final Note on Improving Loop Performance

In the previous sections, you have learned to improve loop performance by eliminating unnecessary operations, considering the order of evaluation for short-circuit operators, making comparisons to 0, employing loop fusion, and using prefix incrementing rather than postfix incrementing. As you become an experienced programmer, you will discover other ways to enhance the operation of the programs you write. You should always be on the lookout for ways to improve program performance. However, almost all business professionals agree that if saving a few milliseconds ends up making your code harder to understand, you have not succeeded. You almost always should err in favor of programs that are more readable and easier to maintain, even if they execute more slowly.

TWO TRUTHS & A LIE

Improving Loop Performance

1. You can improve the performance of a loop by making sure the loop does not include unnecessary operations in the tested expression.

2. You can improve loop performance by making sure the loop does not include unnecessary operations in the body of the loop.

3. You can improve loop performance when two conditions must both be true by testing for the most likely occurrence first.

The false statement is #3. You can improve loop performance when two conditions must both be true by testing for the least likely occurrence first. That way, the second test will need to be performed less frequently.

 You Do It

Comparing Execution Times for Separate and Fused Loops

In this section, you compare the execution times for accomplishing the same tasks using two loops or a single one.

1. Start a new application named **TestFusedLoopTime**.

    ```
    import java.time.*;
    public class TestFusedLoopTime
    {
        public static void main(String[] args)
        {
    ```

2. Create variables to hold starting and ending times for loop execution. Also declare a loop control variable, x, and two named constants that hold a number of times to repeat loops and a factor for converting nanoseconds to milliseconds:

    ```
    int startTime, endTime;
    int x;
    final int REPEAT = 5_000_000;
    final int FACTOR = 1_000_000;
    ```

    Recall that the underscore can be used to make long numbers easier to read. The underscores could be omitted.

(continues)

(continued)

3. Declare a `LocalDateTime` object, initialize it to a starting time, and extract its nanoseconds component.

```
LocalDateTime now;
now = LocalDateTime.now();
startTime = now.getNano();
```

4. In a loop that repeats 5 million times, call a method named `method1()`. When the calls to `method1()` are complete, execute a second loop that also repeats 5 million times, calling another method named `method2()`.

```
for(x = 0; x < REPEAT; ++x)
    method1();
for(x = 0; x < REPEAT; ++x)
    method2();
```

5. When both loops are finished, get the current time, extract the nanoseconds value, and display the difference between the start time and end time, expressed in milliseconds:

```
now = LocalDateTime.now();
endTime = now.getNano();
System.out.println("Time for loops executed separately: " +
    ((endTime - startTime) / FACTOR) + " milliseconds");
```

6. Get a new starting time, and call `method1()` and `method2()` 5 million times each, blocked in a single loop.

```
now = LocalDateTime.now();
startTime = now.getNano();
for(x = 0; x < REPEAT; ++x)
{
    method1();
    method2();
}
```

7. Get the ending time for the loop, and display the value of the elapsed interval. Add a closing curly brace for the method.

```
now = LocalDateTime.now();
endTime = now.getNano();
System.out.println("Time for loops executed in a block: " +
    ((endTime - startTime) / FACTOR) + " milliseconds");
}
```

(continues)

(continued)

8. Create the two methods named method1() and method2(). Each is simply a stub—a method that contains no statements. Add a closing curly brace for the class.

```
public static void method1()
{
}
public static void method2()
{
}
}
```

9. Save the file as **TestFusedLoopTime.java**, and then compile and execute it. Figure 6-33 shows a typical execution. The times might differ on your system, but you should be able to see that using a single loop significantly improves performance over using separate loops.

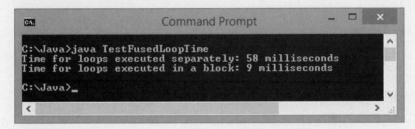

Figure 6-33   Typical execution of the TestFusedLoopTime program

10. Experiment with increasing and decreasing the value of REPEAT, and observe the effects. Experiment with adding statements to method1() and method2(), perhaps including do-nothing loops within one or both of the methods. The time values you observe might also differ when you run the program at different times, depending on what other tasks are running on your system concurrently.

Don't Do It

- Don't insert a semicolon at the end of a `while` clause before the loop body; doing so creates an empty loop body.

- Don't forget to block multiple statements that should execute in a loop.

- Don't make the mistake of checking for invalid data using a decision instead of a loop. Users might enter incorrect data multiple times, so a loop is the superior choice for input validation.

- Don't ignore subtleties in the boundaries used to stop loop performance. For example, looping while interest rates are less than 8% is different than looping while interest rates are no more than 8%.

- Don't repeat steps within a loop that could just as well be placed outside the loop; your program performance will improve.

Key Terms

A **loop** is a structure that allows repeated execution of a block of statements.

A **loop body** is the block of statements that executes when the Boolean expression that controls the loop is `true`.

An **iteration** is one loop execution.

A **while loop** executes a body of statements continually as long as the Boolean expression that controls entry into the loop continues to be `true`.

A **definite loop** or a **counted loop** is one that executes a predetermined number of times.

An **indefinite loop** is one in which the final number of loops is unknown.

A **loop control variable** is a variable whose value determines whether loop execution continues.

An **infinite loop** is a loop that never ends.

An **empty body** is a block with no statements in it.

A **counter-controlled loop** is a definite loop.

Incrementing a variable adds 1 to its value.

Decrementing a variable reduces its value by 1.

An **event-controlled loop** is an indefinite loop in which the number of executions is determined by user actions.

A **sentinel** is a value that stops a loop.

Validating data is the process of ensuring that a value falls within a specified range.

A **priming read** or **priming input** is the first input statement prior to a loop that will execute subsequent input statements for the same variable.

Counting is the process of continually incrementing a variable to keep track of the number of occurrences of some event.

Accumulating is the process of repeatedly increasing a value by some amount to produce a total.

The **add and assign operator** (+=) alters the value of the operand on the left by adding the operand on the right to it.

The **subtract and assign operator** (−=) alters the value of the operand on the left by subtracting the operand on the right from it.

The **multiply and assign operator** (*=) alters the value of the operand on the left by multiplying the operand on the right by it.

The **divide and assign operator** (/=) alters the value of the operand on the left by dividing the operand on the right into it.

The **remainder and assign operator** (%=) alters the value of the operand on the left by assigning the remainder when the left operand is divided by the right operand.

The **prefix ++**, also known as the **prefix increment operator**, adds 1 to a variable, then evaluates it.

The **postfix ++**, also known as the **postfix increment operator**, evaluates a variable, then adds 1 to it.

The **prefix and postfix decrement operators** subtract 1 from a variable.

A **for loop** is a special loop that can be used when a definite number of loop iterations is required.

A **do-nothing loop** is one that performs no actions other than looping.

A **pretest loop** is one in which the loop control variable is tested before the loop body executes.

The **do...while loop** executes a loop body at least one time; it checks the loop control variable at the bottom of the loop after one repetition has occurred.

A **posttest loop** is one in which the loop control variable is tested after the loop body executes.

An **inner loop** is contained entirely within another loop.

An **outer loop** contains another loop.

Loop fusion is the technique of combining two loops into one.

Chapter Summary

- A loop is a structure that allows repeated execution of a block of statements. Within a looping structure, a Boolean expression is evaluated, and if it is true, a block of statements called the loop body executes; then the Boolean expression is evaluated again.

- You can use a while loop to execute a body of statements continually while some condition continues to be true. To correctly execute a while loop, you should initialize a loop control variable, test it in a while statement, and then alter the loop control variable in the loop body.

- The add and assign operator (+=) adds the value on the right to the variable on the left. Similar operations are available for subtraction, multiplication, and division. The prefix and postfix increment operators increase a variable's value by 1. The prefix and postfix decrement operators reduce a variable's value by 1. The prefix operator alters its operand, then uses it; the postfix operator uses the value, then alters it.

- A for loop initializes, tests, and increments in one statement. There are three sections within the parentheses of a for loop that are separated by exactly two semicolons.

- The do...while loop tests a Boolean expression after one repetition has taken place, at the bottom of the loop.

- Loops can be nested, creating inner and outer loops.

- You can improve loop performance by making sure the loop does not include unnecessary operations or statements and by considering factors such as short-circuit evaluation, zero comparisons, loop fusion, and prefix incrementing.

Review Questions

1. A structure that allows repeated execution of a block of statements is a _____ .

   a. cycle   c. ring
   b. loop   d. band

2. A loop that never ends is a(n) _____ loop.

   a. iterative   c. structured
   b. infinite   d. illegal

3. To construct a loop that works correctly, you should initialize a loop control _____ .

   a. variable   c. structure
   b. constant   d. condition

4. What is the output of the following code?

```
b = 1;
while(b < 4)
    System.out.print(b + " ");
```

   a. 1   c. 1 2 3 4

   b. 1 2 3   d. 1 1 1 1 1 1...

5. What is the output of the following code?

```
b = 1;
while(b < 4)
{
    System.out.print(b + " ");
    b = b + 1;
}
```

   a. 1   c. 1 2 3 4

   b. 1 2 3   d. 1 1 1 1 1...

6. What is the output of the following code?

```
e = 1;
while(e < 4);
    System.out.print(e + " ");
```

   a. Nothing   c. 1 2 3 4

   b. 1 1 1 1 1 1...   d. 4 4 4 4 4 4...

7. If `total` = 100 and `amt` = 200, then after the statement `total += amt`, _____ .

   a. `total` is equal to 200   c. `amt` is equal to 100

   b. `total` is equal to 300   d. `amt` is equal to 300

8. The prefix `++` is a _____ operator.

   a. unary   c. tertiary

   b. binary   d. postfix

9. If `g` = 5, then after `h = ++g`, the value of `h` is _____ .

   a. 4   c. 6

   b. 5   d. 7

10. If `m` = 9, then after `n = m++`, the value of `m` is _____ .

   a. 8   c. 10

   b. 9   d. 11

11. If `m` = 9, then after `n = m++`, the value of `n` is _____ .

   a. 8   c. 10

   b. 9   d. 11

12. If j = 5 and k = 6, then the value of j++ == k is _____ .

    a. 5   c. true

    b. 6   d. false

13. You must always include _____ in a for loop's parentheses.

    a. two semicolons   c. two commas

    b. three semicolons   d. three commas

14. What does the following statement output?

```
for(a = 0; a < 5; ++a)
   System.out.print(a + " ");
```

    a. 0 0 0 0 0   c. 0 1 2 3 4 5

    b. 0 1 2 3 4   d. nothing

15. What does the following statement output?

```
for(b = 1; b > 3; ++b)
   System.out.print(b + " ");
```

    a. 1 1 1   c. 1 2 3 4

    b. 1 2 3   d. nothing

16. What does the following statement output?

```
for(f = 1, g = 4; f < g; ++f, --g)
   System.out.print(f + " " + g + " ");
```

    a. 1 4 2 5 3 6 4 7...   c. 1 4 2 3

    b. 1 4 2 3 3 2   d. nothing

17. The loop that performs its conditional check at the bottom of the loop is a _____ loop.

    a. while   c. for

    b. do...while   d. for...while

18. What does the following program segment output?

```
d = 0;
do
{
   System.out.print(d + " ");
   d++;
} while (d < 2);
```

    a. 0   c. 0 1 2

    b. 0 1   d. nothing

19. What does the following program segment output?

```
for(f = 0; f < 3; ++f)
   for(g = 0; g < 2; ++g)
      System.out.print(f + " " + g + " ");
```

a. 0 0 0 1 1 0 1 1 2 0 2 1

b. 0 1 0 2 0 3 1 1 1 2 1 3

c. 0 1 0 2 1 1 1 2

d. 0 0 0 1 0 2 1 0 1 1 1 2 2 0 2 1 2 2

20. What does the following program segment output?

```
for(m = 0; m < 4; ++m);
   for(n = 0; n < 2; ++n);
      System.out.print(m + " " + n + " ");
```

a. 0 0 0 1 1 0 1 1 2 0 2 1 3 0 3 1

b. 0 1 0 2 1 1 1 2 2 1 2 2

c. 4 2

d. 3 1

Exercises

Programming Exercises

1. When you execute the CompareLoopTimes program shown in Figure 6-29, you will occasionally see a negative number output when the nanoseconds values retrieved fall in different seconds. Modify the program to fix this problem, and save the file as **CompareLoopTimes3.java**. (*Hint:* It might take hundreds or thousands of executions for you to "catch" the program near the end of a second in order to test your modifications. For testing purposes, you can assign values to the start and stop times instead of retrieving them from the LocalDateTime class.)

2. a. Write an application that counts by three from 3 through 300 inclusive, and that starts a new line after every multiple of 30 (30, 60, 90, and so on). Save the file as **CountByThrees.java**.

   b. Modify the CountByThrees application so that the user enters the value to count by. Start each new line after 10 values have been displayed. Save the file as **CountByAnything.java**.

3. Write an application that asks a user to type an even number or the sentinel value 999 to stop. When the user types an even number, display the message "Good job!" and then ask for another input. When the user types an odd number, display an error message and then ask for another input. When the user types the sentinel value 999, end the program. Save the file as **EvenEntryLoop.java**.

4. Write an application that displays the factorial for every integer value from 1 to 10. A factorial of a number is the product of that number multiplied by each positive integer lower than it. For example, 4 factorial is 4 * 3 * 2 * 1, or 24. Save the file as **Factorials.java**.

5. Write an application that prompts a user for two integers and displays every integer between them. Display a message if there are no integers between the entered values. Make sure the program works regardless of which entered value is larger. Save the file as **Inbetween.java**.

6. Write an application that displays every perfect number from 1 through 1,000. A perfect number is one that equals the sum of all the numbers that divide evenly into it. For example, 6 is perfect because 1, 2, and 3 divide evenly into it, and their sum is 6; however, 12 is not a perfect number because 1, 2, 3, 4, and 6 divide evenly into it, and their sum is greater than 12. Save the file as **Perfect.java**.

7. Write an application that uses a loop to create the pattern of Os shown in Figure 6-34, in which each O is displayed one additional space to the right. Save the file as **DiagonalOs.java**.

Figure 6-34   Output of the `DiagonalOs` application

8. Write an application that allows a user to enter any number of student test scores until the user enters 999. If the score entered is less than 0 or more than 100, display an appropriate message and do not use the score. After all the scores have been entered, display the number of scores entered, the highest score, the lowest score, and the arithmetic average. Save the file as **TestScoreStatistics.java**.

9. Write an application that computes a business's potential profits each year for 20 years using the following assumptions: (1) Gross profit in the first year is projected to be $20,000. (2) Expenses in the first year are expected to be $35,000. (3) Net profit or loss is gross profit minus expenses. (4) Gross profits are expected to increase 10 percent each year. (5) Expenses are expected to increase 4 percent each year. Display the year, the gross profit, the expenses, and the net profit for each year. Also display the year in which a net profit is first reported. Save the file as **WhenProfitable.java**.

10. a. Write an application that prompts a user for the number of years the user has until retirement and the amount of money the user can save annually. If the user enters 0 or a negative number for either value, reprompt the user until valid entries are made. Assume that no interest is earned on the money. Display the amount of money the user will have at retirement. Save the file as **RetirementGoal.java**.

   b. Modify the RetirementGoal application to display the amount of money the user will have if the user earns 5% interest on the balance every year. Save the file as **RetirementGoal2.java**.

11. Pickering Manufacturing Company randomly selects one of its four factories to inspect each week. Write an application that determines which factory will be selected each week for the next 52 weeks. Use the Math.random() function explained in Appendix D to generate a factory number between 1 and 4; you use a statement similar to:

```
factory = 1 + (int) (Math.random() * 4);
```

After each selection, display the factory to inspect, and after the 52 selections are complete, display the percentage of inspections at each factory for the year. Run the application several times until you are confident that the factory selection is random. Save the file as **Inspections.java**.

12. Assume that the population of Mexico is 121 million and that the population increases 1.01 percent annually. Assume that the population of the United States is 315 million and that the population is reduced 0.15 percent annually. Write an application that displays the populations for the two countries every year until the population of Mexico exceeds that of the United States, and display the number of years it took. Save the file as **Population.java**.

13. The Huntington High School basketball team has five players named Art, Bob, Cal, Dan, and Eli. Accept the number of points scored by each player in a game and create a bar chart that illustrates the points scored, similar to the chart in Figure 6-35. Save the file as **BarChart.java**.

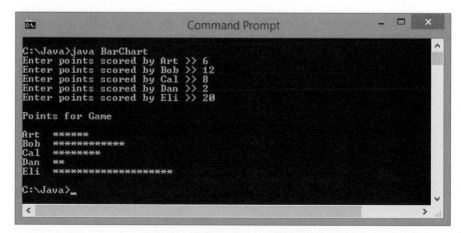

Figure 6-35 Typical execution of the BarChart application

14. a. Create a class named Purchase. Each Purchase contains an invoice number, amount of sale, and amount of sales tax. Include set methods for the invoice number and sale amount. Within the set() method for the sale amount, calculate the sales tax as 5% of the sale amount. Also include a display method that displays a purchase's details. Save the file as **Purchase.java**.

   b. Create an application that declares a Purchase object and prompts the user for purchase details. When you prompt for an invoice number, do not let the user proceed until a number between 1,000 and 8,000 has been entered. When you prompt for a sale amount, do not proceed until the user has entered a nonnegative value. After a valid Purchase object has been created, display the object's invoice number, sale amount, and sales tax. Save the file as **CreatePurchase.java**.

Debugging Exercises

1. Each of the following files in the Chapter06 folder of your downloadable student files has syntax and/or logic errors. In each case, determine the problem and fix the program. After you correct the errors, save each file using the same filename preceded with *Fix*. For example, save DebugSix1.java as **FixDebugSix1.java**.

   a. DebugSix1.java   c. DebugSix3.java
   b. DebugSix2.java   d. DebugSix4.java

Game Zone

1. a. Write an application that creates a quiz. The quiz should contain at least five questions about a hobby, popular music, astronomy, or any other personal interest. Each question should be a multiple-choice question with at least four answer options. When the user answers the question correctly, display a congratulatory message. If the user responds to a question incorrectly, display an appropriate message as well as the correct answer. At the end of the quiz, display the number of correct and incorrect answers, and the percentage of correct answers. Save the file as **Quiz.java**.

   b. Modify the Quiz application so that the user is presented with each question continually until it is answered correctly. Remove the calculation for percentage of correct answers—all users will have 100% correct by the time they complete the application. Save the file as **Quiz2.java**.

2. In Chapter 1, you created a class called RandomGuess. In this game, players guess a number, the application generates a random number, and players determine whether they were correct. In Chapter 5, you improved the application to display a message indicating whether the player's guess was correct, too high, or too low.

Now, add a loop that continuously prompts the user for the number, indicating whether the guess is high or low, until the user enters the correct value. After the user correctly guesses the number, display a count of the number of attempts it took. Save the file as **RandomGuess3.java**.

3. In Chapter 4, you created a Die class from which you could instantiate an object containing a random value from 1 through 6. Now use the class to create a simple dice game in which the user chooses a number between 2 (the lowest total possible from two dice) and 12 (the highest total possible). The user "rolls" two dice up to three times. If the number chosen by the user comes up, the user wins and the game ends. If the number does not come up within three rolls, the computer wins. Save the application as **TwoDice3.java**.

4. a. Using the Die class you created in Chapter 4, create a version of the dice game Pig that a user can play against the computer. The object of the game is to be the first to score 100 points. The user and computer take turns rolling a pair of dice following these rules:

   - On a turn, each player "rolls" two dice. If no 1 appears, the dice values are added to a running total, and the player can choose whether to roll again or pass the turn to the other player.

   - If a *1* appears on one of the dice, nothing more is added to the player's total and it becomes the other player's turn.

   - If a *1* appears on both of the dice, not only is the player's turn over, but the player's entire accumulated score is reset to 0.

   - In this version of the game, when the computer does not roll a 1 and can choose whether to roll again, generate a random value between 0 and 1. Have the computer continue to roll the dice when the value is 0.5 or more, and have the computer quit and pass the turn to the player when the value is not 0.5 or more.

   Save the game as **PigDiceGame.java**.

   b. Modify the PigDiceGame application so that if a player rolls a 1, not only does the player's turn end, but all the player's earned points during that round are eliminated. (Points from earlier rounds are not affected. That is, when either the player or computer rolls a 1, all the points accumulated since the other's turn are subtracted.) Save the game as **PigDiceGame2.java**.

5. Two people play the game of Count 21 by taking turns entering a 1, 2, or 3, which is added to a running total. The player who adds the value that makes the total exceed 21 loses the game. Create a game of Count 21 in which a player competes against the computer, and program a strategy that always allows the computer to win. On any turn, if the player enters a value other than 1, 2, or 3, force the player to reenter the value. Save the game as **Count21.java**.

Case Problems

1. Carly's Catering provides meals for parties and special events. In previous chapters, you developed a class that holds catering event information and an application that tests the methods using four objects of the class. Now modify the EventDemo class to do the following:

    • Continuously prompt for the number of guests for each Event until the value falls between 5 and 100 inclusive.

    • For one of the Event objects, create a loop that displays "Please come to my event!" as many times as there are guests for the Event.

    Save the modified file as **EventDemo.java**.

2. Sammy's Seashore Supplies rents beach equipment to tourists. In previous chapters, you developed a class that holds equipment rental information and an application that tests the methods using four objects of the class. Now modify the RentalDemo class to do the following:

    • Continuously prompt for the number of minutes of each Rental until the value falls between 60 and 7,200 inclusive.

    • For one of the Rental objects, create a loop that displays "Coupon good for 10 percent off next rental" as many times as there are full hours in the Rental.

    Save the modified file as **RentalDemo.java**.

Characters, Strings, and the StringBuilder

In this chapter, you will:

◎ Identify string data problems

◎ Use Character class methods

◎ Declare and compare String objects

◎ Use other String methods

◎ Use the StringBuilder and StringBuffer classes

Understanding String Data Problems

Manipulating characters and strings provides some challenges for the beginning Java programmer. For example, consider the `TryToCompareStrings` application shown in Figure 7-1. The `main()` method declares a `String` named `aName` and assigns "Carmen" to it. The user is then prompted to enter a name. The application compares the two names using the equivalency operator (`==`) and displays one of two messages indicating whether the strings are equivalent.

```java
import java.util.Scanner;
public class TryToCompareStrings
{
    public static void main(String[] args)
    {
        String aName = "Carmen";
        String anotherName;
        Scanner input = new Scanner(System.in);
        System.out.print("Enter your name > ");
        anotherName = input.nextLine();
        if(aName == anotherName)
            System.out.println(aName + " equals " + anotherName);
        else
            System.out.println(aName + " does not equal " + anotherName);
    }
}
```

Don't Do It
Do not use == to compare Strings' contents.

Figure 7-1   The `TryToCompareStrings` application

Figure 7-2 shows a typical execution of the application. When the user types "Carmen" as the value for `anotherName`, the application concludes that the two names are not equal.

```
C:\Java>java TryToCompareStrings
Enter your name > Carmen
Carmen does not equal Carmen

C:\Java>_
```

Figure 7-2   Typical execution of the `TryToCompareStrings` application

The application in Figure 7-1 seems to produce incorrect results. The problem stems from the fact that in Java, `String` is a class, and each created `String` is an object. As an object, a `String` variable name is not a simple data type—it is a **reference**; that is, a variable that holds a memory address. Therefore, when you compare two `String` objects using the `==` operator, you are not comparing their values, but their computer memory locations.

Programmers want to compare the contents of memory locations (the values stored there) more frequently than they want to compare the addresses of the locations. Fortunately, the creators of Java have provided three classes that you can use when working with text data; these classes provide you with many methods that make working with characters and strings easier:

- **Character**—A class whose instances can hold a single character value and whose methods manipulate and inspect single-character data

- **String**—A class for working with fixed-string data—that is, unchanging data composed of multiple characters

- **StringBuilder** and **StringBuffer**—Classes for storing and manipulating changeable data composed of multiple characters

---

TWO TRUTHS & A LIE

Understanding String Data Problems

1. A String is a simple data type that can hold text data.

2. Programmers want to compare the values of Strings more frequently than they want to compare their memory addresses.

3. Character, String, and StringBuilder are useful built-in classes for working with text data.

The false statement is #1. A String variable name is a reference; that is, it holds a memory address.

Using Character Class Methods

You learned in Chapter 2 that the char data type is used to hold any single character—for example, a letter, digit, or punctuation mark. Recall that char literals are surrounded by single quotation marks. Because char is a primitive data type, variables of type char are not references, so you can compare their values using relational operators such as == and >. Comparisons are made using each character's Unicode value. You first learned about Unicode values in Chapter 2. Character comparisons are evaluated how you generally would expect them to be—alphabetically. For example, if yourInitial is 'A' and myInitial is 'B', then yourInitial < myInitial is true.

In addition to the primitive data type char, Java offers a Character class. The Character class contains standard methods for testing the values of characters. Table 7-1 describes many of the Character class methods. The methods that begin with "is", such as isUpperCase(), return a Boolean value that can be used in comparison statements; the methods that begin with "to", such as toUpperCase(), return a character that has been converted to the stated format.

Method	Description
isUpperCase()	Tests if character is uppercase
toUpperCase()	Returns the uppercase equivalent of the argument; no change is made if the argument is not a lowercase letter
isLowerCase()	Tests if character is lowercase
toLowerCase()	Returns the lowercase equivalent of the argument; no change is made if the argument is not an uppercase letter
isDigit()	Returns true if the argument is a digit (0–9) and false otherwise
isLetter()	Returns true if the argument is a letter and false otherwise
isLetterOrDigit()	Returns true if the argument is a letter or digit and false otherwise
isWhitespace()	Returns true if the argument is whitespace and false otherwise; this includes the space, tab, newline, carriage return, and form feed

Table 7-1   Commonly used methods of the `Character` class

The `Character` class is defined in `java.lang` and is automatically imported into every program you write. The `Character` class inherits from `java.lang.Object`. You will learn more about the `Object` class when you study inheritance concepts in the chapter "Introduction to Inheritance."

Figure 7-3 contains an application that uses many of the methods shown in Table 7-1. The application defines the variable aChar as `'C'` and displays information about it.

```java
import java.util.Scanner;
public class CharacterInfo
{
   public static void main(String[] args)
   {
      char aChar = 'C';
      System.out.println("The character is " + aChar);
      if(Character.isUpperCase(aChar))
         System.out.println(aChar + " is uppercase");
      else
         System.out.println(aChar + " is not uppercase");
      if(Character.isLowerCase(aChar))
         System.out.println(aChar + " is lowercase");
      else
         System.out.println(aChar + " is not lowercase");
      aChar = Character.toLowerCase(aChar);
      System.out.println("After toLowerCase(), aChar is " + aChar);
      aChar = Character.toUpperCase(aChar);
      System.out.println("After toUpperCase(), aChar is " + aChar);
```

Figure 7-3   The `CharacterInfo` application *(continues)*

357

(continued)

```
        if(Character.isLetterOrDigit(aChar))
            System.out.println(aChar + " is a letter or digit");
        else
            System.out.println(aChar +
                " is neither a letter nor a digit");
        if(Character.isWhitespace(aChar))
            System.out.println(aChar + " is whitespace");
        else
            System.out.println(aChar + " is not whitespace");
    }
}
```

Figure 7-3   The CharacterInfo application

 You can tell that each of the Character class methods used in the CharacterInfo application in Figure 7-3 is a static method because the method name is used without an object reference—you use only the class name, a dot, and the method name. You learned about the difference between static and instance methods in Chapter 3.

The output of the CharacterInfo application is shown in Figure 7-4, where you can see the following:

- The value returned by the isUpperCase() method is true.

- The value returned by the isLowerCase() method is false.

- The value returned by the toLowerCase() method is 'c'.

- The value returned by the toUpperCase() method is 'C'.

- The value returned by the isLetterOrDigit() method is true.

- The value returned by the isWhitespace() method is false.

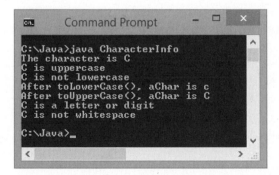

Figure 7-4   Output of the CharacterInfo application

TWO TRUTHS & A LIE

Using Character Class Methods

1. `Character` is a class, but `char` is a simple data type.

2. The `Character` class method `isLowerCase()` returns the lowercase version of any uppercase character.

3. If a `char` variable holds the Unicode value for the Tab key, `isWhitespace()` would be true and `isLetterOrDigit()` would be false.

The false statement is #2. The `Character` class method `isLowerCase()` returns true or false, as do all the `Character` class methods whose names use the `is` prefix.

 You Do It

Testing Characters

In this section, you experiment with the `CharacterInfo` application in order to become comfortable with different character properties.

1. Locate the **CharacterInfo.java** file that is stored in the Chapter07 folder of your Student Files. (If you cannot locate your Student Files, you can type the program shown in Figure 7-3.) Change the value of the `aChar` variable, compile and execute the program, and examine the results. Repeat this task multiple times using a variety of character values, including uppercase and lowercase letters, numbers, punctuation, special characters such as '@' and '[', and whitespace characters, such as a space or Tab. Verify that the output is what you expect in each case.

Examining the Character Class at the Java Web Site

1. Using a Web browser, go to the Java Web site at **www.oracle.com/technetwork/java/index.html**, and select **Java APIs** and **Java SE 8**. Using the alphabetical list of classes, find the `Character` class and select it.

2. Examine the extensive list of methods for the `Character` class. Find one with which you are familiar, such as `toLowerCase()`. Notice that there are two overloaded versions of the method. The one you used in the `CharacterInfo` application accepts a `char` and returns a `char`. The other version that accepts and returns an `int` uses Unicode values. Appendix B provides more information on Unicode.

Declaring and Comparing String Objects

You learned in Chapter 1 that a sequence of characters enclosed within double quotation marks is a literal string. (Programmers might also call it a "string literal.") You have used many literal strings, such as "First Java application", and you have assigned values to String objects and used them within methods, such as println() and showMessageDialog(). A literal string is an unnamed object, or **anonymous object**, of the String class, and a **String variable** is simply a named object of the same class. The class String is defined in java.lang.String, which is automatically imported into every program you write.

You have declared a String array named args in every main() method header that you have written. You will learn about arrays in the next chapter.

When you declare a String object, the String itself—that is, the series of characters contained in the String—is distinct from the identifier you use to refer to it. You can create a String object by using the keyword new and the String constructor, just as you would create an object of any other type. For example, the following statement defines an object named aGreeting, declares it to be of type String, and assigns an initial value of "Hello" to the String:

```
String aGreeting = new String("Hello");
```

The variable aGreeting stores a reference to a String object—it keeps track of where the String object is stored in memory. When you declare and initialize aGreeting, it links to the initializing String value. Because Strings are declared so routinely in programs, Java provides a shortcut, so you can declare a String containing "Hello" with the following statement that omits the keyword new and does not explicitly call the class constructor:

```
String aGreeting = "Hello";
```

Comparing String Values

In Java, String is a class, and each created String is an object. A String variable name is a reference; that is, a String variable name refers to a location in memory, rather than to a particular value.

The distinction is subtle, but when you declare a variable of a basic, primitive type, such as int x = 10;, the memory address where x is located holds the value 10. If you later assign a new value to x, the new value replaces the old one at the assigned memory address. For example, if you code x = 45;, then 45 replaces 10 at the address of x.

By contrast, when you declare a String, such as String aGreeting = "Hello";, aGreeting does not hold the characters "Hello"; instead it holds a memory address where the characters are stored.

The left side of Figure 7-5 shows a diagram of computer memory if aGreeting happens to be stored at memory address 10876 and the String "Hello" happens to be stored at memory address 26040. You cannot choose the memory address where a value is stored. Addresses such as 10876 and 26040 are chosen by the operating system.

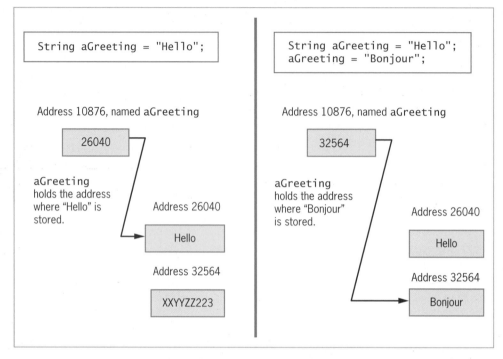

Figure 7-5 Contents of `aGreeting` at declaration and after an assignment

When you refer to `aGreeting`, you are actually accessing the address of the characters you want to use. (In the example on the left side of Figure 7-5, the memory location beginning at address 32564 has not yet been used and holds garbage values.)

If you subsequently assign a new value to `aGreeting`, such as `aGreeting = "Bonjour";`, the address held by `aGreeting` is altered; now, `aGreeting` holds a new address where the characters "Bonjour" are stored. As shown on the right side of Figure 7-5, "Bonjour" is an entirely new object created with its own location. The "Hello" `String` is still in memory, but `aGreeting` no longer holds its address. Eventually, a part of the Java system called the *garbage collector* discards the "Hello" characters so the memory address can be used for something else. `Strings`, therefore, are never actually changed; instead, new `Strings` are created and `String` references hold the new addresses. `Strings` and other objects that can't be changed are **immutable**.

The creators of Java made `String`s immutable for several reasons. For example, in environments where multiple programs (or parts of programs, called *threads of execution*) run concurrently, one logical path cannot change a `String` being used by another path. The compiler can also be made to execute more efficiently with immutable `String` objects. In simple programs, you don't care much about these features. However, immutability leads to performance problems. Later in this chapter, you will learn that if you want to use a *mutable* object to hold strings of characters, you can use the `StringBuilder` class.

Because `String` references hold memory addresses, making simple comparisons between them often produces misleading results. For example, recall the `TryToCompareStrings` application in Figure 7-1. In this example, Java evaluates the `String` variables `aName` and `anotherName` as not equal because even though the variables contain the same series of characters, one set is assigned directly and the other is entered from the keyboard and stored in a different area of memory. When you compare `Strings` with the `==` operator, you are comparing their memory addresses, not their values. Furthermore, when you try to compare `Strings` using the less-than (<) or greater-than (>) operator, the program will not even compile.

If you declare two `String` objects and initialize both to the same value, the value is stored only once in memory and the two object references hold the same memory address. Because the `String` is stored just once, memory is saved. Consider the following example in which the same value is assigned to two `Strings` (as opposed to getting one from user input). The reason for the output in the following example is misleading. When you write the following code, the output is *Strings are the same*.

```
String firstString = "abc";
String secondString = "abc";
if(firstString == secondString)
    System.out.println("Strings are the same");
```

The output is *Strings are the same* because the memory addresses held by `firstString` and `secondString` are the same, not because their contents are the same.

Fortunately, the `String` class provides you with a number of useful methods that compare `Strings` in the way you usually intend. The `String` class `equals()` method evaluates the contents of two `String` objects to determine if they are equivalent. The method returns `true` if the objects have identical contents, no matter how the contents were assigned. For example, Figure 7-6 shows a `CompareStrings` application, which is identical to the `TryToCompareStrings` application in Figure 7-1 except for the shaded comparison.

```java
import java.util.Scanner;
public class CompareStrings
{
    public static void main(String[] args)
    {
        String aName = "Carmen";
        String anotherName;
        Scanner input = new Scanner(System.in);
        System.out.print("Enter your name > ");
        anotherName = input.nextLine();
        if(aName.equals(anotherName))
            System.out.println(aName + " equals " + anotherName);
        else
            System.out.println(aName + " does not equal " + anotherName);
    }
}
```

Figure 7-6 The `CompareStrings` application

When a user runs the `CompareStrings` application and enters "Carmen" for the name, the output appears as shown in Figure 7-7; the contents of the `Strings` are equal. The `String` class `equals()` method returns `true` only if two `Strings` are identical in content. Thus, a `String` that refers to "Carmen" is not equivalent to one that refers to "CARMEN", and a `String` that refers to "Carmen " (with a space after the *n*) is not equivalent to one that refers to "Carmen" (with no space after the *n*).

```
C:\Java>java CompareStrings
Enter your name > Carmen
Carmen equals Carmen

C:\Java>_
```

Figure 7-7   Typical execution of the `CompareStrings` application

Technically, the `equals()` method does not perform an alphabetical comparison with `Strings`; it performs a **lexicographical comparison**—a comparison based on the integer Unicode values of the characters.

Each of the two `String` objects declared in Figure 7-6 (`aName` and `anotherName`) has access to the `String` class `equals()` method. If you analyze how the `equals()` method is used in the application in Figure 7-6, you can tell quite a bit about how the method was written by Java's creators:

- Because you use the `equals()` method with a `String` object and the method uses the unique contents of that object to make a comparison, you can tell that it is not a static method.

- Because the call to the `equals()` method can be used in an `if` statement, you can tell that it returns a Boolean value.

- Because you see a `String` used between the parentheses in the method call, you can tell that the `equals()` method takes a `String` argument.

So, the method header of the `equals()` method within the `String` class must be similar to the following:

```
public boolean equals(String s)
```

The only thing you do not know about the method header is the local name used for the `String` argument—it might be `s`, or it might be any other legal Java identifier. When you use a prewritten method such as `equals()`, you do not know how the code looks inside it. For example, you do not know whether the `equals()` method compares the characters in the `Strings` from left to right or from right to left. All you know is that the method returns `true` if the two `Strings` are completely equivalent and `false` if they are not.

Because both aName and anotherName are Strings in the application in Figure 7-6, the aName object can call equals() with aName.equals(anotherName) as shown, or the anotherName object could call equals() with anotherName.equals(aName). The equals() method can take either a variable String object or a literal string as its argument.

The String class equalsIgnoreCase() method is similar to the equals() method. As its name implies, this method ignores case when determining if two Strings are equivalent. Thus, if you declare a String as String aName = "Carmen";, then aName.equals("caRMen") is false, but aName.equalsIgnoreCase("caRMen") is true. This method is useful when users type responses to prompts in your programs. You cannot predict when a user might use the Shift key or the Caps Lock key during data entry.

When the String class compareTo() method is used to compare two Strings, it provides additional information to the user in the form of an integer value. When you use compareTo() to compare two String objects, the method:

- returns zero if the values of two Strings are exactly the same

- returns a negative number if the calling object is "less than" the argument

- returns a positive number if the calling object is "more than" the argument

Strings are considered "less than" or "more than" each other based on their Unicode values; thus, "a" is less than "b", and "b" is less than "c". For example, if aName refers to "Roger", then aName.compareTo("Robert"); returns a 5. The number is positive, indicating that "Roger" is more than "Robert". This does not mean that "Roger" has more characters than "Robert"; it means that "Roger" is alphabetically "more" than "Robert". The comparison proceeds as follows:

- The *R* in "Roger" and the *R* in "Robert" are compared, and found to be equal.

- The *o* in "Roger" and the *o* in "Robert" are compared, and found to be equal.

- The *g* in "Roger" and the *b* in "Robert" are compared; they are different. The numeric value of *g* minus the numeric value of *b* is 5 (because *g* is five letters after *b* in the alphabet), so the compareTo() method returns the value 5.

Often, you won't care what the specific return value of compareTo() is; you simply want to determine if it is positive or negative. For example, you can use a test such as if(aWord.compareTo(anotherWord) < 0)... to determine whether aWord is alphabetically less than anotherWord. If aWord is a String variable that refers to the value "hamster", and anotherWord is a String variable that refers to the value "iguana", the comparison if(aWord.compareTo(anotherWord) < 0) yields true.

Empty and `null` Strings

Programmers are often confused by the difference between empty Strings and null Strings. You can create an empty String named word1 and two null Strings named word2 and word3 with the following statements:

```
String word1 = "";
String word2 = null;
String word3;
```

The empty `String word1` references a memory address where no characters are stored. The **null String** `word2` uses the Java keyword `null` so that `word2` does not yet hold a memory address. The unassigned `String word3` is also a `null String` by default. A significant difference between these declarations is that `word1` can be used with the `String` methods described in this chapter, but `word2` and `word3` cannot be. For example, assuming a `String` named `someOtherString` has been assigned a value, then the comparison `word1.equals(someOtherString)` is valid, but `word2.equals(someOtherString)` causes an error.

Because `Strings` are set to `null` by default, some programmers think explicitly setting a `String` to `null` is redundant. Other programmers feel that explicitly using the keyword `null` makes your intentions clearer to those reading your program. You should use the style your organization recommends.

Watch the video *Comparing Strings*.

TWO TRUTHS & A LIE

Declaring and Comparing `String` Objects

1. To create a `String` object, you must use the keyword `new` and explicitly call the class constructor.

2. When you compare `Strings` with the `==` operator, you are comparing their memory addresses, not their values.

3. When you compare `Strings` with the `equals()` method, you are comparing their values, not their memory addresses.

The false statement is #1. You can create a `String` object with or without the keyword `new` and without explicitly calling the `String` constructor.

You Do It

Examining the `String` Class at the Java Web Site

In this section, you learn more about the `String` class.

1. Using a Web browser, go to the Java Web site, and select **Java APIs** and **Java SE 8**. Using the alphabetical list of classes, find the `String` class and select it.

(continues)

(continued)

2. Examine the `equals()` method. In the last section you saw this method used in expressions such as `aName.equals(anotherName)`. Because `equals()` is used with the object `aName`, you could predict that the `equals()` method is not `static`. When you look at the documentation for the `equals()` method, you can see this is true. You also can see that it returns a `boolean` value. What you might have predicted is that the `equals()` method takes a `String` argument, because `anotherName` is a `String`. However, the documentation shows that the `equals()` method accepts an `Object` argument. You will learn more about the `Object` class in the chapter "Advanced Inheritance Concepts," but for now understand that a `String` is a type of `Object`. `Object` is a class from which all other classes stem. In Java, every class is a type of `Object`.

Using Other String Methods

A wide variety of additional methods are available with the `String` class. The methods `toUpperCase()` and `toLowerCase()` convert any `String` to its uppercase or lowercase equivalent. For example, if you declare a `String` as `String aWord = "something";`, then the string "something" is created in memory and its address is assigned to `aWord`. The statement `aWord = aWord.toUpperCase();` creates "SOMETHING" in memory and assigns its address to `aWord`. Because `aWord` now refers to "SOMETHING," `aWord = aWord.toLowerCase();` alters `aWord` to refer to "something".

The `length()` method is an accessor method that returns the length of a `String`. For example, the following statements result in the variable `len` that holds the value 5.

```
String greeting = "Hello";
int len = greeting.length();
```

 In Chapter 2, you learned that your own accessor methods often start with the prefix *get*. The creators of Java did not follow this convention when naming the `length()` method.

When you must determine whether a `String` is empty, it is more efficient to compare its length to 0 than it is to use the `equals()` method.

The `indexOf()` method determines whether a specific character occurs within a `String`. If it does, the method returns the position of the character; the first position of a `String` is zero. The return value is −1 if the character does not exist in the `String`. For example, in `String myName = "Stacy";`, the value of `myName.indexOf('S')` is 0, the value of `myName.indexOf('a')` is 2, and the value of `myName.indexOf('q')` is −1.

The `charAt()` method requires an integer argument that indicates the position of the character that the method returns, starting with 0. For example, if `myName` is a `String` that refers to "Stacy", the value of `myName.charAt(0)` is 'S' and the value of `myName.charAt(4)` is 'y'. An error occurs if you use an argument that is negative, or greater than or equal to the length of the calling `String`. Instead of using a constant argument with `charAt()`, frequently you will want to use a variable argument to examine every character in a loop. For example, to count the number of spaces in the `String mySentence`, you might write a loop like the following:

```
for(int x = 0; x < myName.length(); ++x)
    if(mySentence.charAt(x) == ' ')
        ++countOfSpaces;
```

The `charAt()` method is also useful when you want a user to enter a single character from the keyboard. The `nextLine()` method with a `Scanner` object for console input and the `JOptionPane.showInputDialog()` method for GUI input both return `Strings`. For example, if input has been declared as a `Scanner` object, you can extract a character from the user's keyboard input with a statement such as the following:

```
char userLetter = input.NextLine().charAt(0);
```

The `endsWith()` method and the `startsWith()` method each take a `String` argument and return `true` or `false` if a `String` object does or does not end or start with the specified argument. For example, if `String myName = "Stacy";`, then `myName.startsWith("Sta")` is `true`, and `myName.endsWith("z")` is `false`. These methods are case sensitive, so if `String myName = "Stacy";`, then `myName.startsWith("sta")` is `false`.

The `replace()` method allows you to replace all occurrences of some character within a `String`. For example, if `String yourName = "Annette";`, then `String goofyName = yourName.replace('n', 'X');` assigns `"AXXette"` to `goofyName`. The statement `goofyName = yourName.replace('p', 'X');` would assign `"Annette"` to `goofyName` without any changes because `'p'` is not found in `yourName`. The `replace()` method is case sensitive, so if `String yourName = "Annette";`, then `String goofyName = yourName.replace('N', 'X');` results in no change.

Although not part of the `String` class, the `toString()` method is defined for other classes to convert their objects to strings. For example, the `Integer` class `toString()` method converts an integer to a `String`. After the following three statements, `theString` refers to "4":

```
String theString;
int someInt = 4;
theString = Integer.toString(someInt);
```

If you declare another `String` and a `double` as follows, then after the following statements, `anotherString` refers to "8.25"—a `String` of length 4:

```
String anotherString;
double someDouble = 8.25;
anotherString = Double.toString(someDouble);
```

You also can use **concatenation** to convert any primitive type (variable or constant) to a `String` using the + operator. For example, if you declare a variable as `int myAge = 25;`, the following statement results in `aString` that refers to "My age is 25":

```
String aString = "My age is " + myAge;
```

Similarly, if you write the following, then `anotherString` refers to "12.34".

```
String anotherString;
float someFloat = 12.34f;
anotherString = "" + someFloat;
```

The Java interpreter first converts the `float` 12.34f to a `String` "12.34" and adds it to the empty `String` "".

> The `toString()` method originates in the `Object` class; it is a method included in Java that you can use with any type of object. In the chapter "Advanced Inheritance Concepts," you will learn how to construct versions of the method for your own classes. You have been using `toString()` throughout this book without knowing it. When you use `print()` and `println()`, their arguments are automatically converted to `String`s if necessary. You don't need import statements to use `toString()` because it is part of `java.lang`, which is imported automatically. Because the `toString()` method you use with `println()` takes arguments of any primitive type, including `int`, `char`, `double`, and so on, it is a working example of polymorphism.

You already know that you can concatenate `String`s with other `String`s or values by using a plus sign (+); you have used this approach in methods such as `println()` and `showMessageDialog()` since Chapter 1. For example, you can display a `firstName`, a space, and a `lastName` with the following statement:

```
System.out.println(firstName + " " + lastName);
```

In addition, you can extract part of a `String` with the `substring()` method, and use it alone or concatenate it with another `String`. The `substring()` method takes two integer arguments—a start position and an end position—that are both based on the fact that a `String`'s first position is position zero. The length of the extracted substring is the difference between the second integer and the first integer; if you call the method without a second integer argument, the substring extends to the end of the original string.

For example, the application in Figure 7-8 prompts the user for a customer's first and last names. The application then extracts these names so that a friendly business letter can be constructed. After the application prompts the user to enter a name, a loop control variable is initialized to 0. While the variable remains less than the length of the entered name, each character is compared to the space character. When a space is found, two new strings are created. The first, `firstName`, is the substring of the original entry from position 0 to the location where the space was found. The second, `familyName`, is the substring of the original entry from the position after the space to the end of the string. Once the first and last names have been created, the loop control variable is set to the length of the original string so the loop will exit and proceed to the display of the friendly business letter. Figure 7-9 shows the data entry screen as well as the output letter created.

```
import javax.swing.*;
public class BusinessLetter
{
    public static void main(String[] args)
    {
        String name;
        String firstName = "";
        String familyName = "";
        int x;
        char c;
        name = JOptionPane.showInputDialog(null,
            "Please enter customer's first and last name");
        x = 0;
        while(x < name.length())
        {
            if(name.charAt(x) == ' ')
            {
                firstName = name.substring(0, x);
                familyName = name.substring(x + 1, name.length());
                x = name.length();
            }
            ++x;
        }
        JOptionPane.showMessageDialog(null,
            "Dear " + firstName +
            ",\nI am so glad we are on a first name basis" +
            "\nbecause I would like the opportunity to" +
            "\ntalk to you about an affordable insurance" +
            "\nprotection plan for the entire " + familyName +
            "\nfamily. Call A-One Family Insurance today" +
            "\nat 1-800-555-9287.");
    }
}
```

Figure 7-8   The BusinessLetter application

To keep the example simple, the BusinessLetter application in Figure 7-8 displays a letter for just one customer. An actual business application would most likely allow a clerk to enter dozens or even hundreds of customer names and store them in a data file for future use. You will learn to store data permanently in files in the chapter "File Input and Output." For now, just concentrate on the string-handling capabilities of the application.

Figure 7-9   Typical execution of the BusinessLetter application

The regionMatches() method can be used to test whether two String regions are the same. One version of the regionMatches() method takes four arguments—the position at which to start in the calling String, the other String being compared, the position to start in the other String, and the length of the comparison. For example, suppose that you have declared two String objects as follows:

```
String firstString = "abcde";
String secondString = "xxbcdef";
```

Then, the expression firstString.regionMatches(1, secondString, 2, 4) is true because the four-character substring starting at position 1 in firstString is "bcde" and the four-character substring starting at position 2 in secondString is also "bcde". The expression firstString.regionMatches(0, secondString, 3, 2) is false because the two-character substring starting at position 0 in firstString is "ab" and the two-character substring starting at position 3 in secondString is "cd".

A second version of the regionMatches() method takes an additional boolean argument as the first argument. This argument represents whether case should be ignored in deciding whether regions match. For example, suppose that you have declared two Strings as follows:

```
String thirdString = "123 Maple Drive";
String fourthString = "a maple tree";
```

Then the following expression is true because the substring of thirdString that starts at position 4 and continues for five characters is "Maple", the substring of fourthString that starts at position 2 and continues for five characters is "maple", and the argument that ignores case has been set to true:

```
thirdString.regionMatches(true, 4, fourthString, 2, 5)
```

Converting String Objects to Numbers

If a String contains all numbers, as in "649," you can convert it from a String to a number so you can use it for arithmetic, or use it like any other number. For example, suppose you ask a user to enter a salary in an input dialog box. When you accept input using showInputDialog(), the accepted value is always a String. To be able to use the value in arithmetic statements, you must convert the String to a number.

When you use any of the methods described in this section to attempt to convert a `String` to a number, the `String` might not represent a valid number. For example, it might contain a letter, comma, or dollar sign, or it might represent a valid number that is the wrong data type for the conversion. In such cases, an error called a `NumberFormatException` occurs. You will learn about exceptions in the chapter "Exception Handling."

To convert a `String` to an integer, you use the `Integer` class, which is part of `java.lang` and is automatically imported into programs you write. The `Integer` class is an example of a wrapper. A **wrapper** is a class or object that is "wrapped around" a simpler element; the `Integer` wrapper class contains a simple integer and useful methods to manipulate it. In Chapter 2, you were introduced to the `parseInt()` method, which is part of the `Integer` class; the method takes a `String` argument and returns its integer value. For example, the following statement stores the numeric value 649 in the variable `anInt`:

```
int anInt = Integer.parseInt("649");
```

You can then use the integer value just as you would any other integer. You can tell that `parseInt()` is a `static` method because you use it with the class name and not with an object.

It is also easy to convert a `String` object to a `double` value. You must use the `Double` class, which, like the `Integer` class, is a wrapper class and is imported into your programs automatically. The `Double` class `parseDouble()` method takes a `String` argument and returns its `double` value. For example, the following statement stores the numeric value 147.82 in the variable `doubleValue`.

```
double doubleValue = Double.parseDouble("147.82");
```

Besides `Double` and `Integer`, other wrapper classes such as `Float` and `Long` also provide methods such as `parseFloat()` and `parseLong()`.

Watch the video *String Methods*.

TWO TRUTHS & A LIE

Using Other String Methods

1. Assume that `myName` is a `String` defined as "molly". The value of `myName.toUpperCase()` is "Molly".

2. Assume that `myName` is a `String` defined as "molly". The value of `myName.length()` is 5.

3. Assume that `myName` is a `String` defined as "molly". The value of `myName.indexOf('M')` is −1.

The false statement is #1. If myName is "molly", then myName.toUpperCase() is "MOLLY".

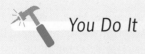

You Do It

Using **String** *Methods*

To demonstrate the use of the **String** methods, in this section you create an application that asks a user for a name and then "fixes" the name so that the first letter of each new word is uppercase, whether the user entered the name that way or not.

1. Open a new text file in your text editor. Enter the following first few lines of a **RepairName** program. The program declares several variables, including two strings that will refer to a name: one will be "repaired" with correct capitalization; the other will be saved as the user entered it so it can be displayed in its original form at the end of the program. After declaring the variables, prompt the user for a name:

    ```
    import javax.swing.*;
    public class RepairName
    {
        public static void main(String[] args)
        {
            String name, saveOriginalName;
            int stringLength;
            int i;
            char c;
            name = JOptionPane.showInputDialog(null,
                "Please enter your first and last name");
    ```

2. Store the name entered in the **saveOriginalName** variable. Next, calculate the length of the name the user entered, then begin a loop that will examine every character in the name. The first character of a name is always capitalized, so when the loop control variable **i** is 0, the character in that position in the name string is extracted and converted to its uppercase equivalent. Then the name is replaced with the uppercase character appended to the remainder of the existing name.

    ```
    saveOriginalName = name;
    stringLength = name.length();
    for(i = 0; i < stringLength; i++)
    {
        c = name.charAt(i);
        if(i == 0)
        {
            c = Character.toUpperCase(c);
            name = c + name.substring(1, stringLength);
        }
    ```

(continues)

372

(continued)

3. After the first character in the name is converted, the program looks through the rest of the name, testing for spaces and capitalizing every character that follows a space. When a space is found at position i, i is increased, the next character is extracted from the name, the character is converted to its uppercase version, and a new name string is created using the old string up to the current position, the newly capitalized letter, and the remainder of the name string. The if...else ends and the for loop ends.

```java
    else
        if(name.charAt(i) == ' ')
        {
            ++i;
            c = name.charAt(i);
            c = Character.toUpperCase(c);
            name = name.substring(0, i) + c +
                name.substring(i + 1, stringLength);
        }
    }
```

4. After every character has been examined, display the original and repaired names, and add closing braces for the main() method and the class.

```java
        JOptionPane.showMessageDialog(null, "Original name was " +
            saveOriginalName + "\nRepaired name is " + name);
    }
}
```

5. Save the application as **RepairName.java**, and then compile and run the program. Figure 7-10 shows a typical program execution. Make certain you understand how all the String methods contribute to the success of this program.

Figure 7-10 Typical execution of the `RepairName` application

You Do It

Converting a String to an Integer

In the next steps, you write a program that prompts the user for a number, reads characters from the keyboard, stores the characters in a String, and then converts the String to an integer that can be used in arithmetic statements.

1. Open a new text file in your text editor. Type the first few lines of a NumberInput class that will accept string input:

```
import javax.swing.*;
public class NumberInput
{
   public static void main(String[] args)
   {
```

2. Declare the following variables for the input String, the integer to which it is converted, and the result:

```
String inputString;
int inputNumber;
int result;
```

3. Declare a constant that holds a multiplier factor. This program will multiply the user's input by 10:

```
final int FACTOR = 10;
```

4. Enter the following input dialog box statement that stores the user keyboard input in the String variable inputString:

```
inputString = JOptionPane.showInputDialog(null,
   "Enter a number");
```

5. Use the following Integer.parseInt() method to convert the input String to an integer. Then multiply the integer by 10 and display the result:

```
inputNumber = Integer.parseInt(inputString);
result = inputNumber * FACTOR;
JOptionPane.showMessageDialog(null,
   inputNumber + " * " + FACTOR + " = " + result);
```

6. Add the final two closing curly braces for the program, then save the program as **NumberInput.java** and compile and test the program. Figure 7-11 shows a typical execution. Even though the user enters a String, it can be used successfully in an arithmetic statement because it was converted using the parseInt() method.

(continues)

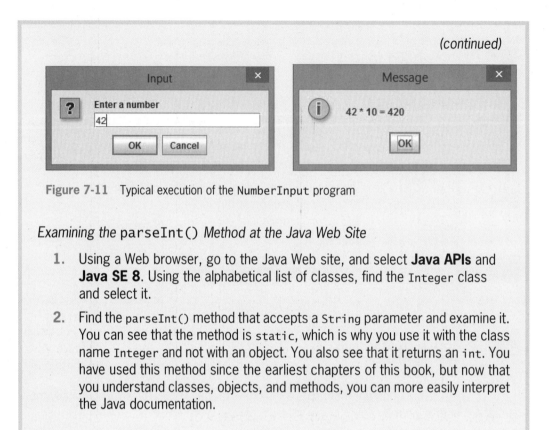

Figure 7-11 Typical execution of the `NumberInput` program

Examining the `parseInt()` *Method at the Java Web Site*

1. Using a Web browser, go to the Java Web site, and select **Java APIs** and **Java SE 8**. Using the alphabetical list of classes, find the `Integer` class and select it.

2. Find the `parseInt()` method that accepts a `String` parameter and examine it. You can see that the method is `static`, which is why you use it with the class name `Integer` and not with an object. You also see that it returns an `int`. You have used this method since the earliest chapters of this book, but now that you understand classes, objects, and methods, you can more easily interpret the Java documentation.

Learning About the `StringBuilder` and `StringBuffer` Classes

In Java, the value of a `String` is fixed after the `String` is created; `Strings` are immutable, or unchangeable. When you write `someString = "Hello";` and follow it with `someString = "Goodbye";`, you have neither changed the contents of computer memory at the address represented by `someString` nor eliminated the characters "Hello". Instead, you have stored "Goodbye" at a new computer memory location and stored the new address in the `someString` variable. If you want to modify `someString` from "Goodbye" to "Goodbye Everybody", you cannot add a space and "Everybody" to the `someString` that contains "Goodbye". Instead, you must create an entirely new `String`, "Goodbye Everybody", and assign it to the `someString` address. If you perform many such operations with `Strings`, you end up creating many different `String` objects in memory, which takes time and resources.

To circumvent these limitations, you can use either the `StringBuilder` or `StringBuffer` class. You use one of these classes, which are alternatives to the `String` class, when you know a `String` will be modified repeatedly. Usually, you can use a `StringBuilder` or `StringBuffer` object anywhere you would use a `String`. Like the `String` class, these two classes are part of the `java.lang` package and are automatically imported into every program. The classes are identical except for the following:

- `StringBuilder` is more efficient.

- `StringBuffer` is thread safe. This means you should use it in applications that run multiple **threads of execution,** which are units of processing that are scheduled by an operating system and that can be used to create multiple paths of control during program execution. Because most programs you write (and all the programs you will write using this book) contain a single thread, usually you should use `StringBuilder`.

The rest of this section discusses `StringBuilder`, but every statement is also true of `StringBuffer`.

You can create a `StringBuilder` object that contains a `String` with a statement such as the following:

```
StringBuilder message = new StringBuilder("Hello there");
```

When you use the `nextLine()` method with a `Scanner` object for console input or a `JOptionPane.showInputDialog()` method for GUI input, user input comes into your program as a `String`. If you want to work with the input as a `StringBuilder` object, you can convert the `String` using the `StringBuilder` constructor. For example, the following two statements get a user's input using a `Scanner` object named `keyboard` and then store it in the `StringBuilder` name:

```
String stringName = keyboard.nextLine();
StringBuilder name = new StringBuilder(stringName);
```

Alternately, you can combine the two statements into one and avoid declaring the variable `stringName`, as in the following:

```
StringBuilder name = new StringBuilder(keyboard.nextLine());
```

When you create a `String`, you have the option of omitting the keyword `new`, but when you initialize a `StringBuilder` object you must use the keyword `new`, the constructor name, and an initializing value between the constructor's parentheses. You can create a null `StringBuilder` variable using a statement such as the following:

```
StringBuilder uninitializedString = null;
```

The variable does not refer to anything until you initialize it with a defined `StringBuilder` object. Generally, when you create a `String` object, sufficient memory is allocated to accommodate the number of Unicode characters in the string. A `StringBuilder` object, however, contains a memory block called a **buffer,** which might or might not contain a string. Even if it does contain a string, the string might not occupy the entire buffer. In other words, the length of a string can be different from the length of the buffer. The actual length of the buffer is the **capacity** of the `StringBuilder` object.

You can change the length of a string in a `StringBuilder` object with the `setLength()` method. The length of a `StringBuilder` object equals the number of characters in the `String` contained in the `StringBuilder`. When you increase a `StringBuilder` object's length to be longer than the `String` it holds, the extra characters contain '\u0000'. If you use the `setLength()` method to specify a length shorter than its `String`, the string is truncated.

To find the capacity of a `StringBuilder` object, you use the `capacity()` method. The `StringBuilderDemo` application in Figure 7-12 demonstrates this method. The application creates a `nameString` object containing the seven characters "Barbara". The capacity of the `StringBuilder` object is obtained and stored in an integer variable named `nameStringCapacity` and displayed.

```java
import javax.swing.JOptionPane;
public class StringBuilderDemo
{
    public static void main(String[] args)
    {
        StringBuilder nameString = new StringBuilder("Barbara");
        int nameStringCapacity = nameString.capacity();
        System.out.println("Capacity of nameString is " +
            nameStringCapacity);
        StringBuilder addressString = null;
        addressString = new
            StringBuilder("6311 Hickory Nut Grove Road");
        int addStringCapacity = addressString.capacity();
        System.out.println("Capacity of addressString is " +
            addStringCapacity);
        nameString.setLength(20);
        System.out.println("The name is " + nameString + "end");
        addressString.setLength(20);
        System.out.println("The address is " + addressString);
    }
}
```

Figure 7-12   The `StringBuilderDemo` application

Figure 7-13 shows the `StringBuilder` capacity is 23, which is 16 characters more than the length of the string "Barbara". Whenever you create a `StringBuilder` object using a `String` as an argument to the constructor, the `StringBuilder`'s capacity is the length of the `String` contained as the argument to the `StringBuilder`, plus 16. The "extra" 16 positions allow for reasonable modification of the `StringBuilder` object after creation without allocating any new memory locations.

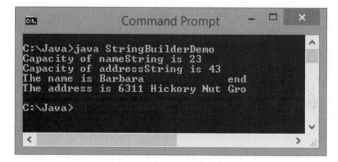

Figure 7-13   Output of the `StringBuilderDemo` application

 The creators of Java chose 16 characters as the "extra" length for a `StringBuilder` object because 16 characters fully occupy four bytes of memory. As you work more with computers in general and programming in particular, you will notice that storage capacities are almost always created in exponential values of 2—4, 8, 16, 32, 64, and so on.

In the application in Figure 7-12, the `addressString` variable is created as `StringBuilder` `addressString = null;`. The variable does not refer to anything until it is initialized with the defined `StringBuilder` object in the following statement:

```
addressString = new StringBuilder("6311 Hickory Nut Grove Road");
```

The capacity of this new `StringBuilder` object is shown in Figure 7-13 as the length of the string plus 16, or 43.

In the application in Figure 7-12, the length of each of the `Strings` is changed to 20 using the `setLength()` method. The application displays the expanded `nameString` and "end", so you can see in the output that there are 13 extra spaces at the end of the `String`. The application also displays the truncated `addressString` so that you can see the effect of reducing its length to 20.

The ability of `StringBuilder` objects to be modified can make using them more efficient than using `Strings` when you know string contents will change repeatedly. However, if your program makes relatively few changes to strings, or requires `String` comparisons, you should not use `StringBuilder`. For example, although the `equals()` method compares `String` object contents, when you use it with `StringBuilder` objects, it compares references. To compare the contents of two `StringBuilder` objects named `obj1` and `obj2`, you must first convert them to `Strings` with an expression such as the following:

```
obj1.toString().equals(obj2.toString())
```

The two most useful methods with `StringBuilder` objects are `append()` and `insert()`. The `append()` method lets you add characters to the end of a `StringBuilder` object. For example, the following two statements together declare `phrase` to hold "Happy" and alter the phrase to hold "Happy birthday":

```
StringBuilder phrase = new StringBuilder("Happy");
phrase.append(" birthday");
```

The insert() method lets you add characters at a specific location within a `StringBuilder` object. For example, if phrase refers to "Happy birthday", then phrase.insert(6, "30th "); alters the `StringBuilder` to contain "Happy 30th birthday". The first character in the `StringBuilder` object occupies position zero.

To alter just one character in a `StringBuilder` object, you can use the setCharAt() method, which allows you to change a character at a specified position. This method requires two arguments: an integer position and a character. If phrase refers to "Happy 30th birthday", then phrase.setCharAt(6,'4'); changes the value into a 40th birthday greeting.

One way you can extract a character from a `StringBuilder` object is to use the charAt() method. The charAt() method accepts an argument that is the offset of the character position from the beginning of a `String` and returns the character at that position. The following statements assign the character 'P' to the variable letter:

```
StringBuilder text = new StringBuilder("Java Programming");
char letter = text.charAt(5);
```

If you try to use an index that is less than 0 or greater than the index of the last position in the `StringBuilder` object, you cause an error known as an exception and your program terminates.

One version of the `StringBuilder` constructor allows you to assign a capacity to a `StringBuilder` object when you create it. For example:

```
StringBuilder prettyBigString = new StringBuilder(300);
```

When you can approximate the eventual size needed for a `StringBuilder` object, assigning sufficient capacity can improve program performance. For example, the program in Figure 7-14 compares the time needed to append "Java" 200,000 times to two `StringBuilder` objects—one that has an initial capacity of 16 characters and another that has an initial capacity of 800,000 characters. Figure 7-15 shows a typical execution; the actual times will vary from execution to execution and will be different on different computers. However, extra time is always needed for the loop that appends to the initially shorter `StringBuilder` because new memory must be allocated for it repeatedly as the object grows in size.

```
import java.time.*;
public class ConcatenationTimeComparison
{
   public static void main(String[] args)
   {
      long startTime, endTime;
      final int TIMES = 200_000;
      final int FACTOR = 1_000_000;
      int x;
      StringBuilder string1 = new StringBuilder("");
      StringBuilder string2 = new StringBuilder(TIMES * 4);
      LocalDateTime now;
      now = LocalDateTime.now();
      startTime = now.getNano();
```

Figure 7-14   The ConcatenationTimeComparison application *(continues)*

(continued)

```
        for(x = 0; x < TIMES; ++x)
            string1.append("Java");
        now = LocalDateTime.now();
        endTime = now.getNano();
        System.out.println("Time with empty StringBuilder: " +
            ((endTime - startTime) / FACTOR + " milliseconds"));
        now = LocalDateTime.now();
        startTime = now.getNano();
        for(x = 0; x < TIMES; ++x)
            string2.append("Java");
        now = LocalDateTime.now();
        endTime = now.getNano();
        System.out.println("Time with empty StringBuilder: " +
            ((endTime - startTime) / FACTOR + " milliseconds"));
    }
}
```

Figure 7-14   The ConcatenationTimeComparison application

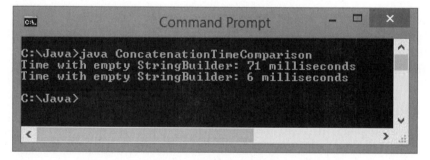

Figure 7-15   Typical execution of the ConcatenationTimeComparison program

   Watch the video *StringBuilder*.

380

TWO TRUTHS & A LIE

Learning About the `StringBuilder` and `StringBuffer` Classes

1. When you create a `String`, you have the option of omitting the keyword `new`, but when you initialize a `StringBuilder` object, you must use the keyword `new`, the constructor name, and an initializing value between the constructor's parentheses.

2. When you create a `StringBuilder` object with an initial value of "Juan", its capacity is 16.

3. If a `StringBuilder` named `myAddress` contains "817", then `myAddress.append(" Maple Lane");` alters `myAddress` to contain "817 Maple Lane".

The false statement is #2. When you create a `StringBuilder` object with an initial value of "Juan", its capacity is the length of the `String` contained in `StringBuilder`, 4, plus 16 more, for a total of 20.

 You Do It

Using `StringBuilder` Methods

In these steps, you write a program that demonstrates some methods in the `StringBuilder` class.

1. Open a new text file, and type the following first lines of a `StringBuilderMethods` class:

    ```
    public class StringBuilderMethods
    {
        public static void main(String[] args)
        {
    ```

2. Use the following code to create a `StringBuilder` object, and then display it:

    ```
    StringBuilder str = new StringBuilder("singing");
    System.out.println(str);
    ```

3. Enter the following `append()` method to add characters to the existing `StringBuilder` and display it again:

    ```
    str.append(" in the dead of ");
    System.out.println(str);
    ```

    (continues)

(continued)

4. Enter the following `insert()` method to insert characters. Then display the `StringBuilder`, insert additional characters, and display it again:

```
str.insert(0, "Black");
System.out.println(str);
str.insert(5, "bird ");
System.out.println(str);
```

5. Add one more append and display sequence:

```
str.append("night");
System.out.println(str);
```

6. Add a closing curly brace for the `main()` method.

7. Type the closing curly brace for the class, and then save the file as **StringBuilderMethods.java**. Compile and execute, and then compare your output to Figure 7-16.

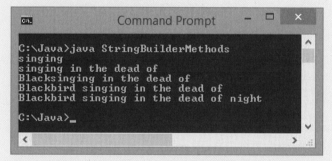

Figure 7-16 Output of the `StringBuilderMethods` application

Don't Do It

- Don't attempt to compare `String` objects using the standard comparison operators. The == operator will only compare the addresses of `Strings`, and the < and > operators will not work.

- Don't forget that `startsWith()`, `endsWith()`, and `replace()` are case sensitive, so you might want to convert participating `Strings` to the same case before using them.

- Don't forget to use the `new` operator and the constructor when declaring initialized `StringBuilder` or `StringBuffer` objects.

- Don't use `StringBuilder` or `StringBuffer` unless you have a good reason; otherwise, use the `String` class.

Key Terms

A **reference** is a variable that holds a memory address.

The **Character** class is one whose instances can hold a single character value. This class also defines methods that can manipulate or inspect single-character data.

The **String** class is for working with fixed-string data—that is, unchanging data composed of multiple characters.

An **anonymous object** is an unnamed object.

A **String variable** is a named object of the String class.

Immutable objects cannot be changed.

A **lexicographical comparison** is based on the integer Unicode values of characters.

A **null String** does not hold a memory address.

Concatenation is the process of joining a value to a string to create a longer string.

A **wrapper** is a class or object that is "wrapped around" a simpler element.

Threads of execution are units of processing that are scheduled by an operating system and that can be used to create multiple paths of control during program execution.

A **buffer** is a block of memory.

The **capacity** of a StringBuilder object is the actual length of the buffer, as opposed to that of the string contained in the buffer.

Chapter Summary

- `String` variables are references, so they require special techniques for making comparisons.

- The `Character` class is one whose instances can hold a single character value. This class also defines methods that can manipulate or inspect single-character data.

- A sequence of characters enclosed within double quotation marks is a literal string. Unlike other classes, you are not required to use the keyword new or explicitly call a constructor when you declare a `String`, although you can do so. `String`s are immutable. Useful `String` class methods include equals(), equalsIgnoreCase(), and compareTo().

- Additional useful `String` methods include toUpperCase(), toLowerCase(), length(), indexOf(), charAt(), endsWith(), startsWith(), and replace(). The toString() method converts any object to a `String`. You can concatenate `String`s using a plus sign (+). You can extract part of a `String` with the substring() method. If a `String` contains appropriate characters, you can convert it to a number with the help of methods such as Integer.parseInt() and Double.parseDouble().

- You can use the `StringBuilder` or `StringBuffer` class to improve performance when a string's contents must change.

Review Questions

1. A sequence of characters enclosed within double quotation marks is a _____ .

   a. symbolic string
   b. literal string
   c. prompt
   d. command

2. To create a `String` object, you can use the keyword _____ before the constructor call, but you are not required to use this format.

   a. `object`
   b. `create`
   c. `char`
   d. `new`

3. A `String` variable name is a _____ .

   a. reference
   b. value
   c. constant
   d. literal

4. The term that programmers use to describe objects that cannot be changed is _____ .

   a. irrevocable
   b. nonvolatile
   c. immutable
   d. stable

5. Suppose that you declare two `String` objects as:

   ```
   String word1 = new String("happy");
   String word2;
   ```

   When you ask a user to enter a value for word2, if the user types "happy", the value of word1 == word2 is _____ .

   a. `true`
   b. `false`
   c. illegal
   d. unknown

6. If you declare two `String` objects as:

   ```
   String word1 = new String("happy");
   String word2 = new String("happy");
   ```

   the value of word1.equals(word2) is _____ .

   a. `true`
   b. `false`
   c. illegal
   d. unknown

7. The method that determines whether two `String` objects are equivalent, regardless of case, is _____ .

   a. `equalsNoCase()`
   b. `toUpperCase()`
   c. `equalsIgnoreCase()`
   d. `equals()`

8. If a `String` is declared as:

   `String aStr = new String("lima bean");`

   then `aStr.equals("Lima Bean")` is ———————.

   a. true

   b. false

   c. illegal

   d. unknown

9. If you create two `String` objects:

   `String name1 = new String("Jordan");`
   `String name2 = new String("Jore");`

   then `name1.compareTo(name2)` has a value of ———————.

   a. true

   b. false

   c. −1

   d. 1

10. If `String myFriend = new String("Ginny");`, which of the following has the value 1?

    a. `myFriend.compareTo("Gabby");`

    b. `myFriend.compareTo("Gabriella");`

    c. `myFriend.compareTo("Ghazala");`

    d. `myFriend.compareTo("Hammie");`

11. If `String movie = new String("West Side Story");`, the value of `movie.indexOf('s')` is ———————.

    a. true

    b. false

    c. 2

    d. 3

12. The `String` class `replace()` method replaces ———————.

    a. a `String` with a character

    b. one `String` with another `String`

    c. one character in a `String` with another character

    d. every occurrence of a character in a `String` with another character

13. The `toString()` method converts a(n) ——————— to a String.

    a. char

    b. int

    c. float

    d. all of the above

14. Joining Strings with a plus sign is called ———————.

    a. chaining

    b. concatenation

    c. parsing

    d. linking

15. The first position in a String _____.

    a. must be alphabetic
    b. must be uppercase
    c. is position zero
    d. is ignored by the compareTo() method

16. The method that extracts a string from within another string is _____.

    a. extract()   c. substring()
    b. parseString()   d. append()

17. The method parseInt() converts a(n) _____.

    a. integer to a String   c. Double to a String
    b. integer to a Double   d. String to an integer

18. The difference between int and Integer is _____.

    a. int is a primitive type; Integer is a class
    b. int is a class; Integer is a primitive type
    c. nonexistent; both are primitive types
    d. nonexistent; both are classes

19. For an alternative to the String class, and so that you can change a String's contents, you can use _____.

    a. char   c. StringBuilder
    b. StringHolder   d. StringMerger

20. Unlike when you create a String, when you create a StringBuilder, you must use the keyword _____.

    a. buffer   c. null
    b. new   d. class

Exercises

 Programming Exercises

1. Modify the CharacterInfo class shown in Figure 7-3 so that the tested character is retrieved from user input. Save the file as **InputCharacterInfo.java**.

2. Write an application that prompts the user for three first names and concatenates them in every possible two-name combination so that new parents can easily compare them to find the most pleasing baby name. Save the file as **BabyNameComparison.java**.

3. a. Create a program that contains a String that holds your favorite movie quote and display the total number of spaces contained in the String. Save the file as **CountMovieSpaces.java**.

   b. Write an application that counts the total number of spaces contained in a movie quote entered by the user. Save the file as **CountMovieSpaces2.java**.

4. Write an application that prompts the user for a password that contains at least two uppercase letters, at least two lowercase letters, and at least two digits. Continuously reprompt the user until a valid password is entered. After each entry, display a message indicating whether the user was successful or the reason the user was not successful. Save the file as **ValidatePassword.java**.

5. Write an application that counts the words in a String entered by a user. Words are separated by any combination of spaces, periods, commas, semicolons, question marks, exclamation points, or dashes. Figure 7-17 shows two typical executions. Save the file as **CountWords.java**.

Figure 7-17 Two typical executions of the CountWords application

6. a. Write an application that accepts three Strings from the user and displays one of two messages depending on whether the user entered the Strings in alphabetical order without regard to case. Save the file as **Alphabetize.java**.

   b. Write an application that accepts three Strings from the user and displays them in alphabetical order without regard to case. Save the file as **Alphabetize2.java**.

7. Three-letter acronyms are common in the business world. For example, in Java you use the IDE (Integrated Development Environment) in the JDK (Java Development Kit) to write programs used by the JVM (Java Virtual Machine) that you might send over a LAN (local area network). Programmers even use the acronym TLA to stand for *three-letter acronym*. Write a program that allows a user to enter three words, and display the appropriate three-letter acronym in all uppercase letters. If the user enters more than three words, ignore the extra words. Save the file as **ThreeLetterAcronym.java**.

8. Write an application that accepts a word from a user and converts it to Pig Latin. If a word starts with a consonant, the Pig Latin version removes all consonants from the beginning of the word and places them at the end, followed by *ay*. For example, *cricket* becomes *icketcray*. If a word starts with a vowel, the Pig Latin version is the original word with *ay* added to the end. For example, *apple* becomes *appleay*. If *y* is the first letter in a word, it is treated as a consonant; otherwise, it is treated as a vowel. For example, *young* becomes *oungyay*, but *system* becomes *ystemsay*. For this program, assume that the user will enter only a single word consisting of all lowercase letters. Save the file as **PigLatin.java**.

9. Write a program that inserts parentheses, a space, and a dash into a string of 10 user-entered numbers to format it as a phone number. For example, *5153458912* becomes *(515) 345-8912*. If the user does not enter exactly 10 digits, display an error message. Continue to accept user input until the user enters *999*. Save the file as **PhoneNumberFormat.java**.

10. Write an application that determines whether a phrase entered by the user is a palindrome. A palindrome is a phrase that reads the same backward and forward without regarding capitalization or punctuation. For example, "Dot saw I was Tod", "Was it a car or a cat I saw?", and "Madam, I'm Adam" are palindromes. Save the file as **Palindrome.java**.

11. Write an application that prompts a user for a full name and street address and constructs an ID from the user's initials and numeric part of the address. For example, the user William Henry Harrison who lives at 34 Elm would have an ID of WHH34, whereas user Addison Mitchell who lives at 1778 Monroe would have an ID of AM1778. Save the file as **ConstructID.java**.

12. Create a TaxReturn class with fields that hold a taxpayer's Social Security number, last name, first name, street address, city, state, zip code, annual income, marital status, and tax liability. Include a constructor that requires arguments that provide values for all the fields other than the tax liability. The constructor calculates the tax liability based on annual income and the percentages in the following table.

Income ($)	Marital status	
	Single	Married
0–20,000	15%	14%
20,001–50,000	22%	20%
50,001 and over	30%	28%

In the TaxReturn class, also include a display method that displays all the TaxReturn data. Save the file as **TaxReturn.java**.

Create an application that prompts a user for the data needed to create a `TaxReturn`. Continue to prompt the user for data as long as any of the following are true:

- The Social Security number is not in the correct format, with digits and dashes in the appropriate positions—for example, 999-99-9999.

- The zip code is not five digits.

- The marital status does not begin with one of the following: "S", "s", "M", or "m".

- The annual income is negative.

After all the input data is correct, create a `TaxReturn` object and then display its values. Save the file as **PrepareTax.java**.

Debugging Exercises

1. Each of the following files in the Chapter07 folder of your downloadable student files has syntax and/or logic errors. In each case, determine the problem and fix the program. After you correct the errors, save each file using the same filename preceded with *Fix*. For example, DebugSeven1.java will become **FixDebugSeven1.java**.

   a. DebugSeven1.java

   b. DebugSeven2.java

   c. DebugSeven3.java

   d. DebugSeven4.java

Game Zone

1. a. In Chapter 3, you designed a `Card` class. The class holds fields that contain a `Card`'s value and suit. Currently, the suit is represented by a single character (s, h, d, or c). Modify the class so that the suit is a string ("Spades", "Hearts", "Diamonds", or "Clubs"). Also, add a new field to the class to hold the string representation of a `Card`'s rank based on its value. Within the `Card` class `setValue()` method, besides setting the numeric value, also set the string rank value as follows.

Numeric value	String value for rank
1	"Ace"
2 through 10	"2" through "10"
11	"Jack"
12	"Queen"
13	"King"

b. In Chapter 5, you created a War Card game that randomly selects two cards (one for the player and one for the computer) and declares a winner (or a tie). Modify the game to set each Card's suit as the appropriate string, then execute the game using the newly modified Card class. Figure 7-18 shows four typical executions. Recall that in this version of War, you assume that the Ace is the lowest-valued card. Save the game as **War2.java**.

```
C:\Java>java War2
My card is the 10 of Diamonds
Your card is the Queen of Hearts
You win

C:\Java>java War2
My card is the Ace of Diamonds
Your card is the 7 of Clubs
You win

C:\Java>java War2
My card is the 10 of Hearts
Your card is the 10 of Spades
It's a tie

C:\Java>java War2
My card is the 9 of Diamonds
Your card is the 3 of Diamonds
I win

C:\Java>
```

Figure 7-18   Four typical executions of the War2 game

2. In Chapter 5, you created a Rock Paper Scissors game. In the game, a player entered a number to represent one of the three choices. Make the following improvements to the game:

- Allow the user to enter a string ("rock", "paper", or "scissors") instead of a digit.

- Make sure the game works correctly, whether the player enters a choice in uppercase or lowercase letters, or a combination of the two.

- To allow for player misspellings, accept the player's entry as long as the first two letters are correct. (In other words, if a player types "scixxrs", you will accept it as "scissors" because at least the first two letters are correct.)

- When the player does not type at least the first two letters of the choice correctly, reprompt the player and continue to do so until the player's entry contains at least the first two letters of one of the options.

- Allow 10 complete rounds of the game. At the end, display counts of the number of times the player won, the number of times the computer won, and the number of tie games.

Save the file as **RockPaperScissors2.java**.

3. Create a simple guessing game, similar to Hangman, in which the user guesses letters and then attempts to guess a partially hidden phrase. Display a phrase in which some of the letters are replaced by asterisks: for example, "G* T***" (for "Go Team"). Each time the user guesses a letter, either place the letter in the correct spot (or spots) in the phrase and display it again or tell the user the guessed letter is not in the phrase. Display a congratulatory message when the entire correct phrase has been deduced. Save the game as **SecretPhrase.java**. In the next chapter, you will modify this program so that instead of presenting the user with the same phrase every time the game is played, the program randomly selects the phrase from a list of phrases.

4. Eliza is a famous 1966 computer program written by Joseph Weizenbaum. It imitates a psychologist (more specifically, a Rogerian therapist) by rephrasing many of a patient's statements as questions and posing them to the patient. This type of therapy (sometimes called nondirectional) is often parodied in movies and television shows, in which the therapist does not even have to listen to the patient, but gives "canned" responses that lead the patient from statement to statement. For example, when the patient says, "I am having trouble with my brother," the therapist might say, "Tell me more about your brother." If the patient says, "I dislike school," the therapist might say, "Why do you say you dislike school?" Eliza became a milestone in the history of computers because it was the first time a computer programmer attempted to create the illusion of human-to-human interaction.

Create a simple version of Eliza by allowing the user to enter statements continually until the user quits by typing "Goodbye". After each statement, have the computer make one of the following responses:

- If the user entered the word "my" (for example, "I am having trouble with my brother"), respond with "Tell me more about your" and insert the noun in question—for example, "Tell me more about your brother". When you search for a word in the user's entry, make sure it is the entire word and not just letters within another word. For example, when searching for *my*, make sure it is not part of another word such as *dummy* or *mystic*.

- If the user entered a strong word, such as "love" or "hate", respond with, "You seem to have strong feelings about that".

- Add a few other appropriate responses of your choosing.

- In the absence of any of the preceding inputs, respond with a random phrase from the following: "Please go on", "Tell me more", or "Continue".

Save the file as **Eliza.java**.

Case Problems

1. Carly's Catering provides meals for parties and special events. In previous chapters, you have developed a class that holds catering event information and an application that tests the methods using four objects of the class. Now modify the Event and EventDemo classes as follows:

   - Modify the method that sets the event number in the Event class so that if the argument passed to the method is not a four-character String that starts with a letter followed by three digits, then the event number is forced to "A000". If the initial letter in the event number is not uppercase, force it to be so.

   - Add a contact phone number field to the Event class.

   - Add a set method for the contact phone number field in the Event class. Whether the user enters all digits or any combination of digits, spaces, dashes, dots, or parentheses for a phone number, store it as all digits. For example, if the user enters *(920) 872-9182*, store the phone number as *9208729182*. If the user enters a number with fewer or more than 10 digits, store the number as *0000000000*.

   - Add a get method for the phone number field. The get method returns the phone number as a String constructed as follows: parentheses surround a three-digit area code, followed by a space, followed by the three-digit phone exchange, followed by a hyphen, followed by the last four digits of the phone number.

   - Modify the EventDemo program so that besides the event number and guests, the program also prompts the user for and retrieves a contact phone number for each of the sample objects. Display the phone number along with the other Event details. Test the EventDemo application to make sure it works correctly with valid and invalid event and phone numbers.

   Save the files as **Event.java** and **EventDemo.java**.

2. Sammy's Seashore Supplies rents beach equipment to tourists. In previous chapters, you have developed a class that holds equipment rental information and an application that tests the methods using four objects of the class. Now modify the Rental and RentalDemo classes as follows:

   - Modify the method that sets the contract number in the Rental class so that if the argument passed to the method is not a four-character String that starts with a letter followed by three digits, then the contract number is forced to "A000". If the initial letter in the contract number is not uppercase, force it to be so.

   - Add a contact phone number field to the Rental class.

- Add a set method for the contact phone number field in the `Rental` class. Whether the user enters all digits or any combination of digits, spaces, dashes, dots, or parentheses for a phone number, store it as all digits. For example, if the user enters *(920) 872-9182*, store the phone number as *9208729182*. If the user enters a number with fewer or more than 10 digits, store the number as *0000000000*.

- Add a get method for the phone number field. The get method returns the phone number as a `String` constructed as follows: parentheses surround a three-digit area code, followed by a space, followed by the three-digit phone exchange, followed by a hyphen, followed by the last four digits of the phone number.

- Modify the `RentalDemo` program so that besides the contract number and minutes, the program also prompts the user for and retrieves a contact phone number for each of the sample objects. Display the phone number along with the other `Rental` details. Test the `RentalDemo` application to make sure it works correctly with valid and invalid contract and phone numbers.

Save the files as **Rental.java** and **RentalDemo.java**.

CHAPTER 8

Arrays

In this chapter, you will:

◎ Declare arrays

◎ Initialize an array

◎ Use variable subscripts with an array

◎ Declare and use arrays of objects

◎ Search an array and use parallel arrays

◎ Pass arrays to and return arrays from methods

Declaring Arrays

While completing the first five chapters in this book, you stored values in variables. In those early chapters, you simply stored a value and used it, usually only once, but never more than a few times. In Chapter 6, you created loops that allow you to "recycle" variables and use them many times; that is, after creating a variable, you can assign a value, use the value, and then, in successive cycles through the loop, reuse the variable as it holds different values.

At times, however, you might encounter situations in which storing just one value at a time in memory does not meet your needs. For example, a sales manager who supervises 20 employees might want to determine whether each employee has produced sales above or below the average amount. When you enter the first employee's sales value into an application, you can't determine whether it is above or below average because you don't know the average until you have all 20 values. Unfortunately, if you attempt to assign 20 sales values to the same variable, when you assign the value for the second employee, it replaces the value for the first employee.

A possible solution is to create 20 separate employee sales variables, each with a unique name, so you can store all the sales until you can determine an average. A drawback to this method is that if you have 20 different variable names to be assigned values, you need 20 separate assignment statements. For 20 different variable names, the statement that calculates total sales will be unwieldy, such as:

```
total = firstAmt + secondAmt + thirdAmt + …
```

This method might work for 20 salespeople, but what if you have 10,000 salespeople?

The best solution is to create an array. An **array** is a named list of data items that all have the same data type. Each data item is an **element** of the array. You declare an array variable in the same way you declare any simple variable, but you insert a pair of square brackets after the type. For example, to declare an array of double values to hold sales figures for salespeople, you can write the following:

```
double[] salesFigures;
```

Similarly, to create an array of integers to hold student ID numbers, you can write the following:

```
int[] idNums;
```

In Java, you can also declare an array variable by placing the square brackets after the array name, as in double salesFigures[];. This format is familiar to C and C++ programmers, but the preferred format among Java programmers is to place the brackets following the variable type and before the variable name.

You can provide any legal identifier you want for an array, but Java programmers conventionally name arrays by following the same rules they use for variables—array names start with a lowercase letter and use uppercase letters to begin subsequent words.

Additionally, many programmers observe one of the following conventions to make it more obvious that the name represents a group of items:

- Arrays are often named using a plural noun such as `salesFigures`.

- Arrays are often named by adding a final word that implies a group, such as `salesList`, `salesTable`, or `salesArray`.

After you create an array variable, you still need to reserve memory space. You use the same procedure to create an array that you use to create an object. Recall that when you create a class named `Employee`, you can declare an `Employee` object with a declaration such as:

```
Employee oneWorker;
```

However, that declaration does not actually create the `oneWorker` object. You create the `oneWorker` object when you use the keyword `new` and a call to the constructor, as in:

```
oneWorker = new Employee();
```

Similarly, declaring an array and reserving memory space for it are two distinct processes. To reserve memory locations for 20 `salesFigures` values, you can declare the array variable and create the array with two separate statements as follows:

```
double[] salesFigures;
salesFigures = new double[20];
```

Alternatively, just as with objects, you can declare and create an array in one statement with the following:

```
double[] salesFigures = new double[20];
```

 In Java, the size of an array follows the data type and is never declared immediately following the array name, as it is in some other languages such as C++. Other languages, such as Visual Basic, BASIC, and COBOL, use parentheses rather than brackets to refer to individual array elements. By using brackets, the creators of Java made it easier for you to distinguish array names from methods.

The statement `double[] salesFigures = new double[20];` reserves 20 memory locations for 20 `double` values. You can distinguish each `salesFigures` item from the others with a subscript. A **subscript** is an integer contained within square brackets that specifies one of an array's elements. In Java, any array's elements are numbered beginning with 0, so you can legally use any subscript from 0 through 19 when working with an array that has 20 elements. In other words, the first `salesFigures` array element is `salesFigures[0]` and the last `salesFigures` element is `salesFigures[19]`. Figure 8-1 shows how the first few and last few elements of an array of 20 `salesFigures` values appear in computer memory.

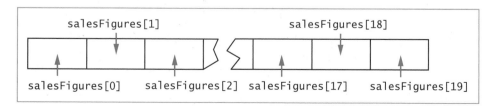

Figure 8-1 The first few and last few elements of an array of 20 `salesFigures` items in memory

A subscript is also called an **index**. In particular, you will see the term *index* in some error messages issued by the compiler.

It is a common mistake to forget that the first element in an array is element 0, especially if you know another programming language in which the first array element is element 1. Making this mistake means you will be "off by one" in your use of any array. It is also common to forget that the last element's subscript is one less than the array's size and not the array's size. For example, the highest allowed subscript for a 100-element array is 99. To remember that array elements begin with element 0, it might help if you think of the first array element as being "zero elements away from" the beginning of the array, the second element as being "one element away from" the beginning of the array, and so on. If you use a subscript that is too small (that is, negative) or too large for an array, the subscript is **out of bounds** and an error message is generated.

When you work with any individual array element, you treat it no differently than you would treat a single variable of the same type. For example, to assign a value to the first salesFigures element in an array, you use a simple assignment statement, such as the following:

```
salesFigures[0] = 2100.00;
```

To display the last salesFigures element in an array of 20, you can write:

```
System.out.println(salesFigures[19]);
```

When programmers talk about these statements, they typically say things like, "salesFigures sub zero is assigned 2100.00," and "salesFigures sub 19 is output." In other words, they use *sub* as shorthand for "with the subscript."

When you declare or access an array, you can use any expression to represent the size, as long as the expression is an integer. Some other programming languages, such as C++, allow only named or unnamed constants to be used for the size when an array is declared. Java allows variables, arithmetic expressions, and method return values to be used as array sizes, which makes array declaration more flexible.

For example, to declare a double array named moneyValues, you might use any of the following:

- A literal integer constant; for example:

  ```
  double[] moneyValues = new double[10];
  ```

- A named integer constant; for example:

  ```
  double[] moneyValues = new double[NUMBER_ELS];
  ```

  In this example, the constant NUMBER_ELS must have been previously declared and assigned a value.

- An integer variable; for example:

```
double[] moneyValues = new double[numberOfEls];
```

In this example, the variable `numberOfEls` must have been previously declared and assigned a value.

- A calculation; for example:

```
double[] moneyValues = new double[x + y * z];
```

In this example, the variables x, y, and z must have been previously declared and assigned values, and the result of the expression x + y * z must be an integer.

- A method's `return` value; for example:

```
double[] moneyValues = new double[getElements()];
```

In this example, the method `getElements()` must return an integer.

TWO TRUTHS & A LIE

Declaring Arrays

1. The statement `int[] idNums = new int[35];` reserves enough memory for exactly 34 integers.

2. The first element in any array has a subscript of 0, no matter what data type is stored.

3. In Java, you can use a variable as well as a constant to declare an array's size.

The false statement is #1. The statement `int[] idNums = new int[35];` reserves enough memory for exactly 35 integers numbered 0 through 34.

You Do It

Declaring an Array

In this section, you create a small array to see how arrays are used. The array holds salaries for four categories of employees.

1. Open a new text file, and begin the class that demonstrates how arrays are used by typing the following class and `main()` headers and their corresponding opening curly braces:

(continues)

(continued)

```java
public class DemoArray
{
    public static void main(String[] args)
    {
```

2. On a new line, declare and create an array that can hold four `double` values by typing the following:

```java
double[] salaries = new double[4];
```

3. One by one, assign four values to the four array elements by typing the following:

```java
salaries[0] = 6.25;
salaries[1] = 6.55;
salaries[2] = 10.25;
salaries[3] = 16.85;
```

4. To confirm that the four values have been assigned, display the salaries one by one using the following code:

```java
System.out.println("Salaries one by one are:");
System.out.println(salaries[0]);
System.out.println(salaries[1]);
System.out.println(salaries[2]);
System.out.println(salaries[3]);
```

5. Add the two closing curly braces that end the `main()` method and the `DemoArray` class.

6. Save the program as **DemoArray.java**. Compile and run the program. The program's output appears in Figure 8-2.

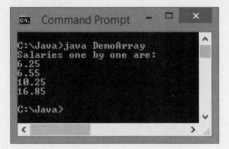

Figure 8-2 Output of the `DemoArray` application

(continues)

(continued)

Using a Subscript that Is Out of Bounds

In this section, you purposely generate an out-of-bounds error so you can familiarize yourself with the error message generated.

1. As the last executable line in the DemoArray.java file, add a new output statement that attempts to display a salaries value using a subscript that is beyond the range of the array:

   ```
   System.out.println(salaries[4]);
   ```

2. Save the file, and then compile and execute it. The output looks like Figure 8-3. The program runs successfully when the subscript used with the array is 0, 1, 2, or 3. However, when the subscript reaches 4, the error in Figure 8-3 is generated. The message indicates that an ArrayIndexOutOfBoundsException has occurred and that the offending index is 4.

Figure 8-3 Output of the DemoArray application when a subscript is out of bounds

 In Chapter 12, you will learn more about the term *exception* and learn new ways to deal with exceptions.

3. Remove the offending statement from the DemoArray class. Save the program, and then compile and run it again to confirm that it again executes correctly.

Initializing an Array

A variable that has a primitive type, such as int, holds a value. A variable with a reference type, such as an array, holds a memory address where a value is stored. In other words, array names contain references, as do all Java object names.

No memory address is assigned when you declare an array using only a data type, brackets, and a name. Instead, the array variable name has the value null, which means the identifier is not associated with a memory address. You can explicitly assign null to an array reference, but it is not required. For example, each of the following statements assigns null to someNums:

```
int[] someNums;
int[] someNums = null;
```

When you use the keyword new to define an array, the array reference acquires a memory address value. For example, when you define someNums in the following statement, a memory address is assigned:

```
int[] someNums = new int[10];
```

When you declare int[] someNums = new int[10];, someNums holds an address, but each element of someNums has a value of 0 by default because someNums is an integer array. Each element in a double or float array is assigned 0.0. By default, char array elements are assigned '\u0000', which is the Unicode value for a null character, and boolean array elements automatically are assigned the value false. In arrays of objects, including Strings, each element is assigned null by default.

You already know how to assign a different value to a single element of an array, as in:

```
someNums[0] = 46;
```

You can also assign nondefault values to array elements upon creation. To initialize an array, you use an **initialization list** of values separated by commas and enclosed within curly braces. Providing values for all the elements in an array also is called **populating the array**.

For example, if you want to create an array named multsOfTen and store the first six multiples of 10 within the array, you can declare the array as follows:

```
int[] multsOfTen = {10, 20, 30, 40, 50, 60};
```

Notice the semicolon at the end of the statement. You don't use a semicolon following a method's closing curly brace, but you do use one following the closing brace of an array initialization list.

When you populate an array upon creation by providing an initialization list, you do not give the array a size—the size is assigned based on the number of values you place in the initializing list. For example, the multsOfTen array just defined has a size of 6. Also, when you initialize an array, you do not need to use the keyword new; instead, new memory is assigned based on the length of the list of provided values.

In Java, you cannot directly initialize part of an array. For example, you cannot create an array of 10 elements and initialize only five; you either must initialize every element or none of them.

 Watch the video *Arrays*.

TWO TRUTHS & A LIE

Initializing an Array

1. When you declare `int[] idNums = new int[35];`, each element of the array has a value of 0.

2. When you declare `double[] salaries = new double[10];`, each element of the array has a value of 0.0.

3. When you declare `int[] scores = {100, 90, 80};`, the first three elements of the array are assigned the values listed, but all the remaining elements are assigned 0.

The false statement is #3. When you provide an initialization list for an array, the array contains exactly the number of elements in the list.

You Do It

Initializing an Array

Next, you alter your `DemoArray` program to initialize the array of `doubles`, rather than declaring the array and assigning values later.

1. Open the **DemoArray.java** file. Immediately save the file as **DemoArray2.java**. Change the class name to `DemoArray2`. Delete the statement that declares the array of four `doubles` named `salaries`, and then replace it with the following initialization statement:

   ```
   double[] salaries = {6.25, 6.55, 10.25, 16.85};
   ```

2. Delete the following four statements that individually assign the values to the array:

   ```
   salaries[0] = 6.25;
   salaries[1] = 6.55;
   salaries[2] = 10.25;
   salaries[3] = 16.85;
   ```

3. Save the file (as **DemoArray2.java**), compile, and test the application. The values that are output are the same as those shown for the `DemoArray` application in Figure 8-2.

Using Variable Subscripts with an Array

If you treat each array element as an individual entity, there isn't much of an advantage to declaring an array over declaring individual primitive type variables, such as those with the type int, double, or char. The power of arrays becomes apparent when you begin to use subscripts that are variables, rather than subscripts that are constant values.

For example, suppose you declare an array of five integers that holds quiz scores, such as the following:

```
int[] scoreArray = {2, 14, 35, 67, 85};
```

You might want to perform the same operation on each array element, such as increasing each score by a constant amount. To increase each scoreArray element by three points, for example, you can write the following:

```
final int INCREASE = 3;
scoreArray[0] += INCREASE;
scoreArray[1] += INCREASE;
scoreArray[2] += INCREASE;
scoreArray[3] += INCREASE;
scoreArray[4] += INCREASE;
```

With five scoreArray elements, this task is manageable, requiring only five statements. However, you can reduce the amount of program code needed by using a variable as the subscript. Then, you can use a loop to perform arithmetic on each array element, as in the following example:

```
final int INCREASE = 3;
for(sub = 0; sub < 5; ++sub)
    scoreArray[sub] += INCREASE;
```

The loop control variable sub is set to 0, and then it is compared to 5. Because the value of sub is less than 5, the loop executes and 3 is added to scoreArray[0]. Then, the variable sub is incremented and it becomes 1, which is still less than 5, so when the loop executes again, scoreArray[1] is increased by 3, and so on. A process that took five statements now takes only one. In addition, if the array had 100 elements, the first method of increasing the array values by 3 in separate statements would result in 95 additional statements. The only changes required using the second method would be to change the array size to 100 by inserting additional initial values for the scores, and to change the middle portion of the for statement to compare sub to 100 instead of to 5. The loop to increase 100 separate scores by 3 each is:

```
for(sub = 0; sub < 100; ++sub)
    scoreArray[sub] += INCREASE;
```

When an application contains an array and you want to use every element of the array in some task, it is common to perform loops that vary the loop control variable from 0 to one less than the size of the array. For example, if you get input values for the elements in the array, alter every value in the array, sum all the values in the array, or display every element in the array, you need to perform a loop that executes the same number of times as there are elements. (If you perform the loop too many times, the subscript will be out of bounds; if you do not perform the loop enough times, you will miss processing some elements in the list.) When there are 10 array elements, the subscript varies from 0 through 9; when there are 800 elements, the subscript varies from 0 through 799. Therefore, in an application that includes an array, it is convenient to declare a named constant equal to the size of the array and use it as a limiting value in every loop that processes the array. That way, if the array size changes in the future, you need to modify only the value stored in the named, symbolic constant, and you do not need to search for and modify the limiting value in every loop that processes the array.

For example, suppose you declare an array and a named constant as follows:

```
int[] scoreArray = {2, 14, 35, 67, 85};
final int NUMBER_OF_SCORES = 5;
```

Then, the following two loops are identical:

```
for(sub = 0; sub < 5; ++sub)
    scoreArray[sub] += INCREASE;
for(sub = 0; sub < NUMBER_OF_SCORES; ++sub)
    scoreArray[sub] += INCREASE;
```

The second format has two advantages. First, by using the named constant, NUMBER_OF_SCORES, the reader understands that you are processing every array element for the size of the entire array. If you use the number 5, the reader must look back to the array declaration to confirm that 5 represents the full size of the array. Second, if the array size changes because you remove or add scores, you change the named constant value only once, and all loops that use the constant are automatically altered to perform the correct number of repetitions.

As an even better option, you can use a field (instance variable) that is automatically assigned a value for every array you create; the length field contains the number of elements in the array. For example, when you declare an array using either of the following statements, the field scoreArray.length is assigned the value 5:

```
int[] scoreArray = {2, 14, 35, 67, 85};
int[] scoreArray = new int[5];
```

Therefore, you can use the following loop to add 3 to every array element:

```
for(sub = 0; sub < scoreArray.length; ++sub)
    scoreArray[sub] += INCREASE;
```

Later, if you modify the size of the array and recompile the program, the value in the length field of the array changes appropriately. When you work with array elements, it is always better to use a named constant or the length field when writing a loop that manipulates an array.

A frequent programmer error is to attempt to use length as an array method, referring to scoreArray.length(). As you learned in the last chapter, length() is a String method. However, length is not an array method; it is a field. An instance variable or object field such as length is also called a **property** of the object.

Using the Enhanced for Loop

In Chapter 6, you learned to use the for loop. Java also supports an **enhanced for loop**. This loop allows you to cycle through an array without specifying the starting and ending points for the loop control variable. For example, you can use either of the following statements to display every element in an array named scoreArray:

```
for(int sub = 0; sub < scoreArray.length; ++sub)
    System.out.println(scoreArray[sub]);
for(int val : scoreArray)
    System.out.println(val);
```

In the second example, val is defined to be the same type as the array named following the colon. Within the loop, val takes on, in turn, each value in the array. You can read the second example as, "For each val in scoreArray, display val." As a matter of fact, you will see the enhanced for loop referred to as a **foreach loop**.

You also can use the enhanced for loop with more complicated Java objects, as you will see in the next section.

Using Part of an Array

Sometimes, you do not want to use every value in an array. For example, suppose that you write a program that allows a student to enter up to 10 quiz scores and then computes and displays the average. To allow for 10 quiz scores, you create an array that can hold 10 values, but because the student might enter fewer than 10 values, you might use only part of the array. Figure 8-4 shows such a program.

```
import java.util.*;
public class AverageOfQuizzes
{
    public static void main(String[] args)
    {
        int[] scores = new int[10];
        int score = 0;
        int count = 0;
        int total = 0;
        final int QUIT = 999;
        final int MAX = 10;
        Scanner input = new Scanner(System.in);
        System.out.print("Enter quiz score or " +
            QUIT + " to quit       >> ");
        score = input.nextInt();
        while(score != QUIT)
        {
            scores[count] = score;
            total += scores[count];
            ++count;
            if(count == MAX)
                score = QUIT;
            else
            {
                System.out.print("Enter next quiz score or " +
                    QUIT + " to quit >> ");
                score = input.nextInt();
            }
        }
    }
```

Figure 8-4   The AverageOfQuizzes application *(continues)*

(continued)

```
        System.out.print("\nThe scores entered were: ");
        for(int x = 0; x < count; ++x)
            System.out.print(scores[x] + " ");
        if(count != 0)
            System.out.println("\n The average is " + (total * 1.0 / count));
        else
            System.out.println("No scores were entered.");
    }
}
```

Figure 8-4 The AverageOfQuizzes application

The AverageOfQuizzes program declares an array that can hold 10 quiz scores. The user is prompted for a first quiz score; then, a while loop starts and continues as long as the user does not enter *999*, as shown in the first shaded line in Figure 8-4. Within the loop, the entered score is placed in the scores array, the score is added to a running total, and the count of scores entered is incremented. If the score just entered is the tenth score, the score is forced to 999 and the loop ends; otherwise, the user is prompted for the next score. The while loop continuously checks to ensure that the user has not entered 999 to quit. When the loop eventually ends, count holds the number of scores entered. The variable count then can be used to control the output loop (in the shaded for statement) and to calculate the average score (the last shaded portion in Figure 8-4). Figure 8-5 shows two typical executions of the program.

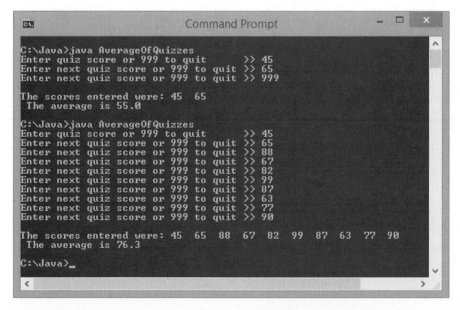

Figure 8-5 Two typical executions of the AverageOfQuizzes application

---

TWO TRUTHS & A LIE

Using Variable Subscripts with an Array

1. When an application contains an array, it is common to perform loops that vary the loop control variable from 0 to one less than the size of the array.

2. An array's `length` field contains the highest value that can be used as the array's subscript.

3. The enhanced `for` loop allows you to cycle through an array without specifying the starting and ending points for the loop control variable.

The false statement is #2. An array's length field contains the number of elements in the array.

You Do It

Using a `for` Loop to Access Array Elements

Next, you modify the `DemoArray2` program to use a `for` loop with the array.

1. Open the **DemoArray2.java** file, and immediately save the file as **DemoArray3.java**. Change the class name to `DemoArray3`. Delete the four `println()` statements that display the four array values, and then replace them with the following `for` loop:

   ```
   for(int x = 0; x < salaries.length; ++x)
       System.out.println(salaries[x]);
   ```

2. Save the program (as **DemoArray3.java**), compile, and run the program. Again, the output is the same as that shown in Figure 8-2.

Declaring and Using Arrays of Objects

Just as you can declare arrays of simple types such as `int` or `double`, you can declare arrays that hold elements of objects. For example, assume you create the `Employee` class shown in Figure 8-6. This class has two data fields (`empNum` and `empSal`), a constructor, and a get method for each field.

```
public class Employee
{
    private int empNum;
    private double empSal;
    Employee(int e, double s)
    {
        empNum = e;
        empSal = s;
    }
    public int getEmpNum()
    {
        return empNum;
    }
    public double getSalary()
    {
        return empSal;
    }
}
```

Figure 8-6 The Employee class

You can create separate Employee objects with unique names, such as the following:

```
Employee painter, electrician, plumber;
Employee firstEmployee, secondEmployee, thirdEmployee;
```

However, in many programs it is far more convenient to create an array of Employee objects. An array named emps that holds seven Employee objects can be defined as:

```
Employee[] emps = new Employee[7];
```

This statement reserves enough computer memory for seven Employee objects named emps[0] through emps[6]. However, the statement does not actually construct those Employee objects; instead, you must call the seven individual constructors. According to the class definition shown in Figure 8-6, the Employee constructor requires two arguments: an employee number and a salary. If you want to number your Employees 101, 102, 103, and so on, and start each Employee at a salary of $15,000, the loop that constructs seven Employee objects is as follows:

```
final int START_NUM = 101;
final double STARTING_SALARY = 15_000;
for(int x = 0; x < emps.length; ++x)
    emps[x] = new Employee(START_NUM + x, STARTING_SALARY);
```

As x varies from 0 through 6, each of the seven emps objects is constructed with an employee number that is 101 more than x, and each of the seven emps objects holds the same salary.

Unlike the Employee class in Figure 8-6, which contains a constructor that requires arguments, some classes contain only a default constructor, which might be supplied automatically when no other constructors are created or might be written explicitly.

To construct an array of objects using a default constructor, you must still call the constructor using the keyword new for each declared array element. For example, suppose you have created a class named InventoryItem but have not written a constructor. To create an array of 1,000 InventoryItem objects, you would write the following:

```
final int NUM_ITEMS = 1000;
InventoryItem[] items = new InventoryItem[NUM_ITEMS];
for(int x = 0; x < NUM_ITEMS; ++x)
    items[x] = new InventoryItem();
```

You could use an initialization list to create an array of objects, as in the following example:

```
InventoryItem[] items = {new InventoryItem(),
    new InventoryItem(), new InventoryItem()};
```

However, even with only a few objects in the array, this approach is unwieldy.

To use a method that belongs to an object that is part of an array, you insert the appropriate subscript notation after the array name and before the dot that precedes the method name. For example, to display data for seven Employees stored in the emps array, you can write the following:

```
for(int x = 0; x < emps.length; ++x)
    System.out.println (emps[x].getEmpNum() + " " +
        emps[x].getSalary());
```

Pay attention to the syntax of the Employee objects' method calls, such as emps[x].getEmpNum(). Although you might be tempted to place the subscript at the end of the expression after the method name—as in emps.getEmpNum[x] or emps.getEmpNum()[x]—you cannot; the values in x (0 through 6) refer to a particular emps object, each of which has access to a single getEmpNum() method. Placement of the bracketed subscript so it follows emps means the method "belongs" to a particular element of emps.

Using the Enhanced for Loop with Objects

You can use the enhanced for loop to cycle through an array of objects. For example, to display data for seven Employees stored in the emps array, you can write the following:

```
for(Employee worker : emps)
    System.out.println(worker.getEmpNum() + " " + worker.getSalary());
```

In this loop, worker is a local variable that represents each element of emps in turn. Using the enhanced for loop eliminates the need to use a limiting value for the loop and eliminates the need for a subscript following each element.

Manipulating Arrays of Strings

As with any other object, you can create an array of String objects. For example, you can store three company department names as follows:

```
String[] deptNames = {"Accounting", "Human Resources", "Sales"};
```

You can access these department names with a subscript like any other array object. For example, you can use the following code to display the list of `Strings` stored in the `deptNames` array:

```
for(int a = 0; a < deptNames.length; ++a)
   System.out.println(deptNames[a]);
```

Notice that `deptNames.length;` refers to the length of the array `deptNames` (three elements) and not to the length of any `String` objects stored in the `deptNames` array. Remember that arrays use a `length` field (no parentheses follow), and `String` objects use a `length()` method. For example, if `deptNames[0]` is "Accounting", then `deptNames[0].length()` is 10 because "Accounting" contains 10 characters.

TWO TRUTHS & A LIE

Declaring and Using Arrays of Objects

1. The following statement declares an array named `students` that holds 10 `Student` objects:

   ```
   Student[] students = new Student[10];
   ```

2. When a class has a default constructor and you create an array of objects from the class, you do not need to call the constructor explicitly.

3. To use a method that belongs to an object that is part of an array, you insert the appropriate subscript notation after the array name and before the dot that precedes the method name.

The false statement is #2. Whether a class has a default constructor or not, when you create an array of objects from the class, you must call the constructor using the keyword new for each declared array element.

 You Do It

Creating a Class that Contains an Array of `Strings`

In this section, you create a class named `BowlingTeam` that contains the name of a bowling team and an array that holds the names of the four team members.

1. Open a new file, and type the header and curly braces for the `BowlingTeam` class:

   ```
   public class BowlingTeam
   {
   }
   ```

(continues)

(continued)

2. Create a field for the team name and an array that holds the team members' names.

```
private String teamName;
private String[] members = new String[4];
```

410

3. Create get and set methods for the teamName field as follows:

```
public void setTeamName(String team)
{
    teamName = team;
}
public String getTeamName()
{
    return teamName;
}
```

4. Add a method that sets a team member's name. The method requires a position and a name, and it uses the position as a subscript to the members array.

```
public void setMember(int number, String name)
{
    members[number] = name;
}
```

5. Add a method that returns a team member's name. The method requires a value used as the subscript that determines which member's name to return.

```
public String getMember(int number)
{
    return members[number];
}
```

6. Save the file as **BowlingTeam.java**. Compile it and correct any errors.

Creating a Program to Demonstrate an Instance of the BowlingTeam *Class*

In this section, you write a program in which you create an instance of the BowlingTeam class and provide values for it.

1. Open a new file, and enter the following code to begin the class.

```
import java.util.*;
public class BowlingTeamDemo
{
    public static void main(String[] args)
    {
```

(continues)

(continued)

2. Add five declarations. These include a `String` that holds user input, a `BowlingTeam` object, an integer to use as a subscript, a constant that represents the number of members on a bowling team, and a `Scanner` object for input.

```
String name;
BowlingTeam bowlTeam = new BowlingTeam();
int x;
final int NUM_TEAM_MEMBERS = 4;
Scanner input = new Scanner(System.in);
```

3. Prompt the user for a bowling team name. Accept it, and then assign it to the `BowlingTeam` object:

```
System.out.print("Enter team name >> ");
name = input.nextLine();
bowlTeam.setTeamName(name);
```

4. In a loop that executes four times, prompt the user for a team member's name. Accept the name and assign it to the `BowlingTeam` object using the subscript to indicate the team member's position in the array in the `BowlingTeam` class.

```
for(x = 0; x < NUM_TEAM_MEMBERS; ++x)
{
    System.out.print("Enter team member's name >> ");
    name = input.nextLine();
    bowlTeam.setMember(x, name);
}
```

5. Display the details of the `BowlingTeam` object using the following code:

```
System.out.println("\nMembers of team " +
    bowlTeam.getTeamName());
for(x = 0; x < NUM_TEAM_MEMBERS; ++x)
    System.out.print(bowlTeam.getMember(x) + " ");
System.out.println();
```

6. Add a closing curly brace for the `main()` method and another for the class.

7. Save the file as **BowlingTeamDemo.java**, and then compile and execute it. Figure 8-7 shows a typical execution.

(continues)

(continued)

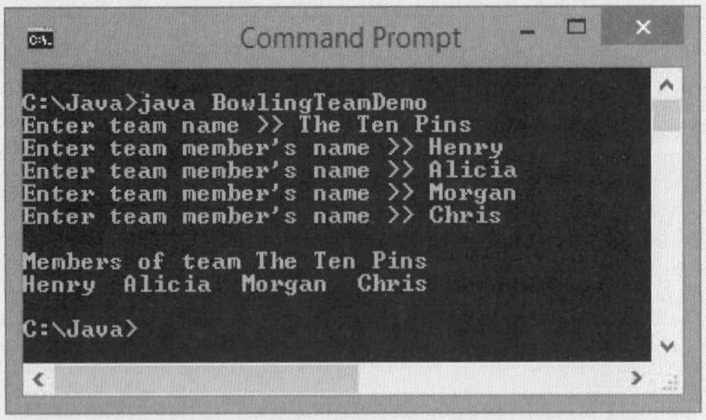

Figure 8-7 Typical execution of the BowlingTeamDemo class

Creating a Program that Declares an Array of BowlingTeam *Objects*

Next, you create and use an array of BowlingTeam objects.

1. Open the **BowlingTeamDemo.java** file. Rename the class
   BowlingTeamDemo2, and immediately save the file as
   BowlingTeamDemo2.java.

2. Above the declaration of the BowlingTeam object, add a new named constant
   that holds a number of BowlingTeams, and then replace the statement that
   declares the single BowlingTeam object with an array declaration of four
   BowlingTeam objects.

   ```
   final int NUM_TEAMS = 4;
   BowlingTeam[] teams = new BowlingTeam[NUM_TEAMS];
   ```

3. The current program declares x, which is used as a subscript to display team
   member names. Now, following the declaration of x, add a variable that is
   used as a subscript to display the teams:

   ```
   int y;
   ```

4. Following the declaration of the Scanner object, and before the team
   name prompt, insert a for loop that executes as many times as there are
   BowlingTeamS. Add the opening curly brace, and within the loop, allocate
   memory for each array element:

   ```
   for(y = 0; y < NUM_TEAMS; ++y)
   {
       teams[y] = new BowlingTeam();
   ```

(continues)

(continued)

5. Delete the statement that uses the `setTeamName()` method with the single `bowlTeam` object. In its place, insert a statement that uses the method with one of the array elements:

```
teams[y].setTeamName(name);
```

6. Within the first `for` loop controlled by `x`, delete the statement that uses the `setMember()` method with the single `bowlTeam` object. In its place, insert a statement that uses the method with one of the array elements:

```
teams[y].setMember(x, name);
```

7. After the closing curly brace for the `for` loop controlled by the variable `x`, add a closing curly brace for the `for` loop controlled by the variable `y`.

8. Adjust the indentation of the program statements so that the program logic is easy to follow with the new nested loops. The nested loops that you just modified should look like the following 13 lines of code:

```
for(y = 0; y < NUM_TEAMS; ++y)
{
   teams[y] = new BowlingTeam();
   System.out.print("Enter team name >> ");
   name = input.nextLine();
   teams[y].setTeamName(name);
   for(x = 0; x < NUM_TEAM_MEMBERS; ++x)
   {
      System.out.print("Enter team member's name >> ");
      name = input.nextLine();
      teams[y].setMember(x, name);
   }
}
```

9. The `for` loop at the end of the current program lists four team members' names. Replace this loop with the following nested version that lists four members' names for each of four teams:

```
for(y = 0; y < NUM_TEAMS; ++y)
{
   System.out.println("\nMembers of team " +
      teams[y].getTeamName());
   for(x = 0; x < NUM_TEAM_MEMBERS; ++x)
      System.out.print(teams[y].getMember(x) + " ");
   System.out.println();
}
```

(continues)

(continued)

10. Save the file, and then compile and execute the program. Figure 8-8 shows a typical execution. The user can enter data into the array of `BowlingTeam` objects, including the array of `Strings` within each object, and then see all the entered data successfully displayed.

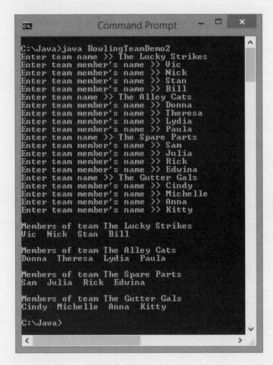

Figure 8-8 Typical execution of the `BowlingTeamDemo2` application

Searching an Array and Using Parallel Arrays

Suppose that a company manufactures 10 items. When a customer places an order for an item, you need to determine whether the item number on the order form is valid. When you want to determine whether a variable holds one of many valid values, one option is to use a series of `if` statements to compare the variable to a series of valid values. If valid item numbers are sequential, such as 101 through 110, the following simple `if` statement that uses a logical AND can verify the order number and set a Boolean field to `true`:

```
final int LOW = 101;
final int HIGH = 110;
boolean validItem = false;
if(itemOrdered >= LOW && itemOrdered <= HIGH)
    validItem = true;
```

In this example, the Boolean field validItem is used as a **flag**—a variable that holds a value as an indicator of whether some condition has been met.

If the valid item numbers are nonsequential—for example, 101, 108, 201, and so on—you can code the following deeply nested if statement or a lengthy OR comparison to determine the validity of an item number:

```
if(itemOrdered == 101)
    validItem = true;
else if(itemOrdered == 108)
    validItem = true;
else if(itemOrdered == 201)
    validItem = true;
// and so on
```

Instead of a long series of if statements, a more elegant solution is to compare the itemOrdered variable to a list of values in an array, a process called **searching an array**. You can initialize the array with the valid values using the following statement, which creates exactly 10 array elements with subscripts 0 through 9:

```
int[] validValues = {101, 108, 201, 213, 266,
    304, 311, 409, 411, 412};
```

After the list of valid values is initialized, you can use a for statement to loop through the array, and set a Boolean variable to true when a match is found:

```
for(int x = 0; x < validValues.length; ++x)
{
    if(itemOrdered == validValues[x])
        validItem = true;
}
```

This simple for loop replaces the long series of if statements; it checks the itemOrdered value against each of the 10 array values in turn. Also, if a company carries 1,000 items instead of 10, nothing changes in the for statement—the value of validValues.length is updated automatically.

Using Parallel Arrays

As an added bonus, if you set up another array with the same number of elements and corresponding data, you can use the same subscript to access additional information. A **parallel array** is one with the same number of elements as another, and for which the values in corresponding elements are related. For example, if the 10 items your company carries have 10 different prices, you can set up an array to hold those prices as follows:

```
double[] prices = {0.29, 1.23, 3.50, 0.69…};
```

The prices must appear in the same order as their corresponding item numbers in the validValues array. Now, the same for loop that finds the valid item number also finds the price, as shown in the application in Figure 8-9. In the shaded portion of the code, notice that when the ordered item's number is found in the validValues array, the itemPrice value is "pulled" from the prices array. In other words, if the item number is found in the second position in the validValues array, you can find the correct price in the second position in the prices array. Figure 8-10 shows a typical execution of the program. A user requests item 409, which is the eighth element in the validValues array, so the price displayed is the eighth element in the prices array.

```java
import javax.swing.*;
public class FindPrice
{
    public static void main(String[] args)
    {
        final int NUMBER_OF_ITEMS = 10;
        int[] validValues = {101, 108, 201, 213, 266,
            304, 311, 409, 411, 412};
        double[] prices = {0.29, 1.23, 3.50, 0.69, 6.79,
            3.19, 0.99, 0.89, 1.26, 8.00};
        String strItem;
        int itemOrdered;
        double itemPrice = 0.0;
        boolean validItem = false;
        strItem = JOptionPane.showInputDialog(null,
            "Enter the item number you want to order");
        itemOrdered = Integer.parseInt(strItem);
        for(int x = 0; x < NUMBER_OF_ITEMS; ++x)
        {
            if(itemOrdered == validValues[x])
            {
                validItem = true;
                itemPrice = prices[x];
            }
        }
        if(validItem)
            JOptionPane.showMessageDialog(null, "The price for item " +
                itemOrdered + " is $" + itemPrice);
        else
            JOptionPane.showMessageDialog(null,
                "Sorry - invalid item entered");
    }
}
```

Figure 8-9   The FindPrice application that accesses information in parallel arrays

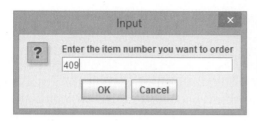

Figure 8-10   Typical execution of the `FindPrice` application

 When you initialize parallel arrays, it is convenient to use spacing so that the values that correspond to each other visually align on the screen or printed page.

 Instead of parallel arrays containing item numbers and prices, you might prefer to create a class named `Item` in which each instance contains two fields—`itemOrdered` and `itemPrice`. Then you could create a single array of objects that encapsulate item numbers and prices. There are almost always multiple ways to approach programming problems.

Within the code shown in Figure 8-9, you compare every `itemOrdered` with each of the 10 `validValues`. Even when an `itemOrdered` is equivalent to the first value in the `validValues` array (101), you always make nine additional cycles through the array. On each of these nine additional cycles, the comparison between `itemOrdered` and `validValues[x]` is always `false`. As soon as a match for an `itemOrdered` is found, it is most efficient to break out of the `for` loop early. An easy way to accomplish this is to set x to a high value within the block of statements executed when there is a match. Then, after a match, the `for` loop does not execute again because the limiting comparison (x < `NUMBER_OF_ITEMS`) is surpassed. Figure 8-11 shows this loop. In an array with many possible matches, it is most efficient to place the more common items first, so they are matched right away. For example, if item 311 is ordered most often, place 311 first in the `validValues` array, and place its price ($0.99) first in the `prices` array.

```
for(int x = 0; x < NUMBER_OF_ITEMS; ++x)
{
    if(itemOrdered == validValues[x])
    {
        validItem = true;
        itemPrice = prices[x];
        x = NUMBER_OF_ITEMS;
    }
}
```

Figure 8-11   A `for` loop with an early exit

In the code in Figure 8-11, the loop control variable is altered within the loop body. Some programmers object to altering a loop control variable within the body of a `for` loop; they feel that the loop control variable should only be altered in the third section of the `for` clause (where x is incremented). These programmers would prefer the loop in Figure 8-12, in which two Boolean expressions appear in the shaded section in the middle portion of the `for` clause. In this example, the loop control variable is not altered within the loop body. Instead, x must be within range before each iteration and `validItem` must not yet have been set to `true`.

```
for(int x = 0; x < NUMBER_OF_ITEMS && !validItem; ++x)
{
    if(itemOrdered == validValues[x])
    {
        validItem = true;
        itemPrice = prices[x];
    }
}
```

Figure 8-12   A for loop that uses a compound test for termination

Searching an Array for a Range Match

Searching an array for an exact match is not always practical. Suppose your company gives customer discounts based on the quantity of items ordered. Perhaps no discount is given for any order of fewer than a dozen items, but there are increasing discounts available for orders of increasing quantities, as shown in Table 8-1.

Total Quantity Ordered	Discount
1 to 12	None
13 to 49	10%
50 to 99	14%
100 to 199	18%
200 or more	20%

Table 8-1   Discount table

One awkward option is to create a single array to store the discount rates. You could use a variable named `numOfItems` as a subscript to the array, but the array would need hundreds of entries, as in the following example:

```
double[] discounts = {0, 0, 0, 0, 0, 0, 0, 0,
    0, 0, 0, 0, 0, 0.10, 0.10, 0.10 …};
```

Thirteen zeroes are listed in the discounts array. The first array element has a 0 subscript and represents a zero discount for zero items. The next 12 discounts (for items 1 through 12) are also zero. When numOfItems is 13, discounts[numOfItems], or discounts[13], is 0.10. The array would store 37 copies of 0.10 for elements 13 through 49. The discounts array would need to be ridiculously large to hold an exact value for each possible quantity ordered.

A better option is to create two corresponding arrays and perform a **range match**, in which you compare a value to the endpoints of numerical ranges to find the category in which a value belongs. For example, one array can hold the five discount rates, and the other array can hold five discount range limits. The Total Quantity Ordered column in Table 8-1 shows five ranges. If you use only the first figure in each range, you can create an array that holds five low limits:

```
int[] discountRangeLimits = {1, 13, 50, 100, 200};
```

A parallel array can hold the five discount rates:

```
double[] discountRates = {0, 0.10, 0.14, 0.18, 0.20};
```

Then, starting at the last discountRangeLimits array element, for any numOfItems greater than or equal to discountRangeLimits[4], the appropriate discount is discounts[4]. In other words, for any numOrdered less than discountRangeLimits[4], you should decrement the subscript and look in a lower range. Figure 8-13 shows an application that uses the parallel arrays, and Figure 8-14 shows a typical execution of the program.

```java
import javax.swing.*;
public class FindDiscount
{
   public static void main(String[] args)
   {
      final int NUM_RANGES = 5;
      int[] discountRangeLimits = { 1, 13, 50, 100, 200};
      double[] discountRates =    {0.00, 0.10, 0.14, 0.18, 0.20};
      double customerDiscount;
      String strNumOrdered;
      int numOrdered;
      int sub = NUM_RANGES - 1;
      strNumOrdered = JOptionPane.showInputDialog(null,
         "How many items are ordered?");
      numOrdered = Integer.parseInt(strNumOrdered);
      while(sub >= 0 && numOrdered < discountRangeLimits[sub])
         --sub;
      customerDiscount = discountRates[sub];
      JOptionPane.showMessageDialog(null, "Discount rate for " +
         numOrdered + " items is " + customerDiscount);
   }
}
```

Figure 8-13   The FindDiscount class

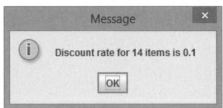

Figure 8-14 Typical execution of the FindDiscount class

In the while loop in the application in Figure 8-13, sub is required to be greater than or equal to 0 before the second half of the statement that compares numOrdered to discountRangeLimits[sub] executes. It is a good programming practice to ensure that a subscript to an array does not fall below zero, causing a runtime error.

Watch the video *Searching an Array*.

TWO TRUTHS & A LIE

Searching an Array and Using Parallel Arrays

1. A parallel array is one with the same number of elements as another, and for which the values in corresponding elements are related.

2. When searching an array, it is usually most efficient to abandon the search as soon as the sought-after element is found.

3. In a range match, you commonly compare a value to the midpoint of each of a series of numerical ranges.

The false statement is #3. In a range match, you commonly compare a value to the low or high endpoint of each of a series of numerical ranges, but not to the midpoint.

You Do It

Searching an Array

In this section, you modify the `BowlingTeamDemo2` program so that after the bowling team data has been entered, a user can request the roster for a specific team.

1. Open the **BowlingTeamDemo2.java** file, and change the class name to `BowlingTeamDemo3`. Immediately save the file as **BowlingTeamDemo3.java**.

2. At the end of the existing application, just before the two final closing curly braces, insert a prompt asking the user to enter a team name. Then accept the entered value.

```
System.out.print("\n\nEnter a team name to see its roster >> ");
name = input.nextLine();
```

3. Next, insert a nested `for` loop. The outer loop varies `y` from 0 through the highest subscript allowed in the `teams` array. Within this loop, the team name requested by the user is compared to each stored team name; when they are equal, another `for` loop displays the four team member names.

```
for(y = 0; y < teams.length; ++y)
   if(name.equals(teams[y].getTeamName()))
      for(x = 0; x < NUM_TEAM_MEMBERS; ++x)
         System.out.print(teams[y].getMember(x) + " ");
```

4. Insert an additional empty `println()` method call.

```
System.out.println();
```

5. Save the file, and then compile and execute the program. Figure 8-15 shows the last part of a typical execution, which contains the output after input is complete.

(continues)

422

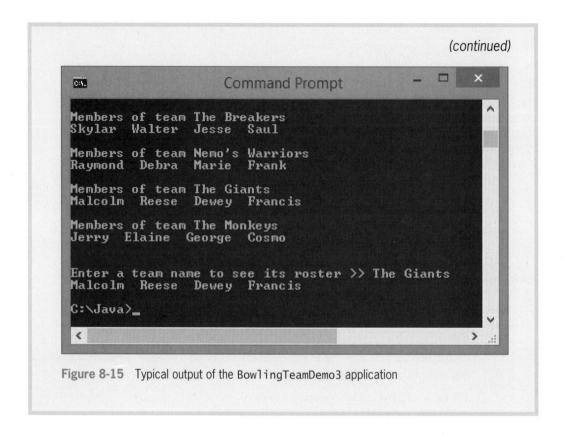

(continued)

Figure 8-15   Typical output of the BowlingTeamDemo3 application

Passing Arrays to and Returning Arrays from Methods

You have already seen that you can use any individual array element in the same manner as you use any single variable of the same type. That is, if you declare an integer array as int[] someNums = new int[12];, you can subsequently display someNums[0], or increment someNums[1], or work with any element just as you do for any integer. Similarly, you can pass a single array element to a method in exactly the same manner as you pass any variable.

Examine the PassArrayElement application shown in Figure 8-16 and the output shown in Figure 8-17. The application creates an array of four integers and displays them. Then, the application calls the methodGetsOneInt() method four times, passing each element in turn. The method displays the number, changes the number to 999, and then displays the number again. Finally, back in the main() method, the four numbers are displayed again.

```
public class PassArrayElement
{
    public static void main(String[] args)
    {
        final int NUM_ELEMENTS = 4;
        int[] someNums = {5, 10, 15, 20};
        int x;
        System.out.print("At start of main: ");
        for(x = 0; x < NUM_ELEMENTS; ++x)
            System.out.print(" " + someNums[x]);
        System.out.println();
        for(x = 0; x < NUM_ELEMENTS; ++x)
            methodGetsOneInt(someNums[x]);
        System.out.print("At end of main: ");
        for(x = 0; x < NUM_ELEMENTS; ++x)
            System.out.print(" " + someNums[x]);
        System.out.println();
    }
    public static void methodGetsOneInt(int one)
    {
        System.out.print("At start of method one is: " + one);
        one = 999;
        System.out.println(" and at end of method one is: " + one);
    }
}
```

Figure 8-16 The PassArrayElement class

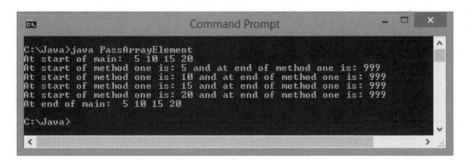

Figure 8-17 Output of the PassArrayElement application

As you can see in Figure 8-17, the four numbers that were changed in the methodGetsOneInt() method remain unchanged back in main() after the method executes. The variable named one is local to the methodGetsOneInt() method, and any changes to variables passed into the method are not permanent and are not reflected in the array in the main() program. Each variable named one in the methodGetsOneInt() method holds only a copy of the array element passed into the method. The individual array elements are passed by value; that is, a copy of the value is made and used within the receiving method. When any primitive type (boolean, char, byte, short, int, long, float, or double) is passed to a method, the value is passed.

Arrays, like all nonprimitive objects, are reference types; this means that the object actually holds a memory address where the values are stored. (You first learned the term *reference types* in Chapter 2, where they were contrasted with *primitive types*.) Because an array name is a reference, you cannot assign another array to it using the = operator, nor can you compare two arrays using the == operator. Additionally, when you pass an array (that is, pass its name) to a method, the receiving method gets a copy of the array's actual memory address. This means that the receiving method has access to, and the ability to alter, the original values in the array elements in the calling method.

The class shown in Figure 8-18 creates an array of four integers. After the integers are displayed, the array name (its address) is passed to a method named methodGetsArray(). Within the method, the numbers are displayed, which shows that they retain their values from main(), but then the value 888 is assigned to each number. Even though methodGetsArray() is a void method—meaning nothing is returned to the main() method—when the main() method displays the array for the second time, all of the values have been changed to 888, as you can see in the output in Figure 8-19. Because the method receives a reference to the array, the methodGetsArray() method "knows" the address of the array declared in main() and makes its changes directly to the original array.

 In some languages, arrays are **passed by reference**, meaning that a receiving method gets the memory address. It is a subtle distinction, but in Java, the receiving method gets a copy of the original address. In other words, in Java, an array is not passed by reference, but a reference to an array is passed by value.

```
public class PassArray
{
    public static void main(String[] args)
    {
        final int NUM_ELEMENTS = 4;
        int[] someNums = {5, 10, 15, 20};
        int x;
        System.out.print("At start of main: ");
        for(x = 0; x < NUM_ELEMENTS; ++x)
            System.out.print(" " + someNums[x]);
        System.out.println();
        methodGetsArray(someNums);
        System.out.print("At end of main: ");
        for(x = 0; x < NUM_ELEMENTS; ++x)
            System.out.print(" " + someNums[x]);
        System.out.println();
    }
```

Figure 8-18   The PassArray class *(continues)*

(continued)

```java
public static void methodGetsArray(int[] arr)
{
    int x;
    System.out.print("At start of method arr holds: ");
    for(x = 0; x < arr.length; ++x)
        System.out.print(" " + arr[x]);
    System.out.println();
    for(x = 0; x < arr.length; ++x)
        arr[x] = 888;
    System.out.print(" and at end of method arr holds: ");
    for(x = 0; x < arr.length; ++x)
        System.out.print(" " + arr[x]);
    System.out.println();
}
}
```

Figure 8-18 The `PassArray` class

Notice that in the first shaded statement in Figure 8-18, the array name is passed to the method and no brackets are used. In the method header, brackets are used to show that the parameter is an array of integers (a reference) and not a simple `int`.

Figure 8-19 Output of the `PassArray` application

 In some other languages, notably C, C++, and C#, you can choose to pass variables to methods by value or reference. In Java, you cannot make this choice. Primitive type variables are always passed by value. When you pass an object, a copy of the reference to the object is always passed.

Returning an Array from a Method

A method can return an array reference. When a method returns an array reference, you include square brackets with the return type in the method header. For example, Figure 8-20 shows a getArray() method that returns a locally declared array of ints. Square brackets are used as part of the return type; the return statement returns the array name without any brackets.

```
public static int[] getArray()
{
    int[] scores = {90, 80, 70, 60};
    return scores;
}
```

Figure 8-20   The getArray() method

When you call the getArray() method in Figure 8-20, you can store its returned value in any integer array reference. For example, you might declare an array and make the method call in the following statement:

```
int[] scoresFromMethod = getArray();
```

 Watch the video *Arrays and Methods*.

TWO TRUTHS & A LIE

Passing Arrays to and Returning Arrays from Methods

1. You pass a single array element to a method using its name, and the method must be prepared to receive the appropriate data type.

2. You pass an array to a method using its name followed by a pair of brackets; arrays are passed by value.

3. When a method returns an array reference, you include square brackets with the return type in the method header.

The false statement is #2. You pass an array to a method using its name; a copy of the array's address is passed to the method.

You Do It

Passing an Array to a Method

Next, you add a method to the BowlingTeamDemo3 application. The improvement allows you to remove the data entry process from the main program and encapsulate the process in its own method.

1. Open the **BowlingTeamDemo3.java** file if it is not already open. Immediately save the file as **BowlingTeamDemo4.java**. Change the class name to match the filename.

2. Just before the closing curly brace for the class, add the following shell for a method that accepts a BowlingTeam array argument.

    ```java
    public static void getTeamData(BowlingTeam[] teams)
    {
    }
    ```

3. Within the getTeamData() method, add the following six declarations (or copy them from the main() method):

    ```java
    String name;
    final int NUM_TEAMS = 4;
    int x;
    int y;
    final int NUM_TEAM_MEMBERS = 4;
    Scanner input = new Scanner(System.in);
    ```

4. Cut the 13 lines of code that assign memory to the BowlingTeam array and obtain all the data values. Place these 13 lines within the getTeamData() method following the declarations.

    ```java
    for(y = 0; y < NUM_TEAMS; ++y)
    {
        teams[y] = new BowlingTeam();
        System.out.print("Enter team name >> ");
        name = input.nextLine();
        teams[y].setTeamName(name);
        for(x = 0; x < NUM_TEAM_MEMBERS; ++x)
        {
            System.out.print("Enter team member's name >> ");
            name = input.nextLine();
            teams[y].setMember(x, name);
        }
    }
    ```

(continues)

427

(continued)

5. In place of the 13 cut lines, insert a method call. This call passes a copy of the array reference to the method. Notice that this call does not assign a return value. The method is a `void` method and returns nothing. Nevertheless, the array in the `main()` method will be updated because the method is receiving access to the array's memory address.

   ```
   getTeamData(teams);
   ```

6. Save the file (as **BowlingTeamDemo4.java**), and then compile and execute the program. Confirm that the program works exactly as it did before the new method was added.

Don't Do It

- Don't forget that the lowest array subscript is 0.
- Don't forget that the highest array subscript is one less than the length of the array.
- Don't forget the semicolon following the closing curly brace in an array initialization list.
- Don't forget that `length` is an array property and not a method. Conversely, `length()` is a `String` method, and not a property.
- Don't place a subscript after an object's field or method name when accessing an array of objects. Instead, the subscript for an object follows the object and comes before the dot and the field or method name.
- Don't assume that an array of characters is a string. Although an array of characters can be treated like a string in languages like C++, you can't do this in Java. For example, if you display the name of a character array, you will see its address, not its contents.
- Don't forget that array names are references. Therefore, you cannot assign one array to another using the = operator, nor can you compare array contents using the == operator.
- Don't use brackets with an array name when you pass it to a method. Do use brackets in the method header that accepts the array.

Key Terms

An **array** is a named list of data items that all have the same type.

An **element** is one variable or object in an array.

A **subscript** is an integer contained within square brackets that indicates one of an array's elements.

An **index** is a subscript.

Out of bounds describes a subscript that is not within the allowed range for an array.

An **initialization list** is a series of values provided for an array when it is declared.

Populating an array is the act of providing values for all the elements.

A **property** of an object is an instance variable or field.

The **enhanced for loop** allows you to cycle through an array without specifying the starting and ending points for the loop control variable.

A **foreach loop** is an enhanced `for` loop.

A **flag** is a variable that holds a value (often `true` or `false`) as an indicator of whether some condition has been met.

Searching an array is the process of comparing a value to a list of values in an array, looking for a match.

A **parallel array** is one with the same number of elements as another, and for which the values in corresponding elements are related.

A **range match** is the process of comparing a value to the endpoints of numerical ranges to find a category in which the value belongs.

Passed by value describes what happens when a variable is passed to a method and a copy is made in the receiving method.

Passed by reference describes what happens when a reference (address) is passed to a method.

Chapter Summary

- An array is a named list of data items that all have the same type. You declare an array variable by inserting a pair of square brackets after the type. To reserve memory space for an array, you use the keyword `new`. You use a subscript contained within square brackets to refer to one of an array's variables, or elements. In Java, any array's elements are numbered beginning with zero.

- Array names represent computer memory addresses. When you declare an array name, no computer memory address is assigned to it, and the array variable name has the value `null`. When you use the keyword `new` or supply an initialization list, an array acquires an actual memory address. When an initialization list is not provided, each data type has a default value for its array elements.

- You can shorten many array-based tasks by using a variable as a subscript. When an application contains an array, it is common to perform loops that execute from 0 to one less than the size of the array. The length field is an automatically created field that is assigned to every array; it contains the number of elements in the array.

- You can declare arrays that hold elements of any type, including Strings and other objects. To use a method that belongs to an object that is part of an array, you insert the appropriate subscript notation after the array name and before the dot that precedes the method name.

- By looping through an array and making comparisons, you can search an array to find a match to a value. You can use a parallel array with the same number of elements to hold related elements. You perform a range match by placing end values of ranges in an array and making greater-than or less-than comparisons to each array element.

- You can pass a single array element to a method, and the array receives a copy of the passed value. You can pass an array name to a method, and the method receives a copy of the array's memory address and has access to the values in the original array.

Review Questions

1. An array is a list of data items that _____.

   a. all have the same type   c. all are integers

   b. all have different names   d. all are null

2. When you declare an array, _____.

   a. you always reserve memory for it in the same statement

   b. you might reserve memory for it in the same statement

   c. you cannot reserve memory for it in the same statement

   d. the ability to reserve memory for it in the same statement depends on the type of the array

3. You reserve memory locations for an array when you _____.

   a. declare the array name   c. use the keyword mem

   b. use the keyword new   d. use the keyword size

4. For how many integers does the following statement reserve room?

   int[] value = new int[34];

   a. 0   c. 34

   b. 33   d. 35

5. Which of the following can be used as an array subscript?

   a. character   c. int

   b. double   d. String

6. If you declare an array as follows, how do you indicate the final element of the array?

   `int[] num = new int[6];`

   a. `num[0]`   c. `num[6]`

   b. `num[5]`   d. impossible to tell

7. If you declare an integer array as follows, what is the value of `num[2]`?

   `int[] num = {101, 202, 303, 404, 505, 606};`

   a. 101   c. 303

   b. 202   d. impossible to tell

8. Array names represent _____.

   a. values   c. references

   b. functions   d. allusions

9. Unicode value '\u0000' is also known as _____.

   a. `nil`   c. `nada`

   b. `void`   d. `null`

10. When you initialize an array by giving it values upon creation, you _____.

    a. do not explicitly give the array a size

    b. also must give the array a size explicitly

    c. must make all the values zero, blank, or `false`

    d. must make certain each value is different from the others

11. In Java, you can declare an array of 12 elements and initialize _____.

    a. only the first one   c. Both of these are true.

    b. all of them   d. Neither of these is true.

12. Assume an array is declared as follows. Which of the following statements correctly assigns the value 100 to each of the array elements?

    `int[] num = new int[4];`

    a. `for(x = 0; x < 3; ++x) num[x] = 100;`

    b. `for(x = 0; x < 4; ++x) num[x] = 100;`

    c. `for(x = 1; x < 4; ++x) num[x] = 100;`

    d. `for(x = 1; x < 5; ++x) num[x] = 100;`

13. Suppose you have declared an array as follows:

    `int[] creditScores = {670, 720, 815};`

    What is the value of `creditScores.length`?

    a. 0   c. 2

    b. 1   d. 3

14. If a class named `Student` contains a method `setID()` that takes an `int` argument and you write an application in which you create an array of 20 `Student` objects named `scholar`, which of the following statements correctly assigns an ID number to the first `Student scholar`?

    a. `Student[0].setID(1234);`   c. `Student.setID[0](1234);`

    b. `scholar[0].setID(1234);`   d. `scholar.setID[0](1234);`

15. A parallel array is one that _____.

    a. holds values that correspond to those in another array

    b. holds an even number of values

    c. is placed adjacent to another array in code

    d. is placed adjacent to another array in memory

16. In which of the following situations would setting up parallel arrays be most useful?

    a. You need to look up an employee's ID number to find the employee's last name.

    b. You need to calculate interest earned on a savings account balance.

    c. You need to store a list of 20 commonly misspelled words.

    d. You need to determine the shortest distance between two points on a map.

17. When you pass an array element to a method, the method receives _____.

    a. a copy of the array   c. a copy of the value in the element

    b. the address of the array   d. the address of the element

18. A single array element of a primitive type is passed to a method by _____.

    a. value   c. address

    b. reference   d. osmosis

19. When you pass an array to a method, the method receives _____.

    a. a copy of the array

    b. a copy of the first element in the array

    c. the address of the array

    d. nothing

20. If a method should return an array to its calling method, _____.

    a. the method's return type must match its parameter type

    b. the return type in the method header is preceded by an ampersand

    c. the return type in the method header is followed by square brackets

    d. A Java method cannot return an array.

Exercises

Programming Exercises

1. Write an application that stores 12 integers in an array. Display the integers from first to last, and then display the integers from last to first. Save the file as **TwelveInts.java**.

2. Allow a user to enter any number of `double` values up to 20. The user should enter 99999 to quit entering numbers. Display an error message if the user quits without entering any numbers; otherwise, display each entered value and its distance from the average. Save the file as **DistanceFromAverage.java**.

3. a. Write an application for Cody's Car Care Shop that shows a user a list of available services: *oil change, tire rotation, battery check*, or *brake inspection*. Allow the user to enter a string that corresponds to one of the options, and display the option and its price as $25, $22, $15, or $5, accordingly. Display an error message if the user enters an invalid item. Save the file as **CarCareChoice.java**.

   b. It might not be reasonable to expect users to type long entries such as "oil change" accurately. Modify the `CarCareChoice` class so that as long as the user enters the first three characters of a service, the choice is considered valid. Save the file as **CarCareChoice2.java**.

4. Create an application containing an array that stores 10 integers. The application should call five methods that in turn (1) display all the integers, (2) display all the integers in reverse order, (3) display the sum of the integers, (4) display all values less than a limiting argument, and (5) display all values that are higher than the calculated average value. Save the file as **ArrayMethodDemo.java**.

5. a. Write an application that accepts up to 10 `Strings`, or fewer if the user enters a terminating value. Divide the entered `Strings` into two lists—one for short `Strings` that are 10 characters or fewer and the other for long `Strings`. After data entry is complete, prompt the user to enter which type of `String` to display, and then output the correct list. For this exercise, you can assume that if the user does not request the list of short strings, the user wants the list of long strings. If there are no `Strings` in a requested list, output an appropriate message. Prompt the user continuously until a sentinel value is entered. Save the file as **CategorizeStrings.java**.

   b. Modify the `CategorizeStrings` application to divide the entered `Strings` into those that contain no spaces, one space, or more. After data entry is complete, continuously prompt the user to enter the type of `String` to display. If the user does not enter one of the three valid choices, display all of the `Strings`. Save the file as **CategorizeStrings2.java**.

6. a. Create a class named `Salesperson`. Data fields for `Salesperson` include an integer ID number and a `double` annual sales amount. Methods include a constructor that requires values for both data fields, as well as get and set methods for each of the

data fields. Write an application named DemoSalesperson that declares an array of 10 Salesperson objects. Set each ID number to 9999 and each sales value to zero. Display the 10 Salesperson objects. Save the files as **Salesperson.java** and **DemoSalesperson.java**.

  b. Modify the DemoSalesperson application so each Salesperson has a successive ID number from 111 through 120 and a sales value that ranges from $25,000 to $70,000, increasing by $5,000 for each successive Salesperson. Save the file as **DemoSalesperson2.java**.

7. a. Create a CollegeCourse class. The class contains fields for the course ID (for example, "CIS 210"), credit hours (for example, 3), and a letter grade (for example, 'A'). Include get and set methods for each field. Create a Student class containing an ID number and an array of five CollegeCourse objects. Create a get and set method for the Student ID number. Also create a get method that returns one of the Student's CollegeCourses; the method takes an integer argument and returns the CollegeCourse in that position (0 through 4). Next, create a set method that sets the value of one of the Student's CollegeCourses; the method takes two arguments—a CollegeCourse and an integer representing the CollegeCourse's position (0 through 4). Save the files as **CollegeCourse.java** and **Student.java**.

  b. Write an application that prompts a professor to enter grades for five different courses each for 10 students. Prompt the professor to enter data for one student at a time, including student ID and course data for five courses. Use prompts containing the number of the student whose data is being entered and the course number—for example, "Enter ID for student #s", where s is an integer from 1 through 10, indicating the student, and "Enter course ID #n", where n is an integer from 1 through 5, indicating the course number. Verify that the professor enters only A, B, C, D, or F for the grade value for each course. Save the file as **InputGrades.java**.

8. Write an application that allows a user to enter the names and birthdates of up to 10 friends. Continue to prompt the user for names and birthdates until the user enters the sentinel value "ZZZ" for a name or has entered 10 names, whichever comes first. When the user is finished entering names, produce a count of how many names were entered, and then display the names. In a loop, continuously ask the user to type one of the names and display the corresponding birthdate or an error message if the name has not been previously entered. The loop continues until the user enters "ZZZ" for a name. Save the application as **BirthdayReminder.java**.

9. A personal phone directory contains room for first names and phone numbers for 30 people. Assign names and phone numbers for the first 10 people. Prompt the user for a name, and if the name is found in the list, display the corresponding phone number. If the name is not found in the list, prompt the user for a phone number, and add the new name and phone number to the list. Continue to prompt the user for names until the user enters *quit*. After the arrays are full (containing 30 names), do not allow the user to add new entries. Save the file as **PhoneNumbers.java**.

10. In the exercises in Chapter 4, you created a CertOfDeposit class. Now, create an application to accept data for an array of five CertOfDeposit objects, and then display the data. Save the application as **CertOfDepositArray.java**.

11. In the exercises in Chapter 6, you created a class named Purchase. Each Purchase contains an invoice number, amount of sale, amount of sales tax, and several methods. Now, write a program that declares an array of five Purchase objects and prompt a user for their values. As each Purchase object is created, continuously prompt until the user enters an invoice number between 1000 and 8000 inclusive and a non-negative sale amount. Prompt the user for values for each object and then display all the values. Save the file as **PurchaseArray.java**.

435

Debugging Exercises

1. Each of the following files in the Chapter08 folder of your downloadable student files has syntax and/or logic errors. In each case, determine the problem and fix the program. After you correct the errors, save each file using the same filename preceded with *Fix*. For example, DebugEight1.java will become **FixDebugEight1.java**.

   a. DebugEight1.java   c. DebugEight3.java

   b. DebugEight2.java   d. DebugEight4.java

Game Zone

1. Write an application that contains an array of 10 multiple-choice quiz questions related to your favorite hobby. Each question contains three answer choices. Also create an array that holds the correct answer to each question—A, B, or C. Display each question and verify that the user enters only A, B, or C as the answer—if not, keep prompting the user until a valid response is entered. If the user responds to a question correctly, display "Correct!"; otherwise, display "The correct answer is" and the letter of the correct answer. After the user answers all the questions, display the number of correct and incorrect answers. Save the file as **Quiz.java**.

2. a. In Chapter 4, you created a Die application that randomly "throws" five dice for the computer and five dice for the player. The application displays the values. Modify the application to decide the winner based on the following hierarchy of Die values. Any higher combination beats a lower one—for example, five of a kind beats four of a kind.

    • Five of a kind

    • Four of a kind

    • Three of a kind

    • A pair

For this game, the dice values do not count; for example, if both players have three of a kind, it's a tie, no matter what the values of the three dice are. Additionally, the game does not recognize a full house (three of a kind plus two of a kind). Figure 8-21 shows a sample execution. Save the application as **FiveDice2.java**.

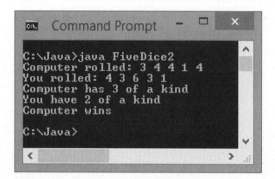

Figure 8-21   Typical execution of the `FiveDice2` application

b. Improve the `FiveDice2` game so that when both players have the same combination of dice, the higher value wins. For example, two 6s beats two 5s. Figure 8-22 shows a sample execution. Save the application as **FiveDice3.java**.

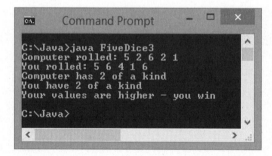

Figure 8-22   Typical execution of the `FiveDice3` application

3. a. In Chapter 7, you modified a previously created `Card` class so that each `Card` would hold the name of a suit ("Spades", "Hearts", "Diamonds", or "Clubs") as well as a value ("Ace", "King", "Queen", "Jack", or a number value). Now, create an array of 52 `Card` objects, assigning a different value to each `Card`, and display each `Card`. Save the application as **FullDeck.java**.

b. In Chapter 7, you created a War2 card game that randomly selects two Card objects (one for the player and one for the computer) and declares a winner or a tie based on the card values. Now create a game that plays 26 rounds of War, dealing a full deck with no repeated cards. Some hints:

- Start by creating an array of all 52 playing cards, as in Part a of this exercise.

- Select a random number for the deck position of the player's first card, and assign the card at that array position to the player.

- Move every higher-positioned card in the deck "down" one to fill in the gap. In other words, if the player's first random number is 49, select the card at position 49, move the card that was in position 50 to position 49, and move the card that was in position 51 to position 50. Only 51 cards remain in the deck after the player's first card is dealt, so the available-card array is smaller by one.

- In the same way, randomly select a card for the computer and "remove" the card from the deck.

- Display the values of the player's and computer's cards, compare their values, and determine the winner.

- When all the cards in the deck are exhausted, display a count of the number of times the player wins, the number of times the computer wins, and the number of ties.

Save the game as **War3.java**.

4. In Chapter 7, you created a Secret Phrase game similar to Hangman, in which the user guesses letters in a partially hidden phrase in an attempt to determine the complete phrase. Modify the program so that:

- The phrase to be guessed is selected randomly from a list of at least 10 phrases.

- The clue is presented to the user with asterisks replacing letters to be guessed but with spaces in the appropriate locations. For example, if the phrase to be guessed is "No man is an island," then the user sees the following as a first clue:

** *** ** ** ******

The spaces provide valuable clues as to where individual words start and end.

- Make sure that when a user makes a correct guess, all the matching letters are filled in, regardless of case.

Save the game as **SecretPhrase2.java**.

Case Problems

1. In previous chapters, you developed classes that work with catering event information for Carly's Catering. Now modify the Event and EventDemo classes as follows:

- Modify the Event class to include an integer field that holds an event type. Add a final String array that holds names of the types of events that Carly's caters—wedding, baptism, birthday, corporate, and other. Include get and set methods for the integer event type field. If the argument passed to the method that sets the event type is larger than the size of the array of String event types, then set the integer to the element number occupied by "other". Include a get method that returns an event's String event type based on the numeric event type.

- To keep the EventDemo class simple, remove all the statements that compare event sizes and that display the invitation Strings.

- Modify the EventDemo class so that instead of creating three single Event objects, it uses an array of three Event objects. Get data for each of the objects, and then display all the details for each object.

Save the files as **Event.java** and **EventDemo.java**.

2. In previous chapters, you developed classes that hold rental contract information for Sammy's Seashore Supplies. Now modify the Rental and RentalDemo classes as follows:

- Modify the Rental class to include an integer field that holds an equipment type. Add a final String array that holds names of the types of equipment that Sammy's rents—jet ski, pontoon boat, rowboat, canoe, kayak, beach chair, umbrella, and other. Include get and set methods for the integer equipment type field. If the argument passed to the method that sets the equipment type is larger than the size of the array of String equipment types, then set the integer to the element number occupied by "other". Include a get method that returns a rental's String equipment type based on the numeric equipment type.

- To keep the RentalDemo class simple, remove all the statements that compare rental times and that display the coupon Strings.

- Modify the RentalDemo class so that instead of creating three single Rental objects, it uses an array of three Rental objects. Get data for each of the objects, and then display all the details for each object.

Save the files as **Rental.java** and **RentalDemo.java**.

Advanced Array Concepts

In this chapter, you will:

◎ Sort array elements using the bubble sort algorithm

◎ Sort array elements using the insertion sort algorithm

◎ Use two-dimensional and other multidimensional arrays

◎ Use the `Arrays` class

◎ Use the `ArrayList` class

◎ Create enumerations

CHAPTER 9   Advanced Array Concepts

Sorting Array Elements Using the Bubble Sort Algorithm

Sorting is the process of arranging a series of objects in some logical order. When you place objects in order beginning with the object that has the lowest value, you are sorting in **ascending order**; conversely, when you start with the object that has the largest value, you are sorting in **descending order**.

The simplest possible sort involves two values that are out of order. To place the values in order, you must swap the two values. Suppose that you have two variables—valA and valB—and further suppose that valA = 16 and valB = 2. To exchange the values of the two variables, you cannot simply use the following code:

```
valA = valB; // 2 goes to valA
valB = valA; // 2 goes to valB
```

If valB is 2, after you execute valA = valB;, both variables hold the value 2. The value 16 that was held in valA is lost. When you execute the second assignment statement, valB = valA;, each variable still holds the value 2.

The solution that allows you to retain both values is to employ a variable to hold valA's value temporarily during the swap:

```
temp = valA; // 16 goes to temp
valA = valB; // 2 goes to valA
valB = temp; // 16 goes to valB
```

Using this technique, valA's value (16) is assigned to the temp variable. The value of valB (2) is then assigned to valA, so valA and valB are equivalent. Then, the temp value (16) is assigned to valB, so the values of the two variables finally are swapped.

If you want to sort any two values, valA and valB, in ascending order so that valA is the lower value, you use the following if statement to make the decision whether to swap. If valA is more than valB, you want to swap the values. If valA is not more than valB, you do not want to swap the values.

```
if(valA > valB)
{
    temp = valA;
    valA = valB;
    valB = temp;
}
```

Sorting two values is a fairly simple task; sorting more values is more complicated, especially if you attempt to use a series of decisions. The task becomes manageable when you know how to use an array.

Using the Bubble Sort Algorithm

Multiple sorting algorithms have been developed; an **algorithm** is a process or set of steps that solve a problem. In the ascending **bubble sort** algorithm, you repeatedly compare pairs of items, swapping them if they are out of order, and eventually creating a sorted list. The bubble sort is neither the fastest nor most efficient sorting technique, but it is one of the simplest to comprehend and provides deeper understanding of array element manipulation.

To use a bubble sort, you place the original, unsorted values in an array. You compare the first two numbers; if they are not in ascending order, you swap them. You compare the second and third numbers; if they are not in ascending order, you swap them. You continue down the list, and for each position x, if the value at position x + 1 is not larger, you want to swap the two values.

Suppose you have declared an array as:

```
int[] someNums = {88, 33, 99, 22, 54};
```

Then, the process proceeds as follows:

- Compare 88 and 33. They are out of order. Swap them. The list becomes 33, 88, 99, 22, 54.

- Compare the second and third numbers in the list—88 and 99. They are in order. Do nothing.

- Compare the third and fourth numbers in the list—99 and 22. They are out of order. Swap them. The list becomes 33, 88, 22, 99, 54.

- Compare the fourth and fifth numbers—99 and 54. They are out of order. Swap them. The list becomes 33, 88, 22, 54, 99.

When you reach the bottom of the list, the numbers are not in ascending order, but the largest number, 99, has moved to the bottom of the list. This feature gives the bubble sort its name—the "heaviest" value has sunk to the bottom of the list as the "lighter" values have bubbled to the top.

Assuming b and temp both have been declared as integer variables, the code so far is as follows:

```
for(b = 0; b < someNums.length - 1; ++b)
    if(someNums[b] > someNums[b + 1])
    {
        temp = someNums[b];
        someNums[b] = someNums[b + 1];
        someNums[b + 1] = temp;
    }
```

 Instead of comparing b to someNums.length - 1 on every pass through the loop, it would be more efficient to declare a variable to which you assign someNums.length - 1 and use that variable in the comparison. That way, the arithmetic is performed just once. That step is omitted here to reduce the number of steps in the example.

Notice that the for statement tests every value of b from 0 through 3. The array someNums contains five integers, so the subscripts in the array range in value from 0 through 4. Within the for loop, each someNums[b] is compared to someNums[b + 1], so the highest legal value for b is 3. For a sort on any size array, the value of b must remain less than the array's length minus 1.

The list of numbers that began as 88, 33, 99, 22, 54 is currently 33, 88, 22, 54, 99. To continue to sort the list, you must perform the entire comparison-swap procedure again.

- Compare the first two values—33 and 88. They are in order; do nothing.

- Compare the second and third values—88 and 22. They are out of order. Swap them so the list becomes 33, 22, 88, 54, 99.

- Compare the third and fourth values—88 and 54. They are out of order. Swap them so the list becomes 33, 22, 54, 88, 99.

- Compare the fourth and fifth values—88 and 99. They are in order; do nothing.

After this second pass through the list, the numbers are 33, 22, 54, 88, and 99—close to ascending order, but not quite. You can see that with one more pass through the list, the values 22 and 33 will swap, and the list is finally placed in order. To fully sort the worst-case list, one in which the original numbers are descending (as out-of-ascending order as they could possibly be), you need to go through the list four times, making comparisons and swaps. At most, you always need to pass through the list as many times as its length minus one. Figure 9-1 assumes that a, b, and temp are integers and shows the entire procedure.

```
for(a = 0; a < someNums.length - 1; ++a)
    for(b = 0; b < someNums.length - 1; ++b)
        if(someNums[b] > someNums[b + 1])
        {
            temp = someNums[b];
            someNums[b] = someNums[b + 1];
            someNums[b + 1] = temp;
        }
```

Figure 9-1   Ascending bubble sort of the someNums array elements

To place the list in descending order, you need to make only one change in the code in Figure 9-1: You change the greater-than sign (>) in if(someNums[b] > someNums[b + 1]) to a less-than sign (<).

Improving Bubble Sort Efficiency

When you use a bubble sort to sort any array into ascending order, the largest value "falls" to the bottom of the array after you have compared each pair of values in the array one time. The second time you go through the array making comparisons, there is no need to check the last pair of values because the largest value is guaranteed to already be at the bottom of the array. You can make the sort process more efficient by using a new control variable to limit the repetitions of the inner for loop and reducing the value by one on each cycle through the array. Figure 9-2 shows how you can use a new variable named comparisonsToMake to control how many comparisons are made in the inner loop during each pass through the list of values to be sorted. In the shaded statement, the comparisonsToMake value is decremented by 1 on each pass through the list.

```
int comparisonsToMake = someNums.length - 1;
for(a = 0; a < someNums.length - 1; ++a)
{
    for(b = 0; b < comparisonsToMake; ++b)
    {
        if(someNums[b] > someNums[b + 1])
        {
            temp = someNums[b];
            someNums[b] = someNums[b + 1];
            someNums[b + 1] = temp;
        }
    }
    --comparisonsToMake;
}
```

Figure 9-2   More efficient ascending bubble sort of the `someNums` array elements

  Watch the video *Sorting*.

Sorting Arrays of Objects

You can sort arrays of objects in much the same way that you sort arrays of primitive types. The major difference occurs when you make the comparison that determines whether you want to swap two array elements. When you sort an array of a primitive element type, you compare the values of two array elements to determine whether they are out of order. When array elements are objects, you usually want to sort based on a particular object field.

Assume that you have created a simple `Employee` class, as shown in Figure 9-3. The class holds four data fields and get and set methods for the fields.

```
public class Employee
{
    private int empNum;
    private String lastName;
    private String firstName;
    private double salary;
    public int getEmpNum()
    {
        return empNum;
    }
    public void setEmpNum(int emp)
    {
        empNum = emp;
    }
    public String getLastName()
    {
        return lastName;
    }
}
```

Figure 9-3   The `Employee` class *(continues)*

(continued)

```java
public void setLastName(String name)
{
    lastName = name;
}
public String getFirstName()
{
    return firstName;
}
public void setFirstName(String name)
{
    firstName = name;
}
public double getSalary()
{
    return salary;
}
public void setSalary(double sal)
{
    salary = sal;
}
}
```

Figure 9-3   The Employee class

You can write a program that contains an array of five Employee objects using the following statement:

```java
Employee[] someEmps = new Employee[5];
```

Assume that after you assign employee numbers and salaries to the Employee objects, you want to sort the Employees in salary order. You can pass the array to a bubbleSort() method that is prepared to receive Employee objects. Figure 9-4 shows the method.

```java
public static void bubbleSort(Employee[] array)
{
    int a, b;
    Employee temp;
    int highSubscript = array.length - 1;
    for(a = 0; a < highSubscript; ++a)
     for(b = 0; b < highSubscript; ++b)
       if(array[b].getSalary() > array[b + 1].getSalary())
       {
           temp = array[b];
           array[b] = array[b + 1];
           array[b + 1] = temp;
       }
}
```

Figure 9-4   The bubbleSort() method that sorts Employee objects by their salaries

Examine Figure 9-4 carefully and notice that the `bubbleSort()` method is very similar to the `bubbleSort()` method you use for an array of any primitive type, but there are three major differences:

- The `bubbleSort()` method header shows that it receives an array of type `Employee`.

- The `temp` variable created for swapping is type `Employee`. The `temp` variable will hold an `Employee` object, not just one number or one field. It is important to note that even though only employee salaries are compared, you do not just swap employee salaries. You do not want to substitute one employee's salary for another's. Instead, you swap each `Employee` object's `empNum` and `salary` as a unit.

- The comparison for determining whether a swap should occur uses method calls to the `getSalary()` method to compare the returned salary for each `Employee` object in the array with the salary of the adjacent `Employee` object.

TWO TRUTHS & A LIE

Sorting Array Elements Using the Bubble Sort Algorithm

1. In an ascending bubble sort, you compare pairs of items, swapping them if they are out of order, so that the largest items "bubble" to the top of the list, eventually creating a sorted list.

2. When you sort objects, you usually want to sort based on a particular object field.

3. When you make a swap while sorting an array of objects, you typically swap entire objects and not just the field on which the comparison is made.

The false statement is #1. In an ascending bubble sort, you compare pairs of items, swapping them if they are out of order, so that the smallest items "bubble" to the top of the list, eventually creating a sorted list.

 You Do It

Using a Bubble Sort

In this section, you create a program in which you enter values that you sort using the bubble sort algorithm. You display the values during each iteration of the outer sorting loop so that you can track the values as they are repositioned in the array.

1. Open a new file in your text editor, and create the shell for a `BubbleSortDemo` program as follows:

(continues)

(continued)

```
import java.util.*;
class BubbleSortDemo
{
    public static void main(String[] args)
    {
    }
}
```

2. Make some declarations between the curly braces of the `main()` method. Declare an array of five integers and a variable to control the number of comparisons to make during the sort. Declare a `Scanner` object, two integers to use as subscripts for handling the array, and a temporary integer value to use during the sort.

```
int[] someNums = new int[5];
int comparisonsToMake = someNums.length - 1;
Scanner keyboard = new Scanner(System.in);
int a, b, temp;
```

3. Write a `for` loop that prompts the user for a value for each array element and accepts them.

```
for(a = 0; a < someNums.length; ++a)
{
    System.out.print("Enter number " + (a + 1) + " >> ");
    someNums[a] = keyboard.nextInt();
}
```

4. Next, call a method that accepts the array and the number of sort iterations performed so far, which is 0. The purpose of the method is to display the current status of the array as it is being sorted.

```
display(someNums, 0);
```

5. Add the nested loops that perform the sort. The outer loop controls the number of passes through the list, and the inner loop controls the comparisons on each pass through the list. When any two adjacent elements are out of order, they are swapped. At the end of the nested loop, the current list is output and the number of comparisons to be made on the next pass is reduced by one.

```
for(a = 0; a < someNums.length - 1; ++a)
{
    for(b = 0; b < comparisonsToMake; ++b)
    {
```

(continues)

(continued)

```java
        if(someNums[b] > someNums[b + 1])
        {
            temp = someNums[b];
            someNums[b] = someNums[b + 1];
            someNums[b + 1] = temp;
        }
    }
    display(someNums, (a + 1));
    --comparisonsToMake;
}
```

6. After the closing brace for the `main()` method, but before the closing brace for the class, insert the `display()` method. It accepts the array and the current outer loop index, and it displays the array contents.

```java
public static void display(int[] someNums, int a)
{
    System.out.print("Iteration " + a + ": ");
    for(int x = 0; x < someNums.length; ++x)
        System.out.print(someNums[x] + " ");
    System.out.println();
}
```

7. Save the file as **BubbleSortDemo.java**, and then compile and execute it. Figure 9-5 shows a typical execution. Notice that after the first iteration, the largest value has sunk to the bottom of the list. After the second iteration, the two largest values are at the bottom of the list, and so on.

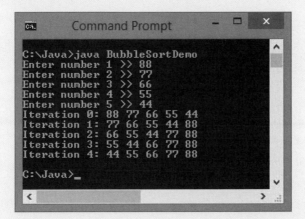

Figure 9-5 Typical execution of the `BubbleSortDemo` application

8. Modify the `BubbleSortDemo` application to any size array you choose. Confirm that no matter how many array elements you specify, the sorting algorithm works correctly and ends with a completely sorted list, regardless of the order of your entered values.

Sorting Array Elements Using the Insertion Sort Algorithm

The bubble sort works well and is relatively easy to understand and manipulate, but many other sorting algorithms have been developed. For example, when you use an **insertion sort**, you look at each list element one at a time. If an element is out of order relative to any of the items earlier in the list, you move each earlier item down one position and then insert the tested element. The insertion sort is similar to the technique you would most likely use to sort a group of objects manually. For example, if a list contains the values 2, 3, 1, and 4, and you want to place them in ascending order using an insertion sort, you test the values 2 and 3, but you do not move them because they are in order. However, when you test the third value in the list, 1, you move both 2 and 3 to later positions and insert 1 at the first position.

Figure 9-6 shows the logic that performs an ascending insertion sort using a five-element integer array named someNums. The logic assumes that a, b, and temp have all been declared as integers.

```
int[] someNums = {90, 85, 65, 95, 75};
a = 1;
while(a < someNums.length)
{
    temp = someNums[a];
    b = a - 1;
    while(b >= 0 && someNums[b] > temp)
    {
        someNums[b + 1] = someNums[b];
        --b;
    }
    someNums[b + 1] = temp;
    ++a;
}
```

Figure 9-6   The insertion sort

The outer loop in Figure 9-6 varies a loop control variable a from 1 through one less than the size of the array. The logic proceeds as follows:

First a is set to 1, and then the while loop begins.

1. The value of temp is set to someNums[1], which is 85, and b is set to 0.

2. Because b is greater than or equal to 0 and someNums[b] (90) is greater than temp, the inner loop is entered. (If you were performing a descending sort, then you would ask whether someNums[b] was less than temp.)

3. The value of someNums[1] becomes 90, and b is decremented, making it −1, so b is no longer greater than or equal to 0, and the inner loop ends.

4. Then someNums[0] is set to temp, which is 85.

After these steps, 90 was moved down one position and 85 was inserted in the first position, so the array values are in slightly better order than they were originally. The values are as follows: 85, 90, 65, 95, 75.

Now, in the outer loop, a becomes 2. The logic in Figure 9-6 proceeds as follows:

1. The value of temp becomes 65, and b is set to 1.

2. The value of b is greater than or equal to 0, and someNums[b] (90) is greater than temp, so the inner loop is entered.

3. The value of someNums[2] becomes 90, and b is decremented, making it 0, so the loop executes again.

4. The value of someNums[1] becomes 85, and b is decremented, making it −1, so the loop ends.

5. Then someNums[0] becomes 65.

After these steps, the array values are in better order than they were originally, because 65 and 85 now both come before 90. The values are: 65, 85, 90, 95, 75. Now, a becomes 3. The logic in Figure 9-6 proceeds to work on the new list as follows:

1. The value of temp becomes 95, and b is set to 2.

2. For the loop to execute, b must be greater than or equal to 0, which it is, and someNums[b] (90) must be greater than temp, which it is *not*. So, the inner loop does not execute.

3. Therefore, someNums[2] is set to 90, which it already was. In other words, no changes are made.

Now, a is increased to 4. The logic in Figure 9-6 proceeds as follows:

1. The value of temp becomes 75, and b is set to 3.

2. The value of b is greater than or equal to 0, and someNums[b] (95) is greater than temp, so the inner loop is entered.

3. The value of someNums[4] becomes 95, and b is decremented, making it 2, so the loop executes again.

4. The value of someNums[3] becomes 90, and b is decremented, making it 1, so the loop executes again.

5. The value of someNums[2] becomes 85, and b is decremented, making it 0; someNums[b] (65) is no longer greater than temp (75), so the inner loop ends. In other words, the values 85, 90, and 95 are each moved down one position, but 65 is left in place.

6. Then someNums[1] becomes 75.

After these steps, all the array values have been rearranged in ascending order as follows: 65, 75, 85, 90, 95.

 Watch the video *The Insertion Sort*.

Many sorting algorithms exist in addition to the bubble sort and insertion sort. You might want to investigate the logic used by the *selection sort, cocktail sort, gnome sort,* and *quick sort.*

TWO TRUTHS & A LIE

Sorting Array Elements Using the Insertion Sort Algorithm

1. When you use an insertion sort, you look at each list element one at a time and move items down if the tested element should be inserted before them.

2. You can create an ascending list using an insertion sort, but not a descending one.

3. The insertion sort is similar to the technique you would most likely use to sort a group of objects manually.

The false statement is #2. You can create both ascending and descending lists using an insertion sort.

You Do It

Using an Insertion Sort

In this section, you modify the `BubbleSortDemo` program so it performs an insertion sort.

1. Open the **BubbleSortDemo.java** file. Change the class name to `InsertionSortDemo`, and immediately save the file as **InsertionSortDemo.java**.

2. Remove the declaration for `comparisonsToMake`.

3. Remove the 14 lines of code that constitute the nested loops that perform the bubble sort. In other words, remove all the lines from the start of the second `for` loop through the closing curly brace following the statement that decrements `comparisonsToMake`.

4. Replace the removed lines with the statements that perform the insertion sort. These are the same statements you saw in Figure 9-6 with the addition of a call to the `display()` method so that you can track the progress of the sort:

(continues)

(continued)

```
a = 1;
while(a < someNums.length)
{
   temp = someNums[a];
   b = a - 1;
   while(b >= 0 && someNums[b] > temp)
   {
      someNums[b + 1] = someNums[b];
      --b;
   }
   someNums[b + 1] = temp;
   display(someNums, a);
   ++a;
}
```

451

5. Save the file as **InsertionSortDemo.java**, and then compile and execute it. Figure 9-7 shows a typical execution. During the first loop, 77 is compared with 88 and inserted at the beginning of the array. In the second loop, 66 is compared with both 77 and 88 and inserted at the beginning of the array. Then the same thing happens with 55 and 44 until all the values are sorted.

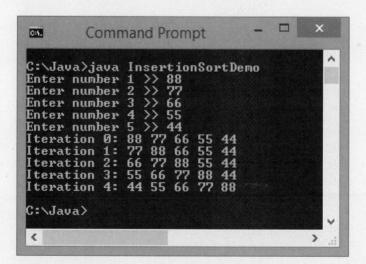

Figure 9-7 Typical execution of the InsertionSortDemo program

6. Try the program with other input values and examine the output so that you understand how the insertion sort algorithm works.

Using Two-Dimensional and Other Multidimensional Arrays

When you declare an array such as `int[] someNumbers = new int[3];`, you can envision the three declared integers as a column of numbers in memory, as shown in Figure 9-8. In other words, you can picture the three declared numbers stacked one on top of the next. An array that you can picture as a column of values, and whose elements you can access using a single subscript, is a **one-dimensional** or **single-dimensional array**. You can think of the size of the array as its height.

Java also supports two-dimensional arrays. **Two-dimensional arrays** have two or more columns of values, as shown in Figure 9-9. The two dimensions represent the height and width of the array. Another way to picture a two-dimensional array is as an array of arrays. It is easiest to picture two-dimensional arrays as having both rows and columns. You must use two subscripts when you access an element in a two-dimensional array. When mathematicians use a two-dimensional array, they often call it a **matrix** or a **table**; you might have used a two-dimensional array called a spreadsheet.

someNumbers[0]
someNumbers[1]
someNumbers[2]

Figure 9-8 View of a single-dimensional array in memory

someNumbers[0][0]	someNumbers[0][1]	someNumbers[0][2]	someNumbers[0][3]
someNumbers[1][0]	someNumbers[1][1]	someNumbers[1][2]	someNumbers[1][3]
someNumbers[2][0]	someNumbers[2][1]	someNumbers[2][2]	someNumbers[2][3]

Figure 9-9 View of a two-dimensional array in memory

When you declare a one-dimensional array, you type a set of square brackets after the array's data type. To declare a two-dimensional array in Java, you type two sets of brackets after the array type. For example, the array in Figure 9-9 can be declared as follows, creating an array named `someNumbers` that holds three rows and four columns:

```
int[][] someNumbers = new int[3][4];
```

Just as with a one-dimensional array, if you do not provide values for the elements in a two-dimensional numeric array, the values default to zero. You can assign other values to the array elements later. For example, `someNumbers[0][0] = 14;` assigns the value 14 to the element of the `someNumbers` array that is in the first column of the first row.

Alternatively, you can initialize a two-dimensional array with values when it is created. For example, the following code assigns values to `someNumbers` when it is created:

```
int[][] someNumbers = { {8, 9, 10, 11},
                        {1, 3, 12, 15},
                        {5, 9, 44, 99} };
```

The someNumbers array contains three rows and four columns. You do not *need* to place each row of values for a two-dimensional array on its own line. However, doing so makes the positions of values easier to understand. You contain the entire set of values within an outer pair of curly braces. The first row of the array holds the four integers 8, 9, 10, and 11. Notice that these four integers are placed within their own inner set of curly braces to indicate that they constitute one row, or the first row, which is row 0. Similarly, 1, 3, 12, and 15 make up the second row (row 1), which you reference with the subscript 1. Next, 5, 9, 44, and 99 are the values in the third row (row 2), which you reference with the subscript 2. The value of someNumbers[0][0] is 8. The value of someNumbers[0][1] is 9. The value of someNumbers[2][3] is 99. The value within the first set of brackets following the array name always refers to the row; the value within the second brackets refers to the column.

As an example of how useful two-dimensional arrays can be, assume that you own an apartment building with four floors—a basement, which you refer to as floor zero, and three other floors numbered one, two, and three. In addition, each of the floors has studio (with no bedroom) and one- and two-bedroom apartments. The monthly rent for each type of apartment is different—the higher the floor, the higher the rent (the view is better), and the rent is higher for apartments with more bedrooms. Table 9-1 shows the rental amounts.

Floor	Zero Bedrooms	One Bedroom	Two Bedrooms
0	400	450	510
1	500	560	630
2	625	676	740
3	1000	1250	1600

Table 9-1 Rents charged (in dollars)

To determine a tenant's rent, you need to know two pieces of information: the floor on which the tenant rents an apartment and the number of bedrooms in the apartment. Within a Java program, you can declare an array of rents using the following code:

```
int[][] rents = { {400, 450, 510},
                  {500, 560, 630},
                  {625, 676, 740},
                  {1000, 1250, 1600} };
```

If you declare two integers named floor and bedrooms, then any tenant's rent can be referred to as rents[floor][bedrooms]. Figure 9-10 shows an application that prompts a user for a floor number and number of bedrooms. Figure 9-11 shows a typical execution.

```
import javax.swing.*;
class FindRent
{
    public static void main(String[] args)
    {
        int[][] rents = { {400, 450, 510},
                          {500, 560, 630},
                          {625, 676, 740},
                          {1000, 1250, 1600} };
        String entry;
        int floor;
        int bedrooms;
        entry = JOptionPane.showInputDialog(null,
            "Enter a floor number ");
        floor = Integer.parseInt(entry);
        entry = JOptionPane.showInputDialog(null,
            "Enter number of bedrooms ");
        bedrooms = Integer.parseInt(entry);
        JOptionPane.showMessageDialog(null,
            "The rent for a " + bedrooms +
                " bedroom apartment on floor " + floor +
                " is $" + rents[floor][bedrooms]);
    }
}
```

Figure 9-10   The FindRent class

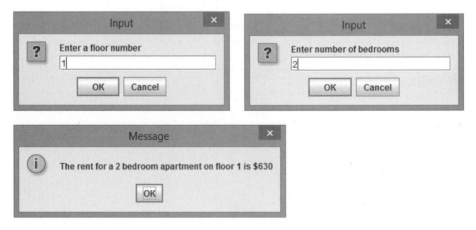

Figure 9-11   Typical execution of the FindRent program

Passing a Two-Dimensional Array to a Method

When you pass a two-dimensional array to a method, you pass the array name just as you do with a one-dimensional array. A method that receives a two-dimensional array uses two bracket pairs following the data type in the parameter list of the method header. For example, the following method headers accept two-dimensional arrays of `int`s, `double`s, and `Employee`s, respectively:

```
public static void displayScores(int[][] scoresArray)
public static boolean areAllPricesHigh(double[][] prices)
public static double computePayrollForAllEmployees(Employee[][] staff)
```

In each case, notice that the brackets indicating the array in the method header are empty. There is no need to insert numbers into the brackets because each passed array name is a starting memory address. The way you manipulate subscripts within the method determines how rows and columns are accessed.

Using the `length` Field with a Two-Dimensional Array

In Chapter 8, you learned that a one-dimensional array has a `length` field that holds the number of elements in the array. With a two-dimensional array, the `length` field holds the number of rows in the array. Each row, in turn, has a `length` field that holds the number of columns in the row. For example, suppose you declare a `rents` array as follows:

```
int[][] rents = { {400, 450, 510},
                  {500, 560, 630},
                  {625, 676, 740},
                  {1000, 1250, 1600} };
```

The value of `rents.length` is 4 because there are four rows in the array. The value of `rents[0].length` is 3 because there are three columns in the first row of the `rents` array. Similarly, the value of `rents[1].length` also is 3 because there are three columns in the second row.

Figure 9-12 shows an application that uses the `length` fields associated with the `rents` array to display all the rents. The `floor` variable varies from 0 through one less than 4 in the outer loop, and the `bdrms` variable varies from 0 through one less than 3 in the inner loop. Figure 9-13 shows the output.

```
class DisplayRents
{
    public static void main(String[] args)
    {
        int[][] rents = { {400, 450, 510},
                          {500, 560, 630},
                          {625, 676, 740},
                          {1000, 1250, 1600} };
        int floor;
        int bdrms;
        for(floor = 0; floor < rents.length; ++floor)
            for(bdrms = 0; bdrms < rents[floor].length; ++bdrms)
                System.out.println("Floor " + floor +
                    " Bedrooms " + bdrms + " Rent is $" +
                        rents[floor][bdrms]);
    }
}
```

Figure 9-12   The `DisplayRents` class

```
Command Prompt                    —  □  ✕

C:\Java>java DisplayRents
Floor 0 Bedrooms 0    Rent is $400
Floor 0 Bedrooms 1    Rent is $450
Floor 0 Bedrooms 2    Rent is $510
Floor 1 Bedrooms 0    Rent is $500
Floor 1 Bedrooms 1    Rent is $560
Floor 1 Bedrooms 2    Rent is $630
Floor 2 Bedrooms 0    Rent is $625
Floor 2 Bedrooms 1    Rent is $676
Floor 2 Bedrooms 2    Rent is $740
Floor 3 Bedrooms 0    Rent is $1000
Floor 3 Bedrooms 1    Rent is $1250
Floor 3 Bedrooms 2    Rent is $1600

C:\Java>_
```

Figure 9-13   Output of the `DisplayRents` program

Watch the video *Two-Dimensional Arrays*.

Understanding Ragged Arrays

In a two-dimensional array, each row also is an array. In Java, you can declare each row to have a different length. When a two-dimensional array has rows of different lengths, it is a **ragged array** because you can picture the ends of each row as uneven. You create a ragged array by defining the number of rows for a two-dimensional array, but not defining the number of columns in the rows. For example, suppose that you have four sales representatives, each of whom covers a different number of states as their sales territory. Further suppose that you want an array to store total sales for each state for each sales representative. You would define the array as follows:

```
double[][] sales = new double[4][];
```

This statement declares an array with four rows, but the rows are not yet created. Then, you can declare the individual rows, based on the number of states covered by each salesperson as follows:

```
sales[0] = new double[12];
sales[1] = new double[18];
sales[2] = new double[9];
sales[3] = new double[11];
```

Using Other Multidimensional Arrays

Besides one- and two-dimensional arrays, Java also supports arrays with three, four, and more dimensions. The general term for arrays with more than one dimension is **multidimensional arrays**. For example, if you own an apartment building with a number of floors and different numbers of bedrooms available in apartments on each floor, you can use a two-dimensional array to store the rental fees. If you own several apartment buildings, you might want to employ a third dimension to store the building number. An expression such as `rents[building][floor][bedrooms]` refers to a specific rent figure for a building whose building number is stored in the `building` variable and whose floor and bedroom numbers are stored in the `floor` and `bedrooms` variables. Specifically, `rents[5][1][2]` refers to a two-bedroom apartment on the first floor of building 5. When you are programming in Java, you can use four, five, or more dimensions in an array. As long as you can keep track of the order of the variables needed as subscripts, and as long as you don't exhaust your computer's memory, Java lets you create arrays of any size.

457

TWO TRUTHS & A LIE

Using Two-Dimensional and Other Multidimensional Arrays

1. Two-dimensional arrays have both rows and columns, so you must use two subscripts when you access an element in a two-dimensional array.

2. The following array contains two columns and three rows:

   ```
   int[][] myArray = { {12, 14, 19},
                       {33, 45, 88} };
   ```

3. With a two-dimensional array, the `length` field holds the number of rows in the array; each row has a `length` field that holds the number of columns in the row.

The false statement is #2. The array shown has two rows and three columns.

 You Do It

Using a Two-Dimensional Array

In this section, you create an application that demonstrates using a two-dimensional array.

1. Open a new file in your text editor, and start a class that will demonstrate a working two-dimensional array:

   ```java
   import java.util.Scanner;
   class TwoDimensionalArrayDemo
   {
       public static void main(String[] args)
       {
   ```

(continues)

(continued)

2. Declare a three-by-three array of integers. By default, the elements will all be initialized to 0.

```
int[][] count = new int[3][3];
```

3. Declare a `Scanner` object for input, variables to hold a row and column, and a constant that can be used to indicate when the user wants to quit the application.

```
Scanner input = new Scanner(System.in);
int row, column;
final int QUIT = 99;
```

4. Prompt the user to enter a row or the QUIT value to quit, then accept the user's input.

```
System.out.print("Enter a row or " + QUIT +
    " to quit > ");
row = input.nextInt();
```

5. In a loop that continues if the user has not entered the QUIT value, prompt the user for a column. If the row and column are both within appropriate ranges, add 1 to the element in the selected position.

```
while(row != QUIT)
{
    System.out.print("Enter a column > ");
    column = input.nextInt();
    if(row < count.length && column < count[row].length)
    {
        count[row][column]++;
```

6. Still within the `if` statement that checks for a valid row and column, add a nested loop that displays each row and column of the newly incremented array. The elements in each row are displayed on the same line, and a new line is started at the end of each row. Add a closing curly brace for the `if` statement.

```
        for(int r = 0; r < count.length; ++r)
        {
            for(int c = 0; c < count[r].length; ++c)
                System.out.print(count[r][c] + " ");
            System.out.println();
        }
    }
```

7. Add an `else` clause to the `if` statement to display an error message when the row or column value is too high.

```
else
    System.out.println("Invalid position selected");
```

(continues)

(continued)

8. At the end of the loop, prompt the user for and accept the next row number. Add closing curly braces for the loop, the `main()` method, and the class.

```
System.out.print("Enter a row or " + QUIT +
    " to quit > ");
row = input.nextInt();
        }
    }
}
```

9. Save the file as **TwoDimensionalArrayDemo.java**. Compile and execute the program. Figure 9-14 shows a typical execution. As the user continues to enter row and column values, the appropriate elements in the array are incremented.

Figure 9-14   Typical execution of the `TwoDimensionalArrayDemo` program

Using the Arrays Class

When you fully understand the power of arrays, you will want to use them to store all kinds of objects. Frequently, you will want to perform similar tasks with different arrays—for example, filling them with values and sorting their elements. Java provides an Arrays class, which contains many useful methods for manipulating arrays. Table 9-2 shows some of the useful methods of the Arrays class. For each method listed in the left column of the table, type stands for a data type; an overloaded version of each method exists for each appropriate data type. For example, there is a version of the sort() method to sort int, double, char, byte, float, long, short, and Object arrays.

You will learn about the Object class in the chapter "Advanced Inheritance Concepts."

Method	Purpose
static int binarySearch(type [] a, type key)	Searches the specified array for the specified key value using the binary search algorithm
static boolean equals(type[] a, type[] a2)	Returns true if the two specified arrays of the same type are equal to one another
static void fill(type[] a, type val)	Assigns the specified value to each element of the specified array
static void sort(type[] a)	Sorts the specified array into ascending order
static void sort(type[] a, int fromIndex, int toIndex)	Sorts the specified range of the array into ascending order
static void parallelSort(type[] a)	Sorts the specified array into ascending order
static void parallelSort(type[] a, int fromIndex, int toIndex)	Sorts the specified range of the array into ascending order

Table 9-2   Useful methods of the Arrays class

The methods in the Arrays class are static methods, which means you use them with the class name without instantiating an Arrays object. The Arrays class is located in the java.util package, so you can use the statement import java.util.*; to access it. The ArraysDemo application in Figure 9-15 demonstrates how you can use some of the methods in the Arrays class. In the ArraysDemo class, the myScores array is created to hold five integers. Then, a message and the array reference are passed to a display() method. The first line of the output in Figure 9-16 shows that the original array is filled with 0s at creation. After the first display, the Arrays.fill() method is called in the first shaded statement in Figure 9-15. Because the arguments are the name of the array and the number 8, when the array is displayed a second time the output is all 8s. In the application, two of the array elements are changed to 6 and 3, and the array is displayed again. Finally, in the second shaded statement, the Arrays.sort() method is called. The output in Figure 9-16 shows that when the display() method executes the fourth time, the array elements have been sorted in ascending order.

```java
import java.util.*;
public class ArraysDemo
{
   public static void main(String[] args)
   {
      int[] myScores = new int [5];
      display("Original array:              ", myScores);
      Arrays.fill(myScores, 8);
      display("After filling with 8s:       ", myScores);
      myScores[2] = 6;
      myScores[4] = 3;
      display("After changing two values:  ", myScores);
      Arrays.sort(myScores);
      display("After sorting:               ", myScores);
   }
   public static void display(String message, int array[])
   {
      int sz = array.length;
      System.out.print(message);
      for(int x = 0; x < sz; ++x)
         System.out.print(array[x] + " ");
      System.out.println();
   }
}
```

Figure 9-15   The ArraysDemo application

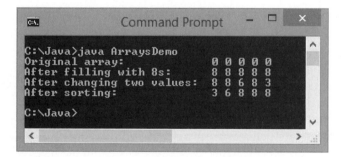

Figure 9-16   Output of the ArraysDemo application

The `Arrays` class `parallelSort()` methods are a new feature in Java 8. You use the methods the same way you use the `sort()` methods, but their algorithms make the sorting more efficient if thousands or millions of objects need to be sorted.

The `Arrays` class `binarySearch()` methods provide convenient ways to search through sorted lists of values of various data types. It is important that the list be in order before you use it in a call to `binarySearch()`; otherwise, the results are unpredictable. You do not have to understand how a binary search works to use the `binarySearch()` method, but basically the operation takes place as follows:

- You have a sorted array and an item for which you are searching within the array. Based on the array size, you determine the middle position. (In an array with an even number of elements, this can be either of the two middle positions.)

- You compare the item you are looking for with the element in the middle position of the array and decide whether your item is above that point in the array—that is, whether your item's value is less than the middle-point value.

- If it is above that point in the array, you next find the middle position of the top half of the array; if it is not above that point, you find the middle position of the bottom half. Either way, you compare your item with that of the new middle position and divide the search area in half again.

- Ultimately, you find the element or determine that it is not in the array.

Programmers often refer to a binary search as a "divide and conquer" procedure. If you have ever played a game in which you tried to guess what number someone was thinking, you might have used a similar technique.

Suppose your organization uses six single-character product codes. Figure 9-17 contains a `VerifyCode` application that verifies a product code entered by the user. The array `codes` holds six values in ascending order. The user enters a code that is extracted from the first `String` position using the `String` class `charAt()` method. Next, the array of valid characters and the user-entered character are passed to the `Arrays.binarySearch()` method. If the character is found in the array, its position is returned. If the character is not found in the array, a negative integer is returned and the application displays an error message. Figure 9-18 shows the program's execution when the user enters *K*; the character is found in position 2 (the third position) in the array.

The negative integer returned by the `binarySearch()` method when the value is not found is the negative equivalent of the array size. In most applications, you do not care about the exact value returned when there is no match; you care only whether it is negative.

```
import java.util.*;
import javax.swing.*;
public class VerifyCode
{
    public static void main(String[] args)
    {
        char[] codes = {'B', 'E', 'K', 'M', 'P', 'T'};
        String entry;
        char usersCode;
        int position;
        entry = JOptionPane.showInputDialog(null,
            "Enter a product code");
        usersCode = entry.charAt(0);
        position = Arrays.binarySearch(codes, usersCode);
        if(position >= 0)
            JOptionPane.showMessageDialog(null, "Position of " +
                usersCode + " is " + position);
        else
            JOptionPane.showMessageDialog(null, usersCode +
                " is an invalid code");
    }
}
```

Figure 9-17   The VerifyCode application

Figure 9-18   Typical execution of the VerifyCode application

 The sort() and binarySearch() methods in the Arrays class are very useful and allow you to achieve results by writing fewer instructions than if you had to write the methods yourself. This does not mean you wasted your time reading about sorting and searching methods earlier in this chapter. The more completely you understand how arrays can be manipulated, the more useful, efficient, and creative your future applications will be.

464

TWO TRUTHS & A LIE

Using the Arrays Class

1. The `Arrays` class contains methods for manipulating arrays, such as `binarySearch()`, `fill()`, and `sort()`.

2. You can use the `Arrays` class `binarySearch()` method successfully on any array as soon as you have assigned values to the array elements.

3. The `binarySearch()` method works by continuously deciding whether the element sought is above or below the halfway point in sublists of the original list.

The false statement is #2. Before you can use the Arrays class binarySearch() method successfully, the array elements must be in order.

You Do It

Using Arrays Class Methods

In this section, you create an application that demonstrates several `Arrays` class methods. The application will allow the user to enter a menu of entrées that are available for the day at a restaurant. Then, the application will present the menu to the user, allow a request, and indicate whether the requested item is on the menu.

1. Open a new file in your text editor, and type the `import` statements you need to create an application that will use the `JOptionPane` and the `Arrays` classes:

   ```
   import java.util.*;
   import javax.swing.*;
   ```

2. Add the first few lines of the `MenuSearch` application class:

   ```
   public class MenuSearch
   {
       public static void main(String[] args)
       {
   ```

(continues)

(continued)

3. Declare an array to hold the day's menu choices; the user is allowed to enter up to 10 entrées. Also declare two **Strings**—one to hold the user's current entry and the other to accumulate the entire menu list as it is entered. The two **String** variables are initialized to empty **Strings** using quotation marks; if you do not initialize these **Strings**, you receive a compiler error because you might attempt to display them without having entered a legitimate value. Also, declare an integer to use as a subscript for the array, another to hold the number of menu items entered, and a third to hold the highest allowable subscript, which is 1 less than the array size:

```
String[] menuChoices = new String[10];
String entry= "", menuString = "";
int x = 0;
int numEntered;
int highestSub = menuChoices.length - 1;
```

4. Use the **Arrays.fill()** method to fill the menu array with *z* characters, as shown in the following line of code. You use this method so that when you perform a search later, actual values will be stored in any unused menu positions. If you ignore this step and fill less than half the array, your search method might generate an error.

```
Arrays.fill(menuChoices, "zzzzzzz");
```

Lowercase *z*s were purposely chosen as the array fill characters because they have a higher value than any other letter. Therefore, when the user's entries are sorted, the *zzzzzzz* entries will be at the bottom of the list.

5. Display an input dialog box into which the user can enter a menu item. Allow the user to quit before entering 10 items by typing "zzz". (Using a value such as "zzz" is a common programming technique to check for the user's desire to stop entering data. If the data items are numeric instead of text, you might use a value such as 999. Values the user enters that are not "real" data, but just signals to stop, are often called **dummy values**.) After the user enters the first menu item, the application enters a loop that continues to add the entered item to the menu list, increase the subscript, and prompt for a new menu item. The loop continues while the user has not entered "zzz" and the subscript has not exceeded the allowable limit. When the loop ends, save the number of menu items entered:

(continues)

(continued)

```
menuChoices[x] = JOptionPane.showInputDialog(null,
    "Enter an item for today's menu, or zzz to quit");
while(!menuChoices[x].equals("zzz") && x < highestSub)
{
    menuString = menuString + menuChoices[x] + "\n";
    ++x;
    if(x < highestSub)
        menuChoices[x] = JOptionPane.showInputDialog(null,
            "Enter an item for today's menu, or zzz to quit");
}
numEntered = x;
```

6. When the menu is complete, display it for the user and allow the user to make a request:

```
entry = JOptionPane.showInputDialog(null,
    "Today's menu is:\n" + menuString +
        "Please make a selection:");
```

7. Sort the array from index position 0 to `numEntered` so that it is in ascending order prior to using the `binarySearch()` method. If you do not sort the array, the result of the `binarySearch()` method is unpredictable. You could sort the entire array, but it is more efficient to sort only the elements that hold actual menu items:

```
Arrays.sort(menuChoices, 0, numEntered);
```

8. Use the `Arrays.binarySearch()` method to search for the requested entry in the previously sorted array. If the method returns a nonnegative value that is less than the `numEntered` value, display the message "Excellent choice"; otherwise, display an error message:

```
x = Arrays.binarySearch(menuChoices, entry);
if(x >= 0 && x < numEntered)
    JOptionPane.showMessageDialog(null, "Excellent choice");
else
    JOptionPane.showMessageDialog(null,
        "Sorry - that item is not on tonight's menu");
```

9. Add the closing curly braces for the `main()` method and the class, and save the file as **MenuSearch.java**. Compile and execute the application. When prompted, enter as many menu choices as you want, and enter "zzz" when you want to quit data entry. When prompted again, enter a menu choice and observe the results. (A choice you enter must match the spelling in the menu exactly.) Figure 9-19 shows a typical menu as it is presented to the user and the results after the user makes a valid choice.

(continues)

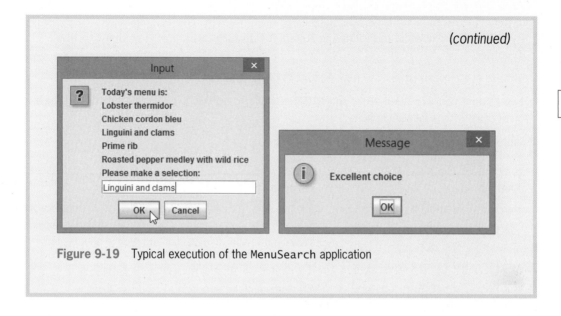

(continued)

Figure 9-19 Typical execution of the MenuSearch application

Using the ArrayList Class

In addition to the Arrays class, Java provides an ArrayList class that can be used to create containers that store lists of objects. The ArrayList class provides some advantages over the Arrays class. Specifically, an ArrayList is **dynamically resizable**, meaning that its size can change during program execution. This means that:

- You can add an item at any point in an ArrayList container, and the array size expands automatically to accommodate the new item.

- You can remove an item at any point in an ArrayList container, and the array size contracts automatically.

To use the ArrayList class, you must use one of the following import statements:

```
import java.util.ArrayList;
import java.util.*;
```

Then, to declare an ArrayList, you can use the default constructor, as in the following example that declares a list of Strings:

```
ArrayList<String> names = new ArrayList<String>();
```

An ArrayList can hold any type of object; adding a data type in angle brackets causes Java to check that you are assigning appropriate types to a list. You can omit the angle brackets and data type following the ArrayList class name, but you receive a warning that you are using an unchecked or unsafe operation.

The default constructor creates an ArrayList with a capacity of 10 items. An ArrayList's **capacity** is the number of items it can hold without having to increase its size. By definition, an ArrayList's capacity is greater than or equal to its size. You can also specify a capacity if you like. For example, the following statement declares an ArrayList that can hold 20 names:

```
ArrayList<String> names = new ArrayList<String>(20);
```

If you know you will need more than 10 items at the outset, it is more efficient to create an ArrayList with a larger capacity.

Table 9-3 summarizes some useful ArrayList methods.

Method	Purpose
public void add(Object)	Adds an item to an ArrayList; the default version adds an
public void add(int, Object)	item at the next available location; an overloaded version allows you to specify a position at which to add the item
public void remove(int)	Removes an item from an ArrayList at a specified location
public void set(int, Object)	Alters an item at a specified ArrayList location
Object get(int)	Retrieves an item from a specified location in an ArrayList
public int size()	Returns the current ArrayList size

Table 9-3   Useful methods of the ArrayList class

In the chapter "Advanced Inheritance Concepts," you will learn that the Object class is the most generic Java class.

To add an item to the end of an ArrayList, you can use the add() method. For example, to add the name *Abigail* to an ArrayList named names, you can make the following statement:

```
names.add("Abigail");
```

You can insert an item into a specific position in an ArrayList by using an overloaded version of the add() method that includes the position. For example, to insert the name *Bob* in the first position of the names ArrayList, you use the following statement:

```
names.add(0, "Bob");
```

With each of the methods described in this section, you receive an error message if the position number is invalid for the ArrayList.

As you can see from Table 9-3, you also can alter and remove items from an ArrayList. The ArrayList class contains a size() method that returns the current size of the ArrayList. Figure 9-20 contains a program that demonstrates each of these methods.

```
import java.util.ArrayList;
public class ArrayListDemo
{
   public static void main(String[] args)
   {
      ArrayList<String> names = new ArrayList<String>();
      names.add("Abigail");
      display(names);
      names.add("Brian");
      display(names);
      names.add("Zachary");
      display(names);
      names.add(2, "Christy");
      display(names);
      names.remove(1);
      display(names);
      names.set(0, "Annette");
      display(names);
   }
   public static void display(ArrayList<String> names)
   {
      System.out.println("\nThe size of the list is " + names.size());
      for(int x = 0; x < names.size(); ++x)
         System.out.println("position " + x + " Name: " +
            names.get(x));
   }
}
```

Figure 9-20 The `ArrayListDemo` program

In the application in Figure 9-20, an `ArrayList` is created and *Abigail* is added to the list. The `ArrayList` is passed to a `display()` method that displays the current list size and all the names in the list. You can see from the output in Figure 9-21 that at this point, the `ArrayList` size is 1, and the array contains just one name. Examine the program in Figure 9-20 along with the output in Figure 9-21 so that you understand how the `ArrayList` is altered as names are added, removed, and replaced.

470

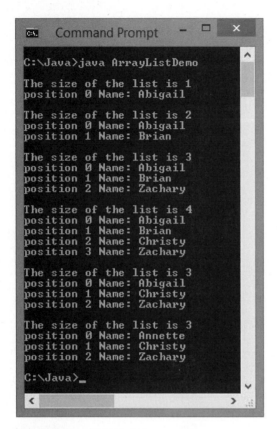

Figure 9-21   Output of the `ArrayListDemo` program

You can display the contents of an `ArrayList` of `Strings` without looping through the values. For example, Figure 9-22 shows an `ArrayList` named `students` that the user populates interactively. Displaying the array name as shown in the shaded statement produces a comma-separated list between square brackets. Figure 9-23 shows a typical execution.

```
import javax.swing.*;
import java.util.ArrayList;
public class ArrayListDemo2
{
    public static void main(String[] args)
    {
        ArrayList<String> students = new ArrayList<String>();
        String name;
        final int LIMIT = 4;
        for(int x = 0; x < LIMIT; ++x)
        {
            name = JOptionPane.showInputDialog(null,
                "Enter a student's name");
            students.add(name);
        }
        System.out.println("The names are " + students);
    }
}
```

Figure 9-22   The ArrayListDemo2 class

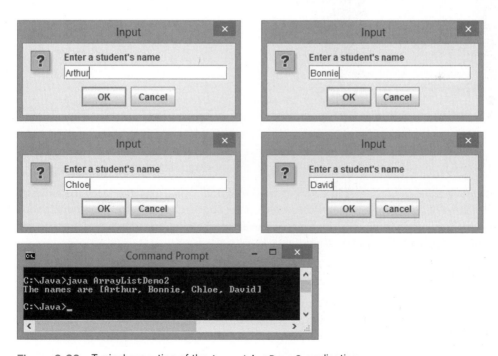

Figure 9-23   Typical execution of the ArrayListDemo2 application

You can sort an `ArrayList` using the `Collections.sort()` method and providing the `ArrayList` as the argument—for example:

```
Collections.sort(students);
```

To use this method, you must import the `java.util.Collections` package at the top of the file.

TWO TRUTHS & A LIE

Using the ArrayList Class

1. An advantage of the `ArrayList` class over the `Arrays` class is that an `ArrayList` is dynamically resizable.

2. An advantage of the `ArrayList` class over the `Arrays` class is that it can hold multiple object types.

3. An advantage of the `ArrayList` class over the `Arrays` class is that it can hold primitive data types such as `int` and `double`.

The false statement is #3. A disadvantage of the ArrayList class is that it cannot hold primitive types.

Creating Enumerations

Data types have a specific set of values. For example, in Chapter 2 you learned that a `byte` cannot hold a value larger than 127 and an `int` cannot hold a value larger than 2,147,483,647. You can also create your own data types that have a finite set of legal values. A programmer-created data type with a fixed set of values is an **enumerated data type**.

In Java, you create an enumerated data type in a statement that uses the keyword `enum`, an identifier for the type, and a pair of curly braces that contain a list of the **enum constants**, which are the allowed values for the type. For example, the following code creates an enumerated type named `Month` that contains 12 values:

```
enum Month {JAN, FEB, MAR, APR, MAY, JUN,
   JUL, AUG, SEP, OCT, NOV, DEC};
```

By convention, the identifier for an enumerated type begins with an uppercase letter. This makes sense because an enumerated type is a class. Also, by convention, the `enum` constants, like other constants, appear in all uppercase letters. The constants are not strings and they are not enclosed in quotes; they are Java identifiers.

After you create an enumerated data type, you can declare variables of that type. For example, you might declare the following:

```
Month birthMonth;
```

You can assign any of the enum constants to the variable. Therefore, you can code a statement such as the following:

```
birthMonth = Month.MAY;
```

An enumeration type like Month is a class, and its enum constants act like objects instantiated from the class, including having access to the methods of the class. These built-in methods include the ones shown in Table 9-4. Each of these methods is nonstatic; that is, each is used with an enum object.

Method	Description	Example if birthMonth = Month.MAY
toString()	The toString() method returns the name of the calling constant object.	birthMonth.toString() has the value "MAY" You can pass birthMonth to print() or println() and it is automatically converted to its string equivalent.
ordinal()	The ordinal() method returns an integer that represents the constant's position in the list of constants. As with arrays, the first position is 0.	birthMonth.ordinal() is 4
equals()	The equals() method returns true if its argument is equal to the calling object's value.	birthMonth.equals(Month.MAY) is true birthMonth.equals(Month.NOV) is false
compareTo()	The compareTo() method returns a negative integer if the calling object's ordinal value is less than that of the argument, 0 if they are the same, and a positive integer if the calling object's ordinal value is greater than that of the argument.	birthMonth.compareTo(Month.JUL) is negative birthMonth.compareTo(Month.FEB) is positive birthMonth.compareTo(Month.MAY) is 0

Table 9-4   Some useful nonstatic enum methods

Several static methods are also available to use with enumerations. These are used with the type and not with the individual constants. Table 9-5 describes two useful static methods.

Method	Description	Example with Month Enumeration
valueOf()	The valueOf() method accepts a string parameter and returns an enumeration constant.	Month.valueOf("DEC") returns the DEC enum constant
values()	The values() method returns an array of the enumerated constants.	Month.values() returns an array with 12 elements that contain the enum constants

Table 9-5   Some static enum methods

You can declare an enumerated type in its own file, in which case the filename matches the type name and has a .java extension. You will use this approach in a "You Do It" exercise later in this chapter. Alternatively, you can declare an enumerated type within a class, but not within a method. Figure 9-24 is an application that declares a Month enumeration and demonstrates its use. Figure 9-25 shows two typical executions.

474

```java
import java.util.Scanner;
public class EnumDemo
{
    enum Month {JAN, FEB, MAR, APR, MAY, JUN,
        JUL, AUG, SEP, OCT, NOV, DEC};
    public static void main(String[] args)
    {
        Month birthMonth;
        String userEntry;
        int position;
        int comparison;
        Scanner input = new Scanner(System.in);
        System.out.println("The months are:");
        for(Month mon : Month.values())
            System.out.print(mon + " ");
        System.out.print("\n\nEnter the first three letters of " +
            "your birth month >> ");
        userEntry = input.nextLine().toUpperCase();
        birthMonth = Month.valueOf(userEntry);
        System.out.println("You entered " + birthMonth);
        position = birthMonth.ordinal();
        System.out.println(birthMonth + " is in position " + position);
        System.out.println("So its month number is " + (position + 1));
        comparison = birthMonth.compareTo(Month.JUN);
        if(comparison < 0)
            System.out.println(birthMonth +
                " is earlier in the year than " + Month.JUN);
        else
            if(comparison > 0)
                System.out.println(birthMonth +
                    " is later in the year than " + Month.JUN);
            else
                System.out.println(birthMonth + " is " + Month.JUN);
    }
}
```

Figure 9-24   The EnumDemo class

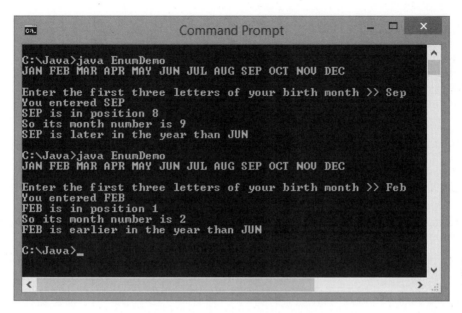

Figure 9-25 Two typical executions of the EnumDemo application

In the application in Figure 9-24, a Month enumeration is declared; in the main() method, a Month variable is declared in the first shaded statement. The second shaded statement uses the enhanced for loop, which you first learned to use with arrays in Chapter 8. The enhanced for loop declares a local Month variable named mon that takes on the value of each element in the Month.value() array in turn so it can be displayed.

In the program in Figure 9-24, the user then is prompted to enter the first three letters for a month, which are converted to their uppercase equivalents. The third shaded statement in the figure uses the valueOf() method to convert the user's string to an enumeration value. The fourth shaded statement gets the position of the month in the enumeration list. The last shaded statement compares the entered month to the JUN constant. This is followed by an if statement that displays whether the user's entered month comes before or after JUN in the list, or is equivalent to it.

In Java 7 and 8, you can use comparison operators with enumeration constants instead of using the compareTo() method to return a number. For example, you can write the following:

```
if(birthMonth < Month.JUN)
   System.out.println(birthMonth +
      " is earlier in the year than " + Month.JUN);
```

You can use enumerations to control a switch structure. Figure 9-26 contains a class that declares a Property enumeration for a real estate company. The program assigns one of the values to a Property variable and then uses a switch structure to display an appropriate message. Figure 9-27 shows the result.

```
import java.util.Scanner;
public class EnumDemo2
{
    enum Property {SINGLE_FAMILY, MULTIPLE_FAMILY,
        CONDOMINIUM, LAND, BUSINESS};
    public static void main(String[] args)
    {
        Property propForSale = Property.MULTIPLE_FAMILY;
        switch(propForSale)
        {
            case SINGLE_FAMILY:
            case MULTIPLE_FAMILY:
                System.out.println("Listing fee is 5%");
                break;
            case CONDOMINIUM:
                System.out.println("Listing fee is 6%");
                break;
            case LAND:
            case BUSINESS:
                System.out.println
                    ("We do not handle this type of property");
        }
    }
}
```

Figure 9-26   The EnumDemo2 class

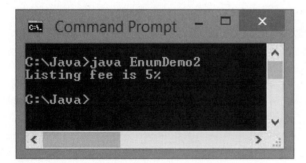

Figure 9-27   Output of the EnumDemo2 application

Creating an enumeration type provides you with several advantages. For example, the Month enumeration improves your programs in the following ways:

- If you did not create an enumerated type for month values, you could use another type—for example, ints or Strings. The problem is that any value could be assigned to an int or String variable, but only the 12 allowed values can be assigned to a Month.

- If you did not create an enumerated type for month values, you could create another type to represent months, but invalid behavior could be applied to the values. For example, if you used integers to represent months, you could add, subtract, multiply, or divide two months, which is not logical. Programmers say using **enums** makes the values type-safe. **Type-safe** describes a data type for which only appropriate behaviors are allowed.

- The **enum** constants provide a form of self-documentation. Someone reading your program might misinterpret what *9* means as a month value, but there is less confusion when you use the identifier OCT.

- As with other classes, you can also add methods and other fields to an **enum** type.

 Watch the video *Enumerations*.

TWO TRUTHS & A LIE

Creating Enumerations

Assume that you have coded the following:

```
enum Color {RED, WHITE, BLUE};
Color myColor = Color.RED;
```

1. The value of myColor.ordinal() is 1.

2. The value of myColor.compareTo(Color.RED) is 0.

3. The value of myColor < Color.WHITE is true.

The false statement is #1. As the first enum constant, the value of myColor.ordinal() is 0.

 You Do It

Creating Enumerations

In this section, you create two enumerations that hold colors and car model types. You will use them as field types in a Car class and write a demonstration program that shows how the enumerations are used.

1. Open a new file in your text editor, and type the following Color enumeration:

   ```
   enum Color {BLACK, BLUE, GREEN, RED, WHITE, YELLOW};
   ```

2. Save the file as **Color.java**.

(continues)

(continued)

3. Open a new file in your text editor, and create the following Model enumeration:

```
enum Model {SEDAN, CONVERTIBLE, MINIVAN};
```

4. Save the file as **Model.java**. Next, open a new file in your text editor, and start to define a Car class that holds three fields: a year, a model, and a color.

```
public class Car
{
    private int year;
    private Model model;
    private Color color;
```

5. Add a constructor for the Car class that accepts parameters that hold the values for year, model, and color as follows:

```
public Car(int yr, Model m, Color c)
{
    year = yr;
    model = m;
    color = c;
}
```

6. Add a display() method that displays a Car object's data, then add a closing curly brace for the class.

```
    public void display()
    {
        System.out.println("Car is a " + year +
            " " + color + " " + model);
    }
}
```

7. Save the file as **Car.java**.

8. Open a new file in your text editor, and write a short demonstration program that instantiates two Car objects and assigns values to them using enumeration values for the models and colors.

```
public class CarDemo
{
    public static void main(String[] args)
    {
        Car firstCar = new Car(2012, Model.MINIVAN, Color.BLUE);
        Car secondcar = new Car(2014, Model.CONVERTIBLE,
            Color.RED);
        firstCar.display();
        secondcar.display();
    }
}
```

(continues)

(continued)

9. Save the file as **CarDemo.java**, and then compile and execute it. Figure 9-28 shows that the values are assigned correctly.

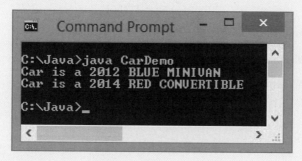

Figure 9-28 Output of the CarDemo program

Don't Do It

- Don't forget that the first subscript used with a two-dimensional array represents the row, and that the second subscript represents the column.

- Don't try to store primitive data types in an ArrayList structure.

- Don't think enum constants are strings; they are not enclosed in quotes.

Key Terms

Sorting is the process of arranging a series of objects in some logical order.

Ascending order describes the order of objects arranged from lowest to highest value.

Descending order describes the order of objects arranged from highest to lowest value.

An **algorithm** is a process or set of steps that solve a problem.

A **bubble sort** operates by comparing pairs of items and swapping them if they are out of order, so that the smallest items "bubble" to the top of the list, eventually creating a sorted list.

An **insertion sort** operates by comparing list elements, and if an element is out of order relative to any of the items earlier in the list, you move each earlier item down one position and then insert the tested element.

A **one-dimensional array** or **single-dimensional array** contains one column of values; you access its elements using a single subscript.

Two-dimensional arrays have two or more columns of values, and you must use two subscripts to access an element.

Matrix and **table** are names used for two-dimensional arrays.

A **ragged array** is a two-dimensional array that has rows of different lengths.

Multidimensional arrays contain two or more dimensions.

Dummy values are values the user enters that are not "real" data; they are just signals to stop data entry.

Dynamically resizable describes an object whose size can change during program execution.

An `ArrayList`'s **capacity** is the number of items it can hold without having to increase its size.

An **enumerated data type** is a programmer-created data type with a fixed set of values.

The **enum constants** are the allowed values for an enumerated data type.

Type-safe describes a data type for which only appropriate behaviors are allowed.

Chapter Summary

- Sorting is the process of arranging a series of objects in ascending or descending order. With a bubble sort, you continue to compare pairs of items, swapping them if they are out of order, so that the smallest items "bubble" to the top of the list, eventually creating a sorted list.

- With an insertion sort, you look at each list element one at a time, and if an element is out of order relative to any of the items earlier in the list, you move each earlier item down one position and then insert the tested element.

- You can sort arrays of objects in much the same way that you sort arrays of primitive types. The major difference occurs when you make the comparison that determines whether you want to swap two array elements. When array elements are objects, you usually want to sort based on a particular object field.

- A one-dimensional or single-dimensional array is accessed using a single subscript. Two-dimensional arrays have both rows and columns and require two subscripts to access. To declare a two-dimensional array, you type two sets of brackets after the array type.

- The Java `Arrays` class contains many useful methods for manipulating arrays. These methods provide ways to easily search, compare, fill, and sort arrays.

- The Java ArrayList class contains useful methods for manipulating dynamically sized arrays. You can add objects to, remove objects from, and replace objects in ArrayList containers.

- An enumerated data type is a programmer-created type with a fixed set of values. In Java, you create an enumerated data type in a statement that uses the keyword enum, an identifier for the type, and a pair of curly braces that contain a list of the enum constants, which are the allowed values for the type.

481

Review Questions

1. When you place objects in order beginning with the object with the highest value, you are sorting in _____ order.

    a. acquiescing

    b. ascending

    c. demeaning

    d. descending

2. Using a bubble sort involves _____ .

    a. comparing parallel arrays

    b. comparing each array element to the average

    c. comparing each array element to the adjacent array element

    d. swapping every array element with its adjacent element

3. When you use a bubble sort to perform an ascending sort, after the first pass through an array the largest value is _____ .

    a. at the beginning of the list

    b. in the middle of the list

    c. at the end of the list

    d. It is impossible to determine the answer without more information.

4. When you use a bubble sort to perform an ascending sort, after the first pass through an array the smallest value is _____ .

    a. at the beginning of the list

    b. in the middle of the list

    c. at the end of the list

    d. It is impossible to determine the answer without more information.

5. When array elements are objects, you usually want to sort based on a particular _____ of the object.

    a. field

    b. method

    c. name

    d. type

6. The following defines a _____ array:

   ```
   int[][] nums = { {1, 2}, {3, 4}, {5, 6} };
   ```

   a. one-dimensional   c. three-dimensional

   b. two-dimensional   d. six-dimensional

7. How many rows are contained in the following array?

   ```
   double[][] prices = { {2.56, 3.57, 4.58, 5.59},
                         {12.35, 13.35, 14.35, 15.00} };
   ```

   a. 1   c. 4

   b. 2   d. 8

8. How many columns are contained in the following array?

   ```
   double[][] prices = { {2.56, 3.57, 4.58, 5.59},
                         {12.35, 13.35, 14.35, 15.00} };
   ```

   a. 1   c. 4

   b. 2   d. 8

9. In the following array, what is the value of `code[2][1]`?

   ```
   char[][] code = { {'A ', 'D ', 'M '},
                     {'P ', 'R ', 'S '},
                     {'U ', 'V ', 'Z '} };
   ```

   a. 'P'   c. 'U'

   b. 'R'   d. 'V'

10. In the following array, what is the value of `address[1][1]`?

    ```
    String address = { {"123 Oak ", "345 Elm "},
                       {"87 Maple ", "901 Linden "} };
    ```

    a. "123 Oak "   c. "87 Maple "

    b. "345 Elm "   d. "901 Linden "

11. In the following array, what is the value of `fees.length`?

    ```
    double[][] fees = { {3.00, 3.50, 4.00, 5.00},
                        {6.35, 7.35, 8.35, 9.00} };
    ```

    a. 2   c. 8

    b. 4   d. none of the above

12. In the following array, what is the value of `fees[1].length`?

    ```
    double[][] fees = { {3.00, 3.50, 4.00, 5.00},
                        {6.35, 7.35, 8.35, 9.00} };
    ```

    a. 2   c. 8

    b. 4   d. none of the above

13. You place _____ after the data type in the parameter list of a method that receives a two-dimensional array.

   a. a pair of empty brackets

   b. two pairs of empty brackets

   c. a pair of brackets that contain the number of rows followed by a pair of empty brackets

   d. a pair of empty brackets followed by brackets that contain the number of columns

14. A _____ array has rows of different lengths.

   a. ragged   c. haggard

   b. jagged   d. tattered

15. If the value of `credits[0].length` is not equal to `credits[1].length`, you know `credits` is _____ .

   a. a three-dimensional array   c. a partially populated array

   b. an uninitialized array   d. a jagged array

16. Which of the following is true if a successfully running program contains the following statement:

   `Arrays.fill(tax, 10);`

   a. `tax` is a two-dimensional array.   c. `tax` is an array with 10 elements.

   b. `fill()` is a nonstatic method.   d. none of the above

17. Which of the following is a requirement when you use a binary search method with an array?

   a. The array must be numeric.

   b. The array must have been sorted in ascending order.

   c. The array must have at least three elements.

   d. none of the above

18. The chief advantage to using the `ArrayList` class instead of the `Arrays` class is that an `ArrayList` _____ .

   a. can be much larger

   b. is easier to search

   c. is dynamically resizable

   d. can be used as an argument to a `static` method

19. The chief disadvantage to using the `ArrayList` class instead of the `Arrays` class is that an `ArrayList` _____.

    a. cannot be sorted

    b. cannot store primitive data types

    c. cannot be accessed using subscripts

    d. All of the above are disadvantages to using an `ArrayList`.

20. An advantage to using an enumerated data type is _____.

    a. errors are reduced because only a limited set of values can be used with the type

    b. time is saved because programs with enumerated types compile faster

    c. coding time is reduced because enumerated types are created automatically by the compiler

    d. All of the above are true.

Exercises

 Programming Exercises

1. a. Write an application containing an array of 20 `String` values, and display them in ascending order. Save the file as **StringSort.java**.

    b. Write an application that accepts any number of `String` values from a user up to 20, and display them in ascending order. Save the file as **StringSort2.java**.

2. a. The mean of a list of numbers is its arithmetic average. The median of a list is its middle value when the values are placed in order. For example, if a list contains 1, 4, 7, 8, and 10, then the mean is 6 and the median is 7. Write an application that allows you to enter five integers and displays the values, their mean, and their median. Save the file as **MeanMedian.java**.

    b. Revise the `MeanMedian` class so that the user can enter any number of values up to 20. If the list has an even number of values, the median is the numeric average of the values in the two middle positions. Save the file as **MeanMedian2.java**.

3. a. Radio station JAVA wants a class to keep track of recordings it plays. Create a class named `Recording` that contains fields to hold methods for setting and getting a `Recording`'s title, artist, and playing time in seconds. Save the file as **Recording.java**.

    b. Write an application that instantiates five `Recording` objects and prompts the user for values for the data fields. Then prompt the user to enter which field the `Recording`s should be sorted by—song title, artist, or playing time. Perform the requested sort procedure, and display the `Recording` objects. Save the file as **RecordingSort.java**.

4. In Chapter 8, you created a Salesperson class with fields for an ID number and sales values. Now, create an application that allows a user to enter values for an array of seven Salesperson objects. Offer the user the choice of displaying the objects in order by either ID number or sales value. Save the application as **SalespersonSort.java**.

5. In Chapter 8, you created a Salesperson class with fields for an ID number and sales values. Now, create an application that allows you to store an array that acts as a database of any number of Salesperson objects up to 20. While the user decides to continue, offer three options: to add a record to the database, to delete a record from the database, or to change a record in the database. Then proceed as follows:

   - If the user selects the add option, issue an error message if the database is full. Otherwise, prompt the user for an ID number. If the ID number already exists in the database, issue an error message. Otherwise, prompt the user for a sales value and add the new record to the database.

   - If the user selects the delete option, issue an error message if the database is empty. Otherwise, prompt the user for an ID number. If the ID number does not exist, issue an error message. Otherwise, do not access the record for any future processing.

   - If the user selects the change option, issue an error message if the database is empty. Otherwise, prompt the user for an ID number. If the requested record does not exist, issue an error message. Otherwise, prompt the user for a new sales value and change the sales value for the record.

   After each option executes, display the updated database in ascending order by Salesperson ID number and prompt the user to select the next action. Save the application as **SalespersonDatabase.java**.

6. Write an application that stores at least five different department and supervisor names in a two-dimensional array. Allow the user to enter a department name (such as "Marketing") and display the corresponding supervisor's name. If the department does not exist, display an error message. Save the file as **Departments.java**.

7. In the exercises in Chapter 6, you created a class named Purchase. Each Purchase contains an invoice number, amount of sale, amount of sales tax, and several methods. Add get methods for the invoice number and sale amount fields so their values can be used in comparisons. Next, write a program that declares an array of five Purchase objects and prompt a user for their values. Then, in a loop that continues until a user inputs a sentinel value, ask the user whether the Purchase objects should be sorted and displayed in invoice number order or sale amount order. Save the file as **SortPurchasesArray.java**.

8. Create an application that contains an enumeration that represents the days of the week. Display a list of the days, then prompt the user for a day. Display business hours for the chosen day. Assume that the business is open from 11 to 5 on Sunday, 9 to 9 on weekdays, and 10 to 6 on Saturday. Save the file as **DayOfWeek.java**.

9. Create a class named `Majors` that includes an enumeration for the six majors offered by a college as follows: ACC, CHEM, CIS, ENG, HIS, PHYS. Display the enumeration values for the user, then prompt the user to enter a major. Display the college division in which the major falls. ACC and CIS are in the Business Division, CHEM and PHYS are in the Science Division, and ENG and HIS are in the Humanities Division. Save the file as **Majors.java**.

10. Morgan's Department Store distributes bonuses to its salespeople after the holiday rush. Table 9-6 shows the bonuses, which are based on full weeks worked during the season and the number of positive online customer reviews. Write a program that allows a user to continuously enter values for the two bonus-determining factors and displays the appropriate bonus. Save the file as **MorgansBonuses.java**.

	Positive Reviews Received				
Full Weeks Worked	**0**	**1**	**2**	**3**	**4 or More**
0	5.00	9.00	16.00	22.00	30.00
1	10.00	12.00	18.00	24.00	36.00
2	20.00	25.00	32.00	42.00	53.00
3	32.00	38.00	45.00	55.00	68.00
4	46.00	54.00	65.00	77.00	90.00
5	60.00	72.00	84.00	96.00	120.00
6 or more	85.00	100.00	120.00	140.00	175.00

Table 9-6   Morgan's Department Store bonuses

Debugging Exercises

1. Each of the following files in the Chapter09 folder in your downloadable student files has syntax and/or logic errors. In each case, determine the problem and fix the program. After you correct the errors, save each file using the same filename preceded with *Fix*. For example, DebugNine1.java will become **FixDebugNine1.java**.

    a. DebugNine1.java

    b. DebugNine2.java

    c. DebugNine3.java

    d. DebugNine4.java

    e. Movie.java, which is used by DebugNine2.java.

 *Game Zone*

1. Create a guessing game called "Does It Have Legs?", in which you think of an animal and the computer tries to guess what it is. The game continually becomes "smarter" as you play because you teach it how to become more specific with its questions. For example, a typical game session might proceed as follows:

    Computer: Does the animal you are thinking of have legs?

    Player: Yes.

    Computer: Is it a dog?

    Player: Yes.

    Computer: Yay! I win. Do you want to play again?

    Player: Yes.

    Computer: Does the animal you are thinking of have legs?

    Player: Yes.

    Computer: Is it a dog?

    Player: No.

    Computer: I give up. What was your animal?

    Player: Horse.

    Computer: Type a question for which the answer is Yes for Dog but No for Horse.

    Player: Does it live in the house?

    Computer: Do you want to play again?

    Player: Yes.

    Computer: Does the animal you are thinking of have legs?

    Player: Yes.

    Computer: Does it live in the house?

    Player: No.

    Computer: Is it a Horse?

    Player: No.

    Computer: I give up. What was your animal?

    Player: Cow.

Computer: Type a question for which the answer is Yes for Horse but No for Cow.

Player: Do people ride it?

Computer: Do you want to play again?

Player: Yes.

Computer: Does the animal you are thinking of have legs?

Player: Yes.

Computer: Does it live in the house?

Player: No.

Computer: Do people ride it?

Player: No.

Computer: Is it a Cow?

Player: Yes.

Computer: Yay! I win. Do you want to play again?

Player: No.

(*Hint*: You might want to look up "binary trees" on the Internet as a method to organize this application.)

Save the application as **DoesItHaveLegs.java**.

2. a. Create a Tic Tac Toe game. In this game, two players alternate placing *X*s and *O*s into a grid until one player has three matching symbols in a row, horizontally, vertically, or diagonally. Create a game in which the user is presented with a three-by-three grid containing the digits 1 through 9. When the user chooses a position by typing a number, place an *X* in the appropriate spot. Generate a random number for the position where the computer will place an *O*. Do not allow the player or the computer to place a symbol where one has already been placed. Figure 9-29 shows the first four windows in a typical game. When either the player or computer has three symbols in a row, declare a winner; if all positions have been exhausted and no one has three symbols in a row, declare a tie. Save the game as **TicTacToe.java**.

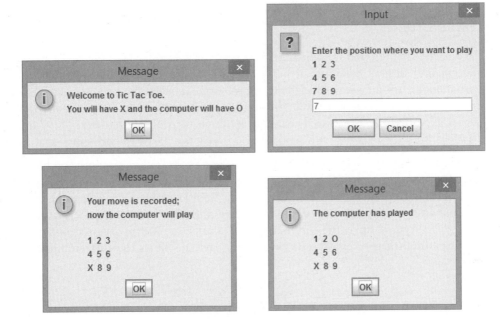

Figure 9-29 Typical game of TicTacToe in progress

    b. In the TicTacToe application, the computer's selection is chosen randomly. Improve the TicTacToe game so that when the computer has two *O*s in any row, column, or diagonal, it selects the winning position for its next move rather than selecting a position randomly. Save the improved game as **TicTacToe2.java**.

3. In Chapter 8, you created an application class named FullDeck that implemented a 52-element array that represented each card in a standard deck of playing cards. Now, create an enumeration that holds the four suits SPADES, HEARTS, DIAMONDS, and CLUBS. Save the enumeration in a file named **Suit.java**. Modify the Card class from Chapter 8 to use the enumeration, and save the class as **Card2.java**. Modify the FullDeck application to use the new Card class, and save the application as **FullDeck2.java**.

4. In Chapter 7, you improved a Rock Paper Scissors game played between a user and the computer. Add an enumeration that holds three values that represent ROCK, PAPER, and SCISSORS, and use it for all comparisons in the program. Save the file as **RockPaperScissors3.java**.

Case Problems

1. In the last chapter, you modified the EventDemo program for Carly's Catering to accept and display data for an array of three Event objects. Now, modify the program to use an array of eight Event objects. Prompt the user to choose an option to sort Events in ascending order by event number, number of guests, or event type. Display the sorted list, and continue to prompt the user for sorting options until the user enters a sentinel value. Save the file as **EventDemo.java**.

2. In the last chapter, you modified the RentalDemo program for Sammy's Seashore Supplies to accept and display data for an array of three Rental objects. Now, modify the program to use an array of eight Rental objects. Prompt the user to choose an option to sort Rentals in ascending order by contract number, price, or equipment type. Display the sorted list, and continue to prompt the user for sorting options until the user enters a sentinel value. Save the file as **RentalDemo.java**.

CHAPTER 10

Introduction to Inheritance

In this chapter, you will:

- ◎ Learn about the concept of inheritance
- ◎ Extend classes
- ◎ Override superclass methods
- ◎ Call constructors during inheritance
- ◎ Access superclass methods
- ◎ Employ information hiding
- ◎ Learn which methods you cannot override

Learning About the Concept of Inheritance

In Java and all object-oriented languages, **inheritance** is a mechanism that enables one class to acquire all the behaviors and attributes of another class, meaning that you can create a new class simply by indicating the ways in which it differs from a class that has already been developed and tested.

You are familiar with the concept of inheritance from all sorts of nonprogramming situations. When you use the term *inheritance*, you might think of genetic inheritance. You know from biology that your blood type and eye color are the product of inherited genes; you can say that many facts about you—your attributes, or "data fields"—are inherited. Similarly, you often can credit your behavior to inheritance. For example, your attitude toward saving money might be the same as your grandmother's, and the odd way that you pull on your ear when you are tired might match what your Uncle Steve does—thus, your methods are inherited, too.

You also might choose plants and animals based on inheritance. You plant impatiens next to your house because of your shady location; you adopt a Doberman Pinscher because you need a watchdog. Every individual plant and pet has slightly different characteristics, but within a species, you can count on many consistent inherited attributes and behaviors. Similarly, the classes you create in object-oriented programming languages can inherit data and methods from existing classes. When you create a class by making it inherit from another class, the new class automatically contains the data fields and methods of the original class.

Diagramming Inheritance Using the UML

Beginning with the first chapter of this book, you have been creating classes and instantiating them. Programmers and analysts sometimes use a graphical language to describe classes and object-oriented processes; this **Unified Modeling Language (UML)** consists of many types of diagrams, some of which can help illustrate inheritance.

For example, consider the simple `Employee` class shown in Figure 10-1. The class contains two data fields, `id` and `salary`, and four methods: a get and set method for each field. Figure 10-2 shows a UML class diagram for the `Employee` class. A **class diagram** is a visual tool that provides you with an overview of a class. It consists of a rectangle divided into three sections—the top section contains the name of the class, the middle section contains the names and data types of the attributes, and the bottom section contains the methods. Only the method return type, name, and arguments are provided in the diagram—the instructions that make up the method body are omitted.

```
public class Employee
{
    private int id;
    private double salary;
    public int getId()
    {
        return id;
    }
    public double getSalary()
    {
        return salary;
    }
    public void setId(int idNum)
    {
        id = idNum;
    }
    public void setSalary(double sal)
    {
        salary = sal;
    }
}
```

Figure 10-1   The Employee class

Employee
-id : int -salary : double
+getId() : int +getSalary() : double +setId(int idNum) : void +setSalary(double sal) : void

Figure 10-2   The Employee class diagram

493

By convention, a class diagram contains the data type following each attribute or method, as shown in Figure 10-2. A minus sign (−) is inserted in front of each private field or method, and a plus sign (+) is inserted in front of each public field or method.

Commonly, UML diagram creators refrain from using Java terminology such as int in a class diagram. Instead, they might use a more general term, such as *integer*. The Employee class is designed in natural language (English) and might be implemented in any programming language, and languages other than Java might use a different keyword to designate integer variables. Because you are studying Java, this book uses the Java keywords in diagrams. For more information on UML, you can go to the Object Management Group's Web site at *www.omg.org*. OMG is an international, nonprofit computer industry consortium.

After you create the Employee class, you can create specific Employee objects, such as the following:

```
Employee receptionist = new Employee();
Employee deliveryPerson = new Employee();
```

These Employee objects can eventually possess different numbers and salaries, but because they are Employee objects, you know that each Employee has *some* ID number and salary.

Suppose that you hire a new type of Employee such as a salesperson or service representative that requires not only an ID number and a salary, but also a data field to indicate the territory served. You can create a class with a name such as EmployeeWithTerritory, and provide the class three fields (idNum, salary, and territory) and six methods (get and set methods for each of the three fields). However, when you do this, you are duplicating much of the work that you have already done for the Employee class. The wise, efficient alternative is to create the class EmployeeWithTerritory so it inherits all the attributes and methods of Employee. Then, you can add just the one field and two methods that are new within EmployeeWithTerritory objects. Figure 10-3 shows a class diagram of the two classes and their relationship. In a UML diagram, an inheritance relationship is indicated with an arrow that points from the descendant class to the original class.

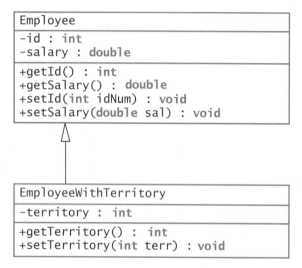

Figure 10-3   Class diagram showing the relationship between Employee and EmployeeWithTerritory

When you use inheritance to create the EmployeeWithTerritory class, you:

- Save time because the Employee fields and methods already exist

- Reduce errors because the Employee methods already have been used and tested

- Reduce the amount of new learning required for programmers to use the new class if they are already familiar with the original class

The ability to use inheritance in Java makes programs easier to write, less error-prone, and more quickly understood. Besides creating EmployeeWithTerritory, you also can create several other specific Employee classes (perhaps EmployeeEarningCommission, including a commission rate, or DismissedEmployee, including a reason for dismissal). By using inheritance, you can develop each new class correctly and more quickly. The concept of inheritance is useful because it makes a class's code more easily reusable. Each defined data field and each method already written and tested in the original class becomes part of the new class that inherits it.

Inheritance Terminology

A class that is used as a basis for inheritance, such as `Employee`, is a **base class**. When you create a class that inherits from a base class (such as `EmployeeWithTerritory`), it is a **derived class**. When considering two classes that inherit from each other, you can tell which is the base class and which is the derived class by using the two classes in a sentence with the phrase "is a(n)." A derived class always "is a" case or example of the more general base class. For example, a `Tree` class can be a base class to an `Evergreen` class. An `Evergreen` "is a" `Tree`, so `Tree` is the base class; however, it is not true for all `Tree`s that "a `Tree` is an `Evergreen`." Similarly, an `EmployeeWithTerritory` "is an" `Employee`—but not the other way around—so `Employee` is the base class.

 Because a derived class object "is an" instance of the base class too, you can assign a derived class object's reference to a base class reference. Similarly, if a method accepts a base class object reference, it also will accept references to its derived classes. The next chapter describes these concepts in greater detail.

Do not confuse "is a" situations with "has a" situations. For example, you might create a `Business` class that contains an array of `Department` objects; in turn, each `Department` object might contain an array of `Employee` objects. You would not say "A department is a business," but that "a business *has* departments." Therefore, this relationship is not inheritance; it is **composition**—the relationship in which a class contains one or more members of another class, when those members would not continue to exist without the object that contains them. (For example, if a `Business` closes, its `Departments` do too.) Similarly, you would not say "an employee is a department," but that "a department *has* employees." This relationship is not inheritance either; it is a specific type of composition known as **aggregation**—the relationship in which a class contains one or more members of another class, when those members *would* continue to exist without the object that contains them. (For example, if a business or department closed, the employees would continue to exist.) On the other hand, if `Employee`s no longer existed, no `EmployeeWithTerritory` would exist either.

You can use the terms **superclass** and **subclass** as synonyms for base class and derived class, respectively. Thus, `Evergreen` can be called a subclass of the `Tree` superclass. You can also use the terms **parent class** and **child class**. An `EmployeeWithTerritory` is a child to the `Employee` parent. Use the pair of terms with which you are most comfortable; all of these terms are used interchangeably throughout this book.

As an alternative way to discover which of two classes is the base class or subclass, you can try saying the two class names together. When people say their names together, they state the more specific name before the all-encompassing family name, as in "Ginny Kroening." Similarly, with classes, the order that "makes more sense" is the child-parent order. "Evergreen Tree" makes more sense than "Tree Evergreen," so `Evergreen` is the child class.

Finally, you usually can distinguish superclasses from their subclasses by size. Although it is not required, in general a subclass is larger than a superclass because it usually has additional fields and methods. A subclass description might look small, but any subclass contains all the fields and methods of its superclass, as well as the new, more specific fields and methods you add to that subclass.

Watch the video *Inheritance*.

496

TWO TRUTHS & A LIE

Learning About the Concept of Inheritance

1. When you use inheritance in Java, you can create a new class that contains all the data and methods of an existing class.

2. When you use inheritance, you save time and reduce errors.

3. A class that is used as a basis for inheritance is called a subclass.

The false statement is #3. A class that is used as a basis for inheritance is called a superclass, base class, or parent class. A subclass is a class that inherits from a superclass.

Extending Classes

You use the keyword **extends** to achieve inheritance in Java. For example, the following class header creates a superclass–subclass relationship between `Employee` and `EmployeeWithTerritory`:

```
public class EmployeeWithTerritory extends Employee
```

Each `EmployeeWithTerritory` automatically receives the data fields and methods of the superclass `Employee`; you then add new fields and methods to the newly created subclass. Figure 10-4 shows an `EmployeeWithTerritory` class.

```
public class EmployeeWithTerritory extends Employee
{
   private int territory;
   public int getTerritory()
   {
      return territory;
   }
   public void setTerritory(int terr)
   {
      territory = terr;
   }
}
```

Figure 10-4   The `EmployeeWithTerritory` class

You can write a statement that instantiates a derived class object, such as the following:

```
EmployeeWithTerritory northernRep = new EmployeeWithTerritory();
```

Then you can use any of the next statements to get field values for the northernRep object:

```
northernRep.getId();
northernRep.getSalary();
northernRep.getTerritory();
```

The northernRep object has access to all three get methods—two methods that it inherits from Employee and one method that belongs to EmployeeWithTerritory.

Similarly, after the northernRep object is declared, any of the following statements are legal:

```
northernRep.setId(915);
northernRep.setSalary(210.00);
northernRep.setTerritory(5);
```

The northernRep object has access to all the parent Employee class set methods, as well as its own class's new set method.

Inheritance is a one-way proposition; a child inherits from a parent, not the other way around. When you instantiate an Employee object, it does not have access to the EmployeeWithTerritory methods. It makes sense that a parent class object does not have access to its child's data and methods. When you create the parent class, you do not know how many future subclasses it might have or what their data fields or methods might look like.

In addition, subclasses are more specific than the superclass they extend. An Orthodontist class and Periodontist class are children of the Dentist parent class. You do not expect all members of the general parent class Dentist to have the Orthodontist's applyBraces() method or the Periodontist's deepClean() method. However, Orthodontist objects and Periodontist objects have access to the more general Dentist methods conductExam() and billPatients().

You can use the instanceof operator to determine whether an object is a member or descendant of a class. For example, if northernRep is an EmployeeWithTerritory object, the value of each of the following expressions is true:

```
northernRep instanceof EmployeeWithTerritory
northernRep instanceof Employee
```

If aClerk is an Employee object, the following is true:

```
aClerk instanceof Employee
```

However, the following is false:

```
aClerk instanceof EmployeeWithTerritory
```

Programmers say that instanceof yields true if the operand on the left can be **upcast** to the operand on the right.

TWO TRUTHS & A LIE

Extending Classes

1. You use the keyword `inherits` to achieve inheritance in Java.

2. A derived class has access to all its parents' nonprivate methods.

3. Subclasses are more specific than the superclass they extend.

The false statement is #1. You use the keyword extends to achieve inheritance in Java.

 You Do It

Demonstrating Inheritance

In this section, you create a working example of inheritance. To see the effects of inheritance, you create this example in four stages:

-   First, you create a `Party` class that holds just one data field and three methods.

-   After you create the general `Party` class, you write an application to demonstrate its use.

-   Then, you create a more specific `DinnerParty` subclass that inherits the fields and methods of the `Party` class.

-   Finally, you modify the demonstration application to add an example using the `DinnerParty` class.

Creating a Superclass and an Application to Use It

1. Open a new file, and enter the following first few lines for a simple `Party` class. The class hosts one integer data field—the number of guests expected at the party:

```
public class Party
{
    private int guests;
```

(continues)

(continued)

2. Add the following methods that get and set the number of `guests`:

```java
public int getGuests()
{
    return guests;
}
public void setGuests(int numGuests)
{
    guests = numGuests;
}
```

3. Add a method that displays a party invitation:

```java
public void displayInvitation()
{
    System.out.println("Please come to my party!");
}
```

4. Add the closing curly brace for the class, and then save the file as **Party.java**. Compile the class; if necessary, correct any errors and compile again.

Writing an Application that Uses the Party Class

Now that you have created a class, you can use it in an application. A very simple application creates a `Party` object, prompts the user for the number of guests at the party, sets the data field, and displays the results.

1. Open a new file, and start to write a `UseParty` application that has one method—a `main()` method. Declare a variable for the number of guests, a `Party` object, and a `Scanner` object to use for input:

```java
import java.util.*;
public class UseParty
{
    public static void main(String[] args)
    {
        int guests;
        Party aParty = new Party();
        Scanner keyboard = new Scanner(System.in);
```

2. Continue the `main()` method by prompting the user for a number of guests and accepting the value from the keyboard. Set the number of guests in the `Party` object, and then display the value.

```java
System.out.print("Enter number of guests for the party >> ");
guests = keyboard.nextInt();
aParty.setGuests(guests);
System.out.println("The party has " + aParty.getGuests() + "
    guests");
```

(continues)

(continued)

3. Add a statement to display the party invitation, and then add the closing curly braces for the `main()` method and for the class:

```
    aParty.displayInvitation();
  }
}
```

4. Save the file as **UseParty.java**, then compile and run the application. Figure 10-5 shows a typical execution.

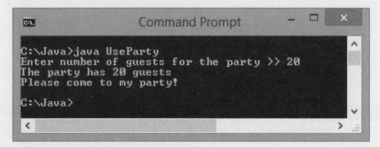

```
C:\Java>java UseParty
Enter number of guests for the party >> 20
The party has 20 guests
Please come to my party!

C:\Java>
```

Figure 10-5   Typical execution of the `UseParty` application

Creating a Subclass from the Party Class

Next, you create a class named `DinnerParty`. A `DinnerParty` "is a" type of `Party` at which dinner is served, so `DinnerParty` is a child class of `Party`.

1. Open a new file, and type the first few lines for the `DinnerParty` class:

```
public class DinnerParty extends Party
{
```

2. A `DinnerParty` contains a number of guests, but you do not have to define the variable here. The variable is already defined in `Party`, which is the superclass of this class. You only need to add any variables that are particular to a `DinnerParty`. Enter the following code to add an integer code for the dinner menu choice:

```
private int dinnerChoice;
```

3. The `Party` class already contains methods to get and set the number of guests, so `DinnerParty` only needs methods to get and set the `dinnerChoice` variable as follows:

```
public int getDinnerChoice()
{
    return dinnerChoice;
}
public void setDinnerChoice(int choice)
{
    dinnerChoice = choice;
}
```

(continues)

(continued)

4. Add a closing curly brace for the class.

5. Save the file as **DinnerParty.java**, and then compile it.

Creating an Application that Uses the DinnerParty Class

Now, you can modify the UseParty application so that it creates a DinnerParty as well as a plain Party.

1. Open the **UseParty.java** file, and change the class name to **UseDinnerParty**. Immediately save the file as **UseDinnerParty.java**.

2. Include a new variable that holds the dinner choice for a DinnerParty:

   ```
   int choice;
   ```

3. After the statement that constructs the Party object, type the following DinnerParty object declaration:

   ```
   DinnerParty aDinnerParty = new DinnerParty();
   ```

4. At the end of the main() method, after the Party object data and invitation are displayed, add a prompt for the number of guests for the DinnerParty. Accept the value the user enters and assign it to the object. Even though the DinnerParty class does not contain a setGuests() method, its parent class does, so aDinnerParty can use the method.

   ```
   System.out.print("Enter number of guests for the dinner party >> ");
   guests = keyboard.nextInt();
   aDinnerParty.setGuests(guests);
   ```

5. Next, prompt the user for a dinner choice. To keep this example simple, the program provides only two choices and does not provide range checking. Accept a response from the user, assign it to the object, and then display all the data for the DinnerParty. Even though the DinnerParty class does not contain a getGuests() method, its parent class does, so aDinnerParty can use the method. The DinnerParty class uses its own setDinnerChoice() and getDinnerChoice() methods.

   ```
   System.out.print
      ("Enter the menu option -- 1 for chicken or 2 for beef >> ");
   choice = keyboard.nextInt();
   aDinnerParty.setDinnerChoice(choice);
   System.out.println("The dinner party has " +
      aDinnerParty.getGuests() + " guests");
   System.out.println("Menu option " +
      aDinnerParty.getDinnerChoice () + " will be served");
   ```

(continues)

(continued)

6. Add a statement to call the `displayInvitation()` method with the `DinnerParty` object. Even though the `DinnerParty` class does not contain a `displayInvitation()` method, its parent class does, so `aDinnerParty` can use the method.

    ```
    aDinnerParty.displayInvitation();
    ```

7. Save the file, compile it, and run it using values of your choice. Figure 10-6 shows a typical execution. The `DinnerParty` object successfully uses the data field and methods of its superclass, as well as its own data field and methods.

Figure 10-6   Typical execution of the `UseDinnerParty` application

Overriding Superclass Methods

When you create a subclass by extending an existing class, the new subclass contains data and methods that were defined in the original superclass. In other words, any child class object has all the attributes of its parent. Sometimes, however, the superclass data fields and methods are not entirely appropriate for the subclass objects; in these cases, you want to override the parent class members. To **override** a field or method in a child class means to use the child's version instead of the parent's version.

When you use the English language, you often use the same method name to indicate diverse meanings. For example, if you think of `MusicalInstrument` as a class, you can think of `play()` as a method of that class. If you think of various subclasses such as `Guitar` and `Drum`, you know that you carry out the `play()` method quite differently for each subclass. Using the same method name to indicate different implementations is called **polymorphism**, a term meaning "many forms"—many different forms of action take place, even though you use the same word to describe the action. In other words, many forms of the same action-describing word exist, depending on the associated object.

You first learned the term *polymorphism* in Chapter 1. Polymorphism is one of the basic principles of object-oriented programming. If a programming language does not support polymorphism, the language is not considered object oriented.

For example, suppose that you create an `Employee` superclass containing data fields such as `firstName`, `lastName`, `socialSecurityNumber`, `dateOfHire`, `rateOfPay`, and so on, and the methods contained in the `Employee` class include the usual collection of get and set methods. If your usual time period for payment to each `Employee` object is weekly, your `displayRateOfPay()` method might include a statement such as:

```
System.out.println("Pay is " + rateOfPay + " per week");
```

Imagine your company has a few `Employees` who are not paid weekly. Maybe some are paid by the hour, and others are `Employees` whose work is contracted on a job-to-job basis. Because each `Employee` type requires different paycheck-calculating procedures, you might want to create subclasses of `Employee`, such as `HourlyEmployee` and `ContractEmployee`.

When you call the `displayRateOfPay()` method for an `HourlyEmployee` object, you want the display to include the phrase "per hour", as in "Pay is $8.75 per hour." When you call the `displayRateOfPay()` method for a `ContractEmployee`, you want to include "per contract", as in "Pay is $2000 per contract." Each class—the `Employee` superclass and the two subclasses—requires its own `displayRateOfPay()` method. Fortunately, if you create separate `displayRateOfPay()` methods for each class, the objects of each class use the appropriate method for that class. When you create a method in a child class that has the same name and parameter list as a method in its parent class, you override the method in the parent class. When you use the method name with a child object, the child's version of the method is used.

It is important to note that each subclass method overrides any method in the parent class that has both the same name and parameter list. If the parent class method has the same name but a different parameter list, the subclass method does not over*ride* the parent class version; instead, the subclass method over*loads* the parent class method, and any subclass object has access to both versions. You learned about overloading methods in Chapter 4. You first saw the term *override* in Chapter 4, when you learned that a variable declared within a block overrides another variable with the same name declared outside the block.

If you could not override superclass methods, you could always create a unique name for each subclass method, such as `displayRateOfPayForHourly()`, but the classes you create are easier to write and understand if you use one reasonable name for methods that do essentially the same thing. Because you are attempting to display the rate of pay for each object, `displayRateOfPay()` is a clear and appropriate method name for all the object types.

A child class object can use an overridden parent's method by using the keyword `super`. You will learn about this word later in this chapter.

Object-oriented programmers use the term *polymorphism* when discussing any operation that has multiple meanings, regardless of whether inheritance is involved. For example, the plus sign (+) is polymorphic because it operates differently depending on its operands. You can use the plus sign to add integers or `double`s, to concatenate strings, or to indicate a positive value. As another example, methods with the same name but different parameter lists are polymorphic because the method call operates differently depending on its arguments. When Java developers refer to methods that work appropriately for subclasses of the same parent class, the more specific term is **subtype polymorphism**.

Using the @Override Tag

When you override a parent class method in a child class, you can insert an override annotation just prior to the method. The **override annotation** lets the compiler know that your intention is to override a method in the parent class rather than create a method with a new signature. For example, if the `Employee` class contains a `displayRateOfPay()` method that displays a weekly pay rate and your intention is to override the method in the child `ContractEmployee` class to display a contractual pay rate, you can write the child class method as follows:

```
@Override
public void displayRateOfPay()
{
    System.out.println("Pay is " + rateOfPay + " per contract ");
}
```

The `@Override` tag before the method header announces your intention to override a parent class method and causes the compiler to issue an error message if you do not—most likely because you made a typographical error in the header of the child class's method so that it does not match the parent class version. A program will work and properly override parent class methods without any `@Override` tags, but using the tags can help you prevent errors and serves as a form of documentation for your intentions.

Some programmers place the `@Override` tag on the same line as the method header. You should use the style that is conventional in your organization.

Watch the video *Handling Methods and Inheritance*.

TWO TRUTHS & A LIE

Overriding Superclass Methods

1. Any child class object has all the attributes of its parent, but all of those attributes might not be directly accessible.

2. You override a parent class method by creating a child class method with the same identifier but a different parameter list or return type.

3. When a child class method overrides a parent class method, and you use the method name with a child class object, the child class method version executes.

The false statement is #2. You override a parent class method by creating a child class method with the same identifier and parameter list. The return type is not a factor in overloading.

 You Do It

Overriding a Superclass Method

In the previous "You Do It" section, you created `Party` and `DinnerParty` classes. The `DinnerParty` class extends `Party`, and so can use its `displayInvitation()` method. Suppose that you want a `DinnerParty` object to use a specialized invitation. In this section, you override the parent class method so that the same method name acts uniquely for the child class object.

1. Open the **DinnerParty.java** class. Change the class name to **DinnerParty2**, and save the file as **DinnerParty2.java**.

2. Create a `displayInvitation()` method that overrides the parent class method with the same name as follows:

```
@Override
public void displayInvitation()
{
    System.out.println("Please come to my dinner party!");
}
```

3. Save the class and compile it.

4. Open the **UseDinnerParty.java** file. Change the class name to **UseDinnerParty2**, and immediately save the file as **UseDinnerParty2.java**.

(continues)

(continued)

5. Change the declaration of the aDinnerParty object so that it uses the DinnerParty2 class as a data type and DinnerParty2 as the constructor name.

6. Save the class, compile it, and execute it. Figure 10-7 shows a typical execution. Each type of object uses its own version of the displayInvitation() method.

```
C:\Java>java UseDinnerParty2
Enter number of guests for the party >> 40
The party has 40 guests
Please come to my party!
Enter number of guests for the dinner party >> 6
Enter the menu option -- 1 for chicken or 2 for beef >> 2
The dinner party has 6 guests
Menu option 2 will be served
Please come to my dinner party!

C:\Java>_
```

Figure 10-7   Typical execution of the UseDinnerParty2 program

7. Purposely introduce an error into the child class displayInvitation() method header. For example, you might make the I lowercase, as in **displayinvitation()**. Save and compile the DinnerParty2.java file. You receive a compiler error message similar to the following:

Method does not override or implement a method from a supertype.

(You will learn about the keyword implements in Chapter 11.)

8. Comment out the @Override annotation by inserting two forward slashes (//) in front of it. Save and compile the DinnerParty2.java file. This time the compilation is successful because displayinvitation() is a valid method name—it's just not one that overrides a parent class method. If you wanted to use this method in an application, you would have to remember to use a lowercase *i* for *invitation* in the method name. However, it would not be recommended because you could easily confuse displayinvitation() with displayInvitation().

9. Remove the comment slashes from the @Override annotation and reinstate the uppercase **I** in the displayInvitation() method header. Save and recompile the class, and confirm it is error-free.

Calling Constructors During Inheritance

When you create any object, as in the following statement, you are calling a constructor:

```
SomeClass anObject = new SomeClass();
```

When you instantiate an object that is a member of a subclass, you are actually calling at least two constructors: the constructor for the base class and the constructor for the extended, derived class. When you create any subclass object, the superclass constructor must execute first, and *then* the subclass constructor executes.

507

In the chapter "Advanced Inheritance Concepts," you will learn that every Java object automatically is a child of a class named Object. So, when you instantiate any object, you call its constructor and Object's constructor, and when you create parent and child classes of your own, the child classes actually use three constructors.

When a superclass contains a default constructor and you instantiate a subclass object, the execution of the superclass constructor usually is transparent—that is, nothing calls attention to the fact that the superclass constructor is executing unless the constructor contains some action such as displaying a message. However, you should realize that when you create an object such as the following (where HourlyEmployee is a subclass of Employee), *both* the Employee() and HourlyEmployee() constructors execute.

```
HourlyEmployee clerk = new HourlyEmployee();
```

For example, Figure 10-8 shows three classes. The class named ASuperClass has a constructor that displays a message. The class named ASubClass descends from ASuperClass, and its constructor displays a different message. The DemoConstructors class contains just one statement that instantiates one object of type ASubClass.

```java
public class ASuperClass
{
   public ASuperClass()
   {
      System.out.println("In superclass constructor");
   }
}
public class ASubClass extends ASuperClass
{
   public ASubClass()
   {
      System.out.println("In subclass constructor");
   }
}
public class DemoConstructors
{
   public static void main(String[] args)
   {
      ASubClass child = new ASubClass();
   }
}
```

Figure 10-8 Three classes that demonstrate constructor calling when a subclass object is instantiated

Figure 10-9 shows the output when DemoConstructors executes. You can see that when DemoConstructors instantiates the ASubClass object, the parent class constructor executes first, displaying its message, and then the child class constructor executes. Even though only one object is created, two constructors execute.

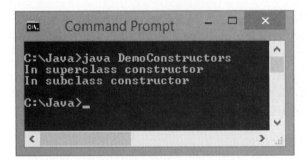

Figure 10-9   Output of the DemoConstructors application

Of course, most constructors perform many more tasks than displaying a message to inform you that they exist. When constructors initialize variables, you usually want the superclass constructor to take care of initializing the data fields that originate in the superclass. Usually, the subclass constructor only needs to initialize the data fields that are specific to the subclass.

Using Superclass Constructors that Require Arguments

When you create a class and do not provide a constructor, Java automatically supplies you with a default constructor—one that never requires arguments. When you write your own constructor, you replace the automatically supplied version. Depending on your needs, a constructor you create for a class might be a default constructor or might require arguments. When you use a class as a superclass and the class has only constructors that require arguments, you must be certain that any subclasses provide the superclass constructor with the arguments it needs.

 Don't forget that a class can have many constructors. As soon as you create at least one constructor for a class, you can no longer use the automatically supplied version.

When a superclass has a default constructor, you can create a subclass with or without its own constructor. This is true whether the default superclass constructor is the automatically supplied one or one you have written. However, when a superclass contains only constructors that require arguments, you must include at least one constructor for each subclass you create. Your subclass constructors can contain any number of statements, but if all superclass constructors require arguments, the first statement within each subclass constructor must call one of the superclass constructors. When a superclass requires constructor arguments upon object instantiation, even if you have no other reason to create a subclass constructor, you must write the subclass constructor so it can call its superclass's constructor.

If a superclass has multiple constructors but one is a default constructor, you do not have to create a subclass constructor unless you want to. If the subclass contains no constructor, all subclass objects use the superclass default constructor when they are instantiated.

The format of the statement that calls a superclass constructor from the subclass constructor is:

```
super(list of arguments);
```

The keyword **super** always refers to the superclass of the class in which you use it.

If a superclass contains only constructors that require arguments, you must create a subclass constructor, but the subclass constructor does not necessarily have to have parameters of its own. For example, suppose that you create an Employee class with a constructor that requires three arguments—a character, a double, and an integer—and you create an HourlyEmployee class that is a subclass of Employee. The following code shows a valid constructor for HourlyEmployee:

```
public HourlyEmployee()
{
    super('P', 12.35, 40);
    // Other statements can go here
}
```

This version of the HourlyEmployee constructor requires no arguments, but it passes three constant arguments to its superclass constructor. A different, overloaded version of the HourlyEmployee constructor can require arguments. It could then pass the appropriate arguments to the superclass constructor. For example:

```
public HourlyEmployee(char dept, double rate, int hours)
{
    super(dept, rate, hours);
    // Other statements can go here
}
```

Except for any comments, the super() statement must be the first statement in any subclass constructor that uses it. Not even data field definitions can precede it. Although it seems that you should be able to use the superclass constructor name to call the superclass constructor—for example, Employee()—Java does not allow this. You must use the keyword super.

In Chapter 4, you learned that you can call one constructor from another using this(). In this chapter, you learned that you can call a base class constructor from a derived class using super(). However, you cannot use both this() and super() in the same constructor because each is required to be the first statement in any constructor in which it appears.

Watch the video *Constructors and Inheritance*.

TWO TRUTHS & A LIE

Calling Constructors During Inheritance

1. When you create any subclass object, the subclass constructor executes first, and then the superclass constructor executes.

2. When constructors initialize variables, you usually want the superclass constructor to initialize the data fields that originate in the superclass and the subclass constructor to initialize the data fields that are specific to the subclass.

3. When a superclass contains only nondefault constructors, you must include at least one constructor for each subclass you create.

The false statement is #1. When you create any subclass object, the superclass constructor must execute first, and *then* the subclass constructor executes.

 You Do It

Understanding the Role of Constructors in Inheritance

Next, you add a constructor to the Party class. When you instantiate a subclass object, the superclass constructor executes before the subclass constructor executes.

1. Open the **Party.java** file, and save it as **PartyWithConstructor.java**. Change the class name to `PartyWithConstructor`.

2. Following the statement that declares the guests data field, type a constructor that does nothing other than display a message indicating it is working:

```
public PartyWithConstructor()
{
    System.out.println("Creating a Party");
}
```

3. Save the file and compile it.

(continues)

(continued)

4. Open the **DinnerParty2.java** file, and change the class name to DinnerPartyWithConstructor. Change the class in the extends clause to PartyWithConstructor. Save the file as **DinnerPartyWithConstructor.java**, and compile it.

5. Open a new file so you can write an application to demonstrate the use of the base class constructor with an extended class object. This application creates only one child class object:

```java
public class UseDinnerPartyWithConstructor
{
   public static void main(String[] args)
   {
      DinnerPartyWithConstructor aDinnerParty =
         new DinnerPartyWithConstructor();
   }
}
```

6. Save the application as **UseDinnerPartyWithConstructor.java**, then compile and run it. The output is shown in Figure 10-10. Even though the application creates only one subclass object (and no superclass objects) and the subclass contains no constructor of its own, the superclass constructor executes.

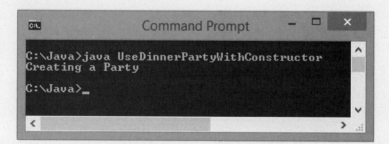

Figure 10-10   Output of the UseDinnerPartyWithConstructor application

Inheritance When the Superclass Requires Constructor Arguments

Next, you modify the PartyWithConstructor class so that its constructor requires an argument. Then, you observe that a subclass without a constructor cannot compile.

1. Open the **PartyWithConstructor.java** file, and then change the class name to **PartyWithConstructor2**.

(continues)

(continued)

2. Replace the existing constructor with a new version using the new class name. This constructor requires an argument, which it uses to set the number of guests who will attend a party:

```java
public PartyWithConstructor2(int numGuests)
{
   guests = numGuests;
}
```

3. Save the file as **PartyWithConstructor2.java**, and then compile it.

4. Open the **DinnerPartyWithConstructor.java** file, and change the class header as follows so that the name of the class is `DinnerPartyWithConstructor2`, and inherits from `PartyWithConstructor2`:

```java
public class DinnerPartyWithConstructor2 extends
   PartyWithConstructor2
```

5. Save the file as **DinnerPartyWithConstructor2.java**, and then compile it. An error message appears, as shown in Figure 10-11. When you attempt to compile the subclass, no parameterless constructor can be found in the superclass, so the compile fails.

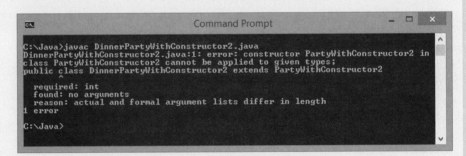

Figure 10-11   Error message generated when compiling the `DinnerPartyWithConstructor2` class

6. To correct the error, open the **DinnerPartyWithConstructor2.java** file. Following the `dinnerChoice` field declaration, insert a constructor for the class as follows:

```java
public DinnerPartyWithConstructor2(int numGuests)
{
   super(numGuests);
}
```

(continues)

(continued)

7. Save the file, and compile it. This time, the compile is successful because the subclass calls its parent's constructor, passing along an integer value. Note that you could have created the `DinnerPartyWithConstructor2` subclass constructor without the integer argument to pass to the parent constructor. For example, it would be acceptable to create a subclass constructor that required no arguments but passed a constant (for example, 0) to its parent. Similarly, the subclass constructor could require several arguments, pass one of them to its parent, and use the others for different purposes. The requirement is not that the subclass constructor must have the same number or types of parameters as its parent; the only requirement is that the subclass constructor calls `super()` and passes to the parent what it needs to execute.

Accessing Superclass Methods

Earlier in this chapter, you learned that a subclass can contain a method with the same name and arguments (the same signature) as a method in its parent class. When this happens and you use the method name with a subclass object, the subclass method overrides the superclass method. However, if a method has been overridden but you want to use the superclass version within the subclass, you can use the keyword `super` to access the parent class method.

For example, examine the `Customer` class in Figure 10-12 and the `PreferredCustomer` class in Figure 10-13. A `Customer` has an `idNumber` and `balanceOwed`. In addition to these fields, a `PreferredCustomer` receives a `discountRate`. In the `PreferredCustomer` `display()` method, you want to display all three fields—`idNumber`, `balanceOwed`, and `discountRate`. Because two-thirds of the code to accomplish the display has already been written for the `Customer` class, it is convenient to have the `PreferredCustomer` `display()` method use its parent's version of the `display()` method before displaying its own discount rate. Figure 10-14 shows a brief application that displays one object of each class, and Figure 10-15 shows the output.

514

```
public class Customer
{
   private int idNumber;
   private double balanceOwed;
   public Customer(int id, double bal)
   {
      idNumber = id;
      balanceOwed = bal;
   }
   public void display()
   {
      System.out.println("Customer #" + idNumber +
         " Balance $" + balanceOwed);
   }
}
```

Figure 10-12   The Customer class

```
public class PreferredCustomer extends Customer
{
   double discountRate;
   public PreferredCustomer(int id, double bal, double rate)
   {
      super(id, bal);
      discountRate = rate;
   }
   @Override
   public void display()
   {
      super.display();
      System.out.println(" Discount rate is " + discountRate);
   }
}
```

Figure 10-13   The PreferredCustomer class

```
public class TestCustomers
{
   public static void main(String[] args)
   {
      Customer oneCust = new Customer(124, 123.45);
      PreferredCustomer onePCust = new
         PreferredCustomer(125, 3456.78, 0.15);
      oneCust.display();
      onePCust.display();
   }
}
```

Figure 10-14   The TestCustomers application

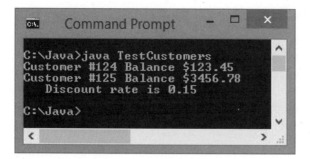

Figure 10-15 Output of the `TestCustomers` application

When you call a superclass constructor from a subclass constructor, the call must be the first statement in the constructor. However, when you call an ordinary superclass method within a subclass method, the call is not required to be the first statement in the method, although it can be, as shown in the `display()` method in Figure 10-13.

Comparing `this` and `super`

In a subclass, the keywords `this` and `super` sometimes refer to the same method, but sometimes they do not.

For example, if a subclass has overridden a superclass method named `someMethod()`, then within the subclass, `super.someMethod()` refers to the superclass version of the method, and both `someMethod()` and `this.someMethod()` refer to the subclass version.

On the other hand, if a subclass has *not* overridden a superclass method named `someMethod()`, the child can use the method name with `super` (because the method is a member of the superclass), with `this` (because the superclass method is a member of the subclass by virtue of inheritance), or alone (again, because the superclass method is a member of the subclass).

TWO TRUTHS & A LIE

Accessing Superclass Methods

1. You can use the keyword `this` within a method in a derived class to access an overridden method in a base class.

2. You can use the keyword `super` within a method in a derived class to access an overridden method in a base class.

3. You can use the keyword `super` within a method in a derived class to access a method in a base class that has not been overridden.

The false statement is #1. You can use the keyword super within a method in a derived class to access an overridden base class method. If you use the keyword this in a method in the derived class, you will access the method defined in the derived class.

Employing Information Hiding

The Student class shown in Figure 10-16 is an example of a typical Java class. Within the Student class, as with most Java classes, the keyword private precedes each data field, and the keyword public precedes each method. In fact, the four get and set methods are public within the Student class specifically because the data fields are private. Without the public get and set methods, there would be no way to access the private data fields.

```java
public class Student
{
    private int idNum;
    private double gpa;
    public int getIdNum()
    {
        return idNum;
    }
    public double getGpa()
    {
        return gpa;
    }
    public void setIdNum(int num)
    {
        idNum = num;
    }
    public void setGpa(double gradePoint)
    {
        gpa = gradePoint;
    }
}
```

Figure 10-16 The Student class

When an application is a client of the Student class (that is, it instantiates a Student object), the client cannot directly alter the data in any private field. For example, suppose that you write a main() method that creates a Student as:

Student someStudent = new Student();

Then you cannot change the Student's idNum with a statement such as:

someStudent.idNum = 812; ⬅

Don't Do It
You cannot access a private data member of an object.

The idNum of the someStudent object is not accessible in the main() method that uses the Student object because idNum is private. Only methods that are part of the Student class itself are allowed to alter private Student data. To alter a Student's idNum, you must use a public method, as in the following:

someStudent.setIdNum(812);

The concept of keeping data private is known as **information hiding**. When you employ information hiding, your data can be altered only by the methods you choose and only in ways that you can control. For example, you might want the setIdNum() method to check to make certain the idNum is within a specific range of values. If a class other than the Student class could alter idNum, idNum could be assigned a value that the Student class couldn't control.

 You first learned about information hiding and using the public and private keywords in Chapter 3. You might want to review these concepts.

When a class serves as a superclass to other classes you create, your subclasses inherit all the data and methods of the superclass. The methods in a subclass can use all of the data fields and methods that belong to its parent, with one exception: private members of the parent class are not accessible within a child class's methods. If a new class could simply extend your Student class and get to its data fields without going through the proper channels, information hiding would not be operating.

 If the members of a base class don't have an explicit access specifier, their access is package by default. Such base class members cannot be accessed within a child class unless the two classes are in the same package. You will learn about packages in the next chapter.

Sometimes, you want to access parent class data within a subclass. For example, suppose that you create two child classes—PartTimeStudent and FullTimeStudent—that extend the Student class. If you want the subclass methods to be able to directly access idNum and gpa, these data fields cannot be private. However, if you don't want other, nonchild classes to access these data fields, they cannot be public. To solve this problem, you can create the fields using the specifier protected. **Protected access** provides you with an intermediate level of security between public and private access. If you create a protected data field or method, it can be used within its own class or in any classes extended from that class, but it cannot be used by "outside" classes. In other words, protected members are those that can be used by a class and its descendants.

You seldom are required to make parent class fields protected. A child class can access its parent's private data fields by using public methods defined in the parent class, just as any other class can. You only need to make parent class fields protected if you want child classes to be able to access parent data directly, but you still want to prohibit other classes from accessing the fields. (For example, perhaps you do not want a parent class to have a public get method for a field, but you do want a child class to be able to access the field. As another example, perhaps a parent class set method enforces limits on a field's value, but a child class object should not have such limits.)

Using the protected access specifier for a field can be convenient, and it also improves program performance because a child class can use an inherited field directly instead of "going through" methods to access the data. However, protected data members should be used sparingly. Whenever possible, the principle of information hiding should be observed, so even child classes usually should have to go through public methods to "get to" their parent's private data. When child classes are allowed direct access to a parent's fields, the likelihood of future errors increases. Classes that directly use fields from parent classes are said to be **fragile** because they are prone to errors—that is, they are easy to "break."

518

TWO TRUTHS & A LIE
Employing Information Hiding

1. Information hiding describes the concept of keeping data private.

2. A subclass inherits all the data and methods of its superclass, except the `private` ones.

3. If a data field is defined as protected, a method in a child class can use it directly.

The false statement is #2. A subclass inherits all the data and methods of its superclass, but it cannot access the `private` ones directly.

Methods You Cannot Override

Sometimes when you create a class, you might choose not to allow subclasses to override some of the superclass methods. For example, an `Employee` class might contain a method that calculates each `Employee`'s ID number based on specific `Employee` attributes, and you might not want any derived classes to be able to provide their own versions of this method. As another example, perhaps a class contains a statement that displays legal restrictions to using the class. You might decide that no derived class should be able to display a different version of the statement.

The three types of methods that you cannot override in a subclass are:

- `static` methods
- `final` methods
- Methods within `final` classes

A Subclass Cannot Override `static` Methods in Its Superclass

A subclass cannot override methods that are declared `static` in the superclass. In other words, a subclass cannot override a class method—a method you use without instantiating an object. A subclass can *hide* a `static` method in the superclass by declaring a `static` method in the subclass with the same signature as the `static` method in the superclass. Then, you can call the new `static` method within the subclass or in another class by using a subclass object. However, this `static` method that hides the superclass `static` method cannot access the parent method using the `super` object.

Figure 10-17 shows a `BaseballPlayer` class that contains a single `static` method named `showOrigins()`. Figure 10-18 shows a `ProfessionalBaseballPlayer` class that extends the `BaseballPlayer` class to provide a salary. Within the `ProfessionalBaseballPlayer` class, an attempt is made to create a nonstatic method that overrides the `static showOrigins()` method to display the general Abner Doubleday message about baseball from the parent class as well as the more specific message about professional baseball. However, the compiler returns the error message shown in Figure 10-19—you cannot override a `static` method with a nonstatic method.

```
public class BaseballPlayer
{
    private int jerseyNumber;
    private double battingAvg;
    public static void showOrigins()
    {
        System.out.println("Abner Doubleday is often " +
            "credited with inventing baseball");
    }
}
```

Figure 10-17   The `BaseballPlayer` class

```
public class ProfessionalBaseballPlayer extends BaseballPlayer
{
    double salary;
    @Override
    public void showOrigins()
    {
        super.showOrigins();
        System.out.println("The first professional " +
            "major league baseball game was played in 1871");
    }
}
```

> **Don't Do It**
> A nonstatic method cannot override a `static` member of a parent class.

Figure 10-18   The `ProfessionalBaseballPlayer` class attempting to override the parent's `static` method

Figure 10-19   Error message when compiling the `ProfessionalBaseballPlayer` class in Figure 10-18

Figure 10-20 shows a second version of the ProfessionalBaseballPlayer class. In this version, the showOrigins() method has been changed to static in an attempt to fix the problem in Figure 10-19. Figure 10-21 shows the error message that appears when this class is compiled. Because this method version is static, the method is not used with an object and does not receive a this reference. The keyword super can be used in child class, nonstatic, and instance methods and constructors, but not in child class static methods.

```
public class ProfessionalBaseballPlayer extends BaseballPlayer
{
    double salary;
    @Override
    public static void showOrigins()
    {
        super.showOrigins();
        System.out.println("The first professional " +
            "major league baseball game was played in 1871");
    }
}
```

Don't Do It
You cannot refer to super in a static method.

Figure 10-20　The ProfessionalBaseballPlayer class with a static method that attempts to reference super

```
C:\Java>javac ProfessionalBaseballPlayer.java
ProfessionalBaseballPlayer.java:6: error: non-static variable super cannot be re
ferenced from a static context
        super.showOrigins();
        ^
1 error

C:\Java>
```

Figure 10-21　Error message when compiling the ProfessionalBaseballPlayer class in Figure 10-20

Finally, Figure 10-22 shows a ProfessionalBaseballPlayer class that compiles without error. The class extends BaseballPlayer, and its showOrigins() method is static. Because this method has the same name as the parent class method, when you use the name with a child class object, this method hides the original. However, it cannot use the super keyword to access the Abner Doubleday method. If you want the ProfessionalBaseballPlayer class to display information about baseball in general as well as professional baseball in particular, you can do either of the following:

- You can repeat the parent class message within the child class using a println() statement.

- You can use the parent class name, a dot, and the method name. Although a child class cannot inherit its parent's static methods, it can access its parent's nonprivate static methods the same way any other class can. The shaded statement in Figure 10-22 uses this approach.

Figure 10-23 shows a class that creates a ProfessionalBaseballPlayer and tests the method; Figure 10-24 shows the output. Notice that the @Override tag is not used with the showOrigins() method because the method does not override the static version in the parent class—it only hides the parent class version.

```java
public class ProfessionalBaseballPlayer extends BaseballPlayer
{
   double salary;
   public static void showOrigins()
   {
      BaseballPlayer.showOrigins();
      System.out.println("The first professional " +
         "major league baseball game was played in 1871");
   }
}
```

Figure 10-22   The ProfessionalBaseballPlayer class

```java
public class TestProPlayer
{
   public static void main(String[] args)
   {
      ProfessionalBaseballPlayer aYankee =
         new ProfessionalBaseballPlayer();
      aYankee.showOrigins();
   }
}
```

Figure 10-23   The TestProPlayer class

```
C:\Java>java TestProPlayer
Abner Doubleday is often credited with inventing baseball
The first professional major league baseball game was played in 1871

C:\Java>_
```

Figure 10-24   Output of the TestProPlayer application

A Subclass Cannot Override `final` Methods in Its Superclass

A subclass cannot override methods that are declared `final` in the superclass. For example, consider the `BasketballPlayer` and `ProfessionalBasketballPlayer` classes in Figures 10-25 and 10-26, respectively. When you attempt to compile the `ProfessionalBasketballPlayer` class, you receive the error message in Figure 10-27, because the class cannot override the `final displayMessage()` method in the parent class.

```
public class BasketballPlayer
{
    private int jerseyNumber;
    public final void displayMessage()
    {
        System.out.println("Michael Jordan is the " +
            "greatest basketball player - and that is final");
    }
}
```

Figure 10-25 The `BasketballPlayer` class

```
public class ProfessionalBasketballPlayer extends BasketballPlayer
{
    double salary;
    @Override
    public void displayMessage()          Don't Do It
    {                                      A child class method
                                           cannot override a final
        System.out.println("I have nothing to say");   parent class method.
    }
}
```

Figure 10-26 The `ProfessionalBasketballPlayer` class that attempts to override a `final` method

Figure 10-27 Error message when compiling the `ProfessionalBasketballPlayer` class in Figure 10-26

If you make the `displayMessage()` method `final` in the `ProfessionalBasketballPlayer` class in Figure 10-26, you receive the same compiler error message as shown in Figure 10-27. If you make the `displayMessage()` method `static` in the `ProfessionalBasketballPlayer` class, the class does not compile, but you do receive an additional error message.

In Chapter 2, you learned that you can use the keyword `final` when you want to create a constant, as in `final double TAXRATE = 0.065;`. You can also use the `final` modifier with methods when you don't want the method to be overridden—that is, when you want every child class to use the original parent class version of a method.

In Java, all instance method calls are **virtual method calls** by default—that is, the method used is determined when the program runs because the type of the object used might not be known until the method executes. For example, with the following method you can pass in a `BasketballPlayer` object, or any object that is a child of `BasketballPlayer`, so the "actual" type of the argument `bbplayer`, and which version of `displayMessage()` to use, is not known until the method executes.

```
public void display(BasketballPlayer bbplayer)
{
    bbplayer.displayMessage();
}
```

In other words, the version of the method used is not determined when the program is compiled; it is determined when the method call is made. Determining the correct method takes a small amount of time. An advantage to making a method `final` is that the compiler knows there is only one version of the method—the parent class version. Therefore, the compiler *does* know which method version to use—the only version—and the program is more efficient.

Because a `final` method's definition can never change—that is, can never be overridden with a modified version—the compiler can optimize a program's performance by removing the calls to `final` methods and replacing them with the expanded code of their definitions at each method call location. This process is called **inlining** the code. When a program executes, you are never aware that inlining is taking place; the compiler chooses to use this procedure to save the overhead of calling a method, and the program runs faster. The compiler chooses to inline a `final` method only if it is a small method that contains just one or two lines of code.

A Subclass Cannot Override Methods in a `final` Superclass

You can declare a class to be `final`. When you do, all of its methods are `final`, regardless of which access specifier precedes the method name. A `final` class cannot be a parent. Figure 10-28 shows two classes: a `HideAndGoSeekPlayer` class that is a `final` class because of the word `final` in the class header, and a `ProfessionalHideAndGoSeekPlayer` class that attempts to extend the `final` class, adding a salary field. Figure 10-29 shows the error message generated when you try to compile the `ProfessionalHideAndGoSeekPlayer` class.

```
public final class HideAndGoSeekPlayer
{
    private int count;
    public void displayRules()
    {
        System.out.println("You have to count to " + count +
            " before you start looking for hiders");
    }
}
public final class ProfessionalHideAndGoSeekPlayer
    extends HideAndGoSeekPlayer
{
    private double salary;
}
```

Notice the keyword `final` in the method header.

Don't Do It
You cannot extend a `final` class.

Figure 10-28   The `HideAndGoSeekPlayer` and `ProfessionalHideAndGoSeekPlayer` classes

```
C:\Java>javac ProfessionalHideAndGoSeekPlayer.java
ProfessionalHideAndGoSeekPlayer.java:2: error: cannot inherit from final HideAnd
GoSeekPlayer
    extends HideAndGoSeekPlayer
            ^
1 error

C:\Java>
```

Figure 10-29   Error message when compiling the `ProfessionalHideAndGoSeekPlayer` class in Figure 10-28

Java's `Math` class, which you learned about in Chapter 4, is an example of a `final` class.

TWO TRUTHS & A LIE

Methods You Cannot Override

1. A subclass cannot override methods that are declared `static` in the superclass.

2. A subclass cannot override methods that are declared `final` in the superclass.

3. A subclass cannot override methods that are declared `private` in the superclass.

The false statement is #3. A subclass can override private methods as well as public or protected ones.

Don't Do It

- Don't capitalize the *o* in the `instanceof` operator. Although the second word in an identifier frequently is capitalized in Java, `instanceof` is an exception.
- Don't try to directly access private superclass members from a subclass.
- Don't forget to call a superclass constructor within a subclass constructor if the superclass does not contain a default constructor.
- Don't try to override a `final` method in an extended class.
- Don't try to extend a `final` class.

Key Terms

Inheritance is a mechanism that enables one class to inherit, or assume, both the behavior and the attributes of another class.

The **Unified Modeling Language** (**UML**) is a graphical language used by programmers and analysts to describe classes and object-oriented processes.

A **class diagram** is a visual tool that provides you with an overview of a class. It consists of a rectangle divided into three sections—the top section contains the name of the class, the middle section contains the names and data types of the attributes, and the bottom section contains the methods.

A **base class** is a class that is used as a basis for inheritance.

A **derived class** is a class that inherits from a base class.

Composition is the relationship in which one class contains one or more members of another class that would not continue to exist without the object that contains them.

Aggregation is a type of composition in which a class contains one or more members of another class that would continue to exist without the object that contains them.

Superclass and **subclass** are synonyms for base class and derived class.

Parent class and **child class** are synonyms for base class and derived class.

The keyword **extends** is used to achieve inheritance in Java.

To **upcast** an object is to change it to an object of a class higher in the object's inheritance hierarchy.

To **override** a field or method in a child class means to use the child's version instead of the parent's version.

Polymorphism is the technique of using the same method name to indicate different implementations.

Subtype polymorphism is the ability of one method name to work appropriately for different subclasses of a parent class.

An **override annotation** notifies the compiler of the programmer's intent to override a parent class method in a child class.

The keyword **super** refers to the parent or superclass of the class in which you use it.

Information hiding is the concept of keeping data private.

Protected access provides an intermediate level of security between public and private; a class's protected members can be used by a class and its descendants, but not by outside classes.

Fragile classes are those that are prone to errors.

Virtual method calls are those in which the method used is determined when the program runs, because the type of the object used might not be known until the method executes.

Inlining the code is an automatic process that optimizes performance by replacing calls to methods with the implementations.

Chapter Summary

- In Java, inheritance is a mechanism that enables one class to inherit both the behavior and the attributes of another class. Using inheritance saves time because the original fields and methods already exist, have been tested, and are familiar to users. A class that is used as a basis for inheritance is a base class. A class you create that inherits from a base class is called a derived class. You can use the terms *superclass* and *subclass* as synonyms for base class and derived class; you can also use the terms *parent class* and *child class*.

- You use the keyword extends to achieve inheritance in Java. A parent class object does not have access to its child's data and methods, but when you create a subclass by extending an existing class, the new subclass contains data and methods that were defined in the original superclass.

- Polymorphism is the act of using the same method name to indicate different implementations for methods based on the type of object. You use polymorphism when you override a superclass method in a subclass by creating a method with the same name and parameter list.

- When you create any subclass object, the superclass constructor must execute first, and *then* the subclass constructor executes. When a superclass contains only constructors that require arguments, you must include at least one constructor for each subclass you create. Subclass constructors can contain any number of statements, but the first statement within each constructor must call the superclass constructor. When a superclass requires parameters upon instantiation, even if you have no other reason to create a subclass constructor, you must write the subclass constructor so it can call its superclass's constructor.

- A subclass can use any nonprivate methods of its superclass, but if the method is overridden in the child class, you can use the keyword `super` to access the parent class method.

- Subclasses inherit all the data and methods of their superclasses, but `private` members of the parent class are not accessible with a child class's methods. However, if you create a `protected` data field or method, it can be used within its own class or in any classes extended from that class, but it cannot be used by "outside" classes. A subclass cannot override methods that are declared `static` in the superclass. A subclass can *hide* a `static` method in the superclass by declaring a `static` method in the subclass with the same signature as the `static` method in the superclass. A subclass cannot override methods that are declared `final` in the superclass or methods declared within a `final` class.

Review Questions

1. A way to discover which of two classes is the base class and which is the subclass is to _____.

   a. look at the class size
   b. try saying the two class names together
   c. use polymorphism
   d. Both a and b are correct.

2. Employing inheritance reduces errors because _____.

   a. the new classes have access to fewer data fields
   b. the new classes have access to fewer methods
   c. you can copy methods that you already created
   d. many of the methods you need have already been used and tested

3. A base class can also be called a _____.

   a. child class   c. derived class
   b. subclass   d. superclass

4. Which of the following choices is the best example of a parent class/child class relationship?

   a. Rose/Flower   c. Dog/Poodle
   b. Present/Gift   d. Sparrow/Bird

5. The Java keyword that creates inheritance is _____.

   a. `static`   c. `extends`
   b. `enlarge`   d. `inherits`

6. A class named `Building` has a `public`, nonstatic method named `getFloors()`. If `School` is a child class of `Building`, and `modelHigh` is an object of type `School`, which of the following statements is valid?

    a. `Building.getFloors();`

    b. `School.getFloors();`

    c. `modelHigh.getFloors();`

    d. All of the previous statements are valid.

7. Which of the following statements is true?

    a. A child class inherits from a parent class.

    b. A parent class inherits from a child class.

    c. Both of the preceding statements are true.

    d. Neither a nor b is true.

8. When a subclass method has the same name and argument types as a superclass method, the subclass method _____ the superclass method.

    a. overrides

    c. overloads

    b. overuses

    d. overcompensates

9. When you instantiate an object that is a member of a subclass, the _____ constructor executes first.

    a. subclass

    c. extended class

    b. child class

    d. parent class

10. The keyword `super` always refers to the _____ of the class in which you use it.

    a. child class

    c. subclass

    b. derived class

    d. parent class

11. If the only constructor in a superclass requires arguments, its subclass _____ .

    a. must contain a constructor

    b. must not contain a constructor

    c. must contain a constructor that requires arguments

    d. must not contain a constructor that requires arguments

12. If a superclass constructor requires arguments, any constructor of its subclasses must call the superclass constructor _____ .

    a. as the first statement

    b. as the last statement

c. at some time

d. multiple times if multiple arguments are involved

13. A child class `Motorcycle` extends a parent class `Vehicle`. Each class constructor requires one `String` argument. The `Motorcycle` class constructor can call the `Vehicle` class constructor with the statement _____.

a. `Vehicle("Honda");`   c. `super("Suzuki");`

b. `Motorcycle("Harley");`   d. none of the above

14. In Java, the concept of keeping data private is known as _____.

a. polymorphism   c. data deception

b. information hiding   d. concealing fields

15. If you create a data field or method that is _____, it can be used within its own class or in any classes extended from that class.

a. `public`   c. `private`

b. `protected`   d. both a and b

16. Within a subclass, you cannot override _____ methods.

a. `public`   c. `static`

b. `private`   d. `constructor`

17. You call a `static` method using _____.

a. the name of its class, a dot, and the method name

b. the name of the class's superclass, a dot, and the method name

c. the name of an object in the same class, a dot, and the method name

d. either a or b

18. You use a _____ method access specifier when you create methods for which you want to prevent overriding in extended classes.

a. `public`   c. `final`

b. `protected`   d. `subclass`

19. A compiler can decide to _____ a `final` method—that is, determine the code of the method call when the program is compiled.

a. duplicate   c. redline

b. inline   d. beeline

20. When a parent class contains a `static` method, child classes _____ override it.

a. frequently   c. must

b. seldom   d. cannot

Exercises

Programming Exercises

1. Create a class named Horse that contains data fields for the name, color, and birth year. Include get and set methods for these fields. Next, create a subclass named RaceHorse, which contains an additional field that holds the number of races in which the horse has competed and additional methods to get and set the new field. Write an application that demonstrates using objects of each class. Save the files as **Horse.java, RaceHorse.java**, and **DemoHorses.java**.

2. Mick's Wicks makes candles in various sizes. Create a class for the business named Candle that contains data fields for color, height, and price. Create get methods for all three fields. Create set methods for color and height, but not for price. Instead, when height is set, determine the price as $2 per inch. Create a child class named ScentedCandle that contains an additional data field named scent and methods to get and set it. In the child class, override the parent's setHeight() method to set the price of a ScentedCandle object at $3 per inch. Write an application that instantiates an object of each type and displays the details. Save the files as **Candle.java, ScentedCandle.java**, and **DemoCandles.java**.

3. Create an ItemSold class for Francis Pet Supply. Fields include an invoice number, description, and price. Create get and set methods for each field. Create a subclass named PetSold that descends from ItemSold and includes three Boolean fields that indicate whether the pet has been vaccinated, neutered, and housebroken, and include get and set methods for these fields. Write an application that creates two objects of each class, and demonstrate that all the methods work correctly. Save the files as **ItemSold.java, PetSold.java**, and **DemoItemsAndPets.java**.

4. Create a class named Poem that contains fields for the name of the poem and the number of lines in it. Include a constructor that requires values for both fields. Also include get methods to retrieve field values. Create three subclasses: Couplet, Limerick, and Haiku. The constructor for each subclass requires only a title; the lines field is set using a constant value. A couplet has two lines, a limerick has five lines, and a haiku has three lines. Create an application that demonstrates usage of an object of each type. Save the files as **Poem.java, Couplet.java, Limerick.java, Haiku.java**, and **DemoPoems.java**.

5. The developers of a free online game named Sugar Smash have asked you to develop a class named SugarSmashPlayer that holds data about a single player. The class contains the following fields: the player's integer ID number, a String screen name, and an array of integers that stores the highest score achieved in each of 10 game levels. Include get and set methods for each field. The get and set methods for the scores should each require two parameters—one that represents the score

achieved and one that represents the game level to be retrieved or assigned. Display an error message if the user attempts to assign or retrieve a score from a level that is out of range for the array of scores. Additionally, no level except the first one should be set unless the user has earned at least 100 points at each previous level. If a user tries to set a score for a level that is not yet available, issue an error message. Create a class named PremiumSugarSmashPlayer that descends from SugarSmashPlayer. This class is instantiated when a user pays $2.99 to have access to 40 additional levels of play. As in the free version of the game, a user cannot set a score for a level unless the user has earned at least 100 points at all previous levels. Create a program that instantiates several objects of each type and demonstrates the methods. Save the files as **SugarSmashPlayer.java, PremiumSugarSmashPlayer.java**, and **DemoSugarSmash.java**.

6. Create a class named BaseballGame that contains data fields for two team names and scores for each team in each of nine innings. Create get and set methods for each field; the get and set methods for the scores should require a parameter that indicates which inning's score is being assigned or retrieved. Do not allow an inning score to be set if all the previous innings have not already been set. If a user attempts to set an inning that is not yet available, issue an error message. Also include a method that determines the winner of the game after scores for the last inning have been entered. (For this exercise, assume that a game might end in a tie.) Create two subclasses from BaseballGame: HighSchoolBaseballGame and LittleLeagueBaseballGame. High school baseball games have seven innings, and Little League games have six innings. Ensure that scores for later innings cannot be accessed for objects of these subtypes. Write three applications that each instantiate one of the object types and demonstrate their methods. Save the files as **BaseballGame.java, HighSchoolBaseballGame.java, LittleLeagueBaseballGame.java, DemoBaseballGame.java, DemoHSBaseballGame.java**, and **DemoLLBaseballGame.java**.

7. Create a class named Package with data fields for weight in ounces, shipping method, and shipping cost. The shipping method is a character: *A* for air, *T* for truck, or *M* for mail. The Package class contains a constructor that requires arguments for weight and shipping method. The constructor calls a calculateCost() method that determines the shipping cost, based on the following table:

Weight (oz.)	Air ($)	Truck ($)	Mail ($)
1 to 8	2.00	1.50	.50
9 to 16	3.00	2.35	1.50
17 and over	4.50	3.25	2.15

The Package class also contains a display() method that displays the values in all four fields. Create a subclass named InsuredPackage that adds an insurance cost to the shipping cost, based on the following table:

Shipping Cost Before Insurance ($)	Additional Cost ($)
0 to 1.00	2.45
1.01 to 3.00	3.95
3.01 and over	5.55

Write an application named UsePackage that instantiates at least three objects of each type (Package and InsuredPackage) using a variety of weights and shipping method codes. Display the results for each Package and InsuredPackage. Save the files as **Package.java, InsuredPackage.java**, and **UsePackage.java**.

8. Create a class named CollegeCourse that includes data fields that hold the department (for example, ENG), the course number (for example, 101), the credits (for example, 3), and the fee for the course (for example, $360). All of the fields are required as arguments to the constructor, except for the fee, which is calculated at $120 per credit hour. Include a display() method that displays the course data. Create a subclass named LabCourse that adds $50 to the course fee. Override the parent class display() method to indicate that the course is a lab course and to display all the data. Write an application named UseCourse that prompts the user for course information. If the user enters a class in any of the following departments, create a LabCourse: BIO, CHM, CIS, or PHY. If the user enters any other department, create a CollegeCourse that does not include the lab fee. Then display the course data. Save the files as **CollegeCourse.java, LabCourse.java**, and **UseCourse.java**.

9. Create a class named Rock that acts as a superclass for rock samples collected and catalogued by a natural history museum. The Rock class contains fields for a number of samples, a description of the type of rock, and the weight of the rock in grams. Include a constructor that accepts parameters for the sample number and weight. The Rock constructor sets the description value to *Unclassified*. Include get methods for each field. Create three child classes named IgneousRock, SedimentaryRock, and MetamorphicRock. The constructors for these classes require parameters for the sample number and weight. Search the Web for a brief description of each rock type and assign it to the description field. Create an application that instantiates an object of each type and demonstrate that the methods work appropriately. Save the files as **Rock.java, IgneousRock.java, SedimentaryRock.java, MetamorphicRock.java**, and **DemoRocks.java**.

10. Develop a set of classes for a college to use in various student service and personnel applications. Classes you need to design include the following:

    • Person—A Person contains a first name, last name, street address, zip code, and phone number. The class also includes a method that sets each data field, using a series of dialog boxes and a display method that displays all of a Person's information on a single line at the command line on the screen.

- CollegeEmployee—CollegeEmployee descends from Person. A CollegeEmployee also includes a Social Security number, an annual salary, and a department name, as well as methods that override the Person methods to accept and display all CollegeEmployee data.

- Faculty—Faculty descends from CollegeEmployee. This class also includes a Boolean field that indicates whether the Faculty member is tenured, as well as methods that override the CollegeEmployee methods to accept and display this additional piece of information.

- Student—Student descends from Person. In addition to the fields available in Person, a Student contains a major field of study and a grade point average as well as methods that override the Person methods to accept and display these additional facts.

Write an application named CollegeList that declares an array of four "regular" CollegeEmployees, three Faculty, and seven Students. Prompt the user to specify which type of person's data will be entered (*C*, *F*, or *S*), or allow the user to quit (*Q*). While the user chooses to continue (that is, does not quit), accept data entry for the appropriate type of Person. If the user attempts to enter data for more than four CollegeEmployees, three Faculty, or seven Students, display an error message. When the user quits, display a report on the screen listing each group of Persons under the appropriate heading of "College Employees," "Faculty," or "Students." If the user has not entered data for one or more types of Persons during a session, display an appropriate message under the appropriate heading.

Save the files as **Person.java, CollegeEmployee.java, Faculty.java, Student.java**, and **CollegeList.java**.

Debugging Exercises

1. Each of the following files in the Chapter10 folder of your downloadable student files has syntax and/or logic errors. In each case, determine the problem and fix the program. After you correct the errors, save each file using the same filename preceded with *Fix*. For example, DebugTen1.java will become **FixDebugTen1.java**.

    a. DebugTen1.java

    b. DebugTen2.java

    c. DebugTen3.java

    d. DebugTen4.java

    e. Eight other Debug files are available in the Chapter10 folder; these files are used by the DebugTen exercises.

Game Zone

1. a. Create an `Alien` class. Include at least three `protected` data members of your choice, such as the number of eyes the `Alien` has. Include a constructor that requires a value for each data field and a `toString()` method that returns a `String` containing a complete description of the `Alien`. Save the file as **Alien.java**.

    b. Create two classes—`Martian` and `Jupiterian`—that descend from `Alien`. Supply each with a constructor that sets the `Alien` data fields with values you choose. For example, you can decide that a `Martian` has four eyes but a `Jupiterian` has only two. Save the files as **Martian.java** and **Jupiterian.java**.

    c. Create an application that instantiates one `Martian` and one `Jupiterian`. Call the `toString()` method with each object and display the results. Save the application as **CreateAliens.java**.

2. a. In Chapter 4, you created a `Die` class that you can use to instantiate objects that hold one of six randomly selected values. Modify this class so its value field is `protected` instead of `private`. This will allow a child class to access the value. Save the file as **Die.java**.

    b. Create a `LoadedDie` class that can be used to give a player a slight advantage over the computer. A `LoadedDie` never rolls a 1; it only rolls values 2 through 6. Save the file as **LoadedDie.java**.

    c. Create a program that rolls two `Die` objects against each other 1,000 times and counts the number of times the first `Die` has a higher value than the other `Die`. Then roll a `Die` object against a `LoadedDie` object 1,000 times, and count the number of times the `Die` wins. Display the results. Save the application as **TestLoadedDie.java**. Figure 10-30 shows two typical executions.

Figure 10-30   Two typical executions of the `TestLoadedDie` application

Case Problems

1. a. In Chapter 8, you created an Event class for Carly's Catering. Now extend the class to create a DinnerEvent class. In the extended class, include four new integer fields that represent numeric choices for an entrée, two side dishes, and a dessert for each DinnerEvent object. Also include three final arrays that contain String menu options for entrées, side dishes, and desserts, and store at least three choices in each array. Create a DinnerEvent constructor that requires arguments for an event number and number of guests, and integer menu choices for one entrée, two side dishes, and one dessert. Pass the first two parameters to the Event constructor, and assign the last four parameters to the appropriate local fields. Also include a getMenu() method that builds and returns a String including the Strings for the four menu choices. Save the file as **DinnerEvent.java**.

    b. In Chapter 9, you created an EventDemo program for Carly's Catering. The program uses an array of Event objects and allows the user to sort Events in ascending order by event number, number of guests, or event type. Now modify the program to use an array of four DinnerEvent objects. Prompt the user for all values for each object, and then allow the user to continuously sort the DinnerEvent descriptions by event number, number of guests, or event type. Save the file as **DinnerEventDemo.java**.

2. a. In Chapter 8, you created a Rental class for Sammy's Seashore Supplies. Now extend the class to create a LessonWithRental class. In the extended class, include a new Boolean field that indicates whether a lesson is required or optional for the type of equipment rented. Also include a final array that contains Strings representing the names of the instructors for each of the eight equipment types, and store names that you choose in the array. Create a LessonWithRental constructor that requires arguments for an event number, minutes for the rental, and an integer equipment type. Pass the first two parameters to the Rental constructor, and assign the last parameter to the equipment type. For the first two equipment types (jet ski and pontoon boat), set the Boolean lesson required field to true; otherwise, set it to false. Also include a getInstructor() method that builds and returns a String including the String for the equipment type, a message that indicates whether a lesson is required, and the instructor's name. Save the file as **LessonWithRental.java**.

    b. In Chapter 9, you created a RentalDemo program for Sammy's Seashore Supplies. The program uses an array of Rental objects and allows the user to sort Rentals in ascending order by contract number, equipment type, or price. Now modify the program to use an array of four LessonWithRental objects. Prompt the user for all values for each object, and then allow the user to continuously sort the LessonWithRental descriptions by contract number, equipment type, or price. Save the file as **LessonWithRentalDemo.java**.

Advanced Inheritance Concepts

Creating and Using Abstract Classes

Developing new classes is easier after you understand the concept of inheritance. When you extend a class, the subclass inherits all the general attributes already defined in the base class; thus, you must create only the new, more specific attributes for the subclass. For example, a `SalariedEmployee` and an `HourlyEmployee` are more specific than an `Employee`. They can inherit general `Employee` attributes, such as an employee number, but they add specific attributes, such as unique pay-calculating methods.

A superclass contains the features that are shared by all of its subclasses. For example, the attributes of the `Dog` class are shared by every `Poodle` and `Spaniel`. The subclasses are more specific examples of the superclass type; they add more features to the shared, general features. Conversely, when you examine a subclass, you see that its parent is more general and less specific; for example, `Animal` is more general than `Dog`.

 Recall from Chapter 10 that the terms *base class*, *superclass*, and *parent* are equivalent. Similarly, the terms *derived class*, *subclass*, and *child* are equivalent. Also recall that a child class contains all the members of its parent, whether those members are `public`, `protected`, or `private`. However, a child object cannot directly access a `private` member inherited from a parent.

A **concrete class** is one from which you can instantiate objects. Sometimes, a class is so general that you never intend to create any specific instances of the class. For example, you might intend never to create an object that is "just" an `Employee`; each `Employee` is more specifically a `SalariedEmployee`, `HourlyEmployee`, or `ContractEmployee`. A class such as `Employee` that you create only to extend from is not a concrete class; it is an **abstract class**. In the last chapter, you learned that you can create `final` classes if you do not want other classes to be able to extend them. Classes that you declare to be `abstract` are the opposite; your only purpose in creating them is to enable other classes to extend them. If you attempt to instantiate an object from an abstract class, you receive an error message from the compiler that you have committed an `InstantiationError`. You use the keyword `abstract` when you declare an abstract class. (In other programming languages, such as C++, abstract classes are known as **virtual classes**.)

 In the last chapter, you learned to create class diagrams. By convention, when you show abstract classes and methods in class diagrams, their names appear in italics.

 `Number` is an abstract, built-in Java class. You cannot create a `Number` object, but you can create objects from its subclasses, including `Double`, `Float`, and `Integer`.

Abstract classes can include two method types:

- **Nonabstract methods**, like those you can create in any class, are implemented in the abstract class and are simply inherited by its children.

- **Abstract methods** have no body and must be implemented in child classes.

Abstract classes usually contain at least one abstract method. When you create an abstract method, you provide the keyword abstract and the rest of the method header, including the method type, name, and parameters. However, the declaration ends there: you do not provide curly braces or any statements within the method—just a semicolon at the end of the declaration. If you create an empty method within an abstract class, the method is abstract even if you do not explicitly use the keyword abstract when defining the method, although programmers often include the keyword for clarity. When making abstract declarations:

539

- If you declare a class to be abstract, each of its methods can be abstract or not.

- If you declare a method to be abstract, you must also declare its class to be abstract.

When you create a subclass that inherits an abstract method, you write a method with the same signature. You are required to code a subclass method to override every empty, abstract superclass method that is inherited. Either the child class method must itself be abstract, or you must provide a body, or implementation, for the inherited method.

Suppose that you want to create classes to represent different animals, such as Dog and Cow. You can create a generic abstract class named Animal so you can provide generic data fields, such as the animal's name, only once. An Animal is generic, but all specific Animals make a sound; the actual sound differs from Animal to Animal. If you code an empty speak() method in the abstract Animal class, you require all future Animal subclasses to code a speak() method that is specific to the subclass. Figure 11-1 shows an abstract Animal class containing a data field for the name, getName() and setName() methods, and an abstract speak() method.

```
public abstract class Animal
{
    private String name;
    public abstract void speak();
    public String getName()
    {
        return name;
    }
    public void setName(String animalName)
    {
        name = animalName;
    }
}
```

Figure 11-1   The abstract Animal class

The Animal class in Figure 11-1 is declared as abstract; the keyword is shaded. You cannot create a class in which you declare an Animal object with a statement such as Animal myPet = new Animal("Murphy");, because a class that attempts to instantiate an Animal object does not compile. Animal is an abstract class, so no Animal objects can exist.

You create an abstract class such as `Animal` only so you can extend it. For example, because a dog is an animal, you can create a `Dog` class as a child class of `Animal`. Figure 11-2 shows a `Dog` class that extends `Animal`.

```
public class Dog extends Animal
{
   @Override
   public void speak()
   {
      System.out.println("Woof!");
   }
}
```

Figure 11-2   The Dog class

The `speak()` method within the `Dog` class is required because you want to create `Dog` objects and the abstract, parent `Animal` class contains an abstract `speak()` method (shaded in Figure 11-1). You can code any statements you want within the `Dog` `speak()` method, but the `speak()` method must exist. If you do not want to create `Dog` objects but want the `Dog` class to be a parent to further subclasses, then the `Dog` class must also be abstract. In that case, you can write code for the `speak()` method within the subclasses of `Dog`. Recall from Chapter 10 that the `@Override` annotation for the `speak()` method is not necessary, but it provides error checking and documentation. Technically, `speak()` *implements* the empty parent class method as well as *overrides* it.

If `Animal` is an abstract class, you cannot instantiate an `Animal` object; however, if `Dog` is a concrete class, instantiating a `Dog` object is perfectly legal. When you code the following, you create a `Dog` object:

`Dog myPet = new Dog("Murphy");`

Then, when you code `myPet.speak();`, the correct `Dog` `speak()` method executes.

The classes in Figures 11-3 and 11-4 also inherit from the `Animal` class and implement `speak()` methods. Figure 11-5 contains a `UseAnimals` application.

```
public class Cow extends Animal
{
   @Override
   public void speak()
   {
      System.out.println("Moo!");
   }
}
```

Figure 11-3   The Cow class

```
public class Snake extends Animal
{
    @Override
    public void speak()
    {
        System.out.println("Ssss!");
    }
}
```

Figure 11-4   The Snake class

```
public class UseAnimals
{
    public static void main(String[] args)
    {
        Dog myDog = new Dog();
        Cow myCow = new Cow();
        Snake mySnake = new Snake();
        myDog.setName("My dog Murphy");
        myCow.setName("My cow Elsie");
        mySnake.setName("My snake Sammy");
        System.out.print(myDog.getName() + " says ");
        myDog.speak();
        System.out.print(myCow.getName() + " says ");
        myCow.speak();
        System.out.print(mySnake.getName() + " says ");
        mySnake.speak();
    }
}
```

Figure 11-5   The UseAnimals application

The output in Figure 11-6 shows that when you create Dog, Cow, and Snake objects, each is an Animal with access to the Animal class getName() and setName() methods, and each uses its own speak() method appropriately.

In Figure 11-6, notice how the myDog.getName() and myDog.speak() method calls produce different output from when the same method names are used with myCow and mySnake.

Recall that using the same method name to indicate different implementations is *polymorphism*. Using polymorphism, one method name causes different and appropriate actions for diverse types of objects.

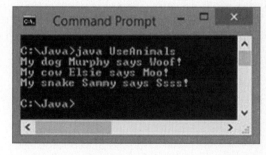

Figure 11-6   Output of the UseAnimals application

Watch the video *Abstract Classes*.

TWO TRUTHS & A LIE

Creating and Using Abstract Classes

1. An abstract class is one from which you cannot inherit, but from which you can create concrete objects.

2. Abstract classes usually have one or more empty abstract methods.

3. An abstract method has no body, curly braces, or statements.

The false statement is #1. An abstract class is one from which you cannot create any concrete objects, but from which you can inherit.

 ## You Do It

Creating an Abstract Class

In this section, you create an abstract Vehicle class. The class includes fields for the power source, the number of wheels, and the price. Vehicle is an abstract class; there will never be a "plain" Vehicle object. Later, you will create two subclasses, Sailboat and Bicycle; these more specific classes include price limits for the vehicle type, as well as different methods for displaying data.

1. Open a new file, and enter the following first few lines to begin creating an abstract Vehicle class:

   ```
   public abstract class Vehicle
   {
   ```

2. Declare the data fields that hold the power source, number of wheels, and price. Declare price as protected rather than private, because you want child classes to be able to access the field.

   ```
   private String powerSource;
   private int wheels;
   protected int price;
   ```

3. The Vehicle constructor accepts three parameters and calls three methods. The first method accepts the powerSource parameter, the second accepts

(continues)

(continued)

the `wheels` parameter, and the third method prompts the user for a vehicle price.

```java
public Vehicle(String powerSource, int wheels)
{
    setPowerSource(powerSource);
    setWheels(wheels);
    setPrice();
}
```

4. Include the following three get methods that return the values for the data fields:

```java
public String getPowerSource()
{
    return powerSource;
}
public int getWheels()
{
    return wheels;
}
public int getPrice()
{
    return price;
}
```

5. Enter the following set methods, which assign values to the `powerSource` and `wheels` fields.

```java
public void setPowerSource(String source)
{
    powerSource = source;
}
public void setWheels(int wls)
{
    wheels = wls;
}
```

6. The `setPrice()` method is an abstract method. Each subclass you eventually create that represents different vehicle types will have a unique prompt for the price and a different maximum allowed price. Type the abstract method definition and the closing curly brace for the class:

```java
    public abstract void setPrice();
}
```

7. Save the file as **Vehicle.java**. At the command prompt, compile the file using the **javac** command.

(continues)

(continued)

Extending an Abstract Class

You just created an abstract class, but you cannot instantiate any objects from this class. Rather, you must extend this class to be able to create any Vehicle-related objects. Next, you create a Sailboat class that extends the Vehicle class. This new class is concrete; that is, you can create actual Sailboat class objects.

1. Open a new file, and then type the following, including a header for a Sailboat class that extends the Vehicle class:

```
import javax.swing.*;
public class Sailboat extends Vehicle
{
```

2. Add the declaration of a length field that is specific to a Sailboat by typing the following code:

```
private int length;
```

3. The Sailboat constructor must call its parent's constructor and send two arguments to provide values for the powerSource and wheels values. It also calls the setLength() method that prompts the user for and sets the length of the Sailboat objects:

```
public Sailboat()
{
    super("wind", 0);
    setLength();
}
```

4. Enter the following setLength() and getLength() methods, which respectively ask for and return the Sailboat's length:

```
public void setLength()
{
    String entry;
    entry = JOptionPane.showInputDialog
        (null, "Enter sailboat length in feet ");
    length = Integer.parseInt(entry);
}
public int getLength()
{
    return length;
}
```

5. The concrete Sailboat class must contain a setPrice() method because the method is abstract in the parent class. Assume that a Sailboat has a maximum price of $100,000. Add the following setPrice() method that

(continues)

(continued)

prompts the user for the price and forces it to the maximum value if the entered value is too high. Include the @Override annotation because the setPrice() method overrides the Vehicle version.

```java
@Override
public void setPrice()
{
    String entry;
    final int MAX = 100000;
    entry = JOptionPane.showInputDialog
        (null, "Enter sailboat price ");
    price = Integer.parseInt(entry);
    if(price > MAX)
        price = MAX;
}
```

6. In Chapter 7, you first used the automatically included Object class toString() method that converts any object to a String. Now, you can override that method for this class by writing your own version as follows. You can include the @Override annotation to indicate that this version of toString() is intended to override the Object class version. When you finish, add a closing curly brace for the class.

```java
@Override
public String toString()
{
    return("The " + getLength() +
        " foot sailboat is powered by " +
        getPowerSource() + "; it has " + getWheels() +
        " wheels and costs $" + getPrice());
}
}
```

7. Save the file as **Sailboat.java**, and then compile the class.

Extending an Abstract Class with a Second Subclass

The Bicycle class inherits from Vehicle, just as the Sailboat class does. Whereas the Sailboat class requires a data field to hold the length of the boat, the Bicycle class does not. Other differences lie in the content of the setPrice() and toString() methods.

1. Open a new file, and then type the following first lines of the Bicycle class:

```java
import javax.swing.*;
public class Bicycle extends Vehicle
{
```

(continues)

(continued)

2. Enter the following `Bicycle` class constructor, which calls the parent constructor, sending it power source and wheel values:

```
public Bicycle()
{
    super("a person", 2);
}
```

3. Enter the following `setPrice()` method that forces a `Bicycle`'s price to be no greater than $4,000:

```
@Override
public void setPrice()
{
    String entry;
    final int MAX = 4000;
    entry = JOptionPane.showInputDialog
        (null, "Enter bicycle price ");
    price = Integer.parseInt(entry);
    if(price > MAX)
        price = MAX;
}
```

4. Enter the following `toString()` method, and add the closing curly brace for the class:

```
@Override
public String toString()
{
    return("The bicycle is powered by " + getPowerSource() +
        "; it has " + getWheels() + " wheels and costs $" +
        getPrice());
}
}
```

5. Save the file as **Bicycle.java**, and then compile the class.

Instantiating Objects from Subclasses

Next, you create a program that instantiates concrete objects from each of the two child classes you just created.

1. Open a new file, and then enter the start of the `DemoVehicles` class as follows:

```
import javax.swing.*;
public class DemoVehicles
{
    public static void main(String[] args)
    {
```

(continues)

(continued)

2. Enter the following statements that declare an object of each subclass type.

```
Sailboat aBoat = new Sailboat();
Bicycle aBike = new Bicycle();
```

3. Enter the following statement to display the contents of the two objects. Add the closing curly braces for the `main()` method and the class:

```
    JOptionPane.showMessageDialog(null,
        "\nVehicle descriptions:\n" +
        aBoat.toString() + "\n" + aBike.toString());
   }
}
```

4. Save the file as **DemoVehicles.java**, and then compile it. After you compile the class with no errors, run this application using the **java DemoVehicles** command. When the application prompts you, enter the length and price for a sailboat, and the price for a bicycle. Figure 11-7 shows output after typical user input.

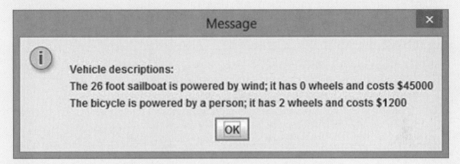

Figure 11-7   Typical output of the DemoVehicles application

Using Dynamic Method Binding

When you create a superclass and one or more subclasses, each object of each subclass "is a" superclass object. Every `SalariedEmployee` "is an" `Employee`; every `Dog` "is an" `Animal`. (The opposite is not true. Superclass objects are not members of any of their subclasses. An `Employee` is not a `SalariedEmployee`. An `Animal` is not a `Dog`.) Because every subclass object "is a" superclass member, you can convert subclass objects to superclass objects.

As you are aware, when a superclass is abstract, you cannot instantiate objects of the superclass; however, you can indirectly create a reference to a superclass abstract object. A reference is not an object, but it points to a memory address. When you create a reference, you do not use the keyword new to create a concrete object; instead, you create a variable name in which you can hold the memory address of a concrete object. So, although a reference to an abstract superclass object is not concrete, you can store a concrete subclass object reference there.

You learned how to create a reference in Chapter 4. When you code SomeClass someObject;, you are creating a reference. If you later code the following statement, including the keyword new and the constructor name, then you actually set aside memory for someObject:

```
someObject = new SomeClass();
```

For example, if you create an Animal class, as shown previously in Figure 11-1, and various subclasses, such as Dog, Cow, and Snake, as shown in Figures 11-2 through 11-4, you can create an application containing a generic Animal reference variable into which you can assign any of the concrete Animal child objects. Figure 11-8 shows an AnimalReference application, and Figure 11-9 shows its output. The variable animalRef is a type of Animal. No superclass Animal object is created (none can be); instead, Dog and Cow objects are created using the new keyword. When the Cow object is assigned to the Animal reference, the animalRef.speak() method call results in "Moo!"; when the Dog object is assigned to the Animal reference, the method call results in "Woof!" Recall that assigning a variable or constant of one type to a variable of another type is called *promotion, implicit conversion,* or *upcasting.*

```
public class AnimalReference
{
    public static void main(String[] args)
    {
        Animal animalRef;
        animalRef = new Cow();
        animalRef.speak();
        animalRef = new Dog();
        animalRef.speak();
    }
}
```

Figure 11-8   The AnimalReference application

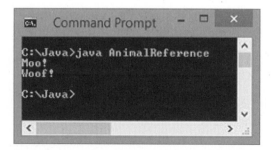

Figure 11-9   Output of the AnimalReference application

The application in Figure 11-8 shows that using a reference polymorphically allows you to extend a base class and use extended objects when a base class type is expected. For example, you could pass a Dog or a Cow to a method that expects an Animal. This means that all methods written to accept a superclass argument can also be used with its children—a feature that saves child-class creators a lot of work.

 Recall from Chapter 10 that you can use the instanceof keyword to determine whether an object is an instance of any class in its hierarchy. For example, both of the following expressions are true if myPoodle is a Dog object and Dog is an Animal subclass:
myPoodle instanceof Animal
myPoodle instanceof Dog

The application in Figure 11-8 demonstrates polymorphic behavior. The same statement, animalRef.speak();, repeats after animalRef is assigned each new animal type. Each call to the speak() method results in different output. Each reference "chooses" the correct speak() method, based on the type of animal referenced. This flexible behavior is most useful when you pass references to methods; you will learn more about this in the next section. In the last chapter, you learned that in Java all instance method calls are virtual method calls by default—the method that is used is determined when the program runs, because the type of the object used might not be known until the method executes. An application's ability to select the correct subclass method depending on the argument type is known as **dynamic method binding**. When the application executes, the correct method is attached (or bound) to the application based on the current, changing (dynamic) context. Dynamic method binding is also called **late method binding**. The opposite of dynamic method binding is **static (fixed) method binding**. In Java, instance methods (those that receive a this reference) use dynamic binding; class methods use static method binding. Dynamic binding makes programs flexible; however, static binding operates more quickly.

 In the example in this section, the objects using speak() happen to be related (Cow and Dog are both Animals). Be aware that polymorphic behavior can apply to nonrelated classes as well. For example, a DebateStudent and a VentriloquistsDummy might also speak(). When polymorphic behavior depends on method overloading, it is called **ad-hoc polymorphism**; when it depends on using a superclass as a method parameter, it is called **pure polymorphism** or **inclusion polymorphism**.

Using a Superclass as a Method Parameter Type

Dynamic method binding is most useful when you want to create a method that has one or more parameters that might be one of several types. For example, the shaded header for the talkingAnimal() method in Figure 11-10 accepts any type of Animal argument. The method can be used in programs that contain Dog objects, Cow objects, or objects of any other class that descends from Animal. The application passes first a Dog and then a Cow to the method. The output in Figure 11-11 shows that the method works correctly no matter which type of Animal descendant it receives.

550

```java
public class TalkingAnimalDemo
{
    public static void main(String[] args)
    {
        Dog dog = new Dog();
        Cow cow = new Cow();
        dog.setName("Ginger");
        cow.setName("Molly");
        talkingAnimal(dog);
        talkingAnimal(cow);
    }
    public static void talkingAnimal(Animal animal)
    {
        System.out.println("Come one. Come all.");
        System.out.println
            ("See the amazing talking animal!");
        System.out.println(animal.getName() +
            " says");
        animal.speak();
        System.out.println("****************");
    }
}
```

Figure 11-10   The `TalkingAnimalDemo` class

Figure 11-11   Output of the `TalkingAnimalDemo` application

TWO TRUTHS & A LIE

Using Dynamic Method Binding

1. If Parent is a parent class and Child is its child, then you can assign a Child object to a Parent reference.

2. If Parent is a parent class and Child is its child, then you can assign a Parent object to a Child reference.

3. Dynamic method binding refers to a program's ability to select the correct subclass method for a superclass reference while a program is running.

The false statement is #2. If Parent is a parent class and Child is its child, then you cannot assign a Parent object to a Child reference; you can only assign a Child object to a Child reference. However, you can assign a Parent object or a Child object to a Parent reference.

Creating Arrays of Subclass Objects

Recall that every array element must be the same data type, which can be a primitive, built-in type or a type based on a more complex class. When you create an array in Java, you are not constructing objects. Instead, you are creating space for references to objects. In other words, although it is convenient to refer to "an array of objects," every array of objects is really an array of object references. When you create an array of superclass references, it can hold subclass references. This is true whether the superclass in question is abstract or concrete.

For example, even though Employee is an abstract class, and every Employee object is either a SalariedEmployee or an HourlyEmployee subclass object, it can be convenient to create an array of generic Employee references. Likewise, an Animal array might contain individual elements that are Dog, Cow, or Snake objects. As long as every Employee subclass has access to a calculatePay() method, and every Animal subclass has access to a speak() method, you can manipulate an array of superclass objects and invoke the appropriate method for each subclass member.

The following statement creates an array of three Animal references:

```
Animal[] animalRef = new Animal[3];
```

The statement reserves enough computer memory for three Animal objects named animalRef[0], animalRef[1], and animalRef[2]. The statement does not actually instantiate Animals; Animal is an abstract class and cannot be instantiated. The Animal array declaration simply reserves memory for three object references. If you instantiate objects from Animal subclasses, you can place references to those objects in the Animal array, as Figure 11-12 illustrates. Figure 11-13 shows the output of the AnimalArrayDemo application. The array of three references is used to access each appropriate speak() method.

```
public class AnimalArrayDemo
{
    public static void main(String[] args)
    {
        Animal[] animalRef = new Animal[3];
        animalRef[0] = new Dog();
        animalRef[1] = new Cow();
        animalRef[2] = new Snake();
        for(int x = 0; x < animalRef.length; ++x)
            animalRef[x].speak();
    }
}
```

Figure 11-12   The AnimalArrayDemo application

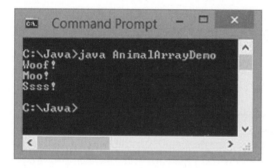

Figure 11-13   Output of the AnimalArrayDemo application

In the AnimalArrayDemo application in Figure 11-12, a reference to an instance of the Dog class is assigned to the first Animal reference, and then references to Cow and Snake objects are assigned to the second and third array elements. After the object references are in the array, you can manipulate them like any other array elements. The application in Figure 11-12 uses a for loop and a subscript to get each individual reference to speak().

TWO TRUTHS & A LIE

Creating Arrays of Subclass Objects

1. You can assign a superclass reference to an array of its subclass type.

2. The following statement creates an array of 10 Table references:

   Table[] table = new Table[10];

3. You can assign subclass objects to an array that is their superclass type.

The false statement is #1. You can assign a subclass reference to an array of its superclass type but not the other way around.

You Do It

Using Object References

Next, you write an application in which you create an array of Vehicle references. Within the application, you assign Sailboat objects and Bicycle objects to the same array. Then, because the different object types are stored in the same array, you can easily manipulate them by using a for loop.

1. Open a new file, and then enter the following first few lines of the VehicleDatabase program:

```
import javax.swing.*;
public class VehicleDatabase
{
    public static void main(String[] args)
    {
```

2. Create the following array of five Vehicle references and an integer subscript to use with the array:

```
Vehicle[] vehicles = new Vehicle[5];
int x;
```

3. Enter the following for loop that prompts you to select whether to enter a sailboat or a bicycle in the array. Based on user input, instantiate the appropriate object type.

```
for(x = 0; x < vehicles.length; ++x)
{
    String userEntry;
    int vehicleType;
    userEntry = JOptionPane.showInputDialog(null,
        "Please select the type of\n " +
        "vehicle you want to enter: \n1 - Sailboat\n" +
        " 2 - Bicycle");
    vehicleType = Integer.parseInt(userEntry);
    if(vehicleType == 1)
        vehicles[x] = new Sailboat();
    else
        vehicles[x] = new Bicycle();
}
```

(continues)

553

(continued)

4. After entering the information for each vehicle, display the array contents by typing the following code. First create a StringBuffer to hold the list of vehicles. Then, in a for loop, build an output String by repeatedly adding a newline character, a counter, and a vehicle from the array to the StringBuffer object. Display the constructed StringBuffer in a dialog box. Then type the closing curly braces for the main() method and the class:

```
StringBuffer outString = new StringBuffer();
for(x = 0; x < vehicles.length; ++x)
{
    outString.append("\n#" + (x + 1) + " ");
    outString.append(vehicles[x].toString());
}
JOptionPane.showMessageDialog(null,
    "Our available Vehicles include:\n" +
    outString);
   }
}
```

5. Save the file as **VehicleDatabase.java**, and then compile it. Run the application, entering five objects of your choice. Figure 11-14 shows typical output after the user has entered data.

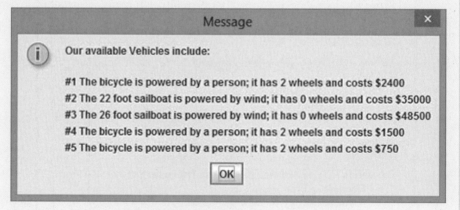

Figure 11-14   Typical output of the VehicleDatabase application

Using the Object Class and Its Methods

Every class in Java is actually a subclass, except one. When you define a class, if you do not explicitly extend another class, your class implicitly is an extension of the Object class. The **Object class** is defined in the java.lang package, which is imported automatically every time you write a program; in other words, the following two class declarations have identical outcomes:

```
public class Animal
{
}
public class Animal extends Object
{
}
```

The `Object` class includes methods that descendant classes can use, overload, or override. Table 11-1 describes the methods built into the `Object` class; every class you create has access to these methods. This chapter describes the `toString()` and `equals()` methods in detail; you will learn about the other methods as you continue to study Java.

Method	Description
`Object clone()`	Creates and returns a copy of this object
`boolean equals` `(Object obj)`	Indicates whether some object is equal to the parameter object (this method is described in detail below)
`void finalize()`	Called by the garbage collector on an object when there are no more references to the object
`Class<?> getClass()`	Returns the class to which this object belongs at run time
`int hashCode()`	Returns a hash code value for the object (this method is described briefly below)
`void notify()`	Wakes up a single thread that is waiting on this object's monitor
`void notifyAll()`	Wakes up all threads that are waiting on this object's monitor
`String toString()`	Returns a string representation of the object (this method is described in detail below)
`void wait()`	Causes the current thread to wait until another thread invokes either the `notify()` method or the `notifyAll()` method for this object
`void wait` `(long timeout)`	Causes the current thread to wait until either another thread invokes the `notify()` method or the `notifyAll()` method for this object, or a specified amount of time has elapsed
`void wait` `(long timeout,` `int nanos)`	Causes the current thread to wait until another thread invokes the `notify()` or `notifyAll()` method for this object, or some other thread interrupts the current thread, or a certain amount of real time has elapsed

Table 11-1   `Object` class methods

Table 11-1 refers to *threads* in several locations. In Chapter 7, you learned about threads in reference to the `StringBuffer` class. Threads of execution are units of processing that are scheduled by an operating system and that can be used to create multiple paths of control during program execution.

Using the `toString()` Method

The `Object` class `toString()` method converts an `Object` into a `String` that contains information about the `Object`. Within a class, if you do not create a `toString()` method that overrides the version in the `Object` class, you can use the superclass version of the method. For example, examine the `Animal` and `Dog` classes originally shown in Figures 11-1 and 11-2 and repeated in Figure 11-15. Notice that neither the `Animal` class nor the `Dog` class in Figure 11-15 defines a `toString()` method. Yet, when you write the `DisplayDog` application in Figure 11-15, it can use a `toString()` method with a `Dog` object in the shaded statement. The output is shown in Figure 11-16. The `Dog` object can use the `toString()` method because `Dog` inherits `toString()` from `Object`.

```
public abstract class Animal
{
    private String name;
    public abstract void speak();
    public String getName()
    {
        return name;
    }
    public void setName(String animalName)
    {
        name = animalName;
    }
}
public class Dog extends Animal
{
    public void speak()
    {
        System.out.println("Woof!");
    }
}
public class DisplayDog
{
    public static void main(String[] args)
    {
        Dog myDog = new Dog();
        String dogString = myDog.toString();
        System.out.println(dogString);
    }
}
```

Figure 11-15   The `Animal` and `Dog` classes and the `DisplayDog` application

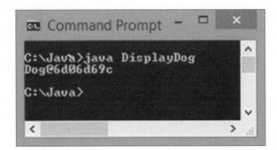

Figure 11-16 Output of the `DisplayDog` application

The output of the `DisplayDog` application in Figure 11-16 is not very useful. It consists of the class name of which the object is an instance (`Dog`), the at sign (@), and a hexadecimal (base 16) identifier. The identifier (*6d06d69c* in Figure 11-16) is an example of a **hash code**—a calculated number used to uniquely identify an object. Even if two objects in an application have the same Java identifier (as might be the case if the same identifier is used in different methods), each will have a unique hash code. Later in this chapter, you learn about the `equals()` method, which also uses a hash code.

Instead of using the automatic `toString()` method with your classes, it is usually more useful to write your own overloaded version that displays some or all of the data field values for the object with which you use it. A good `toString()` method can be very useful in debugging a program; if you do not understand why a class is behaving as it is, you can display the `toString()` value and examine its contents. For example, Figure 11-17 shows a `BankAccount` class that contains a mistake in the shaded line—the `BankAccount balance` value is set to the account number instead of the balance amount. Of course, if you made such a mistake within one of your own classes, there would be no shading or comment to help you find the mistake. In addition, a useful `BankAccount` class would be much larger, so the mistake would be more difficult to locate. However, when you run programs containing `BankAccount` objects, you would notice that the balances of your `BankAccount`s are incorrect. To help you discover why, you could create a short application like the `TestBankAccount` class in Figure 11-18. This application uses the `BankAccount` class `toString()` method to display the relevant details of a `BankAccount` object. The output of the `TestBankAccount` application appears in Figure 11-19.

```
public class BankAccount
{
    private int acctNum;
    private double balance;
    public BankAccount(int num, double bal)
    {
        acctNum = num;
        balance = num;          Don't Do It
    }                           The bal parameter should be
    @Override                   assigned to balance.
    public String toString()
    {
        String info = "BankAccount acctNum = " + acctNum +
            " Balance = $" + balance;
        return info;
    }
}
```

Figure 11-17   The BankAccount class

```
public class TestBankAccount
{
    public static void main(String[] args)
    {
        BankAccount myAccount = new BankAccount(123, 4567.89);
        System.out.println(myAccount.toString());
    }
}
```

Figure 11-18   The TestBankAccount application

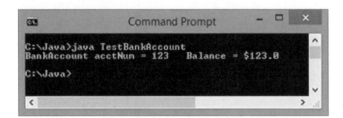

Figure 11-19   Output of the TestBankAccount application

From the output in Figure 11-19, you can see that the account number and balance have the same value, and this knowledge might help you to pin down the location of the incorrect statement in the BankAccount class. Of course, you do not have to use a method named toString() to discover a BankAccount's attributes. If the class had methods such as getAcctNum() and getBalance(), you could use them to create a similar application. The advantage of creating a toString() method for your classes is that toString() is Java's

conventional name for a method that converts an object's relevant details into String format. Because toString() originates in the Object class, you can be assured that toString() compiles with any object whose details you want to see, even if the method has not been rewritten for the subclass in question. In addition, as you write your own applications and use classes written by others, you can hope that those programmers have overridden toString() to provide useful information. You don't have to search documentation to discover a useful method—instead you can rely on the likely usefulness of toString(). In Chapter 7, you learned that you can use the toString() method to convert any object to a String. Now you understand why this works—the String class overloads the Object class toString() method.

Using the equals() Method

The Object class also contains an equals() method with the following header:

```
public boolean equals(Object obj)
```

The method is not static, and it takes a single argument that is compared to the calling object. For example, you might write a statement such as the following:

```
if(someObject.equals(someOtherObject))
    System.out.println("The objects are equal");
```

Other classes, such as the String class, also have their own equals() methods that overload the Object class method. You first used the equals() method to compare String objects in Chapter 7. Two String objects are considered equal only if their String contents are identical.

The Object class equals() method returns a boolean value indicating whether the objects are equal. This equals() method considers two objects to be equal only if they have the same hash code; in other words, they are equal only if one is a reference to the other. For example, two BankAccount objects named myAccount and yourAccount are not automatically equal, even if they have the same account numbers and balances; the inherited equals() method returns true only if they have the same memory address. If you want to consider two objects to be equal only when one is a reference to the other, you can use the built-in Object class equals() method. However, if you want to consider objects to be equal based on their contents, you must write your own equals() method for your classes.

Java's Object class contains a public method named hashCode() that returns an integer representing the hash code. (Discovering this number usually is of little use to you. The default hash code is the internal JVM memory address of the object.)

When you want to create a method that compares two objects based on the values they hold, you have three choices:

- Create a method similar to those you have created for many classes and give it an identifier like areTheyEqual().

- Overload the Object class equals() method.

- Override the Object class equals() method.

The advantage to creating a method with an identifier other than equals() is that programmers will not mistake it for an overridden version of the Object class method. The advantage to using the equals() identifier is that programmers expect it to be used to compare objects. It is easier to overload the equals() method than to override it, so you learn how to overload it in the next section. Then you will read about how to override it.

Overloading equals()

The application shown in Figure 11-20 instantiates two BankAccount objects using the BankAccount class in Figure 11-17. The BankAccount class does not include its own equals() method, so it neither overloads nor overrides the Object equals() method. Thus, the application in Figure 11-20 produces the output in Figure 11-21. Even though the two BankAccount objects have the same account numbers and balances, the BankAccounts are not considered equal because they do not have the same hash code. No two objects you declare in a program will ever have the same hash code unless you change one of them.

```
public class CompareAccounts
{
    public static void main(String[] args)
    {
        BankAccount acct1 = new BankAccount(1234, 500.00);
        BankAccount acct2 = new BankAccount(1234, 500.00);
        if(acct1.equals(acct2))
            System.out.println("Accounts are equal");
        else
            System.out.println("Accounts are not equal");
    }
}
```

Figure 11-20   The CompareAccounts application

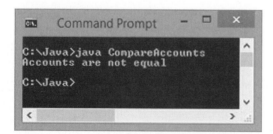

Figure 11-21   Output of the CompareAccounts application

If your intention is that within applications, two BankAccount objects with different hash codes but the same account number and balance should be considered equal, and you want to use the equals() method to make the comparison, you must write your own comparison method within the BankAccount class. For example, Figure 11-22 shows a new version of the BankAccount class containing a shaded `equals()` method. When you reexecute the CompareAccounts application in Figure 11-20, the result appears as in Figure 11-23.

```
public class BankAccount
{
    private int acctNum;
    private double balance;
    public BankAccount(int num, double bal)
    {
        acctNum = num;
        balance = bal;
    }
    @Override
    public String toString()
    {
        String info = "BankAccount acctNum = " + acctNum +
            " Balance = $" + balance;
        return info;
    }
    public boolean equals(BankAccount secondAcct)
    {
        boolean result;
        if(acctNum == secondAcct.acctNum && balance == secondAcct.balance)
            result = true;
        else
            result = false;
        return result;
    }
}
```

Figure 11-22   The BankAccount class containing its own `equals()` method

Figure 11-23   Output of the CompareAccounts application after adding an overloaded `equals()` method to the BankAccount class

The two BankAccount objects described in the output in Figure 11-23 are equal because their account numbers and balances match. Because the `equals()` method in Figure 11-22 is part of the BankAccount class, and because `equals()` is a nonstatic method, the object that calls the method is held by the `this` reference within the method. That is, in the application in Figure 11-22, `acct1` becomes the `this` reference in the `equals()` method. That means the fields acctNum and balance refer to acct1 object values. In the CompareAccounts application, acct2 is the argument to the equals() method, so within the equals() method, acct2 becomes secondAcct, and secondAcct.acctNum and secondAcct.balance refer to acct2's values.

Your organization might consider two BankAccount objects equal if their account numbers match, disregarding their balances. If so, you simply change the if clause in the equals() method. Or, you might decide accounts are equal based on some other criteria. You can implement the equals() method in any way that suits your needs.

The equals() method in the BankAccount class overloads the Object class equals() method. You first learned the term *overload* in Chapter 4; recall that a method overloads another when their parameter lists differ. The BankAccount equals() method has a BankAccount parameter, but the Object equals() method has an Object parameter. Therefore, this equals() method overloads its parent's version, and a BankAccount object has access to two equals() methods—one that takes a BankAccount parameter and one that takes an Object parameter.

 If you change a class (such as changing BankAccount by adding a new method), not only must you recompile the class, you must also recompile any client applications (such as CompareAccounts) so the newly updated class can be relinked to the application and so the clients include the new features of the altered class. If you execute the CompareAccounts application but do not recompile BankAccount, the application continues to use the previously compiled version of the class.

Overriding equals()

When a subclass method overrides a parent's method, the signatures must be the same, as you learned in Chapter 10. Therefore, if you want a BankAccount equals() method to override the parent version, the method header must be written as follows with any identifier you choose for the Object parameter:

```
public boolean equals(Object obj)
```

Within an equals() method with this signature, you must cast the Object parameter to a BankAccount object before comparisons can be made. Figure 11-24 shows the method with the casting statement shaded.

```
@Override
public boolean equals(Object obj)
{
    BankAccount secondAcct = (BankAccount)obj;
    boolean result;
    if(acctNum == secondAcct.acctNum && balance == secondAcct.balance)
        result = true;
    else
        result = false;
    return result;
}
```

Figure 11-24   BankAccount equals() method that overrides Object class version

The method in Figure 11-24 works correctly to compare BankAccount objects in most programs you will write. However, as you start to use more sophisticated Java techniques, you will run into strange errors unless you follow all the recommendations Java's creators have made for overriding equals(). These include the following:

- Determine if the equals() argument is the same object as the calling object by using a comparison such as obj == this, and return true if it is.

- Return false if the Object argument is null.

- Return false if the calling and argument objects are not the same class.

- Cast the Object argument to the same type as the calling object only if they are the same class.

Figure 11-25 shows an equals() method for the BankAccount class that includes all these recommendations.

```java
public boolean equals(Object obj)
{
    boolean result;
    if(obj == this)
        result = true;
    else
        if(obj == null)
            result = false;
        else
            if(obj.getClass() != this.getClass())
                result = false;
    BankAccount secondAcct = (BankAccount)obj;
    if(acctNum == secondAcct.acctNum && balance == secondAcct.balance)
        result = true;
    else
        result = false;
    return result;
}
```

Figure 11-25 Improved BankAccount equals() method that overrides Object class version

Java's creators have one additional recommendation to follow whenever you override the equals() method in a professional class:

- You should override the hashCode() method as well, because equal objects should have equal hash codes.

If you fail to take this step, you won't notice the difference in many programs, but if more complicated programs that use hash-based methods use your class, you will encounter problems. When you override the hashCode() method, you compute a code using a combination of prime numbers and the values of any fields used in the class's equals() method. See the documentation at the Java Web site for more details.

564

 Watch the video *The Object Class.*

TWO TRUTHS & A LIE

Using the Object Class and Its Methods

1. When you define a class, if you do not explicitly extend another class, your class is an extension of the Object class.

2. The Object class is defined in the java.lang package that is imported automatically every time you write a program.

3. The Object class toString() and equals() methods are abstract.

The false statement is #3. The toString() and equals() methods are not abstract—you are not required to override them in a subclass.

Using Inheritance to Achieve Good Software Design

When an automobile company designs a new car model, the company does not build every component of the new car from scratch. The company might design a new feature completely from scratch; for example, at some point someone designed the first air bag. However, many of a new car's features are simply modifications of existing features. The manufacturer might create a larger gas tank or more comfortable seats, but even these new features still possess many properties of their predecessors in the older models. Most features of new car models are not even modified; instead, existing components, such as air filters and windshield wipers, are included in the new model without any changes.

Similarly, you can create powerful computer programs more easily if many of their components are used either "as is" or with slight modifications. Inheritance does not give you the ability to write programs that you could not write otherwise. If Java did not allow you to extend classes, you *could* create every part of a program from scratch. Inheritance simply makes your job easier. Professional programmers constantly create new class libraries for use with Java programs. Having these classes available makes programming large systems more manageable.

You have already used many "as is" classes, such as System and String. In these cases, your programs were easier to write than if you had to write these classes yourself. Now that you have learned about inheritance, you have gained the ability to modify existing classes. When you create a useful, extendable superclass, you and other future programmers gain several advantages:

- Subclass creators save development time because much of the code needed for the class has already been written.

- Subclass creators save testing time because the superclass code has already been tested and probably used in a variety of situations. In other words, the superclass code is reliable.

- Programmers who create or use new subclasses already understand how the superclass works, so the time it takes to learn the new class features is reduced.

- When you create a new subclass in Java, neither the superclass source code nor the superclass bytecode is changed. The superclass maintains its integrity.

When you consider classes, you must think about the commonalities among them; then you can create superclasses from which to inherit. You might be rewarded professionally when you see your own superclasses extended by others in the future.

TWO TRUTHS & A LIE

Using Inheritance to Achieve Good Software Design

1. If object-oriented programs did not support inheritance, programs could still be written, but they would be harder to write.

2. When you create a useful, extendable superclass, you save development and testing time.

3. When you create a new subclass in Java, you must remember to revise and recompile the superclass code.

The false statement is #3. When you create a new subclass in Java, neither the superclass source code nor the superclass bytecode is changed.

Creating and Using Interfaces

Some object-oriented programming languages, such as C++, allow a subclass to inherit from more than one parent class. For example, you might create an InsuredItem class that contains data fields pertaining to each possession for which you have insurance. Data fields might include the name of the item, its value, the insurance policy type, and so on. You might also create an Automobile class that contains data fields such as vehicle identification number, make, model, and year. When you create an InsuredAutomobile class for a car rental agency, you might want to include InsuredItem information and methods, as well as Automobile information and methods. It would be convenient to inherit from both the InsuredItem and Automobile classes. The capability to inherit from more than one class is called **multiple inheritance**.

Many programmers consider multiple inheritance to be a difficult concept, and when inexperienced programmers use it they encounter many problems. Programmers have to deal with the possibility that variables and methods in the parent classes might have identical names, which creates conflict when the child class uses one of the names. Also, you have already learned that a child class constructor must call its parent class

566

constructor. When there are two or more parents, this task becomes more complicated—to which class should super() refer when a child class has multiple parents? For all of these reasons, multiple inheritance is prohibited in Java. A class can inherit from a superclass that has inherited from another superclass—this represents single inheritance with multiple generations. However, Java does not allow a class to inherit directly from two or more parents.

Java, however, does provide an alternative to multiple inheritance—an interface. An **interface** looks much like a class, except that all of its methods (if any) are implicitly public and abstract, and all of its data items (if any) are implicitly public, static, and final. An interface is a description of what a class does, but not how it is done; it declares method headers, but not the instructions within those methods. When you create a class that uses an interface, you include the keyword implements and the interface name in the class header. This notation requires class objects to include code for every method in the interface that has been implemented. Whereas using extends allows a subclass to use nonprivate, nonoverridden members of its parent's class, implements requires the subclass to implement its own version of each method.

 In English, an interface is a device or a system that unrelated entities use to interact. Within Java, an interface provides a way for unrelated objects to interact with each other. An interface is analogous to a protocol, which is an agreed-on behavior. In some respects, an Automobile can behave like an InsuredItem, and so can a House, a TelevisionSet, and a JewelryPiece.

As an example, recall the Animal and Dog classes from earlier in this chapter. Figure 11-26 shows these classes, with Dog inheriting from Animal.

```
public abstract class Animal
{
    private String name;
    public abstract void speak();
    public String getName()
    {
        return name;
    }
    public void setName(String animalName)
    {
        name = animalName;
    }
}
public class Dog extends Animal
{
    public void speak()
    {
        System.out.println("Woof!");
    }
}
```

Figure 11-26   The Animal and Dog classes

You can create a Worker interface, as shown in Figure 11-27. For simplicity, this example gives the Worker interface a single method named work(). When any class implements Worker, it must either include a work() method or the new class must be declared abstract, and then its descendants must implement the method.

```
public interface Worker
{
    public void work();
}
```

Figure 11-27   The Worker interface

The WorkingDog class in Figure 11-28 extends Dog and implements Worker. A WorkingDog contains a data field that a "regular" Dog does not—an integer that holds hours of training received. The WorkingDog class also contains get and set methods for this field. Because the WorkingDog class implements the Worker interface, it also must contain a work() method. In this example, the work() method calls the Dog speak() method, and then produces two more lines of output—a statement about working and the number of training hours.

```
public class WorkingDog extends Dog implements Worker
{
    private int hoursOfTraining;
    public void setHoursOfTraining(int hrs)
    {
        hoursOfTraining = hrs;
    }
    public int getHoursOfTraining()
    {
        return hoursOfTraining;
    }
    public void work()
    {
        speak();
        System.out.println("I am a dog who works");
        System.out.println("I have " + hoursOfTraining +
            " hours of professional training!");
    }
}
```

Figure 11-28   The WorkingDog class

As you know from other classes you have seen, a class can extend another class without implementing any interfaces. A class can also implement an interface even though it does not extend any other class. When a class both extends and implements, like the WorkingDog class, by convention the implements clause follows the extends clause in the class header.

The `DemoWorkingDogs` application in Figure 11-29 instantiates two `WorkingDog` objects. Each object can use the following methods:

- The `setName()` and `getName()` methods that `WorkingDog` inherits from the `Animal` class

- The `speak()` method that `WorkingDog` inherits from the `Dog` class

- The `setHoursOfTraining()` and `getHoursOfTraining()` methods contained within the `WorkingDog` class

- The `work()` method that the `WorkingDog` class was required to contain when it used the phrase `implements Worker`

```
public class DemoWorkingDogs
{
    public static void main(String[] args)
    {
        WorkingDog aSheepHerder = new WorkingDog();
        WorkingDog aSeeingEyeDog = new WorkingDog();
        aSheepHerder.setName("Simon, the Border Collie");
        aSeeingEyeDog.setName("Sophie, the German Shepherd");
        aSheepHerder.setHoursOfTraining(40);
        aSeeingEyeDog.setHoursOfTraining(300);

        System.out.println(aSheepHerder.getName() + " says ");
        aSheepHerder.speak();
        aSheepHerder.work();
        System.out.println(); // outputs a blank line for readability

        System.out.println(aSeeingEyeDog.getName() + " says ");
        aSeeingEyeDog.speak();
        aSeeingEyeDog.work();
    }
}
```

Figure 11-29   The DemoWorkingDogs application

Figure 11-30 shows the output when the `DemoWorkingDogs` application executes. Each animal is introduced, then it "speaks," and then each animal "works," which includes speaking a second time. Each `Animal` can execute the `speak()` method implemented in its own class, and each can execute the `work()` method contained in the implemented interface. Of course, the `WorkingDog` class was not required to implement the `Worker` interface; instead, it could have just contained a `work()` method that all `WorkingDog` objects could use. If `WorkingDog` was the only class that would ever use `work()`, such an approach would probably be the best course of action. However, if many classes will be `Workers`—that is, require a `work()` method—they all can implement `work()`. If you are already familiar with the `Worker` interface and its method, when you glance at a class definition for a `WorkingHorse`, `WorkingBird`, `Employee`, or `Machine` and see that it implements `Worker`, you do not have to guess at the name of the method that shows the work the class objects perform. Notice that when a class implements an interface, it represents a situation similar to inheritance. Just as a `WorkingDog` "is a" `Dog` and "is an" `Animal`, so too it "is a" `Worker`.

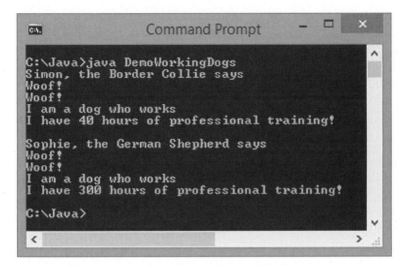

Figure 11-30   Output of the DemoWorkingDogs application

You can compare abstract classes and interfaces as follows:

- Abstract classes and interfaces are similar in that you cannot instantiate concrete objects from either one.

- Abstract classes differ from interfaces because abstract classes can contain nonabstract methods, but all methods within an interface must be abstract.

- A class can inherit from only one abstract superclass, but it can implement any number of interfaces.

Beginning programmers sometimes find it difficult to decide when to create an abstract superclass and when to create an interface. Remember, you create an abstract class when you want to provide data or methods that subclasses can inherit, but at the same time these subclasses maintain the ability to override the inherited methods.

Suppose that you create a CardGame class to use as a base class for different card games. It contains four methods named shuffle(), deal(), displayRules(), and keepScore(). The shuffle() method works the same way for every CardGame, so you write the statements for shuffle() within the superclass, and any CardGame objects you create later inherit shuffle(). The methods deal(), displayRules(), and keepScore() operate differently for every subclass (for example, for TwoPlayerCardGames, FourPlayerCardGames, BettingCardGames, and so on), so you force CardGame children to contain instructions for those methods by leaving them empty in the superclass. The CardGame class, therefore, should be an abstract superclass. When you write classes that extend the CardGame parent class, you inherit the shuffle() method, and write code within the deal(), displayRules(), and keepScore() methods for each specific child.

You create an interface when you know what actions you want to include, but you also want every user to separately define the behavior that must occur when the method executes. Suppose that you create a MusicalInstrument class to use as a base for different musical instrument object classes such as Piano, Violin, and Drum. The parent MusicalInstrument class contains methods such as playNote() and outputSound() that apply to every instrument, but you want to implement these methods differently for each type of instrument. By making MusicalInstrument an interface, you require every nonabstract subclass to code all the methods.

An interface specifies only the messages to which an object can respond; an abstract class can include methods that contain the actual behavior the object performs when those messages are received.

You also create an interface when you want a class to implement behavior from more than one parent. For example, suppose that you want to create an interactive NameThatInstrument card game in which you play an instrument sound from the computer speaker, and ask players to identify the instrument they hear by clicking one of several cards that display instrument images. This game class could not extend from two classes, but it could extend from CardGame and implement MusicalInstrument.

When you create a class and use the implements clause to implement an interface, but fail to code one of the interface's methods, the compiler error generated indicates that you must declare your class to be abstract. If you want your class to be used only for extending, you can make it abstract. However, if your intention is to create a class from which you can instantiate objects, do not make it abstract. Instead, find out which methods from the interface you have failed to implement within your class and code those methods.

Java has many built-in interfaces with names such as Serializable, Runnable, Externalizable, and Cloneable. See the documentation at the Java Web site for more details.

Creating Interfaces to Store Related Constants

Interfaces can contain data fields, but they must be public, static, and final. It makes sense that interface data must not be private because interface methods cannot contain method bodies; without public method bodies, you have no way to retrieve private data. It also makes sense that the data fields in an interface are static because you cannot create interface objects. Finally, it makes sense that interface data fields are final because, without methods containing bodies, you have no way, other than at declaration, to set the data fields' values, and you have no way to change them.

Your purpose in creating an interface containing constants is to provide a set of data that a number of classes can use without having to redeclare the values. For example, the interface class in Figure 11-31 provides a number of constants for a pizzeria. Any class written for the pizzeria can implement this interface and use the permanent values. Figure 11-32 shows an example of one application that uses each value, and Figure 11-33 shows the output. The application in Figure 11-32 only needs a declaration for the current special price; all the constants, such as the name of the pizzeria, are retrieved from the interface.

(continued)

4. Add a variable to hold the amount covered by the insurance:

```
private int coverage;
```

5. Add a constructor that calls the Vehicle superclass constructor, passing arguments for the InsuredCar's power source and number of wheels.

```
public InsuredCar()
{
    super("gas", 4);
    setCoverage();
}
```

6. Implement the setPrice() method required by the Vehicle class. The method accepts the car's price from the user and enforces a maximum value of $60,000.

```
public void setPrice()
{
    String entry;
    final int MAX = 60000;
    entry = JOptionPane.showInputDialog
      (null, "Enter car price ");
    price = Integer.parseInt(entry);
    if(price > MAX)
        price = MAX;
}
```

7. Implement the setCoverage() and getCoverage() methods required by the Insured class. The setCoverage() method sets the coverage value for an insured car to 90 percent of the car's price:

```
public void setCoverage()
{
    coverage = (int)(price * 0.9);
}
public int getCoverage()
{
    return coverage;
}
```

8. Create a toString() method, followed by a closing brace for the class:

```
public String toString()
{
    return("The insured car is powered by " + getPowerSource() +
        "; it has " + getWheels() + " wheels, costs $" +
        getPrice() + " and is insured for $" + getCoverage());
}
}
```

(continues)

(continued)

9. Save the file as **InsuredCar.java** and compile it.

10. Create a demonstration program that instantiates an InsuredCar object and displays its values as follows:

```
import javax.swing.*;
public class InsuredCarDemo
{
    public static void main(String[] args)
    {
        InsuredCar myCar = new InsuredCar();
        JOptionPane.showMessageDialog(null,
            myCar.toString());
    }
}
```

11. Save the file as **InsuredCarDemo.java**. Compile and execute it. You will be prompted to enter the car's price. Figure 11-34 shows the output during a typical execution.

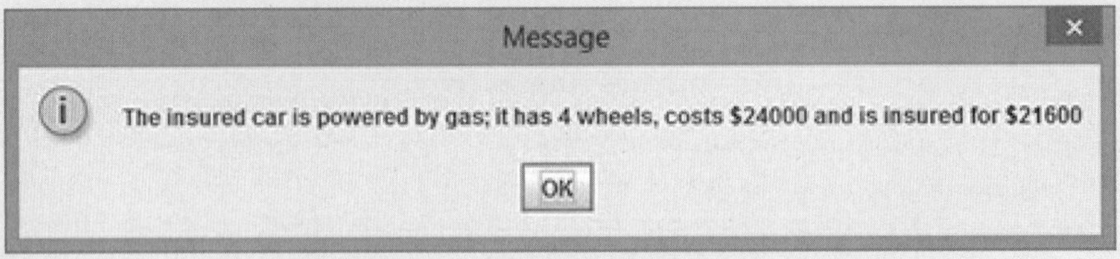

Message ×

ⓘ The insured car is powered by gas; it has 4 wheels, costs $24000 and is insured for $21600

OK

Figure 11-34 Typical output of the InsuredCarDemo program

Creating and Using Packages

Throughout most of this book, you have imported packages into your programs. As you learned in Chapter 4, a package is a named collection of classes; for example, the java.lang package contains fundamental classes and is automatically imported into every program you write. You also have created classes into which you explicitly imported optional packages such as java.util and javax.swing. When you create classes, you can place them in packages so that you or other programmers can easily import your related classes into new programs. Placing classes in packages for other programmers increases the classes' reusability. When you create a number of classes that inherit from each other, as well as multiple interfaces that you want to implement with these classes, you often will find it convenient to place these related classes in a package.

Creating packages encourages others to reuse software because it makes it convenient to import many related classes at once. In Chapter 3, you learned that if you do not use one of the three access specifiers `public`, `private`, or `protected` for a class, then it has default access, which means that the unmodified class is accessible to any other class in the same package.

When you create professional classes for others to use, you most often do not want to provide the users with your source code in the files that have .java extensions. You expend significant effort developing workable code for your programs, and you do not want other programmers to be able to copy your programs, make minor changes, and market the new product themselves. Rather, you want to provide users with the compiled files that have .class extensions. These are the files the user needs to run the program you have developed. Likewise, when other programmers use the classes you have developed, they need only the completed compiled code to import into their programs. The .class files are the files you place in a package so other programmers can import them.

In the Java programming language, a package or class library is often delivered to users as a **Java ARchive (JAR) file**. JAR files compress the data they store, which reduces the size of archived class files. The JAR format is based on the popular Zip file format.

If you do not specify a package for a class, it is placed in an unnamed **default package**. A class that will be placed in a nondefault package for others to use must be `public`. If a class is not `public`, it can be used only by other classes within the same package. To place a class in a package, you include a `package` declaration at the beginning of the source code file that indicates the folder into which the compiled code will be placed. When a file contains a `package` declaration, it must be the first statement in the file (excluding comments). If there are import declarations, they follow the `package` declaration. Within the file, the `package` statement must appear outside the class definition. The `package` statement, `import` statements, and comments are the only statements that appear outside class definitions in Java program files.

For example, the following statement indicates that the compiled file should be placed in a folder named com.course.animals:

```
package com.course.animals;
```

That is, the compiled file should be stored in the animals subfolder inside the course subfolder inside the com subfolder (or com\course\animals). The pathname can contain as many levels as you want.

When you compile a file that you want to place in a package, you can copy or move the compiled .class file to the appropriate folder. Alternatively, you can use a compiler option with the `javac` command. The `-d` (for *directory*) option indicates that you want to place the generated .class file in a folder. For example, the following command indicates that the compiled Animal.java file should be placed in the directory indicated by the `import` statement within the Animal.java file:

```
javac -d . Animal.java
```

The dot (period) in the compiler command indicates that the path shown in the `package` statement in the file should be created within the current directory.

If the `Animal` class file contains the statement `package com.course.animals;`, the Animal. class file is placed in C:\com\course\animals. If any of these subfolders do not exist, Java creates them. Similarly, if you package the compiled files for Dog.java, Cow.java, and so on, future programs need only use the following statements to be able to use all the related classes:

```
import com.course.animals.Dog;
import com.course.animals.Cow;
```

Because Java is used extensively on the Internet, it is important to give every package a unique name. The creators of Java have defined a package-naming convention that uses your Internet domain name in reverse order. For example, if your domain name is course.com, you begin all of your package names with com.course. Subsequently, you organize your packages into reasonable subfolders.

Creating packages using Java's naming convention helps avoid naming conflicts—different programmers might create classes with the same name, but they are contained in different packages. Class naming conflicts are sometimes called **collisions**. Because of packages, you can create a class without worrying that its name already exists in Java or in packages distributed by another organization. For example, if your domain name is course.com, then you might want to create a class named `Scanner` and place it in a package named `com.course.input`. The fully qualified name of your `Scanner` class is `com.course.input.Scanner`, and the fully qualified name of the built-in `Scanner` class is `java.util.Scanner`.

TWO TRUTHS & A LIE

Creating and Using Packages

1. Typically, you place .class files in a package so other programmers can import them into their programs.

2. A class that will be placed in a package for others to use must be `protected` so that others cannot read your source code.

3. Java's creators have defined a package-naming convention in which you use your Internet domain name in reverse order.

The false statement is #2. A class that will be placed in a package for others to use must be `public`. If a class is not `public`, it can be used only by other classes within the same package. To prevent others from viewing your source code, you place compiled .class files in distributed packages.

You Do It

Creating a Package

Next, you place the `Vehicle` family of classes into a package. Assume you work for an organization that sponsors a Web site at *vehicleswesell.com*, so you name the package `com.vehicleswesell`. First, you must create a folder named VehiclePackage in which to store your project. You can use any technique that is familiar to you. For example, in Windows, you can double-click Computer, navigate to the device or folder where you want to store the package, right-click, click New, click Folder, replace "New Folder" with the new folder name (VehiclePackage), and press the Enter key. Alternatively, from the command prompt, you can navigate to the drive and folder where you want the new folder to reside by using the following commands:

- If the command prompt does not indicate the storage device you want, type the name of the drive and a colon to change the command prompt to a different device. For example, to change the command prompt to the F drive on your system, type `F:`.

- If the directory is not the one you want, type `cd\` to navigate to the root directory. The `cd` command stands for "change directory," and the backslash indicates the root directory. Then type `cd` followed by the name of the subdirectory you want. You can repeat this command as many times as necessary to get to the correct subdirectory if it resides many levels down the directory hierarchy.

Next, you can place three classes into a package.

1. Open the **Vehicle.java** file. As the first line in the file, insert the following statement:

   ```
   package com.vehicleswesell.vehicle;
   ```

2. Save the file as **Vehicle.java** in the **VehiclePackage** folder.

3. At the command line, at the prompt for the VehiclePackage folder, compile the file using the following command:

   ```
   javac -d . Vehicle.java
   ```

   Be certain that you type a space between each element in the command, including surrounding the dot. Java creates a folder named com\vehicleswesell\vehicle within the directory from which you compiled the program, and the compiled Vehicle.class file is placed in this folder.

(continues)

577

(continued)

If you see a list of compile options when you try to compile the file, you did not type the spaces within the command correctly. Repeat Step 3 to compile again.

The development tool GRASP generates software visualizations to make programs easier to understand. A copy of this tool is included with your downloadable student files. If you are using jGRASP to compile your Java programs, you also can use it to set compiler options. To set a compiler option to −d, do the following:

- Open a jGRASP project workspace. Click the **Settings** menu, point to **Compiler Settings**, and then click **Workspace**. The Settings for workspace dialog box appears.

- Under the FLAGS or ARGS section of the dialog box, click the dot inside the square next to the Compile option and enter the compiler option (**-d**). Then click the **Apply** button.

- Click the **OK** button to close the dialog box, and then compile your program as usual.

4. Examine the folders on your storage device, using any operating system program with which you are familiar. For example, if you are compiling at the DOS command line, type **dir** at the command-line prompt to view the folders stored in the current directory. You can see that Java created a folder named com. (If you have too many files and folders stored, it might be difficult to locate the com folder. If so, type **dir com*.*** to see all files and folders in the current folder that begin with "com".) Figure 11-35 shows the command to compile the Vehicle class and the results of the dir command, including the com folder.

```
C:\Java\VehiclePackage>javac -d . Vehicle.java

C:\Java\VehiclePackage>dir
 Volume in drive C is Windows8_OS
 Volume Serial Number is 92DA-E9D9

 Directory of C:\Java\VehiclePackage

07/29/2014  04:08 PM    <DIR>          .
07/29/2014  04:08 PM    <DIR>          ..
07/29/2014  04:08 PM    <DIR>          com
07/29/2014  04:07 PM               756 Vehicle.class
07/29/2014  04:08 PM               688 Vehicle.java
               2 File(s)          1,444 bytes
               3 Dir(s)  883,646,189,568 bytes free

C:\Java\VehiclePackage>
```

Figure 11-35   Compiling the Vehicle.java file in a package and viewing the results

(continues)

(continued)

Alternatively, to view the created folders in a Windows 8.1 operating system, you can swipe from the right edge of the screen, tap **Search**, start to type **File Explorer**, and tap **File Explorer**. Then search for the folder. Within the com folder is a vehicleswesell folder, and within vehicleswesell is a vehicle folder. The **Vehicle.class** file is within the vehicle subfolder and not in the same folder as the .java source file where it ordinarily would be placed.

 If you cannot find the com folder on your storage device, you probably are not looking in the same folder where you compiled the class. Repeat Steps 4 and 5, but be certain that you first change to the command prompt for the directory where your source code file resides.

5.   You could now delete the copy of the **Vehicle.java** file from the VehiclePackage folder (although you most likely want to retain a copy elsewhere). There is no further need for this source file in the folder you will distribute to users because the compiled .class file is stored in the com\vehicleswesell\vehicle folder. Don't delete the copy of your code from its original storage location; you might want to retain a copy of the code for modification later.

6.   Open the **Sailboat.java** file in your text editor. For the first line in the file, insert the following statement:

```
package com.vehicleswesell.vehicle;
```

7.   Save the file in the same directory as you saved **Vehicle.java**. At the command line, compile the file using the following command:

```
javac -d . Sailboat.java
```

Then you can delete the **Sailboat.java** source file from the VehiclePackage folder (not from its original location—you want to retain a copy of your original code).

8.   Repeat Steps 6 and 7 to perform the same operations using the **Bicycle.java** file.

9.   Open the **VehicleDatabase.java** file in your text editor. Insert the following statements at the top of the file:

```
import com.vehicleswesell.vehicle.Vehicle;
import com.vehicleswesell.vehicle.Sailboat;
import com.vehicleswesell.vehicle.Bicycle;
```

10. Save the file as **VehiclePackage\VehicleDatabase.java**. Compile the file, and then run the program. The program's output should be the same as it was before you added the import statements. Placing the Vehicle-related class files in a package is not required for the VehicleDatabase program to execute correctly; you ran it in exactly the same manner before you learned about creating packages.

Placing classes in packages gives you the ability to more easily isolate and distribute files.

Don't Do It

- Don't write a body for an abstract method.
- Don't forget to end an abstract method header with a semicolon.
- Don't forget to override any abstract methods in any subclasses you derive.
- Don't mistakenly overload an abstract method instead of overriding it; the subclass method must have the same parameter list as the parent's abstract method.
- Don't try to instantiate an abstract class object.
- Don't forget to override all the methods in an interface that you implement.
- When you create your own packages, don't try to use the wildcard format to import multiple classes. This technique works only with built-in packages.

Key Terms

Concrete classes are nonabstract classes from which objects can be instantiated.

An **abstract class** is one from which you cannot create any concrete objects, but from which you can inherit.

Virtual classes is the name given to abstract classes in other programming languages, such as C++.

A **nonabstract method** is a method that is inherited.

An **abstract method** is declared with the keyword abstract, and has no body; a subclass must override a base class abstract method.

Dynamic method binding is the ability of an application to select the correct method during program execution.

Late method binding is another term for dynamic method binding.

Static or **fixed method binding** is the opposite of dynamic method binding; it occurs when a method is selected when the program compiles rather than while it is running.

Ad-hoc polymorphism occurs when a single method name can be used with a variety of data types because various implementations exist; it is another name for method overloading.

Pure polymorphism or **inclusion polymorphism** occurs when a single method implementation can be used with a variety of related objects because they are objects of subclasses of the parameter type.

The **Object class** is defined in the java.lang package that is imported automatically every time you write a program; every Java class descends from the Object class.

A **hash code** is a calculated number used to identify an object.

Multiple inheritance is the capability to inherit from more than one class.

An **interface** looks much like a class, except that all of its methods must be abstract and all of its data (if any) must be `static final`; it declares method headers, but not the instructions within those methods.

A **Java ARchive (JAR) file** compresses the stored data.

A **default package** is the unnamed one in which a class is placed if you do not specify a package for the class.

Collision is a term that describes a class naming conflict.

Chapter Summary

- A class that you create only to extend from, but not to instantiate from, is an abstract class. Usually, abstract classes contain one or more abstract methods—methods with no method statements. A subclass method overrides any inherited abstract superclass method.

- Every subclass object "is an" instance of its superclass, so you can convert subclass objects to superclass objects. The ability of a program to select the correct method during execution based on argument type is known as dynamic method binding. You can create an array of superclass object references but store subclass instances in it.

- Every class in Java is an extension of the `Object` class, whether or not you explicitly extend it. Every class inherits several methods from `Object`, including `toString()`, which converts an `Object` into a `String`, and `equals()`, which returns a `boolean` value indicating whether one object is a reference to another. You can override or overload these methods to make them more useful for your classes.

- When you create a useful, extendable superclass, you save development time because much of the code needed for the class has already been written. In addition, you save testing time and, because the superclass code is reliable, you reduce the time it takes to learn the new class features. You also maintain superclass integrity.

- An interface is similar to a class, but all of its methods are implicitly `public` and `abstract`, and all of its data (if any) is implicitly `public`, `static`, and `final`. When you create a class that uses an interface, you include the keyword `implements` and the interface name in the class header. This notation serves to require class objects to include code for all the methods in the interface.

- Abstract classes and interfaces are similar in that you cannot instantiate concrete objects from either. Abstract classes differ from interfaces because abstract classes can contain nonabstract methods, but all methods within an interface must be abstract. A class can inherit from only one abstract superclass, but it can implement any number of interfaces.

- You can place classes in packages so you or other programmers can easily import related classes into new classes. The convention for naming packages uses Internet domain names in reverse order to ensure that your package names do not conflict with those of any other Internet users.

Review Questions

1. Parent classes are _____ than their child classes.

   a. less specific   c. easier to understand

   b. more specific   d. more cryptic

2. Abstract classes differ from other classes in that you _____.

   a. must not code any methods within them

   b. must instantiate objects from them

   c. cannot instantiate objects from them

   d. cannot have data fields within them

3. Abstract classes can contain _____.

   a. abstract methods   c. both of the above

   b. nonabstract methods   d. none of the above

4. An abstract class Product has two subclasses, Perishable and NonPerishable. None of the constructors for these classes requires any arguments. Which of the following statements is legal?

   a. Product myProduct = new Product();

   b. Perishable myProduct = new Product();

   c. NonPerishable myProduct = new NonPerishable();

   d. none of the above

5. An abstract class Employee has two subclasses, Permanent and Temporary. The Employee class contains an abstract method named setType(). Before you can instantiate Permanent and Temporary objects, which of the following statements must be true?

   a. You must code statements for the setType() method within the Permanent class.

   b. You must code statements for the setType() method within both the Permanent and Temporary classes.

   c. You must not code statements for the setType() method within either the Permanent or Temporary class.

   d. You can code statements for the setType() method within the Permanent class or the Temporary class, but not both.

6. When you create a superclass and one or more subclasses, each object of the subclass _____ superclass object.

   a. overrides the
   b. "is a"
   c. "is not a"
   d. is a new

7. Which of the following statements is true?

   a. Superclass objects are members of their subclass.
   b. Superclasses can contain abstract methods.
   c. You can create an abstract class object using the new operator.
   d. An abstract class cannot contain an abstract method.

8. When you create a _____ in Java, you create a variable name in which you can hold the memory address of an object.

   a. field
   b. pointer
   c. recommendation
   d. reference

9. An application's ability to select the correct subclass method to execute is known as _____ method binding.

   a. polymorphic
   b. dynamic
   c. early
   d. intelligent

10. Which statement creates an array of five references to an abstract class named Currency?

   a. `Currency[] = new Currency[5];`
   b. `Currency[] currencyref = new Currency[5];`
   c. `Currency[5] currencyref = new Currency[5];`
   d. `Currency[5] = new Currency[5];`

11. You _____ override the `toString()` method in any class you create.

   a. cannot
   b. can
   c. must
   d. must implement `StringListener` to

12. The `Object` class `equals()` method takes _____ .

   a. no arguments
   b. one argument
   c. two arguments
   d. as many arguments as you need

13. Assume the following statement appears in a working Java program and that the equals() method has been correctly overridden in thing's class:

    ```
    if(thing.equals(anotherThing)) x = 1;
    ```

    You know that ―――――――――――.

    a. thing is an object of the Object class
    b. anotherThing is the same type as thing
    c. Every field in thing has the same value as its counterpart in anotherThing.
    d. All of the above are correct.

14. The Object class equals() method considers two object references to be equal if they have the same ―――――――――――.

    a. value in all data fields   c. data type
    b. value in any data field   d. memory address

15. Java subclasses have the ability to inherit from ――――――――――― parent class(es).

    a. one   c. multiple
    b. two   d. no

16. The alternative to multiple inheritance in Java is known as a(n) ―――――――――――.

    a. superobject   c. interface
    b. abstract class   d. none of the above

17. When you create a class that uses an interface, you include the keyword ――――――――――― and the interface's name in the class header.

    a. interface   c. accoutrements
    b. implements   d. listener

18. You can instantiate concrete objects from a(n) ―――――――――――.

    a. abstract class   c. either a or b
    b. interface   d. neither a nor b

19. In Java, a class can ―――――――――――.

    a. inherit from one abstract superclass at most
    b. implement one interface at most
    c. both a and b
    d. neither a nor b

20. When you want to provide some data or methods that subclasses can inherit, but you want the subclasses to override some specific methods, you should write a(n) ―――――――――――.

    a. abstract class   c. final superclass
    b. interface   d. concrete object

Exercises

 Programming Exercises

1. a. Create an abstract class named Book. Include a String field for the book's title and a double field for the book's price. Within the class, include a constructor that requires the book title, and add two get methods—one that returns the title and one that returns the price. Include an abstract method named setPrice(). Create two child classes of Book: Fiction and NonFiction. Each must include a setPrice() method that sets the price for all Fiction Books to $24.99 and for all NonFiction Books to $37.99. Write a constructor for each subclass, and include a call to setPrice() within each. Write an application demonstrating that you can create both a Fiction and a NonFiction Book, and display their fields. Save the files as **Book.java, Fiction.java, NonFiction.java**, and **UseBook.java**.

   b. Write an application named BookArray in which you create an array that holds 10 Books, some Fiction and some NonFiction. Using a for loop, display details about all 10 books. Save the file as **BookArray.java**.

2. a. The Talk-A-Lot Cell Phone Company provides phone services for its customers. Create an abstract class named PhoneCall that includes a String field for a phone number and a double field for the price of the call. Also include a constructor that requires a phone number parameter and that sets the price to 0.0. Include a set method for the price. Also include three abstract get methods—one that returns the phone number, another that returns the price of the call, and a third that displays information about the call. Create two child classes of PhoneCall: IncomingPhoneCall and OutgoingPhoneCall. The IncomingPhoneCall constructor passes its phone number parameter to its parent's constructor and sets the price of the call to 0.02. The method that displays the phone call information displays the phone number, the rate, and the price of the call (which is the same as the rate). The OutgoingPhoneCall class includes an additional field that holds the time of the call in minutes. The constructor requires both a phone number and the time. The price is 0.04 per minute, and the display method shows the details of the call, including the phone number, the rate per minute, the number of minutes, and the total price. Write an application that demonstrates you can instantiate and display both IncomingPhoneCall and OutgoingPhoneCall objects. Save the files as **PhoneCall.java, IncomingPhoneCall.java, OutgoingPhoneCall.java**, and **DemoPhoneCalls.java**.

   b. Write an application in which you assign data to a mix of 10 IncomingPhoneCall and OutgoingPhoneCall objects into an array. Use a for loop to display the data. Save the file as **PhoneCallArray.java**.

3. Create an abstract NewspaperSubscription class with fields for the subscriber name, address, and rate. Include get and set methods for the name field and get methods for the address and subscription rate; the setAddress() method is abstract. Create two subclasses named PhysicalNewspaperSubscription and

OnlineNewspaperSubscription. The parameter for the setAddress() method of the PhysicalNewspaperSubscription class must contain at least one digit; otherwise, an error message is displayed and the subscription rate is set to 0. If the address is valid, the subscription rate is assigned $15. The parameter for the setAddress() method of the OnlineNewspaperSubscription class must contain an at sign (@) or an error message is displayed. If the address is valid, the subscription rate is assigned $9. Finally, write an application that declares several objects of both subscription subtypes and displays their data fields. Save the files as **NewspaperSubscription.java, PhysicalNewspaperSubscription.java, OnlineNewspaperSubscription.java,** and **DemoSubscriptions.java**.

4. Create an abstract Division class with fields for a company's division name and account number, and an abstract display() method. Use a constructor in the superclass that requires values for both fields. Create two subclasses named InternationalDivision and DomesticDivision. The InternationalDivision includes a field for the country in which the division is located and a field for the language spoken; its constructor requires both. The DomesticDivision includes a field for the state in which the division is located; a value for this field is required by the constructor. Write an application named UseDivision that creates InternationalDivision and DomesticDivision objects for two different companies and displays information about them. Save the files as **Division.java, InternationalDivision.java, DomesticDivision.java,** and **UseDivision.java**.

5. Create an abstract class named Element that holds properties of elements, including their symbol, atomic number, and atomic weight. Include a constructor that requires values for all three properties and a get method for each value. (For example, the symbol for carbon is C, its atomic number is 6, and its atomic weight is 12.01. You can find these values by reading a periodic table in a chemistry reference or by searching the Web.) Also include an abstract method named describeElement().

Create two extended classes named MetalElement and NonMetalElement. Each contains a describeElement() method that displays the details of the element and a brief explanation of the properties of the element type. For example, metals are good conductors of electricity, while nonmetals are poor conductors. Write an application named ElementArray that creates and displays an array that holds at least two elements of each type. Save the files as **Element.java, MetalElement.java, NonMetalElement.java,** and **ElementArray.java**.

6. a. Create a class named Blanket with fields for a blanket's size, color, material, and price. Include a constructor that sets default values for the fields as *Twin, white, cotton,* and *$30.00*. Include a set method for each of the first three fields. The method that sets size adds $10 to the base price for a double blanket, $25 for a queen blanket, and $40 for a king. The method that sets the material adds $20 to the price for wool and $45 to the price for cashmere. In other words, the price for a king-sized cashmere blanket is $115. Whenever the size or material is invalid, reset the blanket to the default values. Include a toString() method that returns a description of the blanket. Save the file as **Blanket.java**.

b. Create a child class named ElectricBlanket that extends Blanket and includes two additional fields: one for the number of heat settings and one for whether the electric blanket has an automatic shutoff feature. Default values are one heat setting and no automatic shutoff. Include get and set methods for the fields. Do not allow the number of settings to be fewer than one or more than five; if it is, use the default setting of 1. Add a $5.75 premium to the price if the blanket has the automatic shutoff feature. Also include a toString() method that calls the parent class toString() method and combines the returned value with data about the new fields to return a complete description of features. Save the file as **ElectricBlanket.java**.

c. Create an application that declares a blanket of each type and demonstrates how the methods work. Save the file as **DemoBlankets.java**.

7. The Cullerton Park District holds a mini-Olympics each summer. Create a class named Participant with fields for a name, age, and street address. Include a constructor that assigns parameter values to each field and a toString() method that returns a String containing all the values. Also include an equals() method that determines two Participants are equal if they have the same values in all three fields. Create an application with two arrays of at least eight Participants each—one holds Participants in the mini-marathon, and the other holds Participants in the diving competition. Prompt the user for participant values. After the data values are entered, display values for Participants who are in both events. Save the files as **Participant.java** and **TwoEventParticipants.java**.

8. Create an abstract Student class for Parker University. The class contains fields for student ID number, last name, and annual tuition. Include a constructor that requires parameters for the ID number and name. Include get and set methods for each field; the setTuition() method is abstract. Create three Student subclasses named UndergraduateStudent, GraduateStudent, and StudentAtLarge, each with a unique setTuition() method. Tuition for an UndergraduateStudent is $4,000 per semester, tuition for a GraduateStudent is $6,000 per semester, and tuition for a StudentAtLarge is $2,000 per semester. Write an application that creates an array of at least six objects to demonstrate how the methods work for objects for each Student type. Save the files as **Student.java, UndergraduateStudent.java, GraduateStudent.java, StudentAtLarge.java**, and **StudentDemo.java**.

9. a. Create an interface named Turner, with a single method named turn(). Create a class named Leaf that implements turn() to display "Changing colors". Create a class named Page that implements turn() to display "Going to the next page". Create a class named Pancake that implements turn() to display "Flipping". Write an application named DemoTurners that creates one object of each of these class types and demonstrates the turn() method for each class. Save the files as **Turner.java, Leaf.java, Page.java, Pancake.java**, and **DemoTurners.java**.

b. Think of two more objects that use turn(), create classes for them, and then add objects to the DemoTurners application, renaming it **DemoTurners2.java**. Save the files, using the names of new objects that use turn().

10. Write an application named UseInsurance that uses an abstract Insurance class and Health and Life subclasses to display different types of insurance policies and the cost per month. The Insurance class contains a String representing the type of insurance and a double that holds the monthly price. The Insurance class constructor requires a String argument indicating the type of insurance, but the Life and Health class constructors require no arguments. The Insurance class contains a get method for each field; it also contains two abstract methods named setCost() and display(). The Life class setCost() method sets the monthly fee to $36, and the Health class sets the monthly fee to $196. Write an application named UseInsurance that prompts the user for the type of insurance to be displayed, and then create the appropriate object. Save the files as **Life.java, Health.java, Insurance.java**, and **UseInsurance.java**.

11. Create an abstract class called GeometricFigure. Each figure includes a height, a width, a figure type, and an area. Include an abstract method to determine the area of the figure. Create two subclasses called Square and Triangle. Create an application that demonstrates creating objects of both subclasses, and store them in an array. Save the files as **GeometricFigure.java, Square.java, Triangle.java**, and **UseGeometric.java**.

12. Modify Exercise 11, adding an interface called SidedObject that contains a method called displaySides(); this method displays the number of sides the object possesses. Modify the GeometricFigure subclasses to include the use of the interface to display the number of sides of the figure. Create an application that demonstrates the use of both subclasses. Save the files as **GeometricFigure2.java, Square2.java, Triangle2.java, SidedObject.java**, and **UseGeometric2.java**.

13. Create an interface called Runner. The interface has an abstract method called run() that displays a message describing the meaning of "run" to the class. Create classes called Machine, Athlete, and PoliticalCandidate that all implement Runner. Create an application that demonstrates the use of the classes. Save the files as **Runner.java, Machine.java, Athlete.java, PoliticalCandidate.java**, and **DemoRunners.java**.

14. Create a Building class and two subclasses, House and School. The Building class contains fields for square footage and stories. The House class contains additional fields for number of bedrooms and baths. The School class contains additional fields for number of classrooms and grade level (for example, elementary or junior high). All the classes contain appropriate get and set methods. Place the Building, House, and School classes in a package named com.course.buildings. Create an application that declares objects of each type and uses the package. Save the necessary files as **Building.java, House.java, School.java**, and **CreateBuildings.java**.

15. Sanchez Construction Loan Co. makes loans of up to $100,000 for construction projects. There are two categories of Loans—those to businesses and those to individual applicants.

Write an application that tracks all new construction loans. The application must also calculate the total amount owed at the due date (original loan amount + loan fee). The application should include the following classes:

- Loan—A public abstract class that implements the LoanConstants interface. A Loan includes a loan number, customer last name, amount of loan, interest rate, and term. The constructor requires data for each of the fields except interest rate. Do not allow loan amounts over $100,000. Force any loan term that is not one of the three defined in the LoanConstants class to a short-term, 1-year loan. Create a toString() method that displays all the loan data.

- LoanConstants—A public interface class. LoanConstants includes constant values for short-term (1 year), medium-term (3 years), and long-term (5 years) loans. It also contains constants for the company name and the maximum loan amount.

- BusinessLoan—A public class that extends Loan. The BusinessLoan constructor sets the interest rate to 1 percent over the current prime interest rate.

- PersonalLoan—A public class that extends Loan. The PersonalLoan constructor sets the interest rate to 2 percent over the current prime interest rate.

- CreateLoans—An application that creates an array of five Loans. Prompt the user for the current prime interest rate. Then, in a loop, prompt the user for a loan type and all relevant information for that loan. Store the created Loan objects in the array. When data entry is complete, display all the loans.

Save the files as **Loan.java, LoanConstants.java, BusinessLoan.java, PersonalLoan.java**, and **CreateLoans.java**.

Debugging Exercises

1. Each of the following files in the Chapter11 folder of your downloadable student files has syntax and/or logic errors. In each case, determine the problem and fix the program. After you correct the errors, save each file using the same filename preceded with *Fix*. For example, DebugEleven1.java will become **FixDebugEleven1.java**.

   a. DebugEleven1.java

   b. DebugEleven2.java

   c. DebugEleven3.java

   d. DebugEleven4.java

   e. Three other Debug files in the Chapter11 folder

Game Zone

1. In Chapter 10, you created an `Alien` class as well as two descendant classes, `Martian` and `Jupiterian`. Because you never create any "plain" `Alien` objects, alter the `Alien` class so it is abstract. Verify that the `Martian` and `Jupiterian` classes can still inherit from `Alien` and that the `CreateAliens` program still works correctly. Save the altered `Alien` file as **Alien.java**.

2. a. Create an abstract `CardGame` class similar to the one described in this chapter. The class contains a "deck" of 52 playing cards that uses a `Card` class that holds a suit and value for each `Card` object. It also contains an integer field that holds the number of cards dealt to a player in a particular game. The class contains a constructor that initializes the deck of cards with appropriate values (e.g., "King of Hearts"), and a `shuffle()` method that randomly arranges the positions of the `Cards` in the array. The class also contains two abstract methods: `displayDescription()`, which displays a brief description of the game in each of the child classes, and `deal()`, which deals the appropriate number of `Card` objects to one player of a game. Save the file as **CardGame.java**.

   b. Create two child classes that extend `CardGame`. You can choose any games you prefer. For example, you might create a `Poker` class or a `Bridge` class. Create a constructor for each child class that initializes the field that holds the number of cards dealt to the correct value. (For example, in standard poker, a player receives five cards, but in bridge, a player receives 13.) Create an appropriate `displayDescription()` and `deal()` method for each child class. Save each file using an appropriate name—for example, **Poker.java** or **Bridge.java**.

   c. Create an application that instantiates one object of each game type and demonstrates that the methods work correctly. Save the application as **PlayCardGames.java**.

 Case Problems

1. a. In previous chapters, you have created several classes for Carly's Catering. Now, create a new abstract class named `Employee`. The class contains data fields for an employee's ID number, last name, first name, pay rate, and job title. The class contains get and set methods for each field; the set methods for pay rate and job title are abstract. Save the file as **Employee.java**.

   b. Create three classes that extend `Employee` named `Waitstaff`, `Bartender`, and `Coordinator`. The method that sets the pay rate in each class accepts a parameter and assigns it to the pay rate, but no `Waitstaff` employee can have a rate higher than 10.00, no `Bartender` can have a rate higher than 14.00, and no `Coordinator` can have a rate higher than 20.00. The method that sets the job title accepts no parameters—it simply assigns the string "waitstaff", "bartender", or "coordinator" to the object appropriately. Save the files as **Waitstaff.java, Bartender.java**, and **Coordinator.java**.

c. In Chapter 10, you created a `DinnerEvent` class that holds event information, including menu choices. Modify the class to include an array of 15 `Employee` objects representing employees who might be assigned to work at a `DinnerEvent`. Include a method that accepts an `Employee` array parameter and assigns it to the `Employee` array field, and include a method that returns the `Employee` array. The filename is **DinnerEvent.java**.

d. Write an application that declares a `DinnerEvent` object, prompts the user for an event number, number of guests, menu options, and contact phone number, and then assigns them to the object. Also prompt the user to enter data for as many `Employees` as needed based on the number of guests. A `DinnerEvent` needs one `Waitstaff Employee` for every event, two if an event has 10 guests or more, three if an event has 20 guests or more, and so on. A `DinnerEvent` also needs one `Bartender` for every 25 guests and one `Coordinator` no matter how many guests attend. All of these `Employees` should be stored in the `Employee` array in the `DinnerEvent` object. (For many events, you will have empty `Employee` array positions.) After all the data values are entered, pass the `DinnerEvent` object to a method that displays all of the details for the event, including all the details about the `Employees` assigned to work. Save the program as **StaffDinnerEvent.java**.

2. a. In previous chapters, you have created several classes for Sammy's Seashore Supplies. Now, Sammy has decided to restructure his rates to include different fees for equipment types in addition to the fees based on rental length, and to charge for required lessons for using certain equipment. Create an abstract class named `Equipment` that holds fields for a numeric equipment type, a `String` equipment name, and a fee for renting the equipment. Include a `final` array that holds the equipment names—jet ski, pontoon boat, rowboat, canoe, kayak, beach chair, umbrella, and other. Also include a `final` array that includes the surcharges for each equipment type—$50, $40, $15, $12, $10, $2, $1, and $0, respectively. Include a constructor that requires an equipment type and sets the field to the type unless it is out of range, in which case the type is set to the "other" code. Include get and set methods for each field and include an abstract method that returns a `String` explaining the lesson policy for the type of equipment. Save the file as **Equipment.java**.

b. Create two classes that extend `Equipment`—`EquipmentWithoutLesson` and `EquipmentWithLesson`. The constructor for each class requires that the equipment type be in range—that is, jet skis, pontoon boats, rowboats, canoes, and kayaks are `EquipmentWithLesson` objects, but other equipment types are not. In both subclasses, the constructors set the equipment type to "other" if it is not in range. The constructors also set the equipment fee, as described in part 2a. Each subclass also includes a method that returns a message indicating whether a lesson is required, and the cost ($27) if it is. Save the files as **EquipmentWithoutLesson.java** and **EquipmentWithLesson.java**.

c. In Chapter 8, you created a Rental class. Now, modify it to contain an Equipment data field and an additional price field that holds a base price before equipment fees are added. Remove the array of equipment Strings from the Rental class as well as the method that returns an equipment string. Modify the Rental constructor so that it requires three parameters: contract number, minutes for the rental, and an equipment type. The method that sets the hours and minutes now sets a base price before equipment fees are included. Within the constructor, set the contract number and time as before, but add statements to create either an EquipmentWithLesson object or an EquipmentWithoutLesson object, and assign it to the Equipment data field. Assign the sum of the base price (based on time) and the equipment fee (based on the type of equipment) to the price field. Save the file as **Rental.java**.

d. In Chapter 8, you created a RentalDemo class that displays details for four Rental objects. Modify the class as necessary to use the revised Rental class that contains an Equipment field. Be sure to modify the method that displays details for the Rental to include all the pertinent data for the equipment. Figure 11-36 shows the last part of the output from a typical execution. Save the file as **RentalDemo.java**.

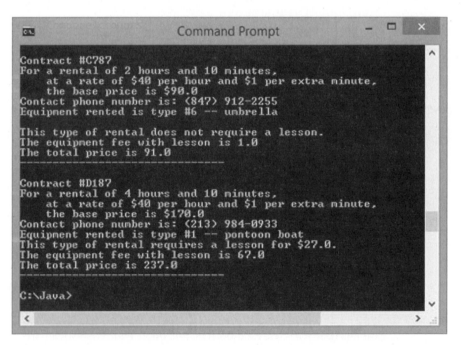

Figure 11-36   End of output of typical execution of RentalDemo application

Exception Handling

In this chapter, you will:

◎ Learn about exceptions

◎ Try code and catch exceptions

◎ Throw and catch multiple exceptions

◎ Use the `finally` block

◎ Understand the advantages of exception handling

◎ Specify the exceptions that a method can throw

◎ Trace exceptions through the call stack

◎ Create your own `Exception` classes

◎ Use an assertion

◎ Learn how to display a virtual keyboard

Learning About Exceptions

An **exception** is an unexpected or error condition. The programs you write can generate many types of potential exceptions:

- A program might issue a command to read a file from a disk, but the file does not exist there.
- A program might attempt to write data to a disk, but the disk is full or unformatted.
- A program might ask for user input, but the user enters an invalid data type.
- A program might attempt to divide a value by 0.
- A program might try to access an array with a subscript that is too large or too small.

These errors are called exceptions because, presumably, they are not usual occurrences; they are "exceptional." **Exception handling** is the name for the object-oriented techniques that manage or resolve such errors. Unplanned exceptions that occur during a program's execution are also called **runtime exceptions**, in contrast with syntax errors that are discovered during program compilation.

Java includes two basic classes of errors: Error and Exception. Both of these classes descend from the Throwable class, as shown in Figure 12-1. Like all other classes in Java, Error and Exception originally descend from the Object class, which is defined in the automatically imported java.lang package.

```
java.lang.Object
|
+--java.lang.Throwable
    |
    +--java.lang.Exception
    |  |
    |  +--java.io.IOException
    |  |
    |  +--java.lang.RuntimeException
    |  |  |
    |  |  +--java.lang.ArithmeticException
    |  |  |
    |  |  +-- java.lang.IndexOutOfBoundsException
    |  |  |  |
    |  |  |  +--java.lang.ArrayIndexOutOfBoundsException
    |  |  |
    |  |  +-- java.util.NoSuchElementException
    |  |  |  |
    |  |  |  +--java.util.InputMismatchException
    |  |  |
    |  |  +--Others..
    |  |
    |  +--Others..
```

Figure 12-1   The Exception and Error class inheritance hierarchy *(continues)*

594

(continued)

```
|  |
   +--java.lang.Error
   |
   +-- java.lang.VirtualMachineError
       |
       +--java.lang.OutOfMemoryError
       |
       +--java.lang.InternalError
       |
       +--Others...
```

Figure 12-1   The Exception and Error class inheritance hierarchy

The Error class represents more serious errors from which your program usually cannot recover. For example, there might be insufficient memory to execute a program. Usually, you do not use or implement Error objects in your programs. A program cannot recover from Error conditions on its own.

The Exception class comprises less serious errors that represent unusual conditions that arise while a program is running and from which the program *can* recover. For example, one type of Exception class error occurs if a program uses an invalid array subscript value, and the program could recover by assigning a valid value to the subscript variable.

Java displays an Exception message when the program code could have prevented an error. For example, Figure 12-2 shows a class named Division that contains a single, small main() method. The method declares three integers, prompts the user for values for two of them, and calculates the value of the third integer by dividing the first two values.

```java
import java.util.Scanner;
public class Division
{
    public static void main(String[] args)
    {
        Scanner input = new Scanner(System.in);
        int numerator, denominator, result;
        System.out.print("Enter numerator >> ");
        numerator = input.nextInt();
        System.out.print("Enter denominator >> ");
        denominator = input.nextInt();
        result = numerator / denominator;
        System.out.println(numerator + " / " + denominator +
            " = " + result);
    }
}
```

Figure 12-2   The Division class

Figure 12-3 shows two typical executions of the Division program. In the first execution, the user enters two usable values and the program executes normally. In the second execution, the user enters 0 as the value for the denominator and an Exception message is displayed. (Java does not allow integer division by 0, but floating-point division by 0 is allowed—the result is displayed as Infinity.) In the second execution in Figure 12-3, most programmers would say that the program experienced a **crash**, meaning that it ended prematurely with an error. The term *crash* probably evolved from the hardware error that occurs when a read/write head abruptly comes into contact with a hard disk, but the term has evolved to include software errors that cause program failure.

Figure 12-3   Two typical executions of the Division application

In Figure 12-3, the Exception is a java.lang.ArithmeticException. ArithmeticException is one of many subclasses of Exception. Java acknowledges more than 75 categories of Exceptions with unusual names such as ActivationException, AlreadyBoundException, AWTException, CloneNotSupportedException, PropertyVetoException, and UnsupportedFlavorException.

Besides the type of Exception, Figure 12-3 also shows some information about the error ("/ by zero"), the method that generated the error (Division.main), and the file and line number for the error (Division.java, line 12).

Figure 12-4 shows two more executions of the Division class. In each execution, the user has entered noninteger data for the denominator—first a string of characters, and second, a floating-point value. In each case, a different type of Exception occurs. You can see from either set of error messages that the Exception is an InputMismatchException. The last line of the messages indicates that the problem occurred in line 11 of the Division program, and the second-to-last error message shows that the problem occurred within the call to nextInt(). Because the user did not enter an integer, the nextInt() method failed. The second-to-last message also shows that the error occurred in line 2076 of the nextInt() method, but clearly you do not want to alter the nextInt() method that resides in the Scanner class—you either want to rerun the program and enter an integer or alter the program so that these errors cannot occur in subsequent executions.

```
C:\Java>java Division
Enter numerator >> 12
Enter denominator >> three
Exception in thread "main" java.util.InputMismatchException
        at java.util.Scanner.throwFor(Scanner.java:864)
        at java.util.Scanner.next(Scanner.java:1485)
        at java.util.Scanner.nextInt(Scanner.java:2117)
        at java.util.Scanner.nextInt(Scanner.java:2076)
        at Division.main(Division.java:11)

C:\Java>java Division
Enter numerator >> 12
Enter denominator >> 3.0
Exception in thread "main" java.util.InputMismatchException
        at java.util.Scanner.throwFor(Scanner.java:864)
        at java.util.Scanner.next(Scanner.java:1485)
        at java.util.Scanner.nextInt(Scanner.java:2117)
        at java.util.Scanner.nextInt(Scanner.java:2076)
        at Division.main(Division.java:11)

C:\Java>
```

Figure 12-4 Two executions of the `Division` application in which the user enters noninteger values

The list of error messages after each attempted execution in Figure 12-4 is called a **stack trace history list**, or more simply, a **stack trace**. (You might also hear the terms *stack backtrace* or *stack traceback*.) The list shows each method that was called as the program ran. You will learn more about tracing the stack later in this chapter.

Just because an exception occurs, you don't necessarily have to deal with it. In the `Division` class, you can simply let the offending program terminate as it did in Figure 12-4. However, the program termination is abrupt and unforgiving. When a program divides two numbers, the user might be annoyed if the program ends abruptly. However, if the program is used for a mission critical task such as air-traffic control or to monitor a patient's vital statistics during surgery, an abrupt conclusion could be disastrous. (The term **mission critical** describes any process that is crucial to an organization.) Object-oriented exception-handling techniques provide more elegant and safer solutions for handling errors.

Of course, you can write programs without using exception-handling techniques—you have already written many such programs as you have worked through this book. Programmers had to deal with error conditions long before object-oriented methods were conceived. Probably the most common error-handling solution has been to use a decision to avoid an error. For example, you can change the `main()` method of the `Division` class to avoid dividing by 0 by adding the decision shown in the shaded portion of Figure 12-5:

```java
import java.util.Scanner;
public class Division2
{
    public static void main(String[] args)
    {
        Scanner input = new Scanner(System.in);
        int numerator, denominator, result;
        System.out.print("Enter numerator >> ");
        numerator = input.nextInt();
        System.out.print("Enter denominator >> ");
        denominator = input.nextInt();
        if(denominator == 0)
            System.out.println("Cannot divide by 0");
        else
        {
            result = numerator / denominator;
            System.out.println(numerator + " / " + denominator +
                " = " + result);
        }
    }
}
```

Figure 12-5   The `Division2` application using a traditional error-handling technique

The application in Figure 12-5 displays a message to the user when 0 is entered for a denominator value, but it is not able to recover when noninteger data such as a string or floating-point value is entered. Object-oriented exception handling enables such error recovery.

Programs that can handle exceptions appropriately are said to be more fault tolerant and robust. **Fault-tolerant** applications are designed so that they continue to operate, possibly at a reduced level, when some part of the system fails. **Robustness** represents the degree to which a system is resilient to stress and able to continue functioning.

Even if you choose never to use object-oriented exception-handling techniques in your own programs, you must understand them because built-in Java methods will throw exceptions.

TWO TRUTHS & A LIE

Learning About Exceptions

1. Exception handling is the name for the object-oriented techniques used to manage runtime errors.

2. The Error class represents serious errors from which your program usually cannot recover, but the Exception class comprises less serious errors from which the program *can* recover.

3. When exceptions occur, object-oriented programs must handle them.

The false statement is #3. Just because an exception occurs, you don't necessarily have to deal with it. You have already written many programs that do not handle exceptions that arise.

Trying Code and Catching Exceptions

In object-oriented terminology, you "try" a procedure that might cause an error. A method that detects an error condition "throws an exception," and if you write a block of code that processes the error, that block is said to "catch the exception."

When you create a segment of code in which something might go wrong, you place the code in a **try block**, which is a block of code you attempt to execute while acknowledging that an exception might occur. A try block consists of the following elements:

- The keyword try followed by a pair of curly braces

- Executable statements lie between the curly braces, including some statements that might cause exceptions

To handle a thrown exception, you can code one or more catch blocks immediately following a try block. A **catch block** is a segment of code that can handle an exception that might be thrown by the try block that precedes it. The exception might be one that is thrown automatically, or you might explicitly write a throw statement. A **throw statement** is one that sends an Exception object out of a block or a method so that it can be handled elsewhere. A thrown Exception can be caught by a catch block. Each catch block can "catch" one type of exception—that is, one object that is an object of type Exception or one of its child classes. You create a catch block by typing the following elements:

- The keyword catch followed by a pair of parentheses

- Between the parentheses, an Exception type and an identifier for an instance

- A pair of curly braces that contain statements that take the actions you want to use to handle the error condition

Figure 12-6 shows the general format of a method that includes a shaded try…catch pair. A catch block looks a lot like a method named catch() that takes an argument that is some type of Exception. However, it is not a method; it has no return type, and you can't call it directly. Some programmers refer to a catch block as a *catch clause*.

```
returnType methodName(optional arguments)
{
   // optional statements prior to code that is tried
   try
   {
      // statement or statements that might generate an exception
   }
   catch(Exception someException)
   {
      // actions to take if exception occurs
   }
   // optional statements that occur after try,
   // whether catch block executes or not
}
```

Figure 12-6   Format of try…catch pair

In Figure 12-6, someException represents an object of the Exception class or any of its subclasses; the name can be any legal Java identifier that the programmer chooses. If an exception occurs during the execution of the try block, the exception is thrown and the statements in the catch block execute. If no exception occurs within the try block, the catch block does not execute. Either way, any statements following the catch block execute normally.

Figure 12-7 shows an application named DivisionMistakeCaught that improves on the Division class. The main() method in the class contains a try block with code that attempts division. When illegal integer division is attempted, an ArithmeticException is automatically created and the catch block executes. Figure 12-8 shows two typical executions, one with a generated Exception and one without.

```
import java.util.Scanner;
public class DivisionMistakeCaught
{
   public static void main(String[] args)
   {
      Scanner input = new Scanner(System.in);
      int numerator, denominator, result;
      System.out.print("Enter numerator >> ");
      numerator = input.nextInt();
      System.out.print("Enter denominator >> ");
      denominator = input.nextInt();
```

Figure 12-7   The DivisionMistakeCaught application *(continues)*

(continued)

```
        try
        {
            result = numerator / denominator;
            System.out.println(numerator + " / " + denominator +
                " = " + result);
        }
        catch(ArithmeticException mistake)
        {
            System.out.println("Arithmetic exception was thrown and caught");
        }
        System.out.println("End of program");
    }
}
```

Figure 12-7 The `DivisionMistakeCaught` application

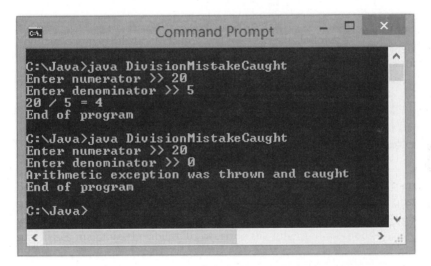

Figure 12-8 Two executions of the `DivisionMistakeCaught` application

In the application in Figure 12-7, the `throw` and `catch` operations reside in the same method. Later in this chapter, you will learn that `throws` and their corresponding `catch` blocks frequently reside in separate methods.

If you want to send error messages to a location other than "normal" output, you can use `System.err` instead of `System.out`. For example, if an application writes a report to a specific disk file, you might want errors to write to a different location—perhaps to a different disk file or to the screen.

The output in Figure 12-8 shows two executions of the DivisionMistakeCaught application.

- When the user enters a valid denominator, the complete try block executes, including the statement that displays the result, and the catch block is bypassed.

- When the user enters *0* for the denominator, the try block is abandoned without displaying the division result, and the catch block executes, displaying the error message.

Whether the denominator is valid or not, the "End of program" message is displayed.

Instead of writing your own message in a catch block, you can use the getMessage() method that ArithmeticException inherits from the Throwable class to retrieve Java's built-in message about an exception. For example, Figure 12-9 shows a DivisionMistakeCaught2 class that uses the getMessage() method (see the shaded statement) to generate the message that "comes with" the caught ArithmeticException argument to the catch block. Figure 12-10 shows the output; the message is "/ by zero".

```java
import java.util.Scanner;
public class DivisionMistakeCaught2
{
    public static void main(String[] args)
    {
        Scanner input = new Scanner(System.in);
        int numerator, denominator, result;
        System.out.print("Enter numerator >> ");
        numerator = input.nextInt();
        System.out.print("Enter denominator >> ");
        denominator = input.nextInt();
        try
        {
            result = numerator / denominator;
            System.out.println(numerator + " / " + denominator +
                " = " + result);
        }
        catch(ArithmeticException mistake)
        {
            System.out.println(mistake.getMessage());
        }
        System.out.println("End of program");
    }
}
```

Figure 12-9   The DivisionMistakeCaught2 application

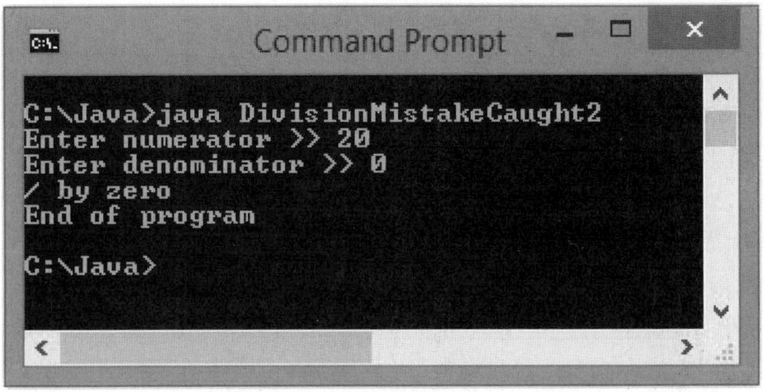

C:\Java>java DivisionMistakeCaught2
Enter numerator >> 20
Enter denominator >> 0
/ by zero
End of program

C:\Java>

Figure 12-10   Output of the DivisionMistakeCaught2 application

It should be no surprise that the automatically generated error message in Figure 12-10 is "/ by zero"; you saw the same message in Figure 12-3 when the programmer provided no exception handling, the exception was automatically thrown, and its message was automatically supplied.

> As an example of another condition that could generate an ArithmeticException, if you create an object using Java's BigDecimal class and then perform a division that results in a nonterminating decimal division such as 1/3, but specify that an exact result is needed, an ArithmeticException is thrown. As another example, you could create your own class containing a method that creates a new instance of the ArithmeticException class and throws it under any conditions you specify.

Of course, you might want to do more in a catch block than display an error message; after all, Java did that for you without requiring you to write the code to catch any exceptions. You also might want to add code to correct the error; for example, such code could force the arithmetic to divide by 1 rather than by 0. Figure 12-11 shows try...catch code in which the catch block computes the result by dividing by 1 instead of by the denominator value. After the catch block, the application could continue with a guarantee that result holds a valid value—either the division worked in the try block and the catch block did not execute, or the catch block remedied the error.

```
try
{
    result = numerator / denominator;
}
catch(ArithmeticException mistake)
{
    result = numerator / 1;
}
// program continues here; result is guaranteed to have a valid value
```

Figure 12-11   A try...catch block in which the catch block corrects the error

In the code in Figure 12-11, you can achieve the same result in the `catch` block by coding `result = numerator;` instead of `result = numerator / 1;`. Explicitly dividing by 1 simply makes the code's intention clearer, but it does require a small amount of time to execute the instruction. As an alternative, you could make the program more efficient by omitting the division by 1 and adding clarity with a comment.

Using a `try` Block to Make Programs "Foolproof"

One of the most common uses for a `try` block is to circumvent user data entry errors. When testing your own programs throughout this book, you might have entered the wrong data type accidentally in response to a prompt. For example, if the user enters a character or floating-point number in response to a `nextInt()` method call, the program crashes. Using a `try` block can allow you to handle potential data conversion exceptions caused by careless users. You can place conversion attempts, such as calling `nextInt()` or `nextDouble()`, in a `try` block and then handle any generated errors.

In Chapter 2, you learned to add a `nextLine()` call after any `next()`, `nextInt()`, or `nextDouble()` call to absorb the Enter key remaining in the input buffer before subsequent `nextLine()` calls. When you attempt to convert numeric data in a `try` block and the effort is followed by another attempted conversion, you also must remember to account for the potential remaining characters left in the input buffer. For example, Figure 12-12 shows a program that accepts and displays an array of six integers. The shaded and commented line is not part of the program when it is executed twice in Figure 12-13.

```
import java.util.Scanner;
public class EnteringIntegers
{
   public static void main(String[] args)
   {
      int[] numberList = {0, 0, 0, 0, 0, 0};
      int x;
      Scanner input = new Scanner(System.in);
      for(x = 0; x < numberList.length; ++x)
      {
         try
         {
            System.out.print("Enter an integer >> ");
            numberList[x] = input.nextInt();
         }
         catch(Exception e)
         {
            System.out.println("Exception occurred");
         }

         // input.nextLine();
      }
}
```

Figure 12-12   The EnteringIntegers program without the extra `nextLine()` call *(continues)*

(continued)

```java
        System.out.print("The numbers are: ");
        for(x = 0; x < numberList.length; ++x)
            System.out.print(numberList[x] + " ");
        System.out.println();
    }
}
```

Figure 12-12   The EnteringIntegers program without the extra nextLine() call

Figure 12-13   Two typical executions of the EnteringIntegers program without the extra nextLine() call

In Figure 12-13, you can see that when a user enters valid data in the first execution, the program runs smoothly. However, in the second execution, the user enters some letters instead of numbers. The program correctly displays *Exception occurred*, but the user is not allowed to enter data for any of the remaining numbers. The problem can be corrected by uncommenting the shaded nextLine() call in the program in Figure 12-12. After the program is recompiled, it executes as shown in Figure 12-14. Now, each data entry exception is noted, but the user can continue entering data for the remaining array elements.

Figure 12-14   A typical execution of the EnteringIntegers program with the extra nextLine() call

Declaring and Initializing Variables in `try...catch` Blocks

You can include any legal Java statements within a `try` block or `catch` block, including variable declarations. However, you must remember that a variable declared within a block is local to that block. In other words, the variable goes out of scope when the `try` or `catch` block ends, so any variable declared within one of the blocks should serve only a temporary purpose.

If you want to use a variable both with a `try` or `catch` block and afterward, then you must declare the variable before the `try` block begins. However, if you declare a variable before a `try` block but wait to assign its initial usable value within the `try...catch` block, you must be careful that the variable receives a useful value; otherwise, when you use the variable after the `try...catch` pair ends, the program will not compile.

Figure 12-15 illustrates this scenario. In the `UninitializedVariableTest` program, x is declared and its value is received from the user in a `try` block. Because the user might not enter an integer, the conversion to an integer might fail, and an exception might be thrown. In this example, the `catch` block only displays a message and does not assign a useful value to x. When the program attempts to display x after the `catch` block, an error message is generated, as shown in Figure 12-16. You have three easy options for fixing this error:

- You can assign a value to x before the `try` block starts. That way, even if an exception is thrown, x will have a usable value to display in the last statement.

- You can assign a usable value to x within the `catch` block. That way, if an exception is thrown, x will again hold a usable value.

- You can move the output statement within the `try` block. If the conversion of the user's entry to an integer is successful, the `try` block finishes execution and the value of x is displayed. However, if the conversion fails, the `try` block is abandoned, the `catch` block executes, the error message is displayed, and x is not used.

```java
import java.util.Scanner;
public class UninitializedVariableTest
{
    public static void main(String[] args)
    {
        int x;
        Scanner input = new Scanner(System.in);
        try
        {
            System.out.print("Enter an integer >> ");
            x = input.nextInt();
        }
        catch(Exception e)
        {
            System.out.println("Exception occurred");
        }
        System.out.println("x is " + x);
    }
}
```

Figure 12-15 The `UninitializedVariableTest` program

Figure 12-16 The error message generated when compiling the UninitializedVariableTest program

 Watch the video *Exceptions*.

TWO TRUTHS & A LIE

Trying Code and Catching Exceptions

1. A try block is a block of code you attempt to execute while acknowledging that an exception might occur.

2. You usually code at least one catch block immediately following a try block to handle an exception that might be thrown by the try block.

3. A throw statement is one that sends an Exception object to a try block so it can be handled.

The false statement is #3. A throw statement sends an Exception object to a catch block.

 You Do It

Throwing and Catching an Exception

In this section, you create an application in which the user enters two values to be divided. The application catches an exception if either of the entered values is not an integer.

(continues)

608

(continued)

1. Open a new file, and type the first few lines of an interactive application named **ExceptionDemo**.

```
import javax.swing.*;
public class ExceptionDemo
{
    public static void main(String[] args)
    {
```

2. Declare three integers—two to be input by the user and a third to hold the result after dividing the first two. The numerator and denominator variables must be assigned starting values because their values will be entered within a try block. The compiler understands that a try block might not complete; that is, it might throw an exception before it is through. Also declare an input String to hold the return value of the JOptionPane showInputDialog() method.

```
int numerator = 0, denominator = 0, result;
String inputString;
```

3. Add a try block that prompts the user for two values, converts each entered String to an integer, and divides the values, producing result.

```
try
{
    inputString = JOptionPane.showInputDialog(null,
        "Enter a number to be divided");
    numerator = Integer.parseInt(inputString);
    inputString = JOptionPane.showInputDialog(null,
        "Enter a number to divide into the first number");
    denominator = Integer.parseInt(inputString);
    result = numerator / denominator;
}
```

4. Add a catch block that catches an ArithmeticException object if division by 0 is attempted. If this block executes, display an error message, and force result to 0.

```
catch(ArithmeticException exception)
{
    JOptionPane.showMessageDialog(null, exception.getMessage());
    result = 0;
}
```

5. Whether the try block succeeds or not, display the result (which might have been set to 0). Include closing curly braces for the main() method and for the class.

(continues)

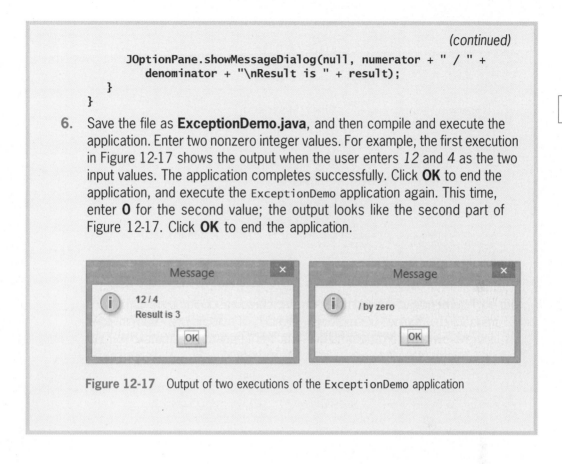

(continued)
```
JOptionPane.showMessageDialog(null, numerator + " / " +
    denominator + "\nResult is " + result);
    }
}
```

6. Save the file as **ExceptionDemo.java**, and then compile and execute the application. Enter two nonzero integer values. For example, the first execution in Figure 12-17 shows the output when the user enters *12* and *4* as the two input values. The application completes successfully. Click **OK** to end the application, and execute the ExceptionDemo application again. This time, enter **0** for the second value; the output looks like the second part of Figure 12-17. Click **OK** to end the application.

Figure 12-17   Output of two executions of the ExceptionDemo application

Throwing and Catching Multiple Exceptions

You can place as many statements as you need within a try block, and you can catch as many exceptions as you want. If you try more than one statement, only the first error-generating statement throws an exception. As soon as the exception occurs, the logic transfers to the catch block, which leaves the rest of the statements in the try block unexecuted.

When a program contains multiple catch blocks, they are examined in sequence until a match is found for the type of exception that occurred. Then, the matching catch block executes, and each remaining catch block is bypassed.

For example, consider the application in Figure 12-18. The main() method in the DivisionMistakeCaught3 class throws two types of Exception objects: an ArithmeticException and an InputMismatchException. The try block in the application surrounds all the statements in which the exceptions might occur.

610

```
import java.util.*;
public class DivisionMistakeCaught3
{
    public static void main(String[] args)
    {
        Scanner input = new Scanner(System.in);
        int numerator, denominator, result;
        try
        {
            System.out.print("Enter numerator >> ");
            numerator = input.nextInt();
            System.out.print("Enter denominator >> ");
            denominator = input.nextInt();
            result = numerator / denominator;
            System.out.println(numerator + " / " + denominator +
                " = " + result);
        }
        catch(ArithmeticException mistake)
        {
            System.out.println(mistake.getMessage());
        }
        catch(InputMismatchException mistake)
        {
            System.out.println("Wrong data type");
        }
        System.out.println("End of program");
    }
}
```

Figure 12-18   The DivisionMistakeCaught3 class

The program in Figure 12-18 must import the java.util.InputMismatchException class to be able to use an InputMismatchException object. The java.util package is also needed for the Scanner class, so it's easiest to import the whole package.

If you use the getMessage() method with the InputMismatchException object, you see that the message is null, because null is the default message value for an InputMismatchException object.

In the main() method of the program in Figure 12-18, the try block executes. Several outcomes are possible:

- If the user enters two usable integers, result is calculated, normal output is displayed, and neither catch block executes.

- If the user enters an invalid (noninteger) value at either the first or second shaded statement, an InputMismatchException object is created and thrown. When the program encounters the first catch block (that catches an ArithmeticException), the block is

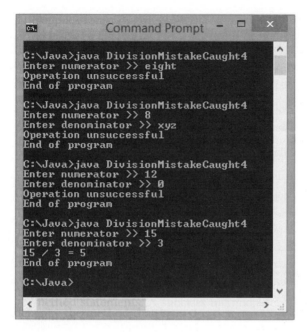

Figure 12-21   Several executions of the `DivisionMistakeCaught4` application

In Java 7 and Java 8, a `catch` block can also be written to catch specific multiple exception types. For example, the following `catch` block catches two `Exception` types. When either is caught, its local identifier is **e**.

```
catch(ArithmeticException, InputMismatchException e)
{
}
```

Although a method can throw any number of `Exception` types, many developers believe that it is poor style for a method to throw and catch more than three or four types. If it does, one of the following conditions might be true:

- Perhaps the method is trying to accomplish too many diverse tasks and should be broken up into smaller methods.

- Perhaps the `Exception` types thrown are too specific and should be generalized, as they are in the `DivisionMistakeCaught4` application in Figure 12-20.

   Watch the video *Catching Multiple Exceptions.*

TWO TRUTHS & A LIE

Throwing and Catching Multiple Exceptions

1. When multiple `try` block statements throw exceptions, multiple `catch` blocks might execute.

2. As soon as an exception occurs, the `try` block that contains it is abandoned and the rest of its statements are unexecuted.

3. When a program contains multiple `catch` blocks, the first one that matches the thrown `Exception` type is the one that executes.

The false statement is #1. If you try more than one statement, only the first error-generating statement throws an exception, and then the rest of the try block is abandoned.

 You Do It

Using Multiple *catch* Blocks

In this section, you add a second `catch` block to the `ExceptionDemo` application.

1. Open the **ExceptionDemo.java** file. Change the class name to `ExceptionDemo2`, and save the file as **ExceptionDemo2.java**.

2. Execute the program, and enter a noninteger value at one of the prompts. Program execution fails. For example, Figure 12-22 shows the error generated when the user types the string "four hundred and seventeen" at the first prompt.

Figure 12-22 Error message generated by the current version of the `ExceptionDemo2` application when a user enters a noninteger value

(continues)

(continued)

3. After the existing `catch` block that catches an `ArithmeticException` object, add a `catch` block that catches a `NumberFormatException` object if neither user entry can be converted to an integer. If this block executes, display an error message, set `numerator` and `denominator` to a default value of 999, and force `result` to 1.

615

```
catch(NumberFormatException exception)
{
    JOptionPane.showMessageDialog(null,
        "This application accepts digits only!");
    numerator = 999;
    denominator = 999;
    result = 1;
}
```

4. Save, compile, and execute the program. This time, if you enter a noninteger value, the output appears as shown in Figure 12-23. Click **OK** to end the application.

Figure 12-23   Error message generated by the improved version of the `ExceptionDemo2` application when a user enters a noninteger value

5. Execute the application a few more times by entering a variety of valid and invalid data. Confirm that the program works appropriately whether you type two usable integers, an unusable 0 for the second integer, or noninteger data such as strings containing alphabetic characters or punctuation.

Using the `finally` Block

When you have actions you must perform at the end of a `try...catch` sequence, you can use a **finally block**. The code within a `finally` block executes regardless of whether the preceding `try` block identifies an exception. Usually, you use a `finally` block to perform cleanup tasks that must happen regardless of whether any exceptions occurred and whether any exceptions that occurred were caught. Figure 12-24 shows the format of a `try...catch` sequence that uses a `finally` block.

```
try
{
    // statements to try
}
catch(Exception e)
{
    // actions that occur if exception was thrown
}
finally
{
    // actions that occur whether catch block executed or not
}
```

Figure 12-24 Format of try...catch...finally sequence

Compare Figure 12-24 to Figure 12-6 shown earlier in this chapter. When the try code works without error in Figure 12-6, control passes to the statements at the end of the method. Also, when the try code fails and throws an exception, and the Exception object is caught, the catch block executes and control again passes to the statements at the end of the method. At first glance, it seems as though the statements at the end of the method in Figure 12-6 always execute. However, the final set of statements might never execute for at least two reasons:

- Any try block might throw an Exception object for which you did not provide a catch block. After all, exceptions occur all the time without your handling them, as one did in the first Division application in Figure 12-2 earlier in this chapter. In the case of an unhandled exception, program execution stops immediately, the exception is sent to the operating system for handling, and the current method is abandoned.

- The try or catch block might contain a System.exit(); statement, which stops execution immediately.

When you include a finally block, you are assured that the finally statements will execute before the method is abandoned, even if the method concludes prematurely. For example, programmers often use a finally block when the program uses data files that must be closed. You will learn more about writing to and reading from data files in the next chapter. For now, however, consider the format shown in Figure 12-25, which represents part of the logic for a typical file-handling program:

```
try
{
    // Open the file
    // Read the file
    // Place the file data in an array
    // Calculate an average from the data
    // Display the average
}
catch(IOException e)
{
    // Issue an error message
    // System exit
}
finally
{
    // If the file is open, close it
}
```

Figure 12-25 Pseudocode that tries reading a file and handles an `IOException`

The pseudocode in Figure 12-25 represents an application that opens a file; in Java, if a file does not exist when you open it, an input/output exception, or `IOException`, is thrown and a `catch` block can handle the error. However, because the application in Figure 12-25 uses an array, an uncaught `IndexOutOfBoundsException` might occur even though the file opened successfully. (An `IndexOutOfBoundsException` occurs, as its name implies, when a subscript is not in the range of valid subscripts for an array.) The `IndexOutOfBoundsException` would not be caught by the existing `catch` block. Also, because the application calculates an average, it might divide by 0 and an `ArithmeticException` might occur; it also would not be caught. In any of these events, you might want to close the file before proceeding. By using the `finally` block, you ensure that the file is closed because the code in the `finally` block executes before control returns to the operating system. The code in the `finally` block executes no matter which of the following outcomes of the `try` block occurs:

- The `try` ends normally.

- The `catch` executes.

- An uncaught exception causes the method to abandon prematurely. An uncaught exception does not allow the `try` block to finish, nor does it cause the `catch` block to execute.

If an application might throw several types of exceptions, you can try some code, catch the possible exception, try some more code and catch the possible exception, and so on. Usually, however, the superior approach is to try all the statements that might throw exceptions, and then include all the needed `catch` blocks and an optional `finally` block. This is the approach shown in Figure 12-25, and it usually results in logic that is easier to follow.

You can avoid using a `finally` block, but you would need repetitious code. For example, instead of using the `finally` block in the pseudocode in Figure 12-25, you could insert the statement "If the file is open, close it" as both the last statement in the `try` block and the second-to-last statement in the `catch` block, just before `System exit`. However, writing code just once in a `finally` block is clearer and less prone to error.

618

If a `try` block calls the `System.exit()` method and the `finally` block calls the same method, the `exit()` method in the `finally` block executes. The `try` block's `exit()` method call is abandoned.

C++ programmers are familiar with `try` and `catch` blocks, but C++ does not provide a `finally` block. C# and Visual Basic contain the keywords `try`, `catch`, and `finally`.

TWO TRUTHS & A LIE

Using the `finally` Block

1. The code within a `finally` block executes when a `try` block identifies an exception that is not caught.

2. Usually, you use a `finally` block to perform cleanup tasks that must happen regardless of whether any exceptions occurred and whether any exceptions that occurred were caught.

3. It's possible that the code that follows a `try...catch...finally` sequence might never execute—for example, if a `try` block throws an unhandled exception.

The false statement is #1. The code within a `finally` block executes whether the preceding `try` block identifies an exception or not, and whether an exception is caught or not.

Understanding the Advantages of Exception Handling

Before the inception of object-oriented programming languages, potential program errors were handled using somewhat confusing, error-prone methods. For example, a traditional, non-object-oriented procedural program might perform three methods that depend on each other using code that provides error checking similar to the pseudocode in Figure 12-26.

```
call methodA()
if methodA() worked
{
    call methodB()
    if methodB() worked
    {
        call methodC()
        if methodC() worked
            everything's okay, so display finalResult
        else
            set errorCode to 'C'
    }
    else
        set errorCode to 'B'
}
else
    set errorCode to 'A'
```

Figure 12-26 Pseudocode representing traditional error checking

Figure 12-26 represents an application in which the logic must pass three tests before finalResult can be displayed. The program executes methodA(); it then calls methodB() only if methodA() is successful. Similarly, methodC() executes only when methodA() and methodB() are both successful. When any method fails, the program sets an appropriate errorCode to 'A', 'B', or 'C'. (Presumably, the errorCode is used later in the application.) The logic is difficult to follow, and the application's purpose and intended usual outcome—to display finalResult—is lost in the maze of if statements. Also, you can easily make coding mistakes within such a program because of the complicated nesting, indenting, and opening and closing of curly braces.

Compare the same program logic using Java's object-oriented, error-handling technique shown in Figure 12-27. Using the try...catch object-oriented technique provides the same results as the traditional method, but the statements of the program that do the "real" work (calling methods A, B, and C and displaying finalResult) are placed together, where their logic is easy to follow. The try steps should usually work without generating errors; after all, the errors are "exceptions." It is convenient to see these business-as-usual steps in one location. The unusual, exceptional events are grouped and moved out of the way of the primary action.

```
try
{
    call methodA() and maybe throw an exception
    call methodB() and maybe throw an exception
    call methodC() and maybe throw an exception
    everything's okay, so display finalResult
}
catch(methodA()'s error)
{
    set errorCode to "A"
}
catch(methodB()'s error)
{
    set errorCode to "B"
}
catch(methodC()'s error)
{
    set errorCode to "C"
}
```

Figure 12-27   Pseudocode representing object-oriented exception handling

Besides clarity, an advantage to object-oriented exception handling is the flexibility it allows in the handling of error situations. When a method you write throws an exception, the same method can catch the exception, although it is not required to do so, and in most object-oriented programs it does not. Often, you don't want a method to handle its own exception. In many cases, you want the method to check for errors, but you do not want to require a method to handle an error if it finds one. Another advantage to object-oriented exception handling is that you gain the ability to appropriately deal with exceptions as you decide how to handle them. When you write a method, it can call another, catch a thrown exception, and you can decide what you want to do. Just as a police officer has leeway to deal with a speeding driver differently depending on circumstances, programs can react to exceptions specifically for their current purposes.

Methods are flexible partly because they are reusable—that is, a well-written method might be used by any number of applications. Each calling application might need to handle a thrown error differently, depending on its purpose. For example, an application that uses a method that divides values might need to terminate if division by 0 occurs. A different program simply might want the user to reenter the data to be used, and a third program might want to force division by 1. The method that contains the division statement can throw the error, but each calling program can assume responsibility for handling the error detected by the method in an appropriate way.

TWO TRUTHS & A LIE

Understanding the Advantages of Exception Handling

1. An advantage to using object-oriented error-handling techniques is that programs are clearer and more flexible.

2. An advantage to using object-oriented error-handling techniques is that when a method throws an exception, it will always be handled in the same, consistent way.

3. In many cases, you want a method to check for errors, but you do not want to require the method to handle an error if it finds one.

The false statement is #2. A well-written method might be used by any number of applications. An advantage of object-oriented exception-handling techniques is that each calling application can handle thrown errors differently, depending on its purpose.

Specifying the Exceptions that a Method Can Throw

If a method throws an exception that it will not catch but that will be caught by a different method, you must create a **throws clause** by using the keyword throws followed by an Exception type in the method header. This practice is known as **exception specification**.

For example, Figure 12-28 shows a PriceList class used by a company to hold a list of prices for items it sells. For simplicity, there are only four prices and a single method that displays the price of a single item. The displayPrice() method accepts a parameter to use as the array subscript, but because the subscript could be out of bounds, the method contains a shaded throws clause, acknowledging it could throw an exception.

```
public class PriceList
{
    private static final double[] price = {15.99, 27.88, 34.56, 45.89};
    public static void displayPrice(int item) throws IndexOutOfBoundsException
    {
        System.out.println("The price is $" + price[item]);
    }
}
```

Figure 12-28   The PriceList class

Figures 12-29 and 12-30 show two applications in which programmers have chosen to handle the potential exception differently. In the first class, PriceListApplication1, the programmer has chosen to handle the exception in the shaded catch block by displaying a price of $0. In the second class, PriceListApplication2, the programmer has chosen to handle the exception by using the highest price in the array. Figure 12-31 shows several executions of each program. Other programmers writing other applications that use the PriceList class could choose still different actions, but they all can use the flexible displayPrice() method because it doesn't limit the calling method's choice of recourse.

```java
import java.util.*;
public class PriceListApplication1
{
    public static void main(String[] args)
    {
        int item;
        Scanner input = new Scanner(System.in);
        System.out.print("Enter item number >> ");
        item = input.nextInt();
        try
        {
            PriceList.displayPrice(item);
        }
        catch(IndexOutOfBoundsException e)
        {
            System.out.println("Price is $0");
        }
    }
}
```

Figure 12-29   The PriceListApplication1 class

```java
import java.util.*;
public class PriceListApplication2
{
    public static void main(String[] args)
    {
        int item;
        Scanner input = new Scanner(System.in);
        final int MAXITEM = 3;
        System.out.print("Enter item number >> ");
        item = input.nextInt();
        try
        {
            PriceList.displayPrice(item);
        }
        catch(IndexOutOfBoundsException e)
        {
            PriceList.displayPrice(MAXITEM);
        }
    }
}
```

Figure 12-30   The PriceListApplication2 class

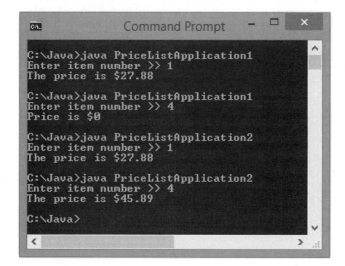

Figure 12-31 Several executions of `PriceListApplication1` and `PriceListApplication2`

For most Java methods that you write, you do not use a `throws` clause. For example, you have not needed to use a `throws` clause in any of the many programs you have written while working through this book; however, in those methods, if you divided by 0 or went beyond an array's bounds, an exception was thrown nevertheless. Most of the time, you let Java handle any exception by shutting down the program. Imagine how unwieldy your programs would become if you were required to provide instructions for handling every possible error, including equipment failures and memory problems. Most exceptions never have to be explicitly thrown or caught, nor do you have to include a `throws` clause in the headers of methods that automatically throw these exceptions. The only exceptions that must be caught or named in a `throws` clause are the type known as *checked* exceptions.

Java's exceptions can be categorized into two types:

- **Unchecked exceptions**—These exceptions inherit from the `Error` class or the `RuntimeException` class. Although you *can* handle these exceptions in your programs, you are not required to do so. For example, dividing by zero is a type of `RuntimeException`, and you are not required to handle this exception—you can simply let the program terminate.

- **Checked exceptions**—These exceptions are the type that programmers should anticipate and from which programs should be able to recover. All exceptions that you explicitly throw and that descend from the `Exception` class are checked exceptions.

Java programmers say that checked exceptions are subject to the **catch or specify requirement**, which means if you throw a checked exception from a method, you must do one of the following:

- *Catch* it within the method.

- *Specify* the exception in your method header's `throws` clause.

Code that uses a checked exception will not compile if the catch or specify rule is not followed.

If you write a method with a throws clause in the header, then any method that uses your method must do one of the following:

- Catch and handle the possible exception.

- Declare the exception in its throws clause. The called method can then rethrow the exception to yet another method that might either catch it or throw it yet again.

In other words, when an exception is a checked exception, client programmers are forced to deal with the possibility that an exception will be thrown.

Some programmers feel that using checked exceptions is an example of "syntactic salt." **Syntactic sugar** is a term coined by Peter J. Landin to describe aspects of a computer language that make it "sweeter," or easier, for programmers to use. For example, you learned in Chapter 1 that you do not have to write import java.lang; at the top of every Java program file because the package is automatically imported for you. The metaphor has been extended by the term **syntactic salt**, which is a language feature designed to make it harder to write bad code.

If you write a method that explicitly throws a checked exception that is not caught within the method, Java requires that you use the throws clause in the header of the method. Using the throws clause does not mean that the method *will* throw an exception—everything might go smoothly. Instead, it means the method *might* throw an exception. You include the throws clause in the method header so applications that use your methods are notified of the potential for an exception.

A method that overrides another cannot throw an exception unless it throws the same type as its parent or a subclass of its parent's thrown type. These rules do not apply to overloaded methods. Any exceptions may (or may not) be thrown from one version of an overloaded method without considering what exceptions are thrown by other versions of an overloaded method.

In Chapter 3, you learned that a method's signature is the combination of the method name and the number, types, and order of arguments. Some programmers argue that any throws clause is also part of the signature, but most authorities disagree. You cannot create a class that contains multiple methods that differ only in their return types; such methods are not overloaded. The same is true for methods with the same signatures that differ only in their throws clauses; the compiler considers the methods to have an identical signature. Instead of saying that the throws clause is part of the method's signature, you might prefer to say that it is part of the method's interface. Whether you consider the throws clause part of a method's signature or not, it is one of the characteristics you should know about every method you use. To be able to use a method to its full potential, you must know the method's name and three additional pieces of information:

- The method's return type
- The type and number of arguments the method requires
- The type and number of exceptions the method throws

You can't call a method without knowing what types of arguments are required, but you can call a method without knowing its return type if you don't want to use the value it returns.

Also, if you use a method without knowing its return type, you probably don't understand the purpose of the method. Likewise, you can't make sound decisions about what to do in case of an error if you don't know what types of exceptions a method might throw.

When a method might throw more than one exception type, you can specify a list of potential exceptions in the method header by separating them with commas. As an alternative, if all the exceptions descend from the same parent, you can specify the more general parent class. For example, if your method might throw either an `ArithmeticException` or an `ArrayIndexOutOfBoundsException`, you can just specify that your method throws a `RuntimeException`. One advantage to this technique is that when your method is modified to include more specific `RuntimeExceptions` in the future, the method header will not change. This saves time and money for users of your methods, who will not have to modify their own methods to accommodate new `RuntimeException` types.

An extreme alternative is simply to specify that your method throws a general `Exception` object, so that all exceptions are included in one clause. Doing this simplifies the exception specification you write. However, using this technique disguises information about the specific types of exceptions that might occur, and such information usually has value to users of your methods.

Usually, you declare only checked exceptions. Remember that runtime exceptions can occur anywhere in a program, and they can be numerous. Programs would be less clear and more cumbersome if you had to account for runtime exceptions in every method declaration. Therefore, the Java compiler does not require that you catch or specify runtime exceptions.

Watch the video *Specifying Exceptions*.

TWO TRUTHS & A LIE

Specifying the Exceptions that a Method Can Throw

1. Exception specification is the practice of listing possible exceptions in a `throws` clause in a method header.

2. Many exceptions never have to be explicitly thrown or caught, nor do you have to include a `throws` clause in the headers of methods that automatically throw these exceptions.

3. If you write a method with a `throws` clause for a checked exception in the header, then any method that uses your method must catch and handle the possible exception.

The false statement is #3. If you write a method with a `throws` clause for a checked exception in the header, then any method that uses your method must catch and handle the possible exception or declare the exception in its `throws` clause so the exception can be rethrown.

Tracing Exceptions Through the Call Stack

When one method calls another, the computer's operating system must keep track of where the method call came from, and program control must return to the calling method when the called method is completed. For example, if methodA() calls methodB(), the operating system has to "remember" to return to methodA() when methodB() ends. Likewise, if methodB() calls methodC(), the computer must "remember" while methodC() executes to return to methodB() and eventually to methodA(). The memory location known as the **call stack** is where the computer stores the list of memory locations to which the system must return when methods end. Programmers sometimes refer to the call stack as the *execution stack*, the *memory stack*, or just the *stack*.

When a method throws an exception and the method does not catch it, the exception is thrown to the next method up the call stack, or in other words, to the method that called the offending method. Figure 12-32 shows how the call stack works. If methodA() calls methodB(), and methodB() calls methodC(), and methodC() throws an exception, Java first looks for a catch block in methodC(). If none exists, Java looks for the same thing in methodB(). If methodB() does not have a catch block, Java looks to methodA(). If methodA() cannot catch the exception, it is thrown to the Java Virtual Machine, which displays a message at the command prompt.

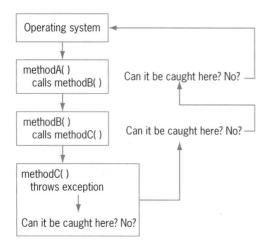

Figure 12-32   Cycling through the call stack

For example, examine the application in Figure 12-33. The main() method of the application calls methodA(), which displays a message and calls methodB(). Within methodB(), another message is displayed and methodC() is called. In methodC(), yet another message is displayed. Then, a three-integer array is declared, and the program attempts to display the fourth element in the array. This program compiles correctly—no error is detected until methodC() attempts to access the out-of-range array element. In Figure 12-33, the comments indicate line numbers so you can more easily follow the sequence of generated error messages. You probably would not add such comments to a working application. Figure 12-34 shows the output when the application executes.

```java
public class DemoStackTrace
{
    public static void main(String[] args)
    {
        methodA(); // line 5
    }
    public static void methodA()
    {
        System.out.println("In methodA()");
        methodB(); // line 10
    }
    public static void methodB()
    {
        System.out.println("In methodB()");
        methodC(); // line 15
    }
    public static void methodC()
    {
        System.out.println("In methodC()");
        int [] array = {0, 1, 2};
        System.out.println(array[3]); // line 21
    }
}
```

Don't Do It
You never would purposely use an out-of-range subscript in a professional program.

Figure 12-33 The DemoStackTrace class

Figure 12-34 Error messages generated by the DemoStackTrace application

As you can see in Figure 12-34, three messages are displayed, indicating that methodA(), methodB(), and methodC() were called in order. However, when methodC() attempts to access the out-of-range element in the array, an ArrayIndexOutOfBoundsException is automatically thrown. The error message generated shows that the exception occurred at line 21 of the file in methodC(), which was called in line 15 of the file by methodB(), which was called in line 10 of the file by methodA(), which was called by the main() method in line 5 of the file. Using this list of error messages, you could track down the location where the error was generated. Of course, in a larger application that contains thousands of lines of code, the stack trace history list would be even more useful.

The technique of cycling through the methods in the stack has great advantages because it allows methods to handle exceptions wherever the programmer has decided it is most appropriate—including allowing the operating system to handle the error. However, when a program uses several classes, the disadvantage is that the programmer finds it difficult to locate the original source of an exception.

You have already used the Throwable method getMessage() to obtain information about an Exception object. Another useful Exception method is the printStackTrace() method. When you catch an Exception object, you can call printStackTrace() to display a list of methods in the call stack so you can determine the location of the statement that caused the exception.

For example, Figure 12-35 shows a DemoStackTrace2 application in which the printStackTrace() method produces a trace of the trail taken by a thrown exception. The differences in the executable statements from the DemoStackTrace application are shaded. The call to methodB() has been placed in a try block so that the exception can be caught. Instead of throwing the exception to the operating system, this application catches the exception, displays a stack trace history list, and continues to execute. The output of the list of methods in Figure 12-36 is similar to the one shown in Figure 12-34, but the application does not end abruptly.

```
public class DemoStackTrace2
{
    public static void main(String[] args)
    {
        methodA(); // line 5
    }
    public static void methodA()
    {
        System.out.println("In methodA()");
        try
        {
            methodB(); // line 12
        }
        catch(ArrayIndexOutOfBoundsException error)
        {
            System.out.println("In methodA() - The stack trace:");
            error.printStackTrace();
        }
        System.out.println("methodA() ends normally.");
        System.out.println("Application could continue " +
            "from this point.");
    }
```

Figure 12-35   The DemoStackTrace2 class *(continues)*

(continued)

```java
    public static void methodB()
    {
        System.out.println("In methodB()");
        methodC(); // line 26
    }
    public static void methodC()
    {
        System.out.println("In methodC()");
        int[] array = {0, 1, 2};
        System.out.println(array[3]); // line 32
    }
}
```

Figure 12-35 The DemoStackTrace2 class

Figure 12-36 Output of the DemoStackTrace2 application

Usually, you do not want to place a `printStackTrace()` method call in a finished program. The typical application user has no interest in the cryptic messages that are displayed. However, while you are developing an application, `printStackTrace()` can be a useful tool for diagnosing your class's problems.

> ## TWO TRUTHS & A LIE
>
> ### Tracing Exceptions Through the Call Stack
>
> 1. The call stack is where the computer stores the list of locations to which the system must return after each method call.
>
> 2. When a method throws an exception and the method does not catch it, the exception is thrown to the next method down the call stack, or in other words, to the next method that the offending method calls.
>
> 3. When you catch an exception, you can call printStackTrace() to display a list of methods in the call stack so you can determine the location of the statement that caused the exception. However, usually you do not want to place a printStackTrace() method call in a finished program.

The false statement is #2. When a method throws an exception and the method does not catch it, the exception is thrown to the next method up the call stack, or in other words, to the method that *called* the offending method.

Creating Your Own Exception Classes

Java provides over 40 categories of Exceptions that you can use in your programs. However, Java's creators could not predict every condition that might be an exception in your applications. For example, you might want to declare an Exception when your bank balance is negative or when an outside party attempts to access your e-mail account. Most organizations have specific rules for exceptional data; for example, an employee number must not exceed three digits, or an hourly salary must not be less than the legal minimum wage. Of course, you can handle these potential error situations with if statements, but Java also allows you to create your own Exception classes.

To create your own throwable Exception class, you must extend a subclass of Throwable. Recall from Figure 12-1 that Throwable has two subclasses, Exception and Error, which are used to distinguish between recoverable and nonrecoverable errors. Because you always want to create your own exceptions for recoverable errors, your classes should extend the Exception class. You can extend any existing Exception subclass, such as ArithmeticException or NullPointerException, but usually you want to inherit directly from Exception. It is conventional to end each Exception subclass name with *Exception*.

The Exception class contains four constructors as follows:

- Exception()—Constructs a new Exception object with null as its detail message

- Exception(String message)—Constructs a new Exception object with the specified detail message

- Exception(String message, Throwable cause)—Constructs a new Exception object with the specified detail message and cause
- Exception(Throwable cause)—Constructs a new Exception object with the specified cause and a detail message of cause.toString(), which typically contains the class and the detail message of cause, or null if the cause argument is null

For example, Figure 12-37 shows a HighBalanceException class. Its constructor contains a single statement that passes a description of an error to the parent Exception constructor. This String would be retrieved if you called the getMessage() method with a HighBalanceException object.

```java
public class HighBalanceException extends Exception
{
    public HighBalanceException()
    {
        super("Customer balance is high");
    }
}
```

Figure 12-37   The HighBalanceException class

Figure 12-38 shows a CustomerAccount class that uses a HighBalanceException. The CustomerAccount constructor header indicates that it might throw a HighBalanceException (see the first shaded statement); if the balance used as an argument to the constructor exceeds a set limit, a new, unnamed instance of the HighBalanceException class is thrown (see the second shaded statement).

```java
public class CustomerAccount
{
    private int acctNum;
    private double balance;
    public static double HIGH_CREDIT_LIMIT = 20000.00;
    public CustomerAccount(int num, double bal) throws HighBalanceException
    {
        acctNum = num;
        balance = bal;
        if(balance > HIGH_CREDIT_LIMIT)
            throw(new HighBalanceException());
    }
}
```

Figure 12-38   The CustomerAccount class

In the CustomerAccount class in Figure 12-38, you could choose to instantiate a named HighBalanceException and throw it when the balance exceeds the credit limit. By waiting and instantiating an unnamed object only when it is needed, you improve program performance.

Figure 12-39 shows an application that instantiates a CustomerAccount. In this application, a user is prompted for an account number and balance. After the values are entered, an attempt is made to construct a CustomerAccount in a try block (as shown in the first shaded section). If the attempt is successful—that is, if the CustomerAccount constructor does not throw an Exception—the CustomerAccount information is displayed in a dialog box. However, if the CustomerAccount constructor does throw a HighBalanceException, the catch block receives it (as shown in the second shaded section) and displays a message. A different application could take any number of different actions; for example, it could display the return value of the getMessage() method, construct a CustomerAccount object with a lower balance, or construct a different type of object—perhaps a child of CustomerAccount called PreferredCustomerAccount that allows a higher balance. Figure 12-40 shows typical output of the application in a case in which a customer's balance is too high.

```java
import javax.swing.*;
public class UseCustomerAccount
{
    public static void main(String[] args)
    {
        int num;
        double balance;
        String input;
        input = JOptionPane.showInputDialog(null,
            "Enter account number");
        num = Integer.parseInt(input);
        input = JOptionPane.showInputDialog(null, "Enter balance due");
        balance = Double.parseDouble(input);
        try
        {
            CustomerAccount ca = new CustomerAccount(num, balance);
            JOptionPane.showMessageDialog(null, "Customer #" +
                num + " has a balance of $" + balance);
        }
        catch(HighBalanceException hbe)
        {
            JOptionPane.showMessageDialog(null, "Customer #" +
                num + " has a balance of $" + balance +
                    " which is higher than the credit limit");
        }
    }
}
```

Figure 12-39   The UseCustomerAccount class

Figure 12-40   Typical output of the `UseCustomerAccount` application

Instead of hard coding error messages into your exception classes, as shown in Figure 12-39, you might consider creating a catalog of possible messages to use. This approach provides several advantages:

- All the messages are stored in one location instead of being scattered throughout the program, making them easier to see and modify.

- The list of possible errors serves as a source of documentation, listing potential problems when running the application.

- Other applications might want to use the same catalog of messages.

- If your application will be used internationally, you can provide messages in multiple languages, and other programmers can use the version that is appropriate for their country.

 You can throw any type of exception at any time, not just exceptions of your own creation. For example, within any program you can code `throw(new RuntimeException());`. Of course, you would want to do so only with good reason because Java handles `RuntimeExceptions` for you by stopping the program. Because you cannot anticipate every possible error, Java's automatic response is often the best course of action.

You should not create an excessive number of special `Exception` types for your classes, especially if the Java development environment already contains an `Exception` class that will catch the error. Extra `Exception` types add complexity for other programmers who use your classes. However, when appropriate, specialized `Exception` classes provide an elegant way for you to handle error situations. They enable you to separate your error code from the usual, nonexceptional sequence of events; they allow errors to be passed up the stack and traced; and they allow clients of your classes to handle exceptional situations in the manner most suitable for their application.

TWO TRUTHS & A LIE

Creating Your Own Exception Classes

1. You must create your own Exception classes for your programs to be considered truly object oriented.

2. To create your own throwable Exception class, you should extend the Exception class.

3. The Exception class contains four constructors, including a default constructor and one that requires a String that contains the message that can be returned by the getMessage() method.

The false statement is #1. You are not required to throw exceptions in object-oriented programs. However, Java does provide many built-in categories of Exceptions that you can use, and you can also create your own Exception classes.

Using Assertions

In Chapter 1, you learned that you might inadvertently create syntax or logic errors when you write a program. Syntax errors are mistakes using the Java language; they are compile-time errors that prevent a program from compiling and creating an executable file with a .class extension.

In Chapter 1, you also learned that a program might contain logic errors even though it is free of syntax errors. Some logic errors cause runtime errors, or errors that cause a program to terminate. In this chapter, you learned how to use exceptions to handle many of these kinds of errors.

Some logic errors do not cause a program to terminate, but nevertheless produce incorrect results. For example, if a payroll program should determine gross pay by multiplying hours worked by hourly pay rate, but you inadvertently divide the numbers, no runtime error occurs and no exception is thrown, but the output is wrong. An **assertion** is a Java language feature that can help you detect such logic errors and debug a program. You use an assert statement to create an assertion; when you use an assert statement, you state a condition that should be true, and Java throws an AssertionError when it is not.

The syntax of an assert statement is:

```
assert booleanExpression : optionalErrorMessage
```

The Boolean expression in the assert statement should always be true if the program is working correctly. The optionalErrorMessage is displayed if the booleanExpression is false.

Figure 12-41 contains an application that prompts a user for a number and passes it to a method that determines whether a value is even. Within the isEven() method, the remainder is taken when the passed parameter is divided by 2. If the remainder after dividing by 2 is 1, result is set to false. For example, 1, 3, and 5 all are odd, and all result in a value of 1 when % 2 is applied to them. If the remainder after dividing by 2 is not 1, result is set to true. For example, 2, 4, and 6 all are even, and all have a 0 remainder when % 2 is applied to them.

```
import java.util.Scanner;
public class EvenOdd
{
    public static void main(String[] args)
    {
        Scanner input = new Scanner(System.in);
        int number;
        System.out.print("Enter a number >> ");
        number = input.nextInt();
        if(isEven(number))
            System.out.println(number + " is even");
        else
            System.out.println(number + " is odd");
    }
    public static boolean isEven(int number)
    {
        boolean result;
        if(number % 2 == 1)
            result = false;
        else
            result = true;
        return result;
    }
}
```

Figure 12-41 The flawed EvenOdd program without an assertion

Figure 12-42 shows several executions of the application in Figure 12-41. The output seems correct until the last two executions. The values −5 and −7 are classified as even although they are odd. An assertion might help you to debug this application.

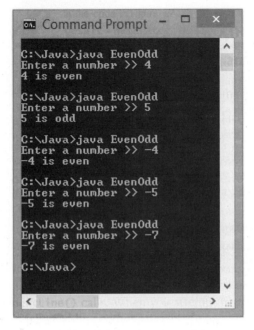

Figure 12-42   Typical executions of the EvenOdd application

Figure 12-43 contains a new version of the isEven() method to which the shaded assert statement has been added. The statement asserts that when the remainder of a number divided by 2 is not 1, it must be 0. If the expression is not true, a message is created using the values of both number and its remainder after dividing by 2.

```java
public static boolean isEven(int number)
{
    boolean result;
    if(number % 2 == 1)
        result = false;
    else
    {
        result = true;
        assert number % 2 == 0 : number + " % 2 is " + number % 2;
    }
    return result;
}
```

Figure 12-43   The flawed isEven() method with an assertion

If you add the assertion shown in Figure 12-43 and then compile and execute the program in the usual way, you get the same incorrect output as in Figure 12-42. To enable the assertion, you must use the -ea option when you execute the program; *ea* stands for *enable assertion*. Figure 12-44 shows the command prompt with an execution that uses the -ea option.

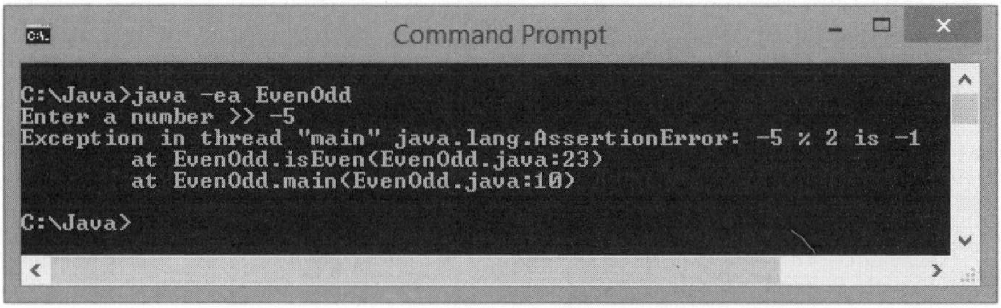

Figure 12-44   Executing an application using the enable assertion option

When the EvenOdd program executes and the user enters –5, the program displays the messages in Figure 12-44 instead of displaying incorrect output. You can see from the message that an AssertionError was thrown and that the value of –5 % 2 is –1, not 1 as you had assumed. The remainder operator results in a negative value when one of its operands is negative, making the output in this program incorrect.

When the programmer sees that –5 % 2 is –1, the reasonable course of action is to return to the source code and change the logic.

Several adjustments are possible:

- The programmer might decide to convert the parameter to the isEven() method to its absolute value before using the remainder operator, as in the following:

  ```
  number = Math.abs(number);
  ```

- Another option would be to change the if statement to test for even values by comparing number % 2 to 0 first, as follows:

  ```
  if(number % 2 == 0)
     result = true;
  else
     result = false;
  ```

  Then values of both 1 and –1 would be classified as not even.

- Other options might include displaying an error message when negative values are encountered, reversing the result values of true and false when the parameter is negative, or throwing an exception.

An experienced programmer might have found the error in the original EvenOdd application without using an assertion. For example, the programmer might have previously used the remainder operator with a negative operand, remembered that the result might be negative, and changed the code accordingly. Alternatively, the programmer could have inserted statements to display values at strategic points in the program. However, after the mistake is found and fixed, any extra display statements should be removed when the final product is ready for distribution to users. By contrast, any assert statements can be left in place, and if the user does not use the -ea option when running the program, the user will see no evidence that the `assert` statements exist. Placing `assert` statements in key program locations can reduce development and debugging time.

You do not want to use assertions to check for every type of error that could occur in a program. For example, if you want to ensure that a user enters numeric data, you should use exception-handling techniques that provide the means for your program to recover from the mistake. If you want to ensure that the data falls within a specific range, you should use a decision or a loop. Assertions are meant to be helpful in the development stage of a program, not when it is in production and in the hands of users.

638

TWO TRUTHS & A LIE

Using Assertions

1. All logic errors cause a program to terminate, and they should be handled by throwing and catching exceptions.

2. The Boolean expression in an `assert` statement should always be `true` if the program is working correctly.

3. To enable an assertion, you must use the `-ea` option when you execute the program.

The false statement is #1. Many logic errors do not cause program termination—they simply produce incorrect results.

 You Do It

Creating a Class that Automatically Throws Exceptions

Next, you create a class that contains two methods that throw exceptions but don't catch them. The `PickMenu` class allows restaurant customers to choose from a dinner menu. Before you create `PickMenu`, you will create the `Menu` class, which lists dinner choices and allows a user to make a selection.

1. Open a new file, and then enter the following `import` statement, class header, and opening curly brace for the `Menu` class:

```
import javax.swing.*;
public class Menu
{
```

(continues)

(continued)

2. Type the following `String` array for three entrée choices. Also include a `String` to build the menu that you will display and an integer to hold the numeric equivalent of the selection.

```
private String[] entreeChoice = {"Rosemary Chicken",
    "Beef Wellington", "Maine Lobster"};
private String menu = "";
private int choice;
```

3. Add the `displayMenu()` method, which lists each entrée option with a corresponding number the customer can type to make a selection. Even though the allowable `entreeChoice` array subscripts are 0, 1, and 2, most users would expect to type 1, 2, or 3. So, you code `x + 1` rather than `x` as the number in the prompt. After the user enters a selection, convert it to an integer. Return the `String` that corresponds to the user's menu selection—the one with the subscript that is 1 less than the entered value. After the closing curly brace for the `displayMenu()` method, add the closing curly brace for the class.

```
public String displayMenu()
{
    for(int x = 0; x < entreeChoice.length; ++x)
    {
        menu = menu + "\n" + (x + 1) + " for " +
            entreeChoice[x];
    }
    String input = JOptionPane.showInputDialog(null,
        "Type your selection, then press Enter." + menu);
    choice = Integer.parseInt(input);
    return(entreeChoice[choice - 1]);
}
}
```

 The curly braces are not necessary in the `for` loop of the `displayMenu()` method because the loop contains only one statement. However, in a later exercise, you will add another statement within this block.

4. Examine the code within the `displayMenu()` method. Consider the exceptions that might occur. The user might not type an integer, so the `parseInt()` method can fail, and even if the user does type an integer, it might not be in the range allowed to access the `entreeChoice` array. Therefore, the `displayMenu()` method, like most methods in which you rely on the user to enter data, might throw exceptions that you can anticipate. (Of course, any method might throw an unanticipated exception.)

5. Save the file as **Menu.java**, and compile the class using the **javac** command.

(continues)

(continued)

Creating a Class that Passes on an Exception Object

Next, you create the PickMenu class, which lets a customer choose from the available dinner entrée options. The PickMenu class declares a Menu and a String named guestChoice that holds the name of the entrée the customer selects.

To enable the PickMenu class to operate with different kinds of Menus in the future, you will pass a Menu to PickMenu's constructor. This technique provides two advantages: First, when the menu options change, you can alter the contents of the Menu.java file without changing any of the code in programs that use Menu. Second, you can extend Menu, perhaps to VegetarianMenu, LowSaltMenu, or KosherMenu, and still use the existing PickMenu class. When you pass any Menu or Menu subclass into the PickMenu constructor, the correct customer options appear.

The PickMenu class is unlikely to directly generate any exceptions because it does not request user input. (Keep in mind that any class might generate an exception for such uncontrollable events as the system not having enough memory available.) However, PickMenu declares a Menu object; the Menu class, because it relies on user input, is likely to generate an exception.

1. Open a new file, and type the following first few lines of the PickMenu class with its data fields (a Menu and a String that reflect the customer's choice):

```java
import javax.swing.*;
public class PickMenu
{
    private Menu briefMenu;
    private String guestChoice = new String();
```

2. Enter the following PickMenu constructor, which receives an argument representing a Menu. The constructor assigns the Menu that is the argument to the local Menu, and then calls the setGuestChoice() method, which prompts the user to select from the available menu. The PickMenu() constructor might throw an exception because it calls setGuestChoice(), which calls displayMenu(), a method that uses keyboard input and might throw an exception.

```java
public PickMenu(Menu theMenu)
{
    briefMenu = theMenu;
    setGuestChoice();
}
```

(continues)

(continued)

3. The following `setGuestChoice()` method displays the menu and reads keyboard data entry (so the method throws an exception). It also displays instructions and then retrieves the user's selection.

```
public void setGuestChoice()
{
    JOptionPane.showMessageDialog(null,
        "Choose from the following menu:");
    guestChoice = briefMenu.displayMenu();
}
```

4. Add the following `getGuestChoice()` method that returns a guest's String selection from the `PickMenu` class. Also, add a closing curly brace for the class.

```
public String getGuestChoice()
{
    return(guestChoice);
}
}
```

5. Save the file as **PickMenu.java**, and compile it using the **javac** command.

Creating an Application that Can Catch Exceptions

You have created a Menu class that simply holds a list of food items, displays itself, and allows the user to make a selection. You also created a PickMenu class with fields that hold a user's specific selection from a given menu and methods to get and set values for those fields. The PickMenu class might throw exceptions, but it contains no methods that catch those exceptions. Next, you write an application that uses the PickMenu class. This application can catch exceptions that PickMenu throws.

1. Open a new file, and start entering the following PlanMenu class, which has just one method—a main() method:

```
import javax.swing.*;
public class PlanMenu
{
    public static void main(String[] args)
    {
```

2. Construct the following Menu named briefMenu, and declare a PickMenu object that you name entree. You do not want to construct a PickMenu object yet because you want to be able to catch the exception that the PickMenu constructor might throw. Therefore, you want to wait and construct the PickMenu object within a try block. For now, you just declare entree and assign it null. Also, you declare a String that holds the customer's menu selection.

(continues)

(continued)

```
Menu briefMenu = new Menu();
PickMenu entree = null;
String guestChoice = new String();
```

3. Write the following `try` block that constructs a `PickMenu` item. If the construction is successful, the next statement assigns a selection to the `entree` object. Because `entree` is a `PickMenu` object, it has access to the `getGuestChoice()` method in the `PickMenu` class, and you can assign the method's returned value to the `guestChoice String`.

```
try
{
    PickMenu selection = new PickMenu(briefMenu);
    entree = selection;
    guestChoice = entree.getGuestChoice();
}
```

4. The `catch` block must immediately follow the `try` block. When the `try` block fails, `guestChoice` will not have a valid value, so recover from the exception by assigning a value to `guestChoice` within the following `catch` block:

```
catch(Exception error)
{
    guestChoice = "an invalid selection";
}
```

5. After the `catch` block, the application continues. Use the following code to display the customer's choice at the end of the `PlanMenu` application, and then add closing curly braces for the `main()` method and the class:

```
        JOptionPane.showMessageDialog(null,
            "You chose " + guestChoice);
    }
}
```

6. Save the file as **PlanMenu.java**, and then compile and execute it. Read the instructions, click **OK**, choose an entrée by typing its number from the menu, and click **OK** again. Confirm that the menu selection displayed is the one you chose, and click **OK** to dismiss the last dialog box. Figure 12-45 shows the first dialog box of instructions, the menu that appears, and the output when the user selects option 3.

(continues)

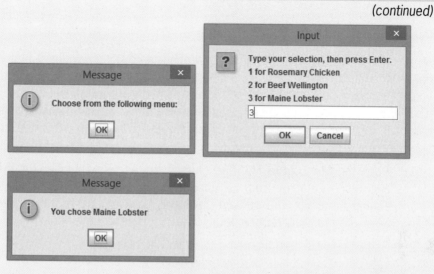

Figure 12-45   Typical execution of the PlanMenu application

7. The PlanMenu application works well when you enter a valid menu selection. One way that you can force an exception is to enter an invalid menu selection at the prompt. Run the PlanMenu application again, and type **4, A**, or any invalid value at the prompt. Entering *4* produces an ArrayIndexOutOfBoundsException, and entering *A* produces a NumberFormatException. If the program lacked the try...catch pair, either entry would halt the program. However, because the setGuestChoice() method in the PickMenu class throws the exception and the PlanMenu application catches it, guestChoice takes on the value "an invalid selection" and the application ends smoothly, as shown in Figure 12-46.

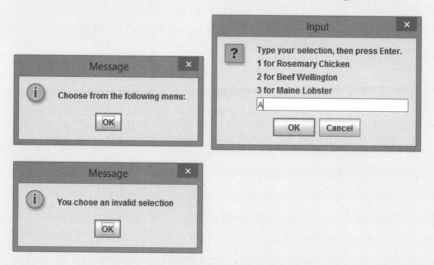

Figure 12-46   Exceptional execution of the PlanMenu application

(continues)

(continued)

Extending a Class that Throws Exceptions

An advantage to using object-oriented exception-handling techniques is that you gain the ability to handle error conditions differently within each program you write. Next, you extend the Menu class to create a class named VegetarianMenu. Subsequently, when you write an application that uses PickMenu with a VegetarianMenu object, you can deal with any thrown exception differently than when you wrote the PlanMenu application.

1. Open the **Menu.java** file, and change the access specifier for the entreeChoice array from private to protected. That way, when you extend the class, the derived class will have access to the array. Save the file, and recompile it using the **javac** command.

2. Open a new file, and then type the following class header for the VegetarianMenu class that extends Menu:

   ```
   public class VegetarianMenu extends Menu
   {
   ```

3. Provide new menu choices for the VegetarianMenu as follows:

   ```
   String[] vegEntreeChoice = {"Spinach Lasagna",
       "Cheese Enchiladas", "Fruit Plate"};
   ```

4. Add the following constructor that calls the superclass constructor and assigns each vegetarian selection to the Menu superclass entreeChoice array, and then add the closing curly brace for the class:

   ```
   public VegetarianMenu()
   {
       super();
       for(int x = 0; x < vegEntreeChoice.length; ++x)
           entreeChoice[x] = vegEntreeChoice[x];
   }
   }
   ```

5. Save the class as **VegetarianMenu.java**, and then compile it.

6. Now write an application that uses VegetarianMenu. You could write any program, but for demonstration purposes, you can simply modify PlanMenu.java. Open the **PlanMenu.java** file, then immediately save it as **PlanVegetarianMenu.java**.

7. Change the class name in the header to **PlanVegetarianMenu**.

8. Change the first statement within the main() method as follows so it declares a VegetarianMenu instead of a Menu:

   ```
   VegetarianMenu briefMenu = new VegetarianMenu();
   ```

(continues)

(continued)

9. Change the `guestChoice` assignment statement in the `catch` block as follows so it is specific to the program that uses the `VegetarianMenu`:

   `guestChoice = "an invalid vegetarian selection";`

10. Save the file, compile it, and run the application. When you see the vegetarian menu, enter a valid selection and confirm that the program works correctly. Run the application again, and enter an invalid selection. The error message shown in Figure 12-47 identifies your invalid entry as "an invalid vegetarian selection". Remember that you did not change the `PickMenu` class. Your new `PlanVegetarianMenu` application uses the `PickMenu` class that you wrote and compiled before a `VegetarianMenu` ever existed. However, because `PickMenu` throws uncaught exceptions, you can handle those exceptions as you see fit in any new applications in which you catch them. Click **OK** to end the application.

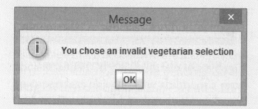

Figure 12-47   Output of the `PlanVegetarianMenu` application when the user makes an invalid selection

Creating an *Exception* Class

Besides using the built-in classes that derive from `Exception` such as `NumberFormatException` and `IndexOutOfBoundsException`, you can create your own `Exception` classes. For example, suppose that although you have asked a user to type a number representing a menu selection, you realize that some users might mistakenly type the initial letter of an option, such as *R* for *Rosemary Chicken*. Although the user has made an error, you want to treat this type of error more leniently than other errors, such as typing a letter that has no discernable connection to the presented menu. In the next section, you create a `MenuException` class that you can use with the `Menu` class to represent a specific type of error.

1. Open a new file, and enter the `MenuException` class. The class extends `Exception`. Its constructor requires a `String` argument, which is passed to the parent class to be used as a return value for the `getMessage()` method.

(continued)

(continued)

```
public class MenuException extends Exception
{
    public MenuException(String choice)
    {
        super(choice);
    }
}
```

2. Save the file as **MenuException.java**, and compile it.

Using an *Exception* You Created

Next, you modify the Menu, PickMenu, and PlanMenu classes to demonstrate how to use a MenuException object.

1. Open the **Menu** file, and immediately save the file as **Menu2.java**.

2. Change the class name to Menu2.

3. At the end of the list of class data fields, add an array of characters that can hold the first letter of each of the entrées in the menu.

   ```
   protected char initial[] = new char[entreeChoice.length];
   ```

4. At the end of the method header for the displayMenu() class, add the following clause:

   ```
   throws MenuException
   ```

   You add this clause because you are going to add code that throws such an exception.

5. Within the displayMenu() method, just before the closing curly brace of the for loop that builds the menu String, add a statement that takes the first character of each entreeChoice and stores it in a corresponding element of the initial array. At the end of the for loop, the initial array holds the first character of each available entrée.

   ```
   initial[x] = entreeChoice[x].charAt(0);
   ```

6. After displaying the JOptionPane dialog box that displays the menu and receives the user's input, add a loop that compares the first letter of the user's choice to each of the initials of valid menu options. If a match is found, throw a new instance of the MenuException class that uses the corresponding entrée as its String argument. In other words, when this thrown MenuException is caught by another method, the assumed entrée is

(continues)

(continued)

the `String` returned by the `getMessage()` method. By placing this test before the call to `parseInt()`, you cause entries of *R*, *B*, or *M* to throw a `MenuException` before they can cause a `NumberFormatException`.

```
for(int y = 0; y < entreeChoice.length; ++y)
   if(input.charAt(0) == initial[y])
      throw (new MenuException(entreeChoice[y]));
```

7. Compare your new class with Figure 12-48, in which all of the changes to the `Menu` class are shaded.

```
import javax.swing.*;
public class Menu2
{
    protected String[] entreeChoice = {"Rosemary Chicken",
        "Beef Wellington", "Maine Lobster"};
    private String menu = "";
    private int choice;
    protected char initial[] = new char[entreeChoice.length];
    public String displayMenu() throws MenuException
    {
        for(int x = 0; x < entreeChoice.length; ++x)
        {
            menu = menu + "\n" + (x + 1) + " for " +
                entreeChoice[x];
            initial[x] = entreeChoice[x].charAt(0);
        }
        String input = JOptionPane.showInputDialog(null,
            "Type your selection, then press Enter." + menu);
        for(int y = 0; y < entreeChoice.length; ++y)
            if(input.charAt(0) == initial[y])
                throw(new MenuException(entreeChoice[y]));
        choice = Integer.parseInt(input);
        return(entreeChoice[choice - 1]);
    }
}
```

Figure 12-48 The Menu2 class

8. Save the class, and compile it.

9. Open the **PickMenu** file, and immediately save it as **PickMenu2.java**.

(continues)

647

(continued)

10. Change the class name to **PickMenu2**, and change the declaration of the Menu object to a **Menu2** object. Change the constructor name to **PickMenu2** and its argument to type **Menu2**. Also add a throws clause to the PickMenu2 constructor header so that it throws a MenuException. This constructor does not throw an exception directly, but it calls the setGuestChoice() method, which calls the displayMenu() method, which throws a MenuException.

11. Add the following throws clause to the setGuestChoice() method header:

    throws MenuException

12. Compare your modifications to the PickMenu2 class in Figure 12-49, in which the changes from the PickMenu class are shaded. Save your file, and compile it.

```
import javax.swing.*;
public class PickMenu2
{
    private Menu2 briefMenu;
    private String guestChoice = new String();
    public PickMenu2(Menu2 theMenu) throws MenuException
    {
        briefMenu = theMenu;
        setGuestChoice();
    }
    public void setGuestChoice() throws MenuException
    {
        JOptionPane.showMessageDialog(null,
            "Choose from the following menu:");
        guestChoice = briefMenu.displayMenu();
    }
    public String getGuestChoice()
    {
        return(guestChoice);
    }
}
```

Figure 12-49 The PickMenu2 class

13. Open the **PlanMenu.java** file, and immediately save it as **PlanMenu2.java**.

14. Change the class name to **PlanMenu2**. Within the main() method, declare a **Menu2** object and a **PickMenu2** reference instead of the current Menu object and PickMenu reference.

(continues)

(continued)

649

15. Within the `try` block, change both references of `PickMenu` to **PickMenu2**.

Using Figure 12-50 as a reference, add a `catch` block after the `try` block and before the existing `catch` block. This `catch` block will catch any thrown `MenuException`s and display their messages. The message will be the name of a menu item, based on the initial the user entered. All other `Exception` objects, including `NumberFormatException`s and `IndexOutOfBoundsException`s, will fall through to the second `catch` block and be handled as before.

```java
import javax.swing.*;
public class PlanMenu2
{
    public static void main(String[] args)
    {
        Menu2 briefMenu = new Menu2();
        PickMenu2 entree = null;
        String guestChoice = new String();
        try
        {
            PickMenu2 selection = new PickMenu2(briefMenu);
            entree = selection;
            guestChoice = entree.getGuestChoice();
        }
        catch(MenuException error)
        {
            guestChoice = error.getMessage();
        }
        catch(Exception error)
        {
            guestChoice = "an invalid selection";
        }
        JOptionPane.showMessageDialog(null,
            "You chose " + guestChoice);
    }
}
```

Figure 12-50   The PlanMenu2 class

16. Save the file, then compile and execute it several times. When you are asked to make a selection, try entering a valid number, an invalid number, an initial letter that is part of the menu, and a letter that is not one of the initial menu letters, and observe the results each time. Whether you enter a valid number or not, the application works as expected. Entering an invalid number still results in an error message. When you enter a letter or a string of letters, the application assumes your selection is valid if you enter the same initial letter, using the same case, as one of the menu options.

Displaying the Virtual Keyboard

You can write many functional Java programs without using exception-handling techniques. After all, you did so when working through the first 11 chapters in this book. However, you will sometimes have to employ exception-handling techniques if you want to use methods written by others that throw exceptions. For example, if you want to display the virtual keyboard of the Windows system, you will have to accommodate a thrown exception.

A **virtual keyboard** is a computer keyboard that appears on the screen. A user operates it by using a mouse to point to and click keys; if the computer has a touch screen, the user touches keys with a finger or stylus. You can use code like that shown in Figure 12-51 to bring up the virtual keyboard in the Windows operating system.

```java
import java.util.Scanner;
import java.io.IOException;
public class VirtualKeyboardDemo
{
    public static void main(String[] args)
    {
        Scanner input = new Scanner(System.in);
        try
        {
            Process proc = Runtime.getRuntime().exec
                ("cmd /c C:\\Windows\\System32\\osk.exe");
        }
        catch(IOException e)
        {
            System.out.println(e.getMessage());
        }
        String name;
        System.out.print("Enter name >> ");
        name = input.nextLine();
        System.out.println("Hello, " + name + "!");
    }
}
```

Figure 12-51   The VirtualKeyboardDemo application

The application in Figure 12-51 contains standard input and output statements that use the Scanner class; you have used statements like these since Chapter 2. The shaded statement that defines a process is the only one that is new to you. Every Java application has a single instance of the Runtime class that allows the program to interface with its environment. The exec() method executes the operating system program named osk.exe. The acronym *osk* stands for *on-screen keyboard*. The exec() method throws an uncaught IOException, so its statement is contained in a try block. You were using Scanner class standard keyboard input and output shortly after you started this book. Now that you understand how exceptions are thrown, you can also use the virtual keyboard.

When you write a program like the one in Figure 12-51, no exception will ever be thrown—an exception is far more likely to occur if you accept the `exec()` method's `String` argument from user input. Therefore, it does not matter what statements you place in the `catch()` block. Instead of using a `try...catch` pair in the `VirtualKeyboardDemo` application, many programmers would eliminate the `try` block, place the phrase `throws IOException` at the end of the `main()` method header, and allow any exceptions to be rethrown to the operating system.

Figure 12-52 shows the `VirtualKeyboardDemo` program during execution. The virtual keyboard appears as soon as the program starts. When the prompt appears at the command line, the user has the option of typing on the standard keyboard or using the on-screen version.

Figure 12-52 The `VirtualKeyboardDemo` program during execution

If you run the program in Figure 12-51 on a machine that does not have the osk.exe file, the program runs correctly but does not display a keyboard.

TWO TRUTHS & A LIE

Displaying the Virtual Keyboard

1. You can write functional Java programs without using exception-handling techniques.

2. You must have a touch screen to be able to display a virtual keyboard on a Windows system.

3. The `Runtime` class `exec()` method throws an `IOException`.

The false statement is #2. A virtual keyboard can be displayed on a standard screen and can be operated with a mouse or a stylus.

You Do It

Displaying the Windows Calculator

In this section, you create a program that asks a user to complete a simple arithmetic problem and displays the Windows calculator to help the user.

1. Open a new file, and then enter the following `import` statements, class header, and opening curly brace for the `CalculatorDemo` class:

    ```
    import java.util.Scanner;
    import java.io.IOException;
    public class CalculatorDemo
    {
    ```

2. Create the `main()` method header. The method throws an `IOException` because it will use the `Runtime exec()` method and not handle the exception the method throws.

    ```
    public static void main(String[] args) throws IOException
    {
    ```

3. Declare a `Scanner` object for input and a `Process` object that invokes the built-in calculator program named calc.exe.

    ```
    Scanner input = new Scanner(System.in);
    Process proc = Runtime.getRuntime().exec
        ("cmd /c C:\\Windows\\System32\\calc.exe");
    ```

4. Declare some values to be used in an arithmetic problem. Also declare a variable to hold the sum of the two numbers and another variable to hold the user's answer.

    ```
    double num1 = 279.6;
    double num2 = 872.8;
    double answer = num1 + num2;
    double usersAnswer;
    ```

5. Prompt the user for an answer, accept it, and then display an appropriate message. Include a closing curly brace for the `main()` method and another for the class.

    ```
            System.out.print("What is the sum of " + num1 +
                " and " + num2 + "? >> ");
            usersAnswer = input.nextDouble();
            if(usersAnswer == answer)
                System.out.println("Correct!");
            else
                System.out.println("Sorry - the answer is " + answer);
        }
    }
    ```

(continues)

(continued)

6. Save the file as **CalculatorDemo.java**, and then compile and execute it. When the program runs, the calculator appears on the screen for use. Figure 12-53 shows a typical execution in progress.

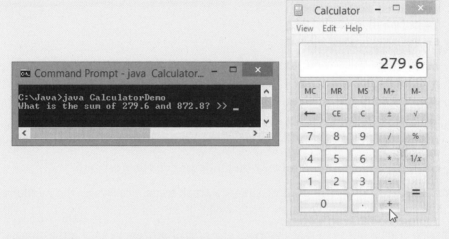

Figure 12-53 Typical execution of `CalculatorDemo` program

7. If you have no further use for the calculator, dismiss it by clicking its **Close** button.

Don't Do It

- Don't forget that all the statements in a `try` block might not execute. If an exception is thrown, no statements after that point in the `try` block will execute.

- Don't forget that you might need a `nextLine()` method call after an attempt to read numeric data from the keyboard throws an exception.

- Don't forget that a variable declared in a `try` block goes out of scope at the end of the block.

- Don't forget that when a variable gets its usable value within a `try` block, you must ensure that it has a valid value before attempting to use it.

- Don't forget to place more specific `catch` blocks before more general ones.

- Don't forget to write a `throws` clause for a method that throws a checked exception but does not handle it.

- Don't forget to handle any checked exception thrown to your method either by writing a `catch` block or by listing it in your method's `throws` clause.

Key Terms

An **exception** is an unexpected or error condition.

Exception handling is an object-oriented technique for managing or resolving errors.

Runtime exceptions are unplanned exceptions that occur during a program's execution. The term is also used more specifically to describe members of the `RuntimeException` class.

A **crash** is a premature, unexpected, and inelegant end to a program.

A **stack trace history list**, or more simply a **stack trace**, displays all the methods that were called during program execution.

Mission critical is a term that describes any crucial process in an organization.

Fault-tolerant applications are designed so that they continue to operate, possibly at a reduced level, when some part of the system fails.

Robustness represents the degree to which a system is resilient to stress, maintaining correct functioning.

A **try block** is a block of code that might throw an exception that can be handled by a subsequent `catch` block.

A **catch block** is a segment of code that can handle an exception that might be thrown by the `try` block that precedes it.

A **throw statement** is one that sends an exception out of a block or a method so it can be handled elsewhere.

A **`finally` block** is a block of code that holds statements that must execute at the end of a `try`…`catch` sequence, whether an exception was thrown or not.

A **throws clause** is an exception specification in a method header.

Exception specification is the practice of using a `throws` clause in a method header; this practice is required if a method throws a checked `Exception` object that it will not catch.

Unchecked exceptions are those from which an executing program cannot reasonably be expected to recover.

Checked exceptions are those that a programmer should plan for and from which a program should be able to recover.

The **catch or specify requirement** is the Java rule that checked exceptions require catching or declaration.

Syntactic sugar is a term to describe aspects of a computer language that make it "sweeter," or easier, for programmers to use.

Syntactic salt describes a language feature designed to make it harder to write bad code.

The **call stack** is where the computer stores the list of memory locations to which the system must return when methods end.

An **assertion** is a Java language feature that can help you detect logic errors and debug a program.

A **virtual keyboard** is a computer keyboard that appears on the screen. A user operates it by using a mouse to point to and click keys; if the computer has a touch screen, the user touches keys with a finger or stylus.

Chapter Summary

- An exception is an unexpected or error condition. Exception handling is the name for the object-oriented techniques that manage or resolve such errors. In Java, the two basic classes of errors are Error and Exception; both descend from the Throwable class.

- In object-oriented terminology, a try block holds code that might cause an error and throw an exception, and a catch block processes the error.

- You can place as many statements as you need within a try block, and you can catch as many exceptions as you want. If you try more than one statement, only the first error-generating statement throws an exception. As soon as the exception occurs, the logic transfers to the catch block, which leaves the rest of the statements in the try block unexecuted. When a program contains multiple catch blocks, the first matching catch block executes, and each remaining catch block is bypassed.

- When you have actions you must perform at the end of a try…catch sequence, you can use a finally block that executes regardless of whether the preceding try block identifies an exception. Usually, you use a finally block to perform cleanup tasks.

- Besides clarity, an advantage to object-oriented exception handling is the flexibility it allows in the handling of error situations. Each calling application might need to handle the same error differently, depending on its purpose.

- When you write a method that might throw a checked exception that is not caught within the method, you must type the clause throws <name>Exception after the method header to indicate the type of Exception that might be thrown. Methods in which you explicitly throw a checked exception require a catch or a declaration.

- The call stack is the memory location where the computer stores the list of method locations to which the system must return. When you catch an exception, you can call printStackTrace() to display a list of methods in the call stack so you can determine the location of the exception.

- Java provides over 40 categories of Exceptions that you can use in your programs. However, Java's creators could not predict every condition that might be an Exception in your applications, so Java also allows you to create your own Exceptions. To create your own throwable Exception class, you must extend a subclass of Throwable.

- An assertion is a Java language feature that can help you detect logic errors and debug a program. When you use an assertion, you state a condition that should be true, and Java throws an AssertionError when it is not.

- You can call up Windows operating system programs such as the virtual keyboard using the exec() method in the Runtime class.

Review Questions

1. In object-oriented programming terminology, an unexpected or error condition is a(n) _____ .

   a. anomaly

   b. aberration

   c. deviation

   d. exception

2. All Java Exceptions are _____ .

   a. Errors

   b. RuntimeExceptions

   c. Throwables

   d. Omissions

3. Which of the following statements is true?

   a. Exceptions are more serious than Errors.

   b. Errors are more serious than Exceptions.

   c. Errors and Exceptions are equally serious.

   d. Exceptions and Errors are the same thing.

4. The method that ends the current application and returns control to the operating system is _____ .

   a. System.end()

   b. System.done()

   c. System.exit()

   d. System.abort()

5. In object-oriented terminology, you _____ a procedure that might not complete correctly.

   a. try

   b. catch

   c. handle

   d. encapsulate

6. A method that detects an error condition or `Exception` —————— an `Exception`.

   a. throws   c. handles

   b. catches   d. encapsulates

7. A `try` block includes all of the following elements except —————— .

   a. the keyword `try`

   b. the keyword `catch`

   c. curly braces

   d. statements that might cause `Exceptions`

8. The segment of code that handles or takes appropriate action following an exception is a —————— block.

   a. `try`   c. `throws`

   b. `catch`   d. `handles`

9. You —————— within a `try` block.

   a. must place only a single statement

   b. can place any number of statements

   c. must place at least two statements

   d. must place a `catch` block

10. If you include three statements in a `try` block and follow the block with three `catch` blocks, and the second statement in the `try` block throws an `Exception`, then —————— .

   a. the first `catch` block executes

   b. the first two `catch` blocks execute

   c. only the second `catch` block executes

   d. the first matching `catch` block executes

11. When a `try` block does not generate an `Exception` and you have included multiple `catch` blocks, —————— .

   a. they all execute   c. only the first matching one executes

   b. only the first one executes   d. no `catch` blocks execute

12. The `catch` block that begins `catch(Exception e)` can catch `Exceptions` of type —————— .

   a. `IOException`   c. both of the above

   b. `ArithmeticException`   d. none of the above

13. The code within a `finally` block executes when the `try` block _____.

     a.   identifies one or more `Exceptions`

     b.   does not identify any `Exceptions`

     c.   either a or b

     d.   neither a nor b

14. An advantage to using a `try...catch` block is that exceptional events are _____.

     a.   eliminated   c.   integrated with regular events

     b.   reduced   d.   isolated from regular events

15. Which methods can throw an `Exception`?

     a.   methods with a `throws` clause

     b.   methods with a `catch` block

     c.   methods with both a `throws` clause and a `catch` block

     d.   any method

16. A method can _____.

     a.   check for errors but not handle them

     b.   handle errors but not check for them

     c.   either of the above

     d.   neither of the above

17. Which of the following is least important to know if you want to be able to use a method to its full potential?

     a.   the method's return type

     b.   the type of arguments the method requires

     c.   the number of statements within the method

     d.   the type of `Exceptions` the method throws

18. The memory location where the computer stores the list of method locations to which the system must return is known as the _____.

     a.   registry   c.   chronicle

     b.   call stack   d.   archive

19. You can get a list of the methods through which an `Exception` has traveled by using the _____ method.

     a.   `getMessage()`   c.   `getPath()`

     b.   `callStack()`   d.   `printStackTrace()`

20. A(n) _____ is a statement used in testing programs that should be true; if it is not true, an Exception is thrown.

a. assertion

c. verification

b. throwable

d. declaration

Exercises

 Programming Exercises

1. Write an application named BadSubscriptCaught in which you declare an array of 10 first names. Write a try block in which you prompt the user for an integer and display the name in the requested position. Create a catch block that catches the potential ArrayIndexOutOfBoundsException thrown when the user enters a number that is out of range. The catch block should also display an error message. Save the file as **BadSubscriptCaught.java**.

2. The Double.parseDouble() method requires a String argument, but it fails if the String cannot be converted to a floating-point number. Write an application in which you try accepting a double input from a user and catch a NumberFormatException if one is thrown. The catch block forces the number to 0 and displays an appropriate error message. Following the catch block, display the number. Save the file as **TryToParseDouble.java**.

3. In Chapter 2, you created an application named QuartsToGallonsInteractive that accepts a number of quarts from a user and converts the value to gallons. Now, add exception-handling capabilities to this program and continuously reprompt the user while any nonnumeric value is entered. Save the file as **QuartsToGallonsWithExceptionHandling.java**.

4. In Chapter 8, you wrote an application named DistanceFromAverage that allows a user to enter up to 20 double values and then displays each entered value and its distance from the average. Now, modify that program to first prompt the user to enter a number that represents the array size. Java generates a NegativeArraySizeException if you attempt to create an array with a negative size, and it creates a NumberFormatException if you attempt to create an array using a nonnumeric value for the size. Handle these exceptions using a catch block that displays an appropriate message. If the array is created successfully, use exception-handling techniques to ensure that each entered array value is a double before the program calculates each element's distance from the average. Save the file as **DistanceFromAverageWithExceptionHandling.java**.

5. Write an application that throws and catches an ArithmeticException when you attempt to take the square root of a negative value. Prompt the user for an input value and try the Math.sqrt() method on it. The application either displays the square root or catches the thrown Exception and displays an appropriate message. Save the file as **SqrtException.java**.

6. Create an `ApartmentException` class whose constructor receives a `String` that holds a street address, an apartment number, a number of bedrooms, and a rent value for an apartment. Save the file as **ApartmentException.java**. Create an `Apartment` class with those fields. The `Apartment` constructor requires values for each field. Upon construction, throw an `ApartmentException` if the apartment number does not consist of three digits, if the number of bedrooms is less than 1 or more than 4, or if the rent is less than $500 or over $2,500. Save the class as **Apartment.java**. Write an application that establishes an array of at least six `Apartment` objects with valid and invalid values. Display an appropriate message when an `Apartment` object is created successfully and when one is not. Save the file as **ThrowApartmentException.java**.

7. Create a `UsedCarException` class that extends `Exception`; its constructor receives a value for a vehicle identification number (VIN) that is passed to the parent constructor so it can be used in a `getMessage()` call. Save the class as **UsedCarException.java**. Create a `UsedCar` class with fields for VIN, make, year, mileage, and price. The `UsedCar` constructor throws a `UsedCarException` when the VIN is not four digits; when the make is not *Ford, Honda, Toyota, Chrysler*, or *Other*; when the year is not between 1990 and 2014 inclusive; or either the mileage or price is negative. Save the class as **UsedCar.java**. Write an application that establishes an array of at least seven `UsedCar` objects and handles any `Exceptions`. Display a list of only the `UsedCar` objects that were constructed successfully. Save the file as **ThrowUsedCarExceptions.java**.

8. Write an application that displays a series of at least five student ID numbers (that you have stored in an array) and asks the user to enter a numeric test score for the student. Create a `ScoreException` class, and throw a `ScoreException` for the class if the user does not enter a valid score (less than or equal to 100). Catch the `ScoreException`, and then display an appropriate message. In addition, store a *0* for the student's score. At the end of the application, display all the student IDs and scores. Save the files as **ScoreException.java** and **TestScore.java**.

9. Write an application that displays a series of at least 10 student ID numbers (that you have stored in an array) and asks the user to enter a test letter grade for the student. Create an `Exception` class named `GradeException` that contains a `static public` array of valid grade letters ('A', 'B', 'C', 'D', 'F', and 'I') that you can use to determine whether a grade entered from the application is valid. In your application, throw a `GradeException` if the user does not enter a valid letter grade. Catch the `GradeException`, and then display an appropriate message. In addition, store an 'I' (for Incomplete) for any student for whom an exception is caught. At the end of the application, display all the student IDs and grades. Save the files as **GradeException.java** and **TestGrade.java**.

10. Create a `DataEntryException` class whose `getMessage()` method returns information about invalid integer data. Write a program named `GetIDAndAge` that continually prompts the user for an ID number and an age until a terminal *0* is entered for both. Throw a `DataEntryException` if the ID is not in the range of valid ID numbers (0 through 999), or if the age is not in the range of valid

ages (0 through 119). Catch any DataEntryException or InputMismatchException that is thrown, and display an appropriate message. Save the files as **DataEntryException.java** and **GetIDAndAge.java**.

11. Create an application that accepts employee data interactively. Users might make any of the following errors as they enter data:

- The employee number is not numeric, less than 1000, or more than 9999.

- The hourly pay rate is not numeric, less than $9.00, or more than $25.00.

Create a class that stores an array of six usable error messages that describe the preceding mistakes; save the file as **EmployeeMessages.java**. Create an EmployeeException class; each object of this class will store one of the messages. Save the file as **EmployeeException.java**. Create an application that prompts the user for employee data, and display the appropriate message when an error occurs. If no error occurs, display the message "Valid employee data". Save the program as **EmployeeDataEntry.java**.

12. A company accepts user orders for its products interactively. Users might make the following errors as they enter data:

- The item number ordered is not numeric, too low (less than 0), or too high (more than 9999).

- The quantity is not numeric, too low (less than 1), or too high (more than 12).

- The item number is not a currently valid item.

Although the company might expand in the future, its current inventory consists of the items listed in Table 12-1.

Item Number	Price ($)
111	0.89
222	1.47
333	2.43
444	5.99

Table 12-1   Item numbers and prices

Create a class that stores an array of usable error messages; save the file as **OrderMessages.java**. Create an OrderException class that stores one of the messages; save the file as **OrderException.java**. Create an application that contains prompts for an item number and quantity. Allow for the possibility of nonnumeric entries as well as out-of-range entries and entries that do not match any of the currently available item numbers. The program should display an appropriate message if an error has occurred. If no errors exist in the entered data, compute the user's total amount due (quantity times price each) and display it. Save the program as **PlaceAnOrder.java**.

13. In a "You Do It" section of this chapter, you created a `CalculatorDemo` program that asked the user to solve an arithmetic problem and provided the system calculator for assistance. Now modify that program to include the following improvements:

- Both numbers in the arithmetic problem should be random integers between 1 and 5,000.

- The program should ask the user to solve five problems.

- The program should handle any noninteger data entry by displaying an appropriate message and continuing with the next problem.

Save the file as **CalculatorDemo2.java**.

Debugging Exercises

1. Each of the following files in the Chapter12 folder of your downloadable student files has syntax and/or logic errors. In each case, determine the problem and fix the program. After you correct the errors, save each file using the same filename preceded with *Fix*. For example, DebugTwelve1.java will become **FixDebugTwelve1.java**. You will also use a file named DebugEmployeeIDException.java with the DebugTwelve4.java file.

   a. DebugTwelve1.java   c. DebugTwelve3.java

   b. DebugTwelve2.java   d. DebugTwelve4.java

Game Zone

1. In Chapter 1, you created a class called `RandomGuess`. In this game, the application generates a random number for a player to guess. In Chapter 5, you improved the application to display a message indicating whether the player's guess was correct, too high, or too low. In Chapter 6, you further improved the game by adding a loop that continually prompts the user to enter the correct value, if necessary. As written, the game should work as long as the player enters numeric guesses. However, if the player enters a letter or other nonnumeric character, the game throws an exception. Discover the type of `Exception` thrown, then improve the game by handling the exception so that the user is informed of the error and allowed to attempt to enter the correct data again. Save the file as **RandomGuess4.java**.

2. In Chapter 8, you created a `Quiz` class that contains an array of 10 multiple-choice questions to which the user was required to respond with an *A*, *B*, or *C*. At the time, you knew how to handle the user's response if an invalid character was entered. Rerun the program now to determine whether an exception is thrown if the user enters nothing—that is, the user just presses the Enter key without making an entry. If so, improve the program by catching the exception, displaying an appropriate error message, and presenting the same question to the user again. Save the file as **QuizWithExceptionsCaught.java**.

Case Problems

1. In Chapter 11, you created an interactive StaffDinnerEvent class that obtains all the data for a dinner event for Carly's Catering, including details about the staff members required to work at the event. Now, modify the class so that it becomes immune to user data entry errors by handling exceptions for each numeric entry. Each time the program requires numeric data—for example, for the number of guests, selected menu options, and staff members' salaries—continuously prompt the user until the data entered is the correct type. Save the revised program as **StaffDinnerEvent.java**.

2. In Chapter 11, you created an interactive RentalDemo class that obtains all the data for four rentals from Sammy's Seashore Rentals, including details about the contract number, length of the rental, and equipment type. Now, modify the class so that it becomes immune to user data entry errors by handling exceptions for each numeric entry. Each time the program requires numeric data—for example, for the rental period—continuously prompt the user until the data entered is the correct type. Save the revised program as **RentalDemo.java**.

File Input and Output

In this chapter, you will:

◎ Learn about computer files

◎ Use the Path and Files classes

◎ Learn about file organization, streams, and buffers

◎ Use Java's IO classes to write to and read from a file

◎ Create and use sequential data files

◎ Learn about random access files

◎ Write records to a random access data file

◎ Read records from a random access data file

Understanding Computer Files

Data items can be stored on two broad types of storage devices in a computer system:

- **Volatile storage** is temporary; values that are volatile, such as those stored in variables, are lost when a computer loses power. **Random access memory (RAM)** is the temporary storage within a computer. When you write a Java program that stores a value in a variable, you are using RAM. Most computer professionals simply call nonvolatile storage *memory*.

- **Nonvolatile storage** is permanent storage; it is not lost when a computer loses power. When you write a Java program and save it to a disk, you are using permanent storage.

> When discussing computer storage, *temporary* and *permanent* refer to volatility, not length of time. For example, a *temporary* variable might exist for several hours in a large program or one that the user forgets to close, but a *permanent* piece of data might be saved and then deleted within a few seconds. In recent years, the distinction between memory and storage has blurred because many systems automatically save data to a nonvolatile device and retrieve it after a power interruption. Because you can erase data from files, some programmers prefer the term "persistent storage" to permanent storage. In other words, you can remove data from a file stored on a device such as a disk drive, so it is not technically permanent. However, the data remains in the file even when the computer loses power; so, unlike with RAM, the data persists, or perseveres.

A **computer file** is a collection of data stored on a nonvolatile device. Files exist on **permanent storage devices**, such as hard disks, Zip disks, USB drives, reels or cassettes of magnetic tape, and compact discs.

You can categorize files by the way they store data:

- **Text files** contain data that can be read in a text editor because the data has been encoded using a scheme such as ASCII or Unicode. (See Appendix B for more information on Unicode.) Some text files are **data files** that contain facts and figures, such as a payroll file that contains employee numbers, names, and salaries; some files are **program files** or **application files** that store software instructions. You have created many such files throughout this book.

- **Binary files** contain data that has not been encoded as text. Their contents are in binary format, which means that you cannot understand them by viewing them in a text editor. Examples include images, music, and the compiled program files with a .class extension that you have created using this book.

Although their contents vary, files have many common characteristics—each file has a size that specifies the space it occupies on a section of disk or other storage device, and each file has a name and a specific time of creation.

When you store a permanent file, you can place it in the main or **root directory** of your storage device. If you compare computer storage to using a file cabinet drawer, saving to the root directory is equivalent to tossing a loose document into the drawer. However, for better organization, most office clerks place documents in folders, and most computer users organize their files into **folders** or **directories**. Users also can create folders within folders to form a hierarchy. A complete list of the disk drive plus the hierarchy of directories in which a file resides is its **path**. For example, the following is the complete path for a Windows file named Data.txt, which is saved on the C drive in a folder named Chapter.13 within a folder named Java:

```
C:\Java\Chapter.13\Data.txt
```

In the Windows operating system, the backslash (\ ) is the **path delimiter**—the character used to separate path components. In the Solaris (UNIX) operating system, a slash (/) is used as the delimiter.

When you work with stored files in an application, you typically perform the following tasks:

- Determining whether and where a path or file exists
- Opening a file
- Writing to a file
- Reading from a file
- Closing a file
- Deleting a file

Java provides built-in classes that contain methods to help you with these tasks.

TWO TRUTHS & A LIE

Understanding Computer Files

1. An advantage of modern computer systems is that both internal computer memory and disk storage are nonvolatile.

2. Data files contain facts and figures; program files store software instructions that might use data files.

3. A complete list of the disk drive plus the hierarchy of directories in which a file resides is the file's path.

The false statement is #1. Internal computer memory (RAM) is volatile; disk storage is nonvolatile.

Using the `Path` and `Files` Classes

You can use Java's `Path` and `Files` classes to work with stored files.

- The `Path` class is used to create objects that contain information about files and directories, such as their locations, sizes, creation dates, and whether they even exist.

- The `Files` class is used to perform operations on files and directories, such as deleting them, determining their attributes, and creating input and output streams.

You can include the following statement in a Java program to use both the `Path` and `Files` classes:

```
import java.nio.file.*;
```

The *nio* in java.nio stands for *new input/output* because its classes are "new" in that they were not developed until Java 7.

Creating a Path

To create a `Path`, you first determine the default file system on the host computer by using a statement such as the following:

```
FileSystem fs = FileSystems.getDefault();
```

This statement creates a `FileSystem` object using the `getDefault()` method in the `FileSystems` class. The statement uses two different classes. The `FileSystem` class, without an ending *s*, is used to instantiate the object. `FileSystems`, with an ending *s*, is a class that contains **factory methods**, which assist in object creation.

After you create a `FileSystem` object, you can define a `Path` using the `getPath()` method with it:

```
Path path = fs.getPath("C:\\Java\\Chapter.13\\Data.txt");
```

Recall that the backslash is used as part of an escape sequence in Java. (For example, `'\n'` represents a newline character.) So, to enter a backslash as a path delimiter within a string, you must type two backslashes to indicate a single backslash. An alternative is to use the `FileSystem` method `getSeparator()`. This method returns the correct separator for the current operating system. For example, you can create a `Path` that is identical to the previous one using a statement such as the following:

```
Path filePath = fs.getPath("C:" + fs.getSeparator() + "Java" +
    fs.getSeparator() + "Chapter.13" + fs.getSeparator()  +
    "Data.txt");
```

Another way to create a `Path` is to use the `Paths` class (notice the name ends with *s*). The `Paths` class is a helper class that eliminates the need to create a `FileSystem` object. The `Paths` class `get()` method calls the `getPath()` method of the default file system without requiring you to instantiate a `FileSystem` object. You can create a `Path` object by using the following statement:

```
Path filePath = Paths.get("C:\\Java\\Chapter.13\\SampleFile.txt");
```

After the `Path` is created, you use its identifier (in this case, `filePath`) to refer to the file and perform operations on it. C:\Java\Chapter.13\SampleFile.txt is the full name of a stored file when the operating system refers to it, but the path is known as `filePath` within the application. The idea of a file having one name when referenced by the operating system and a different name within an application is similar to the way a student known as "Arthur" in school might be "Junior" at home. When an application declares a path and you want to use the application with a different file, you would change only the `String` passed to the instantiating method.

Every `Path` is either absolute or relative.

- An **absolute path** is a complete path; it does not need any other information to locate a file on a system. A full path such as C:\Java\Chapter.13\SampleFile.txt is an absolute path.

- A **relative path** depends on other path information. A simple path such as SampleFile.txt is relative. When you work with a path that contains only a filename, the file is assumed to be in the same folder as the program using it. Similarly, when you refer to a relative path such as Chapter.13\SampleFile.txt (without the drive letter or the top-level Java folder), the Chapter.13 folder is assumed to be a subfolder of the current directory, and SampleFile.txt is assumed to be within the folder.

669

 For Microsoft Windows platforms, the prefix of an absolute pathname that contains a disk-drive specifier consists of the drive letter followed by a colon. For UNIX platforms, the prefix of an absolute pathname is always a forward slash.

Retrieving Information About a Path

Table 13-1 summarizes several useful `Path` methods. As you have learned with other classes, the `toString()` method is overridden from the `Object` class; it returns a `String` representation of the `Path`. Basically, this is the list of path elements separated by copies of the default separator for the operating system. The `getFileName()` method returns the last element in a list of pathnames; frequently this is a filename, but it might be a folder name.

Method	Description
`String toString()`	Returns the `String` representation of the `Path`, eliminating double backslashes
`Path getFileName()`	Returns the file or directory denoted by this `Path`; this is the last item in the sequence of name elements
`int getNameCount()`	Returns the number of name elements in the `Path`
`Path getName(int)`	Returns the name in the position of the `Path` specified by the integer parameter

Table 13-1 Selected `Path` class methods

A `Path`'s elements are accessed using an index. The top-level element in the directory structure is located at index 0; the lowest element in the structure is accessed by the `getName()` method, and has an index that is one less than the number of items on the list. You can use the `getNameCount()` method to retrieve the number of names in the list and the `getName(int)` method to retrieve the name in the position specified by the argument.

Figure 13-1 shows a demonstration program that creates a `Path` and uses some of the methods in Table 13-1. Figure 13-2 shows the output when the file named in the `Path` declaration exists.

```java
import java.nio.file.*;
public class PathDemo
{
    public static void main(String[] args)
    {
        Path filePath =
            Paths.get("C:\\Java\\Chapter.13\\Data.txt");
        int count = filePath.getNameCount();
        System.out.println("Path is " + filePath.toString());
        System.out.println("File name is " + filePath.getFileName());
        System.out.println("There are " + count +
            " elements in the file path");
        for(int x = 0; x < count; ++x)
          System.out.println("Element " + x + " is " +
              filePath.getName(x));
    }
}
```

Figure 13-1   The `PathDemo` class

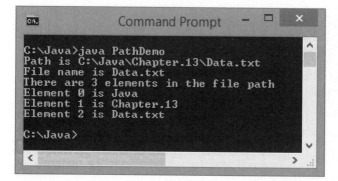

Figure 13-2   Output of the `PathDemo` application

Converting a Relative Path to an Absolute One

The `toAbsolutePath()` method converts a relative path to an absolute path. For example, Figure 13-3 shows a program that asks a user for a filename and converts it to an absolute path, if necessary.

```
import java.util.Scanner;
import java.nio.file.*;
public class PathDemo2
{
    public static void main(String[] args)
    {
        String name;
        Scanner keyboard = new Scanner(System.in);
        System.out.print("Enter a file name >> ");
        name = keyboard.nextLine();
        Path inputPath = Paths.get(name);
        Path fullPath = inputPath.toAbsolutePath();
        System.out.println("Full path is " + fullPath.toString());
    }
}
```

Figure 13-3   The PathDemo2 class

When the PathDemo2 program executes and the filename that is input represents an absolute Path, the program does not modify the input. However, if the input represents a relative Path, this program then creates an absolute path by assigning the file to the current directory. Figure 13-4 shows a typical program execution.

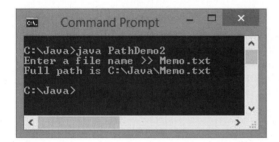

Command Prompt

```
C:\Java>java PathDemo2
Enter a file name >> Memo.txt
Full path is C:\Java\Memo.txt

C:\Java>
```

Figure 13-4   Output of the PathDemo2 program

Checking File Accessibility

To verify that a file exists and that the program can access it as needed, you can use the checkAccess() method. The following import statement allows you to access constants that can be used as arguments to the method:

```
import static java.nio.file.AccessMode.*;
```

Assuming that you have declared a Path named filePath, the syntax you use with checkAccess() is as follows:

```
filePath.getFileSystem().provider().checkAccess();
```

You can use any of the following as arguments to the checkAccess() method:

- No argument—Checks that the file exists
- READ—Checks that the file exists and that the program has permission to read the file
- WRITE—Checks that the file exists and that the program has permission to write to the file
- EXECUTE—Checks that the file exists and that the program has permission to execute the file

Java's **static import feature** takes effect when you place the keyword static between import and the name of the package being imported. This feature allows you to use static constants without their class name. For example, if you remove static from the import statement for java.nio.file.AccessMode, you must refer to the READ constant by its full name as AccessMode.READ; when you use static, you can refer to it just as READ.

As an alternative to using checkAccess() with no argument to determine whether a file exists, you can substitute the Files.exists() method and pass it a Path argument.

You can use multiple arguments to the checkAccess() method, separated by commas. If the file named in the method call cannot be accessed, an IOException is thrown. (Notice in Figure 13-5 that the java.io.IOException package must be imported.) Figure 13-5 shows an application that declares a Path and checks whether a file named there can both be read and executed. Figure 13-6 shows the output when the PathDemo.class file is available in the specified location.

```java
import java.nio.file.*;
import static java.nio.file.AccessMode.*;
import java.io.IOException;
public class PathDemo3
{
    public static void main(String[] args)
    {
        Path filePath =
            Paths.get("C:\\Java\\Chapter.13\\PathDemo.class");
        System.out.println("Path is " + filePath.toString());
        try
        {
            filePath.getFileSystem().provider().checkAccess
                (filePath, READ, EXECUTE);
            System.out.println("File can be read and executed");
        }
        catch(IOException e)
        {
            System.out.println
                ("File cannot be used for this application");
        }
    }
}
```

Figure 13-5   The PathDemo3 class

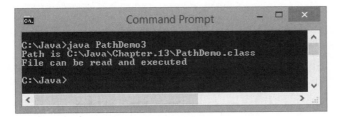

Figure 13-6 Output of the PathDemo3 application

 A program might find a file usable, but then the file might become unusable before it is actually used in a later statement. This type of program bug is called a **TOCTTOU bug** (pronounced *tock too*)—it happens when changes occur from Time Of Check To Time Of Use.

Deleting a Path

The Files class delete() method accepts a Path parameter and deletes the last element (file or directory) in a path or throws an exception if the deletion fails. For example:

- If you try to delete a file that does not exist, a NoSuchFileException is thrown.

- A directory cannot be deleted unless it is empty. If you attempt to delete a directory that contains files, a DirectoryNotEmptyException is thrown.

- If you try to delete a file but you don't have permission, a SecurityException is thrown.

- Other input/output errors cause an IOException.

Figure 13-7 shows a program that displays an appropriate message in each of the preceding scenarios after attempting to delete a file.

```java
import java.nio.file.*;
import java.io.IOException;
public class PathDemo4
{
    public static void main(String[] args)
    {
        Path filePath =
            Paths.get("C:\\Java\\Chapter.13\\Data.txt");
        try
        {
            Files.delete(filePath);
            System.out.println("File or directory is deleted");
        }
```

Figure 13-7 The PathDemo4 class *(continues)*

(continued)

```
        catch (NoSuchFileException e)
        {
            System.out.println("No such file or directory");
        }
        catch (DirectoryNotEmptyException e)
        {
            System.out.println("Directory is not empty");
        }
        catch (SecurityException e)
        {
            System.out.println("No permission to delete");
        }
        catch (IOException e)
        {
            System.out.println("IO exception");
        }
    }
}
```

Figure 13-7   The `PathDemo4` class

The `Files` class `deleteIfExists()` method also can be used to delete a file, but if the file does not exist, no exception is thrown.

Determining File Attributes

You can use the `readAttributes()` method of the `Files` class to retrieve useful information about a file. The method takes two arguments—a `Path` object and `BasicFileAttributes.class`—and returns an instance of the `BasicFileAttributes` class. You might create an instance with a statement such as the following:

```
BasicFileAttributes attr =
    Files.readAttributes(filePath, BasicFileAttributes.class);
```

After you have created a `BasicFileAttributes` object, you can use a number of methods for retrieving information about a file. For example, the `size()` method returns the size of a file in bytes. Methods such as `creationTime()` and `lastModifiedTime()` return important file times. Figure 13-8 contains a program that uses these methods.

```java
import java.nio.file.*;
import java.nio.file.attribute.*;
import java.io.IOException;
public class PathDemo5
{
   public static void main(String[] args)
   {
      Path filePath =
         Paths.get("C:\\Java\\Chapter.13\\Data.txt");
      try
      {
         BasicFileAttributes attr =
            Files.readAttributes(filePath, BasicFileAttributes.class);
         System.out.println("Creation time " + attr.creationTime());
         System.out.println("Last modified time " +
            attr.lastModifiedTime());
         System.out.println("Size " + attr.size());
      }
      catch(IOException e)
      {
         System.out.println("IO Exception");
      }
   }
}
```

Figure 13-8   The PathDemo5 class

The time methods in the PathDemo5 program each return a FileTime object that is converted to a String in the println() method calls. FileTime objects are represented in the following format:

yyyy-mm-ddThh:mm:ss.

In a FileTime object, the four-digit year is followed by the two-digit month and two-digit day. Following a *T* for *Time*, the hour, minute, and seconds (including fractions of a second) are separated by colons. You can see from the output in Figure 13-9 that the file was created in October 2012 and last modified in May 2014.

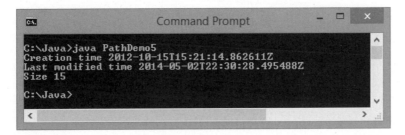

Figure 13-9   Output of the PathDemo5 program

Frequently, you don't care about a file's exact `FileTime` value, but you are interested in comparing two files. You can use the `compareTo()` method to determine the time relationships between files. For example, Figure 13-10 shows how you might compare the creation times of two files. As shown in the shaded statement, the `compareTo()` method returns a value of less than 0 if the first `FileTime` comes before the argument's `FileTime`. The method returns a value of greater than 0 if the first `FileTime` is later than the argument's, and it returns 0 if the `FileTime` values are the same.

```java
import java.nio.file.*;
import java.nio.file.attribute.*;
import java.io.IOException;
public class PathDemo6
{
    public static void main(String[] args)
    {
        Path file1 =
            Paths.get("C:\\Java\\Chapter.13\\Data.txt");
        Path file2 =
            Paths.get("C:\\Java\\Chapter.13\\Data2.txt");
        try
        {
            BasicFileAttributes attr1 =
                Files.readAttributes(file1, BasicFileAttributes.class);
            BasicFileAttributes attr2 =
                Files.readAttributes(file2, BasicFileAttributes.class);
            FileTime time1 = attr1.creationTime();
            FileTime time2 = attr2.creationTime();
            System.out.println("file1's creation time is: " + time1);
            System.out.println("file2's creation time is: " + time2);
            if(time1.compareTo(time2) < 0)
                System.out.println("file1 was created before file2");
            else
                if(time1.compareTo(time2) > 0)
                    System.out.println("file1 was created after file2");
                else
                    System.out.println
                        ("file1 and file2 were created at the same time");
        }
        catch(IOException e)
        {
            System.out.println("IO Exception");
        }
    }
}
```

Figure 13-10   The PathDemo6 class

Figure 13-11 shows the output of the application in Figure 13-10. The file named file1 was created in October 2012, and file2 was created in April 2015, so the program correctly determines that file1 was created first.

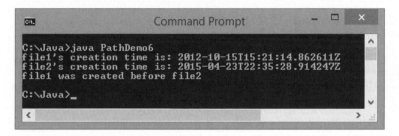

```
C:\Java>java PathDemo6
file1's creation time is: 2012-10-15T15:21:14.862611Z
file2's creation time is: 2015-04-23T22:35:28.914247Z
file1 was created before file2

C:\Java>_
```

Figure 13-11　Output of the PathDemo6 program

Besides BasicFileAttributes, Java supports specialized classes for DOS file attributes used on DOS systems and POSIX file attributes used on systems such as UNIX. For example, DOS files might be *hidden* or *read only* and UNIX files might have a group owner. For more details on specialized file attributes, visit the Java Web site.

Watch the video *Paths and Attributes*.

TWO TRUTHS & A LIE

Using the Path and Files Classes

1. Java's Path class is used to create objects that contain information to specify the location of files or directories.

2. A relative path is a complete path; it does not need any other information to locate a file on a system.

3. You can use the readAttributes() method of the Files class to retrieve information about a file, such as its size and when it was created.

The false statement is #2. A relative path depends on other path information. An absolute path is a complete path; it does not need any other information to locate a file on a system.

File Organization, Streams, and Buffers

Most businesses generate and use large quantities of data every day. You can store data in variables within a program, but such storage is temporary. When the application ends, the variables no longer exist and the data values are lost. Variables are stored in the computer's main or primary memory (RAM). When you need to retain data for any significant amount of time, you must save the data on a permanent, secondary storage device, such as a disk.

Businesses organize data in a hierarchy, as shown in Figure 13-12. The smallest useful piece of data to most users is the character. A **character** can be any letter, number, or other special symbol (such as a punctuation mark) that comprises data. Characters are made up of bits (the zeros and ones that represent computer circuitry), but people who use data typically do not care whether the internal representation for an *A* is 01000001 or 10111110. Rather, they are concerned with the meaning of *A*—for example, it might represent a grade in a course, a person's initial, or a company code. In computer terminology, a character can be any group of bits, and it does not necessarily represent a letter or number; for example, some "characters" produce a sound or control the display. Also, characters are not necessarily created with a single keystroke; for example, escape sequences are used to create the ' \n' character, which starts a new line, and ' \\', which represents a single backslash. Sometimes, you can think of a character as a unit of information instead of data with a particular appearance. For example, the mathematical character pi (π) and the Greek letter pi look the same, but have two different Unicode values.

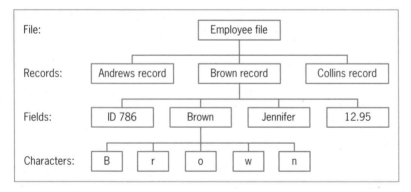

Figure 13-12   Data hierarchy

When businesses use data, they group characters into fields. A **field** is a group of characters that has some meaning. For example, the characters *T, o,* and *m* might represent your first name. Other data fields might represent items such as last name, Social Security number, zip code, and salary.

Fields are grouped together to form records. A **record** is a collection of fields that contain data about an entity. For example, a person's first and last names, Social Security number, zip code, and salary represent that person's record. When programming in Java, you have created many classes, such as an `Employee` class or a `Student` class. You can think of the data typically stored in each of these classes as a record. These classes contain individual variables that represent data fields. A business's data records usually represent a person, item, sales transaction, or some other concrete object or event.

Records are grouped to create files. Data files consist of related records, such as a company's personnel file that contains one record for each employee. Some files have only a few records; perhaps your professor maintains a file for your class with 25 records—one record for each student. Other files contain thousands or even millions of records. For example, an insurance company maintains a file of policyholders, and a mail-order catalog company maintains a file of available items.

A data file can be used as a **sequential access file** when each record is accessed one after another in the order in which it was stored. Most frequently, each record is stored in order based on the value in some field; for example, employees might be stored in Social Security number order, or inventory items might be stored in item number order. When records are not used in sequence, the file is used as a random access file. You learn more about random access files later in this chapter.

When records are stored in a data file, their fields can be organized one to a line, or a character can be used to separate them. A file of **comma-separated values (CSV)** is one in which each value in a record is separated from the next by a comma; CSV is a widely used format for files used in all sorts of applications, including databases and spreadsheets. Later in this chapter, you will see examples of CSV files.

Before an application can use a data file, it must open the file. A Java application **opens a file** by creating an object and associating a stream of bytes with it. Similarly, when you finish using a file, the program should **close the file**—that is, make it no longer available to your application. If you fail to close an input file—a file from which you are reading data—there usually are no serious consequences; the data still exists in the file. However, if you fail to close an output file—a file to which you are writing data—the data might become inaccessible. You should always close every file you open, and usually you should close the file as soon as you no longer need it. When you leave a file open for no reason, you use computer resources, and your computer's performance suffers. Also, particularly within a network, another program might be waiting to use the file.

Whereas people view a file as a series of records, with each record containing data fields, Java does not automatically attribute such meaning to a file's contents. Instead, Java simply views a file as a series of bytes. When you perform an input operation in an application, you can picture bytes flowing into your program from an input device through a **stream**, which functions as a pipeline or channel. When you perform output, some bytes flow out of your application through another stream to an output device, as shown in Figure 13-13. A stream is an object, and like all objects, streams have data and methods. The methods allow you to perform actions such as opening, closing, reading, and writing.

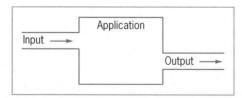

Figure 13-13 File streams

680

Most streams flow in only one direction; each stream is either an input or output stream. (Random access files use streams that flow in two directions. You will use a random access file later in this chapter.) You might open several streams at once within an application. For example, an application that reads a data disk and separates valid records from invalid ones might require three streams. The data arrives via an input stream; one output stream writes some records to a file of valid records, and another output stream writes other records to a file of invalid records.

Input and output operations are usually the slowest in any computerized system because of limitations imposed by the hardware. For that reason, professional programs often employ buffers. In Chapter 7, you learned that the `StringBuilder` object sets aside a memory block called a *buffer*. The same term describes a memory location where bytes are held after they are logically output but before they are sent to the output device. Using a buffer to accumulate input or output before issuing the actual IO command improves program performance. When you use an output buffer, you sometimes flush it before closing it. **Flushing** clears any bytes that have been sent to a buffer for output but have not yet been output to a hardware device.

 Watch the video *File Organization, Streams, and Buffers.*

TWO TRUTHS & A LIE

File Organization, Streams, and Buffers

1. A field is a group of characters that has some meaning; a record is a collection of fields.

2. A data file is used as a sequential access file when the first field for each record is stored first in a file, the second field for each record is stored next, and so on.

3. Java views files as a series of bytes that flow into and out of your applications through a stream.

The false statement is #2. A data file is used as a sequential access file when each record is stored in order based on the value in some field.

Using Java's IO Classes

Figure 13-14 shows a partial hierarchical relationship of some of the classes Java uses for input and output (IO) operations; it shows that `InputStream`, `OutputStream`, and `Reader` are subclasses of the `Object` class. All three of these classes are abstract. As you learned in Chapter 11, abstract classes contain methods that must be overridden in their child classes. The figure also shows the major IO child classes that you will study in this chapter. The capabilities of these classes are summarized in Table 13-2.

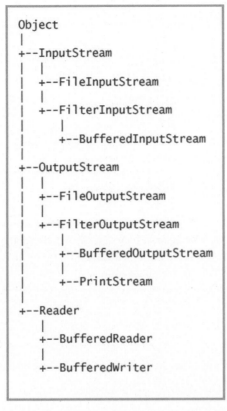

```
Object
|
+--InputStream
|   |
|   +--FileInputStream
|   |
|   +--FilterInputStream
|       |
|       +--BufferedInputStream
|
+--OutputStream
|   |
|   +--FileOutputStream
|   |
|   +--FilterOutputStream
|       |
|       +--BufferedOutputStream
|       |
|       +--PrintStream
|
+--Reader
    |
    +--BufferedReader
    |
    +--BufferedWriter
```

Figure 13-14 Relationship of selected IO classes

Class	Description
InputStream	Abstract class that contains methods for performing input
FileInputStream	Child of InputStream that provides the capability to read from disk files
BufferedInputStream	Child of FilterInputStream, which is a child of InputStream; BufferedInputStream handles input from a system's standard (or default) input device, usually the keyboard
OutputStream	Abstract class that contains methods for performing output
FileOutputStream	Child of OutputStream that allows you to write to disk files
BufferedOutputStream	Child of FilterOutputStream, which is a child of OutputStream; BufferedOutputStream handles input from a system's standard (or default) output device, usually the monitor
PrintStream	Child of FilterOutputStream, which is a child of OutputStream; System.out is a PrintStream object

Table 13-2   Description of selected classes used for input and output *(continues)*

(continued)

Class	Description
Reader	Abstract class for reading character streams; the only methods that a subclass must implement are read(char[], int, int) and close()
BufferedReader	Reads text from a character-input stream, buffering characters to provide for efficient reading of characters, arrays, and lines
BufferedWriter	Writes text to a character-output stream, buffering characters to provide for the efficient writing of characters, arrays, and lines

Table 13-2   Description of selected classes used for input and output

As its name implies, the OutputStream class can be used to produce output. Table 13-3 shows some of the class's common methods. You can use OutputStream to write all or part of an array of bytes. When you finish using an OutputStream, you usually want to flush and close it.

OutputStream Method	Description
void close()	Closes the output stream and releases any system resources associated with the stream
void flush()	Flushes the output stream; if any bytes are buffered, they will be written
void write(byte[] b)	Writes all the bytes to the output stream from the specified byte array
void write(byte[] b, int off, int len)	Writes bytes to the output stream from the specified byte array starting at offset position off for a length of len characters

Table 13-3   Selected OutputStream methods

Java's System class contains a PrintStream object named System.out; you have used this object extensively in the book, along with its print() and println() methods. Besides System.out, the System class defines a PrintStream object named System.err. The output from System.err and System.out can go to the same device; in fact, System.err and System.out are both directed by default to the command line on the monitor. The difference is that System.err is usually reserved for error messages, and System.out is reserved for valid output. You can direct either System.err or System.out to a new location, such as a disk file or printer. For example, you might want to keep a hard copy (printed) log of the error messages generated by a program, but direct the standard output to a disk file.

Although you usually have no need to do so, you can create your own OutputStream object and assign System.out to it. Figure 13-15 shows how this works. The application declares a String of letter grades allowed in a course. Then, the getBytes() method converts the String to an array of bytes. An OutputStream object is declared, and System.out is assigned to the OutputStream reference in a try block. The write() method accepts the byte array and sends it to the output device, and then the output stream is flushed and closed. Figure 13-16 shows the execution.

```java
import java.io.*;
public class ScreenOut
{
    public static void main(String[] args)
    {
        String s = "ABCDF";
        byte[] data = s.getBytes();
        OutputStream output = null;
        try
        {
            output = System.out;
            output.write(data);
            output.flush();
            output.close();
        }
        catch(Exception e)
        {
            System.out.println("Message: " + e);
        }
    }
}
```

Figure 13-15 The ScreenOut class

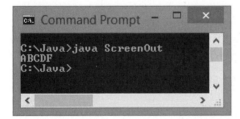

Figure 13-16 Output of the ScreenOut program

Writing to a File

The output in Figure 13-16 is not very impressive. Before you knew about streams, you wrote applications that displayed a string on the monitor by using the automatically created System.out object, so the application in Figure 13-15 might seem to contain a lot of unnecessary work at first. However, other output devices can be assigned to OutputStream references, allowing your applications to save data to them.

Instead of assigning the standard output device to OutputStream, you can assign a file. To accomplish this, you can construct a BufferedOutputStream object and assign it to the OutputStream. If you want to change an application's output device, you don't have to modify the application except to assign a new object to the OutputStream; the rest of the logic remains the same. Java lets you assign a file to a Stream object so that screen output and file output work in exactly the same manner.

You can create a writeable file by using the Files class newOutputStream() method. You pass a Path and a StandardOpenOption argument to this method. The method creates a file if it does not already exist, opens the file for writing, and returns an OutputStream that can be used to write bytes to the file. Table 13-4 shows the StandardOpenOption arguments you can use as the second argument to the newOutputStream() method. If you do not specify any options and the file does not exist, a new file is created. If the file exists, it is truncated. In other words, specifying no option is the same as specifying both CREATE and TRUNCATE_EXISTING.

StandardOpenOption	Description
WRITE	Opens the file for writing
APPEND	Appends new data to the end of the file; use this option with WRITE or CREATE
TRUNCATE_EXISTING	Truncates the existing file to 0 bytes so the file contents are replaced; use this option with the WRITE option
CREATE_NEW	Creates a new file only if it does not exist; throws an exception if the file already exists
CREATE	Opens the file if it exists or creates a new file if it does not
DELETE_ON_CLOSE	Deletes the file when the stream is closed; used most often for temporary files that exist only for the duration of the program

Table 13-4   Selected StandardOpenOption constants

Figure 13-17 shows an application that writes a String of bytes to a file. The only differences from the preceding ScreenOut class are shaded in the figure and summarized here:

- Additional import statements are used.

- The class name is changed.

- A Path is declared for a Grades.txt file.

- Instead of assigning System.out to the OutputStream reference, a BufferedOutputStream object is assigned.

```
import java.nio.file.*;
import java.io.*;
import static java.nio.file.StandardOpenOption.*;

public class FileOut
{
    public static void main(String[] args)
    {
        Path file =
            Paths.get("C:\\Java\\Chapter.13\\Grades.txt");
        String s = "ABCDF";
```

Figure 13-17   The FileOut class *(continues)*

(continued)

```
        byte[] data = s.getBytes();
        OutputStream output = null;
        try
        {
            output = new
                BufferedOutputStream(Files.newOutputStream(file, CREATE));
            output.write(data);
            output.flush();
            output.close();
        }
        catch(Exception e)
        {
            System.out.println("Message: " + e);
        }
    }
}
```

Figure 13-17   The FileOut class

When the FileOut program executes, no output appears on the monitor, but a file is created at the location specified in the Path statement. Figure 13-18 shows the file when it is opened in Notepad.

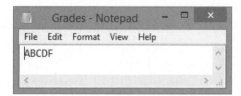

Figure 13-18   Contents of the Grades.txt file created by the FileOut program

Reading from a File

You use an InputStream like you use an OutputStream. If you want, you can create an InputStream, assign System.in to it, and use the class's read() method with the created object to retrieve keyboard input. Usually, however, it is more efficient to use the Scanner class for keyboard input and to use the InputStream class to input data that has been stored in a file.

To open a file for reading, you can use the Files class newInputStream() method. This method accepts a Path parameter and returns a stream that can read bytes from a file. Figure 13-19 shows a ReadFile class that reads from the Grades.txt file created earlier. The Path is declared, an InputStream is declared using the Path, and, in the first shaded statement in the figure, a stream is assigned to the InputStream reference.

686

```
import java.nio.file.*;
import java.io.*;
public class ReadFile
{
    public static void main(String[] args)
    {
        Path file = Paths.get("C:\\Java\\Chapter.13\\Grades.txt");
        InputStream input = null;
        try
        {
            input = Files.newInputStream(file);
            BufferedReader reader = new
                BufferedReader(new InputStreamReader(input));
            String s = null;
            s = reader.readLine();
            System.out.println(s);
            input.close();
        }
        catch (IOException e)
        {
            System.out.println(e);
        }
    }
}
```

Figure 13-19   The ReadFile class

If you needed to read multiple lines from the file in the program in Figure 13-19, you could use a loop such as the following:

```
while(s = reader.readLine() != null)
    System.out.println(s);
```

This loop continuously reads and displays lines from the file until the readLine() method returns null, indicating that no more data is available.

In the second shaded statement in the ReadFile class, a BufferedReader is declared. A BufferedReader reads a line of text from a character-input stream, buffering characters so that reading is more efficient. Figure 13-20 shows the ReadFile program's execution. The readLine() method gets the single line of text from the Grades.txt file, and then the line is displayed.

Figure 13-20   Execution of the ReadFile program

When you use the BufferedReader class, you must import the java.io package into your program. Table 13-5 shows some useful BufferedReader methods.

BufferedReader Method	Description
close()	Closes the stream and any resources associated with it
read()	Reads a single character
read(char[] buffer, int off, int len)	Reads characters into a portion of an array from position off for len characters
readLine()	Reads a line of text
skip(long n)	Skips the specified number of characters

Table 13-5 Selected BufferedReader methods

TWO TRUTHS & A LIE

Using Java's IO Classes

1. Java's InputStream, OutputStream, and Reader classes are used for handling input and output.

2. You can create your own OutputStream object, assign System.out to it, and use it for writing output to the screen, or you can use the Files class newOutputStream() method to create a file and open it for writing.

3. To open a file for reading, you can use the newOutputStream() method to get a stream that can read bytes from a file.

The false statement is #3. To open a file for reading, you can use the newInputStream() method to get a stream that can read bytes from a file.

Creating and Using Sequential Data Files

Frequently, you want to save more than a single String to a file. For example, you might have a data file of personnel records that include an ID number, name, and pay rate for each employee in your organization. Figure 13-21 shows a program that reads employee ID numbers, names, and pay rates from the keyboard and sends them to a comma-separated file.

```java
import java.nio.file.*;
import java.io.*;
import static java.nio.file.StandardOpenOption.*;
import java.util.Scanner;
public class WriteEmployeeFile
{
    public static void main(String[] args)
    {
        Scanner input = new Scanner(System.in);
        Path file =
            Paths.get("C:\\Java\\Chapter.13\\Employees.txt");
        String s = "";
        String delimiter = ",";
        int id;
        String name;
        double payRate;
        final int QUIT = 999;
        try
        {
            OutputStream output = new
                BufferedOutputStream(Files.newOutputStream(file, CREATE));
            BufferedWriter writer = new
                BufferedWriter(new OutputStreamWriter(output));
            System.out.print("Enter employee ID number >> ");
            id = input.nextInt();
            while(id != QUIT)
            {
                System.out.print("Enter name for employee #" +
                    id + " >> ");
                input.nextLine();
                name = input.nextLine();
                System.out.print("Enter pay rate >> ");
                payRate = input.nextDouble();
                s = id + delimiter + name + delimiter + payRate;
                writer.write(s, 0, s.length());
                writer.newLine();
                System.out.print("Enter next ID number or " +
                    QUIT + " to quit >> ");
                id = input.nextInt();
            }
            writer.close();
        }
        catch(Exception e)
        {
            System.out.println("Message: " + e);
        }
    }
}
```

Figure 13-21   The WriteEmployeeFile class

In Figure 13-21, notice the extra nextLine() call after the employee's ID number is entered. Recall from Chapter 2 that this extra call is necessary to consume the newline character that remains in the input buffer after the ID number is accepted.

The first shaded statement in the WriteEmployeeFile program creates a BufferedWriter named writer. The BufferedWriter class is the counterpart to BufferedReader. It writes text to an output stream, buffering the characters. The class has three overloaded write() methods that provide for efficient writing of characters, arrays, and strings, respectively. Table 13-6 contains all the methods defined in the BufferedWriter class.

BufferedWriter Method	Description
close()	Closes the stream, flushing it first
flush()	Flushes the stream
newline()	Writes a line separator
write(String s, int off, int len)	Writes a String from position off for length len
write(char[] array, int off, int len)	Writes a character array from position off for length len
write(int c)	Writes a single character

Table 13-6   BufferedWriter methods

In the WriteEmployeeFile program, Strings of employee data are constructed within a loop that executes while the user does not enter the QUIT value. When a String is complete—that is, when it contains an ID number, name, and pay rate separated with commas—the String is sent to writer in the second shaded statement in the class. The write() method accepts the String from position 0 for its entire length.

After the String is written, the system's newline character is also written. Although a data file would not require a newline character after each record (each new record could be separated with a comma or any other unique character that was not needed as part of the data), placing each record on a new line makes the output file easier for a person to read and interpret. Because not all platforms use '\n' to separate lines, the BufferedWriter class contains a newLine() method that uses the current platform's line separator. Alternatively, you could write the value of System.getProperty("line.separator "). This method call returns the default line separator for a system; the same separator is supplied either way because the newLine() method actually calls the System.getProperty() method for you.

Any of the input or output methods in the WriteEmployeeFile program might throw an exception, so all the relevant code in the class is placed in a try block. Figure 13-22 shows a typical program execution, and Figure 13-23 shows the output file when it is opened in Notepad.

```
C:\Java>java WriteEmployeeFile
Enter employee ID number >> 145
Enter name for employee #145 >> Harris
Enter pay rate >> 12.55
Enter next ID number or 999 to quit >> 289
Enter name for employee #289 >> Gorman
Enter pay rate >> 15.65
Enter next ID number or 999 to quit >> 364
Enter name for employee #364 >> Parker
Enter pay rate >> 19.95
Enter next ID number or 999 to quit >> 999

C:\Java>
```

Figure 13-22   Typical execution of the WriteEmployeeFile program

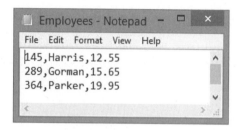

```
145,Harris,12.55
289,Gorman,15.65
364,Parker,19.95
```

Figure 13-23   Output file following the program execution in Figure 13-22

Figure 13-24 shows a program that reads the Employees.txt file created by the WriteEmployeeFile program. The program declares an InputStream for the file, then creates a BufferedReader using the InputStream. The first line is read into a String; as long as the readLine() method does not return null, the String is displayed and a new line is read.

```java
import java.nio.file.*;
import java.io.*;
public class ReadEmployeeFile
{
    public static void main(String[] args)
    {
        Path file =
            Paths.get("C:\\Java\\Chapter.13\\Employees.txt");
        String s = "";
```

Figure 13-24   The ReadEmployeeFile class (continues)

(continued)

```java
    try
    {
        InputStream input = new
            BufferedInputStream(Files.newInputStream(file));
        BufferedReader reader = new
            BufferedReader(new InputStreamReader(input));
        s = reader.readLine();
        while(s != null)
        {
            System.out.println(s);
            s = reader.readLine();
        }
        reader.close();
    }
    catch(Exception e)
    {
        System.out.println("Message: " + e);
    }
    }
}
```

Figure 13-24   The ReadEmployeeFile class

Figure 13-25 shows the output of the ReadEmployeeFile program when it uses the file that was created during the execution in Figure 13-22. Each comma-separated String is displayed on its own line.

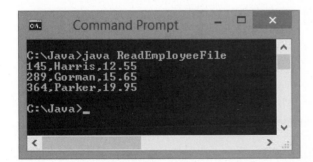

Figure 13-25   Output of the ReadEmployeeFile program

Many applications would not want to use the file data only as a String like the ReadEmployeeFile program does. Figure 13-26 shows a more useful program in which the retrieved file Strings are split into usable fields. The String class split() method accepts an argument that identifies the field delimiter (in this case, a comma) and returns an array of Strings. Each array element holds one field. Then methods such as parseInt() and parseDouble() can be used to reformat the split Strings into their respective data types.

```
import java.nio.file.*;
import java.io.*;
public class ReadEmployeeFile2
{
    public static void main(String[] args)
    {
        Path file =
            Paths.get("C:\\Java\\Chapter.13\\Employees.txt");
        String[] array = new String[3];
        String s = "";
        String delimiter = ",";
        int id;
        String name;
        double payRate;
        double gross;
        final double HRS_IN_WEEK = 40;
        double total = 0;
        try
        {
            InputStream input = new
                BufferedInputStream(Files.newInputStream(file));
            BufferedReader reader = new
                BufferedReader(new InputStreamReader(input));
            System.out.println();
            s = reader.readLine();
            while(s != null)
            {
                array = s.split(delimiter);
                id = Integer.parseInt(array[0]);
                name = array[1];
                payRate = Double.parseDouble(array[2]);
                gross = payRate * HRS_IN_WEEK;
                System.out.println("ID#" + id + " " + name +
                    "    $" + payRate + "    $" + gross);
                total += gross;
                s = reader.readLine();
            }
            reader.close();
        }
        catch(Exception e)
        {
            System.out.println("Message: " + e);
        }
        System.out.println("  Total gross payroll is $" + total);
    }
}
```

Figure 13-26   The ReadEmployeeFile2 class

As each record is read and split in the ReadEmployeeFile2 class, its pay rate field is used to calculate gross pay for the employee based on a 40-hour workweek. Then the gross is accumulated to produce a total gross payroll that is displayed after all the data has been processed. Figure 13-27 shows the program's execution.

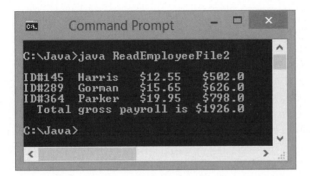

Figure 13-27   Execution of the ReadEmployeeFile2 program

TWO TRUTHS & A LIE

Creating and Using Sequential Data Files

1. A BufferedWriter writes text to an output stream, buffering the characters.

2. A data file does not require a newline character after each record, but adding a newline makes the output file easier for a person to read and interpret.

3. The String class split() method converts parts of a String to ints, doubles, and other data types.

The false statement is #3. The String class split() method accepts an argument that identifies a field delimiter and returns an array of Strings in which each array element holds one field. Then you can use methods such as parseInt() and parseDouble() to convert the split Strings to other data types.

Learning About Random Access Files

The file examples in the first part of this chapter have been sequential access files, which means that you work with the records in sequential order from beginning to end. For example, in the ReadEmployeeFile programs, if you write an employee record with an ID number of 145, and then write a second record with an ID number of 289, the records remain in the original data-entry order when you retrieve them. Businesses store data in sequential order when they use the records for **batch processing**, which involves performing the same tasks with many records, one after the other. For example, when a company produces customer bills, the records for the billing period are gathered in a batch and the bills are calculated and printed in sequence. It really doesn't matter whose bill is produced first because none are distributed to customers until all bills in a group have been printed and mailed.

Besides indicating a system that works with many records, the term *batch processing* can refer to a system in which you issue many operating-system commands as a group.

For many applications, sequential access is inefficient. These applications, known as **real-time** applications, require that a record be accessed immediately while a client is waiting. A program in which the user makes direct requests is an **interactive program**. For example, if a customer telephones a department store with a question about a monthly bill, the customer service representative does not want to access every customer account in sequence. Suppose that the store's database contains tens of thousands of account records to read, and that the customer record in question is near the end of the list. It would take too long to access the customer's record if all the records had to be read sequentially. Instead, customer service representatives require **random access files**—files in which records can be retrieved directly in any order. Random files are also called **direct access files** or **instant access files**.

You can use Java's FileChannel class to create your own random access files. A **file channel** object is an avenue for reading and writing a file. A file channel is **seekable**, meaning you can search for a specific file location and operations can start at any specified position. Table 13-7 describes some FileChannel methods.

FileChannel Method	Description
FileChannel open(Path file, OpenOption... options)	Opens or creates a file, returning a file channel to access the file
long position()	Returns the channel's file position
FileChannel position(long newPosition)	Sets the channel's file position
int read(ByteBuffer buffer)	Reads a sequence of bytes from the channel into the buffer
long size()	Returns the size of the channel's file
int write(ByteBuffer buffer)	Writes a sequence of bytes to the channel from the buffer

Table 13-7   Selected FileChannel methods

Several methods in Table 13-7 use a ByteBuffer object. As its name describes, a ByteBuffer is simply a holding place for bytes waiting to be read or written. An array of bytes can be **wrapped**, or encompassed, into a ByteBuffer using the ByteBuffer wrap() method. Wrapping a byte array into a buffer causes changes made to the buffer to change the array as well, and causes changes made to the array to change the buffer. Creating a usable FileChannel for randomly writing data requires creating a ByteBuffer and several other steps:

- You can use the Files class newByteChannel() method to get a ByteChannel for a Path. The newByteChannel() method accepts Path and StandardOpenOption arguments that specify how the file will be opened.

- The ByteChannel returned by the newByteChannel() method can then be cast to a FileChannel using a statement similar to the following:

```
FileChannel fc = (FileChannel)Files.newByteChannel(file, READ, WRITE);
```

- You can create a byte array. For example, a byte array can be built from a String using the getBytes() method as follows:

```
String s = "XYZ";
byte[] data = s.getBytes();
```

- The byte array can be wrapped into a ByteBuffer as follows:

```
ByteBuffer out = ByteBuffer.wrap(data);
```

- Then the filled ByteBuffer can be written to the declared FileChannel with a statement such as the following:

```
fc.write(out);
```

- You can test whether a ByteBuffer's contents have been used up by checking the hasRemaining() method.

- After you have written the contents of a ByteBuffer, you can write the same ByteBuffer contents again by using the rewind() method to reposition the ByteBuffer to the beginning of the buffer.

Figure 13-28 employs all these steps to declare a file and write some bytes in it randomly at positions 0, 22, and 12, in that order.

```
import java.nio.file.*;
import java.io.*;
import java.nio.channels.FileChannel;
import java.nio.ByteBuffer;
import static java.nio.file.StandardOpenOption.*;
public class RandomAccessTest
{
   public static void main(String[] args)
   {
      Path file =
         Paths.get("C:\\Java\\Chapter.13\\Numbers.txt");
      String s = "XYZ";
      byte[] data = s.getBytes();
      ByteBuffer out = ByteBuffer.wrap(data);
      FileChannel fc = null;
```

Figure 13-28   The RandomAccessTest class (continues)

(continued)

```
    try
    {
        fc = (FileChannel)Files.newByteChannel(file, READ, WRITE);
        fc.position(0);
        while(out.hasRemaining())
            fc.write(out);
        out.rewind();
        fc.position(22);
        while(out.hasRemaining())
            fc.write(out);
        out.rewind();
        fc.position(12);
        while(out.hasRemaining())
            fc.write(out);
        fc.close();
    }
    catch (Exception e)
    {
        System.out.println("Error message: " + e);
    }
    }
}
```

Figure 13-28 The RandomAccessTest class

Figure 13-29 shows the Numbers.txt text file before and after executing the RandomAccessTest program in Figure 13-28. The String "XYZ" has been written at positions 0, 8, and 12.

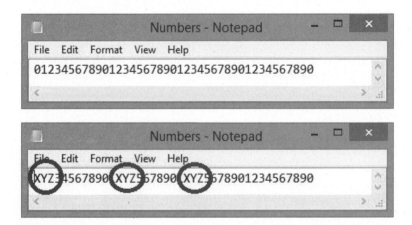

Figure 13-29 The Numbers.txt file before and after execution of RandomAccessTest

---

TWO TRUTHS & A LIE

Learning About Random Access Files

1. Businesses store data in random order when they use the records for batch processing.

2. Real-time applications are interactive and require using random access data files.

3. A `FileChannel` object is a seekable channel for reading and writing a file.

The false statement is #1. Businesses store data in sequential order when they use the records for batch processing.

Writing Records to a Random Access Data File

Writing characters at random text file locations, as in the `RandomAccessTest` program, is of limited value. When you store records in a file, it is often more useful to be able to access the eighth or 12th record rather than the eighth or 12th byte. In such a case, you multiply each record's size by the position you want to access. For example, if you store records that are 50 bytes long, the first record is at position 0, the second record is at position 50, the third record is at position 100, and so on. In other words, you can access the nth record in a `FileChannel` named `fc` using the following statement:

```
fc.position((n - 1) * 50);
```

One approach to writing a random access file is to place records into the file based on a key field. A **key field** is the field in a record that makes the record unique from all others. For example, suppose you want to store employee ID numbers, last names, and pay rates in a random access file. In a file of employees, many records might have the same last name or pay rate, but each record has a unique employee ID number, so that field can act as the key field.

The first step in creating the random access employee file is to create a file that holds default records—for example, using zeroes for the ID numbers and pay rates and blanks for the names. For this example, assume that each employee ID number is three digits; in other words, you cannot have more than 1,000 employees because the ID number cannot surpass 999. Figure 13-30 contains a program that creates 1,000 such records.

```
import java.nio.file.*;
import java.io.*;
import java.nio.ByteBuffer;
import static java.nio.file.StandardOpenOption.*;
public class CreateEmptyEmployeesFile
{
    public static void main(String[] args)
    {
        Path file =
            Paths.get("C:\\Java\\Chapter.13\\RandomEmployees.txt");
        String s = "000,         ,00.00" +
            System.getProperty("line.separator");
        byte[] data = s.getBytes();
        ByteBuffer buffer = ByteBuffer.wrap(data);
        final int NUMRECS = 1000;
        try
        {
            OutputStream output = new
                BufferedOutputStream(Files.newOutputStream(file, CREATE));
            BufferedWriter writer = new
                BufferedWriter(new OutputStreamWriter(output));
            for(int count = 0; count < NUMRECS; ++count)
                writer.write(s, 0, s.length());
            writer.close();
        }
        catch(Exception e)
        {
            System.out.println("Error message: " + e);
        }
    }
}
```

Figure 13-30   The `CreateEmptyEmployeesFile` class

In the first shaded statement in Figure 13-30, a `String` that represents a default record is declared. The three-digit employee number is set to zeros, the name consists of seven blanks, the pay rate is 00.00, and the `String` ends with the system's line separator value. A `byte` array is constructed from the `String` and wrapped into a buffer. Then a file is opened in `CREATE` mode and a `BufferedWriter` is established.

In the last shaded statement in Figure 13-30, a loop executes 1,000 times. Within the loop, the default employee string is passed to the `BufferedWriter` object's `write()` method. Figure 13-31 shows a few records from the created file when it is opened in Notepad.

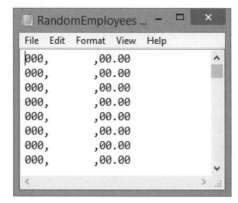

Figure 13-31 The RandomEmployees.txt file created by the
`CreateEmptyEmployeesFile` program

The default fields in the base random access file don't have to be zeros and blanks. For example, if you wanted 000 to be a legitimate employee ID number or you wanted blanks to represent a correct name, you could use different default values such as 999 and "XXXXXXX". The only requirement is that the default records be recognizable as such.

After you create the base default file, you can replace any of its records with data for an actual employee. You can locate the correct position for the new record by performing arithmetic with the record's key field.

For example, the application in Figure 13-32 creates a single employee record defined in the first shaded statement. The record is for employee 002 with a last name of Newmann and a pay rate of 12.25. In the second shaded statement, the length of this string is assigned to RECSIZE. (In this case, RECSIZE is 19, which includes one character for each character in the sample record string, including the delimiting commas, plus two bytes for the line separator value returned by the System.getProperty() method.) After the FileChannel is established, the record is written to the file at the position that begins at two times the record size. The value 2 is hard coded in this demonstration program because the employee's ID number is 002.

```
import java.nio.file.*;
import java.io.*;
import java.nio.channels.FileChannel;
import java.nio.ByteBuffer;
import static java.nio.file.StandardOpenOption.*;
public class CreateOneRandomAccessRecord
{
    public static void main(String[] args)
    {
        Path file =
            Paths.get("C:\\Java\\Chapter.13\\RandomEmployees.txt");
        String s = "002,Newmann,12.25" +
            System.getProperty("line.separator");
```

Figure 13-32 The CreateOneRandomAccessRecord class *(continues)*

(continued)

```
        final int RECSIZE = s.length();
        byte[] data = s.getBytes();
        ByteBuffer buffer = ByteBuffer.wrap(data);
        FileChannel fc = null;
        try
        {
            fc = (FileChannel)Files.newByteChannel(file, READ, WRITE);
            fc.position(2 * RECSIZE);
            fc.write(buffer);
            fc.close();
        }
        catch (Exception e)
        {
            System.out.println("Error message: " + e);
        }
    }
}
```

Figure 13-32   The `CreateOneRandomAccessRecord` class

Figure 13-33 shows the RandomEmployees.txt file contents after the `CreateOneRandomAccessRecord` program runs. The employee's data record is correctly placed in the third position in the file. Later, if employees are added that have ID numbers 000 and 001, they can be inserted as the first two records in the file.

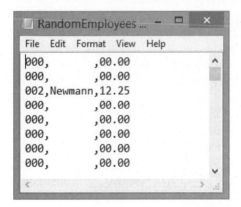

Figure 13-33   The RandomEmployees.txt file after running the `CreateOneRandomAccessRecord` program

A program that inserts one hard-coded employee record into a data file is not very useful. The program in Figure 13-34 accepts any number of records as user input and writes records to a file in a loop. As shown in the first shaded line in the figure, each employee's data value is accepted from the keyboard as a `String` and converted to an integer using the `parseInt()` method. Then, as shown in the second shaded statement, the record's desired position is computed by multiplying the ID number value by the record size.

700

```java
import java.nio.file.*;
import java.io.*;
import java.nio.channels.FileChannel;
import java.nio.ByteBuffer;
import static java.nio.file.StandardOpenOption.*;
import java.util.Scanner;
public class CreateEmployeesRandomFile
{
    public static void main(String[] args)
    {
        Scanner input = new Scanner(System.in);
        Path file =
            Paths.get("C:\\Java\\Chapter.13\\RandomEmployees.txt");
        String s = "000,         ,00.00" +
            System.getProperty("line.separator");
        final int RECSIZE = s.length();
        FileChannel fc = null;
        String delimiter = ",";
        String idString;
        int id;
        String name;
        String payRate;
        final String QUIT = "999";
        try
        {
            fc = (FileChannel)Files.newByteChannel(file, READ, WRITE);
            System.out.print("Enter employee ID number >> ");
            idString = input.nextLine();
            while(!(idString.equals(QUIT)))
            {
                id = Integer.parseInt(idString);
                System.out.print("Enter name for employee #" +
                    id + " >> ");
                name = input.nextLine();
                System.out.print("Enter pay rate >> ");
                payRate = input.nextLine();
                s = idString + delimiter + name + delimiter +
                    payRate + System.getProperty("line.separator");
                byte[] data = s.getBytes();
                ByteBuffer buffer = ByteBuffer.wrap(data);
                fc.position(id * RECSIZE);
                fc.write(buffer);
                System.out.print("Enter next ID number or " +
                    QUIT + " to quit >> ");
                idString = input.nextLine();
            }
            fc.close();
        }
        catch (Exception e)
        {
            System.out.println("Error message: " + e);
        }
    }
}
```

Figure 13-34   The CreateEmployeesRandomFile class

Figure 13-35 shows a typical execution of the program, and Figure 13-36 shows the resulting file. (This program was executed after rerunning the CreateEmptyEmployeesFile program, so all records started with default values, and the record created by the program shown in Figure 13-33 is not part of the file.) In Figure 13-36, you can see that each employee record is not stored based on the order in which it was entered, but is located in the correct spot based on its key field.

```
C:\Java>java CreateEmployeesRandomFile
Enter employee ID number >> 004
Enter name for employee #4 >> Lincoln
Enter pay rate >> 11.65
Enter next ID number or 999 to quit >> 014
Enter name for employee #14 >> Greeley
Enter pay rate >> 21.15
Enter next ID number or 999 to quit >> 003
Enter name for employee #3 >> Calhoon
Enter pay rate >> 21.45
Enter next ID number or 999 to quit >> 012
Enter name for employee #12 >> Winters
Enter pay rate >> 17.25
Enter next ID number or 999 to quit >> 999

C:\Java>
```

Figure 13-35   Typical execution of the CreateEmployeesRandomFile program

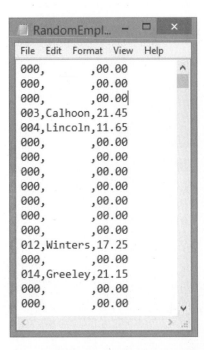

```
000,        ,00.00
000,        ,00.00
000,        ,00.00
003,Calhoon,21.45
004,Lincoln,11.65
000,        ,00.00
000,        ,00.00
000,        ,00.00
000,        ,00.00
000,        ,00.00
000,        ,00.00
000,        ,00.00
012,Winters,17.25
000,        ,00.00
014,Greeley,21.15
000,        ,00.00
000,        ,00.00
```

Figure 13-36   File created during the execution in Figure 13-35

To keep this example brief and focused on the random access file writing, the `CreateEmployeesFile` application makes several assumptions:

- An employee record contains only an ID number, name, and pay rate. In a real application, each employee would require many more data fields, such as address, phone number, date of hire, and so on.

- Each employee ID number is three digits. In many real applications, ID numbers would be longer to ensure unique values. (Three-digit numbers provide only 1,000 unique combinations.)

- The user will enter valid ID numbers and pay rates. In a real application, this would be a foolhardy assumption because users might type too many digits or type nonnumeric characters. However, to streamline the code and concentrate on the writing of a random access file, error checking for valid ID numbers and pay rates is eliminated from this example.

- The user will not duplicate employee ID numbers. In a real application, a key field should be checked against all existing key fields to ensure that a record is unique before adding it to a file.

- The names entered are all seven characters. This permits each record to be the same size. Only when record sizes are uniform can they be used to arithmetically calculate offset positions. In a real application, you would have to pad shorter names with spaces and truncate longer names to achieve a uniform size.

- Each employee's record is placed in the random access file position that is one less than the employee's ID number. In many real applications, the mathematical computations performed on a key field to determine file placement are more complicated.

TWO TRUTHS & A LIE

Writing Records to a Random Access Data File

1. You can set a `FileChannel`'s reading position based on a key field in a record and the record size.

2. A key field is the field in a record that holds the most sensitive information.

3. A useful technique for creating random access files involves first setting up a file with default records in each position.

The false statement is #2. A key field is the field in a record that makes the record unique from all others.

Reading Records from a Random Access Data File

Just because a file is created as a random access file does not mean it has to be used as one. You can process a random access file either sequentially or randomly.

Accessing a Random Access File Sequentially

The RandomEmployees.txt file created in the previous section contains 1,000 records. However, only four of them contain valuable data. Displaying every record in the file would result in many irrelevant lines of output. It makes more sense to display only those records for which an ID number has been inserted. The application in Figure 13-37 reads through the 1,000-record file sequentially in a `while` loop. The shaded statements check for valid ID numbers. This example assumes that no employee has a valid ID number of 000, so the program displays a record only when the ID is not 000. If 000 could be a valid ID number, then you would want to check for a name that was blank, a pay rate that was 0, or both. Figure 13-38 shows the application's output—a list of the entered records, conveniently in ID number order, which reflects their relative positions within the file.

```
import java.nio.file.*;
import java.io.*;
import static java.nio.file.AccessMode.*;
public class ReadEmployeesSequentially
{
    public static void main(String[] args)
    {
        Path file =
            Paths.get("C:\\Java\\Chapter.13\\RandomEmployees.txt");
        String[] array = new String[3];
        String s = "";
        String delimiter = ",";
        int id;
        String stringId;
        String name;
        double payRate;
        double gross;
        final double HRS_IN_WEEK = 40;
        double total = 0;
        try
        {
            InputStream input = new
                BufferedInputStream(Files.newInputStream(file));
            BufferedReader reader = new
                BufferedReader(new InputStreamReader(input));
            System.out.println();
            s = reader.readLine();
```

Figure 13-37   The ReadEmployeesSequentially class *(continues)*

(continued)

```
        while(s != null)
        {
            array = s.split(delimiter);
            stringId = array[0];
            id = Integer.parseInt(array[0]);
            if(id != 0)
            {
                name = array[1];
                payRate = Double.parseDouble(array[2]);
                gross = payRate * HRS_IN_WEEK;
                System.out.println("ID#" + stringId + "  " +
                    name + " $" + payRate + " $" + gross);
                total += gross;
            }
            s = reader.readLine();
        }
        reader.close();
    }
    catch(Exception e)
    {
        System.out.println("Message: " + e);
    }
    System.out.println("  Total gross payroll is $" + total);
  }
}
```

Figure 13-37   The ReadEmployeesSequentially class

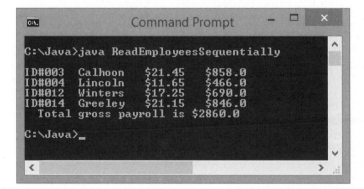

Figure 13-38   Output of the ReadEmployeesSequentially application

Accessing a Random Access File Randomly

If you simply want to display records in order based on their key field, you do not need to create a random access file and waste unneeded storage. Instead, you could sort the records using one of the techniques you learned in Chapter 9. The benefit of using a random access file is the ability to retrieve a specific record from a file directly, without reading through other records to locate the desired one.

In the ReadEmployeesRandomly application in Figure 13-39, the user is prompted for an employee ID number, which is converted to an integer with the parseInt() method. (To keep this example brief, the application does not check for a valid ID number, so the parseInt() method might throw an exception to the operating system, ending the execution of the application.) In the shaded portion of the application in Figure 13-39, the position of the desired record is calculated by multiplying the ID number by the record size and then positioning the file pointer at the desired location. (Again, to keep the example short, the ID number is not checked to ensure that it is 999 or less.) The employee record is retrieved from the data file and displayed, and then the user is prompted for the next desired ID number. Figure 13-40 shows a typical execution.

```java
import java.nio.file.*;
import java.io.*;
import java.nio.channels.FileChannel;
import java.nio.ByteBuffer;
import static java.nio.file.StandardOpenOption.*;
import java.util.Scanner;
public class ReadEmployeesRandomly
{
    public static void main(String[] args)
    {
        Scanner keyBoard = new Scanner(System.in);
        Path file =
            Paths.get("C:\\Java\\Chapter.13\\RandomEmployees.txt");
        String s = "000,        ,00.00" +
            System.getProperty("line.separator");
        final int RECSIZE = s.length();
        byte[] data = s.getBytes();
        ByteBuffer buffer = ByteBuffer.wrap(data);
        FileChannel fc = null;
        String idString;
        int id;
        final String QUIT = "999";
        try
        {
            fc = (FileChannel)Files.newByteChannel(file, READ, WRITE);
            System.out.print("Enter employee ID number or " +
                QUIT + " to quit >> ");
            idString = keyBoard.nextLine();
```

Figure 13-39   The ReadEmployeesRandomly class *(continues)*

(continued)

```
        while(!idString.equals(QUIT))
        {
            id = Integer.parseInt(idString);
            buffer= ByteBuffer.wrap(data);
            fc.position(id * RECSIZE);
            fc.read(buffer);
            s = new String(data);
            System.out.println("ID #" + id + "   " + s);
            System.out.print("Enter employee ID number or " +
                QUIT + " to quit >> ");
            idString = keyBoard.nextLine();
        }
        fc.close();
    }
    catch (Exception e)
    {
        System.out.println("Error message: " + e);
    }
  }
}
```

Figure 13-39   The ReadEmployeesRandomly class

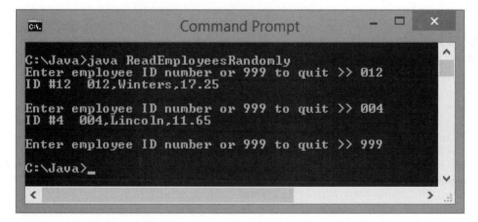

Figure 13-40   Typical execution of the ReadEmployeesRandomly program

Watch the video *Random Access Data Files.*

708

TWO TRUTHS & A LIE

Reading Records from a Random Access Data File

1. When a file is created as a random access file, you also must read it randomly.

2. The benefit of using a random access file is the ability to retrieve a specific record from a file directly, without reading through other records to locate the desired one.

3. When you access a record from a random access file, you usually calculate its position based on a key.

The false statement is #1. Just because a file is created as a random access file does not mean it has to be used as one. You can process the file sequentially or randomly.

 You Do It

Creating Multiple Random Access Files

In this section, you write a class that prompts the user for customer data and assigns the data to one of two files depending on the customer's state of residence. This program assumes that Wisconsin (WI) records are assigned to an in-state file and that all other records are assigned to an out-of-state file. First you will create empty files to store the records, and then you will write the code that places each record in the correct file.

1. Open a new file, and type the following required `import` statements:

```
import java.nio.file.*;
import java.io.*;
import java.nio.channels.FileChannel;
import java.nio.ByteBuffer;
import static java.nio.file.StandardOpenOption.*;
import java.util.Scanner;
import java.text.*;
```

2. Enter the beginning lines of the program, which include a `Scanner` class object to accept user input:

```
public class CreateFilesBasedOnState
{
    public static void main(String[] args)
    {
        Scanner input = new Scanner(System.in);
```

(continues)

(continued)

3. This program uses two `Path` objects to hold records for in-state and out-of-state customers. You can use a different `String` value for your `Path`s based on your `System` and the location where you want to save your files.

```java
Path inStateFile =
    Paths.get("C:\\Java\\Chapter.13\\InStateCusts.txt");
Path outOfStateFile =
    Paths.get("C:\\Java\\Chapter.13\\OutOfStateCusts.txt");
```

4. Build a `String` that can be used to format the empty files that are created before any actual customer data is written. Include constants for the format of the account number (three digits), the customer name (10 spaces), the customer's state, and the customer's balance (up to 9999.99). After defining the field delimiter (a comma), you can build a generic customer string by assembling the pieces. The record size is then calculated from the dummy record. A consistent record size is important so it can be used to calculate a record's position when the files are accessed randomly.

```java
final String ID_FORMAT = "000";
final String NAME_FORMAT = "          ";
final int NAME_LENGTH = NAME_FORMAT.length();
final String HOME_STATE = "WI";
final String BALANCE_FORMAT = "0000.00";
String delimiter = ",";
String s = ID_FORMAT + delimiter + NAME_FORMAT +
    delimiter + HOME_STATE + delimiter + BALANCE_FORMAT +
    System.getProperty("line.separator");
final int RECSIZE = s.length();
```

5. The last declarations are for two `FileChannel` references; `String` and integer representations of the customer's account number; the customer's `name`, `state`, and `balance` fields; and a `QUIT` constant that identifies the end of data entry.

```java
FileChannel fcIn = null;
FileChannel fcOut = null;
String idString;
int id;
String name;
String state;
double balance;
final String QUIT = "999";
```

6. Next, you call a method that creates the empty files into which the randomly placed data records can eventually be written. The method accepts the `Path` for a file and the `String` that defines the record format.

```java
createEmptyFile(inStateFile, s);
createEmptyFile(outOfStateFile, s);
```

(continues)

(continued)

7. Add closing curly braces for the main() method and the class. Then save the file as **CreateFilesBasedOnState.java**, compile it, and correct any syntax errors before proceeding.

Writing a Method to Create an Empty File

In this section, you write the method that creates empty files using the default record format string. The method will create 1,000 records with an account number of 000.

1. Just before the closing curly brace of the CreateFilesBasedOnState class, insert the header and opening brace for a method that will create an empty file to hold random access records. The method accepts a Path argument and the default record String.

```
public static void createEmptyFile(Path file, String s)
{
```

2. Define a constant for the number of records to be written:

```
final int NUMRECS = 1000;
```

3. In a try block, declare a new OutputStream using the method's Path parameter. Then create a BufferedWriter using the OutputStream.

```
try
{
   OutputStream outputStr = new
      BufferedOutputStream(Files.newOutputStream(file,CREATE));
   BufferedWriter writer = new BufferedWriter(new
      OutputStreamWriter(outputStr));
```

4. Use a for loop to write 1,000 default records using the parameter String. Then close the BufferedWriter, and add a closing brace for the try block.

```
for(int count = 0; count < NUMRECS; ++count)
   writer.write(s, 0, s.length());
writer.close();
}
```

5. Add a catch block to handle any Exception thrown from the try block, and add a closing curly brace for the method.

```
catch(Exception e)
{
   System.out.println("Error message: " + e);
}
}
```

6. Save the file and compile it. Correct any errors.

(continues)

(continued)

Adding Data-Entry Capability to the Program

In these steps, you add the code that accepts data from the keyboard and writes it to the correct location (based on the customer's account number) within the correct file (based on the customer's state).

1. After the calls to the `createEmptyFile()` method, but before the method header, start a `try` block that will handle all the data entry and file writing for customer records:

   ```
   try
   {
   ```

2. Set up the `FileChannel` references for both the in-state and out-of-state files.

   ```
   fcIn = (FileChannel)Files.newByteChannel(inStateFile, CREATE, WRITE);
   fcOut = (FileChannel)Files.newByteChannel(outOfStateFile, CREATE, WRITE);
   ```

3. Prompt the user for a customer account number, and accept it from the keyboard. Then start a loop that will continue as long as the user does not enter the `QUIT` value. Next, convert the entered account number to an integer so it can be used to calculate the file position for the entered record. In a full-blown application, you would add code to ensure that the account number is three digits, but to keep this example shorter, this program assumes that the user will enter valid account numbers.

   ```
   System.out.print("Enter customer account number >> ");
   idString = input.nextLine();
   while(!(idString.equals(QUIT)))
   {
       id = Integer.parseInt(idString);
   ```

4. Prompt the user for and accept the customer's name. To ensure that entered names are stored using a uniform length, assign the name to a `StringBuilder` object, and set the length to the standard length. Then assign the newly sized `StringBuilder` back to the `String`.

   ```
   System.out.print("Enter name for customer >> ");
   name = input.nextLine();
   StringBuilder sb = new StringBuilder(name);
   sb.setLength(NAME_LENGTH);
   name = sb.toString();
   ```

5. Prompt the user for and accept the customer's state of residence. (In a fully developed program, you would check the entered state against a list of valid states, but this step is omitted to keep the program shorter.)

   ```
   System.out.print("Enter state >> ");
   state = input.nextLine();
   ```

(continues)

(continued)

6. Prompt the user for and accept the customer's balance. Because you use the `nextDouble()` method to retrieve the balance, you follow it with a call to `nextLine()` to absorb the Enter key value left in the input stream. Then you can use the `DecimalFormat` class to ensure that the balance meets the format requirements of the file. Because the `BALANCE_FORMAT` String's value is 0000.00, zeros will be added to the front or back of any `double` that would not otherwise meet the standard. For example, 200.99 will be stored as 0200.99 and 0.1 will be stored as 0000.10. Appendix C contains more information on the `DecimalFormat` class and describes other potential formats.

```
System.out.print("Enter balance >> ");
balance = input.nextDouble();
input.nextLine();
DecimalFormat df = new DecimalFormat(BALANCE_FORMAT);
```

7. Construct the String to be written to the file by concatenating the entered fields with the comma delimiter and the line separator.

```
s = idString + delimiter + name + delimiter +
    state + delimiter + df.format(balance) +
    System.getProperty("line.separator");
```

8. Convert the constructed String to an array of bytes, and wrap the array into a ByteBuffer.

```
byte data[] = s.getBytes();
ByteBuffer buffer = ByteBuffer.wrap(data);
```

9. Depending on the customer's state, use the in-state or out-of-state FileChannel. Position the file pointer to start writing a record in the correct position based on the account number, and write the data String.

```
if(state.equals(HOME_STATE))
{
    fcIn.position(id * RECSIZE);
    fcIn.write(buffer);
}
else
{
    fcOut.position(id * RECSIZE);
    fcOut.write(buffer);
}
```

10. Prompt the user for the next customer account number, and add a closing curly brace for the `while` loop.

```
    System.out.print("Enter next customer account number or " +
        QUIT + " to quit >> ");
    idString = input.nextLine();
}
```

(continues)

(continued)

11. Close the `FileChannels`, and add a closing curly brace for the class.

```
fcIn.close();
fcOut.close();
}
```

12. Add a `catch` block that can handle any exceptions thrown from the `try` block you started in the first step of this section.

```
catch (Exception e)
{
    System.out.println("Error message: " + e);
}
```

13. Save the file, and compile it. Execute the program, and enter several records. Make sure to include names that are longer and shorter than 10 characters and to include a variety of balance values. Figure 13-41 shows a typical execution.

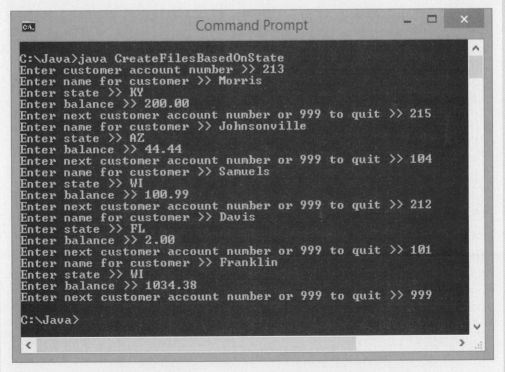

```
C:\Java>java CreateFilesBasedOnState
Enter customer account number >> 213
Enter name for customer >> Morris
Enter state >> KY
Enter balance >> 200.00
Enter next customer account number or 999 to quit >> 215
Enter name for customer >> Johnsonville
Enter state >> AZ
Enter balance >> 44.44
Enter next customer account number or 999 to quit >> 104
Enter name for customer >> Samuels
Enter state >> WI
Enter balance >> 100.99
Enter next customer account number or 999 to quit >> 212
Enter name for customer >> Davis
Enter state >> FL
Enter balance >> 2.00
Enter next customer account number or 999 to quit >> 101
Enter name for customer >> Franklin
Enter state >> WI
Enter balance >> 1034.38
Enter next customer account number or 999 to quit >> 999

C:\Java>
```

Figure 13-41   Typical execution of the `CreateFilesBasedOnState` program

(continues)

(continued)

14. Locate and open the **InStateCusts.txt** and **OutOfStateCusts.txt** files. Scroll through the files until you find the records you created. Figure 13-42 shows part of both files that contains the records added using the execution in Figure 13-41. Confirm that each record is placed in the correct file location, that each name and balance is in the correct format, and that the records with a `state` value of "WI" are placed in one file while all the other records are placed in the other file.

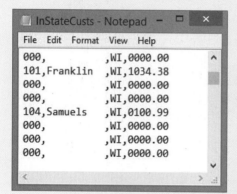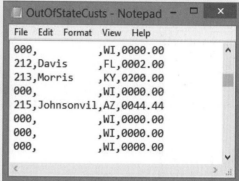

Figure 13-42   Part of the contents of the files created by the program execution in Figure 13-41

Setting Up a Program to Read the Created Files

Now, you can write a program that can use either of the files you just created. The program has four parts:

- The program will prompt the user to enter the filename to be used and set up all necessary variables and constants.

- A few statistics about the file will be displayed.

- The nondefault contents of the file will be displayed sequentially.

- A selected record from the file will be accessed directly.

1. Open a new file. Enter all the required import statements and the class header for the `ReadStateFile` application.

```
import java.nio.file.*;
import java.io.*;
import java.nio.file.attribute.*;
import static java.nio.file.StandardOpenOption.*;
import java.nio.ByteBuffer;
import java.nio.channels.FileChannel;
import java.util.Scanner;
public class ReadStateFile
{
```

(continues)

(continued)

2. Start a `main()` method in which you declare a `Scanner` object to handle keyboard input. Then declare a `String` that will hold the name of the file the program will use. Prompt the user for the filename, concatenate it with the correct path, and create a `Path` object.

```java
public static void main(String[] args)
{
   Scanner kb = new Scanner(System.in);
   String fileName;
   System.out.print("Enter name of file to use >> ");
   fileName = kb.nextLine();
   fileName = "C:\\Java\\Chapter.13\\" + fileName;
   Path file = Paths.get(fileName);
```

3. Add the `String` formatting constants and build a sample record `String` so that you can determine the record size. To save time, you can copy these declarations from the `CreateFilesBasedOnState` program.

```java
final String ID_FORMAT = "000";
final String NAME_FORMAT = "        ";
final int NAME_LENGTH = NAME_FORMAT.length();
final String HOME_STATE = "WI";
final String BALANCE_FORMAT = "0000.00";
String delimiter = ",";
String s = ID_FORMAT + delimiter + NAME_FORMAT + delimiter +
   HOME_STATE + delimiter + BALANCE_FORMAT +
   System.getProperty("line.separator");
final int RECSIZE = s.length();
```

4. The last set of declarations includes a byte array that you will use with a `ByteBuffer` later in the program, a `String` that represents the account number in an empty account, and an array of strings that can hold the pieces of a split record after it is read from the input file. Add a variable for the numeric customer balance, which will be converted from the `String` stored in the file. Also, declare a total and initialize it to 0 so the total customer balance due value can be accumulated.

```java
byte data[] = s.getBytes();
final String EMPTY_ACCT = "000";
String[] array = new String[4];
double balance;
double total = 0;
```

5. Add two closing curly braces for the method and the class. Save the file as **ReadStateFile.java**. Compile the file and correct any errors.

(continues)

716

(continued)

Displaying File Statistics

In the next section of the program, you display the creation time and size of the file.

1. Just before the two closing curly braces you just added to the program, insert a `try` block in which you declare a `BasicFileAttributes` object. Then add statements to display the file's creation time and size. Include a `catch` block to handle any thrown exceptions.

```
try
{
    BasicFileAttributes attr =
        Files.readAttributes(file, BasicFileAttributes.class);
    System.out.println("\nAttributes of the file:");
    System.out.println("Creation time " + attr.creationTime());
    System.out.println("Size " + attr.size());
}
catch(IOException e)
{
    System.out.println("IO Exception");
}
```

2. Save the file, then compile and execute it. When prompted, you can type the name of either the **InStateCusts.txt** file or the **OutOfStateCusts.txt** file. Figure 13-43 shows a typical execution.

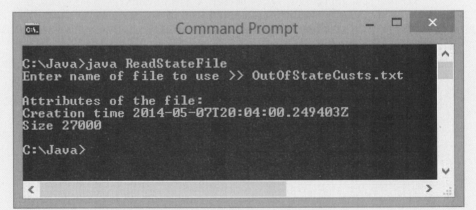

Figure 13-43 Typical execution of the `ReadStateFile` program

Reading a File Sequentially and Randomly

In these steps, you first display all the entered records in a file sequentially, and then you display one record that is accessed randomly.

1. Start a new `try…catch` pair after the first one ends, but before the two closing curly braces in the program. Declare an `InputStream` and `BufferedReader` to handle reading the file.

(continues)

(continued)

```
try
{
    InputStream iStream = new
        BufferedInputStream(Files.newInputStream(file));
    BufferedReader reader = new
        BufferedReader(new InputStreamReader(iStream));
```

2. Display a heading, and then read the first record from the file into a `String`.

```
System.out.println("\nAll non-default records:\n");
s = reader.readLine();
```

3. In a loop that continues while there is more data to read, split the `String` using the comma delimiter. Test the first split element, the account number, and proceed only if it is not "000". If the record was entered in the previous program, display the split `String` elements. Add the balance to a running total. As the last action in the loop, read the next record.

```
while(s != null)
{
    array = s.split(delimiter);
    if(!array[0].equals(EMPTY_ACCT))
    {
        balance = Double.parseDouble(array[3]);
        System.out.println("ID #" + array[0] + " " +
            array[1] + array[2] + " $" + array[3]);
        total += balance;
    }
    s = reader.readLine();
}
```

4. After all the records have been processed, display the total and close the reader. Add a closing curly brace for the `try` block.

```
    System.out.println("Total of all balances is $" + total);
    reader.close();
}
```

5. Create a `catch` block to handle any thrown exceptions.

```
catch(Exception e)
{
    System.out.println("Message: " + e);
}
```

6. After the closing brace of the last `catch` block, but before the two final closing braces in the class, add a new `try` block that declares a `FileChannel` and `ByteBuffer` and then prompts the user for and accepts an account to search for in the file.

(continues)

718

(continued)

```
try
{
    FileChannel fc = (FileChannel)Files.newByteChannel(file, READ);
    ByteBuffer buffer = ByteBuffer.wrap(data);
    int findAcct;
    System.out.print("\nEnter account to seek >> ");
    findAcct = kb.nextInt();
```

7. Calculate the position of the desired record in the file by multiplying the record number by the file size. Read the selected record into the ByteBuffer, and convert the associated byte array to a String that you can display. Add a closing curly brace for the try block.

```
    fc.position(findAcct * RECSIZE);
    fc.read(buffer);
    s = new String(data);
    System.out.println("Desired record: " + s);
}
```

8. Add a catch block to handle any exceptions.

```
catch(Exception e)
{
    System.out.println("Message: " + e);
}
```

9. Save the file, and then compile and execute it. Figure 13-44 shows a typical execution. First, the file attributes are displayed, then all the records are displayed, and then a record selected by the user is displayed.

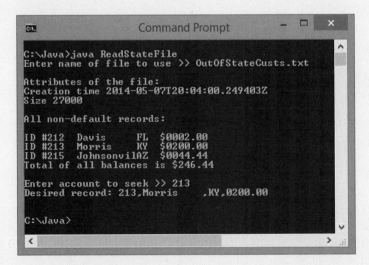

Figure 13-44   Typical execution of the ReadStateFile program after code has been completed

Don't Do It

- Don't forget that a `Path` name might be relative and that you might need to make the `Path` absolute before accessing it.

- Don't forget that the backslash character starts the escape sequence in Java, so you must use two backslashes in a string that describes a `Path` in the DOS operating system.

Key Terms

Volatile storage is temporary storage that is lost when a computer loses power.

Random access memory (**RAM**) is the temporary storage within a computer.

Nonvolatile storage is permanent storage; it is not lost when a computer loses power.

A **computer file** is a collection of data stored on a nonvolatile device in a computer system.

Permanent storage devices, such as hard disks, Zip disks, USB drives, reels or cassettes of magnetic tape, and compact discs, are nonvolatile and hold files.

Text files contain data that can be read in a text editor because the data has been encoded using a scheme such as ASCII or Unicode.

Data files contain facts and figures, such as a payroll file that contains employee numbers, names, and salaries.

Program files or **application files** store software instructions.

Binary files contain data that has not been encoded as text; their contents are in binary format.

The **root directory** of a storage device is the main directory.

Folders or **directories** are used to organize stored files.

A **path** is the complete list of the disk drive plus the hierarchy of directories in which a file resides.

A **path delimiter** is the character used to separate path components.

Factory methods are methods that assist in object creation.

An **absolute path** is a complete path; it does not need any other information to locate a file on a system.

A **relative path** is one that depends on other path information.

Java's **static import feature** allows you to use `static` constants without their class name.

A **TOCTTOU bug** is an error that occurs when changes take place from Time Of Check To Time Of Use.

A **character** can be any letter, number, or other special symbol (such as a punctuation mark) that comprises data.

A **field** is a group of characters that has some meaning.

A **record** is a collection of fields that contain data about an entity.

A **sequential access file** is a file that contains records that are accessed one after another in the order in which they were stored.

Comma-separated values (**CSV**) are fields that are separated by a comma.

To **open a file** is to create an object and associate a stream of bytes with it.

To **close the file** is to make it no longer available to an application.

A **stream** is a data pipeline or channel.

Flushing clears any bytes that have been sent to a buffer for output but that have not yet been output to a hardware device.

Batch processing involves performing the same tasks with many records, one after the other.

Real-time applications require that a record be accessed immediately while a client is waiting.

An **interactive program** is a program in which a user makes direct requests.

Random access files are files in which records can be retrieved directly in any order.

Direct access files and **instant access files** are alternate names for *random access files*.

A **file channel** object is an avenue for reading and writing a file.

Seekable describes a file channel in which you can search for a specific file location and in which operations can start at any specified position.

To be **wrapped** is to be encompassed in another type.

A **key field** is the field in a record that makes the record unique from all others.

Chapter Summary

- Data items can be stored on two broad types of storage devices—temporary, volatile storage, or permanent, nonvolatile storage. A computer file is a collection of data stored on a nonvolatile device. Files can be text files or binary files, but all files share characteristics, such as a size, name, and time of creation.

- Java's Path class is used to gather file information, such as its location, size, and creation date. You can use the Files class to perform operations on files and directories, such as deleting them, determining their attributes, and creating input and output streams.

- Businesses organize data in a hierarchy of character, field, record, and file. When a program performs input and output operations, bytes flow into a program stream, which functions as a pipeline or channel. A buffer is a memory location where bytes are held after they are logically output but before they are sent to the output device. Using a buffer to accumulate input or output improves program performance. Flushing clears any bytes that have been sent to a buffer for output but that have not yet been output to a hardware device.

- `InputStream`, `OutputStream`, and `Reader` are subclasses of the `Object` class that are used for input and output. Output devices can be assigned to `OutputStream` references, allowing applications to save data to them. You can create a file and write to it by using the `Files` class `newOutputStream()` method. To open a file for reading, you can use the `newInputStream()` method.

- The `BufferedWriter` class contains `write()` methods that are used to create data files. Files can be read using the `BufferedReader` class. The `String` class `split()` method accepts an argument that identifies a field delimiter and returns an array of `Strings` in which each array element holds one field.

- Businesses store data in sequential order when they use the records for batch processing. Real-time applications require interactive processing with random access files. Java's `FileChannel` class creates random access files. A file channel is seekable, meaning you can search for a specific file location and operations can start at any specified position.

- One approach to writing a random file is to place records into the file based on a key field that makes a record unique from all others. The first step in creating the random access file is to create a file that holds default records. Then you can replace any default record with actual data by setting the file channel position.

- You can process a random access file either sequentially or randomly. The benefit of using a random access file is the ability to retrieve a specific record from a file directly, without reading through other records to locate the desired one.

Review Questions

1. Which of the following statements is true?

   a. Volatile storage lasts only a few seconds.
   b. Volatile storage is lost when a computer loses power.
   c. Computer disks are volatile storage devices.
   d. All of the above are true.

2. A collection of data stored on a nonvolatile device in a computer system is _____ .

   a. a file   c. volatile
   b. an application   d. a type of binary file

721

3. A complete list of the disk drive plus the hierarchy of directories in which a file resides is ——————.

   a. directory

   b. folder

   c. delimiter

   d. path

4. Which of the following statements creates a `Path` named p to a `FileStream` named f?

   a. `Path p = new Path("C:\\Java\\MyFile.txt");`

   b. `Path p = f("C:\\Java\\MyFile.txt");`

   c. `Path p = f.getPath("C:\\Java\\MyFile.txt");`

   d. `Path p = getPath(new f("C:\\Java\\MyFile.txt"));`

5. A path that needs no additional information to locate a file is ——————.

   a. an absolute path

   b. a relative path

   c. a final path

   d. a constant path

6. The `Path` class `getFileName()` method returns ——————.

   a. the `String` representation of a `Path`

   b. an absolute `Path`

   c. the first item in a `Path`'s list of name elements

   d. the last item in a `Path`'s list of name elements

7. Which of the following statements always returns the same value as `Files.exists(file)`?

   a. `file.checkAccess()`

   b. `file.checkAccess(EXISTS)`

   c. `file.checkAccess(READ, WRITE)`

   d. `file.checkAccess(file.exists())`

8. You cannot delete a `Path` ——————.

   a. under any circumstances

   b. if it represents a directory

   c. if it represents a directory that is not empty

   d. if it represents more than five levels

9. The data hierarchy occurs in the following order from the smallest to largest piece of data: ——————.

   a. character, field, record, file

   b. character, file, record, field

   c. character, record, field, file

   d. record, character, field, file

10. When records are accessed one after the other in the order in which they were stored, their file is being used as a —————— access file.

   a. random

   b. binary

   c. chronological

   d. sequential

11. If you fail to close an output file, —————————.

    a. there are usually no serious consequences

    b. you might lose access to the written data

    c. Java will close it for you automatically

    d. Two of the above are correct.

12. Which of the following is true of streams?

    a. Streams are channels through which bytes flow.

    b. Streams always flow in two directions.

    c. Only one stream can be open in a program at a time.

    d. All of the above are true.

13. A buffer —————————.

    a. holds bytes that are scheduled for input or output

    b. deteriorates program performance

    c. cannot be flushed in Java

    d. All of the above are true.

14. `InputStream` is —————————.

    a. a child of `OutputStream`

    b. an abstract class

    c. used for screen output as opposed to file output

    d. All of the above are true.

15. Java's `print()` and `println()` methods are defined in the ————————— class.

    a. `BufferedOutputStream`   c. `PrintStream`

    b. `System`   d. `Print`

16. The `newOutputStream()` method —————————.

    a. is defined in the `Files` class

    b. creates a file if it does not already exist

    c. opens a file for writing

    d. All of the above are true.

17. Which of the following does the same thing as the `BufferedWriter` class `newLine()` method?

    a. `System.getProperty("line.separator ")`

    b. `Path.getProperty("line.separator ")`

    c. `System.out.println()`

    d. `System.out.print("\n")`

18. Which of the following systems is most likely to use batch processing?

    a. an airline reservation system   c. point-of-sale credit checking

    b. payroll   d. an e-mail application

19. Real-time applications _____ .

    a. use sequential access files   c. use random access files

    b. use batch processing   d. seldom are interactive

20. A file channel _____ .

    a. can be read from   c. is seekable

    b. can be written to   d. All of the above are true.

Exercises

Programming Exercises

1. Create a file using any word-processing program or text editor. Write an application that displays the file's name, containing folder, size, and time of last modification. Save the file as **FileStatistics.java**.

2. Create three files of any type you choose—for example, word-processing documents, spreadsheets, or pictures. Write an application that determines whether the first two files are located in the same folder as the third one. Test the program when the files are in the same folder and when they are not. Save the file as **CompareFolders.java**.

3. Create a file that contains your favorite song lyric. Use a text editor such as Notepad, and save the file. Copy the file contents, and paste them into a word-processing program such as Word. Write an application that displays the sizes of the two files as well as the ratio of their sizes to each other. Save the file as **FileSizeComparison.java**.

4. Write an application that determines which, if any, of the following files are stored in the folder where you have saved the exercises created in this chapter: autoexec.bat, CompareFolders.java, FileStatistics.class, and Hello.doc. Save the file as **FindSelectedFiles.java**.

5. a. Create a program that allows a user to input customer records (ID number, first name, last name, and balance owed) and save each record to a file. Save the program as **WriteCustomerList.java**. When you execute the program, be sure to enter multiple records that have the same last name because you will search for repeated first names in part d of this exercise.

    b. Write an application that reads the file created by the `WriteCustomerList` application and displays the records. Save the file as **DisplaySavedCustomerList.java**.

c. Write an application that allows you to enter any ID number, reads the customer data file created in Exercise 5a, and displays the data for the customer. Display an appropriate message if the ID number cannot be found in the input file. Save the file as **DisplaySelectedCustomer.java**.

d. Write an application that allows you to enter any last name and displays all the data for customers with the given last name. Display an appropriate message if the name cannot be found in the input file. Save the file as **DisplaySelectedCustomersByName.java**.

e. Write an application that allows you to enter any purchase amount and displays all the data for customers with balances greater than the entered value. Display an appropriate message if no customers meet the criteria. Save the file as **DisplaySelectedCustomersByBalance.java**.

6. Using a text editor, create a file that contains a list of at least 10 six-digit account numbers. Read in each account number and display whether it is valid. An account number is valid only if the last digit is equal to the sum of the first five digits divided by 10. For example, the number 223355 is valid because the sum of the first five digits is 15, the remainder when 15 is divided by 10 is 5, and the last digit is 5. Write only valid account numbers to an output file, each on its own line. Save the application as **ValidateCheckDigits.java**.

7. a. Write an application that allows a user to enter a filename and an integer representing a file position. Assume that the file is in the same folder as your executing program. Access the requested position within the file, and display the next 20 characters there. Save the file as **SeekPosition.java**.

   b. Modify the SeekPosition application so that instead of displaying 20 characters, the user enters the number of characters to display, beginning with the requested position. Save the file as **SeekPosition2.java**.

8. a. Create an application that allows you to enter student data that consists of an ID number, first name, last name, and grade point average. Depending on whether the student's grade point average is at least 2.0, output each record either to a file of students in good standing or those on academic probation. Save the program as **StudentsStanding.java**.

   b. Create an application that displays each record in the two files created in the StudentsStanding application in Exercise 8a. Display a heading to introduce the list produced from each file. For each record, display the ID number, first name, last name, grade point average, and the amount by which the grade point average exceeds or falls short of the 2.0 cutoff. Save the program as **StudentsStanding2.java**.

9. a. The Rochester Bank maintains customer records in a random access file. Write an application that creates 10,000 blank records and then allows the user to enter customer account information, including an account number that is 9999 or less, a last name, and a balance. Insert each new record into a data file at a location that is equal to the account number. Assume that the user will not enter invalid account numbers. Force each name to eight characters, padding it with spaces

or truncating it if necessary. Also assume that the user will not enter a bank balance greater than 99,000.00. Save the file as **CreateBankFile.java**.

b. Create an application that uses the file created by the user in Exercise 9a and displays all existing accounts in account-number order. Save the file as **ReadBankAccountsSequentially.java**.

c. Create an application that uses the file created by the user in Exercise 9a and allows the user to enter an account number to view the account balance. Allow the user to view additional account balances until entering an application-terminating value. Save the file as **ReadBankAccountsRandomly.java**.

10. a. Write a program that allows you to create a file of customers for a company. The first part of the program should create an empty file suitable for writing a three-digit ID number, six-character last name, and five-digit zip code for each customer. The second half of the program accepts user input to populate the file. For this exercise, assume that the user will correctly enter ID numbers and zip codes, but force the customer name to seven characters if it is too long or too short. Issue an error message, and do not save the records if the user tries to save a record with an ID number that has already been used. Save the program as **CreateCustomerFile.java**.

b. Write a program that creates a file of items carried by the company. Include a three-digit item number and up to a 20-character description for each item. Issue an error message if the user tries to store an item number that has already been used. Save the program as **CreateItemFile.java**.

c. Write an application that takes customer orders. Allow a user to enter a customer number and item ordered. Display an error message if the customer number does not exist in the customer file or the item does not exist in the item file; otherwise, display all the customer information and item information. Save the program as **CustomerItemOrder.java**.

Debugging Exercises

1. Each of the following files in the Chapter13 folder of your downloadable student files has syntax and/or logic errors. In each case, determine the problem and fix the program. After you correct the errors, save each file using the same filename preceded with *Fix*. For example, DebugThirteen1.java will become **FixDebugThirteen1.java**.

a. DebugThirteen1.java
b. DebugThirteen2.java

c. DebugThirteen3.java
d. DebugThirteen4.java

The Chapter13 folder contains four additional data files named DebugData1.txt, DebugData2.txt, DebugData3.txt, and DebugData4.txt. These files are used by the Debug programs.

Game Zone

1. In several Game Zone assignments earlier in this book, you created games similar to Hangman in which the user guesses a secret phrase by selecting a series of letters. These versions had limited appeal because each contained only a few possible phrases to guess; after playing the games a few times, the user would have memorized all the phrases. Now create a version in which any number of secret phrases can be saved to a file before the game is played. Use a text editor such as Notepad to type any number of phrases into a file, one per line. Save the file as **Phrases.txt**. Then, create a game that randomly selects a phrase from the file and allows a user to guess the phrase letter by letter. Save the game as **SecretPhraseUsingFile.java**.

2. In Chapter 8, you created a game named Quiz in which the user could respond to multiple-choice questions. Modify the game so that it stores the player's highest score from any previous game in a file and displays the high score at the start of each new game. (The first time you play the game, the high score is 0.) Save the game as **QuizUsingFile.java**.

3. Use a text editor to create a comma-delimited file of user IDs and passwords. Revise any one of the games you have created throughout this book so the user must first enter a correct ID and its associated password before playing. Save the program as **GameWithPassword.java**.

 Case Problems

1. a. In Chapter 12, you created an interactive StaffDinnerEvent class that obtains all the data for a dinner event for Carly's Catering, including details about the event and all the staff members required to work at the event. Now, modify the program to prompt the user for data for three dinner events and to create a data file that contains each event number, event type code, number of guests, and price. Save the program as **StaffDinnerEventAndCreateFile.java**.

   b. Write a program that displays the data saved in the file created in part 1a. Save the program as **DisplayDinnerEventFile.java**.

2. a. In Chapter 12, you created an interactive RentalDemo class that obtains all the data for four rentals from Sammy's Seashore Rentals, including details about the contract number, length of the rental, and equipment type. Now, modify the program to create a data file that contains each contract number, rental time in hours and minutes, equipment type code and name, and price. Save the program as **RentalDemoAndCreateFile.java**.

   b. Write a program that displays the data saved in the file created in part 2a. Save the program as **DisplayRentalFile.java**.

CHAPTER 14

Introduction to Swing Components

In this chapter, you will:

- ◎ Understand `Swing` components
- ◎ Use the `JFrame` class
- ◎ Use the `JLabel` class
- ◎ Use a layout manager
- ◎ Extend the `JFrame` class
- ◎ Add `JTextFields`, `JButtons`, and tool tips to a `JFrame`
- ◎ Learn about event-driven programming
- ◎ Understand `Swing` event listeners
- ◎ Use the `JCheckBox`, `ButtonGroup`, and `JComboBox` classes

Understanding Swing Components

Computer programs usually are more user friendly (and more fun to use) when they contain graphical user interface (GUI) components. **GUI components** are buttons, text fields, and other components with which the user can interact. Java contains two sets of prewritten GUI components—the **Abstract Windows Toolkit (AWT)** and Swing. AWT components are older, not as portable as Swing components, and do not have a consistent appearance when used with different operating systems. This chapter focuses on Swing components because they are now used more frequently in new program development. In the AWT, components have simple names, such as Frame and Button. When Java's creators designed new, improved classes, they needed new names for the classes, so they used a *J* in front of each new class name. Hence, Swing components have names like JFrame and JButton.

Swing components were named after a musical style that was popular in the 1940s. The name is meant to imply that the components have style and pizzazz. You have already used the JOptionPane component that is part of the Swing class. The Swing classes are part of a more general set of GUI programming capabilities that are collectively called the **Java Foundation Classes (JFC)**. JFC includes Swing component classes and selected classes from the java.awt package.

GUI components are also called *controls* or *widgets*. Each Swing component is a descendant of JComponent, which in turn inherits from the java.awt.Container class. You can insert the statement import javax.swing.*; at the beginning of your Java program files so you can take advantage of all the Swing GUI components and their methods. The *x* in *javax* originally stood for *extension*, so named because the Swing classes were an extension of the original Java language specifications.

Almost all Swing components are said to be **lightweight components** because they are written completely in Java and do not have to rely on the local operating system code. This means the components are not "weighed down" by having to interact with the operating system (for example, Windows or Macintosh) in which the application is running. Some Swing components, such as JFrames, are known as **heavyweight components** because they do require interaction with the local operating system. A lightweight component reuses the native (original) window of its closest heavyweight ancestor; a heavyweight component has its own opaque native window. The only heavyweight components used in Swing are swing.JFrame, swing.JDialog, swing.JWindow, swing.JApplet, awt.Component, awt.Container, and awt.JComponent.

When you use Swing components, you usually place them in containers. A **container** is a type of component that holds other components so you can treat a group of them as a single entity. Containers are defined in the Container class. Often, a container takes the form of a window that you can drag, resize, minimize, restore, and close.

As you know from reading about inheritance in Chapters 10 and 11, all Java classes descend from the Object class. The Component class is a child of the Object class, and the Container class is a child of the Component class. Therefore, every Container object "is a" Component, and every Component object (including every Container) "is an" Object.

The Container class is also a parent class, and the Window class is a child of Container. A **window** is a rectangular container that can hold GUI controls. However, Java programmers often prefer to create a frame instead of a window. A **frame** is a window that has a title bar and border. In Java, Frame is a child of Window, and JFrame is the Swing object that is a child of Frame.

TWO TRUTHS & A LIE

Understanding Swing Components

1. Swing components are elements such as buttons; you can usually recognize their names because they contain the word *Swing*.

2. Each Swing component is a descendant of JComponent, which in turn inherits from the java.awt.Container class.

3. You insert the import statement import javax.swing.*; at the beginning of your Java program files so you can use Swing components.

The false statement is #1. You can usually recognize Swing component names because they begin with J.

Using the JFrame Class

You usually create a JFrame so that you can place other objects within it for display. Figure 14-1 shows the JFrame's inheritance tree. Recall that the Object class is defined in the java.lang package, which is imported automatically every time you write a Java program. However, Object's descendants (shown in Figure 14-1) are not automatically imported.

```
java.lang.Object
  !--java.awt.Component
        !--java.awt.Container
              !--java.awt.Window
                    !--java.awt.Frame
                          !--javax.swing.JFrame
```

Figure 14-1   Relationship of the JFrame class to its ancestors

The JFrame class has four constructors:

- JFrame() constructs a new frame that initially is invisible and has no title.

- JFrame(String title) creates a new, initially invisible JFrame with the specified title.

- JFrame(GraphicsConfiguration gc) creates a JFrame in the specified GraphicsConfiguration of a screen device with a blank title. (You will learn about the GraphicsConfiguration class as you continue to study Java.)

- JFrame(String title, GraphicsConfiguration gc) creates a JFrame with the specified title and the specified GraphicsConfiguration of a screen.

You can construct a JFrame as you do other objects, using the class name, an identifier, the assignment operator, the new operator, and a constructor call. For example, the following two statements construct two JFrames: one with the title *Hello* and another with no title:

```
JFrame firstFrame = new JFrame("Hello");
JFrame secondFrame = new JFrame();
```

After you create a JFrame object, you can use the now-familiar object-dot-method format you have used with other objects to call methods that manipulate a JFrame's features. Table 14-1 describes some useful JFrame class methods.

The methods in Table 14-1 represent only a small portion of the available methods you can use with a JFrame. Each of the methods listed in Table 14-1 is inherited from either JFrame's Component or Frame parent class. These classes contain many useful methods in addition to the few listed here. You can read the documentation for all the methods at *http://docs.oracle.com/javase/8/docs/api/*.

Method	Purpose
void setTitle(String)	Sets a JFrame's title using the String argument
void setSize(int, int)	Sets a JFrame's size in pixels with the width and height as arguments
void setSize(Dimension)	Sets a JFrame's size using a Dimension class object; the Dimension(int, int) constructor creates an object that represents both a width and a height
String getTitle()	Returns a JFrame's title
void setResizable(boolean)	Sets the JFrame to be resizable by passing true to the method, or sets the JFrame not to be resizable by passing false to the method
boolean isResizable()	Returns true or false to indicate whether the JFrame is resizable
void setVisible(boolean)	Sets a JFrame to be visible using the boolean argument true and invisible using the boolean argument false
void setBounds(int, int, int, int)	Overrides the default behavior for the JFrame to be positioned in the upper-left corner of the computer screen's desktop; the first two arguments are the horizontal and vertical positions of the JFrame's upper-left corner on the desktop, and the final two arguments set the width and height

Table 14-1   Useful methods inherited by the JFrame class

Figure 14-2 shows a program that declares a JFrame named aFrame, sets its size to 250 pixels horizontally by 100 pixels vertically, and sets its title to display a String. **Pixels** are the picture elements, or tiny dots of light, that make up the image on your computer monitor.

 When you set a JFrame's size, you do not have the full area available to use because part of the area is consumed by the JFrame's title bar and borders.

```
import javax.swing.*;
public class JFrame1
{
    public static void main(String[] args)
    {
        JFrame aFrame = new JFrame("First frame");
        aFrame.setSize(250, 100);
        aFrame.setVisible(true);
    }
}
```

Figure 14-2 The JFrame1 application

The application in Figure 14-2 produces the JFrame shown in Figure 14-3. It resembles frames that you have probably seen when using GUI programs. One reason to use similar frame objects in your own programs is that users are already familiar with the frame environment. When users see frames on their computer screens, they expect to see a title bar at the top containing text information (such as "First frame"). Users also expect to see Minimize, Maximize or Restore, and Close buttons in the frame's upper-right corner. Most users assume that they can change a frame's size by dragging its border or reposition the frame on their screen by dragging the frame's title bar to a new location. The JFrame in Figure 14-3 has all of these capabilities.

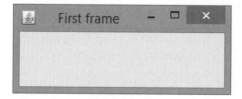

Figure 14-3 Output of the JFrame1 application

In the application in Figure 14-2, all three statements in the main() method are important. After you instantiate the JFrame object, you will not see it if you do not use setVisible(true). If you do not set its size, you see only the title bar of the JFrame because the JFrame size is 0 × 0 by default. It might seem unusual that the default state for a JFrame is invisible. However, consider that you might want to construct a JFrame in the background while other actions are occurring and that you might want to make it visible later, when appropriate (for example, after the user has taken an action such as selecting an option).

When a user closes a JFrame by clicking the Close button in the upper-right corner, the default behavior is for the JFrame to be hidden and for the application to keep running. This makes sense when there are other tasks for the program to complete after the main frame is closed—for example, displaying additional frames, closing open data files, or printing an activity report. To change this behavior, you can call a JFrame's setDefaultCloseOperation() method and use one of the following four values as an argument:

- JFrame.EXIT_ON_CLOSE exits the program when the JFrame is closed.

- WindowConstants.DISPOSE_ON_CLOSE closes the frame, disposes of the JFrame object, and keeps running the application.

- WindowConstants.DO_NOTHING_ON_CLOSE keeps the JFrame and continues running. In other words, it disables the Close button.

- WindowConstants.HIDE_ON_CLOSE closes the JFrame and continues running; this is the default operation that you frequently want to override.

 Each of the four usable setDefaultCloseOperation() arguments represents an integer; for example, the value of JFrame.EXIT_ON_CLOSE is 3. However, it is easier to remember the constant names than the numeric values they represent, and other programmers more easily understand your intentions if you use the named constant identifier.

If you are testing an application and you want to end the program when the user closes a JFrame, but you forget to change the default close operation, you can end the program by typing *Ctrl+C*.

Customizing a JFrame's Appearance

The appearance of the JFrame in Figure 14-3 is provided by the operating system in which the program is running (in this case, Windows). For example, the coffee-cup icon in the frame's title bar and the Minimize, Restore, and Close buttons look and act as they do in other Windows applications. The icon and buttons are known as **window decorations**; by default, window decorations are supplied by the operating system. However, you can request that Java's look and feel provide the decorations for a frame. **Look and feel** comprises the elements of design, style, and functionality in any user interface.

Optionally, you can set a JFrame's look and feel using the setDefaultLookAndFeelDecorated() method. For example, Figure 14-4 shows an application that calls this method.

```
import javax.swing.*;
public class JFrame2
{
    public static void main(String[] args)
    {
        JFrame.setDefaultLookAndFeelDecorated(true);
        JFrame aFrame = new JFrame("Second frame");
        aFrame.setSize(250, 100);
        aFrame.setVisible(true);
    }
}
```

Figure 14-4   The JFrame2 class

 You can provide a custom icon for a frame instead of using your operating system's default icon or the Java look-and-feel icon. For details, go to the Java Web site and search for "How to Make Frames."

The program in Figure 14-4 differs from Figure 14-2 only in the shaded areas, which show the class name, the text in the title bar, and the look-and-feel statement. Figure 14-5 shows the output. If you compare the frame in Figure 14-5 with the one in Figure 14-3, you can see that Java's look and feel has similar features to that of Windows, but their appearance is different. Java's look and feel is also known by the name *Metal*.

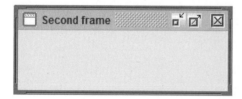

Figure 14-5   Output of the JFrame2 application

 Look and feel is a legal issue because some software companies claim that competitors are infringing on their copyright protection by copying the look and feel of their products.

 Watch the video *Using the JFrame class.*

736

TWO TRUTHS & A LIE
Using the JFrame Class

1. The JFrame class contains overloaded constructors; for example, you can specify a title or not.

2. An advantage of using a JFrame is that it resembles traditional frames that people are accustomed to using.

3. When a user closes a JFrame by clicking the Close button in the upper-right corner, the default behavior is for the application to end.

The false statement is #3. When a user closes a JFrame by clicking the Close button in the upper-right corner, the default behavior is for the JFrame to be hidden and for the application to keep running.

 You Do It

Creating a JFrame

In this section, you create a JFrame object that appears on the screen.

1. Open a new file, and type the following statement to import the javax.swing classes:

   ```
   import javax.swing.*;
   ```

2. On the next lines, type the following class header for the JDemoFrame class, its opening curly brace, the main() method header, and its opening curly brace:

   ```
   public class JDemoFrame
   {
       public static void main(String[] args)
       {
   ```

3. Within the body of the main() method, enter the following code to declare a JFrame with a title, set its size, and make it visible. If you neglect to set a JFrame's size, you see only the title bar of the JFrame (because the size is 0 × 0 by default); if you neglect to make the JFrame visible, you do not see anything. Add two closing curly braces—one for the main() method and one for the JDemoFrame class.

(continues)

(continued)

```
        JFrame aFrame = new JFrame("This is a frame");
        final int WIDTH = 250;
        final int HEIGHT = 250;
        aFrame.setSize(WIDTH, HEIGHT);
        aFrame.setVisible(true);
    }
}
```

4. Save the file as **JDemoFrame.java**. Compile and then run the program. The output looks like Figure 14-6—an empty JFrame with a title bar, a little taller than it is wide. The JFrame has all the properties of frames you have seen in applications you have used. For example, click the JFrame's **Minimize** button, and the JFrame minimizes to an icon on the Windows taskbar.

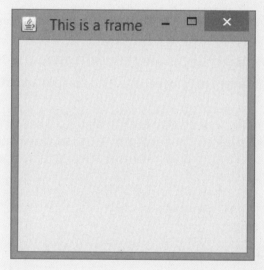

Figure 14-6   Output of the JDemoFrame application

5. Click the JFrame's **icon** on the taskbar. The JFrame returns to its previous size.

6. Click the JFrame's **Maximize** button. The JFrame fills the screen.

7. Click the JFrame's **Restore** button. The JFrame returns to its original size.

8. Position your mouse pointer on the JFrame's title bar, and then drag the JFrame to a new position on your screen.

9. Click the JFrame's **Close** button. The JFrame disappears or hides. The default behavior of a JFrame is simply to hide when the user clicks the Close button—not to end the program.

(continues)

737

(continued)

10. To end the program and return control to the command line, click the **Command Prompt** window, and then press **Ctrl+C**. In Chapter 6, you learned to press Ctrl+C to stop a program that contains an infinite loop. This situation is similar—you want to stop a program that does not have a way to end automatically.

Ending an Application When a JFrame Closes

Next, you modify the JDemoFrame program so that the application ends when the user clicks the JDemoFrame Close button.

1. Within the JDemoFrame class file, change the class name to JDemoFrameThatCloses.

2. Add a new line of code as the final executable statement within the main() method, as follows:

```
aFrame.setDefaultCloseOperation(JFrame.EXIT_ON_CLOSE);
```

3. Save the file as **JDemoFrameThatCloses.java**, and compile and execute the application.

4. When the JFrame appears on your screen, confirm that it still has Minimize, Maximize, and Restore capabilities. Then click the JFrame's **Close** button. The JFrame closes, and the command prompt returns as the program relinquishes control to the operating system.

Using the JLabel Class

In a GUI environment, a **label** is an uneditable component that is most often used to provide information for a user. (**Editable** describes a component that can accept keystrokes.) JLabel is a built-in Java Swing class that allows you to create a label that you can display in a JFrame. The inheritance hierarchy of the JLabel class is shown in Figure 14-7.

```
java.lang.Object
    |
  +--java.awt.Component
        |
      +--java.awt.Container
            |
          +--javax.swing.JComponent
                |
              +--javax.swing.JLabel
```

Figure 14-7   The JLabel class inheritance hierarchy

Available constructors for the JLabel class include the following:

- JLabel() creates a JLabel instance with no image and with an empty string for the title.

- JLabel(Icon image) creates a JLabel instance with the specified image.

- JLabel(Icon image, int horizontalAlignment) creates a JLabel instance with the specified image and horizontal alignment.

- JLabel(String text) creates a JLabel instance with the specified text.

- JLabel(String text, Icon icon, int horizontalAlignment) creates a JLabel instance with the specified text, image, and horizontal alignment.

- JLabel(String text, int horizontalAlignment) creates a JLabel instance with the specified text and horizontal alignment.

For example, you can create a JLabel named greeting that holds the words *Good day* by writing the following statement:

```
JLabel greeting = new JLabel("Good day");
```

You then can add the greeting object to the JFrame object named aFrame using the add() method as follows:

```
aFrame.add(greeting);
```

Figure 14-8 shows an application in which a JFrame is created and its size, visibility, and close operation are set. Then a JLabel is created and added to the JFrame. Figure 14-9 shows the output.

```
import javax.swing.*;
public class JFrame3
{
   public static void main(String[] args)
   {
      final int FRAME_WIDTH = 250;
      final int FRAME_HEIGHT = 100;
      JFrame aFrame = new JFrame("Third frame");
      aFrame.setSize(FRAME_WIDTH, FRAME_HEIGHT);
      aFrame.setVisible(true);
      aFrame.setDefaultCloseOperation(JFrame.EXIT_ON_CLOSE);
      JLabel greeting = new JLabel("Good day");
      aFrame.add(greeting);
   }
}
```

Figure 14-8 The JFrame3 class

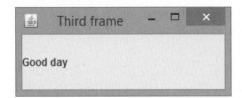

740

Figure 14-9   Output of the JFrame3 application

The counterpart to the add() method is the remove() method. The following statement removes greeting from aFrame:

```
aFrame.remove(greeting);
```

If you add or remove a component from a container after it has been made visible, you should also call the invalidate(), validate(), and repaint() methods, or else you will not see the results of your actions. Each performs slightly different functions, but all three together guarantee that the results of changes in your layout will take effect. The invalidate() and validate() methods are part of the Container class, and the repaint() method is part of the Component class.

 If you add or remove a component in a JFrame *during* construction, you do not have to call repaint() if you later alter the component—for example, by changing its text. You only need to call repaint() if you add or remove a component after construction. You will learn more about the repaint() method in the "Graphics" chapter.

You can change the text in a JLabel by using the Component class setText() method with the JLabel object and passing a String to it. For example, the following code changes the value displayed in the greeting JLabel:

```
greeting.setText("Howdy");
```

You can retrieve the text in a JLabel (or other Component) by using the getText() method, which returns the currently stored String.

Changing a JLabel's Font

You probably are not very impressed with the simple application displayed in Figure 14-9. You might think that the string *Good day* is plain and lackluster. Fortunately, you can change the font of strings displayed in GUI components. A **font** is the size, weight, and style of a typeface, and Java provides you with a Font class from which you can create an object that holds typeface and size information. The setFont() method requires a Font object argument. To construct a Font object, you need three arguments: typeface, style, and point size.

- The *typeface argument* to the Font constructor is a String representing a font. Common fonts have names such as *Arial, Century, Monospaced,* and *Times New Roman*. The typeface argument in the Font constructor is only a request; the system on which your program runs might not have access to the requested font, and if necessary, it substitutes a default font.

- The *style argument* applies an attribute to displayed text and is one of three values: Font.PLAIN, Font.BOLD, or Font.ITALIC.

- The *point size argument* is an integer that represents about 1/72 of an inch. Printed text is commonly 12 points; a headline might be 30 points.

 In printing, point size defines a measurement between lines of text in a single-spaced text document. The point size is based on typographic points, which are approximately 1/72 of an inch. Java adopts the convention that one point on a display is equivalent to one unit in user coordinates. For more information, see the Font documentation at the Java Web site.

To give a JLabel object a new font, you can create a Font object, as in the following:

Font headlineFont = new Font("Monospaced", Font.BOLD, 36);

The typeface name is a String, so you must enclose it in double quotation marks.

You can use the setFont() method to assign the Font to a JLabel with a statement such as:

greeting.setFont(headlineFont);

Figure 14-10 shows a class named JFrame4. All the changes from JFrame3 are shaded.

```java
import javax.swing.*;
import java.awt.*;
public class JFrame4
{
    public static void main(String[] args)
    {
        final int FRAME_WIDTH = 250;
        final int FRAME_HEIGHT = 100;
        Font headlineFont = new Font("Arial", Font.BOLD, 36);
        JFrame aFrame = new JFrame("Fourth frame");
        aFrame.setSize(FRAME_WIDTH, FRAME_HEIGHT);
        aFrame.setVisible(true);
        aFrame.setDefaultCloseOperation(JFrame.EXIT_ON_CLOSE);
        JLabel greeting = new JLabel("Good day");
        greeting.setFont(headlineFont);
        aFrame.add(greeting);
    }
}
```

Figure 14-10 The JFrame4 program

The program in Figure 14-10 includes a new import statement for the package that contains the Font class. The program contains a Font object named headlineFont that is applied to the greeting. Figure 14-11 shows the execution of the JFrame4 program; the greeting appears in a 36-point, bold, Arial font.

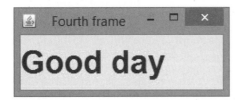

Figure 14-11   Output of the JFrame4 program

You are not required to provide an identifier for a Font. For example, you could omit the shaded statement that declares headlineFont in Figure 14-10 and set the greeting Font with the following statement that uses an anonymous Font object:

```
greeting.setFont(new Font("Arial", Font.BOLD, 36));
```

After you create a Font object, you can create a new object with a different type and size using the deriveFont() method with appropriate arguments. For example, the following two statements create a headlineFont object and a textBodyFont object that is based on the first object:

```
Font headlineFont = new Font("Arial", Font.BOLD, 36);
Font textBodyFont = headlineFont.deriveFont(Font.PLAIN, 14);
```

TWO TRUTHS & A LIE

Using the JLabel Class

1. JLabel is a built-in Java Swing class that holds text you can display.

2. You can change a JLabel's text by using its JFrame's name, a dot, and the add() method, and then using the desired text as the argument to the method.

3. If you add or remove a component from a container after it has been made visible, you should also call the validate() and repaint() methods, or else you will not see the results of your actions.

The false statement is #2. You change a JLabel's text using the setText() method, including the new text as the argument. You add a JLabel to a JFrame by using the JFrame's name, a dot, and the add() method, and then by using the JLabel's name as an argument to the method.

Using a Layout Manager

When you want to add multiple components to a JFrame or other container, you usually need to provide instructions for the layout of the components. For example, Figure 14-12 shows an application in which two JLabels are created and added to a JFrame in the final shaded statements.

```java
import javax.swing.*;
import java.awt.*;
public class JFrame5
{
    public static void main(String[] args)
    {
        final int FRAME_WIDTH = 250;
        final int FRAME_HEIGHT = 100;
        JFrame aFrame = new JFrame("Fifth frame");
        aFrame.setSize(FRAME_WIDTH, FRAME_HEIGHT);
        aFrame.setVisible(true);
        aFrame.setDefaultCloseOperation(JFrame.EXIT_ON_CLOSE);
        JLabel greeting = new JLabel("Hello");
        JLabel greeting2 = new JLabel("Who are you?");
        aFrame.add(greeting);
        aFrame.add(greeting2);
    }
}
```

Figure 14-12   The JFrame5 program

Figure 14-13 shows the output of the application in Figure 14-12. Although two JLabels are added to the frame, only the last one added is visible. The second JLabel has been placed on top of the first one, totally obscuring it. If you continued to add more JLabels to the program, only the last one added to the JFrame would be visible.

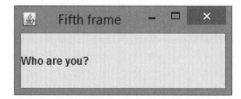

Figure 14-13   Output of the JFrame5 program

To place multiple components at specified positions in a container so they do not hide each other, you must explicitly use a **layout manager**—an object that controls component positioning. The normal (default) behavior of a JFrame is to use a **border layout manager**, which divides a container into regions. The Java class that provides this type of layout is named BorderLayout. When you use BorderLayout but do not specify a region in which to place a component (as the JFrame5 program fails to do), all the components are placed in the same region, and they obscure each other.

When you use a **flow layout manager**, components do not lie on top of each other. Instead, the flow layout manager places components in rows; after any row is filled, additional components automatically spill into the next row. The Java class that provides this type of layout is FlowLayout.

Three constants are defined in the FlowLayout class that specify how components are positioned in each row of their container. These constants are FlowLayout.LEFT, FlowLayout.RIGHT, and FlowLayout.CENTER. For example, to create a layout manager named flow that positions components to the right, you can use the following statement:

FlowLayout flow = new FlowLayout(FlowLayout.RIGHT);

If you do not specify how components are laid out, by default they are centered in each row.

Suppose that you create a FlowLayout object named flow as follows:

FlowLayout flow = new FlowLayout();

Then the layout of a JFrame named aFrame can be set to the newly created FlowLayout using the statement:

aFrame.setLayout(flow);

A more compact syntax that uses an anonymous FlowLayout object is:

aFrame.setLayout(new FlowLayout());

Figure 14-14 shows an application in which the JFrame's layout manager has been set so that multiple components are visible.

```
import javax.swing.*;
import java.awt.*;
public class JFrame6
{
   public static void main(String[] args)
   {
      final int FRAME_WIDTH = 250;
      final int FRAME_HEIGHT = 100;
      JFrame aFrame = new JFrame("Sixth frame");
      aFrame.setSize(FRAME_WIDTH, FRAME_HEIGHT);
      aFrame.setVisible(true);
      aFrame.setDefaultCloseOperation(JFrame.EXIT_ON_CLOSE);
      JLabel greeting = new JLabel("Hello");
      JLabel greeting2 = new JLabel("Who are you?");
      aFrame.setLayout(new FlowLayout());
      aFrame.add(greeting);
      aFrame.add(greeting2);
   }
}
```

Figure 14-14   The JFrame6 program

Figure 14-15 shows the execution of the JFrame6 program. Because a FlowLayout is used, the two JLabels appear side by side. If there were more JLabels or other components, they would continue to be placed side by side across the JFrame until there was no more room. Then, the additional components would be placed in a new row beneath the first row of components.

745

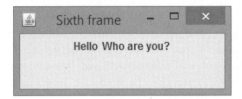

Figure 14-15   Output of the JFrame6 program

Other layout managers allow you to position components in a container more precisely. You will learn about these in the "Graphics" chapter. The examples in this chapter will use FlowLayout because it is the easiest of the layout managers to use.

Watch the video *Using a Layout Manager*.

TWO TRUTHS & A LIE

Using a Layout Manager

1. If you do not provide a layout manager for a JFrame, you cannot add multiple components to it.

2. The normal (default) behavior of a JFrame is to use a layout format named BorderLayout.

3. The flow layout manager places components in a row, and when a row is filled, it automatically spills components into the next row.

The false statement is #1. If you do not provide a layout manager for a JFrame, you can add multiple components to it, but only the most recently added one is visible.

Extending the JFrame Class

You can instantiate a simple JFrame object within an application's main() method or with any other method of any class you write. Alternatively, you can create your own class that descends from the JFrame class. The advantage of creating a child class of JFrame is that you can set the JFrame's properties within your object's constructor; then, when you create your JFrame child object, it is automatically endowed with the features you have specified, such as title, size, and default close operation.

You already know that you create a child class by using the keyword extends in the class header, followed by the parent class name. You also know that you can call the parent class's constructor using the keyword super, and that when you call super(), the call must be the first statement in the constructor. For example, the JMyFrame class in Figure 14-16 extends JFrame. Within the JMyFrame constructor, the super() JFrame constructor is called; it accepts a String argument to use as the JFrame's title. (Alternatively, the setTitle() method could have been used.) The JMyFrame constructor also sets the size, visibility, and default close operation for every JMyFrame. Each of the methods—setSize(), setVisible(), and setDefaultCloseOperation()—appears in the constructor in Figure 14-16 without an object, because the object is the current JMyFrame being constructed. Each of the three methods could be preceded with a this reference with exactly the same meaning. That is, within the JMyFrame constructor, the following two statements have identical meanings:

```
setSize(WIDTH, HEIGHT);
this.setSize(WIDTH, HEIGHT);
```

Each statement sets the size of "this" current JMyFrame instance.

```
import javax.swing.*;
public class JMyFrame extends JFrame
{
    final int WIDTH = 200;
    final int HEIGHT = 120;
    public JMyFrame()
    {
        super("My frame");
        setSize(WIDTH, HEIGHT);
        setVisible(true);
        setDefaultCloseOperation(JFrame.EXIT_ON_CLOSE);
    }
}
```

Figure 14-16   The JMyFrame class

Figure 14-17 shows an application that declares two JMyFrame objects. Each has the same set of attributes, determined by the JMyFrame constructor.

```
public class CreateTwoJMyFrameObjects
{
    public static void main(String[] args)
    {
        JMyFrame myFrame = new JMyFrame();
        JMyFrame mySecondFrame = new JMyFrame();
    }
}
```

Figure 14-17 The CreateTwoJMyFrameObjects application

When you execute the application in Figure 14-17, the two JMyFrame objects are displayed with the second one on top of, or obscuring, the first. Figure 14-18 shows the output of the CreateTwoJMyFrameObjects application after the top JMyFrame has been dragged to partially expose the bottom one.

Figure 14-18 Output of the CreateTwoJMyFrameObjects application after dragging the top frame

You could use the setBounds() method with one of the JMyFrame objects that produces the output in Figure 14-18 so that you don't have to move one JMyFrame object to view the other. See Table 14-1 for details.

You exit the application when you click the Close button on either of the two JMyFrame objects shown in Figure 14-18. Each object has the same default close operation because each uses the same constructor that specifies this operation. To allow only one JMyFrame to control the program's exit, you could use the setDefaultCloseOperation() method with one or both of the objects in the application to change its close behavior. For example, you could use DISPOSE_ON_CLOSE to dismiss one of the frames but keep the application running.

When you extend a JFrame to create a new custom class, you must remember to make decisions as to which attributes you want to set within the class and which you want to leave to the applications that will use the class. For example, you can place the setVisible()

statement within the JFrame child class constructor (using either an explicit or implied this reference), or you can allow the application to use a setVisible() statement (using the name of an instantiated object followed by a dot and the method name). Either one works, but if you fail to do either, the frame will not be visible.

Programmers frequently place a main() method within a class such as JMyFrame. Then the class provides the option to be used to instantiate objects, as in the CreateTwoJMyFrameObjects application, or to be used to execute as a program that creates an object.

TWO TRUTHS & A LIE

Extending the JFrame Class

1. The advantage of creating a child class of JFrame is that you can set the JFrame's properties within your object's constructor so it is automatically endowed with the features that you have specified.

2. When a class descends from JFrame, you can use super() or setTitle() to set the title within any of the child's methods.

3. When you extend a JFrame to create a new custom class, you can decide which attributes you want to set within the class and which you want to leave to the applications that will use the class.

The false statement is #2. When a class descends from JFrame, you can use super() or setTitle() to set the title within the child's constructor. However, super() does not work in other methods.

Adding JTextFields, JButtons, and Tool Tips to a JFrame

In addition to including JLabel objects, JFrames often contain other window features, such as JTextFields, JButtons, and tool tips.

Adding JTextFields

A **text field** is a component into which a user can type a single line of text data. (Text data comprises any characters you can enter from the keyboard, including numbers and punctuation.) The Swing class that creates a text field is JTextField. Figure 14-19 shows the inheritance hierarchy of the JTextField class.

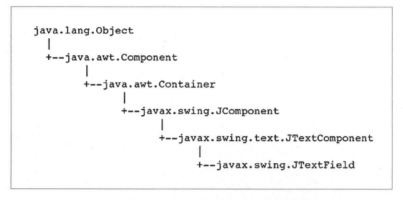

```
java.lang.Object
   |
   +--java.awt.Component
          |
          +--java.awt.Container
                 |
                 +--javax.swing.JComponent
                        |
                        +--javax.swing.text.JTextComponent
                               |
                               +--javax.swing.JTextField
```

Figure 14-19 The JTextField class inheritance hierarchy

Typically, a user types a line into a JTextField and then presses Enter on the keyboard or clicks a button with the mouse to enter the data. You can construct a JTextField object using one of several constructors:

- public JTextField() constructs a new JTextField.

- public JTextField(int columns) constructs a new, empty JTextField with a specified number of columns.

- public JTextField(String text) constructs a new JTextField initialized with the specified text.

- public JTextField(String text, int columns) constructs a new JTextField initialized with the specified text and columns.

For example, to provide a JTextField that allows enough room for a user to enter approximately 10 characters, you can code the following:

```
JTextField response = new JTextField(10);
```

To add the JTextField named response to a JFrame named frame, you write:

```
frame.add(response);
```

The number of characters a JTextField can display depends on the font being used and the actual characters typed. For example, in most fonts, *w* is wider than *i*, so a JTextField of size 10 using the Arial font can display 24 *i* characters, but only eight *w* characters.

Try to anticipate how many characters your users might enter when you create a JTextField. The user can enter more characters than those that display, but the extra characters scroll out of view. It can be disconcerting to try to enter data into a field that is not large enough. It is usually better to overestimate than underestimate the size of a text field.

Several other methods are available for use with JTextFields. The setText() method allows you to change the text in a JTextField (or other Component) that has already been created, as in the following:

```
response.setText("Thank you");
```

After a user has entered text in a JTextField, you can clear it out with a statement such as the following, which assigns an empty string to the text:

```
response.setText("");
```

The getText() method allows you to retrieve the String of text in a JTextField (or other Component), as in:

```
String whatUserTyped = response.getText();
```

A JTextField is editable by default. If you do not want the user to be able to enter data in a JTextField, you can send a boolean value to the setEditable() method to change the JTextField's editable status. For example, if you want to give a user a limited number of chances to answer a question correctly, you can count data-entry attempts and then prevent the user from replacing or editing the characters in the JTextField by using a statement similar to the following:

```
if(attempts > LIMIT)
    response.setEditable(false);
```

Adding JButtons

In a GUI environment, a **button** is a component typically used to trigger an action or make a selection when the user clicks it. The Java class that creates a button is JButton. A JButton is even easier to create than a JTextField. There are five JButton constructors:

- public JButton() creates a button with no set text.
- public JButton(Icon icon) creates a button with an icon of type Icon or ImageIcon.
- public JButton(String text) creates a button with text.
- public JButton(String text, Icon icon) creates a button with initial text and an icon of type Icon or ImageIcon.
- public JButton(Action a) creates a button in which properties are taken from the Action supplied. (Action is a Java class.)

The inheritance hierarchy of the JButton class is shown in Figure 14-20.

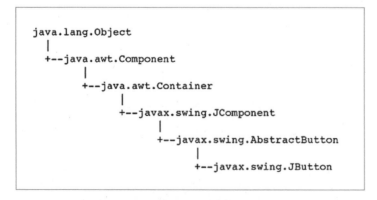

```
java.lang.Object
   |
   +--java.awt.Component
          |
          +--java.awt.Container
                 |
                 +--javax.swing.JComponent
                        |
                        +--javax.swing.AbstractButton
                               |
                               +--javax.swing.JButton
```

Figure 14-20   The JButton class inheritance hierarchy

To create a JButton with the text *Press when ready*, you can write the following:

```
JButton readyJButton = new JButton("Press when ready");
```

You can add a JButton to a JFrame (or other container) using the add() method. You can change a JButton's text with the setText() method, as in:

```
readyJButton.setText("Don't press me again!");
```

You can retrieve the text from a JButton and assign it to a String object with the getText() method, as in:

```
String whatsOnJButton = readyJButton.getText();
```

Figure 14-21 shows a class that extends JFrame and holds several components. As the components (two JLabels, a JTextField, and a JButton) are added to the JFrame, they are placed from left to right in horizontal rows across the JFrame's surface. Figure 14-22 shows the program that instantiates an instance of the JFrame.

```
import javax.swing.*;
import java.awt.*;
public class JFrameWithManyComponents extends JFrame
{
    final int FRAME_WIDTH = 300;
    final int FRAME_HEIGHT = 150;
    public JFrameWithManyComponents()
    {
        super("Demonstrating many components");
        setSize(FRAME_WIDTH, FRAME_HEIGHT);
        setDefaultCloseOperation(JFrame.EXIT_ON_CLOSE);
        JLabel heading = new JLabel("This frame has many components");
        heading.setFont(new Font("Arial", Font.BOLD, 16));
        JLabel namePrompt = new JLabel("Enter your name:");
        JTextField nameField = new JTextField(12);
        JButton button = new JButton("Click to continue");
        setLayout(new FlowLayout());
        add(heading);
        add(namePrompt);
        add(nameField);
        add(button);
    }
}
```

Figure 14-21   The JFrameWithManyComponents class

```
public class ComponentDemo
{
    public static void main(String[] args)
    {
        JFrameWithManyComponents frame =
            new JFrameWithManyComponents();
        frame.setVisible(true);
    }
}
```

Figure 14-22   A ComponentDemo application that instantiates a JFrameWithManyComponents

When you execute the ComponentDemo program, the JFrame contains all the components that were added in the frame's constructor, as shown in Figure 14-23. A user can minimize or restore the frame and alter its size by dragging the frame borders. The user can type characters in the JTextField and click the JButton. When the button is clicked, it appears to be pressed just like buttons you have used in professional applications. However, when the user types characters or clicks the button, no resulting actions occur because code has not yet been written to handle those user-initiated events.

Figure 14-23   Execution of the ComponentDemo program

Using Tool Tips

Tool tips are popup windows that can help a user understand the purpose of components in an application; the tool tip appears when a user hovers the mouse pointer over the component. You define the text to be displayed in a tool tip by using the setToolTipText() method and passing an appropriate String to it. For example, in the JFrameWithManyComponents program in Figure 14-21, you can add a tool tip to the button component by using the following statement in the JFrame constructor:

```
button.setToolTipText("Click this button");
```

Figure 14-24 shows the result when the JFrame is displayed and the user's mouse pointer is placed over the button.

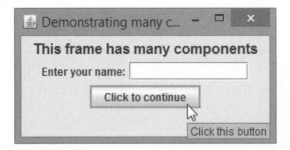

Figure 14-24 JFrame with added tool tip

The JFrameWithToolTip.java file in your downloadable student files contains a revised version of JFrameWithManyComponents with the tool tip added. The ToolTipDemo.java file contains an application that instantiates a JFrameWithToolTip object.

TWO TRUTHS & A LIE

Adding JTextFields, JButtons, and Tool Tips to a JFrame

1. A JTextField is a component into which a user can type a single line of text data; typically, a user types a line into a JTextField and then presses Enter on the keyboard or clicks a button with the mouse to enter the data.

2. A JButton is a Component the user can click to make a selection.

3. Tool tips are the different symbols you can select to display as a cursor in your applications.

The false statement is #3. Tool tips are popup windows that can help a user understand the purpose of components in an application; the tool tip appears when a user hovers the mouse pointer over the component.

You Do It

Adding Components to a JFrame

Next, you create a Swing application that displays a JFrame that holds a JLabel, JTextField, and JButton.

1. Open a new file, and then type the following first few lines of an application. The import statements make the Swing and AWT components available, and the class header indicates that the class is a JFrame. The class contains several components: a label, field, and button.

    ```
    import javax.swing.*;
    import java.awt.*;
    public class JFrameWithComponents extends JFrame
    {
        JLabel label = new JLabel("Enter your name");
        JTextField field = new JTextField(12);
        JButton button = new JButton("OK");
    ```

2. In the JFrameWithComponents constructor, set the JFrame title to "Frame with Components" and the default close operation to exit the program when the JFrame is closed. Set the layout manager. Add the label, field, and button to the JFrame.

    ```
    public JFrameWithComponents()
    {
        super("Frame with Components");
        setDefaultCloseOperation(JFrame.EXIT_ON_CLOSE);
        setLayout(new FlowLayout());
        add(label);
        add(field);
        add(button);
    }
    ```

3. Add a closing curly brace for the class, and then save the file as **JFrameWithComponents.java**.

4. Compile the class and correct any errors.

5. Next, write an application that creates a new JFrameWithComponents named aFrame, sizes it using the setSize() method, and then sets its visible property to true.

(continues)

(continued)

```java
import javax.swing.*;
public class CreateJFrameWithComponents
{
    public static void main(String[] args)
    {
        JFrameWithComponents aFrame =
            new JFrameWithComponents();
        final int WIDTH = 350;
        final int HEIGHT = 100;
        aFrame.setSize(WIDTH, HEIGHT);
        aFrame.setVisible(true);
    }
}
```

6. Save the file as **CreateJFrameWithComponents.java**. Compile and then execute the application. The output is shown in Figure 14-25.

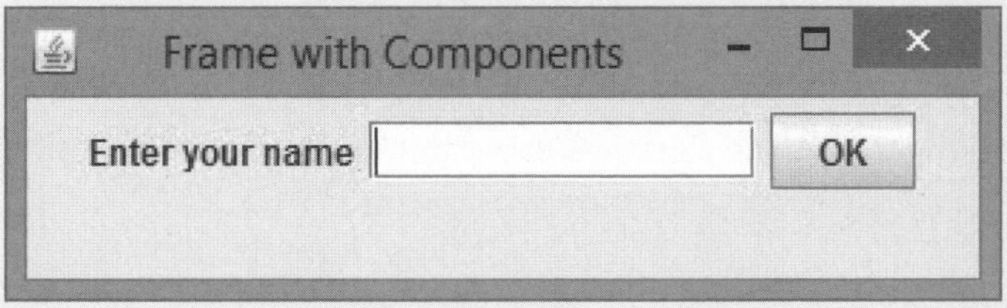

Figure 14-25   Output of the `CreateJFrameWithComponents` application

7. Click the `JButton`. It acts like a button should—that is, it appears to be pressed when you click it, but nothing happens because you have not yet written instructions for the button clicks to execute.

8. Close the application.

Learning About Event-Driven Programming

An **event** occurs when a user takes action on a component, such as clicking the mouse on a JButton object. In an **event-driven program**, the user might initiate any number of events in any order. For example, if you use a word-processing program, you have dozens of choices at your disposal at any time. You can type words, select text with the mouse, click a button to change text to bold, click a button to change text to italic, choose a menu item, and so on. With each word-processing document you create, you choose options in any order that seems appropriate at the time. The word-processing program must be ready to respond to any event you initiate.

Within an event-driven program, a component on which an event is generated is the **source** of the event. An object that is interested in an event is a **listener**. Programmers sometimes say a source *triggers* an event or *fires* an event. For example, if a label appears or changes color when the user clicks a button, the button is the source of the event and the label is a listener. When the source fires an event, an event-handling method contained in the listener object's class responds to the event. A source and a listener can be the same object. For example, you might program a button to change its own text when a user clicks it.

Not all objects listen for all possible events—you probably have used programs in which clicking many areas of the screen has no effect. If you want an object to be a listener for an event, you must **register** or sign up the object as a listener for the source. Social networking sites maintain lists of people in whom you are interested and notify you each time a person on your list posts a comment or picture. Similarly, a Java component source object (such as a button) maintains a list of registered listeners and notifies all of them when an event occurs.

To respond to user events within any class you create, you must do the following:

- Prepare your class to accept event messages by importing and implementing the appropriate listener interface.

- Tell your class to expect events to happen by registering it as a listener.

- Tell your class how to respond to events by writing necessary action statements in a method.

Preparing Your Class to Accept Event Messages

The `java.awt.event` package includes event classes that provide the capability to work with user-generated events such as an `ActionEvent`, which is the type of event that occurs when a user clicks a button. You import the `event` package to gain access to the methods in the event classes, and then you prepare a class to work with events by adding an `implements` phrase to the class header. For example, implementing the `ActionListener` interface provides you with standard event method specifications that allow a listener to work with `ActionEvents`.

You learned to create and implement interfaces in Chapter 11. You can identify interfaces such as `ActionListener` because they are used in phrases with the keyword `implements`. In ordinary language, an item that is implemented is put into service, or used. Implementation has a similar meaning when applied to interfaces. By contrast, packages that are *imported* are brought into an application, and classes that are added onto are *extended*.

If you declare a class that extends a class that implements a listener, you do not need to include `implements` in the child class header because the new class inherits the implementation.

Telling Your Class to Expect Events to Happen

You tell your class to expect an event using a method name that begins with the appropriate listener-registering method. The method that registers an ActionEvent is the addActionListener() method. (You learn about other listener-registering methods later in this chapter.) For example, suppose that you are creating a class that represents a frame; within the class, you have declared a JButton named aButton, and you want to perform an action when a user clicks aButton. In this case, aButton is the source of a message, and your class is a listener.

The following code in the frame class causes any ActionEvent messages (button clicks) that come from aButton to be sent to the frame:

```
aButton.addActionListener(this);
```

You learned in Chapter 4 that the this reference means "this current object." In this case, this refers to the frame class in which this statement appears.

Not all Events are ActionEvents with an addActionListener() method. For example, KeyListeners have an addKeyListener() method, and FocusListeners have an addFocusListener() method. Additional event types and methods are covered in more detail in the next chapter.

Telling Your Class How to Respond to Events

You tell your class what to do when an event is generated by writing statements in a specific method that is part of the listener interface. For example, the ActionListener interface contains the actionPerformed() method specification that executes when an event occurs. The method is an example of an **event handler**—it reacts to and takes care of generated events. When you implement the ActionListener interface, you must write the actionPerformed() method to overload the empty version in the interface. (In Chapter 11, you learned that all the methods in an interface are abstract, and therefore must be given a body in classes that use them.)

Suppose that you have created a class that extends JFrame, and that you have registered it as a listener for events triggered by a JButton. When a user clicks the JButton, the actionPerformed() method executes automatically. The actionPerformed() method must have the following header, in which e represents any name you choose for the Event:

```
public void actionPerformed(ActionEvent e)
```

The body of the method contains any statements that you want to execute when the action occurs. You might want to perform mathematical calculations, construct new objects, produce output, or execute any other operation.

An Event-Driven Program

For example, Figure 14-26 shows a JFrame that reacts to a button click. The class contains a JLabel that prompts the user for a name, a JTextField into which the user can type a response, a JButton to click, and a second JLabel that displays the name entered by the user. The first shaded section imports the event package, the second shaded section shows the phrase that implements the event listener, the third shaded section is the statement that registers the frame as a listener for button clicks, and the last shaded section is the method that executes when the button is clicked. Within the actionPerformed() method, the String that a user has typed into the JTextField is retrieved and stored in the name variable and then used in the text of a second JLabel. Figure 14-27 shows an application that instantiates a JHelloFrame object and makes it visible.

```java
import javax.swing.*;
import java.awt.*;
import java.awt.event.*;
public class JHelloFrame extends JFrame implements ActionListener
{
    JLabel question = new JLabel("What is your name?");
    Font bigFont = new Font("Arial", Font.BOLD, 16);
    JTextField answer = new JTextField(10);
    JButton pressMe = new JButton("Press me");
    JLabel greeting = new JLabel("");
    final int WIDTH = 275;
    final int HEIGHT = 225;
    public JHelloFrame()
    {
        super("Hello Frame");
        setSize(WIDTH, HEIGHT);
        setLayout(new FlowLayout());
        question.setFont(bigFont);
        greeting.setFont(bigFont);
        add(question);
        add(answer);
        add(pressMe);
        add(greeting);
        setDefaultCloseOperation(JFrame.EXIT_ON_CLOSE);
        pressMe.addActionListener(this);
    }
    @Override
    public void actionPerformed(ActionEvent e)
    {
        String name = answer.getText();
        String greet = "Hello, " + name;
        greeting.setText(greet);
    }
}
```

Figure 14-26   The JHelloFrame class that produces output when the user clicks the JButton

```
public class JHelloDemo
{
    public static void main(String[] args)
    {
        JHelloFrame frame = new JHelloFrame();
        frame.setVisible(true);
    }
}
```

Figure 14-27 An application that instantiates a JHelloFrame object

Figure 14-28 shows a typical execution of the JHelloDemo program. The user enters *Lindsey* into the JTextField, and the greeting with the name is displayed after the user clicks the button.

Figure 14-28 Typical execution of the JHelloDemo program

Using Multiple Event Sources

You can add more than one event source component to a listener. For example, in the JHelloFrame class in Figure 14-26, you might want the user to be able to see the message after either clicking the button or pressing Enter in the JTextField. In that case, you would designate both the pressMe button and the answer text field to be message sources by using the addActionListener() method with each, as follows:

```
pressMe.addActionListener(this);
answer.addActionListener(this);
```

These two statements make the JFrame a listener for messages from either object. The actionPerformed() method then executes when either the pressMe button or the answer text field generates an event.

If you want different actions to occur depending on whether the user clicks the button or presses Enter, you must determine the source of the event. Within the `actionPerformed()` method, you can use the `getSource()` method with the event parameter to determine which component generated the event. For example, when the parameter to the `actionPerformed()` method is named e, you can use the following statement to determine which object generated the `ActionEvent`:

```
Object source = e.getSource();
```

For example, if a `JFrame` contains two `JButtons` named `option1` and `option2`, you can use the decision structure in the method in Figure 14-29 to take different courses of action based on which button is clicked. Whether an event's source is a `JButton`, `JTextField`, or other `Component`, it can be assigned to an `Object` because all components descend from `Object`.

```java
@Override
public void actionPerformed(ActionEvent e)
{
    Object source = e.getSource();
    if(source == option1)
        //execute these statements when user clicks option1
    else
        //execute these statements when user clicks any other option
}
```

Figure 14-29   An `actionPerformed()` method that takes one of two possible actions

Alternatively, you can also use the `instanceof` keyword to determine the source of the event. The `instanceof` keyword is used when it is necessary to know only the component's type, rather than what component triggered the event. For example, if you want to take some action when a user enters data into any `JTextField`, but not when an event is generated by a different `Component` type, you could use the method format shown in Figure 14-30.

```java
@Override
void actionPerformed(ActionEvent e)
{
    Object source = e.getSource();
    if(source instanceof JTextField)
    {
        // execute these statements when any JTextField
        // generates the event
        // but not when a JButton or other Component does
    }
}
```

Figure 14-30   An `actionPerformed()` method that executes a block of statements when a user generates an event from any `JTextField`

Using the `setEnabled()` Method

You probably have used computer programs in which a component becomes disabled or unusable. For example, a `JButton` might become dim and unresponsive when the programmer no longer wants the user to have access to the `JButton`'s functionality. Components are enabled by default, but you can use the `setEnabled()` method to make a component available or unavailable by passing `true` or `false` to it, respectively. For example, Figure 14-31 shows a `JFrame` with two `JButton` objects. The one on top is enabled, but the one on the bottom has been disabled.

Figure 14-31   A `JFrame` with an enabled `JButton` and a disabled `JButton`

 Your downloadable student files contain a file named JTwoButtons.java that produces the `JFrame` shown in Figure 14-31.

TWO TRUTHS **& A LIE**

Learning About Event-Driven Programming

1. Within an event-driven program, a component on which an event is generated is a listener.

2. You prepare your class to accept button-press events by importing the `java.awt.event` package into your program and adding the phrase `implements ActionListener` to the class header.

3. A class that can react to `ActionEvents` includes an `actionPerformed()` method.

The false statement is #1. Within an event-driven program, a component on which an event is generated is the source of the event, and an object that is interested in an event is a listener.

You Do It

Adding Functionality to a *JButton* and a *JTextField*

Next, you add functionality to the JButton and JTextField that you created in the JFrameWithComponents class.

1. Open the **JFrameWithComponents.java** file. Immediately save the file as **JAction.java**.

2. After the existing import statements at the top of the file, add the following import statement that will allow event handling:

   import java.awt.event.*;

3. Change the class name to **JAction** to match the new filename. Also change the constructor header to match the new class name. Within the constructor, change the string argument to the super() method from "Frame with Components" to "Action".

4. After extends JFrame at the end of the JAction class header, add the following phrase so that the class can respond to ActionEventS:

   implements ActionListener

5. Register the JAction class as a listener for events generated by either the button or the text field by adding the following statements at the end of, but within, the JAction() constructor:

   button.addActionListener(this);
   field.addActionListener(this);

6. Just prior to the closing curly brace for the class, add the following actionPerformed() method that overrides the one defined in the ActionListener interface. The method changes the text on both the label and the button whenever the user clicks the button or presses Enter in the text field.

   @Override
   public void actionPerformed(ActionEvent e)
   {
       label.setText("Thank you");
       button.setText("Done");
   }

7. Just after the actionPerformed() method, and just before the closing curly brace for the class, add a main() method to the class so that you can instantiate a JAction object for demonstration purposes.

(continues)

(continued)

```
public static void main(String[] args)
{
    JAction aFrame = new JAction();
    final int WIDTH = 250;
    final int HEIGHT = 100;
    aFrame.setSize(WIDTH, HEIGHT);
    aFrame.setVisible(true);
}
```

8. Save the file, then compile and execute it. The output looks like the frame on the left side of Figure 14-32. Type a name in the text field, and then click the **OK** button. Its text changes to "Done", and its size increases slightly because the label "Done" requires more space than the label "OK". The other label requires less space than it did because "Thank you" is a shorter message than "Enter your name". Therefore, all the components are redistributed because the FlowLayout manager places as many components as will fit horizontally in the top row before adding components to subsequent rows. The output looks like the right side of Figure 14-32.

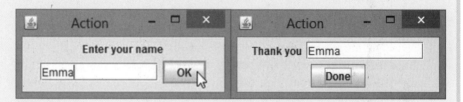

Figure 14-32 Typical execution of the JAction application after the user clicks the OK button

9. Close the application and then execute it again. This time, enter a name in the text field and press **Enter**. Again, the button text changes, showing that the actionPerformed() method reacts to actions that take place on either the button or the text field.

10. Close the application.

Distinguishing Event Sources

Next, you will modify the actionPerformed() method of the JAction class so that different results occur depending on which action a user takes.

1. Open the **JAction.java** file if it is not still open. Immediately save the file as **JAction2.java**.

(continues)

(continued)

2. Change the class name and the constructor name to match the new filename by adding **2** to each name.

3. In the `main()` method, change the statement that instantiates the `JFrame` object to the following:

   ```
   JAction2 aFrame = new JAction2();
   ```

4. Within the `actionPerformed()` method, you can use the named `ActionEvent` argument and the `getSource()` method to determine the source of the event. Using an `if` statement, you can take different actions when the argument represents different sources. For example, you can change the label in the frame to indicate the event's source. Change the `actionPerformed()` method to:

   ```
   @Override
   public void actionPerformed(ActionEvent e)
   {
      Object source = e.getSource();
      if(source == button)
         label.setText("You clicked the button");
      else
         label.setText("You pressed Enter");
   }
   ```

5. Save the file (as JAction2.java), then compile and execute it. Type a name, press **Enter** or click the **button**, and notice the varying results in the frame's label. For example, Figure 14-33 shows the application after the user has typed a name and pressed Enter.

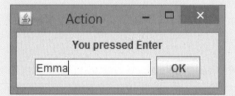

Figure 14-33   Typical execution of the `JAction2` application

6. Close the application.

Understanding Swing Event Listeners

Many types of listeners exist in Java, and each of these listeners can handle a specific event type. A class can implement as many event listeners as it needs—for example, a class might need to respond to both a mouse button press and a keyboard key press, so you might implement both ActionListener and KeyListener interfaces. Table 14-2 lists some event listeners and the types of events for which they are used.

 As a shorthand, programmers sometimes refer to all the listener classes as a group using *XXXListener* or *<name>Listener*.

Listener	Type of Events	Example
ActionListener	Action events	Button clicks
AdjustmentListener	Adjustment events	Scroll bar moves
ChangeListener	Change events	Slider is repositioned
FocusListener	Keyboard focus events	Text field gains or loses focus
ItemListener	Item events	Check box changes status
KeyListener	Keyboard events	Text is entered
MouseListener	Mouse events	Mouse clicks
MouseMotionListener	Mouse movement events	Mouse rolls
WindowListener	Window events	Window closes

Table 14-2   Alphabetical list of some event listeners

An event occurs every time a user types a character, clicks a mouse button, taps a touch screen, or takes a similar action. Any object can be notified of an event as long as it implements the appropriate interface and is registered as an event listener on the appropriate event source. You already know that you establish a relationship between a JButton and a JFrame that contains it by using the addActionListener() method. Similarly, you can create relationships between other Swing components and the classes that react to users' manipulations of them. In Table 14-3, each component listed on the left is associated with a method on the right. For example, when you want a JCheckBox to respond to a user's clicks, you can use the addItemListener() method to register the JCheckBox as the type of object that can create an ItemEvent. (You learn more about JCheckBox objects later in this chapter.) The argument you place within the parentheses of the call to the addItemListener() method is the object that should respond to the event. The format is:

```
theSourceOfTheEvent.addListenerMethod(theClassThatShouldRespond);
```

As you have already learned, the class that should respond is frequently the this class.

Component(s)	Associated Listener-Registering Method(s)
JButton, JCheckBox, JComboBox, JTextField, and JRadioButton	addActionListener()
JScrollBar	addAdjustmentListener()
All Swing components	addFocusListener(), addKeyListener(), addMouseListener(), and addMouseMotionListener()
JButton, JCheckBox, JComboBox, and JRadioButton	addItemListener()
All JWindow and JFrame components	addWindowListener()
JSlider and JCheckBox	addChangeListener()

Table 14-3   Some Swing components and their associated listener-registering methods

Programmers sometimes use the shorthand *addXXXListener()* or *add<name>Listener()* to refer to all the add listener methods as a group.

Any event source can have multiple listeners registered on it. Conversely, a single listener can be registered with multiple event sources. In other words, a single instance of JCheckBox might generate ItemEvents and FocusEvents, and a single instance of the JFrame class might respond to ActionEvents generated by a JButton and ItemEvents generated by a JCheckBox.

The class of the object that responds to an event must contain an event-handling method that accepts the event object created by the user's action. You cannot choose your own name for event handlers—specific method identifiers react to specific event types. Table 14-4 lists just some of the methods that react to events.

Listener	Method
ActionListener	actionPerformed(ActionEvent)
AdjustmentListener	adjustmentValueChanged(AdjustmentEvent)
FocusListener	focusGained(FocusEvent) and focusLost(FocusEvent)
ItemListener	itemStateChanged(ItemEvent)

Table 14-4   Selected methods that respond to events

Each listener in Table 14-4 is associated with only one or two methods. Other listeners, such as KeyListener and MouseListener, are associated with multiple methods. You will learn how to use these more complicated listeners in the chapter "Advanced GUI Topics."

Until you become familiar with the event-handling model, it can seem quite confusing. For now, remember these tasks you must perform when you declare a class that handles an event:

- You must import the java.awt.event package in the class that handles the event.

- The class that handles an event must either implement a listener interface or extend a class that implements a listener interface.

- You must register each instance of the event-handling class as a listener for one or more components using an addXXXListener() method.

- You must write an event handler method with an appropriate identifier (as shown in Table 14-4) that accepts the generated event and reacts to it.

 Watch the video *Event-Driven Programming*.

TWO TRUTHS & A LIE

Understanding Swing Event Listeners

1. A class can implement as many event listeners as it needs.

2. Any object can be notified of a mouse click or keyboard press as long as it implements the appropriate interface and is registered as an event listener on the appropriate event source.

3. Every event-handling method accepts a parameter that represents the listener for the event.

The false statement is #3. Every event-handling method accepts a parameter that represents the generated event.

Using the JCheckBox, ButtonGroup, and JComboBox Classes

Besides JButtons and JTextFields, several other Java components allow a user to make selections in a GUI environment. These include JCheckBoxes, ButtonGroups, and JComboBoxes.

The JCheckBox Class

A **check box** consists of a label positioned beside a square; you can click the square to display or remove a check mark. Usually, you use a check box to allow the user to turn an option on or off. The Java Swing class that creates a check box is JCheckBox. For example, Figure 14-34 shows the code for an application that uses four JCheckBox objects, and Figure 14-35 shows the output.

```java
import java.awt.*;
import javax.swing.*;
import java.awt.event.*;
public class CheckBoxDemonstration
    extends JFrame implements ItemListener
{
    FlowLayout flow = new FlowLayout();
    JLabel label = new JLabel("What would you like to drink?");
    JCheckBox coffee = new JCheckBox("Coffee", false);
    JCheckBox cola = new JCheckBox("Cola", false);
    JCheckBox milk = new JCheckBox("Milk", false);
    JCheckBox water = new JCheckBox("Water", false);
    public CheckBoxDemonstration()
    {
        super("CheckBox Demonstration");
        setDefaultCloseOperation(JFrame.EXIT_ON_CLOSE);
        setLayout(new FlowLayout());
        label.setFont(new Font("Arial", Font.ITALIC, 22));
        coffee.addItemListener(this);
        cola.addItemListener(this);
        milk.addItemListener(this);
        water.addItemListener(this);
        add(label);
        add(coffee);
        add(cola);
        add(milk);
        add(water);
    }
    @Override
    public void itemStateChanged(ItemEvent check)
    {
        // Actions based on choice go here
    }
    public static void main(String[] arguments)
    {
        final int FRAME_WIDTH = 350;
        final int FRAME_HEIGHT = 120;
        CheckBoxDemonstration frame =
            new CheckBoxDemonstration();
        frame.setSize(FRAME_WIDTH, FRAME_HEIGHT);
        frame.setVisible(true);
    }
}
```

Figure 14-34 The CheckBoxDemonstration class

In the application in Figure 14-34, the CheckBoxDemonstration class and the main() method that instantiates an instance of it are part of the same class. You could also store the two parts in separate classes, as in previous examples.

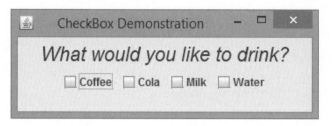

Figure 14-35   Output of the CheckBoxDemonstration class

The inheritance hierarchy of the JCheckBox class is shown in Figure 14-36; frequently used JCheckBox methods appear in Table 14-5.

```
java.lang.Object
  !--java.awt.Component
        !--java.awt.Container
              !--javax.swing.JComponent
                    !--javax.swing.AbstractButton
                          !--javax.swing.JToggleButton
                                !--javax.swing.JCheckBox
```

Figure 14-36   The inheritance hierarchy of the JCheckBox class

Method	Purpose
void setText(String)	Sets the text for the JCheckBox
String getText()	Returns the JCheckBox text
void setSelected(boolean)	Sets the state of the JCheckBox to true for selected or false for unselected
boolean isSelected()	Gets the current state (checked or unchecked) of the JCheckBox

Table 14-5   Frequently used JCheckBox methods

Several constructors can be used with JCheckBoxes. When you construct a JCheckBox, you can choose whether to assign it a label; you can also decide whether the JCheckBox appears selected (JCheckBoxes start unselected by default). The following statements create four JCheckBox objects—one with no label and unselected, two with labels and unselected, and one with a label and selected.

- JCheckBox box1 = new JCheckBox();
      // No label, unselected

- JCheckBox box2 = new JCheckBox("Check here");
      // Label, unselected

- JCheckBox box3 = new JCheckBox("Check here", false);
      // Label, unselected

- JCheckBox box4 = new JCheckBox("Check here", true);
      // Label, selected

If you do not initialize a JCheckBox with a label and you want to assign one later, or if you want to change an existing label, you can use the setText() method, as in the following example:

```
box1.setText("Check this box now");
```

You can set the state of a JCheckBox with the setSelected() method; for example, you can use the following statement to ensure that box1 is unchecked:

```
box1.setSelected(false);
```

The isSelected() method is most useful in Boolean expressions, as in the following example, which adds one to a voteCount variable if box2 is currently checked.

```
if(box2.isSelected())
    ++voteCount;
```

When the status of a JCheckBox changes from unchecked to checked (or from checked to unchecked), an ItemEvent is generated, and the itemStateChanged() method executes. You can use the getItem() method to determine which object generated the event and the getStateChange() method to determine whether the event was a selection or a deselection. The getStateChange() method returns an integer that is equal to one of two class variables—ItemEvent.SELECTED or ItemEvent.DESELECTED. For example, in Figure 14-37 the itemStateChanged() method calls the getItem() method, which returns the object named source. Then, the value of source is tested in an if statement to determine if it is equivalent to a JCheckBox object named checkBox. If the two references are to the same object, the code determines whether the checkBox was selected or deselected, and in each case appropriate actions are taken.

```
@Override
public void itemStateChanged(ItemEvent e)
{
    Object source = e.getItem();
    if(source == checkBox)
    {
        int select = e.getStateChange();
        if(select == ItemEvent.SELECTED)
            // statements that execute when the box is checked
        else
            // statements that execute when the box is unchecked
    }
    else
    {
        // statements that execute when the source of the event is
        // some component other than the checkBox object
    }
}
```

Figure 14-37 Typical itemStateChanged() method

The ButtonGroup Class

Sometimes, you want options to be mutually exclusive—that is, you want the user to be able to select only one of several choices. When you create a **button group** using the ButtonGroup class, you can group several components, such as JCheckBoxes, so a user can select only one at a time. When you group JCheckBox objects, all of the other JCheckBoxes are automatically turned off when the user selects any one check box. The inheritance hierarchy for the ButtonGroup class is shown in Figure 14-38. You can see that ButtonGroup descends directly from the Object class. Even though it does not begin with a *J*, the ButtonGroup class is part of the javax.swing package.

```
java.lang.Object
   !--javax.swing.ButtonGroup
```

Figure 14-38 The inheritance hierarchy for the ButtonGroup class

A group of JCheckBoxes in which a user can select only one at a time also acts like a set of radio buttons (for example, those used to select preset radio stations on an automobile radio), which you can create using the JRadioButton class. The JRadioButton class is very similar to the JCheckBox class, and you might prefer to use it when you have a list of mutually exclusive user options. It makes sense to use ButtonGroups with items that can be selected (that is, those that use an isSelected() method). You can find more information about the JRadioButton class at the Java Web site.

To create a ButtonGroup in a JFrame and then add a JCheckBox, you must perform four steps:

- Create a ButtonGroup, such as ButtonGroup aGroup = new ButtonGroup();.
- Create a JCheckBox, such as JCheckBox aBox = new JCheckBox();.
- Add aBox to aGroup with aGroup.add(aBox);.
- Add aBox to the JFrame with add(aBox); or this.add(aBox);.

You can create a ButtonGroup and then create the individual JCheckBox objects, or you can create the JCheckBoxes and then create the ButtonGroup. If you create a ButtonGroup but forget to add any JCheckBox objects to it, then the JCheckBoxes act as individual, nonexclusive check boxes.

A user can set one of the JCheckBoxes within a group to "on" by clicking it, or the programmer can select a JCheckBox within a ButtonGroup with a statement such as the following:

aGroup.setSelected(aBox);

Only one JCheckBox can be selected within a group. If you assign the selected state to a JCheckBox within a group, any previous assignment is negated.

You can determine which, if any, of the JCheckBoxes in a ButtonGroup is selected using the isSelected() method.

After a JCheckBox in a ButtonGroup has been selected, one in the group will always be selected. In other words, you cannot "clear the slate" for all the items that are members of a ButtonGroup. A trick that you can use to cause all the JCheckBoxes in a ButtonGroup to initially appear unselected is to add one JCheckBox that is not visible (using the setVisible() method). Then, you can use the setSelected() method to select the invisible JCheckBox, and all the others appear to be deselected.

The JComboBox Class

A **combo box** is a component that combines a button or an editable field and a drop-down list. The Swing class JComboBox creates a combo box. When a JComboBox appears on the screen, the default option is displayed in a field at the top of the box, and the list is not displayed. When the user clicks the button on the JComboBox, a list drops down; if the user selects an item from this list, it replaces the box's displayed item. If the field at the top of the combo box is editable, the user can also type in it. The biggest advantage to using a JComboBox over displaying a series of choices with check boxes or buttons is that a combo box doesn't take up much room in a frame until its list is expanded. Figure 14-39 shows a JComboBox as it looks when first displayed and after a user clicks it.

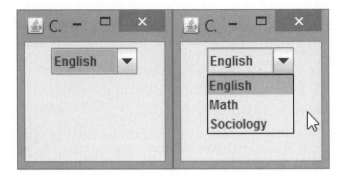

Figure 14-39   A JComboBox before and after the user clicks it

 The code that produces the JComboBox in Figure 14-39 is contained in the file named ComboBoxDemonstration.java in your downloadable student files.

Users often expect to view JComboBox options in alphabetical order. If it makes sense for your application, consider displaying your options this way. Other reasonable approaches are to place choices in logical order, such as "small", "medium", and "large", or to position the most frequently selected options first.

The inheritance hierarchy of the JComboBox class is shown in Figure 14-40.

```
java.lang.Object
    !--java.awt.Component
        !--java.awt.Container
            !--javax.swing.JComponent
                !--javax.swing.JComboBox
```

Figure 14-40   The inheritance hierarchy of the JComboBox class

You can build a JComboBox by using a constructor with no arguments and then adding items (for example, Strings) to the list with the addItem() method. The following statements create a JComboBox named majorChoice that contains three options from which a user can choose:

```
JComboBox<String> majorChoice = new JComboBox<String>();
majorChoice.addItem("English");
majorChoice.addItem("Math");
majorChoice.addItem("Sociology");
```

In the declaration of the JComboBox, notice the use of String following the constructor call. By default, a JComboBox expects items that are added to be Object types. Adding the angle brackets and String notifies the compiler of the expected data types in the JComboBox and allows the compiler to check for errors if invalid items are added. If you do not insert a data type for a JComboBox, the program compiles, but a warning message is issued with each addItem() method call. Programmers say that JComboBox uses *generics*. **Generic programming** is a feature of modern languages that allows multiple data types to be used safely with methods.

As an alternative, you can construct a JComboBox using an array of Objects as the constructor argument; the Objects in the array become the listed items within the JComboBox. For example, the following code creates the same majorChoice JComboBox as the preceding code:

```
String[] majorArray = {"English", "Math", "Sociology"};
JComboBox majorChoice = new JComboBox(majorArray);
```

Table 14-6 lists some methods you can use with a JComboBox object. For example, you can use the setSelectedItem() or setSelectedIndex() method to choose one of the items in a JComboBox to be the initially selected item. You also can use the getSelectedItem() or getSelectedIndex() method to discover which item is currently selected.

Method	Purpose
void addItem(Object)	Adds an item to the list
void removeItem(Object)	Removes an item from the list
void removeAllItems()	Removes all items from the list
Object getItemAt(int)	Returns the list item at the index position specified by the integer argument
int getItemCount()	Returns the number of items in the list
int getMaximumRowCount()	Returns the maximum number of items the combo box can display without a scroll bar
int getSelectedIndex()	Returns the position of the currently selected item
Object getSelectedItem()	Returns the currently selected item
Object[] getSelectedObjects()	Returns an array containing selected Objects
void setEditable(boolean)	Sets the field to be editable or not editable
void setMaximumRowCount(int)	Sets the number of rows in the combo box that can be displayed at one time
void setSelectedIndex(int)	Sets the index at the position indicated by the argument
void setSelectedItem(Object)	Sets the selected item in the combo box display area to be the Object argument

Table 14-6   Some JComboBox class methods

You can treat the list of items in a JComboBox object as an array; the first item is at position 0, the second is at position 1, and so on. It is convenient to use the getSelectedIndex() method to determine the list position of the currently selected item; then you can use the index to access corresponding information stored in a parallel array. For example, if a JComboBox named historyChoice has been filled with a list of historical events, such as "Declaration of Independence," "Pearl Harbor," and "Man walks on moon," you can code the following to retrieve the user's choice:

```
int positionOfSelection = historyChoice.getSelectedIndex();
```

The variable positionOfSelection now holds the position of the selected item, and you can use the variable to access an array of dates so you can display the date that corresponds to the selected historical event. For example, if you declare the following, then dates[positionOfSelection] holds the year for the selected historical event:

```
int[] dates = {1776, 1941, 1969};
```

A JComboBox does not have to hold items declared as Strings; it can hold an array of Objects and display the results of the toString() method used with those objects. In other words, instead of using parallel arrays to store historical events and dates, you could design a HistoricalEvent class that encapsulates Strings for the event and ints for the date.

In addition to JComboBoxes for which users click items presented in a list, you can create JComboBoxes into which users type text. To do this, you use the setEditable() method. A drawback to using an editable JComboBox is that the text a user types must exactly match an item in the list box. If the user misspells the selection or uses the wrong case, a negative value is returned from the getSelectedIndex() method. You can use an if statement to test the value returned or take action such as forcing a default option or issuing an appropriate error message.

TWO TRUTHS & A LIE

Using the JCheckBox, ButtonGroup, and JComboBox Classes

1. A JCheckBox consists of a label positioned beside a square; you can click the square to display or remove a check mark.

2. When you create a ButtonGroup, you can group several components, such as JCheckBoxes, so a user can select multiple options simultaneously.

3. When a user clicks a JComboBox, a list of alternative items drops down; if the user selects one, it replaces the box's displayed item.

The false statement is #2. When you create a ButtonGroup, you can group several components, such as JCheckBoxes, so a user can select only one at a time.

You Do It

Including JCheckBoxes in an Application

Next, you create an interactive program for a resort. The base price for a room is $200, and a guest can choose from several options. Reserving a room for a weekend night adds $100 to the price, including breakfast adds $20, and including a round of golf adds $75. A guest can select none, some, or all of these premium additions. Each time the user changes the option package, the price is recalculated.

1. Open a new file, and then type the following first few lines of a Swing application that demonstrates the use of a JCheckBox. Note that the JResortCalculator class implements the ItemListener interface:

    ```
    import javax.swing.*;
    import java.awt.*;
    import java.awt.event.*;
    public class JResortCalculator extends
       JFrame implements ItemListener
    {
    ```

2. Declare the named constants that hold the base price for a resort room and the premium amounts for a weekend stay, including breakfast and a round of golf. Also include a variable that holds the total price for the stay, and initialize it to the value of the base price. Later, depending on the user's selections, premium fees might be added to totalPrice, making it more than BASE_PRICE.

    ```
    final int BASE_PRICE = 200;
    final int WEEKEND_PREMIUM = 100;
    final int BREAKFAST_PREMIUM = 20;
    final int GOLF_PREMIUM = 75;
    int totalPrice = BASE_PRICE;
    ```

3. Declare three JCheckBox objects. Each is labeled with a String that contains a description of the option and the cost of the option. Each JCheckBox starts unchecked or deselected.

    ```
    JCheckBox weekendBox = new JCheckBox
       ("Weekend premium $" + WEEKEND_PREMIUM, false);
    JCheckBox breakfastBox = new
       JCheckBox("Breakfast $" + BREAKFAST_PREMIUM, false);
    JCheckBox golfBox = new JCheckBox
       ("Golf $" + GOLF_PREMIUM, false);
    ```

(continues)

(continued)

4. Include `JLabels` to hold user instructions and information and a `JTextField` in which to display the total price:

```
JLabel resortLabel = new JLabel("Resort Price Calculator");
JLabel priceLabel = new JLabel("The price for your stay is");
JTextField totPrice = new JTextField(4);
JLabel optionExplainLabel = new JLabel
    ("Base price for a room is $" + BASE_PRICE + ".");
JLabel optionExplainLabel2 = new JLabel
    ("Check the options you want.");
```

5. Begin the `JResortCalculator` class constructor. Include instructions to set the title by passing it to the `JFrame` parent class constructor, to set the default close operation, and to set the layout manager. Then add all the necessary components to the `JFrame`.

```
public JResortCalculator()
{
       super("Resort Price Estimator");
       setDefaultCloseOperation(JFrame.EXIT_ON_CLOSE);
       setLayout(new FlowLayout());
       add(resortLabel);
       add(optionExplainLabel);
       add(optionExplainLabel2);
       add(weekendBox);
       add(breakfastBox);
       add(golfBox);
       add(priceLabel);
       add(totPrice);
```

6. Continue the constructor by setting the text of the `totPrice` `JTextField` to display a dollar sign and the `totalPrice` value. Register the class as a listener for events generated by each of the three `JCheckBoxes`. Finally, add a closing curly brace for the constructor.

```
       totPrice.setText("$" + totalPrice);
       weekendBox.addItemListener(this);
       breakfastBox.addItemListener(this);
       golfBox.addItemListener(this);
}
```

(continues)

(continued)

7. Begin the `itemStateChanged()` method that executes when the user selects or deselects a `JCheckBox`. Use the appropriate methods to determine which `JCheckBox` is the source of the current `ItemEvent` and whether the event was generated by selecting a `JCheckBox` or by deselecting one.

```java
@Override
public void itemStateChanged(ItemEvent event)
{
    Object source = event.getSource();
    int select = event.getStateChange();
```

8. Write a nested `if` statement that tests whether the source is equivalent to the `weekendBox`, `breakfastBox`, or, by default, the `golfBox`. In each case, depending on whether the item was selected or deselected, add or subtract the corresponding premium fee from the `totalPrice`. Display the total price in the `JTextField`, and add a closing curly brace for the method.

```java
if(source == weekendBox)
    if(select == ItemEvent.SELECTED)
        totalPrice += WEEKEND_PREMIUM;
    else
        totalPrice -= WEEKEND_PREMIUM;
else if(source == breakfastBox)
{
    if(select == ItemEvent.SELECTED)
        totalPrice += BREAKFAST_PREMIUM;
    else
        totalPrice -= BREAKFAST_PREMIUM;
}
else // if(source == golfBox) by default
    if(select == ItemEvent.SELECTED)
        totalPrice += GOLF_PREMIUM;
    else
        totalPrice -= GOLF_PREMIUM;
    totPrice.setText("$" + totalPrice);
}
```

9. Add a `main()` method that creates an instance of the `JFrame` and sets its size and visibility. Then add a closing curly brace for the class.

```java
public static void main(String[] args)
{
    JResortCalculator aFrame = new JResortCalculator();
    final int WIDTH = 300;
    final int HEIGHT = 200;
    aFrame.setSize(WIDTH, HEIGHT);
    aFrame.setVisible(true);
}
}
```

(continues)

10. Save the file as **JResortCalculator.java**. Compile and execute the application. The output appears in Figure 14-41 with the base price initially set to $200.

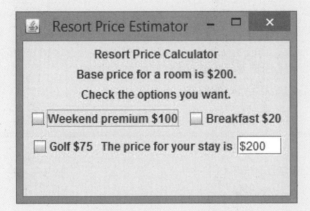

Figure 14-41   Initial output of the JResortCalculator application

11. Select the **Weekend premium** JCheckBox, and note the change in the total price of the event. Experiment with selecting and deselecting options to ensure that the price changes correctly. For example, Figure 14-42 shows the application with the weekend and golf options selected, adding a total of $175 to the $200 base price. After testing all the option combinations, close the application.

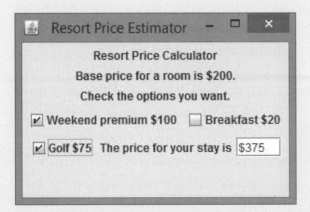

Figure 14-42   Output of the JResortCalculator application after the user has made selections

Don't Do It

- Don't forget the *x* in javax when you import Swing components into an application.

- Don't forget to use a JFrame's setVisible() method if you want the JFrame to be visible.

- Don't forget to use setLayout() when you add multiple components to a JFrame.

- Don't forget to call validate() and repaint() after you add or remove a component from a container that has been made visible.

- Don't forget that creating a ButtonGroup does not cause components to be grouped; each component that should be in the group must be added explicitly.

- Don't forget that the ButtonGroup class does not begin with a *J*.

Key Terms

GUI components are graphical user interface components, such as buttons and text fields, with which the user can interact.

The **Abstract Windows Toolkit** (**AWT**) contains GUI components that are older and not as portable as Swing components.

Swing is a toolkit that contains GUI components that are more portable than AWT components; you can usually recognize their names because they begin with *J*.

Java Foundation Classes (**JFC**) include Swing component classes and selected classes from the java.awt package.

Lightweight components are written completely in Java and do not have to rely on the code written to run the local operating system.

Heavyweight components require interaction with the local operating system.

A **container** is a type of component that holds other components so you can treat a group of them as a single entity. Often, a container takes the form of a window that you can drag, resize, minimize, restore, and close.

A **window** is a rectangular container that can hold GUI components.

A **frame** is a GUI component that is similar to a window, but that has a title bar and border.

Pixels are the picture elements, or tiny dots of light, that make up the image on your computer monitor.

Window decorations are the icons and buttons that are part of a window or frame.

Look and feel comprises the elements of design, style, and functionality in a user interface.

A **label** is an uneditable GUI component that is most often used to provide information for a user.

Editable describes a component that can accept keystrokes.

A **font** is the size, weight, and style of a typeface.

A **layout manager** is a class that controls component positioning.

A **border layout manager** is a layout manager that divides a container into regions.

A **flow layout manager** is a layout manager that places components in rows; when any row is filled, additional components automatically spill into the next row.

A **text field** is a GUI component into which a user can type a single line of text data.

A **button** is a GUI component typically used to trigger an action or make a selection when the user clicks it.

Tool tips are popup windows that can help a user understand the purpose of components in an application; a tool tip appears when a user hovers the mouse pointer over the component.

An **event** occurs when a user takes action on a component.

In an **event-driven program**, the user might initiate any number of events in any order.

The **source** of an event is the component on which an event is generated.

A **listener** is an object that is interested in an event.

To **register** an object as an event listener is to sign it up as one.

An **event handler** is a method that executes automatically when an appropriate event occurs.

A **check box** consists of a label positioned beside a clickable square; frequently you use a check box to allow the user to turn an option on or off.

A **button group** groups several components, such as check boxes, so a user can select only one at a time.

A **combo box** is a GUI component that combines a display area showing a default option and a list box containing additional options.

Generic programming is a feature of languages that allows methods to be used safely with multiple data types.

Chapter Summary

- Swing components are GUI elements such as dialog boxes and buttons. Each Swing component is a descendant of a JComponent, which in turn inherits from the java.awt.Container class. Swing components usually are placed in a container—a type of component that holds other components. Containers are defined in the Container class. Often, a container takes the form of a window that you can drag, resize, minimize, restore, and close.

- A JFrame holds and displays other objects. Useful methods include setSize(), setTitle(), setVisible(), setBounds(), and setDefaultCloseOperation(). JFrames include a title bar at the top containing text information, and Minimize, Maximize or Restore, and Close buttons in the frame's upper-right corner. When a user closes a JFrame by clicking the Close button in the upper-right corner, the default behavior is for the JFrame to be hidden and for the application to keep running.

- JLabel is a built-in Java Swing class that holds text. The setFont() method changes the font typeface, style, and point size.

- A layout manager is a class that controls component positioning in a container. The normal (default) behavior of a JFrame is to use a layout format named BorderLayout. With FlowLayout, components are placed in rows; when any row is filled, additional components automatically spill into the next row.

- The advantage to creating a child class of JFrame is that you can set the JFrame's properties within your object's constructor; then, when you create your JFrame child object, it is automatically endowed with the features you have specified, such as title, size, and default close operation.

- A JTextField is a component into which a user can type a single line of text data. A JButton is a Component the user can click to make a selection. Tool tips are popup windows that can help a user understand the purpose of components in an application; the tool tip appears when a user hovers the mouse pointer over the component.

- Within an event-driven program, a component on which an event is generated is the source of the event, and an object that is interested in an event is a listener. You prepare your class to accept button-press events by importing the java.awt.event package into your program and adding the phrase implements ActionListener to the class header. You register your class as a listener with the addActionListener() method, and then you implement the actionPerformed() method to contain the actions that should occur in response to the event. Within the actionPerformed() method, you can use the getSource() method to determine which component generated the event.

- A class can implement as many event listeners as it needs. Examples of event listeners are ActionListener, ItemListener, KeyListener, and MouseListener. Any object can be notified of an event as long as it implements the appropriate interface and is registered as an event listener on the appropriate event source. Specific methods react to specific event types.

- A JCheckBox consists of a label positioned beside a checkable square and frequently is used to allow the user to turn an option on or off. A ButtonGroup groups components so a user can select only one at a time. A JComboBox is a component that combines a display area showing a default option and a drop-down list box containing additional options.

Review Questions

1. A JFrame is a descendant of each of the following classes except the ——————— class.

   a. Component
   b. Jar

   c. Container
   d. Window

2. Unlike a Window, a JFrame ———————.

   a. can hold other objects
   b. can be made visible

   c. can have descendants
   d. has a title bar and border

3. The statement JFrame myFrame = new JFrame(); creates a JFrame that is ———————.

   a. invisible and has no title
   b. invisible and has a title

   c. visible and has no title
   d. visible and has a title

4. To create a JFrame named aFrame that is 300 pixels wide by 200 pixels tall, you can ———————.

   a. use the declaration JFrame aFrame = new JFrame(300, 200);
   b. declare a JFrame named aFrame and then code aFrame.setSize(300, 200);
   c. declare a JFrame named aFrame and then code aFrame.setBounds(300, 200);
   d. use any of the above

5. When a user closes a JFrame, the default behavior is for ———————.

   a. the JFrame to close and the application to keep running
   b. the JFrame to be hidden and the application to keep running
   c. the JFrame to close and the application to exit
   d. nothing to happen

6. An advantage of extending the JFrame class is ———————.

   a. you can set the child class properties within the class constructor
   b. there is no other way to cause an application to close when the user clicks a JFrame's Close button
   c. there is no other way to make a JFrame visible
   d. all of the above

7. Suppose that you create an application in which you instantiate a JFrame named frame1 and a JLabel named label1. Which of the following statements within the application adds label1 to frame1?

   a. label1.add(frame1);
   b. frame1.add(label1);

   c. this.add(label1);
   d. two of the above

8. The arguments required by the Font constructor include all of the following except ――――――――― .

    a. typeface   c. mode

    b. style   d. point size

9. A class that controls component positioning in a JFrame is a ――――――――― .

    a. container   c. formatter

    b. layout manager   d. design supervisor

10. Which of the following is not true of a JTextField?

    a. A user can type text data into it.

    b. Its data can be set in the program instead of by the user.

    c. A program can set its attributes so that a user cannot type in it.

    d. It is a type of Container.

11. ――――――――― are popup windows that appear when a user hovers the mouse pointer over a component.

    a. Navigation notes   c. Help icons

    b. Tool tips   d. Graphic suggestions

12. Within an event-driven program, a component on which an event is generated is the ――――――――― .

    a. performer   c. source

    b. listener   d. handler

13. A class that will respond to button-press events must use which phrase in its header?

    a. import java.event   c. extends JFrame

    b. extends Action   d. implements ActionListener

14. A JFrame contains a JButton named button1 that should execute an actionPerformed() method when clicked. Which statement is needed in the JFrame class?

    a. addActionListener(this);

    b. addActionListener(button1);

    c. button1.addActionListener(this);

    d. this.addActionListener(button1);

15. When you use the getSource() method with an ActionEvent object, the result is a(n) ――――――――― .

    a. Object   c. Component

    b. ActionEvent   d. TextField

16. A class can implement ———————.

    a. one listener

    b. two listeners

    c. as many listeners as it needs

    d. any number of listeners as long as they are not conflicting listeners

17. When you write a method that reacts to `JCheckBox` changes, you name the method ———————.

    a. `itemStateChanged()`   c. `checkBoxChanged()`

    b. `actionPerformed()`   d. any legal identifier you choose

18. If a class contains two components that might each generate a specific event type, you can determine which component caused the event by using the ——————— method.

    a. `addActionListener()`   c. `whichOne()`

    b. `getSource()`   d. `identifyOrigin()`

19. To group several components such as `JCheckBox`es so that a user can select only one at a time, you create a ———————.

    a. `JCheckBoxGroup`   c. `JButtonGroup`

    b. `CheckBoxGroup`   d. `ButtonGroup`

20. Suppose that you have declared a `ButtonGroup` named `twoOptions` and added two `JCheckBox`es named `box1` and `box2` to it. Which box is selected after the following statements execute?

```
twoOptions.setSelected(box1);
twoOptions.setSelected(box2);
```

    a. `box1`   c. both `box1` and `box2`

    b. `box2`   d. none of these

Exercises

 Programming Exercises

1. a. Write an application that displays a `JFrame` containing the opening sentence or two from your favorite book. Save the file as **JBookQuote.java**.

    b. Add a button to the frame in the `JBookQuote` program. When the user clicks the button, display the title of the book that contains the quote. Save the file as **JBookQuote2.java**.

2. a. Write an application that instantiates a `JFrame` that contains a `JButton`. Disable the `JButton` after the user clicks it. Save the file as **JFrameDisableButton.java**.

b. Modify the JFrameDisableButton program so that the JButton is not disabled until the user has clicked at least eight times. At that point, display a JLabel that indicates "That's enough!". Save the file as **JFrameDisableButton2.java**.

3. Create an application with a JFrame and at least five labels that contain interesting historical facts. Every time the user clicks a JButton, remove one of the labels and add a different one. Save the file as **JHistoricalFacts.java**.

4. Write an application for Lambert's Vacation Rentals. Use separate ButtonGroups to allow a client to select one of three locations, the number of bedrooms, and whether meals are included in the rental. Assume that the locations are parkside for $600 per week, poolside for $750 per week, or lakeside for $825 per week. Assume that the rentals have one, two, or three bedrooms and that each bedroom over one adds $75 to the base price. Assume that if meals are added, the price is $200 more per rental. Save the file as **JVacationRental.java**.

5. a. Write an application that allows a user to select one of at least five television shows to watch on demand. When the user selects a show, display a brief synopsis. Save the file as **JTVDownload.java**.

   b. Change the JTVDownload application to include an editable combo box. Allow the user to type the name of a television show and display an appropriate error message if the desired show is not available. Save the file as **JTVDownload2.java**.

6. Design an application for a pizzeria. The user makes pizza order choices from list boxes, and the application displays the price. The user can choose a pizza size of small ($7), medium ($9), large ($11), or extra large ($14), and one of any number of toppings. There is no additional charge for cheese, but any other topping adds $1 to the base price. Offer at least five different topping choices. Save the file as **JPizza.java**.

7. Write an application that allows a user to select a country from a list box that contains at least seven options. After the user makes a selection, display the country's capital city. Save the file as **JCapitals.java**.

8. Write an application that allows the user to choose insurance options in JCheckBoxes. Use a ButtonGroup to allow the user to select only one of two insurance types—HMO (health maintenance organization) or PPO (preferred provider organization). Use regular (single) JCheckBoxes for dental insurance and vision insurance options; the user can select one option, both options, or neither option. As the user selects each option, display its name and price in a text field; the HMO costs $200 per month, the PPO costs $600 per month, the dental coverage adds $75 per month, and the vision care adds $20 per month. When a user deselects an item, make the text field blank. Save the file as **JInsurance.java**.

9. a. Search the Java Web site for information on how to use a JTextArea, its constructors, and its setText() and append() methods. Write an application that allows the user to select options for a dormitory room. Use JCheckBoxes for options such as private room, Internet connection, cable TV connection, microwave, refrigerator, and so on. When the application starts, use a text area to display a message listing the options that are not yet selected. As the user selects

and deselects options, add appropriate messages to the common text area so it accumulates a running list that reflects the user's choices. Save the file as **JDorm.java**.

b. Modify the JDorm application so that instead of a running list of the user's choices, the application displays only the current choices. Save the file as **JDorm2.java**.

10. Create an application for Paula's Portraits, a photography studio. The application allows users to compute the price of a photography session. Paula's base price is $40 for an in-studio photo session with one person. The in-studio fee is $75 for a session with two or more subjects, and $95 for a session with a pet. A $90 fee is added to take photos on location instead of in the studio. Include a set of mutually exclusive check boxes to select the portrait subject and another set of mutually exclusive check boxes for the session location. Include labels as appropriate to explain the application's functionality. Save the file as **JPhotoFrame.java**.

Debugging Exercises

1. Each of the following files in the Chapter14 folder of your downloadable student files has syntax and/or logic errors. In each case, determine the problem and fix the program. After you correct the errors, save each file using the same filename preceded with *Fix*. For example, DebugFourteen1.java will become **FixDebugFourteen1.java**.

   a. DebugFourteen1.java   c. DebugFourteen3.java
   b. DebugFourteen2.java   d. DebugFourteen4.java

Game Zone

1. a. Create a quiz game that displays, in turn, five questions about any topic of your choice. All five questions should have the same three possible multiple-choice answers. For example, you might ask trivia questions about U.S. states for which the correct response is either California, Florida, or New York. After each question is displayed, allow the user to choose one, two, or all three answers by selecting JCheckBoxes. In other words, if the user is sure of an answer, he will select just one box, but if he is uncertain, he might select two or three boxes. When the user is ready to submit the answer(s), he clicks a button. If the user's answer to the question is correct and he has selected just one box, award 5 points. If the user is correct but has selected two boxes, award 2 points. If the user has selected all three boxes, award 1 point. If the user has selected fewer than three boxes but is incorrect, the user receives 0 points. A total of 25 points is possible. If the user has accumulated more than 21 points at the end of the quiz, display the message *Fantastic!* If the user has accumulated more than 15 points, display the message *Very good*, and if the user has accumulated fewer points, display *OK*. Save the file as **HedgeYourBet.java**.

b. Modify the HedgeYourBet game so that it stores the player's score from the last game in a file and displays the previous score at the start of each new game. (The first time you play the game, the previous score should be 0.) Save the game as **HedgeYourBetUsingFile.java**.

2. In Chapter 5, you created a lottery game application. Create a similar game using check boxes. For this game, generate six random numbers, each between 0 and 30 inclusive. Allow the user to choose six check boxes to play the game. (Do not allow the user to choose more than six boxes.) After the player has chosen six numbers, display the randomly selected numbers, the player's numbers, and the amount of money the user has won, as follows:

Matching Numbers	Award ($)
Three matches	100
Four matches	10,000
Five matches	50,000
Six matches	1,000,000
Zero, one, or two matches	0

Save the file as **JLottery2.java**.

3. a. Create a game called Last Man Standing in which the objective is to select the last remaining JCheckBox. The game contains 10 JCheckBoxes. The player can choose one, two, or three boxes, and then click a JButton to indicate the turn is complete. The computer then randomly selects one, two, or three JCheckBox objects. When the last JCheckBox is selected, display a message indicating the winner. Save the game as **LastManStanding.java**.

b. In the current version of the Last Man Standing game, the computer might seem to make strategic mistakes because of its random selections. For example, when only two JCheckBox objects are left, the computer might randomly choose to check only one, allowing the player to check the last one and win. Modify the game to make it as smart as possible, using a random value for the number of the computer's selections only when there is no superior alternative. Save the improved game as **SmarterLastManStanding.java**.

Case Problems

1. In previous chapters, you have created a number of programs for Carly's Catering. Now, create an interactive GUI program that allows the user to enter the number of guests for an event into a text field; if the value entered is not numeric, set the event price to 0. Also allow the user to choose one entree from a group of at least four choices, up to two side dishes from a group of at least four choices, and

one dessert from a group of at least three choices. Display the cost of the event as $35 per person; as the user continues to make selection changes, display a list of the current items chosen. If a user attempts to choose more than two side dishes, remove all the current side dish selections so that the user can start over. Save the program as **JCarlysCatering.java**.

2. In previous chapters, you have created a number of programs for Sammy's Seashore Rentals. Now, create an interactive GUI program that allows the user to enter a rental time in hours into a text field; if the value entered is not numeric, set the rental price to 0. Also allow the user to choose one equipment type to rent from a group of seven choices. The rental fee is $40 per hour for a jet ski or pontoon boat; $20 per hour for a rowboat, canoe, or kayak; and $7 per hour for a beach chair or umbrella. Let the user add an equipment lesson for an extra $5. Display a message that indicates all the details for the rental, including the total price. Save the program as **JSammysSeashore.java**.

Advanced GUI Topics

In this chapter, you will:

◎ Use content panes

◎ Use color

◎ Learn more about layout managers

◎ Use `JPanel`s to increase layout options

◎ Create `JScrollPane`s

◎ Understand events and event handling more thoroughly

◎ Use the `AWTEvent` class methods

◎ Handle mouse events

◎ Use menus

Understanding the Content Pane

Every Java `Swing` component that appears on the screen must be part of a **containment hierarchy**, which is a tree of components that has a top-level container at its uppermost level. `JFrame`, `JDialog`, and `JApplet` are Java's three **top-level container** classes. Every top-level container has a **content pane** that contains all the visible components in the container's user interface. So, for example, any of the following techniques causes a `JButton` to appear onscreen in a `JFrame`:

- The button can be placed directly on the content pane of the `JFrame`.

- The button can be placed on a container, like a `JPanel`, that is on the content pane of the `JFrame`. (You learn about the `JPanel` class later in this chapter.)

- The button can be placed on a container that is on another container that is on the content pane of a `JFrame`.

- And so on, with the content pane always at the top of the hierarchy.

A top-level container can contain a menu bar. A **menu bar** is a horizontal strip that conventionally is placed at the top of a container and contains user options. The menu bar, if there is one, is just above (and separate from) the content pane. A **glass pane** resides above the content pane. Figure 15-1 shows the relationship between a `JFrame` and its root, content, and glass panes.

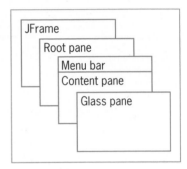

Figure 15-1   Parts of a `JFrame`

 The glass pane is a powerful container feature. Tool tips, which you learned about in Chapter 14, reside on the glass pane. You also can draw your own graphics on the glass pane "on top of" components on a `JFrame`. (You will learn about drawing in the "Graphics" chapter.) If you add a `MouseListener` to the glass pane, it prevents the mouse from triggering events on the components below the glass pane on the `JFrame`.

An additional layered pane exists above the root pane, but it is not often used explicitly by Java programmers. For more details, see the Java Web site.

Whenever you create a `JFrame` (or other top-level container), you can get a reference to its content pane using the `getContentPane()` method. In Chapter 14, you added and removed components from `JFrames` and set their layout managers without understanding you were using the content pane. You had this ability because Java automatically converts `add()`, `remove()`, and `setLayoutManager()` statements to more complete versions. For example, the following three statements are equivalent within a class that descends from `JFrame`:

```
this.getContentPane().add(aButton);
getContentPane().add(aButton);
add(aButton);
```

In the first statement, this refers to the JFrame class in which the statement appears, and getContentPane() provides a reference to the content pane. In the second statement, the this reference is implied. In the third statement, both the this reference and the getContentPane() call are implied.

Although you do not need to worry about the content pane if you only add components to, remove components from, or set the layout manager of a JFrame, you must refer to the content pane for all other actions, such as setting the background color.

When you write an application that adds multiple components to a content pane, it is more efficient to declare an object that represents the content pane than to keep calling the getContentPane() method. For example, consider the following code in a JFrame class that adds three buttons:

```
getContentPane().add(button1);
getContentPane().add(button2);
getContentPane().add(button3);
```

You might prefer to write the following statements. The call to getContentPane() is made once, its reference is stored in a variable, and the reference name is used repeatedly with the call to the add() method:

```
Container con = getContentPane();
con.add(button1);
con.add(button2);
con.add(button3);
```

As an example, the class in Figure 15-2 creates a JFrame like the ones you created throughout Chapter 14, although to keep the example simple, no tasks are assigned to the button.

```java
import java.awt.*;
import javax.swing.*;
public class JFrameWithExplicitContentPane extends JFrame
{
    private final int SIZE = 180;
    private Container con = getContentPane();
    private JButton button = new JButton("Press Me");
    public JFrameWithExplicitContentPane()
    {
        setSize(SIZE, SIZE);
        con.setLayout(new FlowLayout());
        con.add(button);
    }
    public static void main(String[] args)
    {
        JFrameWithExplicitContentPane frame =
            new JFrameWithExplicitContentPane();
        frame.setVisible(true);
    }
}
```

Figure 15-2   The JFrameWithExplicitContentPane class

To keep the examples simple, many programs shown in the figures in this chapter do not set a title or a default close operation. Recall that you can end a program without a specified close operation by pressing *Ctrl+C* at the command line.

In Figure 15-2, the getContentPane() method assigns a reference to a Container named con, and the Container reference is used later with the setLayout() and add() methods. Figure 15-3 shows the result. The frame constructed from the class in Figure 15-2 is identical to the one that would be constructed if the shaded parts were omitted.

When you want to use methods other than add(), remove(), or setLayout(), you must use a content pane. In the next section, you will learn about the setBackground() and setForeground() methods, which are used to change colors in a JFrame. If you use these methods without a content pane reference, the user will not see the results.

Figure 15-3 Output of the JFrameWithExplicitContentPane application

---

TWO TRUTHS & A LIE

Understanding the Content Pane

1. Every Java component has a content pane that contains all the visible parts a user sees.

2. Whenever you create a JFrame, you can get a reference to its content pane using the getContentPane() method.

3. When you change the background color or layout of a JFrame, you should change the content pane and not the JFrame directly.

The false statement is #1. Every *top-level container* has a content pane that contains all the visible components in the container's user interface.

Using Color

The Color class defines colors for you to use in your applications. The Color class can be used with the setBackground() and setForeground() methods of the Component class to make your applications more attractive and interesting. When you use the Color class, you include the statement import java.awt.Color; at the top of your class file.

 The statement import java.awt.*; uses the wildcard to import all of the types in the java.awt package, but it does not import java.awt.Color, java.awt.Font, or any other packages within awt. If you plan to use the classes from java.awt and from java.awt.Color, you must use both import statements.

The Color class defines named constants that represent 13 colors, as shown in Table 15-1. Although Java constants are usually written in all uppercase letters, as you learned in Chapter 2, Java's creators declared two constants for every color in the Color class—an uppercase version, such as BLUE, and a lowercase version, such as blue. Earlier versions of Java contained only the lowercase Color constants. (Two uppercase Color constants use an underscore in DARK_GRAY and LIGHT_GRAY; the lowercase versions are a single word: darkgray and lightgray.)

BLACK	GREEN	RED
BLUE	LIGHT_GRAY	WHITE
CYAN	MAGENTA	YELLOW
DARK_GRAY	ORANGE	
GRAY	PINK	

Table 15-1 Color class constants

You can also create your own Color object with the following statement:

```
Color someColor = new Color(r, g, b);
```

In this statement, r, g, and b are numbers representing the intensities of red, green, and blue you want in your color. The numbers can range from 0 to 255. For example, the color black is created using r, g, and b values 0, 0, 0, and white is created by 255, 255, 255. The following statement produces a dark purple color that has red and blue components, but no green.

```
Color darkPurple = new Color(100, 0, 100);
```

You can create more than 16 million custom colors using this approach. Some computers cannot display each of the 16 million possible colors; each computer displays the closest color it can to the requested color.

You also can create a Color object using four arguments. The fourth argument is the **alpha value**, which indicates the color's level of transparency and can be a value from 0.0 to 1.0. If you use no fourth argument or 1.0, the color is completely opaque. If you use 0.0 as the fourth argument, the color is completely transparent.

You can discover the red, green, or blue components of any existing color with the methods getRed(), getGreen(), and getBlue(). Each of these methods returns an integer. For example, you can discover the amount of red in MAGENTA by displaying the value of Color.MAGENTA.getRed().

Figure 15-4 shows a short application that sets the background color of a JFrame's content pane and sets both the foreground and background colors of a JButton. Figure 15-5 shows the output.

```java
import java.awt.*;
import javax.swing.*;
import java.awt.Color;
public class JFrameWithColor extends JFrame
{
    private final int SIZE = 180;
    private Container con = getContentPane();
    private JButton button = new JButton("Press Me");
    public JFrameWithColor()
    {
        setSize(SIZE, SIZE);
        con.setLayout(new FlowLayout());
        con.add(button);
        con.setBackground(Color.YELLOW);
        button.setBackground(Color.RED);
        button.setForeground(Color.WHITE);
    }
    public static void main(String[] args)
    {
        JFrameWithColor frame = new JFrameWithColor();
        frame.setVisible(true);
    }
}
```

Figure 15-4   The JFrameWithColor class

Figure 15-5   Execution of the JFrameWithColor application

 Because this book is printed in only two colors, you can't see the full effect of setting applications' colors in the figures. However, when you work through the "You Do It" exercises later in this chapter, you can observe the effect of color changes on your own monitor.

TWO TRUTHS & A LIE

Using Color

1. The Color class can be used with the setBackground() and setForeground() methods of the Component class to make your applications more attractive and interesting.

2. The Color class defines named constants that represent 256 colors.

3. You can create your own Color object using values that represent the intensities of red, green, and blue you want in your color.

The false statement is #2. The Color class defines named constants that represent 13 colors.

Learning More About Layout Managers

As you learned in Chapter 14, a layout manager is an object that controls the size and position of components inside a Container object. The layout manager that you assign to a Container determines how its components are sized and positioned. Layout manager classes are interfaces that are part of the JDK; they align your components so the components neither crowd each other nor overlap. For example, you have already learned that the FlowLayout layout manager positions components in rows from left to right across their container. Other layout managers arrange components in equally spaced columns and rows or center components within their container. Each component you place within a Container can also be a Container itself, so you can assign layout managers within layout managers. The Java platform supplies layout managers that range from the very simple (FlowLayout and GridLayout) to the special purpose (BorderLayout and CardLayout) to the very flexible (GridBagLayout and BoxLayout). Table 15-2 lists each layout manager and situations in which each is commonly used.

Layout Manager	When to Use
BorderLayout	Use when you add components to a maximum of five sections arranged in north, south, east, west, and center positions
FlowLayout	Use when you need to add components from left to right; FlowLayout automatically moves to the next row when needed, and each component takes its preferred size
GridLayout	Use when you need to add components into a grid of rows and columns; each component is the same size
CardLayout	Use when you need to add components that are displayed one at a time
BoxLayout	Use when you need to add components into a single row or a single column
GridBagLayout	Use when you need to set size, placement, and alignment constraints for every component that you add

Table 15-2   Java layout managers

Using BorderLayout

The BorderLayout manager is the default manager class for all content panes. You can use the BorderLayout class with any container that has five or fewer components. (However, any of the components could be a container that holds even more components.) When you use the BorderLayout manager, the components fill the screen in five regions: north, south, east, west, and center. If you do not specify a region when you add a component to a BorderLayout, the component is placed in the center region. In Chapter 14, when you placed multiple components in a BorderLayout without specifying a region, each new component obscured the previous one in the center region.

Figure 15-6 shows a JFrame that uses BorderLayout; each of the five regions in the content pane contains a JButton object with descriptive text.

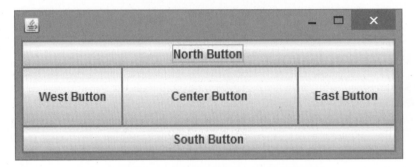

Figure 15-6   Output of the JDemoBorderLayout application

When you add a component to a container that uses BorderLayout, the add() method uses two arguments: the component and the region to which the component is added. The BorderLayout class provides five named constants for the regions—BorderLayout.NORTH, .SOUTH, .EAST, .WEST, and .CENTER—or you can use the Strings those constants represent: "North", "South", "East", "West", or "Center". Figure 15-7 shows the class that creates the output in Figure 15-6.

```
import javax.swing.*;
import java.awt.*;
public class JDemoBorderLayout extends JFrame
{
    private JButton nb = new JButton("North Button");
    private JButton sb = new JButton("South Button");
    private JButton eb = new JButton("East Button");
    private JButton wb = new JButton("West Button");
    private JButton cb = new JButton("Center Button");
    private Container con = getContentPane();
```

Figure 15-7   The JDemoBorderLayout class *(continues)*

(continued)

```java
public JDemoBorderLayout()
{
    con.setLayout(new BorderLayout());
    con.add(nb, BorderLayout.NORTH);
    con.add(sb, BorderLayout.SOUTH);
    con.add(eb, BorderLayout.EAST);
    con.add(wb, BorderLayout.WEST);
    con.add(cb, BorderLayout.CENTER);
    setSize(400, 150);
}
public static void main(String[] args)
{
    JDemoBorderLayout frame = new JDemoBorderLayout();
    frame.setVisible(true);
}
}
```

Figure 15-7 The `JDemoBorderLayout` class

The `JDemoBorderLayout` program in Figure 15-7 uses the `setLayout()` and `add()` methods with the content pane reference. The reference could also be omitted.

When using `BorderLayout`, you can use the constants PAGE_START, PAGE_END, LINE_START, LINE_END, and CENTER instead of NORTH, SOUTH, EAST, WEST, and CENTER. Rather than using geographical references, these constants correspond to positions as you might picture them on a printed page. Also, if you add the following import statement at the top of your file, you can simply refer to CENTER instead of `BorderLayout.CENTER`:

```java
import static java.awt.BorderLayout.*;
```

When you place exactly five components in a container and use a different region for each in a `BorderLayout`, each component fills one entire region, as illustrated in Figure 15-6. When the application runs, Java determines the exact size of each component based on the component's contents. When you resize a `Container` that uses `BorderLayout`, the regions also change in size. If you drag the `Container`'s border to make it wider (using a mouse, or a finger or stylus on a touch screen), the north, south, and center regions become wider, but the east and west regions do not change. If you increase the `Container`'s height, the east, west, and center regions become taller, but the north and south regions do not change.

In Figure 15-7, an anonymous `BorderLayout` object is created when the constructor is called within the `setLayout()` method. Instead, you could declare a named `BorderLayout` object and use its identifier in the `setLayout()` call. However, it's not necessary to use either technique to specify `BorderLayout` because it is the default layout manager for all content panes. You must use `setLayout()` with other managers such as `FlowLayout`.

When you use `BorderLayout`, you are not required to add components into each of the five regions. If you add fewer components, any empty component regions disappear, and the remaining components expand to fill the available space. If any or all of the north, south, east, or west areas are left out, the center area spreads into the missing area or areas. However, if the center area is left out, the north, south, east, or west areas do not change.

Using FlowLayout

Recall from Chapter 14 that you can use the FlowLayout manager class to arrange components in rows across the width of a Container. With FlowLayout, each Component that you add is placed to the right of previously added components in a row; or, if the current row is filled, the Component is placed to start a new row.

When you use BorderLayout, the Components you add fill their regions—that is, each Component expands or contracts based on its region's size. However, when you use FlowLayout, each Component retains its default size, or **preferred size**. For example, a JButton's preferred size is the one that is large enough to hold the JButton's text comfortably. Unlike BorderLayout, when you use FlowLayout and then resize the window, each component retains its size, but it might become partially obscured or change position.

The FlowLayout class contains three constants you can use to align Components with a Container:

- FlowLayout.LEFT
- FlowLayout.CENTER
- FlowLayout.RIGHT

If you do not specify alignment, Components are center-aligned in a FlowLayout Container by default. Figure 15-8 shows an application that uses the FlowLayout.LEFT and FlowLayout.RIGHT constants to reposition JButtons. In this example, a FlowLayout object named layout is used to set the layout of the content pane. When the user clicks a button, the shaded code in the actionPerformed() method changes the alignment to left or right using the FlowLayout class setAlignment() method. Figure 15-9 shows the application when it starts, how the JButton Components are repositioned after the user clicks the "L" button, and how the Components are repositioned after the user clicks the "R" button.

```java
import javax.swing.*;
import java.awt.*;
import java.awt.event.*;
public class JDemoFlowLayout extends JFrame implements ActionListener
{
    private JButton leftButton = new JButton("L Button");
    private JButton rightButton = new JButton("R Button");
    private Container con = getContentPane();
    private FlowLayout layout = new FlowLayout();
    public JDemoFlowLayout()
    {
        con.setLayout(layout);
        con.add(leftButton);
        con.add(rightButton);
        leftButton.addActionListener(this);
        rightButton.addActionListener(this);
        setSize(500, 100);
    }
```

Figure 15-8 The JDemoFlowLayout application *(continues)*

(continued)

```java
    @Override
    public void actionPerformed(ActionEvent event)
    {
        Object source = event.getSource();
        if(source == leftButton)
            layout.setAlignment(FlowLayout.LEFT);
        else
            layout.setAlignment(FlowLayout.RIGHT);
        con.invalidate();
        con.validate();
    }
    public static void main(String[] args)
    {
        JDemoFlowLayout frame = new JDemoFlowLayout();
        frame.setVisible(true);
    }
}
```

801

Figure 15-8   The JDemoFlowLayout application

 The last statements in the JDemoFlowLayout class call invalidate() and validate(). The invalidate() call marks the container (and any of its parents) as needing to be laid out. The validate() call causes the components to be rearranged based on the newly assigned layout.

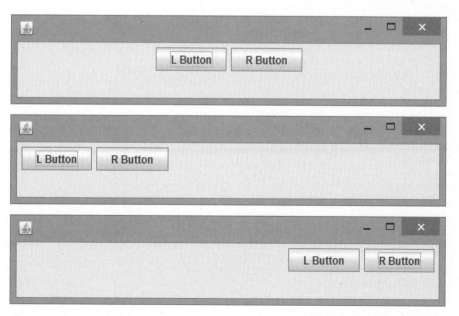

Figure 15-9   The JDemoFlowLayout application as it first appears on the screen, after the user chooses the "L" button, and after the user chooses the "R" button

Using GridLayout

If you want to arrange components into equal rows and columns, you can use the GridLayout manager class. When you create a GridLayout object, you indicate the numbers of rows and columns you want, and then the container surface is divided into a grid, much like the screen you see when using a spreadsheet program. For example, the following statement establishes an anonymous GridLayout with four horizontal rows and five vertical columns in a Container named con:

```
con.setLayout(new GridLayout(4, 5));
```

Specifying rows and then columns when you use GridLayout might seem natural to you, because this is the approach you take when defining two-dimensional arrays.

As you add new Components to a GridLayout, they are positioned in sequence from left to right across each row. Unfortunately, you can't skip a position or specify an exact position for a component. (However, you can add a blank component such as a label or panel to a grid position to give the illusion of skipping a position.) You also can specify a vertical and horizontal gap measured in pixels, using two additional arguments. For example, Figure 15-10 shows a JDemoGridLayout program that uses the shaded statement to establish a GridLayout with three horizontal rows and two vertical columns, and horizontal and vertical gaps of five pixels each. Five JButton Components are added to the JFrame's automatically retrieved content pane.

```java
import javax.swing.*;
import java.awt.*;
public class JDemoGridLayout extends JFrame
{
    private JButton b1 = new JButton("Button 1");
    private JButton b2 = new JButton("Button 2");
    private JButton b3 = new JButton("Button 3");
    private JButton b4 = new JButton("Button 4");
    private JButton b5 = new JButton("Button 5");
    private GridLayout layout = new GridLayout(3, 2, 5, 5);
    private Container con = getContentPane();
    public JDemoGridLayout()
    {
        con.setLayout(layout);
        con.add(b1);
        con.add(b2);
        con.add(b3);
        con.add(b4);
        con.add(b5);
        setSize(200, 200);
    }
    public static void main(String[] args)
    {
        JDemoGridLayout frame = new JDemoGridLayout();
        frame.setVisible(true);
    }
}
```

Figure 15-10   The JDemoGridLayout class

Figure 15-11 shows the output of the JDemoGridLayout application. The Components are placed into the pane across the three rows. Because there are six positions but only five Components, one spot remains unused.

With GridLayout, you can specify the number of rows and use 0 for the number of columns to let the layout manager determine the number of columns, or you can use 0 for the number of rows, specify the number of columns, and let the layout manager calculate the number of rows.

Figure 15-11   Output of the JDemoGridLayout program

When trying to decide whether to use GridLayout or FlowLayout, remember the following:

- Use GridLayout when you want components in fixed rows and columns and you want the components' size to fill the available space.

- Use FlowLayout if you want Java to determine the rows and columns, do not want a rigid row and column layout, and want components to retain their "natural" size when their container is resized so their contents are fully visible.

Using CardLayout

The CardLayout manager generates a stack of containers or components, one on top of another, much like a blackjack dealer reveals playing cards one at a time from the top of a deck. Each component in the group is referred to as a card, and each card can be any component type—for example, a JButton, JLabel, or JPanel. You use a CardLayout when you want multiple components to share the same display space.

A card layout is created from the CardLayout class using one of two constructors:

- CardLayout() creates a card layout without a horizontal or vertical gap.

- CardLayout(int hgap, int vgap) creates a card layout with the specified horizontal and vertical gaps. The horizontal gaps are placed at the left and right edges. The vertical gaps are placed at the top and bottom edges.

For example, Figure 15-12 shows a JDemoCardLayout class that uses a CardLayout manager to create a stack of JButtons that contain the labels *Ace of Hearts, Three of Spades,* and *Queen of Clubs*. In the class constructor, you need a slightly different version of the add() method to add a component to a content pane whose layout manager is CardLayout. The format of the method is:

```
add(aString, aContainer);
```

In this statement, aString represents a name you want to use to identify the Component card that is added.

804

```
import javax.swing.*;
import java.awt.*;
import java.awt.event.*;
public class JDemoCardLayout extends JFrame implements ActionListener
{
    private CardLayout cards = new CardLayout();
    private JButton b1 = new JButton("Ace of Hearts");
    private JButton b2 = new JButton("Three of Spades");
    private JButton b3 = new JButton("Queen of Clubs");
    private Container con = getContentPane();
    public JDemoCardLayout()
    {
        con.setLayout(cards);
        con.add("ace", b1);
        b1.addActionListener(this);
        con.add("three", b2);
        b2.addActionListener(this);
        con.add("queen", b3);
        b3.addActionListener(this);
        setSize(200, 100);
    }
    @Override
    public void actionPerformed(ActionEvent e)
    {
        cards.next(getContentPane());
    }
    public static void main(String[] args)
    {
        JDemoCardLayout frame = new JDemoCardLayout();
        frame.setVisible(true);
    }
}
```

Figure 15-12   The JDemoCardLayout class

In a program that has a CardLayout manager, a change of cards is usually triggered by a user's action. For example, in the JDemoCardLayout program, each JButton can trigger the actionPerformed() method. Within this method, the statement next(getContentPane()) flips to the next card of the container. (The order of the cards depends on the order in which you add them to the container.) You also can use previous(getContentPane());, first(getContentPane());, and last(getContentPane()); to flip to the previous, first, and last card, respectively. You can go to a specific card by using the String name assigned in the add() method call. For example, in the application in Figure 15-12, the following statement would display "Three of Spades" because "three" is used as the first argument when the b2 object is added to the content pane in the JDemoCardLayout constructor:

```
cards.show(getContentPane(), "three");
```

Figure 15-13 shows the output of the JDemoCardLayout program when it first appears on the screen, after the user clicks the button or taps it on a touch screen once, and after the user clicks or taps the button a second time. Because each JButton is a card, each JButton consumes the entire viewing area in the container that uses the CardLayout manager. If the user continued to click or tap the card buttons in Figure 15-13, the cards would continue to cycle in order.

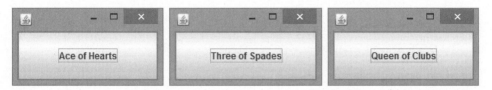

Figure 15-13 Output of JDemoCardLayout when it first appears on the screen, after the user clicks or taps once, and after the user clicks or taps twice

The JTabbedPane class operates like a container with a CardLayout, but folder-type tabs are in place for the user to select the various components. You can find out more about the class at the Java Web site.

Using Advanced Layout Managers

Just as professional Java programmers are constantly creating new Components, they also create new layout managers. You can search the Web for *third-party layout managers* to find some interesting layout managers that have been created for Java. During your programming career, you might even create your own.

For example, when GridLayout is not sophisticated enough for your purposes, you can use GridBagLayout. The GridBagLayout manager allows you to add Components to precise locations within the grid, as well as to indicate that specific Components should span multiple rows or columns within the grid. For example, if you want to create a JPanel with six JButtons, in which two of the JButtons are twice as wide as the others, you can use GridBagLayout. This class is difficult to use because you must set the position and size for each component, and more than 20 methods are associated with the class. Visit the Java Web site for details on how to use this class.

Another layout manager option is the BoxLayout manager, which allows multiple components to be laid out either vertically or horizontally. The components do not wrap, so a vertical arrangement of components, for example, stays vertically arranged when the frame is resized. The Java Web site can provide you with details.

Watch the video *Layout Managers*.

806

TWO TRUTHS & A LIE

Learning More About Layout Managers

1. The FlowLayout manager is the default manager class for all content panes.

2. The BorderLayout manager can directly hold only up to five components.

3. The GridLayout manager arranges components in rows and columns.

The false statement is #1. The BorderLayout manager is the default manager class for all content panes.

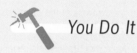 *You Do It*

Using BorderLayout

Using layout managers in the containers in your applications allows flexibility in arranging the components that users see on the screen. In this section, you create a JFrame that uses a BorderLayout with components placed in each region. In the following sections, you will observe how the same components appear when other layout managers are used.

1. Open a new file, and then type the following first few lines of a program that demonstrates BorderLayout with five objects:

```
import javax.swing.*;
import java.awt.*;
public class JBorderLayout extends JFrame
{
```

2. Instantiate five JButton objects, each with a label that is the name of one of the regions used by BorderLayout:

```
private JButton nb = new JButton("North");
private JButton sb = new JButton("South");
private JButton eb = new JButton("East");
private JButton wb = new JButton("West");
private JButton cb = new JButton("Center");
```

3. Write the constructor that sets the JFrame's layout manager and adds each of the five JButtons to the appropriate region. Also set the default close operation for the JFrame.

(continues)

(continued)

```java
public JBorderLayout()
{
    setLayout(new BorderLayout());
    add(nb, BorderLayout.NORTH);
    add(sb, BorderLayout.SOUTH);
    add(eb, BorderLayout.EAST);
    add(wb, BorderLayout.WEST);
    add(cb, BorderLayout.CENTER);
    setDefaultCloseOperation(JFrame.EXIT_ON_CLOSE);
}
```

4. Add a `main()` method that instantiates a `JBorderLayout` object and sets its size and visibility, and include a closing curly brace for the class:

```java
public static void main(String[] args)
{
    JBorderLayout jbl = new JBorderLayout();
    jbl.setSize(250, 250);
    jbl.setVisible(true);
}
}
```

5. Save the file as **JBorderLayout.java**, and then compile and execute it. The output looks like Figure 15-14. Each `JButton` entirely fills its region. (If you click the `JButton`s, they appear to be pressed, but because you have not implemented `ActionListener`, no other action is taken.)

Figure 15-14   Output of the JBorderLayout program

(continues)

(continued)

6. So you can observe the effects of changing the size of the viewing area, use your mouse to drag the right border of the JFrame to increase the width to approximately that shown in Figure 15-15. (You can use your touch screen if you have one.) Notice that the center region expands, while the east and west regions retain their original size.

Figure 15-15 Output of the JBorderLayout program after the user drags the right border to increase the width

7. Experiment with resizing both the width and height of the JFrame. Close the JFrame when you finish.

Using Fewer than Five Components with the *BorderLayout* Manager

When you use JBorderLayout, you are not required to place components in every region. For example, you might use only four components, leaving the north region empty. Next, you remove one of the objects from the JBorderLayout JFrame to observe the effect.

1. Open the **JBorderLayout.java** file, and immediately save it as **JBorderLayoutNoNorth.java**.

2. Change the class name to JBorderLayoutNoNorth. Also change the constructor name and the two instances of the class name in the main() method.

3. Remove the declaration of the "North" button, and within the constructor, remove the statement that adds the "North" button to the JFrame.

(continues)

(continued)

4. Save the file, compile it, and then run the program. The output appears as shown in Figure 15-16. The center region occupies the space formerly held by the north region.

5. Experiment with removing some of the other components from the JBorderLayoutNoNorth program.

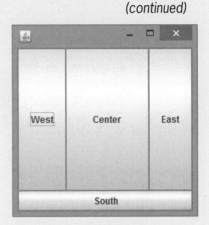

Using FlowLayout

Next, you modify the JBorderLayout program to demonstrate how the same components appear when using FlowLayout.

Figure 15-16 Output of the JBorderLayoutNoNorth program

1. Open the **JBorderLayout.java** file, and immediately save it as **JFlowLayoutRight.java**.

2. Change the class name from JBorderLayout to **JFlowLayoutRight**. Also change the constructor name and the references to the name in the main() method.

3. Within the constructor, change the setLayout() statement to use FlowLayout and right alignment:

   setLayout(new FlowLayout(FlowLayout.RIGHT));

4. Alter each of the five add() statements so that just the button name appears within the parentheses and the region is omitted. For example, add(nb, BorderLayout.NORTH); becomes the following:

   add(nb);

5. Save the file, and then compile and execute it. Your output should look like Figure 15-17. The components have their "natural" size (or preferred size)— the minimum size the buttons need to display their labels. The buttons flow across the JFrame surface in a row until no more can fit; in Figure 15-17 the last two buttons added cannot fit in the first row, so they appear in the second row, right-aligned.

(continues)

810

(continued)

Figure 15-17   Output of the `JFlowLayoutRight` program

6. Experiment with widening and narrowing the `JFrame`, and observe how the components realign. Then close the `JFrame`.

Using *GridLayout*

Next, you modify a `JFrame` to demonstrate `GridLayout`.

1. Open the **JFlowLayoutRight.java** file, and save the file as **JGridLayout.java**.

2. Change the class name from `JFlowLayoutRight` to **JGridLayout**. Change the constructor name and the two references to the class in the `main()` method.

3. Within the constructor, change the `setLayout()` statement to establish a `GridLayout` with two rows, three columns, a horizontal space of two pixels, and a vertical space of four pixels:

   ```
   setLayout(new GridLayout(2, 3, 2, 4));
   ```

4. Save the file, and then compile and execute it. The components are arranged in two rows and three columns from left to right across each row, in the order they were added to their container. Because there are only five components, one grid position still is available. See Figure 15-18.

(continues)

(continued)

Figure 15-18 Output of the JGridLayout program

5. Close the program.

Using CardLayout

Next, you create a CardLayout with five cards, each holding one of the JButtons used in the previous examples.

1. Open the **JGridLayout.java** file, and save the file as **JCardLayout.java**.

2. Change the class name from JGridLayout to **JCardLayout**. Also change the constructor name and the two references in the main() method.

3. Within the constructor, change the setLayout() statement to establish a CardLayout:

   ```
   setLayout(new CardLayout());
   ```

4. Change the five add() statements that add the buttons to the content pane so that each includes a String that names the added component, as follows:

   ```
   add("north", nb);
   add("south", sb);
   add("east", eb);
   add("west", wb);
   add("center", cb);
   ```

5. Save the file, and then compile and execute it. The output looks like Figure 15-19. You see only the "North" JButton because, as the first one added, it is the top card. You can click the button, but no actions take place because you have not implemented ActionListener.

(continues)

(continued)

6. Close the program.

Viewing All the Cards in CardLayout

Next, you modify the JCardLayout program so that its buttons can initiate events that allow you to view all five JButtons you add to the content pane.

Figure 15-19 Output of the JCardLayout program

1. Open the **JCardLayout.java** file, and save the file as **JCardLayout2.java**.

2. Change the class name, constructor name, and two main() method references from JCardLayout to **JCardLayout2**.

3. At the top of the file, add the import statement that adds the classes and methods that allow the class to respond to events:

```
import java.awt.event.*;
```

4. At the end of the class header, insert the following phrase so the JFrame can respond to button clicks:

```
implements ActionListener
```

5. Instead of an anonymous layout manager, you need to create a CardLayout manager with an identifier that you can use with the next() method when the user clicks a button. Immediately after the five JButton declaration statements, insert the following statement:

```
CardLayout cardLayout = new CardLayout();
```

6. Within the constructor, change the setLayout() statement so it uses the named layout manager:

```
setLayout(cardLayout);
```

7. At the end of the constructor, add five statements that allow each of the buttons to initiate an ActionEvent:

```
nb.addActionListener(this);
sb.addActionListener(this);
eb.addActionListener(this);
wb.addActionListener(this);
cb.addActionListener(this);
```

(continues)

(continued)

8. After the constructor's closing curly brace, add an `actionPerformed()` method that responds to user clicks. The method uses the `next()` method to display the next card (next button) in the collection.

```
@Override
public void actionPerformed(ActionEvent e)
{
    cardLayout.next(getContentPane());
}
```

9. Save, compile, and run the program. The output looks the same as in Figure 15-19: you see only the "North" JButton. However, when you click it, the button changes to "South", "East", "West", and "Center" in succession. Close the JFrame when you finish.

813

Using the JPanel Class

Using the BorderLayout, FlowLayout, GridLayout, and CardLayout managers would provide a limited number of screen arrangements if you could place only one Component in a section of the layout. Fortunately, you can greatly increase the number of possible component arrangements by using the JPanel class to create a **panel**, which is a plain, borderless surface that can hold lightweight GUI components such as buttons, check boxes, or other panels. Figure 15-20 shows the inheritance hierarchy of the JPanel class. You can see that every JPanel is a Container. By using JPanels within JPanels, you can create an infinite variety of screen layouts. The default layout manager for every JPanel is FlowLayout.

```
java.lang.Object
   !--java.awt.Component
         !--java.awt.Container
               !--javax.swing.JComponent
                     !--javax.swing.JPanel
```

Figure 15-20 The inheritance hierarchy of the JPanel class

To add a component to a JPanel, you call the container's add() method, using the component as the argument. For example, Figure 15-21 shows the code that creates a JFrameWithPanels class that extends JFrame. A JButton is added to a JPanel named panel1, and two more JButtons are added to another JPanel named panel2. Then panel1 and panel2 are added to the JFrame's content pane.

```java
import javax.swing.*;
import java.awt.*;
import java.awt.Color;
public class JFrameWithPanels extends JFrame
{
    private final int WIDTH = 250;
    private final int HEIGHT = 120;
    private JButton button1 = new JButton("One");
    private JButton button2 = new JButton("Two");
    private JButton button3 = new JButton("Three");
    public JFrameWithPanels()
    {
        JPanel panel1 = new JPanel();
        JPanel panel2 = new JPanel();
        Container con = getContentPane();
        con.setLayout(new FlowLayout());
        con.add(panel1);
        con.add(panel2);
        panel1.add(button1);
        panel1.setBackground(Color.BLUE);
        panel2.add(button2);
        panel2.add(button3);
        panel2.setBackground(Color.BLUE);
        setSize(WIDTH, HEIGHT);
    }
    public static void main(String[] args)
    {
        JFrameWithPanels frame = new JFrameWithPanels();
        frame.setVisible(true);
    }
}
```

Figure 15-21   The JFrameWithPanels class

Figure 15-22 shows the output of the JFrameWithPanels program. Two JPanels have been added to the JFrame. Because this application uses the setBackground() method to make each JPanel's background blue, you can see where one panel ends and the other begins. The first JPanel contains a single JButton, and the second one contains two JButtons.

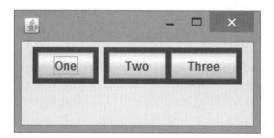

Figure 15-22   Output of the JFrameWithPanels application

When you create a `JPanel` object, you can use one of four constructors. In Chapters 7 and 13, you learned that a *buffer* is a block of memory set aside for a special purpose, such as creating a `StringBuilder` object or holding file output. A `JPanel` also is created in a buffer. The different constructors allow you to use default values or to specify a layout manager and whether the `JPanel` is double buffered. If you indicate **double buffering**, which is the default buffering strategy, you specify that additional memory space will be used to draw the `JPanel` offscreen when it is updated. With double buffering, a redrawn `JPanel` is displayed only when it is complete; this provides the viewer with updated screens that do not flicker while being redrawn. The four constructors are as follows:

- `JPanel()` creates a `JPanel` with double buffering and a flow layout.

- `JPanel(LayoutManager layout)` creates a `JPanel` with the specified layout manager and double buffering.

- `JPanel(Boolean isDoubleBuffered)` creates a `JPanel` with a flow layout and the specified double-buffering strategy.

- `JPanel(LayoutManager layout, Boolean isDoubleBuffered)` creates a `JPanel` with the specified layout manager and the specified buffering strategy.

 When you employ double buffering, the visible screen surface is called the **primary surface**, and the offscreen image is called the **back buffer**. The act of copying the contents from one surface to another is frequently referred to as a **block line transfer**, or **blitting**, because of the acronym *blt*, pronounced *blit*. Double buffering prevents "tearing," the visual effect that occurs when you see parts of different images because the redrawing rate is not fast enough. As with most beneficial features, double buffering has a cost: additional memory requirements.

As with many aspects of Java, there are multiple ways to achieve the same results. For example, each of the following techniques creates a `JPanel` that uses a `BorderLayout` manager and double buffering:

- You can create a named layout and use it as an argument in a `JPanel` constructor:

```
BorderLayout border = new BorderLayout();
JPanel myPanel = new JPanel(border);
```

- You can use an anonymous layout manager in the `JPanel` constructor:

```
JPanel myPanel = new JPanel(new BorderLayout());
```

- You can create a `JPanel` and then set its layout manager using the `setLayout()` method and an anonymous layout manager:

```
JPanel myPanel = new JPanel();
myPanel.setLayout(new BorderLayout());
```

- You can create a `JPanel` and then set its layout manager using the `setLayout()` method and a named layout manager:

```
JPanel myPanel = new JPanel();
BorderLayout border = new BorderLayout();
myPanel.setLayout(border);
```

- You can create a JPanel with two constructor arguments, explicitly indicating double buffering:

```
JPanel myPanel = new JPanel(new BorderLayout(), true);
```

When a JPanel will have a layout other than FlowLayout, specifying the layout manager when you create the JPanel is preferable for performance reasons. If you create the JPanel first and then change its layout, you automatically create an unnecessary FlowLayout object for the original instantiation.

You add components to a JPanel with the add() method. Figure 15-23 shows a JDemoManyPanels program in which the JFrame contains four JPanels and 12 JButtons that each display a single spelled-out number so you can better understand their positions. The automatically supplied content pane for the JFrame is assigned a BorderLayout, and each JPanel is assigned either a GridLayout or FlowLayout and placed in one of the regions (leaving the north region empty). One or more JButtons are then placed on each JPanel. Figure 15-24 shows the output as the user adjusts the borders of the JFrame to change its size. Using the code as a guide, be certain you understand why each JButton appears as it does in the JFrame.

```
import javax.swing.*;
import java.awt.*;
public class JDemoManyPanels extends JFrame
{
// Twelve buttons
   private JButton button01 = new JButton("One");
   private JButton button02 = new JButton("Two");
   private JButton button03 = new JButton("Three");
   private JButton button04 = new JButton("Four");
   private JButton button05 = new JButton("Five");
   private JButton button06 = new JButton("Six");
   private JButton button07 = new JButton("Seven");
   private JButton button08 = new JButton("Eight");
   private JButton button09 = new JButton("Nine");
   private JButton button10 = new JButton("Ten");
   private JButton button11 = new JButton("Eleven");
   private JButton button12 = new JButton("Twelve");

// Four panels
   private JPanel panel01 = new JPanel(new GridLayout(2, 0));
   private JPanel panel02 = new JPanel(new FlowLayout());
   private JPanel panel03 = new JPanel(new FlowLayout());
   private JPanel panel04 = new JPanel(new GridLayout(2, 0));
```

Figure 15-23   The JDemoManyPanels class (continues)

(continued)

```java
    public JDemoManyPanels()
    {
        setLayout(new BorderLayout());
        add(panel01, BorderLayout.WEST);
        add(panel02, BorderLayout.CENTER);
        add(panel03, BorderLayout.SOUTH);
        add(panel04, BorderLayout.EAST);

        panel01.add(button01);
        panel01.add(button02);
        panel01.add(button03);

        panel02.add(button04);
        panel02.add(button05);
        panel02.add(button06);

        panel03.add(button07);

        panel04.add(button08);
        panel04.add(button09);
        panel04.add(button10);
        panel04.add(button11);
        panel04.add(button12);

        setSize(400, 250);
    }
    public static void main(String[] args)
    {
        JDemoManyPanels frame = new JDemoManyPanels();
        frame.setVisible(true);
    }
}
```

Figure 15-23   The JDemoManyPanels class

If you were creating a program with as many buttons and panels as the one in Figure 15-23, you might prefer to create arrays of the components instead of so many individually named ones. This example does not use an array so you can more easily see how each component is placed.

818

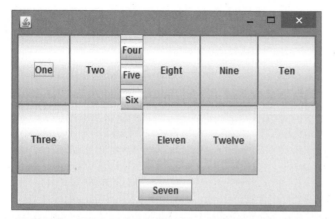

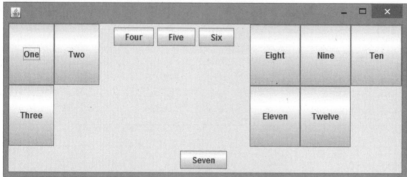

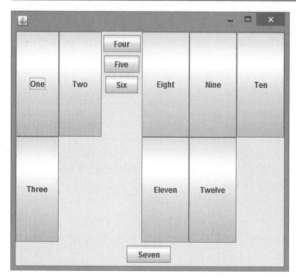

Figure 15-24   Output of the JDemoManyPanels program: three views as the user adjusts the JFrame borders

Swing containers other than JPanel and content panes generally provide Application Program Interface (API) methods that you should use instead of the add() method. See the Java Web site for details.

GridLayout provides you with rows and columns that are similar to a two-dimensional array. Therefore, it particularly lends itself to displaying arrays of objects. For example, Figure 15-25 contains a Checkerboard class that displays a pattern of eight rows and columns in alternating colors. The JPanel placed in the content pane has a GridLayout of eight by eight. Sixty-four JPanels are declared, and in a loop, one by one, they are instantiated and assigned to a section of the grid (see shaded statements). After each set of eight JPanels is assigned to the grid (when x is evenly divisible by 8), the first and second color values are reversed, so that the first row starts with a blue square, the second row starts with a white square, and so on. Within each row, all the even-positioned squares are filled with one color, and the odd-positioned squares are filled with the other. Figure 15-26 shows the output.

```java
import java.awt.*;
import javax.swing.*;
import java.awt.Color;
public class Checkerboard extends JFrame
{
    private final int ROWS = 8;
    private final int COLS = 8;
    private final int GAP = 2;
    private final int NUM = ROWS * COLS;
    private int x;
    private JPanel pane = new JPanel
        (new GridLayout(ROWS, COLS, GAP, GAP));
    private JPanel[] panel = new JPanel[NUM];
    private Color color1 = Color.WHITE;
    private Color color2 = Color.BLUE;
    private Color tempColor;
    public Checkerboard()
    {
        add(pane);
        for(x = 0; x < NUM; ++x)
        {
            panel[x] = new JPanel();
            pane.add(panel[x]);
            if(x % COLS == 0)
            {
                tempColor = color1;
                color1 = color2;
                color2 = tempColor;
            }
```

Figure 15-25 The Checkerboard class *(continues)*

(continued)

```
            if(x % 2 == 0)
                panel[x].setBackground(color1);
            else
                panel[x].setBackground(color2);
        }
    }
    public static void main(String[] args)
    {
        Checkerboard frame = new Checkerboard();
        final int SIZE = 300;
        frame.setSize(SIZE, SIZE);
        frame.setVisible(true);
    }
}
```

Figure 15-25   The Checkerboard class

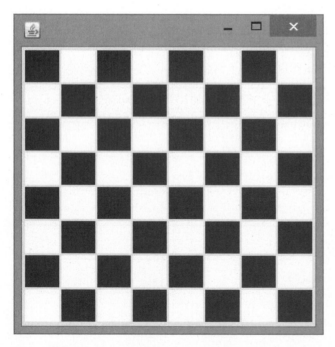

Figure 15-26   Output of the Checkerboard application

When creating the Checkerboard class, you might be tempted to create just two JPanels, one blue and one white, and add them to the content pane multiple times. However, each GUI component can be contained only once. If a component is already in a container and you try to add it to another container, the component will be removed from the first container and then added to the second.

 Watch the video *The JPanel Class*.

TWO TRUTHS & A LIE

Using the JPanel Class

1. A JPanel is a plain, borderless surface that can hold lightweight GUI components.

2. To add a component to a JPanel, you call the component's add() method, using the JPanel as the argument.

3. Different JPanel constructors allow you to use default values or to specify a layout manager and whether the JPanel is double buffered.

The false statement is #2. To add a component to a JPanel, you call the container's add() method, using the component as the argument.

Creating JScrollPanes

When components in a Swing application require more display area than they have been allocated, you can use a JScrollPane container to hold the components in a way that allows a user to scroll initially invisible parts of the pane into view. A **scroll pane** provides scroll bars along the side or bottom of a pane, or both, with a viewable area called a **viewport**. Figure 15-27 displays the inheritance hierarchy of the JScrollPane class.

```
java.lang.Object
   !--java.awt.Component
        !--java.awt.Container
             !--javax.swing.JComponent
                  !--javax.swing.JScrollPane
```

Figure 15-27   The inheritance hierarchy of the JScrollPane class

The JScrollPane constructor takes one of four forms:

- JScrollPane() creates an empty JScrollPane in which both horizontal and vertical scroll bars appear when needed.

- JScrollPane(Component) creates a JScrollPane that displays the contents of the specified component.

- JScrollPane(Component, int, int) creates a JScrollPane that displays the specified component and includes both vertical and horizontal scroll bar specifications.

- JScrollPane(int, int) creates a JScrollPane with both vertical and horizontal scroll bar specifications.

When you create a simple scroll pane using the constructor that takes no arguments, as in the following example, horizontal and vertical scroll bars appear only if they are needed; that is, if the contents of the pane cannot be fully displayed without them:

```
JScrollPane aScrollPane = new JScrollPane();
```

To force the display of a scroll bar, you can use class variables defined in the ScrollPaneConstants class, as follows:

```
ScrollPaneConstants.HORIZONTAL_SCROLLBAR_AS_NEEDED
ScrollPaneConstants.HORIZONTAL_SCROLLBAR_ALWAYS
ScrollPaneConstants.HORIZONTAL_SCROLLBAR_NEVER
ScrollPaneConstants.VERTICAL_SCROLLBAR_AS_NEEDED
ScrollPaneConstants.VERTICAL_SCROLLBAR_ALWAYS
ScrollPaneConstants.VERTICAL_SCROLLBAR_NEVER
```

For example, the following code creates a scroll pane that displays an image named picture, a vertical scroll bar, and no horizontal scroll bar:

```
JScrollPane scroll = new JScrollPane(picture,
    ScrollPaneConstants.VERTICAL_SCROLLBAR_ALWAYS,
    ScrollPaneConstants.HORIZONTAL_SCROLLBAR_NEVER);
```

Figure 15-28 shows a JScrollDemo class in which a label with a large font is added to a panel. The scroll pane named scroll includes the panel and two scroll bars.

```
import javax.swing.*;
import java.awt.*;
public class JScrollDemo extends JFrame
{
    private JPanel panel = new JPanel();
    private JScrollPane scroll = new JScrollPane(panel,
        ScrollPaneConstants.VERTICAL_SCROLLBAR_ALWAYS,
        ScrollPaneConstants.HORIZONTAL_SCROLLBAR_ALWAYS);
```

Figure 15-28   The JScrollDemo application (continues)

(continued)

```java
    private JLabel label = new JLabel("Four score and seven");
    private Font bigFont = new Font("Arial", Font.PLAIN, 20);
    private Container con;
    public JScrollDemo()
    {
        con = getContentPane();
        label.setFont(bigFont);
        con.add(scroll);
        panel.add(label);
    }
    public static void main(String[] args)
    {
        final int WIDTH = 180;
        final int HEIGHT = 100;
        JScrollDemo aFrame = new JScrollDemo();
        aFrame.setSize(WIDTH, HEIGHT);
        aFrame.setVisible(true);
    }
}
```

Figure 15-28   The `JScrollDemo` application

The `JScrollDemo` object in the program in Figure 15-28 is purposely set small enough
(180 × 100) so that only part of the label it contains is visible at a time. A user can slide the
scroll bars to view the entire label. Figure 15-29 shows the output with the scroll bar in
two positions.

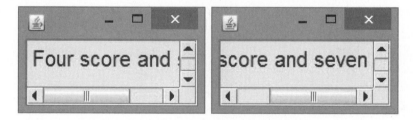

Figure 15-29   Output of the `JScrollDemo` application

> **TWO TRUTHS & A LIE**
>
> ### Creating JScrollPanes
>
> 1. A `JScrollPane` can provide scroll bars along the side or bottom of a pane, or both.
>
> 2. When you create a simple scroll pane using the constructor that takes no arguments, horizontal and vertical scroll bars appear only if they are needed.
>
> 3. You cannot force the display of a scroll bar in a `JScrollPane` unless the components it contains require too much room.
>
> The false statement is #3. You can use class variables defined in the ScrollPaneConstants class to force the display of a scroll bar.

A Closer Look at Events and Event Handling

In Chapter 14, you learned that an `ActionEvent` is generated when a user clicks a button and an `ItemEvent` is generated when a user clicks a check box. Both of those event types descend from the abstract class `AWTEvent`, which is contained in the package `java.awt.event`. `AWTEvent` descends from `EventObject`, which descends from the `Object` class. Although you might think it would have been logical for the developers to name the event base class `Event` rather than `EventObject`, there is no currently active, built-in Java class named `Event` (although there was one in Java 1.0). Figure 15-30 illustrates the inheritance hierarchy of these relationships.

```
java.lang.Object
  !--java.util.EventObject
       !--java.awt.AWTEvent
             !--java.awt.event.ActionEvent
             +--java.awt.event.AdjustmentEvent
             +--java.awt.event.ItemEvent
             +--java.awt.event.TextEvent
             +--java.awt.event.ComponentEvent
                     !--java.awt.event.ContainerEvent
                     +--java.awt.event.FocusEvent
                     +--java.awt.event.PaintEvent
                     +--java.awt.event.WindowEvent
                     +--java.awt.event.InputEvent
                             !--java.awt.event.KeyEvent
                             +--java.awt.event.MouseEvent
```

Figure 15-30   The inheritance hierarchy of event classes

You can see in Figure 15-30 that ComponentEvent is a parent to several event classes, including InputEvent, which is a parent of KeyEvent and MouseEvent. The family tree for events has roots that go fairly deep, but the class names are straightforward, and they share basic roles within your programs. For example, ActionEvents are generated by components that users can click, such as JButtons and JCheckBoxes, and TextEvents are generated by components into which the user enters text, such as a JTextField. MouseEvents include determining the location of the mouse pointer and distinguishing between a single- and double-click. Table 15-3 lists some common user actions and the events that are generated from them.

User Action	Resulting Event Type
Click a button	ActionEvent
Click a component	MouseEvent
Click an item in a list box	ItemEvent
Click an item in a check box	ItemEvent
Change text in a text field	TextEvent
Open a window	WindowEvent
Iconify a window	WindowEvent
Press a key	KeyEvent

Table 15-3   Examples of user actions and their resulting event types

Because ActionEvents involve the mouse, it is easy to confuse ActionEvents and MouseEvents. If you are interested in ActionEvents, you focus on changes in a component (for example, a JButton on a JFrame being pressed); if you are interested in MouseEvents, your focus is on what the user does manually with the mouse (for example, clicking the left mouse button).

When you write programs with GUIs, you are always handling events that originate with the mouse or keys on specific Components or Containers. Just as your telephone notifies you when you have a call, the computer's operating system notifies the user when an AWTEvent occurs—for example, when the mouse is clicked. Just as you can ignore your phone when you're not expecting or interested in a call, you can ignore AWTEvents. If you don't care about an event, such as when your program contains a component that produces no effect when clicked, you simply don't look for a message to occur.

When you care about events—that is, when you want to listen for an event—you can implement an appropriate interface for your class. Each event class shown in Table 15-3 has a listener interface associated with it, so that for every event class, <name>Event, there is a similarly named <name>Listener interface. For example, ActionEvent has an ActionListener interface. (The MouseEvent class has an additional listener besides MouseListener: MouseMotionListener.)

Remember that an interface contains only abstract methods, so all interface methods are empty. If you implement a listener, you must provide your own methods for all the methods that are part of the interface. Of course, you can leave the methods empty in your implementation, providing a header and curly braces but no statements.

Every <name>Listener interface method has the return type void, and each takes one argument: an object that is an instance of the corresponding <name>Event class. Thus, the ActionListener interface has an event handler method named actionPerformed(), and its header is void actionPerformed(ActionEvent e). When an action takes place, the actionPerformed() method executes, and e represents an instance of that event. Instead of implementing a listener class, you can extend an adapter class. An **adapter class** implements all the methods in an interface, providing an empty body for each method. For example, the MouseAdapter class provides an empty method for all the methods contained in MouseListener. The advantage to extending an adapter class instead of implementing a listener class is that you need to write only the methods you want to use, and you do not have to bother creating empty methods for all the others. (If a listener has only one method, there is no need for an adapter. For example, the ActionListener class has one method, actionPerformed(), so there is no ActionAdapter class.)

Whether you use a listener or an adapter, you create an event handler when you write code for the listener methods; that is, you tell your class how to handle the event. After you create the handler, you must also register an instance of the class with the component that you want the event to affect. For any <name>Listener, you must use the form object.add<name>Listener(Component) to register an object with the Component that will listen for objects emanating from it. The add<name>Listener() methods, such as addActionListener() and addItemListener(), all work the same way. They register a listener with a Component, return void, and take a <name>Listener object as an argument. For example, if a JFrame is an ActionListener and contains a JButton named pushMe, then the following statement registers this JFrame as a listener for the pushMe JButton:

pushMe.addActionListener(this);

Table 15-4 lists the events with their listeners and handlers.

Event	Listener(s)	Handler(s)
ActionEvent	ActionListener	actionPerformed(ActionEvent)
ItemEvent	ItemListener	itemStateChanged(ItemEvent)
TextEvent	TextListener	textValueChanged(TextEvent)
AdjustmentEvent	AdjustmentListener	adjustmentValueChanged (AdjustmentEvent)
ContainerEvent	ContainerListener	componentAdded(ContainerEvent) componentRemoved(ContainerEvent)
ComponentEvent	ComponentListener	componentMoved(ComponentEvent) componentHidden(ComponentEvent) componentResized(ComponentEvent) componentShown(ComponentEvent)
FocusEvent	FocusListener	focusGained(FocusEvent) focusLost(FocusEvent)
MouseEvent	MouseListener MouseMotionListener	mousePressed(MouseEvent) mouseReleased(MouseEvent) mouseEntered(MouseEvent) mouseExited(MouseEvent) mouseClicked(MouseEvent) mouseDragged(MouseEvent) mouseMoved(MouseEvent)
KeyEvent	KeyListener	keyPressed(KeyEvent) keyTyped(KeyEvent) keyReleased(KeyEvent)
WindowEvent	WindowListener	windowActivated(WindowEvent) windowClosing(WindowEvent) windowClosed(WindowEvent) windowDeiconified(WindowEvent) windowIconified(WindowEvent) windowOpened(WindowEvent)
MouseWheelEvent	MouseWheelListener	mouseWheelMoved(MouseWheelEvent)

Table 15-4   Events with their related listeners and handlers

827

An Event-Handling Example: KeyListener

You use the KeyListener interface when you are interested in actions the user initiates from the keyboard. The KeyListener interface contains three methods: keyPressed(), keyTyped(), and keyReleased(). For most keyboard applications in which the user must press a keyboard key, it is probably not important whether you take resulting action when a user first presses a key, during the key press, or upon the key's release; most likely, these events occur in quick sequence. However, on those occasions when you don't want to take action while the user holds down the key, you can place the actions in the keyReleased() method. It is best to use the keyTyped() method when you want to discover which character was typed. When the user presses a key that does not generate a character, such as a function key (sometimes called an **action key**), keyTyped() does not execute. The methods keyPressed() and keyReleased() provide the only ways to get information about keys that don't generate characters. The KeyEvent class contains constants known as **virtual key codes** that represent keyboard keys that have been pressed. For example, when you type *A*, two virtual key codes are generated: Shift and "a". The virtual key code constants have names such as VK_SHIFT and VK_ALT. See the Java Web site for a complete list of virtual key codes. Figure 15-31 shows a JDemoKeyFrame class that uses the keyTyped() method to discover which key the user typed last.

 Java programmers call keyTyped() events "higher-level" events because they do not depend on the platform or keyboard layout. (For example, the key that generates VK_Q on a U.S. keyboard layout generates VK_A on a French keyboard layout.) By contrast, keyPressed() and keyReleased() events are "lower-level" events and do depend on the platform and keyboard layout. According to the Java documentation, using keyTyped() is the preferred way to find out about character input.

```java
import javax.swing.*;
import java.awt.*;
import java.awt.event.*;
public class JDemoKeyFrame extends JFrame
    implements KeyListener
{
    private JLabel prompt = new JLabel("Type keys below:");
    private JLabel outputLabel = new JLabel();
    private JTextField textField = new JTextField(10);
    public JDemoKeyFrame()
    {
        setLayout(new BorderLayout());
        add(prompt, BorderLayout.NORTH);
        add(textField, BorderLayout.CENTER);
        add(outputLabel, BorderLayout.SOUTH);
        addKeyListener(this);
        textField.addKeyListener(this);
    }
    @Override
    public void keyTyped(KeyEvent e)
    {
        char c = e.getKeyChar();
        outputLabel.setText("Last key typed: " + c);
    }
```

Figure 15-31 The JDemoKeyFrame class *(continues)*

(continued)

```java
    @Override
    public void keyPressed(KeyEvent e)
    {
    }
    @Override
    public void keyReleased(KeyEvent e)
    {
    }
    public static void main(String[] args)
    {
        JDemoKeyFrame keyFrame = new JDemoKeyFrame();
        final int WIDTH = 250;
        final int HEIGHT = 100;
        keyFrame.setSize(WIDTH, HEIGHT);
        keyFrame.setVisible(true);
    }
}
```

Figure 15-31 The `JDemoKeyFrame` class

A prompt in the north border area asks the user to type in the text field in the center area. With each key press by the user, the `keyTyped()` method changes the label in the south border area of the frame to display the key that generated the most recent `KeyEvent`. Figure 15-32 shows the output after the user has typed several characters into the text field.

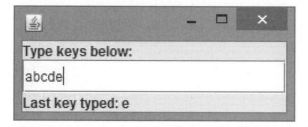

Figure 15-32 Output of the `JDemoKeyFrame` application after the user has typed several characters

 Watch the video *Event Handling*.

TWO TRUTHS & A LIE

A Closer Look at Events and Event Handling

1. ActionEvents are generated by components that users can click, TextEvents are generated by components into which the user enters text, and MouseEvents are generated by mouse actions.

2. Every <name>Listener interface method has a return type that refers to an instance of the corresponding <name>Event class.

3. An adapter class implements all the methods in an interface, providing an empty body for each method.

The false statement is #2. Every <name>Listener interface method has the return type void, and each takes one argument: an object that is an instance of the corresponding <name>Event class.

Using AWTEvent Class Methods

In addition to the handler methods included with the event listener interfaces, the AWTEvent classes themselves contain many other methods that return information about an event. For example, the ComponentEvent class contains a getComponent() method that allows you to determine which of multiple Components generates an event. The WindowEvent class contains a similar method, getWindow(), that returns the Window that is the source of an event. Table 15-5 lists some useful methods for many of the event classes. All Components have these methods:

- addComponentListener()
- addFocusListener()
- addMouseListener()
- addMouseMotionListener()

Class	Method	Purpose
EventObject	Object getSource()	Returns the Object involved in the event
ComponentEvent	Component getComponent()	Returns the Component involved in the event
WindowEvent	Window getWindow()	Returns the Window involved in the event
ItemEvent	Object getItem()	Returns the Object that was selected or deselected
ItemEvent	int getStateChange()	Returns an integer named ItemEvent.SELECTED or ItemEvent.DESELECTED
InputEvent	int getModifiers()	Returns an integer to indicate which mouse button was clicked
InputEvent	int getWhen()	Returns a time indicating when the event occurred
InputEvent	boolean isAltDown()	Returns whether the Alt key was pressed when the event occurred
InputEvent	boolean isControlDown()	Returns whether the Ctrl key was pressed when the event occurred
InputEvent	boolean isShiftDown()	Returns whether the Shift key was pressed when the event occurred
KeyEvent	int getKeyChar()	Returns the Unicode character entered from the keyboard
MouseEvent	int getClickCount()	Returns the number of mouse clicks; lets you identify the user's double-clicks
MouseEvent	int getX()	Returns the x-coordinate of the mouse pointer
MouseEvent	int getY()	Returns the y-coordinate of the mouse pointer
MouseEvent	Point getPoint()	Returns the Point Object that contains the x- and y-coordinates of the mouse location

Table 15-5   Useful event class methods

You can call any of the methods listed in Table 15-5 by using the object-dot-method format that you use with all class methods. For example, if you have a KeyEvent named inputEvent and an integer named unicodeVal, the following statement is valid:

```
unicodeVal = inputEvent.getKeyChar();
```

When you use an event, you can use any of the event's methods, and through the power of inheritance, you can also use methods that belong to any superclass of the event. For example, any KeyEvent has access to the InputEvent, ComponentEvent, AWTEvent, EventObject, and Object methods, as well as to the KeyEvent methods.

Understanding x- and y-Coordinates

Table 15-5 refers to x- and y-coordinates of a mouse pointer. A window or frame consists of a number of horizontal and vertical pixels on the screen. Any component you place on the screen has a horizontal, or **x-axis**, position as well as a vertical, or **y-axis**, position in the window. The upper-left corner of any display is position 0, 0. The first, or **x-coordinate**, value increases as you travel from left to right across the window. The second, or **y-coordinate**, value increases as you travel from top to bottom. Figure 15-33 illustrates some screen coordinate positions.

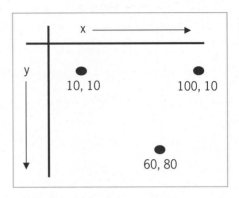

Figure 15-33 Screen coordinate positions

TWO TRUTHS & A LIE

Using AWTEvent Class Methods

1. You use many of the AWTEvent class methods to determine the nature of and facts about an event.

2. The getSource() method returns the Object involved in an event, and the getComponent() method returns the Component involved in an event.

3. The methods isAltDown() and isShiftDown() are ActionEvent methods.

The false statement is #3. The methods isAltDown() and isShiftDown() are KeyEvent methods.

Handling Mouse Events

Even though Java program users sometimes type characters from a keyboard, when you write GUI programs you probably expect users to spend most of their time operating a mouse. The MouseMotionListener interface provides you with methods named mouseDragged() and mouseMoved() that detect the mouse being rolled or dragged across a component surface. The MouseListener interface provides you with methods named mousePressed(), mouseClicked(), and mouseReleased() that are analogous to the keyboard event methods keyPressed(), keyTyped(), and keyReleased(). With a mouse, however, you are interested in more than its button presses; you sometimes simply want to know where a mouse is pointing. The additional interface methods mouseEntered() and mouseExited() inform you when the user positions the mouse over a component (entered) or moves the mouse off a component (exited). The MouseInputListener interface implements all the methods in both the

MouseListener and MouseMotionListener interfaces; although it has no methods of its own, it is a convenience when you want to handle many different types of mouse events. Tables 15-6 and 15-7 show the methods of the MouseListener and MouseMotionListener classes, respectively.

Method	Description
void mouseClicked(MouseEvent e)	Invoked when the mouse button has been clicked (pressed and released) on a component
void mouseEntered(MouseEvent e)	Invoked when the mouse pointer enters a component
void mouseExited(MouseEvent e)	Invoked when the mouse pointer exits a component
void mousePressed(MouseEvent e)	Invoked when a mouse button has been pressed on a component
void mouseReleased(MouseEvent e)	Invoked when a mouse button has been released on a component

Table 15-6 MouseListener methods

Many of the methods in Tables 15-6 and 15-7 also appear in tables earlier in this chapter. They are organized by interface here so you can better understand the scope of methods that are available for mouse actions. Don't forget that because MouseListener, MouseMotionListener, and MouseInputListener are interfaces, you must include each method in every program that implements them, even if you choose to place no instructions within some of the methods.

Method	Description
void mouseDragged(MouseEvent e)	Invoked when a mouse button is pressed on a component and then dragged
void mouseMoved(MouseEvent e)	Invoked when the mouse pointer has been moved onto a component but no buttons have been pressed

Table 15-7 MouseMotionListener methods

The MouseWheelListener interface contains just one method named mouseWheelMoved(), and it accepts a MouseWheelEvent argument.

Each of the methods in Tables 15-6 and 15-7 accepts a MouseEvent argument. A MouseEvent is the type of event generated by mouse manipulation. Figure 15-34 shows the inheritance hierarchy of the MouseEvent class. From this diagram, you can see that a MouseEvent is a type of InputEvent, which is a type of ComponentEvent. The MouseEvent class contains many instance methods and fields that are useful in describing mouse-generated events. Table 15-8 lists some of the more useful methods of the MouseEvent class, and Table 15-9 lists some fields.

```
java.lang.Object
   |--java.util.EventObject
        |--java.awt.AWTEvent
             |--java.awt.event.ComponentEvent
                  |--java.awt.event.InputEvent
                       |--java.awt.event.MouseEvent
```

Figure 15-34   The inheritance hierarchy of the MouseEvent class

Method	Description
int getButton()	Returns which, if any, of the mouse buttons has changed state; uses fields NOBUTTON, BUTTON1, BUTTON2, and BUTTON3
int getClickCount()	Returns the number of mouse clicks associated with the current event
int getX()	Returns the horizontal x-position of the event relative to the source component
int getY()	Returns the vertical y-position of the event relative to the source component

Table 15-8   Some useful MouseEvent methods

Field	Description
static int BUTTON1	Indicates mouse button #1; used by getButton()
static int BUTTON2	Indicates mouse button #2; used by getButton()
static int BUTTON3	Indicates mouse button #3; used by getButton()
static int NOBUTTON	Indicates no mouse buttons; used by getButton()
static int MOUSE_CLICKED	The "mouse clicked" event
static int MOUSE_DRAGGED	The "mouse dragged" event
static int MOUSE_ENTERED	The "mouse entered" event
static int MOUSE_EXITED	The "mouse exited" event

Table 15-9   Some useful MouseEvent fields

Figure 15-35 shows a JMouseActionFrame application that demonstrates several of the mouse listener and event methods. JMouseActionFrame extends JFrame, and because it implements the MouseListener interface, it must include all five methods— mouseClicked(), mouseEntered(), mouseExited(), mousePressed(), and mouseReleased()—even though no actions are included in the mousePressed() or mouseReleased() methods.

```java
import javax.swing.*;
import java.awt.*;
import java.awt.event.*;
public class JMouseActionFrame extends JFrame implements MouseListener
{
    private int x, y;
    private JLabel label= new JLabel("Do something with the mouse");
    String msg = "";

    public JMouseActionFrame()
    {
        setLayout(new FlowLayout());
        addMouseListener(this);
        add(label);
    }
    @Override
    public void mouseClicked(MouseEvent e)
    {
        int whichButton = e.getButton();
        msg = "You pressed mouse ";
        if(whichButton == MouseEvent.BUTTON1)
            msg += "button 1.";
        else
            if(whichButton == MouseEvent.BUTTON2)
                msg += "button 2.";
            else
                msg += "button 3.";
        msg += " You are at position " +
            e.getX() + ", " + e.getY() + ".";
        if(e.getClickCount() == 2)
            msg += " You double-clicked.";
        else
            msg += " You single-clicked.";
        label.setText(msg);
    }
    @Override
    public void mouseEntered(MouseEvent e)
    {
        msg = "You entered the frame.";
        label.setText(msg);
    }
}
```

Figure 15-35   The JMouseActionFrame application (continues)

(continued)

```
    @Override
    public void mouseExited(MouseEvent e)
    {
        msg = "You exited the frame.";
        label.setText(msg);
    }
    @Override
    public void mousePressed(MouseEvent e)
    {
    }
    @Override
    public void mouseReleased(MouseEvent e)
    {
    }
    public static void main(String[] args)
    {
        JMouseActionFrame mFrame = new JMouseActionFrame();
        final int WIDTH = 600;
        final int HEIGHT = 100;
        mFrame.setSize(WIDTH, HEIGHT);
        mFrame.setVisible(true);
    }
}
```

Figure 15-35　The JMouseActionFrame application

The JMouseActionFrame application in Figure 15-35 displays messages as the user generates mouse actions. At the start of the class, two integers are declared to hold the mouse position x- and y-coordinates. A JLabel and a String are also declared to hold messages that inform the user of the mouse actions taken. In the first shaded section of Figure 15-35, the constructor sets the layout manager, enables the frame to listen for mouse events, and adds the JLabel to the JFrame.

In Figure 15-35, most of the action occurs in the mouseClicked() method (the second unshaded area in the figure). The method builds a String that is ultimately assigned to the JLabel. The same actions could have been placed in the mousePressed() or mouseReleased() method because the statements could be placed in the frame just as well at either of those times. Within the mouseClicked() method, the MouseEvent object named e is used several times. It is used with the getButton() method to determine which mouse button the user clicked, getX() and getY() are used to retrieve the mouse position, and getClickCount() is used to distinguish between single- and double-clicks.

In Figure 15-35, different messages also are generated in the mouseEntered() and mouseExited() methods, so the user is notified when the mouse pointer has "entered"—that is, passed over the surface area of—the JFrame, the component that is listening for actions.

The main() method at the end of the class creates one instance of the JMouseActionFrame class and sets its size and visibility.

Figure 15-36 shows the JMouseActionFrame application during execution. At this point, the user has just clicked the left mouse button near the lower-left corner of the frame. Of course, in your own applications you might not want only to notify users of their mouse actions; instead, you might want to perform calculations, create files, or generate any other programming tasks.

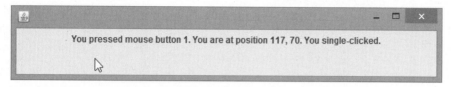

You pressed mouse button 1. You are at position 117, 70. You single-clicked.

Figure 15-36   Typical execution of the JMouseActionFrame application

837

TWO TRUTHS & A LIE

Handling Mouse Events

1. The MouseMotionListener interface provides you with methods that detect the mouse being rolled or dragged across a component surface.

2. The MouseListener interface provides you with methods that are analogous to the keyboard event methods keyPressed(), keyTyped(), and keyReleased().

3. The MouseListener interface implements all the methods in the MouseInputListener interface.

The false statement is #3. The MouseInputListener interface implements all the methods in both the MouseListener and MouseMotionListener interfaces.

Using Menus

Menus are lists of user options; they are commonly added features in GUI programs. Application users are used to seeing horizontal menu bars across the tops of frames, and they expect to be able to click those options to produce drop-down lists that display more choices. The horizontal list of JMenus is a JMenuBar. Each JMenu can contain options, called JMenuItems, or can contain submenus that also are JMenus. For example, Figure 15-37 shows a JFrame that illustrates the use of the following components:

- A JMenuBar that contains two JMenus named File and Colors.

- Three items within the Colors JMenu: Bright, Dark, and White. Dark and White are JMenuItems. Bright is a JMenu that holds a submenu. You can tell that Bright is a submenu because an arrow sits to the right of its name, and when the mouse hovers over Bright, two additional JMenuItems appear: Pink and Yellow.

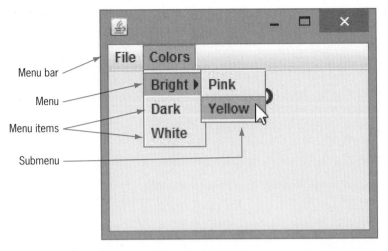

Figure 15-37   A JFrame with a horizontal JMenuBar that holds two JMenus

To create the output shown in Figure 15-37, a series of JMenuBar, JMenu, and JMenuItem objects were created and put together in stages. You can create each of the components you see in the menus in Figure 15-37 as follows:

- You can create a JMenuBar much like other objects—by using the new operator and a call to the constructor, as follows:

  ```
  JMenuBar mainBar = new JMenuBar();
  ```

- You can create the two JMenus that are part of the JMenuBar:

  ```
  JMenu menu1 = new JMenu("File");
  JMenu menu2 = new JMenu("Colors");
  ```

- The three components within the Colors JMenu are created as follows:

  ```
  JMenu bright = new JMenu("Bright");
  JMenuItem dark = new JMenuItem("Dark");
  JMenuItem white = new JMenuItem("White");
  ```

- The two JMenuItems that are part of the Bright JMenu are created as follows:

  ```
  JMenuItem pink = new JMenuItem("Pink");
  JMenuItem yellow = new JMenuItem("Yellow");
  ```

Once all the components are created, you assemble them.

- You add the JMenuBar to a JFrame using the setJMenuBar() method as follows:

  ```
  setJMenuBar(mainBar);
  ```

Using the setJMenuBar() method assures that the menu bar is anchored to the top of the frame and looks like a conventional menu bar. Notice that the JMenuBar is not added to a JFrame's content pane; it is added to the JFrame itself.

- The JMenus are added to the JMenuBar using the add() method. For example:

```
mainBar.add(menu1);
mainBar.add(menu2);
```

- A submenu and two JMenuItems are added to the Colors menu as follows:

```
menu2.add(bright);
menu2.add(dark);
menu2.add(white);
```

- A submenu can contain its own JMenuItems. For example, the Bright JMenu that is part of the Colors menu in Figure 15-37 contains its own two JMenuItem objects:

```
bright.add(pink);
bright.add(yellow);
```

Figure 15-38 shows a complete working program that creates a frame with a greeting and the JMenu shown in Figure 15-37.

```
import javax.swing.*;
import java.awt.*;
import java.awt.event.*;
import java.awt.Color;
public class JMenuFrame extends JFrame implements
    ActionListener
{
    private JMenuBar mainBar = new JMenuBar();
    private JMenu menu1 = new JMenu("File");
    private JMenu menu2 = new JMenu("Colors");
    private JMenuItem exit = new JMenuItem("Exit");
    private JMenu bright = new JMenu("Bright");
    private JMenuItem dark = new JMenuItem("Dark");
    private JMenuItem white = new JMenuItem("White");
    private JMenuItem pink = new JMenuItem("Pink");
    private JMenuItem yellow = new JMenuItem("Yellow");
    private JLabel label = new JLabel("Hello");
```

Figure 15-38 The JMenuFrame class *(continues)*

(continued)

```java
    public JMenuFrame()
    {
        setLayout(new FlowLayout());
        setJMenuBar(mainBar);
        mainBar.add(menu1);
        mainBar.add(menu2);
        menu1.add(exit);
        menu2.add(bright);
        menu2.add(dark);
        menu2.add(white);
        bright.add(pink);
        bright.add(yellow);
        exit.addActionListener(this);
        dark.addActionListener(this);
        white.addActionListener(this);
        pink.addActionListener(this);
        yellow.addActionListener(this);
        add(label);
        label.setFont(new Font("Arial", Font.BOLD, 26));
    }
    @Override
    public void actionPerformed(ActionEvent e)
    {
        Object source = e.getSource();
        Container con = getContentPane();
        if(source == exit)
            System.exit(0);
        else if(source == dark)
            con.setBackground(Color.BLACK);
        else if(source == white)
            con.setBackground(Color.WHITE);
        else if(source == pink)
            con.setBackground(Color.PINK);
        else con.setBackground(Color.YELLOW);
    }
    public static void main(String[] args)
    {
        JMenuFrame mFrame = new JMenuFrame();
        final int WIDTH = 250;
        final int HEIGHT = 200;
        mFrame.setSize(WIDTH, HEIGHT);
        mFrame.setVisible(true);
    }
}
```

Figure 15-38 The JMenuFrame class

In the application in Figure 15-38, each JMenuItem becomes a source for an ActionEvent, and the JFrame is assigned the role of listener for each. The actionPerformed() method determines the source of any generated event. If the user selects the Exit option from the

File menu, the application ends. If the user selects any of the colors from the Colors menu, the background color of the JFrame is altered accordingly.

Using Specialized Menu Items

The JCheckBoxMenuItem and JRadioButtonMenuItem classes derive from the JMenuItem class. Each provides more specific menu items as follows:

- JCheckBoxMenuItem objects appear with a check box next to them. An item can be selected (displaying a check mark in the box) or not. Usually, you use check box items to turn options on or off.

- JRadioButtonMenuItem objects appear with a round radio button next to them. Users usually expect radio buttons to be mutually exclusive, so you usually make radio buttons part of a ButtonGroup. Then, when any radio button is selected, the others are all deselected.

The state of a JCheckBoxMenuItem or JRadioButtonMenuItem can be determined with the isSelected() method, and you can alter the state of the check box with the setSelected() method.

Figure 15-39 shows a JMenuFrame2 application in which two JCheckBoxMenuItems and three JRadioButtonMenuItems have been added to a JMenu. The controls have not yet been assigned any tasks, but Figure 15-40 shows how the menu looks when the application executes.

```java
import javax.swing.*;
import java.awt.*;
import java.awt.event.*;
public class JMenuFrame2 extends JFrame
{
   private JMenuBar mainBar = new JMenuBar();
   private JMenu menu1 = new JMenu("File");
   private JCheckBoxMenuItem check1 = new
      JCheckBoxMenuItem("Check box A");
   private JCheckBoxMenuItem check2 = new
      JCheckBoxMenuItem("Check box B");
   private JRadioButtonMenuItem radio1 = new
      JRadioButtonMenuItem("Radio option 1");
   private JRadioButtonMenuItem radio2 = new
      JRadioButtonMenuItem("Radio option 2");
   private JRadioButtonMenuItem radio3 = new
      JRadioButtonMenuItem("Radio option 3");
   private ButtonGroup group = new ButtonGroup();
```

Figure 15-39 The JMenuFrame2 application *(continues)*

(continued)

```java
public JMenuFrame2()
{
    setLayout(new FlowLayout());
    setJMenuBar(mainBar);
    mainBar.add(menu1);
    menu1.add(check1);
    menu1.add(check2);
    menu1.addSeparator();
    menu1.add(radio1);
    menu1.add(radio2);
    menu1.add(radio3);
    group.add(radio1);
    group.add(radio2);
    group.add(radio3);
}
public static void main(String[] args)
{
    JMenuFrame2 frame = new JMenuFrame2();
    final int WIDTH = 150;
    final int HEIGHT = 200;
    frame.setSize(WIDTH, HEIGHT);
    frame.setVisible(true);
}
}
```

Figure 15-39   The JMenuFrame2 application

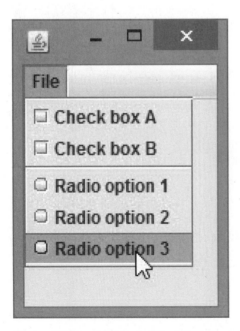

Figure 15-40   Execution of the JMenuFrame2 application

Using addSeparator()

The shaded statement in Figure 15-39 calls the addSeparator() method. This method adds a horizontal line to menus in order to visually separate groups for your users. In Figure 15-40, you can see that the separator falls between the JCheckBoxMenuItems and the JRadioButtonMenuItems because that's the order in which the shaded addSeparator() method call was made. The separator does not change the functionality of the menu; it simply makes the menu more visually organized for the user.

Using setMnemonic()

A **mnemonic** is a key that causes an already visible menu item to be chosen. You can use the setMnemonic() method to provide a shortcut menu key for any visible menu item. For example, when you add the following statement to the JMenuFrame2 constructor in Figure 15-39, the menu appears as in Figure 15-41:

```
menu1.setMnemonic('F');
```

The mnemonic for the File menu is set to *F*, so the *F* in *File* is underlined. When a user presses Alt+F on the keyboard, the result is the same as if the user had clicked File on the menu: the menu list is opened and displayed.

 Your downloadable student files contain a JMenuFrame3 application that includes the setMnemonic() instruction that produces the output in Figure 15-41.

Figure 15-41   The File menu with a mnemonic applied

You should use a different mnemonic for each menu item that has one; if you use the same mnemonic multiple times, only the first assignment works. Usually, you use the first letter of the option—for example, *F* for *File*. If multiple menu items start with the same letter, the convention is to choose the next most prominent letter in the name. For example, *X* is often chosen as the mnemonic for *Exit*.

An **accelerator** is similar to a mnemonic. It is a key combination that causes a menu item to be chosen whether it is visible or not. For example, many word-processing programs allow you to press Ctrl+P to print from anywhere in the program. Only **leaf menu items**—menus that don't bring up other menus—can have accelerators. (They are called "leaves" because they are at the end of a branch with no more branches extending from them.) See the Java Web site for more details.

TWO TRUTHS & A LIE

Using Menus

1. The horizontal list of JMenus at the top of a JFrame is also a JMenu.

2. Each JMenu can contain options, called JMenuItems, or it can contain submenus that also are JMenus.

3. You add a JMenuBar to a JFrame using the setJMenuBar() method.

The false statement is #1. The horizontal list of JMenus at the top of a JFrame is a JMenuBar.

 You Do It

Using a Menu Bar and JPanels

Next, you create an application for a party planning company that uses a menu bar with multiple user options, and that uses separate JPanels with different layout managers to organize components.

1. Open a new file, and enter the following first few lines of the EventSelector class. The class extends JFrame and implements ActionListener because the JFrame contains potential user mouse selections.

```
import javax.swing.*;
import java.awt.*;
import java.awt.event.*;
import java.awt.Color;
public class EventSelector extends JFrame implements ActionListener
{
```

2. Create a JMenuBar and its two JMenus as follows:

```
private JMenuBar mainBar = new JMenuBar();
private JMenu menu1 = new JMenu("File");
private JMenu menu2 = new JMenu("Event types");
```

3. Next, create the items that will appear within the menus. The File menu contains an Exit option. The Event types menu contains two submenus: Adult and Child. Each of those submenus contains more options. For example, Figure 15-42 shows the expanded Adult event types menu in the finished program.

(continues)

```
                                                                     (continued)
private JMenuItem exit = new JMenuItem("Exit");
private JMenu adult = new JMenu("Adult");
private JMenu child = new JMenu("Child");
private JMenuItem adultBirthday = new JMenuItem("Birthday");
private JMenuItem anniversary = new JMenuItem("Anniversary");
private JMenuItem retirement = new JMenuItem("Retirement");
private JMenuItem adultOther = new JMenuItem("Other");
private JMenuItem childBirthday = new JMenuItem("Birthday");
private JMenuItem childOther = new JMenuItem("Other");
```

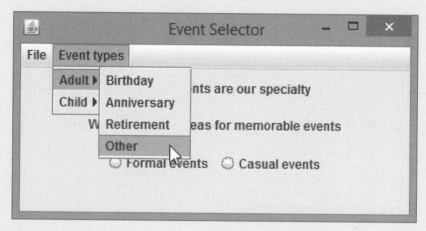

Figure 15-42   The Adult menu

4. Declare several other components that will be used to show how JFrames are composed:

```
private JPanel birthdayPanel = new JPanel();
private JPanel otherPanel = new JPanel();
private JLabel birthdayLabel = new
   JLabel("Birthday events are our specialty");
private JLabel otherLabel = new
   JLabel("We have lots of ideas for memorable events");
private JPanel buttonPanel = new JPanel();
private JRadioButton radButton1 = new
   JRadioButton("Formal events");
private JRadioButton radButton2 = new
   JRadioButton("Casual events");
```

5. Write the constructor for the JFrame. Set the title, the default close operation, and the layout. Call separate methods to compose the menu, to add the necessary action listeners to the menu items, and to lay out the JFrame's components. These tasks could be performed directly within the constructor, but you can place them in separate methods to better organize the application.

(continues)

(continued)

```java
public EventSelector()
{
    setTitle("Event Selector");
    setDefaultCloseOperation(JFrame.EXIT_ON_CLOSE);
    setLayout(new FlowLayout());
    composeMenus();
    addActionListeners();
    layoutComponents();
}
```

6. Add the `composeMenus()` method. Set the main menu bar, and add two menus to it. Then add one option to the first menu and two submenus to the second menu. Finally, add four items to the first submenu and two items to the other one.

```java
public void composeMenus()
{
    setJMenuBar(mainBar);
    mainBar.add(menu1);
    mainBar.add(menu2);
    menu1.add(exit);
    menu2.add(adult);
    menu2.add(child);
    adult.add(adultBirthday);
    adult.add(anniversary);
    adult.add(retirement);
    adult.add(adultOther);
    child.add(childBirthday);
    child.add(childOther);
}
```

7. Add the `addActionListeners()` method, which makes the `JFrame` become a listener for each menu item:

```java
public void addActionListeners()
{
    exit.addActionListener(this);
    adultBirthday.addActionListener(this);
    anniversary.addActionListener(this);
    retirement.addActionListener(this);
    adultOther.addActionListener(this);
    childBirthday.addActionListener(this);
    childOther.addActionListener(this);
}
```

8. The `layoutComponents()` method arranges all the components that appear in the content pane. The `birthdayPanel` object contains a single label. The `otherPanel` object contains a label and another panel (`buttonPanel`) in a grid. The `buttonPanel` contains two radio buttons. For this demonstration, the

(continues)

(continued)

radio buttons are not functional, but in a more complicated application, an `addActionListener()` method could be applied to them. Also, in a more complicated application, you could continue to place panels within another panel to achieve complex designs.

```java
public void layoutComponents()
{
    birthdayPanel.setLayout(new FlowLayout());
    otherPanel.setLayout(new GridLayout(2, 1, 3, 3));
    birthdayPanel.add(birthdayLabel);
    otherPanel.add("other", otherLabel);
    otherPanel.add("buttons", buttonPanel);
    buttonPanel.add(radButton1);
    buttonPanel.add(radButton2);
    add(birthdayPanel);
    add(otherPanel);
}
```

9. Add an `actionPerformed()` method that responds to menu selections. Different background colors are set depending on the user's choices.

```java
@Override
public void actionPerformed(ActionEvent e)
{
    Object source = e.getSource();
    Container con = getContentPane();
    if(source == exit)
        System.exit(0);
    else if(source == childBirthday || source == childOther)
        con.setBackground(Color.PINK);
    else
        con.setBackground(Color.WHITE);
    if(source == adultBirthday || source == childBirthday)
    {
        birthdayPanel.setBackground(Color.YELLOW);
        otherPanel.setBackground(Color.WHITE);
    }
    else
    {
        birthdayPanel.setBackground(Color.WHITE);
        otherPanel.setBackground(Color.YELLOW);
    }
}
```

10. Add the `main()` method, which instantiates an `EventSelector` object and sets its size and visibility. Add a closing curly brace for the class.

(continues)

848

(continued)

```
        public static void main(String[] args)
        {
            EventSelector frame = new EventSelector();
            final int WIDTH = 400;
            final int HEIGHT = 200;
            frame.setSize(WIDTH, HEIGHT);
            frame.setVisible(true);
        }
    }
```

11. Save the application as **EventSelector.java**, and then compile and run it. Make various selections and observe the effects. Figure 15-43 shows the running application after the user has made a selection. After you experiment with the application, dismiss the frame.

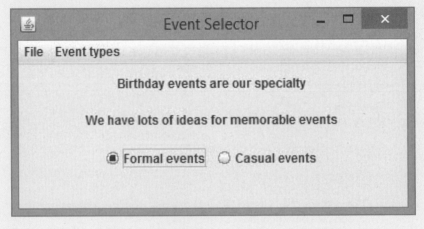

Figure 15-43　Typical execution of the EventSelector application

12. Experiment by making changes to the EventSelector application. For example, some menu selections could change the JFrame background to a different color, and others could add a new JLabel to the JFrame content pane.

Don't Do It

- Don't forget that the content pane is operating behind the scenes when you use a top-level container and that, depending on the operations you want to perform, you might need to get a reference to it.

- Don't forget that when you create a custom Color object, 0 represents the darkest shade and 255 represents the lightest.

- Don't forget to set a layout manager if you do not want to use the default one for a container.

- Don't forget to use a region when adding a component to a BorderLayout if you do not want the component to be placed in the center region by default.

- Don't use add() to place a JFrame's menu bar. You must use the setMenuBar() method to place a menu bar correctly.

- Don't use the same mnemonic for multiple menu items.

Key Terms

A **containment hierarchy** is a tree of components that has a top-level container as its root (that is, at its uppermost level).

A **top-level container** is one at the top of a containment hierarchy. The Java top-level containers are JFrame, JDialog, and JApplet.

A **content pane** contains all the visible components in a top-level container's user interface.

A **menu bar** is a horizontal strip that is placed at the top of a container and that contains user options.

A **glass pane** resides above the content pane in a container. It can contain tool tips.

The **alpha value** of a color indicates the level of transparency.

The **preferred size** of a Component is its default size.

A **panel** is a plain, borderless surface that can hold other GUI components.

Double buffering is the default buffering strategy in which JPanels are drawn offscreen when they are updated and displayed only when complete.

The **primary surface** is the visible screen surface during double buffering.

The **back buffer** is the offscreen image during double buffering.

A **block line transfer**, or **blitting**, is the act of copying the contents from one surface to another.

A **scroll pane** provides scroll bars along the side or bottom of a pane, or both, so that the user can scroll initially invisible parts of the pane into view.

The **viewport** is the viewable area in a scroll pane.

An **adapter class** implements all the methods in an interface, providing an empty body for each method.

An **action key** is a keyboard key that does not generate a character.

Virtual key codes represent keyboard keys that have been pressed.

The **x-axis** is an imaginary horizontal line that indicates screen position.

The **y-axis** is an imaginary vertical line that indicates screen position.

The **x-coordinate** is a value that increases as you travel from left to right across a window.

The **y-coordinate** is a value that increases as you travel from top to bottom across a window.

Menus are lists of user options.

A **mnemonic** is a key that causes an already visible menu item to be chosen.

An **accelerator** is a key combination that causes a menu item to be chosen, whether or not the menu item is visible.

A **leaf menu item** is a menu item that does not bring up another menu; in other words, it is at the end of a branch.

Chapter Summary

- Every top-level container has a content pane that contains all the visible components in the container's user interface. The content pane can contain components and other containers. Whenever you create a top-level container, you can get a reference to its content pane using the `getContentPane()` method.

- The `Color` class defines 13 colors for you to use in your applications; you also can create more than 16 million custom colors. The class can be used with the `setBackground()` and `setForeground()` methods of the `Component` class to make your applications more attractive and interesting.

- The layout manager assigned to a `Container` determines how its components are sized and positioned. The `BorderLayout` manager is the default manager class for all content panes; when you use it, the components fill the screen in five regions. The `FlowLayout` manager arranges components in rows across the width of a `Container`. The `GridLayout` manager arranges components in rows and columns. The `CardLayout` manager generates a stack of components.

- A `JPanel` is a plain, borderless surface that can hold lightweight GUI components.

- A `JScrollPane` provides scroll bars along the side or bottom of a pane, or both, so that the user can scroll initially invisible parts of the pane into view.

- `ActionEvents` are generated by components that users can click, and `TextEvents` are generated by components into which the user enters text. `MouseEvents` include determining the location of the mouse pointer and distinguishing between a single- and double-click. For every event class, such as <name>Event, there is a similarly named <name>Listener interface. Instead of implementing a listener class, you can extend an adapter class.

- In addition to the handler methods included with the event listener interfaces, the `AWTEvent` classes themselves contain methods that return information about an event.

- The MouseMotionListener interface provides you with methods that react to the mouse being rolled or dragged across a component surface. The MouseListener interface provides you with methods that react when a mouse button is pressed, clicked, or released and then the user enters or exits a component using the mouse. The MouseInputListener interface implements all the methods in both the MouseListener and MouseMotionListener interfaces.

- Menus are lists of user options. You use JMenuBar, JMenu, JMenuItem, and other classes in menu creation.

Review Questions

1. If you add fewer than five components to a BorderLayout, _____.

   a. any empty component regions disappear

   b. the remaining components expand to fill the available space

   c. both a and b

   d. none of the above

2. When you resize a Container that uses BorderLayout, _____.

   a. the Container and the regions both change in size

   b. the Container changes in size, but the regions retain their original sizes

   c. the Container retains its size, but the regions change or might disappear

   d. nothing happens

3. When you create a JFrame named myFrame, you can set its layout manager to BorderLayout with the statement _____.

   a. myFrame.setLayout = new BorderLayout();

   b. myFrame.setLayout(new BorderLayout());

   c. setLayout(myFrame = new BorderLayout());

   d. setLayout(BorderLayout(myFrame));

4. Which of the following is the correct syntax for adding a JButton named b1 to a Container named con when using CardLayout?

   a. con.add(b1);   c. con.add("Options", b1);

   b. con.add("b1");   d. none of the above

5. You can use the _____ class to arrange components in a single row or column of a container.

   a. FlowLayout   c. CardLayout

   b. BorderLayout   d. BoxLayout

6. When you use _____ , the components you add fill their region; they do not retain their default size.

   a. FlowLayout

   b. BorderLayout

   c. FixedLayout

   d. RegionLayout

7. The statement _____ ensures that components are placed from left to right across a JFrame surface until the first row is full, at which point a second row is started at the frame surface's left edge.

   a. setLayout(FlowLayout.LEFT);

   b. setLayout(new FlowLayout(LEFT));

   c. setLayout(new FlowLayout(FlowLayout.LEFT));

   d. setLayout(FlowLayout(FlowLayout.LEFT));

8. The GridBagLayout class allows you to _____ .

   a. add components to precise locations within the grid

   b. indicate that specific components should span multiple rows or columns within the grid

   c. both a and b

   d. none of the above

9. The statement setLayout(new GridLayout(2,7)); establishes a GridLayout with _____ horizontal row(s).

   a. zero

   b. one

   c. two

   d. seven

10. As you add new components to a GridLayout, _____ .

    a. they are positioned from left to right across each row in sequence

    b. you can specify exact positions by skipping some positions

    c. both of the above

    d. none of the above

11. A JPanel is a _____ .

    a. Window

    b. Container

    c. both of the above

    d. none of the above

12. The _____ class allows you to arrange components as if they are stacked like index or playing cards.

    a. GameLayout

    b. CardLayout

    c. BoxLayout

    d. GridBagLayout

13. AWTEvent is the child class of _____.

    a. EventObject   c. ComponentEvent

    b. Event   d. ItemEvent

14. When a user clicks a JPanel or JFrame, the action generates a(n) _____.

    a. ActionEvent   c. PanelEvent

    b. MouseEvent   d. KeyboardEvent

15. Event handlers are _____.

    a. abstract classes   c. listeners

    b. concrete classes   d. methods

16. The return type of getComponent() is _____.

    a. Object   c. int

    b. Component   d. void

17. The KeyEvent method getKeyChar() returns a(n) _____.

    a. int   c. KeyEvent

    b. char   d. AWTEvent

18. The MouseEvent method that allows you to identify double-clicks is _____.

    a. getDouble()   c. getDoubleClick()

    b. isClickDouble()   d. getClickCount()

19. You can use the _____ method to determine the Object in which an ActionEvent originates.

    a. getObject()   c. getOrigin()

    b. getEvent()   d. getSource()

20. Which of the following is true in a standard menu application?

    a. A JMenuItem holds a JMenu.   c. A JMenuBar holds a JMenu.

    b. A JMenuItem holds a JMenuBar.   d. A JMenu holds a JMenuBar.

Exercises

Programming Exercises

1. Create a JFrame and set the layout to BorderLayout. In each region, place a JButton that displays the name of a classic movie that has the region name in its title. For example, the east button might indicate the movie *East of Eden*. When the user clicks the button, display the year of the movie's release and the name of one of its stars. Save the file as **JMovieFrame.java**.

2. Create an educational program for children that distinguishes between vowels and consonants as the user clicks buttons. Create 26 JButtons, each labeled with a different letter of the alphabet. Create a JFrame to hold three JPanels in a two-by-two grid. Randomly select eight of the 26 JButtons and place four in each of the first two JPanels. Add a JLabel to the third JPanel. When the user clicks a JButton, the text of the JLabel identifies the button's letter as a vowel or consonant, and then a new randomly selected letter replaces the letter on the JButton. Save the file as **JVowelConsonant.java**.

3. Create a JFrame that holds five buttons with the names of five different fonts. Include a sixth button that the user can click to make a font larger or smaller. Display a demonstration JLabel using the font and size that the user selects. Save the file as **JFontSelector.java**.

4. Create a JFrame that uses BorderLayout. Place a JButton in the center region. Each time the user clicks the JButton, change the background color in one of the other regions. Save the file as **JColorFrame.java**.

5. Create a JFrame with JPanels, a JButton, and a JLabel. When the user clicks the JButton, reposition the JLabel to a new location in a different JPanel. Save the file as **JMovingFrame.java**.

6. Create a class that extends JPanel and whose constructor accepts two colors, a Font, and a String. Use the colors for the background and foreground of the panel and display the string using the font parameter. Create an application named JPanelDemo. Use GridLayout to display four sample panels. Save the files as **JFlexiblePanel.java** and **JPanelDemo.java**.

7. Write an application that lets you determine the integer value returned by the InputEvent method getModifiers() when you click your left, right, or—if you have one—middle mouse button on a JFrame. Save the file as **JLeftOrRight.java**.

8. a. Search the Java Web site for information on how to use a JTextArea. Write an application for the WebBuy Company that allows a user to compose the three parts of a complete e-mail message: the "To:", "Subject:", and "Message:" text. The "To:" and "Subject:" text areas should provide a single line for data entry. The "Message:" area should allow multiple lines of input and be able to scroll if necessary to accommodate a long message. The user clicks a button to send the e-mail message. When the message is complete and the Send button is clicked, the application should display "Mail has been sent!" on a new line in the message area. Save the file as **JEMail.java**.

   b. Modify the JEMail application to include a Clear button that the user can click at any time to clear the "To:", "Subject:", and "Message:" fields. Save the file as **JEMail2.java**.

9. a. Create an application that uses a graphic interface to capture employee data and writes that data to a random access output file. The data required for each employee includes an employee ID number from 1 through 99 inclusive, the first and last names of the employee, and the employee's hourly pay rate. Allow the

user to enter data one record at a time and to click a button to save each record. Save the class as **CreateRandomEmployeeFile.java**.

b. Create an application that allows the user to enter an employee ID number. When the user clicks a button, display all the stored data for the employee. Save the file as **ReadRandomEmployeeFile.java**.

10. Create a `JFrame` for Java Junior College. Use menus to allow the user to access information about different campuses, major fields of study offered, and activities. Include at least two options in each menu. Save the file as **JavaJuniorCollege.java**.

Debugging Exercises

1. Each of the following files in the Chapter15 folder of your downloadable student files has syntax and/or logic errors. In each case, determine the problem and fix the program. After you correct the errors, save each file using the same filename preceded with *Fix*. For example, DebugFifteen1.java will become **FixDebugFifteen1.java**.

    a. DebugFifteen1.java   c. DebugFifteen3.java

    b. DebugFifteen2.java   d. DebugFifteen4.java

Game Zone

As you create some of the games in this section, you might find it convenient to add or remove components in a container after construction. Recall from Chapter 14 that in order for the user to see your changes, you might need to call the `validate()`, `invalidate()`, and `repaint()` methods. You will learn more about the `repaint()` method in the next chapter, "Graphics."

1. a. Create a Mine Field game in which the user attempts to click 10 panels of a grid before hitting the "bomb." Set up a `JFrame` using `BorderLayout`, use the `NORTH` region for a congratulatory message, and use the `CENTER` region for the game. In the `CENTER` region, create a four-by-five grid using `GridLayout` and populate the grid with `JPanel`s. Set the background color for all the `JPanel`s to `Color.BLUE`. Randomly choose one of the panels to be the bomb; the other 19 panels are "safe." Allow the player to click on grids. If the player chooses a safe panel, turn the panel to `Color.WHITE`. If the player chooses the bomb panel, turn the panel to `Color.RED` and turn all the remaining panels white. If the user successfully chooses 10 safe panels before choosing the bomb, display a congratulatory message in the `NORTH` JFrame region. Save the game as **MineField.java**.

856

b. Improve the Mine Field game by allowing the user to choose a difficulty level before beginning. Place three buttons labeled "Easy", "Intermediate", and "Difficult" in one region of the JFrame, and place the game grid and congratulatory message in other regions. Require the user to select a difficulty level before starting the game, and then disable the buttons. If the user chooses "Easy", the user must select only five safe panels to win the game. If the user selects "Intermediate", require 10 safe panels, as in the original game. If the user selects "Difficult", require 15 safe panels. Save the game as **MineField2.java**.

2. a. Create a game that helps new mouse users improve their hand-eye coordination. Within a JFrame, display an array of 48 JPanels in a GridLayout using eight rows and six columns. Randomly display an *X* on one of the panels. When the user clicks the correct panel (the one displaying the *X*), remove the *X* and display it on a different panel. After the user has successfully "hit" the correct panel 10 times, display a congratulatory message that includes the user's percentage (hits divided by clicks). Save the file as **JCatchTheMouse.java**.

b. Review how to use the LocalDateTime class from Chapter 4, and then revise the JCatchTheMouse game to conclude by displaying the number of seconds it takes the user to click all 10 *X*s. (For this program, assume that the user starts and stops the game during the same hour. That way, you only have to compare the minute and second values of the start and stop times.) Save the file as **JCatchTheMouseTimed.java**.

If you were writing a professional timed game, you would test the timer's accuracy regardless of when the user decided to play, even if the game's duration fell into different days or years. To make sure that the game's timer works correctly, you would either have to test it over the midnight hour on New Year's Eve (which is impractical), or you would have to reset your system's clock to simulate New Year's Eve. If you are writing the programs in this book on a school's computer network, you might be blocked by the administrator from changing the date and time. Even if you are working on your own computer, do not attempt to change the date and time unless you understand the impact on other installed applications. For example, your operating system might assume that an installed virus-protection program is expired, or a financial program might indicate that automatically paid bills are overdue.

3. The game Corner the King is played on a checkerboard. To begin, a checker is randomly placed in the bottom row. The player can move one or two squares to the left or upwards, and then the computer can move one or two squares left or up. The first to reach the upper-left corner wins. Design a game in which the computer's moves are chosen randomly. When the game ends, display a message that indicates the winner. Save the game as **CornerTheKing.java**.

4. Create a target practice game that allows the user to click moving targets and displays the number of hits in a 10-second period. (In Chapter 4, you learned how to use the LocalDateTime class to measure elapsed time.) Create a grid of at least 100 JPanels. Randomly display an *X* on five panels to indicate targets. As the user clicks each *X*, change the label to indicate a hit. When all five *X*s have been hit, randomly display a new set of five targets. Continue with as many sets as the user can hit in 10 seconds. When the time is up, display a count of the number of targets hit. Save the file as **JTargetPractice.java**.

5. You set up the card game Concentration by placing pairs of cards face down in a grid. The player turns up two cards at a time, exposing their values. If the cards match, they are removed from the grid. If the cards do not match, they are turned back over so their values are hidden again, and the player selects two more cards to expose. Using the knowledge gained by the previously exposed cards, the player attempts to remove all the pairs of cards from play. Create a Java version of this game using a `GridLayout` that is four rows high and five columns wide. Randomly assign two of the numbers 0 through 9 to each of 20 `JPanels`, and place each of the 20 `JPanels` in a cell of the grid. Initially, show only "backs" of cards by setting each panel's background to a solid color. When the user clicks a first card, change its color and expose its value. After the user clicks a second card, change its color to the same color as the first exposed card, expose the second card's value, and keep both cards exposed until the user's mouse pointer exits the second card. If the two exposed cards are different, hide the cards again. If the two turned cards match, then "remove" the pair from play by setting their background colors to white. When the user has matched all 20 cards into 10 pairs, display a congratulatory message. Save the game as **JConcentration.java**.

6. Create a Mine Sweeper game by setting up a grid of rows and columns in which "bombs" are randomly hidden. You choose the size and difficulty of the game; for example, you might choose to create a fairly simple game by displaying a four-by-five grid that contains four bombs. If a player clicks a panel in the grid that contains a bomb, then the player loses the game. If the clicked panel is not a bomb, display a number that indicates how many adjacent panels contain a bomb. For example, if a user clicks a panel containing a 0, the user knows it is safe to click any panel above, below, beside, or diagonally adjacent to the cell, because those cells cannot possibly contain a bomb. If the player loses by clicking a bomb, display all the numeric values as well as the bomb positions. If the player succeeds in clicking all the panels except those containing bombs, the player wins and you should display a congratulatory message. Figure 15-44 shows the progression of a typical game. In the first screen, the user has clicked a panel, and the display indicates that no adjacent cells contain a bomb. In the second screen, the user has clicked a second panel, and the display indicates that one adjacent cell contains a bomb. In the last screen, the user has clicked a bomb panel, and all the bomb positions are displayed. Save the game as **MineSweeper.java**.

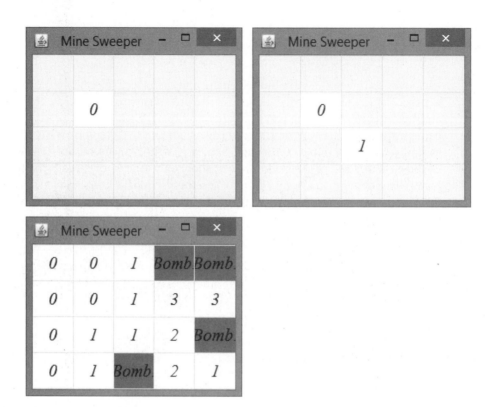

Figure 15-44   Typical progression of `MineSweeper` game

7. Create the game Lights Out using a `BorderLayout`. Place a five-by-five grid of panels in one region, and reserve another region for a congratulatory message. Randomly set each panel in the grid to a dark color or light color. The object of the game is to force all the panels to be dark, thus turning the "lights out." When the player clicks a panel, turn all the panels in the same row and column, including the clicked panel, to the opposite color. For example, if the user clicks the panel in the second row, third column, then darken all the light-colored panels in the second row and third column, and lighten all the dark-colored panels in that row and column. When all the panels in the grid are dark, all the lights are out, so display a congratulatory message. Save the game as **LightsOut.java**.

8. The game StopGate is played on a checkerboard with a set of dominoes; each domino is large enough to cover two checkerboard squares. One player places a domino horizontally on the checkerboard, covering any two squares. The other player then places a domino vertically to cover any other two squares. When a player has no more moves available, that player loses. Create a computerized version of the game in which the player places the horizontal pieces and the computer randomly selects a position for the vertical pieces. (Game construction will be simpler if you allow the player to select only the left square of a two-square area and assume that the domino covers that position plus the position immediately to the right.) Use a different color

for the player's dominoes and the computer's dominoes. Display a message naming the winner when no more moves are possible. Figure 15-45 shows a typical game after the player (blue) and computer (black) have each made one move, and near the end of the game when the player is about to win—the player has one move remaining, but the computer has none. Save the file as **StopGate.java**.

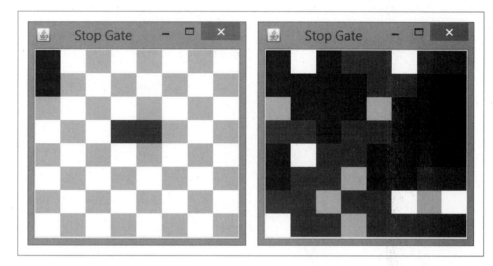

Figure 15-45   A typical game of StopGate just after play begins and near the end of the game

Case Problems

1. In Chapter 14, you created an interactive GUI application for Carly's Catering that allows the user to enter a number of guests for an event and to choose an entrée, two side dishes, and a dessert from groups of choices. Then, the application displays the cost of the event and a list of the chosen items. Now, modify the interface to include separate panels for the guest number entry, each group of menu choices, and the output. Use at least two different layout managers and at least two different colors in your application. Save the program as **JCarlysCatering.java**.

2. In Chapter 14, you created an interactive GUI application for Sammy's Seashore Rentals that allows the user to enter a rental time in hours, an equipment type, and a lesson option. Then, the application displays the cost of the rental and rental details. Now, modify the interface to include separate panels for the hour entry, each group of menu choices, and the output. Use at least two different layout managers and at least two different colors in your application. Save the program as **JSammysSeashore.java**.

Graphics

In this chapter, you will:

- ◎ Learn about rendering methods
- ◎ Draw strings
- ◎ Draw lines and shapes
- ◎ Learn more about fonts
- ◎ Draw with Java 2D graphics

Learning About Rendering Methods

When you run a Java program that contains graphics, such as the JFrame applications in the previous chapters, the display surface frequently must be displayed repeatedly, or **rendered** and **rerendered**. Rendering and rerendering a surface also is called **painting**. Painting operations fall into two broad categories based on what causes them:

- **System-triggered painting** occurs when the system asks a component to render its contents. This request happens when the component is first made visible, if it is resized, or if it is damaged. For example, a component becomes damaged when another component that covered part of it is moved, revealing a portion that was not visible.

- **Application-triggered painting** occurs when a program requests it, usually because the internal state of a component has changed. For example, you might want to change a component's text or color when a user clicks a button.

In Java, whether a paint request is triggered by the system or an application, a Component's paint() method is invoked. The header for the paint() method is:

```
public void paint(Graphics g)
```

The parameter to the method is a Graphics object. The Graphics class is an abstract class that descends directly from Object and holds data about graphics operations and methods for drawing shapes, text, and images. You learn more about this class later in this chapter.

You can override the paint() method in your programs if you want specific actions to take place when components must be rendered. For example, a window might need to be updated because it contains new images or you have moved a new object onto the screen. You don't usually call the paint() method directly. Instead, the repaint() method calls paint(). The Java system calls the repaint() method automatically when it needs to update a window, or you can call it yourself when you want painting to occur.

When a Swing object such as a JPanel calls the repaint() method, it not only calls paint(), it calls three other methods named paintComponent(), paintBorder(), and paintChildren(). Java's creators recommend that classes that extend Swing components should place all drawing code in a paintComponent() method that overrides the parent class version of the method. You generally should not write your own versions of paintBorder() or paintChildren(). The paintComponent() method where you place drawing code has the following header:

```
public void paintComponent(Graphics g)
```

The first statement you place in this method is most often the following:

```
super.paintComponent(g);
```

This statement uses the Graphics object that is automatically created as a parameter to paintComponent() and passes it up to the parent class version of the method, which makes sure that the component is erased before new drawing occurs. If you omit this statement, the component is not erased between updates and new output appears to "pile up" on top of previous output.

Figure 16-1 shows a class that demonstrates how component painting executes automatically. The figure contains a class that extends JPanel. The constructor requires a color parameter so that you can easily see the panel when it is eventually placed on a frame. For simplicity, the constructor assumes that the color is either red or blue, and it assigns the appropriate value to a string and sets the panel's background color. The JColorPanel class also contains a paintComponent() method that will be called automatically and that overrides the JPanel version of the method. In it, count is incremented and displayed so that you can keep track of the number of times the method has been called with each object created from the class. Notice that the paintComponent() method is never called from this class.

```java
import javax.swing.*;
import java.awt.*;
import java.awt.Color;
public class JColorPanel extends JPanel
{
    int count = 0;
    String colorString;
    public JColorPanel(Color color)
    {
        if(color.equals(Color.RED))
            colorString = "red";
        else
            colorString = "blue";
        setBackground(color);
    }
    @Override
    public void paintComponent(Graphics g)
    {
        super.paintComponent(g);
        ++count;
        System.out.println("In paintComponent() method -- " +
            colorString + " " + count);
    }
}
```

Figure 16-1   The JColorPanel class

Figure 16-2 shows a class that extends JFrame. Two JColorPanel objects are declared—a red one and a blue one. The background of the frame is set to yellow and the blue and red panels are added to different regions of the frame. The main() method simply declares a frame object and sets its size and visibility. Notice that the paintComponent() method is not called from this class either.

864

```
import javax.swing.*;
import java.awt.*;
import java.awt.Color;
public class JDemoPaintComponent extends JFrame
{
    JColorPanel p1 = new JColorPanel(Color.RED);
    JColorPanel p2 = new JColorPanel(Color.BLUE);
    public JDemoPaintComponent()
    {
        setLayout(new BorderLayout());
        setDefaultCloseOperation(JFrame.EXIT_ON_CLOSE);
        getContentPane().setBackground(Color.YELLOW);
        add(p1, BorderLayout.EAST);
        add(p2, BorderLayout.SOUTH);
    }
    public static void main(String[] args)
    {
        JDemoPaintComponent frame = new JDemoPaintComponent();
        frame.setSize(150, 100);
        frame.setVisible(true);
    }
}
```

Figure 16-2 The JDemoPaintComponent class

Figure 16-3 shows a typical execution of the JDemoPaintComponent program. The frame contains red and blue panels in its east and south regions, respectively, and the command line displays output from multiple calls to the paintComponent() method, alternating between the method associated with the blue panel and the red one. To create this sample output, the user started the program and then minimized and restored the frame several times. Although the paintComponent() method is never explicitly called in the program, it executes every time the system decides the panels need to be rerendered, including multiple times before the user takes any action on the frame. Each time the user resizes the frame by dragging its borders or minimizes and restores the frame, the paintComponent() method executes additional times for each panel.

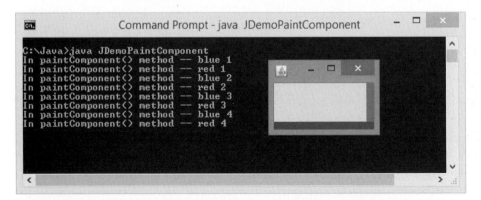

Figure 16-3 Typical execution of the JDemoPaintComponent program

If you want to call paintComponent() before the system calls it automatically, you should call repaint() and let it call paintComponent(). For example, if you want to change graphic output on a panel in response to a user's mouse click, you would place a call to repaint() in the actionPerformed() method. This technique is shown in a program later in this chapter.

TWO TRUTHS & A LIE

Learning About Rendering Methods

1. In Java, painting can be system triggered or application triggered.

2. The parameter to paintComponent() is a Graphics object.

3. In a Java Swing program, graphics drawing instructions should be placed in a method named paint().

The false statement is #3. Drawing instructions belong in the paintComponent() method.

Drawing Strings

The drawString() method in the Graphics class allows you to draw a String on a JPanel or other component. The drawString() method requires three arguments: a String, an x-axis coordinate, and a y-axis coordinate. (You learned about the x- and y-axes in Chapter 15. The x-axis represents horizontal position and the y-axis represents vertical position.)

When you use x- and y-coordinates with drawString(), the lower-left corner of the String appears at the coordinates.

The drawString() method is an instance method in the Graphics class, so you need to use a Graphics object to call it. For example, if you create a class that extends JPanel and implement a method with the header public void paintComponent(Graphics brush), you can draw a String within your method by using a statement such as:

```
brush.drawString("Hi ", 50, 80);
```

Figure 16-4 contains a class named JPanelWithButton that extends JPanel and contains a JButton. The constructor sets the panel's background color to red and activates the button. The actionPerformed() method that executes when the user clicks the button sets the panel's color to blue if it is currently red and to red if it is blue. The paintComponent() method that is automatically called when the panel needs repainting calls drawString(), which displays the current color name at position 20, 80.

```
import javax.swing.*;
import java.awt.*;
import java.awt.event.*;
import java.awt.Color;
public class JPanelWithButton extends JPanel implements ActionListener
{
    JButton button = new JButton("Press me");
    Color color;
    String colorString;
    public JPanelWithButton()
    {
        color = Color.RED;
        colorString = "red";
        setBackground(color);
        add(button);
        button.addActionListener(this);
    }
    public void actionPerformed(ActionEvent e)
    {
        if(color.equals(Color.RED))
        {
            color = Color.BLUE;
            colorString = "blue";
        }
        else
        {
            color = Color.RED;
            colorString = "red";
        }
        setBackground(color);
    }
    public void paintComponent(Graphics g)
    {
        super.paintComponent(g);
        g.drawString("The panel is " + colorString, 20, 80);
    }
}
```

Figure 16-4   The JPanelWithButton program

 The equals() method is overridden in the Color class to compare colors. Colors are equal only if their red, green, blue, and alpha (transparency) values are all the same.

Figure 16-5 contains a short demonstration program that extends JFrame, adds a JPanelWithButton object to it, and displays it. When you execute the program, the frame looks like Figure 16-6. When the user clicks the button, the background color of the panel changes from red to blue, and when the user clicks again, it changes from blue to red. The string changes appropriately because the paintComponent() method executes automatically in response to the color change.

```
import javax.swing.*;
import java.awt.*;
public class JDemoPanelWithButton extends JFrame
{
    JPanelWithButton p1 = new JPanelWithButton();
    public JDemoPanelWithButton()
    {
        setDefaultCloseOperation(JFrame.EXIT_ON_CLOSE);
        add(p1, BorderLayout.CENTER);
    }
    public static void main(String[] args)
    {
        JDemoPanelWithButton frame = new JDemoPanelWithButton();
        frame.setSize(200, 200);
        frame.setVisible(true);
    }
}
```

Figure 16-5   The JDemoPanelWithButton program

Figure 16-6   Typical execution of the JDemoPanelWithButton program

Interestingly, when you use the drawString() method with a negative font size, the string appears upside down. The coordinates then indicate the lower-right corner of the string.

Repainting

In the JPanelWithButton program in Figure 16-4, the paintComponent() method executed automatically and displayed a string because the panel's color changed, creating a need for the panel to be repainted. However, you might want to execute paintComponent() even when no draw-triggering changes have been made to a panel.

Consider the JPanelWithButton2 class in Figure 16-7. This class is similar to the JPanelWithButton class, except that the color has been removed. When the user clicks the button, a count variable is incremented and then displayed with the drawString() method call in the paintComponent() method. Because the color doesn't change, nothing in this program calls paintComponent() automatically, so the shaded call to repaint() is necessary. Without it, paintComponent() would never execute, and the new value of count would not be displayed with each button press. Instead, it would be displayed only after the next time the panel was repainted automatically—for example, after the application was minimized and restored.

```
import javax.swing.*;
import java.awt.*;
import java.awt.event.*;
public class JPanelWithButton2 extends JPanel implements ActionListener
{
    JButton button = new JButton("Press me");
    int count = 0;
    public JPanelWithButton2()
    {
        add(button);
        button.addActionListener(this);
    }
    public void actionPerformed(ActionEvent e)
    {
        ++count;
        repaint();
    }
    @Override
    public void paintComponent(Graphics g)
    {
        super.paintComponent(g);
        g.drawString("The count is " + count, 20, 80);
    }
}
```

Figure 16-7   The JPanelWithButton2 class

Figure 16-8 contains a program that extends JFrame and demonstrates the
JDemoPanelWithButton2 class. The only changes from the JDemoPanelWithButton class
in Figure 16-5 are the shaded additions of 2 to the class names.

```
import javax.swing.*;
import java.awt.*;
public class JDemoPanelWithButton2 extends JFrame
{
    JPanelWithButton2 p1 = new JPanelWithButton2();
    public JDemoPanelWithButton2()
    {
        setDefaultCloseOperation(JFrame.EXIT_ON_CLOSE);
        add(p1, BorderLayout.CENTER);
    }
    public static void main(String[] args)
    {
        JDemoPanelWithButton2 frame = new JDemoPanelWithButton2();
        frame.setSize(200, 200);
        frame.setVisible(true);
    }
}
```

Figure 16-8   The JDemoPanelWithButton2 application

Figure 16-9 The
JDemoPanelWithButton2
program during execution

Figure 16-9 shows the frame after the user has clicked the button three times. The display on the panel is rerendered after each button click in response to the call to repaint() in the button's actionPerformed() method.

Setting a Font

You can improve the appearance of strings drawn using Graphics objects by using the setFont() method. The setFont() method requires a Font argument. (You learned about the Font class in Chapter 14.) You can instruct a Graphics object to use a font by inserting it as the argument in a setFont() method call. For example, if a Graphics object is named artist, its font can be set with the following:

```
Font smallFont = new Font("Arial", Font.PLAIN, 8);
artist.setFont(smallFont);
```

Instead of creating a named Font object, you can use an anonymous object in the setFont() method call, as in the following example:

```
artist.setFont(new Font("Arial", Font.PLAIN, 8);
```

Figure 16-10 shows a panel class that creates a Font object used to draw a string. Figure 16-11 is a frame application that displays the panel, and Figure 16-12 shows the output.

```
import javax.swing.*;
import java.awt.*;
public class JFontPanel extends JPanel
{
   Font fancyFont = new Font("Serif", Font.ITALIC, 40);
   @Override
   public void paintComponent(Graphics g)
   {
      super.paintComponent(g);
      g.setFont(fancyFont);
      g.drawString("Hello", 20, 80);
   }
}
```

Figure 16-10 The JFontPanel class

```
import javax.swing.*;
import java.awt.*;
public class JDemoFontPanel extends JFrame
{
    JFontPanel p1 = new JFontPanel();
    public JDemoFontPanel()
    {
        setDefaultCloseOperation(JFrame.EXIT_ON_CLOSE);
        add(p1);
    }
    public static void main(String[] args)
    {
        JDemoFontPanel frame = new JDemoFontPanel();
        frame.setSize(200, 200);
        frame.setVisible(true);
    }
}
```

Figure 16-11 The JDemoFontPanel application

Figure 16-12 Output of the JDemoFontPanel class

Using Color

You can improve the appearance of graphics output by designating a Graphics object's color with the setColor() method. As you learned in Chapter 15, the Color class contains 13 constants; you can use any of these constants as an argument to the setColor() method. For example, you can instruct a Graphics object named g to produce green output by using the following statement:

g.setColor(Color.GREEN);

Until you change the color, subsequent graphics output appears in green.

TWO TRUTHS & A LIE

Drawing Strings

1. The `drawString()` method requires three arguments: a `String`, an x-axis coordinate, and a y-axis coordinate.

2. The upper-left corner of a `String` appears at the location indicated by the x- and y-coordinate arguments to `drawString()`.

3. The `drawString()` method is an instance method of the `Graphics` class.

The false statement is #2. The x- and y-coordinate arguments to `drawString()` indicate the lower-left corner of the `String`.

 You Do It

Using the drawString() Method

In the next steps, you write a class that extends `JPanel` and uses the `drawString()` method.

1. Open a new file, and begin a definition for a `JStringPanel` class by typing the following:

   ```
   import javax.swing.*;
   import java.awt.*;
   import java.awt.Color;
   public class JStringPanel extends JPanel
   {
   ```

2. Declare five variables that can hold a string's contents, font, color, and horizontal and vertical positions:

   ```
   String string;
   Font font;
   Color color;
   int horizontal;
   int vertical;
   ```

3. Add a constructor that assigns parameters to each of the panel's properties and sets the panel's background color to white:

(continues)

(continued)

```
public JStringPanel(String s, Font f, Color c, int x, int y)
{
    string = s;
    font = f;
    color = c;
    horizontal = x;
    vertical = y;
    setBackground(Color.WHITE);
}
```

4. Type the following `paintComponent()` method that calls the `JPanel` class version of the method and then sets the font and color of the `Graphics` parameter. Draw a string at the position indicated, and add a closing curly brace for the class.

```
@Override
public void paintComponent(Graphics g)
{
    super.paintComponent(g);
    g.setFont(font);
    g.setColor(color);
    g.drawString(string, horizontal, vertical);
}
}
```

5. Save the file as **JStringPanel.java**, and then compile it and fix any errors.

Creating a *JFrame* to Hold *JStringPanel* Objects

Next, you create a `JFrame` that holds four `JStringPanel` objects so you can observe how different string colors, fonts, and positions look.

1. Open a new file and write the first few lines of a class that creates a `JFrame` that can hold four `JStringPanel` objects.

```
import javax.swing.*;
import java.awt.*;
import java.awt.Color;
public class JDemoStringPanels extends JFrame
{
```

2. The frame will have a grid layout, so create a constant to hold the gap between the panels that will appear in the grid:

```
final int GAP = 15;
```

3. Instantiate a `JStringPanel` object. The constructor requires a string, a font, a color, and x- and y-axis positions:

```
JStringPanel p1 = new JStringPanel("abc",
    new Font("TimesRoman", Font.BOLD, 16), Color.BLACK, 20, 20);
```

(continues)

(continued)

4. Create three additional panels, each with different values:

```
JStringPanel p2 = new JStringPanel("def",
    new Font("Arial", Font.ITALIC, 26), Color.RED, 20, 60);
JStringPanel p3 = new JStringPanel("ghi",
    new Font("Boopee", Font.BOLD, 32), Color.BLUE, 20, 80);
JStringPanel p4 = new JStringPanel("jkl",
    new Font("Serif", Font.PLAIN, 40), Color.MAGENTA, 20, 120);
```

873

5. Start the `JFrame` constructor, which contains statements to set the close operation, set the layout to a 2-by-2 grid, and set the background color to black. The background of the frame will appear in the gaps between sections of the grid layout.

```
public JDemoStringPanels()
{
    setDefaultCloseOperation(JFrame.EXIT_ON_CLOSE);
    setLayout(new GridLayout(2, 2, GAP, GAP));
    getContentPane().setBackground(Color.BLACK);
```

6. Next, add the four `JStringPanel` objects to the frame and include a closing curly brace for the constructor.

```
    add(p1);
    add(p2);
    add(p3);
    add(p4);
}
```

7. Complete the class with a `main()` method that instantiates a `JDemoStringPanels` `JFrame` and sets its size and visibility. Include a closing curly brace for the class.

```
public static void main(String[] args)
{
    JDemoStringPanels frame = new JDemoStringPanels();
    frame.setSize(400, 400);
    frame.setVisible(true);
}
}
```

8. Save the file as **JDemoStringPanels.java**, compile it, and execute it. The program's output appears in Figure 16-13. You can see the four panels that are separated by the black gaps. You can see that different fonts, sizes, and positions are used for the string in each panel. Although the figure is shown in black and white in this book, notice that the strings on your screen are displayed in different colors. The fonts that appear in your program might be different from those shown in the figure, depending on your computer's installed fonts. (Later in this chapter, you will learn how to view a list of all available fonts on your computer.)

(continues)

(continued)

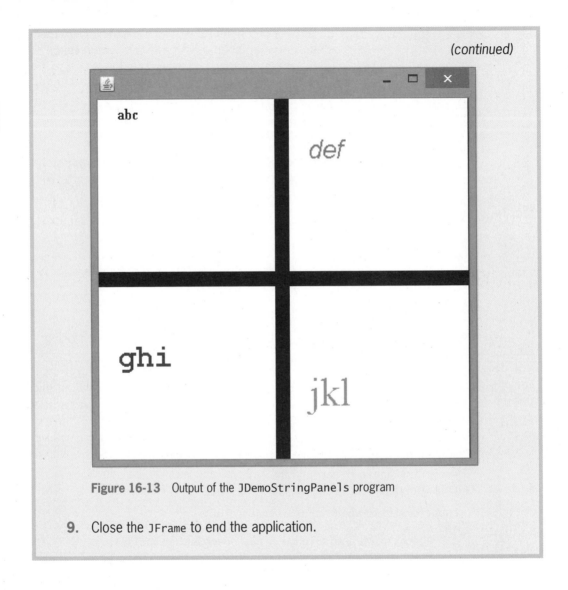

Figure 16-13   Output of the JDemoStringPanels program

9. Close the JFrame to end the application.

Drawing Lines and Shapes

Much like you can draw strings using a Graphics object, Java provides you with several methods for drawing a variety of lines and geometric shapes. Any line or shape is drawn in the color you set with the setColor() method. When you do not set a color, lines are drawn in black by default.

Drawing Lines

You can use the drawLine() method to draw a straight line between any two points on the screen. The drawLine() method takes four arguments: the x- and y-coordinates of the line's

starting point and the x- and y-coordinates of the line's ending point. For example, if you create a Graphics object named pen, the following statement draws a straight line that slants down and to the right from position 50, 50 to position 100, 200, as shown in Figure 16-14.

```
pen.drawLine(50, 50, 100, 200);
```

Because you can start at either end when you draw a line, an identical line would be created with the following code:

```
pen.drawLine(100, 200, 50, 50);
```

Figure 16-14 A line created with drawLine(50, 50, 100, 200);

 Your downloadable student files contain a JDemoLine.java file with a working program that draws the line shown in Figure 16-14.

Drawing Unfilled and Filled Rectangles

You could draw a rectangle by drawing four lines. Alternatively, you can use the drawRect() and fillRect() methods, respectively, to draw the outline of a rectangle or a solid, or filled, rectangle. Each of these methods requires four arguments. The first two arguments represent the x- and y-coordinates of the upper-left corner of the rectangle. The last two arguments represent the width and height of the rectangle. For example, the following statement uses a Graphics object named g to draw a short, wide rectangle that begins at position 20, 100 and is 200 pixels wide by 10 pixels tall:

```
g.drawRect(20, 100, 200, 10);
```

Drawing Clear Rectangles

The clearRect() method also requires four arguments and draws a rectangle. The difference between using the drawRect() and fillRect() methods and the clearRect() method is that the first two methods use the current drawing color, whereas the clearRect() method draws what appears to be an empty or "clear" rectangle. A rectangle created with the clearRect() method is not really clear; in other words, it is not transparent. When you create a rectangle, you do not see objects that might be hidden behind it. Instead, the clearRect() method clears anything drawn from view, showing the original content pane.

For example, the program shown in Figure 16-15 displays several rectangles. In the paintComponent() method, the background of the panel is set to blue, the Graphics object is set to red, and a filled red rectangle is painted. Then, the Graphics object is changed to yellow, and a larger filled rectangle is drawn further to the right and further down on the panel. Then a clear rectangle is drawn overlapping the other two rectangles.

```java
import javax.swing.*;
import java.awt.*;
import java.awt.Color;
public class JDemoRectangles extends JPanel
{
    @Override
    public void paintComponent(Graphics gr)
    {
        super.paintComponent(gr);
        setBackground(Color.BLUE);
        gr.setColor(Color.RED);
        gr.fillRect(40, 40, 120, 120);
        gr.setColor(Color.YELLOW);
        gr.fillRect(80, 80, 160, 160);
        gr.clearRect(50, 60, 50, 50);
    }
    public static void main(String[] args)
    {
        JFrame frame = new JFrame();
        frame.add(new JDemoRectangles());
        frame.setSize(300, 300);
        frame.setVisible(true);
    }
}
```

Figure 16-15   The JDemoRectangles class

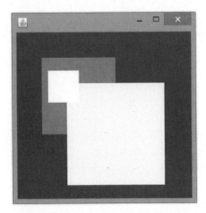

Figure 16-16   Output of the
JDemoRectangles program

Although you have seen several JPanel examples in which a separate JFrame class was created to hold one or more panels, a main() method that declares a JFrame is included in the JDemoRectangles class for convenience. This approach is frequently used to test a JPanel class because all the code for the panel and a frame that holds it is contained in a single file. In this example, the main() method instantiates a JFrame and adds a JDemoRectangles panel to it. The output appears in Figure 16-16. You cannot see the boundaries of the original rectangles in the "clear" area of the figure—you simply see that portions of the red and yellow filled rectangles have been removed from the drawing.

Drawing Rounded Rectangles

The drawRoundRect() method creates rectangles with rounded corners. The method requires six arguments. The first four arguments match the four arguments required to draw a rectangle: the x- and y-coordinates of the upper-left corner, the width, and the height. The two additional arguments represent the arc width and height associated with the rounded corners. (An **arc** is a portion of a circle's circumference.) If you assign zeros to the arc coordinates, the rectangle is not rounded; instead, the corners are square. At the other extreme, if you assign values to the arc coordinates that are at least the width and height of the rectangle, the rectangle is so rounded that it is a circle. The `paintComponent()` method in Figure 16-17 draws four rectangles with increasingly large corner arcs. The first rectangle is drawn at coordinates 20, 40, and the horizontal coordinate is increased by 100 for each subsequent rectangle. Each rectangle is the same width and height, but each set of arc values becomes larger, producing rectangles that are not rounded, slightly rounded, very rounded, and completely rounded in sequence. Figure 16-18 shows the program's output.

```java
import javax.swing.*;
import java.awt.*;
public class JDemoRoundedRectangles extends JPanel
{
    @Override
    public void paintComponent(Graphics gr)
    {
        super.paintComponent(gr);
        int x = 20;
        int y = 40;
        final int WIDTH = 80, HEIGHT = 80;
        final int ARC_INCREASE = 20;
        final int HORIZONTAL_GAP = 100;
        for(int size = x; size <= HEIGHT; size += ARC_INCREASE)
        {
            gr.drawRoundRect(x, y, WIDTH, HEIGHT, size, size);
            x += HORIZONTAL_GAP;
        }
    }
    public static void main(String[] args)
    {
        JFrame frame = new JFrame();
        frame.add(new JDemoRoundedRectangles());
        frame.setSize(430, 180);
        frame.setVisible(true);
    }
}
```

Figure 16-17 The JDemoRoundedRectangles class

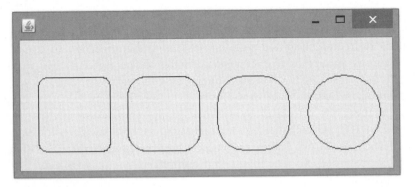

Figure 16-18   Output of the JDemoRoundedRectangles program

Java also contains a fillRoundRect() method that creates a filled rounded rectangle and a clearRoundRect() method that creates a clear rounded rectangle.

Drawing Shadowed Rectangles

The draw3DRect() method is a minor variation on the drawRect() method. You use the draw3DRect() method to draw a rectangle that appears to have dark "shadowing" on two of its edges and light "highlights" on two others. The draw3DRect() method requires a fifth argument in addition to the x- and y-coordinates, width, and height required by the drawRect() method. The fifth argument is a Boolean value, which is true if you want the raised rectangle effect (darker on the right and bottom) and false if you want the lowered rectangle effect (lighter on the right and bottom). You see a rectangle that has shadowing on the bottom as it is raised because objects are lit from the top when struck by sunlight in nature.

The fill3DRect() method creates filled three-dimensional (3D) rectangles; this method is used in the program in Figure 16-19.

```
import javax.swing.*;
import java.awt.*;
import java.awt.Color;
public class JDemo3DRectangles extends JPanel
{
    @Override
    public void paintComponent(Graphics gr)
    {
        super.paintComponent(gr);
        final int WIDTH = 60, HEIGHT = 80;
        gr.setColor(Color.PINK);
        gr.fill3DRect(20, 40, WIDTH, HEIGHT, true);
        gr.fill3DRect(100, 40, WIDTH, HEIGHT, false);
    }
}
```

Figure 16-19   The JDemo3DRectangles class *(continues)*

(continued)

```
    public static void main(String[] args)
    {
        JFrame frame = new JFrame();
        frame.add(new JDemo3DRectangles());
        frame.setSize(200, 180);
        frame.setVisible(true);
    }
}
```

Figure 16-19   The JDemo3DRectangles class

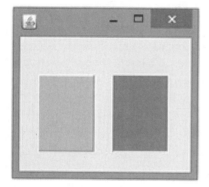

Figure 16-20   Output of the JDemo3DRectangles() program

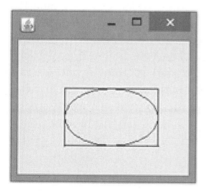

Figure 16-21   Demonstration of the drawOval() method

The program in Figure 16-19 creates two filled 3D rectangles in pink. (The 3D methods work best with lighter drawing colors.) You can see that the shadowing effect on the output in Figure 16-20 is very subtle; the shadowing is only one pixel wide.

Drawing Ovals

You can draw an oval using the drawRoundRect() or fillRoundRect() method, but it is usually easier to use the drawOval() and fillOval() methods. Both methods draw ovals using the same four arguments that rectangles use. When you supply drawOval() or fillOval() with x- and y-coordinates for the upper-left corner and width and height measurements, you can picture an imaginary rectangle that uses the four arguments. The oval is then placed within the rectangle so the oval touches the center of each of the rectangle's sides. For example, suppose that you create a Graphics object named tool and draw a rectangle with the following statement:

```
tool.drawRect(50, 50, 100, 60);
```

Suppose that then you create an oval with the same coordinates as follows:

```
tool.drawOval(50, 50, 100, 60);
```

The output appears as shown in Figure 16-21, with the oval edges just skimming the rectangle's sides.

 Your downloadable student files contain a JDemoOval.java file that produces the frame in Figure 16-21.

If you draw a rectangle with identical height and width, you draw a square. If you draw an oval with identical height and width, you draw a circle.

Drawing Arcs

In Java, you can draw an arc using the Graphics drawArc() method. To use the drawArc() method, you provide six arguments:

- The x- and y-coordinates of the upper-left corner of an imaginary rectangle that represents the bounds of the imaginary circle that contains the arc

- The width and height of the imaginary rectangle that represents the bounds of the imaginary circle that contains the arc

- The beginning arc position and the arc angle

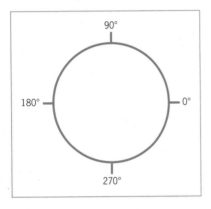

Figure 16-22   Arc positions

Arc positions and angles are measured in degrees; there are 360 degrees in a circle. The 0° position for any arc is the three o'clock position, as shown in Figure 16-22. The other 359 degree positions increase as you move counterclockwise around an imaginary circle, so 90° is at the top of the circle in the 12 o'clock position, 180° is opposite the starting position at nine o'clock, and 270° is at the bottom of the circle in the six o'clock position.

The arc angle is the number of degrees over which you want to draw the arc, traveling counterclockwise from the starting position. For example, you can draw a half circle by indicating an arc angle of 180° or a quarter circle by indicating an arc angle of 90°. If you want to travel clockwise from the starting position, you express the degrees as a negative number. Just as when you draw a line, you can take one of two approaches when drawing an arc: either start at point A and travel to point B, or start at point B and travel to point A. For example, if you create an arc object using a Graphics object named g that looks like the top half of a circle, the following statements produce identical results:

```
g.drawArc(x, y, w, h, 0, 180);
g.drawArc(x, y, w, h, 180, -180);
```

The first statement starts an arc at the three o'clock position and travels 180 degrees counterclockwise to the nine o'clock position. The second statement starts at nine o'clock and travels clockwise to three o'clock.

The fillArc() method creates a solid arc. The arc is drawn, and two straight lines are drawn from the arc endpoints to the center of the imaginary circle whose perimeter the arc occupies. For example, assuming you have declared a Graphics object named g, the following two statements together produce the output shown in Figure 16-23:

```
g.fillArc(20, 50, 100, 100, 20, 320);
g.fillArc(60, 50, 100, 100, 340, 40);
```

881

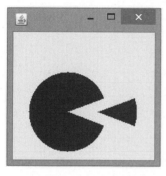

Each of the two arcs is in a circle that has a size of 100 by 100. The first arc almost completes a full circle, starting at position 20 (near two o'clock) and ending 320 degrees around the circle (at position 340, near four o'clock). The second filled arc more closely resembles a pie slice, starting at position 340 and extending 40 degrees to end at position 20.

 Your downloadable student files contain a program named JDemoFilledArcs.java that produces Figure 16-23.

Figure 16-23   Two filled arcs

Creating Polygons

A **polygon** is a geometric figure with straight sides. A rectangle is a type of polygon with four sides and all right angles. It's easiest to draw a rectangle using the drawRect() method, but if you want to create a shape that is more complex, you have the following options:

- You can use a sequence of calls to the drawLine() method.

- You can use the drawPolygon() method.

The drawPolygon() method requires three arguments: two integer arrays and a single integer. The first integer array holds a series of x-coordinate positions, and the second array holds a series of corresponding y-coordinate positions. These positions represent points that are connected to form the polygon. The third integer argument is the number of pairs of points you want to connect. If you don't want to connect all the points represented by the array values, you can assign the third argument a value that is smaller than the number of elements in each array. An error occurs if the third argument has a greater value than the available number of coordinate pairs.

For example, examine the code shown in Figure 16-24, which is a JPanel that draws a star-shaped polygon.

882

```
import javax.swing.*;
import java.awt.*;
public class JStar extends JPanel
{
    int xPoints[] = {42, 52, 72, 52, 60, 40, 15, 28, 9, 32, 42};
    int yPoints[] = {38, 62, 68, 80, 105, 85, 102, 75, 58, 60, 38};
    @Override
    public void paintComponent(Graphics g)
    {
        super.paintComponent(g);
        g.drawPolygon(xPoints, yPoints, xPoints.length);
    }
    public static void main(String[] args)
    {
        JFrame frame = new JFrame();
        frame.add(new JStar());
        frame.setSize(140, 160);
        frame.setVisible(true);
    }
}
```

Figure 16-24   The JStar class

Figure 16-25   Output of the JStar program

In the JStar program, two parallel arrays are assigned x- and y-coordinates. It is almost impossible to create a program like this without sketching the desired shape on a piece of graph paper to discover appropriate coordinate values. The drawPolygon() method uses the two arrays and the length of one array for the number of points. The program's output appears in Figure 16-25.

You can use the fillPolygon() method to draw a solid shape. The major difference between the drawPolygon() and fillPolygon() methods is that if the beginning and ending points used with the fillPolygon() method are not identical, the two endpoints are connected by a straight line before the polygon is filled with color.

Rather than providing the fillPolygon() method with three arguments, you can also create a Polygon object and pass the constructed object as a single argument to the fillPolygon() method. The Polygon constructor requires an array of x-coordinates, an array of y-coordinates, and a size. For example, you can create a filled polygon using the following statements:

```
Polygon someShape = new Polygon(xPoints, yPoints, xPoints.length);
gr.fillPolygon(someShape);
```

The `Polygon` class also has a default constructor, so you can instantiate an empty `Polygon` object (with no points) using the following statement:

```
Polygon someFutureShape = new Polygon();
```

Whether you use the default constructor or not, you can add points to a polygon after construction. For example, you might want to add points that are determined by user input or mathematical calculations. You use the `addPoint()` method in statements such as the following to add points to the polygon after construction:

```
someFutureShape.addPoint(100, 100);
someFutureShape.addPoint(150, 200);
someFutureShape.addPoint(50, 250);
```

Points can be added to a polygon indefinitely.

Copying an Area

After you create a graphics image, you might want to create copies of the image. For example, you might want a company logo to appear several times in an application. Of course, you can redraw the picture, but you can also use the `copyArea()` method to copy any rectangular area to a new location. The `copyArea()` method requires six parameters:

- The x- and y-coordinates of the upper-left corner of the area to be copied
- The width and height of the area to be copied
- The horizontal and vertical displacement of the destination of the copy

For example, the following line of code causes a `Graphics` object named `gr` to copy an area 20 pixels wide by 30 pixels tall from the upper-left corner of your `JFrame` (coordinates 0, 0) to an area that begins 100 pixels to the right and 50 pixels down:

```
gr.copyArea(0, 0, 20, 30, 100, 50);
```

Using the `paint()` Method with `JFrames`

Java's creators recommend that you create graphics on a `JPanel` (or other `JComponent`), but you might see programs in which graphics are drawn on a `JFrame`. When you place graphics on a `JFrame`, you should override the `paint()` method rather than the `paintComponent()` method.

For example, Figure 16-26 shows a `JFrameDrawingDemo` class that extends `JFrame`. Its `paint()` method calls the parent class `paint()` method, and then draws three shapes on the `JFrame` surface. Figure 16-27 shows the output.

```
import java.awt.*;
import javax.swing.*;
public class JFrameDrawingDemo extends JFrame
{
    final int SIZE = 40;
    @Override
    public void paint(Graphics g)
    {
        super.paint(g);
        g.drawRect(50, 50, SIZE, SIZE);
        g.drawOval(80, 80, SIZE, SIZE);
        g.drawRect(110, 110, SIZE, SIZE);
    }
    public static void main(String[] args)
    {
        JFrameDrawingDemo frame = new JFrameDrawingDemo();
        frame.setDefaultCloseOperation(JFrame.EXIT_ON_CLOSE);
        frame.setSize(170, 210);
        frame.setVisible(true);
    }
}
```

Figure 16-26   The JFrameDrawingDemo class

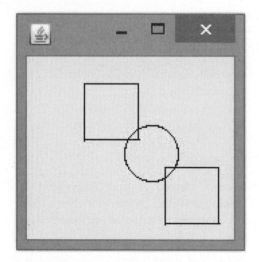

Figure 16-27   Output of the JFrameDrawingDemo class

 Watch the video *Drawing Lines and Shapes.*

TWO TRUTHS & A LIE

Drawing Lines and Shapes

1. You can use the drawLine() method to draw a straight line between any two points on the screen.

2. You can use methods named drawRect(), fillRect(), clearRect(), drawOval(), and fillOval() to create a variety of shapes.

3. When you draw an arc, the zero-degree position is at 12 o'clock on an imaginary clock, and the 90-degree position is at three o'clock.

The false statement is #3. When you draw an arc, the zero-degree position is at three o'clock, and the degree values increase as you move counterclockwise in a 360-degree circle, so the 90-degree position is at 12 o'clock.

 You Do It

Creating a JPanel with a JButton and Graphics

In this section, you create a panel that alternates drawing a red circle and a blue square in a series of positions from the top left to the bottom right in response to each user button click.

1. Start a new program named JShapePanel as follows:

```
import javax.swing.*;
import java.awt.*;
import java.awt.event.*;
import java.awt.Color;
public class JShapePanel extends JPanel implements ActionListener
{
```

2. Instantiate a JButton, a Color object that holds the current drawing color, and three integers to hold the horizontal and vertical position of each shape that will be drawn and a count of the number of shapes drawn:

```
JButton button = new JButton("Press me");
Color color = Color.RED;
String shape = "circle";
int x = 0;
int y = 0;
int count = 0;
```

(continues)

(continued)

3. Add three constants. The SIZE constant holds the width and height of each circle and square that will be drawn. The INCREASE constant holds the value by which the horizontal and vertical position variables will increase each time the user clicks the panel's button. The TIMES constant holds the number of times the circles and squares will be drawn on the panel from the top left to the bottom right before starting over again from the top left.

```
final int SIZE = 40;
final int INCREASE = 15;
final int TIMES = 14;
```

4. Add a constructor to the class. It sets the background color, adds the button to the panel, and activates the button.

```
public JShapePanel()
{
    setBackground(Color.WHITE);
    add(button);
    button.addActionListener(this);
}
```

5. Start the actionPerformed() method that will respond to button clicks. Each time the user clicks the button, count is incremented. After 14 clicks, shapes will have been drawn from the top left to the bottom right of the panel, so the method sets the horizontal and vertical position for the next drawing back to the top-left corner of the panel and resets the count of clicks to 0.

```
public void actionPerformed(ActionEvent e)
{
    ++count;
    if(count == TIMES)
    {
        x = 0;
        y = 0;
        count = 0;
    }
```

6. If the current shape is a circle, change it to a blue square for the next rendering. Otherwise, change it to a red circle.

```
if(shape.equals("circle"))
{
    color = Color.BLUE;
    shape = "rect";
}
```

(continues)

(continued)

```
else
{
    shape = "circle";
    color = Color.RED;
}
```

7. Change the position where the next shape will be drawn—a little further right and a little further down. Then, to render the new shape at its new position, call `repaint()`, which calls `paintComponent()`. Add a closing curly brace for the `actionPerformed()` method.

```
    x += INCREASE;
    y += INCREASE;
    repaint();
}
```

8. The `paintComponent()` method calls the parent class's version of the method, then sets the painting color to the current color. If the current shape is a circle, the method uses `fillOval()` to draw a circle at the current position. Otherwise, it uses `fillRect()` to draw a square at the current position.

```
@Override
public void paintComponent(Graphics g)
{
    super.paintComponent(g);
    g.setColor(color);
    if(shape.equals("circle"))
        g.fillOval(x, y, SIZE, SIZE);
    else
        g.fillRect(x, y, SIZE, SIZE);
}
```

9. The `main()` method for the class instantiates a frame to hold the panel and sets the close operation, size, and visibility. The class ends with a closing curly brace.

```
public static void main(String[] args)
{
    JFrame frame = new JFrame();
    frame.setDefaultCloseOperation(JFrame.EXIT_ON_CLOSE);
    frame.add(new JShapePanel());
    frame.setSize(300, 300);
    frame.setVisible(true);
}
}
```

10. Save the file as **JShapePanel.java**, and compile and execute it. The left side of Figure 16-28 shows the application when it starts. The first shape displayed is a red circle at position 15, 15. The image on the right shows the frame after the

(continues)

(continued)

user has clicked the button one time. The shape becomes a blue square
at position 30, 30, slightly below and to the right of the red circle's original
position.

Figure 16-28   Execution of the `JShapePanel` program before and after the `JButton` is clicked

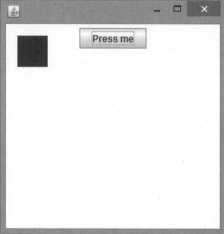

11. Continue to click the button and observe
    alternating circles and squares in new
    positions on the panel. After the thirteenth
    click, the frame looks like Figure 16-29.
    With the fourteenth click, the shape
    appears at the top of the panel again
    and resumes its journey down and to
    the right.

12. Close the application.

Figure 16-29   Execution of the
`JShapePanel` program after the
button is clicked 13 times

Observing the Effect of the
super.paintComponent() Call

Next, you will observe the effect of omitting
the call to the superclass `paintComponent()` method.

1. Locate the call to `super.paintComponent()` in the `paintComponent()` method
   in the `JShapePanel` class. Comment out the statement by placing two forward
   slashes at the start of its line.

(continues)

(continued)

2. Save the program, and then compile and execute it. With this version of the class, the panel is not redrawn each time you click the button, so the shapes "pile up" on top of each other. Additionally, an unwanted second version of the button appears at the top of the panel. Figure 16-30 shows the output after the user has clicked the button 10 times.

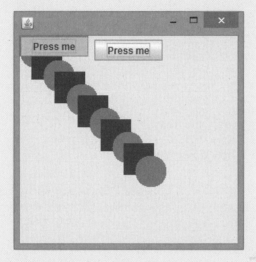

Figure 16-30 Execution of the `JShapePanel` class after the call to the parent class `paintComponent()` method is removed

3. Restore the `super.paintComponent()` call to active status by removing the comment slashes, and then compile and execute the program. Make sure it works correctly again.

Copying an Area

Next, you learn how to copy an area containing a shape that you want to display several times on a `JPanel`. By copying, you do not have to re-create the shape each time.

1. Open a new file, and then enter the beginning statements for a `JPanel` that uses the `copyArea()` method:

```
import javax.swing.*;
import java.awt.*;
public class JCopyShape extends JPanel
{
```

(continues)

(continued)

2. Add the following statements, which create a polygon in the shape of a star:

```
int xPoints[] = {42, 52, 72, 52,
    60, 40, 15, 28, 9, 32, 42};
int yPoints[] = {38, 62, 68, 80,
    105, 85, 102, 75, 58, 60, 38};
Polygon aStar = new Polygon(xPoints, yPoints, xPoints.length);
```

3. Add the following `paintComponent()` method, which draws a star and then draws four additional identical stars in different positions:

```
@Override
public void paintComponent(Graphics g)
{
    super.paintComponent(g);
    g.drawPolygon(aStar);
    g.copyArea(0, 0, 75, 105, 80, 40);
    g.copyArea(0, 0, 75, 105, 40, 150);
    g.copyArea(0, 0, 75, 105, 170, 0);
    g.copyArea(0, 0, 75, 105, 150, 110);
}
```

4. Add a `main()` method that instantiates a `JFrame` that holds a `JCopyShape` panel and sets a close operation, size, and visibility. Add a closing brace to end the class:

```
public static void main(String[] args)
{
    JFrame frame = new JFrame();
    frame.setDefaultCloseOperation(JFrame.EXIT_ON_CLOSE);
    frame.add(new JCopyShape());
    frame.setSize(300, 300);
    frame.setVisible(true);
}
}
```

5. Save the file as **JCopyShape.java**, and then compile the program. When you run the program, the output looks like Figure 16-31. Although the program lists point coordinates for only one star, five identical stars are drawn.

6. Close the frame to end the application.

Figure 16-31   Output of the JCopyShape program

Learning More About Fonts

As you add more components in your GUI applications, positioning becomes increasingly important. In particular, when you draw strings using different fonts, it is difficult to place them correctly so they don't overlap, making them difficult or impossible to read. In addition, the number of available fonts varies greatly across operating systems, so even when you define a font using a string argument such as "Arial" or "Courier", you have no guarantee that the font will be available on every computer that runs your application. If a user's computer does not have the requested font installed, Java chooses a default replacement font, so you can never be completely certain how your output will look. Fortunately, Java provides many useful methods for obtaining information about the fonts you use.

You can discover which fonts are available on your system by using the `getAvailableFontFamilyNames()` method, which is part of the `GraphicsEnvironment` class defined in the `java.awt` package. The `GraphicsEnvironment` class describes the collection of `Font` objects and `GraphicsDevice` objects available to a Java application on a particular platform. The `getAvailableFontFamilyNames()` method returns an array of `String` objects that are the names of available fonts. For example, the following statements declare a `GraphicsEnvironment` object named `ge`, and then use the object with the method to store the font names in a string array:

```
GraphicsEnvironment ge =
    GraphicsEnvironment.getLocalGraphicsEnvironment();
String[] fontNames = ge.getAvailableFontFamilyNames();
```

Notice in the preceding example that you can't instantiate the `GraphicsEnvironment` object directly. Instead, you must get a reference object to the current computer environment by calling the static `getLocalGraphicsEnvironment()` method. (This technique is similar to the one you used when calling `getRuntime()` in Chapter 12 and `getContentPane()` in Chapter 15.) Figure 16-32 shows a class that extends `JPanel` and lists all the available font names on the computer on which the program is executed. A `GraphicsEnvironment` object is created and the `getAvailableFontFamilyNames()` method is used to retrieve the array of font names. Then, in the `paintComponent()` method, the names are displayed using `drawString()` in a `for` loop. After each string is drawn, the vertical position is increased by 10 so the next string will be a little lower on the panel surface. After a column is full, the horizontal position is increased so the next output appears in a new column. The panel is displayed in a `JFrame`. Typical output is shown in Figure 16-33.

```java
import javax.swing.*;
import java.awt.*;
import java.awt.Color;
public class JFontList extends JPanel
{
    int i, x, y;
    final int VERTICAL_SPACE = 10;
    final int HORIZONTAL_SPACE = 180;
    final int NUM_IN_COLUMN = 63;
    GraphicsEnvironment ge =
        GraphicsEnvironment.getLocalGraphicsEnvironment();
    String[] fontNames = ge.getAvailableFontFamilyNames();
    public JFontList()
    {
        setBackground(Color.WHITE);
    }
    @Override
    public void paintComponent(Graphics gr)
    {
        super.paintComponent(gr);
        x = 10;
        y = 20;
        gr.setFont(new Font("Arial", Font.PLAIN, 10));
        for(i = 0; i < fontNames.length; ++i)
        {
            gr.drawString(fontNames[i], x, y);
            y += VERTICAL_SPACE;
            if(y > VERTICAL_SPACE * NUM_IN_COLUMN)
            {
                x += HORIZONTAL_SPACE;
                y = 20;
            }
        }
    }
    public static void main(String[] args)
    {
        JFrame frame = new JFrame();
        frame.add(new JFontList());
        frame.setSize(940, 680);
        frame.setVisible(true);
    }
}
```

Figure 16-32   The JFontList class

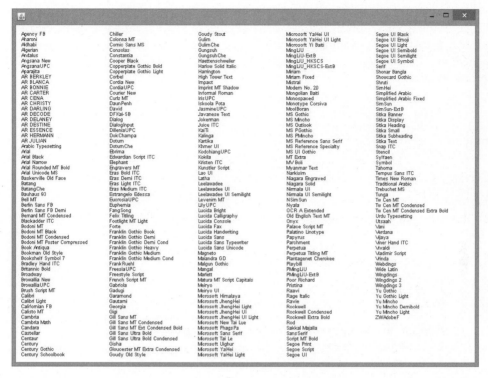

Figure 16-33 Typical output of the `JFontList` program

Discovering Screen Statistics

Frequently, before you can determine the best Font size to use, it is helpful to know more about the screen on which the Font will be displayed. For example, you can discover the resolution and screen size on your system by using programs that are part of the Toolkit class.

The `getDefaultToolkit()` method returns a Toolkit object that contains information about the system in use. The `getScreenResolution()` method returns the number of pixels as an integer. You can create a Toolkit object and get the screen resolution by using the following code:

```
Toolkit tk = Toolkit.getDefaultToolkit();
int resolution = tk.getScreenResolution();
```

The Dimension class is useful for representing the width and height of a user interface component, such as a JFrame or a JButton. The Dimension class has three constructors:

- The `Dimension()` method creates an instance of Dimension with a width of 0 and a height of 0.

- `Dimension(Dimension d)` creates an instance of Dimension whose width and height equal those in the Dimension argument.

- `Dimension(int width, int height)` constructs a Dimension and initializes it to the specified width and height.

The getScreenSize() method returns an object of type Dimension, which specifies the width and height of the screen in pixels. Knowing the number of pixels for the width and height of your display is useful if you want to determine a component's maximum size or place a component at a specific position. The following code stores the width and height of a screen in separate variables:

```
Toolkit tk = Toolkit.getDefaultToolkit();
Dimension screen = tk.getScreenSize();
int width = screen.width;
int height = screen.height;
```

Discovering Font Statistics

Typesetters and desktop publishers measure the height of every font in three parts: ascent, descent, and leading. **Ascent** is the height of an uppercase character from a baseline to the top of the character. **Descent** measures the part of characters that "hang below" the baseline, such as the tails on the lowercase letters *g* and *j*. **Leading** (pronounced *ledding*) is the amount of space between the bottom of the descent of one line and the top of the characters in the successive line of type. The **height of a font** is the sum of the leading, ascent, and descent. Figure 16-34 illustrates each of these measurements.

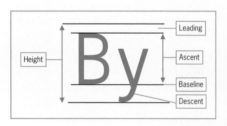

Figure 16-34   Parts of a font's height

You can discover a font's statistics by using the Graphics class getFontMetrics() method to return a FontMetrics object and then using one of the following FontMetrics class methods with the object to return the information you want:

- public int getLeading()

- public int getAscent()

- public int getDescent()

- public int getHeight()

Another method, getLineMetrics(), is more complicated to use, but it returns similar font statistics. For more details, see the Java Web site.

Each of these methods returns an integer value representing the font size in points of the requested portion of the Font object. (One point measures 1/72 of an inch.) For example, if you define a Font object named myFont and a Graphics object named paintBrush, you can set the current font for the Graphics object by using the following statements:

```
paintBrush.setFont(myFont);
int heightOfFont = paintBrush.getFontMetrics().getHeight();
```

Then the heightOfFont variable holds the total height of myFont characters.

When you define a Font object, you use point size. However, when you use the FontMetrics get methods, the sizes are returned in pixels.

A practical use for discovering the height of a font is to space Strings correctly as you display them. For example, you could draw a series of Strings in a loop with a statement such as the following:

```
g.drawString("Some string", x, y += INCREASE);
```

In this statement, g is a Graphics object and INCREASE is a numeric constant. Instead, you can make the actual increase in the vertical position dependent on the font. If you code the following, you are assured that each String has enough room, regardless of which font is currently in use by the Graphics object:

```
pen.drawString("Some string",
    x, y += pen.getFontMetrics().getHeight());
```

When you create a String, you know how many characters are in it. However, you cannot be certain which font Java will use or substitute, and because fonts have different measurements, it is difficult to know the exact width of the String that appears in a JFrame. Fortunately, the FontMetrics class contains a stringWidth() method that returns the integer width of a String argument. For example, if you create a String named myString, you can retrieve the width of myString with the following code:

```
int width = g.getFontMetrics().stringWidth(myString);
```

Watch the video *Font Methods*.

TWO TRUTHS & A LIE

Learning More About Fonts

1. One reason for Java's popularity is that its fonts are guaranteed to look the same on all computers.

2. You can discover the resolution and screen size on your system by using the getScreenResolution() and getScreenSize() methods, which are part of the Toolkit class.

3. Ascent is the height of an uppercase character from a baseline to the top of the character, and descent measures the part of characters that "hang below" the baseline, such as the tail on the lowercase letter y.

The false statement is #1. If a user's computer does not have a font you request, Java chooses a default replacement font, so you can never be completely certain how your output will look.

896

You Do It

Using *FontMetrics* Methods to Compare Fonts

Next, you write a program to demonstrate FontMetrics methods. You will create three Font objects and display their metrics.

1. Open a new file, and then enter the first few lines of the JDemoFontMetrics program. Include any movie quote you choose.

```
import javax.swing.*;
import java.awt.*;
public class JDemoFontMetrics extends JPanel
{
    String movieQuote =
    new String("Go ahead, make my day");
```

2. Type the following code to create a few fonts to use for demonstration purposes:

```
Font courierItalic = new Font("Courier New", Font.ITALIC, 16),
    timesPlain = new Font("Times New Roman", Font.PLAIN, 16),
    scriptBold = new Font("Freestyle Script", Font.BOLD, 16);
```

3. Add the following code to define four integer variables that hold the four font measurements and two integer variables to hold the horizontal and vertical positions for output:

```
int ascent, descent, height, leading;
int x, y;
```

4. Create a paintComponent() method that calls the parent version of the method, gives x and y starting values, sets the font to each of the declared fonts, and passes the Graphics object to a method that displays the font statistics.

```
@Override
public void paintComponent(Graphics g)
{
    super.paintComponent(g);
    x = 20;
    y = 30;
    g.setFont(courierItalic);
    displayMetrics(g);
    g.setFont(timesPlain);
    displayMetrics(g);
    g.setFont(scriptBold);
    displayMetrics(g);
}
```

(continues)

(continued)

5. Start a `displayMetrics()` method with a `Graphics` parameter passed from the `paintComponent()` method. Obtain values for the four font statistics fields.

```
public void displayMetrics(Graphics g)
{
    leading = g.getFontMetrics().getLeading();
    ascent = g.getFontMetrics().getAscent();
    descent = g.getFontMetrics().getDescent();
    height = g.getFontMetrics().getHeight();
```

6. Finish the `displayMetrics()` method by displaying the movie quote and statistics about the current font. Each string is drawn at the appropriate increased vertical distance based on the font's height. After the statistics are displayed, increase the vertical coordinate again so that double spacing will appear between each font's set of five statements. Include a closing curly brace for the method.

```
    g.drawString(movieQuote, x, y += height);
    g.drawString("Leading is " + leading,
        x, y += height);
    g.drawString("Ascent is " + ascent,
        x, y += height);
    g.drawString("Descent is " + descent,
        x, y += height);
    g.drawString("Height is " + height,
        x, y += height);
    y += height * 2;
}
```

7. To demonstrate the `JPanel`'s operation, write a `main()` method that declares a `JFrame` and adds the `JPanel` to it. After you set the close operation, size, and visibility of the `JFrame`, end the method and the class.

```
public static void main(String[] args)
{
    JFrame frame = new JFrame();
    frame.add(new JDemoFontMetrics());
    frame.setDefaultCloseOperation(JFrame.EXIT_ON_CLOSE);
    frame.setSize(300, 460);
    frame.setVisible(true);
    }
}
```

8. Save the file as **JDemoFontMetrics.java**, and then compile it. When you run the program, the output should look like Figure 16-35. Notice that even though each `Font` object was constructed with a size of 16, the individual statistics vary.

(continues)

(continued)

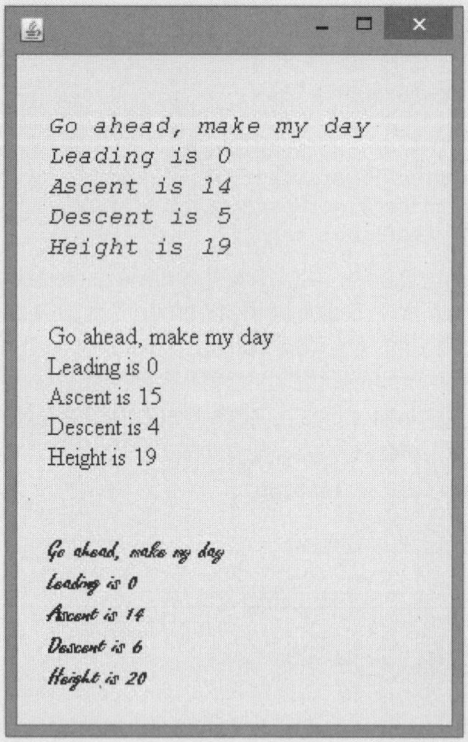

898

Figure 16-35   Output of the `JDemoFontMetrics` program

9. Close the frame to end the program. Modify the program to use other fonts and observe the results.

Drawing with Java 2D Graphics

Drawing operations earlier in this chapter were called using a `Graphics` object, but you can also call drawing operations using an object of the `Graphics2D` class. The advantage of using Java 2D objects is the higher-quality two-dimensional (2D) graphics, images, and text they provide.

Features of some of the 2D classes include:

● Fill patterns, such as gradients

● Strokes that define the width and style of a drawing stroke

● Anti-aliasing, a graphics technique for producing smoother screen graphics

Graphics2D is found in the java.awt package. A Graphics2D object is produced by casting, or converting and promoting, a Graphics object. For example, in a paintComponent() method that automatically receives a Graphics object, you can cast the object to a Graphics2D object using the following code:

```
public void paintComponent(Graphics pen)
{
    Graphics2D newPen = (Graphics2D)pen;
```

The process of drawing with Java 2D objects includes:

* Specifying the rendering attributes

* Setting a drawing stroke

* Creating objects to draw

Specifying the Rendering Attributes

The first step in drawing a 2D object is to specify how a drawn object is rendered. Drawings that are not 2D can only use the attribute Color, but with 2D you can designate other attributes, such as line width and fill patterns. You specify 2D colors by using the setColor() method, which works like the Graphics method of the same name. Using a Graphics2D object named g, you can set the color to black using the following code:

```
g.setColor(Color.BLACK);
```

Fill patterns control how a drawing object is filled in. In addition to using a solid color, 2D fill patterns can be a gradient fill, a texture, or even a pattern that you devise. A fill pattern is created by using the setPaint() method of Graphics2D with a fill pattern object as the only argument. Classes from which you can construct a fill pattern include Color, TexturePaint, and GradientPaint.

A **gradient fill** is a gradual shift from one color at one coordinate point to a different color at a second coordinate point. If the color shift occurs once between the points—for example, slowly changing from yellow to red—you are using an **acyclic gradient**, one that does not cycle between the colors. If the shift occurs repeatedly, such as from yellow to red and back to yellow again, you are using a **cyclic gradient**, one that cycles between the colors.

Figure 16-36 shows an application that demonstrates acyclic and cyclic gradient fills. The program operates as follows:

* The first shaded setPaint() method call sets a gradient that begins at coordinates 20, 40 in LIGHT_GRAY and ends at coordinates 180, 100 in DARK_GRAY. The last argument to the GradientPaint() constructor is false, indicating an acyclic gradient. After the Graphics2D object's paint is applied, a filled rectangle is drawn over the same area. These statements produce the rectangle on the left in Figure 16-37, which gradually shifts from light gray to dark gray, moving down and to the right.

- The second shaded setPaint() statement in Figure 16-36 establishes a new gradient beginning farther to the right. In this statement, the final argument to GradientPaint() is true, creating a cyclic gradient. As you can see on the right side in Figure 16-37, this rectangle's shading changes gradually across its surface.

Later in this chapter, you will learn about the Rectangle2D.Double class used to create the rectangles in this application.

```java
import javax.swing.*;
import java.awt.*;
import java.awt.geom.*;
import java.awt.Color;
public class JGradient extends JPanel
{
    int x, y, x2, y2;
    public void paintComponent(Graphics gr)
    {
        super.paintComponent(gr);
        x = 20;
        y = 40;
        x2 = 180;
        y2 = 100;
        Graphics2D gr2D = (Graphics2D)gr;
        gr2D.setPaint(new GradientPaint(x, y, Color.LIGHT_GRAY,
            x2, y2, Color.DARK_GRAY, false));
        gr2D.fill(new Rectangle2D.Double(x, y, x2, y2));
        x = 210;
        gr2D.setPaint(new GradientPaint(x, y, Color.LIGHT_GRAY,
            x2, y2, Color.DARK_GRAY, true));
        gr2D.fill(new Rectangle2D.Double(x, y, x2, y2));
    }
    public static void main(String[] args)
    {
        JFrame frame = new JFrame();
        frame.add(new JGradient());
        frame.setSize(440, 200);
        frame.setVisible(true);
    }
}
```

Figure 16-36   The JGradient class

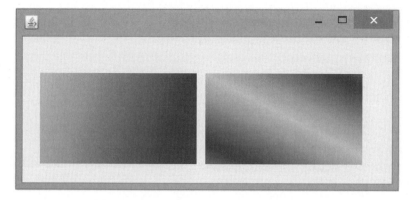

Figure 16-37 Output of the JGradient application

Setting a Drawing Stroke

All lines in non-2D graphics operations are drawn to be solid with square ends and to have a line width of one pixel. With 2D methods, the drawing line is a **stroke**, which represents a single movement as if you were using a drawing tool, such as a pen or a pencil. In Java 2D, you can change a stroke's width using the setStroke() method. Stroke is actually an interface; the class that defines line types and implements the Stroke interface is named BasicStroke. A BasicStroke constructor takes three arguments:

- A float value representing the line width
- An int value that determines the type of cap decoration at the end of a line
- An int value that determines the style of juncture between two line segments

BasicStroke class variables determine the endcap and juncture style arguments. **Endcap styles** apply to the ends of lines that do not join with other lines, and include CAP_BUTT, CAP_ROUND, and CAP_SQUARE. **Juncture styles**, for lines that join, include JOIN_MITER, JOIN_ROUND, and JOIN_BEVEL.

The following statements create a BasicStroke object and make it the current stroke:

```
BasicStroke aLine = new BasicStroke(1.0f,
    BasicStroke.CAP_ROUND, BasicStroke.JOIN_ROUND);
```

Figure 16-38 shows a program that draws a rectangle using a very wide stroke.

902

```java
import javax.swing.*;
import java.awt.*;
import java.awt.geom.*;
public class JStroke extends JPanel
{
    public void paintComponent(Graphics gr)
    {
        super.paintComponent(gr);
        Graphics2D gr2D = (Graphics2D)gr;
        BasicStroke aStroke = new BasicStroke(15.0f,
            BasicStroke.CAP_ROUND, BasicStroke.JOIN_ROUND);
        gr2D.setStroke(aStroke);
        gr2D.draw(new Rectangle2D.Double(20, 20, 100, 100));
    }
    public static void main(String[] args)
    {
        JFrame frame = new JFrame();
        frame.add(new JStroke());
        frame.setSize(160, 180);
        frame.setVisible(true);
    }
}
```

Figure 16-38 The JStroke class

The shaded statement in the JStroke class sets the BasicStroke width to 15 pixels using round endcap and juncture parameters. Notice that the line width value is followed by an f, making the value a float instead of a double. Figure 16-39 shows the rectangle.

Creating Objects to Draw

After you have created a Graphics2D object and specified the rendering attributes, you can create different objects to draw. Objects that are drawn in Java 2D are first created by defining them as geometric shapes using the java.awt.geom package classes. You can define the shapes of lines, rectangles, ovals, and arcs; after you define a shape, you can use it as an argument to the draw() or fill() method. The Graphics2D class does not have different methods for each shape you can draw.

Figure 16-39 Output of the JStroke program

Lines

Lines are created using the Line2D.Float class or the Line2D.Double class. Each of these classes has a constructor that takes four arguments, which are the x- and y-coordinates of the line endpoints. For example, to create a line from the endpoint 60, 5 to the endpoint 13, 28, you could write the following:

```java
Line2D.Float line = new Line2D.Float(60F, 5F, 13F, 28F);
```

You can also create lines based on points. You can use the `Point2D.Float` or `Point2D.Double` class to create points that have both x- and y-coordinates. For example, you could create two `Point2D.Float` points using the following code:

```
Point2D.Float pos1 = new Point2D.Float(60F, 5F);
Point2D.Float pos2 = new Point2D.Float(13F, 28F);
```

Then the code to create a line might be:

```
Line2D.Float line = new Line2D.Float(pos1, pos2);
```

Rectangles

You can create rectangles by using a `Rectangle2D.Float` or a `Rectangle2D.Double` class. As with the `Line` and `Point` classes, the two rectangle classes are distinguished by the type of argument used to call their constructors: `float` or `double`. Both `Rectangle2D.Float` and `Rectangle2D.Double` can be created using four arguments representing the x-coordinate, y-coordinate, width, and height. For example, the following code creates a `Rectangle2D.Float` object named `rect` at 10, 10 with a width of 50 and height of 40:

```
Rectangle2D.Float rect = new Rectangle2D.Float(10F, 10F, 50F, 40F);
```

In this example, the *F* following each argument is optional because the integers would be promoted to `floats` automatically.

Ovals

You can create `Oval` objects with the `Ellipse2D.Float` or `Ellipse2D.Double` class. The `Ellipse2D.Float` constructor requires four arguments representing the x-coordinate, y-coordinate, width, and height. The following code creates an `Ellipse2D.Float` object named `ell` at 10, 73 with a width of 40 and height of 20:

```
Ellipse2D.Float ell = new Ellipse2D.Float(10F, 73F, 40F, 20F);
```

Arcs

You can create arcs with the `Arc2D.Float` or `Arc2D.Double` class. The `Arc2D.Float` constructor takes seven arguments. The first four arguments represent the x-coordinate, y-coordinate, width, and height that apply to the ellipse of which the arc is a part. The remaining three arguments are as follows:

- The starting position of the arc
- The number of degrees it travels
- An integer field indicating how it is closed

The starting position is expressed in degrees, in the same way it is in the `Graphics` class `drawArc()` method; for example, 0 is the three o'clock position. The number of degrees traveled by the arc is specified in a counterclockwise direction using positive numbers. The final argument uses one of the three class fields:

- `Arc2D.PIE` connects the arc to the center of an ellipse and looks like a pie slice.

- `Arc2D.CHORD` connects the arc's endpoints with a straight line.

- `Arc2D.OPEN` is an unclosed arc.

The following statement creates an `Arc2D.Float` object named `ac` at position 10, 133. Its width is 30 and its height is 33. The starting degree is 30, and the arc travels for 120 degrees using the variable `Arc2D.PIE`.

```
Arc2D.Float ac = new Arc2D.Float(10F, 133F, 30F, 33F, 30F, 120F, Arc2D.PIE);
```

Polygons

You create a `Polygon` object by defining movements from one point to another. The movement that creates a polygon is a `GeneralPath` object; the `GeneralPath` class is found in the `java.awt.geom` package.

You can instantiate a `GeneralPath` object with a statement such as the following:

```
GeneralPath poly = new GeneralPath();
```

Then you use the `moveTo()` method to define the beginning point of a polygon. For example, the following statement starts a polygon at the coordinates 10, 100.

```
poly.moveTo(10F, 100F);
```

The `lineTo()` method is used to create a line that ends at a new point. After the preceding `moveTo()` statement, the following statement draws a connecting line from 10, 100 to 50, 200:

```
poly.lineTo(50F, 200F);
```

You can use as many `lineTo()` statements as you need to create the shape you want. For a closed shape, the `lineTo()` method can help you connect the line to the original point. Alternatively, you can use the `closePath()` method without any arguments to complete the shape. You will create a polygon in the next "You Do It" section.

TWO TRUTHS & A LIE

Drawing with Java 2D Graphics

1. The advantage of using Java 2D objects is the higher-quality 2D graphics, images, and text they provide.

2. With Java's 2D graphics, you can designate attributes such as color, line width, and fill patterns.

3. With Java's 2D methods, the drawing line is a brush that represents a single movement as if you were using a drawing tool, such as a pen or a pencil.

The false statement is #3. With Java's 2D methods, the drawing line is a stroke that represents a single movement as if you were using a drawing tool, such as a pen or a pencil.

You Do It

Using Drawing Strokes

Next, you create a line with a drawing stroke to illustrate how it can have different end types and juncture types where lines intersect.

1. Open a new file, and then enter the first few lines of a J2DLine class that extends JPanel. (Note that you are importing the java.awt.geom package.)

```
import javax.swing.*;
import java.awt.*;
import java.awt.geom.*;
public class J2DLine extends JPanel
{
```

2. Start a paintComponent() method by calling the superclass version of the method and declaring a Graphics2D object. Then declare points for the beginning and end of the line.

```
@Override
public void paintComponent(Graphics gr)
{
    super.paintComponent(gr);
    Graphics2D gr2D = (Graphics2D)gr;
    Point2D.Float pos1 = new Point2D.Float(80, 20);
    Point2D.Float pos2 = new Point2D.Float(20, 100);
```

3. Create a BasicStroke object, and then create a drawing stroke named aStroke. Note that the line width is set to 15 pixels, and the endcap style and juncture style are set to CAP_ROUND and JOIN_MITER, respectively.

```
BasicStroke aStroke = new BasicStroke(15.0f,
    BasicStroke.CAP_ROUND, BasicStroke.JOIN_MITER);
gr2D.setStroke(aStroke);
```

4. Add the following code to create a line between the points pos1 and pos2, and draw the line. Add a closing curly brace for the method.

```
    gr2D.setStroke(aStroke);
    Line2D.Float line = new Line2D.Float(pos1, pos2);
    gr2D.draw(line);
}
```

(continues)

(continued)

5. Add a main() method and the closing curly brace for the class:

```
public static void main(String[] args)
{
    JFrame frame = new JFrame();
    frame.add(new J2DLine());
    frame.setDefaultCloseOperation(JFrame.EXIT_ON_CLOSE);
    frame.setSize(90, 160);
    frame.setVisible(true);
}
}
```

6. Save the file as **J2DLine.java**, and then compile and execute it. Your output should look like Figure 16-40.

7. Experiment by making the JFrame larger and adding more lines to create an interesting design.

Working with Shapes

Next, you use the Java 2D drawing object types to create a JFrame that illustrates sample rectangles, ovals, arcs, and polygons.

Figure 16-40   Output of the J2DLine program

1. Open a new file, and then enter the first few lines of a JShapes2D program:

```
import javax.swing.*;
import java.awt.*;
import java.awt.geom.*;
public class JShapes2D extends JPanel
{
```

2. Enter the following statements to start a paintComponent() method and call its parent. Create a Graphics environment gr, and cast the Graphics environment to a Graphics2D environment gr2D:

```
public void paintComponent(Graphics gr)
{
    super.paintComponent(gr);
    Graphics2D gr2D = (Graphics2D)gr;
```

3. Create two Rectangle2D.Float objects named rect and rect2. Draw the rect object and fill the rect2 object:

(continues)

(continued)

```
Rectangle2D.Float rect =
    new Rectangle2D.Float(20F, 40F, 40F, 40F);
Rectangle2D.Float rect2 =
    new Rectangle2D.Float(20F, 70F, 40F, 40F);
gr2D.draw(rect);
gr2D.fill(rect2);
```

907

4. Create two `Ellipse2D.Float` objects named `ellipse` and `ellipse2`. Draw the `ellipse` object and fill the `ellipse2` object:

```
Ellipse2D.Float ellipse = new
    Ellipse2D.Float(20F, 120F, 40F, 40F);
Ellipse2D.Float ellipse2 = new
    Ellipse2D.Float(20F, 170F, 40F, 40F);
gr2D.draw(ellipse);
gr2D.fill(ellipse2);
```

5. Create two `Arc2D.Float` objects named `ac` and `ac2`. Draw the `ac` object and fill the `ac2` object:

```
Arc2D.Float ac = new
    Arc2D.Float(20F, 220F, 50F, 50F, 30F, 120F, Arc2D.PIE);
Arc2D.Float ac2 = new
    Arc2D.Float(20F, 270F, 50F, 50F, 30F, 120F, Arc2D.PIE);
gr2D.draw(ac);
gr2D.fill(ac2);
```

6. Create a new `GeneralPath` object named `pol`. Set the starting point of the polygon and create two additional points. Use the `closePath()` method to close the polygon by connecting the current point to the starting point. Draw the `pol` object, and then end the method with a curly brace:

```
GeneralPath pol = new GeneralPath();
pol.moveTo(20F, 300F);
pol.lineTo(40F, 360F);
pol.lineTo(100F, 380F);
pol.closePath();
gr2D.draw(pol);
}
```

7. Add a `main()` method and the final curly brace for the class:

```
public static void main(String[] args)
{
    JFrame frame = new JFrame();
    frame.add(new JShapes2D());
    frame.setDefaultCloseOperation(JFrame.EXIT_ON_CLOSE);
    frame.setSize(100, 430);
    frame.setVisible(true);
}
}
```

(continues)

(continued)

8. Save the file as **JShapes2D.java**, and compile and execute the program.

    Your output should look like Figure 16-41. When you are ready, close the window, and then experiment with making changes to the program to produce different shapes.

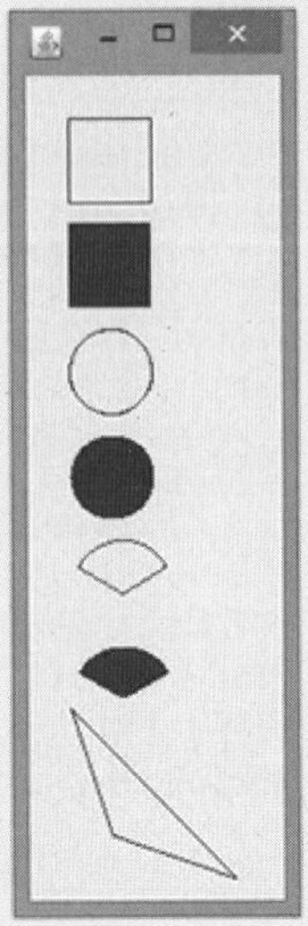

Figure 16-41   Output of the JShapes2D program

Creating an Interactive Program that Draws Lines

In this section, you create a sketch pad that draws lines on a panel in response to a user's mouse movements.

1. Open a new file and start a program that allows a user to draw 2D lines on a JPanel. The program implements MouseListener and MouseMotionListener so it can respond to both clicks and drags.

   ```
   import javax.swing.*;
   import java.awt.*;
   import java.awt.event.*;
   import java.awt.geom.*;
   public class SketchPad extends JPanel implements MouseListener,
       MouseMotionListener
   {
   ```

2. Add the following fields to the class: horizontal and vertical positions for each end of the line the user will draw and a BasicStroke object.

   ```
   int xStart, yStart;
   int xStop, yStop;
   BasicStroke aStroke = new BasicStroke(5.0f,
       BasicStroke.CAP_ROUND, BasicStroke.JOIN_ROUND);
   ```

3. The constructor makes the JPanel respond to mouse events:

   ```
   public SketchPad()
   {
       addMouseListener(this);
       addMouseMotionListener(this);
   }
   ```

4. Each time the mouse is pressed, store its coordinates in the horizontal and vertical start positions.

   ```
   public void mousePressed(MouseEvent e)
   {
       xStart = e.getX();
       yStart = e.getY();
   }
   ```

(continues)

(continued)

5. Each time the mouse is dragged, store its coordinates in the horizontal and vertical end positions and call `repaint()` to draw a line between the start and stop positions. Then update the start coordinates to hold the current end coordinates so the next line will start where the last one ended.

```
public void mouseDragged(MouseEvent e)
{
    xStop = e.getX();
    yStop = e.getY();
    repaint();
    xStart = xStop;
    yStart = yStop;
}
```

6. Implementing `MouseListener` and `MouseMotionListener` requires the coding of five additional methods as follows:

```
public void mouseClicked(MouseEvent e)
{
}
public void mouseEntered(MouseEvent e)
{
}
public void mouseExited(MouseEvent e)
{
}
public void mouseReleased(MouseEvent e)
{
}
public void mouseMoved(MouseEvent e)
{
}
```

7. The `paintComponent()` method casts the `Graphics` object parameter to a 2D object. A `Line2D.Float` object is declared using the stored stop and start coordinates. Notice that each coordinate is cast to a `float` for clarity; if no cast was performed, the integers would be promoted to `float`s automatically. Also notice that, unlike other programs in this chapter, this program does not call the superclass `paintComponent()` method—the lines the user creates should not be erased with each new `paintComponent()` call.

```
public void paintComponent(Graphics g)
{
    Graphics2D gr2D = (Graphics2D)g;
    Line2D.Float line = new Line2D.Float((float)xStart,
        (float)yStart, (float)xStop, (float)yStop);
    gr2D.setStroke(aStroke);
    gr2D.draw(line);
}
```

(continues)

909

(continued)

8. Add a `main()` method that declares a frame and adds the `SketchPad` panel to it. Set the frame attributes, and after the closing brace for the `main()` method, add a closing curly brace for the class.

```
public static void main(String[] args)
{
    JFrame frame = new JFrame();
    frame.add(new SketchPad());
    frame.setSize(400, 400);
    frame.setVisible(true);
    frame.setDefaultCloseOperation(JFrame.EXIT_ON_CLOSE);
}
}
```

9. Save the file as **SketchPad.java**, and compile and execute it. Figure 16-42 shows a typical execution. You can drag your mouse across the panel surface and draw any number of lines.

10. Dismiss the frame. Experiment with the program by adding the panel to new frames that allow the user to choose options such as color and line thickness, and to erase a sketch and start over.

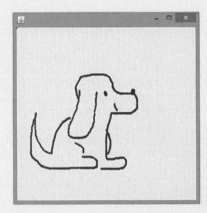

Figure 16-42   Typical execution of the SketchPad application

Don't Do It

- Don't forget to call `super.paintComponent()` as the first statement in the `paintComponent()` method when you write a class that uses graphics and extends `JPanel` and you want the panel erased before each new graphical output.

- Don't forget that the lower-left corner of a `String` is placed at the coordinates used when you call `drawString()`.

- Don't forget that the name of the `Graphics` method that draws rectangles is `drawRect()` and not `drawRectangle()`.

Key Terms

To **render** a drawing is to paint or display it.

To **rerender** a drawing is to repaint or redisplay it.

Painting is the act of redisplaying a surface.

System-triggered painting occurs when the system asks a component to render its contents.

Application-triggered painting occurs when a program requests it, usually because the internal state of a component has changed.

An **arc** is a portion of a circle's circumference.

A **polygon** is a geometric figure with straight sides.

Ascent is one of three measures of a Font's height; it is the height of an uppercase character from a baseline to the top of the character.

Descent is one of three measures of a Font's height; it measures the part of characters that "hang below" the baseline, such as the tails on the lowercase letters *g* and *j*.

Leading is one of three measures of a Font's height; it is the amount of space between the bottom of the descent of one line and the top of the characters in the successive line of type.

The **height of a font** is the sum of its leading, ascent, and descent.

Fill patterns control how a drawing object is filled in.

A **gradient fill** is a gradual shift from one color at one coordinate point to a different color at a second coordinate point.

An **acyclic gradient** is a fill pattern in which a color shift occurs once between two points.

A **cyclic gradient** is a fill pattern in which a shift between colors occurs repeatedly between two points.

A **stroke** is a line-drawing feature in Java 2D that represents a single movement as if you were using a drawing tool, such as a pen or a pencil.

Endcap styles apply to the ends of lines that do not join with other lines, and include CAP_BUTT, CAP_ROUND, and CAP_SQUARE.

Juncture styles, for lines that join, include JOIN_MITER, JOIN_ROUND, and JOIN_BEVEL.

Chapter Summary

- Painting operations can be triggered by the system or the application. Java's creators recommend that you create most graphics on a JPanel by overriding the paintComponent() method and using the automatically supplied Graphics parameter to render output.

- The drawString() method allows you to draw a String using a Graphics object. The method requires three arguments: a String, an x-axis coordinate, and a y-axis coordinate. You can improve the appearance of strings drawn with Graphics objects by using the setFont() and setColor() methods.

- Java provides several methods for drawing a variety of lines and geometric shapes, such as drawLine(), drawRect(), drawOval(), and drawPolygon(). You can also use the copyArea() method to copy any rectangular area to a new location.

- If a user's computer does not have a requested font, Java chooses a default replacement font. You can discover which fonts are available on your system by using the getAvailableFontFamilyNames() method, which is part of the GraphicsEnvironment class. You can discover the resolution and screen size on your system by using the getScreenResolution() and getScreenSize() methods, which are part of the Toolkit class. The height of every font is the sum of three parts: ascent, descent, and leading.

- Graphics2D objects provide high-quality 2D graphics, images, and text. With 2D you can designate attributes such as line width and fill patterns.

Review Questions

1. In Java, repainting of a visible surface is triggered by _____.

   a. the operating system
   b. the application
   c. either of these
   d. none of these

2. The method where you should place drawing code for Swing objects is _____.

   a. callPaint()
   b. paint()
   c. requestPaint()
   d. paintComponent()

3. The paintComponent() method header requires a(n) _____ argument.

   a. Graphics
   b. int
   c. String
   d. Color

4. The three arguments to the drawString() method represent _____.

   a. a String and horizontal and vertical positions
   b. a String, a Color, and a Font
   c. a Graphics object, a String, and a Point position
   d. a JPanel, a Graphics object, and a Font

5. The statement g.drawString(someString, 50, 100); places someString's _____ corner at position 50, 100.

   a. upper-left
   b. lower-left
   c. upper-right
   d. lower-right

6. If you use the `setColor()` method to change a `Graphics` object's color to yellow, ──────── .

    a. only the next output from the object appears in yellow

    b. all output from the object for the remainder of the method always appears in yellow

    c. all output from the object for the remainder of the application always appears in yellow

    d. all future output from the object appears in yellow until you change the color

7. In the statement `x.drawString greeting("Hi ", 10, 10);`, x is a ────────── object.

    a. `Graphics`　　　　　　　　　c. `JPanel`

    b. `String`　　　　　　　　　　d. `Font`

8. The statement `g.drawRoundRect(100, 100, 100, 100, 0, 0);` draws a shape that looks most like a ──────── .

    a. square　　　　　　　　　　c. circle

    b. round-edged rectangle　　　d. straight line

9. If you draw an oval with the same value for width and height, you draw a(n) ──────── .

    a. circle　　　　　　　　　　c. rounded square

    b. square　　　　　　　　　　d. ellipsis

10. The zero-degree position for any arc is at the ──────── o'clock position.

    a. three　　　　　　　　　　c. nine

    b. six　　　　　　　　　　　d. twelve

11. The method you use to create a solid arc is ──────── .

    a. `solidArc()`　　　　　　　c. `arcSolid()`

    b. `fillArc()`　　　　　　　d. `arcFill()`

12. You use the ──────── method to copy any rectangular area to a new location.

    a. `copyRect()`　　　　　　　c. `repeatRect()`

    b. `copyArea()`　　　　　　　d. `repeatArea()`

13. The measurement of an uppercase character from the baseline to the top of the character is its ──────── .

    a. ascent　　　　　　　　　　c. leading

    b. descent　　　　　　　　　d. height

14. To be certain that a vertical series of `Strings` drawn with object g has enough room to appear on a `JPanel`, which of the following expressions should you use for the vertical coordinate?

    a. `y += g.getFontMetrics().getHeight();`
    b. `y += g.getFontMetrics().getLeading();`
    c. `g.getFontMetrics().getAscent();`
    d. `y += g.getFontMetrics().getDescent();`

15. You can discover which fonts are available on your system by using the _____.

    a. `getAvailableFontFamilyNames()` method of the `GraphicsEnvironment` class
    b. `getFonts()` method of the `Graphics` class
    c. `getMyFonts()` method of the `GraphicsFonts` class
    d. `getAllFonts()` method of the `Fonts` class

16. The data types returned by the `getScreenResolution()` and `getScreenSize()` methods are _____.

    a. both `ints`
    b. an `int` and an object of type `Dimension`
    c. both objects of type `Dimension`
    d. both `doubles`

17. A `Graphics2D` object can be produced by _____.

    a. calling `setGraphics2D()`   c. casting a `Graphics2D` object
    b. calling `getGraphics2D()`   d. casting a `Graphics` object

18. The process of drawing with Java 2D objects includes _____.

    a. specifying the rendering attributes
    b. setting a drawing stroke
    c. both of the above
    d. none of the above

19. A gradient fill is a gradual change in _____.

    a. color   c. drawing style
    b. font size   d. line thickness

20. With 2D methods, the drawing line is known as a _____.

    a. brush   c. belt
    b. stroke   d. draw

Exercises

Programming Exercises

1. Write an application that extends JPanel and displays a phrase in every font size from 6 through 20. Save the file as **JFontSizesPanel.java**.

2. a. Write an application that extends JPanel and displays a phrase in a large font. Each time the user clicks a JButton, display the same phrase in a different color, a little further to the right, and in a slightly smaller font. Allow only three clicks. Save the file as **JChangeSizeAndColorPanel.java**.

   b. Modify the JChangeSizeAndColorPanel application so that it continuously changes the size, color, and location of a phrase as long as the user continues to click the button. Save the application as **JChangeSizeAndColorPanel2.java**.

3. Write an application that extends JPanel and displays a phrase. Each time the user clicks a button, alternate between displaying the phrase upside down and right-side up. Save the application as **JUpsideDownPanel.java**.

4. Write an application that extends JPanel and displays eight nested rectangles, like those in the first panel in Figure 16-43. You may use only one drawRect() statement in the program. (*Hint*: Use it in a loop.) Save the file as **JNestedBoxesPanel.java**.

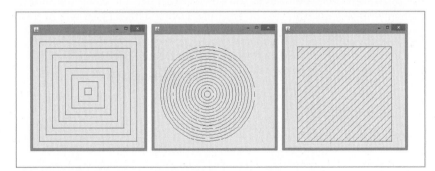

Figure 16-43   Output of the programs described in exercises 4, 5, and 6

5. Write an application that extends JPanel and displays 15 nested circles, like those in the center panel in Figure 16-43. You may use only one drawOval() statement in the program. Save the file as **JNestedCirclesPanel.java**.

6. Write an application that extends JPanel and displays diagonal lines in a square, like those in the last panel in Figure 16-43. Save the file as **JDiagonalLinesPanel.java**.

7. a. Write an application that extends JPanel and displays a yellow smiling face on the screen. Save the file as **JSmileFacePanel.java**.

   b. Add a JButton to the JSmileFacePanel program so the smile changes to a frown and then back to a smile each time the user clicks the JButton. Save the file as **JSmileFacePanel2.java**.

8. Use polygons and lines to create a graphics image that looks like a fireworks display. Write an application that extends JPanel and displays the fireworks. Save the file as **JFireworksPanel.java**.

9. a. Write an application that extends JPanel and displays your name. Place boxes of different colors around your name at intervals of 10, 20, 30, and 40 pixels. Save the file as **JBorderPanel.java**.

   b. Modify the JBorderPanel program so that when the user enters any name in a JTextField, the name is displayed with borders at intervals of 10, 20, 30, and 40 pixels. Save the file as **JBorderPanel2.java**.

10. Write an application that extends JPanel and uses the Graphics2D environment to create a GeneralPath object. Use the GeneralPath object to create the outline of your favorite state. Display the state's name at the approximate center of its boundaries. Save the file as **JStatePanel.java**.

Debugging Exercises

1. Each of the following files in the Chapter16 folder of your downloadable student files has syntax and/or logic errors. In each case, determine the problem and fix the program. After you correct the errors, save each file using the same filename preceded with *Fix*. For example, DebugSixteen1.java will become **FixDebugSixteen1.java**.

   a. DebugSixteen1.java   c. DebugSixteen3.java
   b. DebugSixteen2.java   d. DebugSixteen4.java

Game Zone

1. a. In Chapter 9, you created a Tic Tac Toe game in which you used a 2D array of characters to hold *X*s and *O*s for a player and the computer. Now create a JPanel that uses an array of nine JButtons to represent the Tic Tac Toe grid. When the user clicks a button that has not already been taken, place an *X* on the button and then allow the computer to place an *O* on a different button. Announce the winner when either the computer or the player achieves three marks in sequence, or announce that the game was a tie. Figure 16-44 shows a typical game in progress and after the player has won. Save the game as **JTicTacToe.java**.

Figure 16-44 Typical execution of the JTicTacToe program

b. Add a graphic that displays a large letter representing the winning player of the JTicTacToe game. Draw a large *X*, *O*, or, in case of a tie, an overlapping *X* and *O* in different colors. Save the game as **JTicTacToe2.java**.

2. Create an application that plays a card game named Lucky Seven. In real life, the game can be played with seven cards, each containing a number from 1 through 7. The cards are shuffled and dealt number-side down. To start the game, a player turns over any card. The exposed number on the card determines the position (reading from left to right) of the next card that must be turned over. For example, if the player turns over the first card and its number is 7, the next card turned must be the seventh card (counting from left to right). If the player turns over a card whose number denotes a position that was already turned, the player loses the game. If the player succeeds in turning over all seven cards, the player wins.

Instead of cards, you will use seven buttons on a JPanel. The buttons are labeled *1* through *7* from left to right. Randomly associate one of the seven values 1 through 7 with each button. (In other words, the associated value might or might not be equivalent to the button's labeled value.) When the player clicks a button, reveal the associated hidden value. If the value represents the position of a button already clicked, the player loses. If the revealed number represents an available button, force the user to click it; that is, do not take any action until the user clicks the correct button. After a player clicks a button, remove the button from play.

For example, a player might click Button 7, revealing a 4. Then the player clicks Button 4, revealing a 2. Then the player clicks Button 2, revealing a 7. The player loses because Button 7 was already used. Save the game as **JLuckySeven.java**.

3. a. In Chapters 7 and 8, you created a game named Secret Phrase in which the user guesses a randomly selected secret phrase by entering one letter at a time. Now create a GUI application that plays the game, allowing users to choose a letter by selecting one of 26 buttons. (*Hint*: Consider creating an array of buttons rather than 26 individually named buttons.)

Disable a letter button once it has been guessed, and after the puzzle is complete, disable all the letters. Figure 16-45 shows a typical execution after the user has guessed an *E*, which is in the phrase. Save the file as **JSecretPhrase.java**.

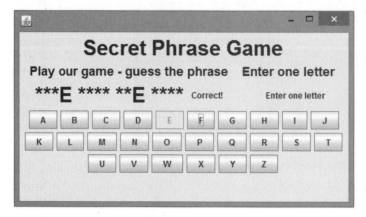

Figure 16-45   Typical execution of the JSecretPhrase program

b. Make the JSecretPhrase game more like the traditional letter-guessing game Hangman by drawing a "hanged" person piece by piece with each missed letter. For example, when the user chooses a correct letter, place it in the appropriate position or positions in the phrase, but the first time the user chooses a letter that is not in the target phrase, draw a head for the "hanged" man. The second time the user makes an incorrect guess, add a torso. Continue with arms and legs. If the complete body is drawn before the user has guessed all the letters in the phrase, display a message indicating that the player has lost the game. If the user completes the phrase before all the body parts are drawn, display a message that the player has won. Save the game as **JSecretPhrase2.java**.

Case Problems

1. In Chapters 14 and 15, you developed an interactive GUI application for Carly's Catering. Now, design a JPanel that uses graphics to display a logo for the company, and modify the GUI application to include it. Save the JPanel class as **JCarlysLogoPanel.java**, and save the GUI application as **JCarlysCatering.java**.

2. In Chapters 14 and 15, you developed an interactive GUI application for Sammy's Seashore Rentals. Now, design a JPanel that uses graphics to display a logo for the company, and modify the GUI application to include it. Save the JPanel class as **JSammysLogoPanel.java**, and save the GUI application as **JSammysSeashore.java**.

Working with the Java Platform

In this appendix, you will:

◎ Learn about the Java SE Development Kit

◎ Configure Windows to work with the JDK

◎ Compile and execute a Java program

Learning about the Java SE Development Kit

Several versions of Java are available for free at the Java Web site (*www.oracle.com/technetwork/java/index.html*). The official name of the most recent version is Java Platform, Standard Edition 8, often called **Java SE 8** for short. Two version numbers (for example, 1.8.0 and 8) are used to identify each release of the Java Platform. Version 8 is the product version, and 1.8.0 is the developer version. The number 8 is used to reflect Java's evolving level of maturity. As updates to existing versions emerge or entirely new versions containing advanced features are released, you can download them. For example, a recent update as this book was being written is Java SE 8u11, which is short for *version 8, update 11*.

Java's Web site was *http://java.sun.com* before Java was purchased by Oracle. Now the Web site is *http://www.oracle.com/technetwork/java/index.html*. However, the shorter URL redirects you to the longer one, so you can use the shorter address if it is more convenient. Traditionally, each new version of Java has had a code name. The code names for versions 5, 6, and 7 were Tiger, Mustang, and Dolphin, respectively. With version 8, code names have been discontinued, but some Java developers refer to it as Spider.

Over the years, Java has been inconsistent in numbering new versions. Before version 6, the standard editions were called JDK 1.0.3, JDK 1.1.2 through 1.1.8, J2SE 1.2.0 through 1.4.2, and J2SE 5.0. With versions 6, 7, and 8, Java is attempting to simplify the name and number changes. Java sometimes adds a "half step" for minor revisions in a version, such as JDK 1.8.0_05.

The different names for Java configurations are somewhat confusing and frequently misused. If you download Java to use with this book, you want to acquire the Java Standard Edition (SE) Development Kit, also known as the **JDK**. Java also supports the **Java Enterprise Edition (EE)**, which includes all of the classes in the Java SE, plus a number of classes that are more useful to programs running on servers than on workstations. The Java EE Development Kit is known as **SDK**. The names of the development kits have changed frequently; originally, JDK meant "Java Development Kit," but that interpretation was used with the earliest Java versions and is no longer used officially.

The **Java Micro Edition (ME)** is another Java platform, which is used for devices such as cell phones and other small consumer appliances.

Configuring Windows to Use the JDK

To configure your Windows operating system with the JDK, you must add the Java bin directory to the command path of your operating system (OS). That way, your OS will know where to look for the Java commands that you use.

One way to update the OS path for Windows is to edit or set the OS path in the autoexec.bat file. This file is automatically executed every time you start your computer. A simpler and less error-prone alternative is to type two commands at the OS prompt when you want to begin a session of working on Java programs. (These two commands are described later in this appendix.)

You do not need to be an operating system expert to issue operating system commands. Learning just a few commands allows you to create and run all the examples in this book.

Finding the Command Prompt

To locate the command prompt on your Windows 8.1 computer, you can swipe from the right of the screen, click Search, and start to type *Command Prompt*. When *Command Prompt* appears in the list, click it. Alternately, you can select the *Win* and *X* keys together to bring up the Power User Menu, and then click Command Prompt. With older Windows versions, you can click Start, point to Programs, point to Accessories, and then click Command Prompt.

 In earlier versions of Windows, the console window was called the MS-DOS *(Microsoft Disk Operating System)* prompt, or more simply, the *DOS prompt*. Many people still use this term instead of *command prompt*.

Command Prompt Anatomy

The Windows command prompt contains at least a disk drive name followed by a colon, a backslash, and a greater-than sign (for example, C:\>). You might also see folder or directory names within the command prompt just before the greater-than sign, as shown in the following examples:

C:\Documents and Settings>

C:\Documents and Settings\Administrator>

Each directory in the path is separated by a backslash.

Changing Directories

You can back up one directory level by typing cd for "change directory," followed by two periods:

`cd..`

For example, if your OS prompt contains C:\Users\<*your name*> and you type `cd..`, the command prompt changes to C:\Users>. If you type `cd..` again, the prompt changes to C:\>, indicating the root directory.

When you have multiple directories to back through, it is easier to use the following command:

`cd\`

This takes you immediately to the root directory instead of backing up one level at a time.

At the command prompt, you can change the directory by typing cd followed by the name of the directory. For example, if you have a folder named Java and it contains a folder named Chapter.01, you can change the command prompt to the Chapter.01 folder by backing up to the root directory and typing the following:

```
cd Java
cd Chapter.01
```

After these commands, the command prompt reads *C:\Java\Chapter.01>*. When you compile and execute your Java programs, you should start from the command prompt where the files are stored.

When your command prompt display is filled with commands, it can look confusing. If you want, you can type cls (for Clear Screen) to remove old commands.

Setting the `class` and `classpath` Variables

When you start a Java session, you might need to set the `class` and `classpath` options. These settings tell the operating system where to find the Java compiler and your classes. If you or someone else has altered your autoexec.bat file to contain these commands, you do not need to type them. Otherwise, every time you want to compile and execute Java programs, you need to type statements similar to the following:

```
path = c:\program files\java\jdk1.8.0\bin
set classpath=.
```

After you have typed the `class` and `classpath` statements, you can compile and run as many Java programs as you want without typing these commands again. You must type them again if you close the Command Prompt window or restart your computer.

The first statement sets the path and allows the OS to recognize the `javac` command you use when compiling programs. Consider the following example:

```
path = c:\program files\java\jdk1.8.0\bin
```

This example assumes that you are using JDK 1.8.0 and that it is stored in the java folder in the program files folder. These are the defaults when you download Java from the Java Web site; if you installed Java in a different location, you need to alter the command accordingly.

The command `set classpath=.` tells Java to find your compiled classes in the current directory when you execute your applications. There must be no space between `classpath` and the equal sign, or between the equal sign and the period.

After you set the path correctly, you should be able to use the `javac` command. If you attempt to compile a Java class and see an error message that `javac` is not a recognized command, either Java was not properly installed or the path command was incorrect. If classes compile successfully but do not execute, you might have entered the `classpath` command incorrectly.

Changing a File's Name

When working through the examples in this book, you will often find it convenient to change the name of an existing file—for example, when you want to experiment with altering code without losing the original version, or if you find that when you previously saved a file, you mistyped a filename so that it did not match the class name within the .java file you created. You can take at least three approaches:

- Open the existing file using the appropriate software application (for example, Notepad), click File on the menu bar, and then click Save As. Select the folder you want, then type a new filename for the file. Now you have two versions—one with the old name and one with the new.

- Open the folder where the file is located and find the misnamed file. Select the file and then click the filename. (Do not double-click the filename unless you want to open the file.) You can then edit the filename by using a combination of the Backspace, Delete, and character keys. Press Enter when the filename is correct. Alternately, you can right-click the filename and choose *Rename* from the menu that appears.

- At the command prompt, use the rename command. You type rename, a space, the old filename, another space, and the new filename. For example, to change a file named xyz.java to abc.java, type the following at the command prompt for the directory containing the existing file:

```
rename xyz.java abc.java
```

Compiling and Executing a Java Program

At the command prompt, change from the default drive prompt to the drive where your application is stored. Then change the directory (or folder) to the directory that holds your application.

To compile an application, you type the javac command to start the Java compiler, then type a space and the complete name of the .java file—for example, First.java. If the application doesn't compile successfully, the path might not be set correctly to the Java JDK bin directory where the javac.exe file is located. Also, you might have failed to use the same spelling as the Java filename.

When you compile a .java file correctly, the Java compiler creates a .class file that has the same filename as the .java file. Thus, a successful compilation of the First.java file creates a file named First.class. To run a Java application, you use the java command and the class name without the .class extension. For example, after an application named First.java is compiled, producing First.class, you execute the program using the following command:

```
java First
```

After the program executes, control is returned to the command prompt. If a program does not end on its own, or you want to end it prematurely, you can press Ctrl+C to return to the command prompt.

After you compile a Java program, you can execute it as many times as you want without recompiling. If you change the source code, you must save and compile again before you can see the changed results in an executed application.

 When you are testing a Java program, you often issue the commands to compile and execute it many times before you are satisfied with the results. If you press the Up Arrow key at the command line, the previous commands appear in reverse succession. When you find the command you want to repeat, just press Enter.

Key Terms

Java SE 8 is the most recent version of Java. The full, official name is Java Platform, Standard Edition 8.

The **JDK** is the Java Standard Edition Development Kit.

The **Java Enterprise Edition (EE)** includes all of the classes in the Java SE, plus a number of classes that are more useful to programs running on servers.

The **SDK** is the Java EE Development Kit.

The **Java Micro Edition (ME)** is a Java platform used for small devices such as cell phones.

Data Representation

In this appendix, you will:

◎ Work with numbering systems

◎ Learn how numeric values are represented

◎ Learn how character values are represented

Understanding Numbering Systems

You can use devices such as computers, cell phones, microwave ovens, and automobiles without understanding how they work internally. Likewise, you can write many Java programs without understanding how the data items they use are represented internally. However, once you learn how data items are stored, you gain a deeper understanding of computer programming in general and Java in particular. You also can more easily troubleshoot some types of problems that arise in your programs.

The numbering system you know best is the **decimal numbering system**, which is based on 10 digits, 0 through 9. When you use the decimal system, no other symbols are available; if you want to express a value larger than 9, you must use multiple digits from the same pool of 10, placing them in columns. Decimal numbers are also called base 10 numbers.

When you use the decimal system, you analyze a multicolumn number by mentally assigning place values to each column. The value of the rightmost column is 1, the value of the next column to the left is 10, the next column's value is 100, and so on; you multiply the column value by 10 as you move to the left. There is no limit to the number of columns you can use; you simply add them to the left as you need to express higher values. For example, Figure B-1 shows how the value 305 is represented in the decimal system. You simply multiply the digit in each column by the value of the column, and then add the values together.

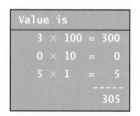

Figure B-1   Representing 305 in the decimal system

The **binary numbering system** works in the same way as the decimal numbering system, except that it uses only two digits, *0* and *1*. When you use the binary system and you want to express a value greater than 1, you must use multiple columns because no single symbol represents any value other than 0 or 1. Instead of each new column to the left being 10 times greater than the previous column, each new binary column is only two times the value of the previous column. Binary numbers are called base 2 numbers.

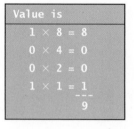

Figure B-2   Representing decimal value 9 in the binary system

For example, Figure B-2 shows how the decimal number 9 is represented in the binary system. Notice that both the binary and decimal systems allow you to create numbers with 0 in one or more columns. As with the decimal system, the binary system has no limit to the number of columns—you

Value is
1 × 32 = 32
1 × 16 = 16
0 × 8 = 0
0 × 4 = 0
1 × 2 = 2
0 × 1 = 0

50

32s	16s	8s	4s	2s	1s
1	1	0	0	1	0

Figure B-3 Representing decimal value 50 in the binary system

can use as many as it takes to express a value. For example, Figure B-3 shows that the decimal number 50 requires six binary system columns.

A computer stores every piece of data it uses as a set of 0s and 1s. Each 0 or 1 is known as a **bit**, which is short for *binary digit*. Every computer uses 0s and 1s because all its values are stored as electronic signals that are either on or off. This two-state system is most easily represented using just two digits.

Representing Numeric Values

In Chapter 2, you learned that a floating-point number contains decimal positions. The term *floating point* comes from the fact that the decimal point can be at any location in the stored value, allowing a much larger range of possible values to be stored in the same amount of memory. For example, assume that a computer could store only four digits and that the decimal point had to fall after the first two. The positive values that could be stored would then range from 00.00 through 99.99. However, if the decimal point could fall anywhere, the values could range from .0000 through 9999. Computers use more storage for each value, and store negative values as well, but the principle is the same.

Because of the binary nature of computers, representing floating-point numbers is imprecise. For example, suppose you want to represent the value 1/10 (0.10). You could try using each of the following techniques:

- If you use two bits to store the value, only four combinations are available (00, 01, 10, and 11), so they can only represent 0/4, 1/4, 2/4 (or 1/2), and 3/4. None of these is exactly 1/10, but 0/4 is the closest.

- Suppose you use three bits. This allows twice as many combinations, or eight, and the closest to 1/10 is 1/8. The approximation is closer than with two bits, but still not exact.

- Suppose you use four bits, which allows 16 combinations. The closest value to 1/10 is 2/16. This value is no closer to 1/10 than you could achieve with three bits.

- Suppose you use eight bits. Now, there are 256 bit combinations from 0/256 through 255/256. The value of 26/256, at 0.1015625, is closer than any of the other values so far, but it's still not exact.

- No matter how many bits you add to the representation, doubling the number of combinations each time, you can never express 0.1 exactly.

Although you cannot store 0.1 exactly, you can still display it. For example, the following two lines of code display 0.1 as expected:

```
double oneTenth = 0.1;
System.out.println(oneTenth);
```

When Java displays a floating-point number, it always displays at least one digit after the decimal. After that, it uses only as many digits as necessary to distinguish the number from the nearest floating-point value it can represent.

However, when you use 0.1 in an arithmetic statement, the imprecision becomes evident. Figure B-4 shows a simple program that declares two variables named oneTenth and threeTenths; the variables contain the values 0.1 and 0.3, respectively. Figure B-5 shows the result of summing oneTenth three times and of comparing that sum to threeTenths. Because of floating-point imprecision, the first value is calculated to be slightly more than 0.3, so the comparison of oneTenth + oneTenth + oneTenth to threeTenths is false.

```
import java.util.Scanner;
public class FloatingPointTest
{
    public static void main(String[] args)
    {
        double oneTenth = 0.1;
        double threeTenths = 0.3;
        System.out.println(oneTenth + oneTenth + oneTenth);
        System.out.println(oneTenth + oneTenth + oneTenth ==
            threeTenths);
    }
}
```

Figure B-4   The FloatingPointTest class

Figure B-5   Output of the FloatingPointTest program

For many purposes, you do not care about the small imprecisions generated by floating-point calculations, but sometimes they can make a difference. For example, several popular movies have used the idea that small amounts of extra money can be sliced off bank balances when compounding interest and then siphoned to a criminal's account. Many programmers recommend that you use the Java class BigDecimal when working with monetary or scientific values where precision is important. Additionally, be aware that when you test two floating-point values for equivalency, you might not get the expected results.

When precision is not an issue, but better-looking output is important, you can format the output to eliminate the small imprecisions that occur far to the right of the decimal point. Appendix C teaches you many techniques for formatting output to a desired number of decimal places.

Representing Character Values

The characters used in Java are represented in **Unicode**, which is a 16-bit coding scheme for characters. For example, the letter *A* actually is stored in computer memory as a set of 16 zeros and ones as 0000 0000 0100 0001 (a space is inserted after each set of four digits for readability). Because 16-digit numbers are difficult to read, programmers often use a shorthand notation called the **hexadecimal numbering system,** or base 16. The hexadecimal system uses 16 values, 0 through 9 and A through F, to represent the decimal values 0 through 15. In hexadecimal shorthand, 0000 becomes 0, 0100 becomes 4, and 0001 becomes 1, so the letter *A* is represented in hexadecimal as 0041. You tell the compiler to treat the four-digit hexadecimal 0041 as a single character by preceding it with the \u escape sequence. Therefore, each of the following declarations stores the character *A*:

```
char letter = 'A';
char letter = '\u0041';
char letter = 65;
```

 Two-digit, base 16 numbers can be converted to base 10 numbers by multiplying the left digit by 16 and adding the right digit. For example, hexadecimal 41 is 4 times 16 plus 1, or 65.

The options that use hexadecimal and decimal values are more difficult and confusing to use than the first method, so it is not recommended that you store letters of the alphabet using numeric values. However, you can produce some interesting output using the Unicode format. For example, the sequence '\u0007' produces a bell-like noise if you send it to output. Letters from foreign alphabets that use characters instead of letters (Greek, Hebrew, Chinese, and so on) and other special symbols (foreign currency symbols, mathematical symbols, geometric shapes, and so on) are available using Unicode, but not on a standard keyboard, so it may be important that you know how to use Unicode characters. For more information about Unicode, go to *www.unicode.org*.

In the United States, the most widely used character set traditionally has been **ASCII** (American Standard Code for Information Interchange). The ASCII character set contains 128 characters. You can create any Unicode character by adding eight 0s to the beginning of its ASCII character equivalent. This means that the decimal value of any ASCII character is the same as that of the corresponding Unicode character. For example, *B* has the value 66 in both character sets. The decimal values are important because they allow you to show nonprintable characters, such as a carriage return, in decimal codes. Also, the numeric values of the coding schemes are used when a computer sorts numbers and strings. When you sort characters in ascending order, for example, numbers are sorted first (because their Unicode values begin with decimal code 48), followed by capital letters (starting with decimal 65) and then lowercase letters (starting with decimal 97).

Chapter 2 contains a list of Unicode values for some commonly used characters. For a complete list, see *www.unicode.org/charts*. There you will find Greek, Armenian, Hebrew, Tagalog, Cherokee, and a host of other character sets. Unicode also contains characters for mathematical symbols, geometric shapes, and other unusual characters. The ASCII character set is more limited than Unicode; it contains only letters and symbols used in the English language.

Key Terms

The **decimal numbering system** is based on 10 digits, 0 through 9, in which each column represents a value 10 times higher than the column to its right.

The **binary numbering system** is based on two digits, 0 and 1, in which each column represents a value two times higher than the column to its right.

A **bit** is each binary digit, 0 or 1, used to represent computerized values.

Unicode is a 16-bit coding scheme for representing characters.

The **hexadecimal numbering system** is based on 16 digits, 0 through F, in which each column represents a value 16 times higher than the column to its right.

ASCII (American Standard Code for Information Interchange) is a character set widely used to represent computer data.

Formatting Output

In this appendix, you will:

- ◎ Round numbers
- ◎ Use the `printf()` method
- ◎ Use the `DecimalFormat` class

Rounding Numbers

In Chapter 2 and Appendix B, you learned about the imprecision of floating-point numbers. For example, if you write a program that subtracts 2.00 from 2.20, the result is not 0.20—it is 0.20000000000000018. To eliminate odd-looking output and nonintuitive comparisons caused by imprecise calculations in floating-point numbers, you can take the approach shown in the class in Figure C-1. If you want to round a number to two decimal places, note the shaded steps in the figure:

- Multiply the value by 100. So, for example, 0.20000000000000018 becomes 20.000000000000018.

- Add 0.5. This increases a value's whole number part by 1 if the fractional part is 0.5 or greater. For example, 41.6 would become 42.1. In this case, 20.000000000000018 becomes 20.500000000000018.

- Cast the value to an integer. In this case, 20.500000000000018 becomes 20.

- Divide by 100. In this case, the value becomes 0.20.

```java
public class RoundingDemo1
{
    public static void main(String[] args)
    {
        double answer = 2.20 - 2.00;
        boolean isEqual;
        isEqual = answer == 0.20;
        System.out.println("Before conversion");
        System.out.println("answer is " + answer);
        System.out.println("isEqual is " + isEqual);
        answer = answer * 100;
        answer = answer + 0.5;
        answer = (int) answer;
        answer = answer / 100;
        isEqual = answer == 0.20;
        System.out.println("After conversion");
        System.out.println("answer is " + answer);
        System.out.println("isEqual is " + isEqual);
    }
}
```

Figure C-1   The RoundingDemo1 class

Figure C-2 shows the output of the program. Without rounding, the displayed difference between 2.20 and 2.00 is 0.20000000000000018. However, after applying the rounding technique, the result is displayed as 0.2 as expected.

As an alternative, you can use the round() method that is supplied with Java's Math class. The round() method returns the nearest long value. Figure C-3 shows a program that multiplies the double answer by 100, rounds it, and then divides by 100.0. The output is identical to that shown in Figure C-2.

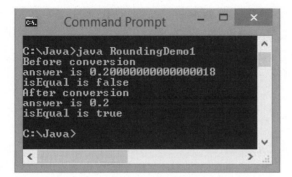

Figure C-2 Output of the RoundingDemo1 program

```java
public class RoundingDemo2
{
    public static void main(String[] args)
    {
        double answer = 2.20 - 2.00;
        boolean isEqual;
        isEqual = answer == 0.20;
        System.out.println("Before conversion");
        System.out.println("answer is " + answer);
        System.out.println("isEqual is " + isEqual);
        answer = answer * 100;
        long roundedAnswer = Math.round(answer);
        answer = roundedAnswer / 100.0;
        isEqual = answer == 0.20;
        System.out.println("After conversion");
        System.out.println("answer is " + answer);
        System.out.println("isEqual is " + isEqual);
    }
}
```

Figure C-3 The RoundingDemo2 class

Using the `printf()` Method

When you display numbers using the `println()` method in Java applications, it sometimes is difficult to make numeric values appear as you want. For example, in the output in Figure C-2, the difference between 2.20 and 2.00 is displayed as 0.2. By default, Java eliminates trailing zeros when floating-point numbers are displayed because they do not add any mathematical information. You might prefer to see 0.20 because the original numbers were both expressed to two decimal places, or, in particular, if the values represent currency.

Additionally, you frequently want to align columns of numeric values. For example, Figure C-4 shows a `NumberList` application that contains an array of floating-point values. The application displays the values using a `for` loop, but as the output in Figure C-5 shows, the numbers are not aligned by the decimal point as you usually would want numbers to be aligned. Because the println() method displays values as Strings, the displayed values are left-aligned, just as series of words would be. The numeric values are accurate; they just are not attractively arranged.

```java
public class NumberList
{
    public static void main(String[] args)
    {
        double[] list = {0.20, 2.00, 2.20, 22.22,
            22.20, 222.00, 222.22};
        int x;
        for(x = 0; x < list.length; ++x)
            System.out.println(list[x]);
    }
}
```

Figure C-4   The NumberList application

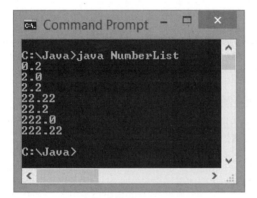

Figure C-5   Output of the NumberList application

The System.out.printf() method is used to format numeric values. It is a newer Java feature that was first included in the Formatter class in Java 1.5.0. (This is the internal version number of the Java Development Kit; the external version number is 5.0.) Because this class is contained in the java.util package, you do not need to include any import statements to use it. The printf() method allows you to format numeric values in two useful ways:

- By specifying the number of decimal places to display

- By specifying the field size in which to display values

The Formatter class contains many formats that are not covered here. To view the details of formatting data types such as BigDecimal and Calendar, visit the Java Web site.

C programmers use a printf() function that is very similar to Java's printf() method. Although the printf() method is used in these examples, in Java, you can substitute System.out.format() for System.out.printf(). There is no difference in the way you use these two methods.

When creating numeric output, you can specify a number of decimal places to display by using the `printf()` method with two types of arguments that represent the following:

- A format string
- A list of arguments

A **format string** is a string of characters; it includes optional text (that is displayed literally) and one or more format specifiers. A **format specifier** is a placeholder for a numeric value. Within a call to `printf()`, you include one argument (either a variable or a constant) for each format specifier.

The format specifiers for general, character, and numeric types contain the following elements, in order:

- A percent sign (%), which indicates the start of every format specifier

- An optional argument index, which is an integer indicating the position of the argument in the argument list. The integer is followed by a dollar sign. You will learn more about this option later in this appendix.

- Optional flags that modify the output format. The set of valid flags depends on the data type you are formatting. You can find more details about this feature at the Java Web site.

- An optional field width, which is an integer indicating the minimum number of characters to be written to the output. You will learn more about this option later in this appendix.

- An optional precision factor, which is a decimal point followed by a number and typically used to control the number of decimal places displayed. You will learn more about this option in the next section.

- The required conversion character, which indicates how its corresponding argument should be formatted. Java supports a variety of conversion characters, but the three you want to use most frequently are d, f, and s, the characters that represent decimal (base 10 integer), floating-point (`float` and `double`), and string values, respectively.

 Other conversion characters include those used to display hexadecimal numbers and scientific notation. If you need these display formats, you can find more details at the Java Web site.

For example, you can use the `ConversionCharacterExamples` class in Figure C-6 to display a declared integer and `double`. The `main()` method of the class contains three `printf()` statements. The three calls to `printf()` in this class each contain a format string; the first two calls contain a single additional argument, and the last `printf()` statement contains two arguments after the string. None of the format specifiers in this class use any of the optional parameters—only the required percent sign and conversion character. The first `printf()` statement uses `%d` in its format string as a placeholder for the integer argument at the end. The second `printf()` statement uses `%f` as a placeholder for the floating-point argument at the end. The last `printf()` statement uses both a `%d` and `%f` to indicate the positions of the integer and floating-point values at the end, respectively. If you attempt to use a conversion character that is invalid for the data type, the program will compile, but it will throw an exception during execution when it encounters the wrong conversion character for the value being displayed.

```
public class ConversionCharacterExamples
{
    public static void main(String[] args)
    {
        int age = 23;
        double money = 123.45;
        System.out.printf("Age is %d\n", age);
        System.out.printf("Money is $%f\n", money);
        System.out.printf
            ("Age is %d and money is $%f\n", age, money);
    }
}
```

Figure C-6 The ConversionCharacterExamples application

Figure C-7 shows the output of the program, in which the values are inserted in the appropriate places in their strings. Note that floating-point values are displayed with six decimal positions by default.

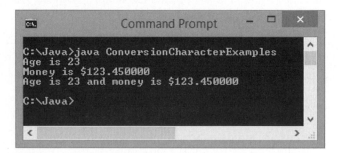

Figure C-7 Output of the ConversionCharacterExamples application

Notice that in the ConversionCharacterExamples class, the output appears on three separate lines only because the newline character ('\n') has been included at the end of each printf() format string. Unlike the println() statement, printf() does not include an automatic new line.

Specifying a Number of Decimal Places to Display with printf()

You can control the number of decimal places displayed when you use a floating-point value in a printf() statement by adding the optional precision factor to the format specifier. Between the percent sign and the conversion character, you can add a decimal point and the number of decimal positions to display. For example, the following statements produce the output "Money is $123.45", displaying the money value with just two decimal places instead of six, which would occur without the precision factor:

```
double money = 123.45;
System.out.printf("Money is $%.2f\n", money);
```

Similarly, the following statements display 8.10. If you use the `println()` equivalent with `amount`, only 8.1 is displayed; if you use a `printf()` statement without inserting the `.2` precision factor, 8.100000 is displayed.

```
double amount = 8.1;
System.out.printf("%.2f",amount);
```

When you use a precision factor on a value that contains more decimal positions than you want to display, the result is rounded. For example, the following statements produce 100.457 (not 100.456), displaying three decimals because of the precision factor.

```
double value = 100.45678;
System.out.printf("%.3f",value);
```

You cannot use the precision factor with an integer value; if you do, your program will throw an `IllegalFormatConversionException`.

Specifying a Field Size with `printf()`

You can indicate a field size in which to display output by using an optional integer as the field width. For example, the `NumberList2` class in Figure C-8 displays each array element in a field with a size of 6, using two decimal places. Figure C-9 shows the output of the application. Each value is displayed right-aligned in its field; for example, 0.20 is preceded by two blank spaces, and 22.20 is preceded by one blank space. If a numeric value contains more positions than you indicate for its `printf()` field size, the field size is ignored, and the entire value is displayed.

```
public class NumberList2
{
    public static void main(String[] args)
    {
        double[] list = {0.20, 2.00, 2.20, 22.22,
            22.20, 222.00, 222.22};
        int x;
        for(x = 0; x < list.length; ++x)
            System.out.printf("%6.2f\n", list[x]);
    }
}
```

Figure C-8   The `NumberList2` class

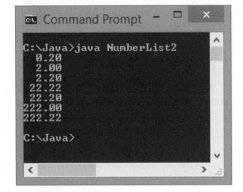

Figure C-9 Output of the
NumberList2 class

Throughout this book, you have been encouraged to use named constants for numeric values instead of literal constants, so that your programs are clearer. In the program in Figure C-9, you could define constants such as:

```
final int DISPLAY_WIDTH = 6;
final int DISPLAY_DECIMALS = 2;
```

Then the `printf()` statement would be:

```
System.out.printf("%" + DISPLAY_WIDTH + "." +
    DISPLAY_DECIMALS + "f\n", list[x]);
```

Another, perhaps clearer alternative is to define a format string such as the following:

```
final String FORMAT = "%6.2f\n";
```

Then the `printf()` statement would be:

```
System.out.printf(FORMAT, list[x]);
```

You can specify that a value be left-aligned in a field instead of right-aligned by inserting a negative sign in front of the width. Although you can do this with numbers, most often you choose to left-align strings. For example, the following code displays five spaces followed by "hello" and then five spaces followed by "there". Each string is left-aligned in a field with a size of 10.

```
String string1 = "hello";
String string2 = "there";
System.out.printf("%-10s%-10s", string1, string2);
```

Using the Optional Argument Index with `printf()`

The **argument index** is an integer that indicates the position of an argument in the argument list of a `printf()` statement. To separate it from other formatting options, the argument index is followed by a dollar sign ($). The first argument is referenced by "1$", the second by "2$", and so on.

For example, the `printf()` statement in the following code contains four format specifiers but only two variables in the argument list:

```
int x = 56;
double y = 78.9;
System.out.printf("%1$6d%2$6.2f%1$6d%2$6.2f", x, y);
```

The `printf()` statement displays the value of the first argument, x, in a field with a size of 6, and then it displays the second argument, y, in a field with a size of 6 with two decimal places. Then, the value of x is displayed again, followed by the value of y. The output appears as follows:

```
    56 78.90     56 78.90
```

938

Using the DecimalFormat Class

The DecimalFormat class provides ways to easily convert numbers into strings, allowing you to control the display of leading and trailing zeros, prefixes and suffixes, grouping (thousands) separators, and the decimal separator. You specify the formatting properties of DecimalFormat with a pattern String. The **pattern String** is composed of symbols that determine what the formatted number looks like; it is passed to the DecimalFormat class constructor.

The symbols you can use in a pattern String include:

- A pound sign (#), which represents a digit
- A period (.), which represents a decimal point
- A comma (,), which represents a thousands separator
- A zero (0), which represents leading and trailing zeros when it replaces the pound sign

 The pound sign is typed using Shift+3 on standard computer keyboards. It also is called an **octothorpe**, a number sign, a hash sign, square, tic-tac-toe, gate, and crunch.

For example, the following lines of code result in value being displayed as 12,345,678.90.

```
double value = 12345678.9;
DecimalFormat aFormat = new DecimalFormat("#,###,###,###.00");
System.out.printf("%s\n", aFormat.format(value));
```

A DecimalFormat object is created using the pattern #,###,###,###.00. When the object's format() method is used in the printf() statement, the first two pound signs and the comma between them are not used because value is not large enough to require those positions. The value is displayed with commas inserted where needed, and the decimal portion is displayed with a trailing *0* because the *0*s at the end of the pattern indicate that they should be used to fill out the number to two places.

When you use the DecimalFormat class, you must use the import statement import java.text.*;. Figure C-10 shows a class that creates a String pattern that it passes to the DecimalFormat constructor to create a moneyFormat object. The class displays an array of values, each in a field that is 10 characters wide. Some of the values require commas, and some do not. Figure C-11 shows the output.

```
import java.text.*;
public class DecimalFormatTest
{
    public static void main(String[] args)
    {
        String pattern = "###,###.00";
        DecimalFormat moneyFormat = new DecimalFormat(pattern);
        double[] list = {1.1, 23.23, 456.249, 7890.1, 987.5678, 65.0};
        int x;
        for(x = 0; x < list.length; ++x)
            System.out.printf("%10s\n", moneyFormat.format(list[x]));
    }
}
```

Figure C-10   The DecimalFormatTest class

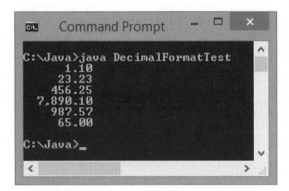

Figure C-11   Output of the DecimalFormatTest program

Key Terms

A **format string** in a printf() statement is a string of characters; it includes optional text (that is displayed literally) and one or more format specifiers.

A **format specifier** in a printf() statement is a placeholder for a numeric value.

The **argument index** in a printf() statement is an integer that indicates the position of an argument in the argument list.

A **pattern String** is composed of symbols that determine what a formatted number looks like.

An **octothorpe** is a pound sign.

Generating Random Numbers

In this appendix, you will:

- ◎ Understand computer-generated random numbers
- ◎ Use the `Math.random()` method
- ◎ Use the `Random` class

Understanding Computer-Generated Random Numbers

A **random number** is a number whose value cannot be predicted. Many types of programs use random numbers. For example, simulations that predict phenomena such as urban traffic patterns, crop production, and weather systems typically use random numbers. You might want to use random numbers to change your screen's appearance; for example, screen savers often use random numbers to define graphics so that a changing pattern remains interesting.

Random numbers are also used in many computer game applications. When you play games with human opponents, their choices are often unpredictable (and sometimes even irrational). Computers usually are predictable and rational, so when you play a game against a computer opponent, you frequently need to generate random numbers. For example, a guessing game would not be very interesting if you were asked to guess the same number every time you played.

Most computer programming languages, including Java, come with built-in methods that generate random numbers. The random numbers are calculated based on a starting value, called a **seed**. The random numbers generated using these methods are not truly random; they are **pseudorandom** in that they produce the same set of numbers whenever the seed is the same. Therefore, if you seed a random-number generator with a constant, you always receive the same sequence of values. Many computer programs use the time of day as a random number-generating seed. For game applications, this method works well, as a player is unlikely to reset his computer's clock and attempt to replay a game beginning at exactly the same moment in time.

 For applications in which randomness is more crucial than in game playing, you can use other methods (such as using the points in time at which a radioactive source decays) to generate truly random starting numbers.

There are two approaches to generating random numbers in Java. Both techniques are explained in this appendix and summarized in Table D-1.

Method/Class	Advantages
`Math.random()` method	You do not need to create an object
	You do not need to understand constructors and multiple methods
`Random` class and its methods	You can generate numbers in the format you need without arithmetic manipulation
	You can create reproducible results if necessary

Table D-1   Generating random numbers in Java

Using the Math.random() Method

Java's Math class provides a random() method that returns a double value in the range of 0.0 up to, but not including, 1.0. For example, the application in Figure D-1 generates three random numbers and displays them. Figure D-2 shows three successive executions of the program.

```java
public class SomeRandomNumbers
{
    public static void main (String[] args)
    {
        double ran;
        ran = Math.random();
        System.out.println(ran);
        ran = Math.random();
        System.out.println(ran);
        ran = Math.random();
        System.out.println(ran);
    }
}
```

Figure D-1   The SomeRandomNumbers class

Figure D-2   Three executions of the SomeRandomNumbers program

The values displayed in Figure D-2 appear to be random, but they are not typical of the values you need in a game-playing program. Usually, you need a relatively small number of whole values. For example, a game that involves a coin flip might only need two values to represent heads or tails, and a dice game might need only six values to represent rolls of a single die. Even in a complicated game in which 40 types of space aliens might attack the player, you need only 40 whole numbers generated to satisfy the program requirements.

For example, suppose you need a random number from 1 to 10. To change any value generated by the Math.random() method to fall between 0 and 10, you can multiply the generated number by 10. For example, the last three numbers in Figure D-2 would become approximately 2.53, 1.86, and 9.07. Then, you can eliminate the fractional part of each number by casting it to an int; after this step, every generated number will be a value from 0 to 9 inclusive. Finally, you can add 1 to a value so it falls in the range from 1 to 10 instead of 0 to 9. In short, the following statement generates a random number from 1 through 10 inclusive, and assigns it to ran:

```
int ran = 1 + (int)(Math.random() * 10);
```

Suppose that, instead of 1 through 10, you need random numbers from 1 through 13. (For example, standard decks of playing cards have 13 values from which you might want to select.) When you use the modulus operator (%) to find a remainder, the remainder is always a value from 0 to one less than the number. For example, if you divide any number by 4, the remainder is always a value from 0 through 3. Therefore, to find a number from 1 through 13, you can use a statement like the following:

```
int ranCardValue = ((int)(Math.random() * 100) % 13 + 1);
```

In this statement, a randomly generated value (for example, 0.447) is multiplied by 100 (producing 44.7). The result is converted to an int (44). The remainder after dividing by 13 is 5. Finally, 1 is added so the result is 1 through 13 instead of 0 through 12 (giving 6). In short, the general format for assigning a random number to a variable is:

```
int result = ((int)(Math.random() * 100) %
   HIGHEST_VALUE_WANTED + LOWEST_VALUE_WANTED);
```

 Instead of using 100 as the multiplier, you might prefer to use a higher value such as 1,000 or 10,000. For most games, the randomness generated using 100 is sufficient.

Using the Random Class

The Random class provides a generator that creates a list of random numbers. To use this class, you must use one of the following import statements:

```
import java.util.*;
import java.util.Random;
```

You also must instantiate a random-number generator object using one of the following constructors:

- Random(), in which the seed comes from the operating system; this constructor sets the seed of the random-number generator to a value that is probably distinct from any other invocation of this constructor

- Random(long seed), in which you provide a starting seed so that your results are reproducible

After you create a random-number generator object, you can use any of the methods in Table D-2 to get the next random number from the generator.

Method	Explanation
nextInt(int n)	Returns a pseudorandom int value between 0 (inclusive) and the specified value *n* (exclusive), drawn from the random-number generator's sequence
nextInt()	Returns a pseudorandom int value between 0 (inclusive) and 1.0 (exclusive), drawn from the random-number generator's sequence
nextLong()	Returns the next pseudorandom long value from the generator's sequence
nextFloat()	Returns the next pseudorandom float value between 0.0 and 1.0 from the generator's sequence
nextDouble()	Returns the next pseudorandom double value between 0.0 and 1.0 from the generator's sequence
nextBoolean()	Returns the next pseudorandom boolean value from the generator's sequence

Table D-2 Selected Random class methods

For example, Figure D-3 contains an application that declares a Random generator named ran, using the version of the constructor that takes no arguments. This ensures that the results are different each time the application runs. The program then defines LIMIT as 10, and calls ran.nextInt(LIMIT) three times, displaying the results (see Figure D-4).

```java
import java.util.*;
public class SomeRandomNumbers2
{
    public static void main(String[] args)
    {
        Random ran = new Random();
        final int LIMIT = 10;
        System.out.print(ran.nextInt(LIMIT) + " ");
        System.out.print(ran.nextInt(LIMIT) + " ");
        System.out.println(ran.nextInt(LIMIT));
    }
}
```

Figure D-3 The SomeRandomNumbers2 class

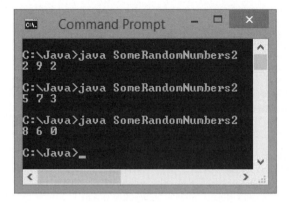

Figure D-4 Three executions of the SomeRandomNumbers2 program

In Figure D-4, each displayed value falls between 0 and LIMIT. (Of course, to select values between 1 and LIMIT inclusive, you could add 1 to each result.)

Figure D-5 shows a class using the version of the Random constructor that takes an argument (shaded). In this example, a value between 0 and 6 inclusive is generated 15 times. Figure D-6 shows the output when the program is run three times. Although the 15 numbers displayed for each execution constitute a random list, the list is identical in each program execution. You use a seed when you want random but reproducible results. For games, you usually want to use the no-argument version of the Random constructor.

```java
import java.util.*;
public class SomeRandomNumbers3
{
    public static void main(String[] args)
    {
        Random ran = new Random(129867L);
        final int TIMES = 15;
        final int LIMIT = 7;
        for(int x = 0; x < TIMES; ++x)
            System.out.print(ran.nextInt(LIMIT) + " ");
        System.out.println();
    }
}
```

Figure D-5 The SomeRandomNumbers3 class

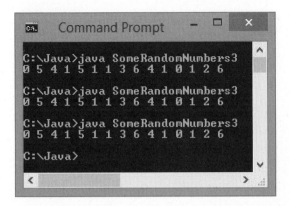

Figure D-6 Three executions of the SomeRandomNumbers3 program

Key Terms

A **random number** is a number whose value cannot be predicted.

A **seed** is a starting value.

Pseudorandom numbers appear to be random, but are the same set of numbers whenever the seed is the same.

Javadoc

In this appendix, you will:

- ◎ Learn about the Javadoc documentation generator
- ◎ Understand Javadoc comment types
- ◎ Generate Javadoc documentation

The Javadoc Documentation Generator

Javadoc is a documentation generator created by Sun Microsystems that allows you to generate Application Programming Interface (API) documentation in **HTML (Hypertext Markup Language)** format. HTML is a relatively simple language used to create Web pages; you can also use it to create Java documentation from source code. In Chapter 1, you learned that you can place both line and block comments anywhere in a program to provide documentation that can be useful both to yourself and others. A **Javadoc comment** is a special form of block comment that provides a standard way to document Java code. After you write Javadoc comments, they can be interpreted by special utility programs that generate an HTML document. The resulting HTML document provides an attractive format for the documentation when you open it in a browser. Most class libraries, both commercial and open source, provide Javadoc documents. If you have visited the Java Web site to research how to use a class, you most likely have viewed documentation created by the Javadoc utility.

In Chapter 1, you learned that block comments start with /* and end with */, that Javadoc comments start with /** and end with */, and that both comment types can span as many lines as necessary. For symmetry, many developers end their Javadoc comments with **/. By convention, asterisks start intermediate lines in a Javadoc comment. This is not required, but it helps you more easily distinguish comments from code.

Javadoc comments can contain tags. A **Javadoc tag** is a keyword within a comment that the Javadoc tool can process. Tags begin with an at-sign (@) and use a limited vocabulary of keywords. Some commonly used Javadoc tags include:

- @author: Describes the author of a document
- @param: Describes a parameter of a method or constructor
- @return: Describes the return type of a method
- @throws: Describes an exception a method may throw
- @exception: Describes an exception

Javadoc Comment Types

There are two types of Javadoc comments:

- Class-level comments that provide a description of a class
- Member-level comments that describe the purposes of class members

Class-level Javadoc comments provide a description of a class; you place class-level comments above the code that declares a class. Class-level comments frequently contain author tags and a description of the class. Figure E-1 shows a shaded class-level comment in a class.

```
/**
 * @author Joyce Farrell.
 * The Employee class contains data about one employee.
 * Fields include an ID number and an hourly pay rate.
 */
public class Employee
{
    private int idNum;
    private double hourlyPay;
    public Employee(int id, double pay)
    {
        idNum = id;
        hourlyPay = pay;
    }
    int getIdNum()
    {
        return idNum;
    }
    void setIdNum(int id)
    {
        idNum = id;
    }
}
```

Figure E-1 An Employee class with class-level comments

Member-level Javadoc comments describe the fields, methods, and constructors of a class. Method and constructor comments may contain tags that describe the parameters, and method comments may also contain return tags. Figure E-2 shows a class with some shaded member-level comments.

```
/**
 * @author Joyce Farrell.
 * The Employee2 class contains data about one employee.
 * Fields include an ID number and an hourly pay rate.
 */
public class Employee2
{
    /**
     * Employee ID number
     */
    private int idNum;
    /**
     * Employee hourly pay
     */
```

Figure E-2 An Employee2 class with class-level and member-level comments *(continues)*

(continued)

```java
    private double hourlyPay;
    /**
     * Sole constructor for Employee2
     */
    public Employee2(int id, double pay)
    {
        idNum = id;
        hourlyPay = pay;
    }
    /**
     * Returns the Employee2 ID number
     *
     * @return int
     */
    int getIdNum()
    {
        return idNum;
    }
    /**
     * Sets the Employee2 ID number
     *
     * @param id employee ID number
     */
    void setIdNum(int id)
    {
        idNum = id;
    }
}
```

Figure E-2   An `Employee2` class with class-level and member-level comments

Like all program comments, Javadoc comments *can* contain anything. However, you should follow the conventions for Javadoc comments. For example, developers expect all Javadoc comments to begin with an uppercase letter, and they recommend that method comments start with a verb such as "Returns" or "Sets." For more information, go to the Java Web site.

Generating Javadoc Documentation

To generate the Javadoc documentation from your class, you should do the following:

1. Create a folder in which to store your class. For example, you might store the Employee2.java file in a folder named Employee2.

2. Within the folder, you can create a Documents subfolder to hold the documentation that you generate. However, if you omit this step and use the syntax described in Step 3, the folder is created for you automatically.

3. Go to the command prompt and navigate to the directory that holds the Employee2.java file. (See Appendix A for information on finding the command prompt and changing directories.) From the command prompt, run the following command:

```
javadoc -d Documents *.java
```

The –d is the directory option. If you omit it, all the generated files are saved in the current directory. By including this option, you indicate that the files should be saved in the Documents directory.

 To see the author's name in the resulting documentation, change the Javadoc command to the following:
```
javadoc -d Documents -author *.java
```

 If you are using the jGRASP development environment to create your Java programs, you can execute the Javadoc command with a button click. You can download the jGRASP program from *http://jGRASP.org*.

4. Navigate to the Documents folder. You will see a number of generated files, as shown in Figure E-3. The list includes HTML documents with information about all the constants in your class, all the deprecated methods in your class, and so on. (The Employee2 class has no constants or deprecated methods, but you can open the files and view the format that the contents would take if they existed.)

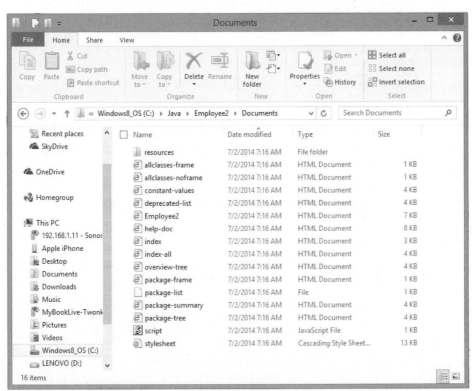

Figure E-3 Contents of the Employee2 Documents folder in File Explorer

On your computer, you might see a different name for the file type for HTML documents, depending on how your default options have been set.

The index.html file provides an index of all class interface, constructor, field, and method names; when you double-click it, the file opens in your default browser. Figure E-4 shows how the first part of the index.html file for Employee2 appears in Internet Explorer. If you have searched the Java Web site for documentation, the format of the page in Figure E-4 is familiar to you. The class name and other information appear in a font and style consistent with other classes in the Java API. You can see information about the class constructor and the notes that you added in your comments. You see inheritance information—Employee2 descends directly from Object. The format of this documentation is familiar to users, making it much easier for them to find what they need than if each developer created documentation formats independently.

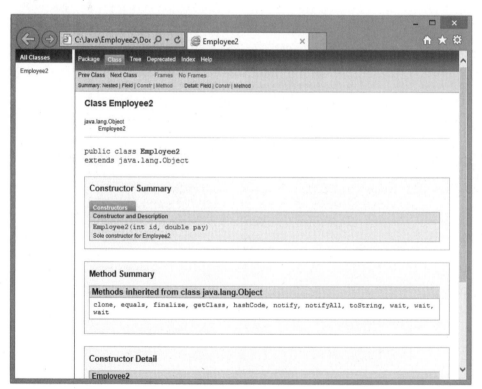

Figure E-4   The Employee2 class documentation in Internet Explorer

The Javadoc tool will run on .java source files that are stub files with no method bodies. This means you can write documentation comments and run the Javadoc tool when you are first designing classes, before you have written implementations for the class's methods.

Writing acceptable Javadoc comments requires adherence to some style standards. For example, professionals recommend that multiple @author tags should be listed in chronological order, with the creator of the class listed at the top, and that multiple @param tags should be listed in argument-declaration order. Additionally, Javadoc comments can provide hyperlinks that allow navigation from one document to another. For example, when a class contains a field that is an object of another class, you might want to link to the other class's documentation. For more information, see the recommendations from Java developers at the Java Web site.

Specifying Visibility of Javadoc Documentation

By default, Javadoc documents only `public` and `protected` members of an API. In other words, even if you write Javadoc comments for `private` members, the comments do not appear in the generated documentation unless you take special action to make them visible. Although the index.html file contains details about the `Employee2` class's constructor and methods, there is no information about the `private` fields `idNum` and `hourlyPay`. To generate that documentation, you must specify `private` visibility by using the following `javadoc` command:

```
javadoc -d Documents -private *.java
```

Figure E-5 shows the documentation generated by this command. You can see that the newly generated documentation includes a Field Summary section. It lists the fields in alphabetical order preceded by their access specifiers and data types. Each field identifier is followed by the appropriate description that was provided in the Javadoc comment in the source code.

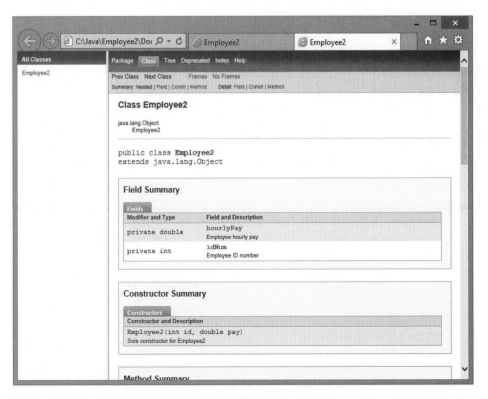

Figure E-5 The `Employee2` class documentation when `private` members are included

You can specify four types of visibility:

- `public`—Displays `public` members only

- `protected`—Displays `public` and `protected` members only. This is the default option.

- `package`—Displays package classes and members in addition to `public` and `protected` members

- `private`—Displays all members

Key Terms

Javadoc is a documentation generator created by Sun Microsystems that allows you to generate Application Programming Interface (API) documentation in HTML format from Java source code.

HTML (Hypertext Markup Language) is a relatively simple language used to create Web pages.

A **Javadoc comment** is a special form of block comment that provides a standard way to document Java code.

A **Javadoc tag** is a keyword within a comment that the Javadoc tool can process.

Class-level Javadoc comments provide a description of a class.

Member-level Javadoc comments describe the fields, methods, and constructors of a class.

Glossary

A

absolute path—a complete file path that does not require any other information to locate a file on a system.

abstract class—a class from which no concrete objects can be instantiated, but which can serve as a basis for inheritance. Abstract classes usually have one or more empty abstract methods. Contrast with *concrete class*.

abstract data type—a type whose implementation is hidden and accessed through its public methods.

abstract method—a method declared with the keyword abstract and that has no body; a subclass must override each base class abstract method.

Abstract Windows Toolkit (AWT)—a set of GUI components that predates Swing and is less portable than the set of Swing components.

abstraction—the programming feature that allows a method name to encapsulate multiple statements.

accelerator—a key combination that causes a menu item to be chosen, whether or not the menu item is visible.

access modifier—defines the circumstances under which a class can be accessed; often used interchangeably with *access specifier*.

access specifier—defines the circumstances under which a class can be accessed; often used interchangeably with *access modifier*.

accessor methods—methods that return information about an object.

accumulating—the process of repeatedly increasing a value by some amount to produce a total.

action key—a keyboard key that does not generate a character.

actual parameters—the arguments in a method call. Contrast with *formal parameters*.

acyclic gradient—a fill pattern in which a color shift occurs once between two points.

adapter class—a class that implements all the methods in an interface, providing an empty body for each method.

add and assign operator—an operator that alters the value of the operand on the left by adding the operand on the right to it; it is composed of a plus sign and an equal sign (+=).

ad-hoc polymorphism—polymorphism that occurs when a single method name can be used with a variety of data types because various implementations exist; it is another name for method overloading.

aggregation—a type of composition in which a class contains one or more members of another class that would continue to exist without the object that contains them.

algorithm—a process or set of steps that solves a problem.

Allman style—the indent style in which curly braces are aligned and each occupies its own line; it is named for Eric Allman, a programmer who popularized the style. Contrast with *K & R style*.

alpha value—the level of a color's transparency.

ambiguous—describes a situation in which the compiler cannot determine which method to use.

anonymous classes—nested, local classes that have no identifier.

anonymous object—an unnamed object.

applet—a Java program that is called from within another application, frequently a Web page.

application files—files that store software instructions.

application software—programs that perform tasks for users. Contrast with *system software*.

application-triggered painting—describes a painting operation that occurs when a program requests it, usually because the internal state of a component has changed. Contrast with *system-triggered painting*.

arc—a portion of a circle's circumference.

architecturally neutral—describes the feature of Java that allows a program to run on any platform.

argument index—in a `printf()` statement, an integer that indicates the position of an argument in the argument list.

arguments—data items sent to methods in a method call.

arithmetic operators—operators used to perform calculations with values.

array—a named list of data items that all have the same type.

ascending order—the order of objects arranged from lowest to highest value. See also *descending order*.

ascent—one of three measures of a Font's height; it is the height of an uppercase character from a baseline to the top of the character. See also *leading* and *descent*.

ASCII—an acronym for American Standard Code for Information Interchange, a character set widely used to represent computer data.

assertion—a Java language feature that can help detect logic errors and debug a program.

assignment—the act of providing a value for a variable.

assignment operator—the equal sign (=); any value to the right of the equal sign is assigned to the variable on the left of the equal sign.

associativity—describes the order in which operands are used with operators.

at run time—describes the period of time during which a program executes.

attributes—the characteristics that define an object as part of a class.

B

back buffer—the offscreen image during double buffering.

base class—a class that is used as a basis for inheritance.

batch processing—processing that involves performing the same tasks with many records, one after the other.

binary files—files that contain data that has not been encoded as text; their contents are in binary format.

binary numbering system—a numbering system based on two digits, 0 and 1, in which each column represents a value two times higher than the column to its right.

binary operators—operators that require two operands.

bit—a binary digit, 0 or 1, used to represent computerized values.

black box—a device that can be used solely in terms of input and output without regard to how it works internally.

blank `final`—a `final` variable that has not yet been assigned a value.

block—the code between a pair of curly braces.

block comments—comments that start with a forward slash and an asterisk (/*) and end with an asterisk and a forward slash (*/). Block comments can appear on a line by themselves, on a line before executable code, or on a line after executable code. Block comments can also extend across as many lines as needed. Contrast with *line comments*.

block line transfer or **blitting**—the act of copying contents from one surface to another.

Boolean values—true or false values; every computer decision results in a Boolean value.

`boolean` variable—a variable of the `boolean` data type that can hold only one of two values—`true` or `false`.

border layout manager—a layout manager that divides a container into regions.

bubble sort—a type of sort that operates by comparing pairs of items and swapping them if they are out of order so that the smallest items "bubble" to the top of the list, eventually creating a sorted list.

buffer—a memory location that holds data temporarily—for example, when creating a `StringBuilder` object or during input and output operations.

bug—a flaw or mistake in a computer program.

button—a GUI component typically used to trigger an action or make a selection when the user clicks it.

button group—a GUI component that groups other components, such as check boxes, so a user can select only one at a time.

byte—the data type that holds very small integers, from –128 to 127.

bytecode—programming statements that have been compiled into binary format.

C

call a procedure—to invoke a method.

call stack—the memory location where the computer stores the list of memory locations to which the system must return when methods end.

called method—a term used to describe the relationship between two methods; a method that is invoked by another.

calling method—a term used to describe the relationship between two methods; a method that invokes another.

camel casing—a naming style in which an identifier begins with a lowercase letter and subsequent words within the identifier are capitalized. Contrast with *Pascal casing*.

capacity—an attribute of an `ArrayList` whose value is the number of items it can hold without having to increase its size. Also, with a `StringBuilder` object, the actual length of the buffer, as opposed to that of the string contained in the buffer.

cast operator—an operator that performs an explicit type conversion; it is created by placing the desired result type in parentheses before the expression to be converted.

catch block—a segment of code that can handle an exception that might be thrown by the `try` block that precedes it.

catch or specify requirement—the Java rule that checked exceptions require catching or declaration.

char—the data type that holds any single character.

character—any letter, number, or special symbol (such as a punctuation mark) that comprises data.

Character class—a class whose instances can hold a single character value. This class also defines methods that can manipulate or inspect single-character data.

check box—a GUI element with a label and a clickable square that is frequently used to turn an option on or off.

checked exceptions—exceptions that a programmer should plan for and from which a program should be able to recover. Contrast with *unchecked exceptions*.

child class—a derived class.

class—a group or collection of objects with common properties.

class body—the set of data items and methods between the curly braces that follow the class header.

class client—an application or class that instantiates objects of another class. See also *class user*.

class definition—a description of attributes and methods of objects instantiated from a class.

class diagram—a visual tool that provides an overview of a class. It consists of a rectangle divided into three sections—the top section contains the name of the class, the middle section contains the names and data types of the attributes, and the bottom section contains the methods.

class methods—static methods that do not have a `this` reference (because they have no object associated with them).

class user—an application or class that instantiates objects of another prewritten class. See also *class client*.

class variables—static variables that are shared by every instantiation of a class.

class-level Javadoc comments—Javadoc comments that provide a description of a class.

clean build—a compilation that is created after deleting all previously compiled versions of a class.

client method—a method that calls another method.

close the file—to make a file no longer available to an application.

closer in scope—a term that describes the status of a local variable over others that it shadows.

collision—describes a class naming conflict.

combo box—a GUI component that combines a display area showing a default option and a list box containing additional options.

comes into scope—describes what happens to a variable when it is declared. Contrast with *goes out of scope*.

comma-separated values (CSV)—fields that are separated with a comma.

commands—program statements.

comment out—the technique of turning a program statement into a comment so the compiler will not execute its command.

comparison operator—a relational operator.

compiler—a program that translates language statements into machine code. A compiler translates an entire program before executing it. Contrast with *interpreter*.

compile-time error—an error for which the compiler detects a violation of language syntax rules and is unable to translate the source code to machine code.

composition—describes the relationship between classes when an object of one class is a data field within another class. See also *has-a relationship*.

compound Boolean expression—an expression that contains an AND or OR operator.

compound condition—the condition that is tested in a compound Boolean expression.

computer file—a collection of stored information in a computer system.

computer program—a set of instructions that tells a computer what to do; software.

computer simulations—programs that attempt to mimic real-world activities so that their processes can be improved or so that users can better understand how the real-world processes operate.

concatenated—describes values that are added onto the end of another value.

concatenation—the process of joining a variable to a string to create a longer string.

concrete class—a nonabstract class from which objects can be instantiated. Contrast with *abstract class*.

conditional operator—an operator that requires three expressions separated with a question mark and a colon; the operator is used as an abbreviated version of the `if...else` structure.

confirm dialog box—a window that can be created using the `showConfirmDialog()` method in the `JOptionPane` class and that displays the options Yes, No, and Cancel.

console applications—programs that support character or text output to a computer screen.

constant—describes values that cannot be changed during the execution of an application.

constructor—a method that establishes an object.

consume—to retrieve and discard an entry without using it.

container—a type of component that holds other components so they can be treated as a single entity.

containment hierarchy—a tree of components that has a top-level container as its root (that is, at its uppermost level).

content pane—a component that contains all the visible components in a top-level container's user interface.

counted loop—a definite loop.

counter-controlled loop—a definite loop. Contrast with *event-controlled loop*.

counting—the process of continually incrementing a variable to keep track of the number of occurrences of some event.

crash—a premature, unexpected, and inelegant end to a program.

cyclic gradient—a fill pattern in which a shift between colors occurs repeatedly between two points.

D

data fields—data variables declared in a class outside of any method.

data files—files that consist of related records that contain facts and figures, such as employee numbers, names, and salaries.

data type—describes the type of data that can be stored in a variable, how much memory the item occupies, and what types of operations can be performed on the data.

dead code—unreachable statements.

debugging—the process of locating and repairing a program's error.

decimal numbering system—the numbering system based on 10 digits, 0 through 9, in which each column value is 10 times the value of the column to its right.

decision structure—a logical structure that involves choosing between alternative courses of action based on some value within a program.

declaration—another name for a method header; also, the statement that assigns a data type and identifier to a variable.

decrementing—the act of subtracting 1 from a variable.

default constructor—a constructor that requires no arguments.

default package—the unnamed package in which a class is placed if no package is specified.

definite loop—a loop that executes a predetermined number of times; a counted loop. Contrast with *indefinite loop*.

derived class—a class that inherits from a base class.

descending order—the order of objects arranged from highest to lowest value. See also *ascending order*.

descent—one of three measures of a Font's height; it measures the part of characters that "hang below" the baseline, such as the tails on the lowercase letters *g* and *j*. See also *ascent* and *leading*.

development environment—a set of tools that helps programmers by providing such features as displaying a language's keywords in color.

dialog box—a GUI object resembling a window that displays messages.

direct access files—random access files.

directories—elements in a storage organization hierarchy. See also *folders*.

divide and assign operator—an operator that alters the value of the operand on the left by dividing the operand on the right into it; it is composed of a slash and an equal sign (/=).

documentation comments—comments that automatically generate well-formatted program documentation.

do-nothing loop—a loop that performs no actions other than looping.

do...while loop—a loop that executes a loop body at least one time; it checks the loop control variable at the bottom of the loop after one repetition has occurred.

double—a data type that can hold a floating-point value of up to 14 or 15 significant digits of accuracy. Contrast with *float*.

double buffering—the default buffering strategy in which JPanels are drawn offscreen when they are updated and displayed only when complete.

double-precision floating-point number—a type of value that is stored in a double.

dual-alternative selection—a selection that results in one of two possible courses of action.

dummy values—values the user enters that are not "real" data, but just signals to stop data entry.

dynamic method binding—the ability of an application to select the correct subclass method when the program executes. See also *late method binding*.

dynamically resizable—describes an object whose size can change during program execution.

E

echoing the input—the act of repeating the user's entry as output so the user can visually confirm the entry's accuracy.

editable—describes a component that can accept keystrokes.

element—one variable or object in an array.

else clause—the part of an if...else statement that executes when the evaluated Boolean expression is false.

else...if clause—a format used in nested if statements in which each instance of else and its subsequent if are placed on the same line.

empty body—a block with no statements in it.

empty statement—a statement that contains only a semicolon.

encapsulation—the act of hiding data and methods within an object.

endcap styles—styles applied to the ends of lines that do not join with other lines; they include CAP_BUTT, CAP_ROUND, and CAP_SQUARE.

enhanced for loop—a language construct that cycles through an array without specifying the starting and ending points for the loop control variable.

enum constants—the allowed values for an enumerated data type.

enumerated data type—a programmer-created data type with a fixed set of values.

enumeration—a data type that consists of a list of values.

equivalency operator—the operator composed of two equal signs that compares values and returns true if they are equal.

escape sequence—a sequence that begins with a backslash followed by a character; the pair frequently represents a nonprinting character.

event—a result when a user takes action on a component.

event-controlled loop—an indefinite loop in which the number of executions is determined by user actions. Contrast with *counter-controlled loop*.

event-driven program—a program in which the user might initiate any number of events in any order.

event handler—a method that executes because it is called automatically when an appropriate event occurs.

exception—in object-oriented terminology, an unexpected or error condition.

exception handling—an object-oriented technique for managing or resolving errors.

exception specification—the practice of using the keyword throws followed by an Exception type in the method header. An exception specification is required when a method throws a checked Exception that it will not catch but will be caught by a different method.

executing—the act of carrying out a program statement or program.

explicit conversion—the data type transformation caused by using a cast operator.

extended—describes classes that have descended from another class.

extends—a keyword used to achieve inheritance in Java.

F

factory methods—methods that assist in object creation.

FAQs—frequently asked questions.

fault-tolerant—describes applications that are designed so that they continue to operate, possibly at a reduced level, when some part of the system fails.

field—a data variable declared in a class outside of any method. In reference to storage, a group of characters that has some meaning.

file channel—an object that is an avenue for reading and writing a file.

fill patterns—patterns that describe how drawing objects are filled in.

final—the keyword that precedes named constants, that describes superclass methods that cannot be overridden in a subclass, and describes classes in which all methods are final.

finally block—a block of code that executes at the end of a try...catch sequence.

fixed method binding—the opposite of dynamic method binding; it occurs when a subclass method is selected while the program compiles rather than while it is running. See also *static method binding*.

flag—a variable that holds a value (often true or false) to indicate whether some condition has been met.

float—a data type that can hold a floating-point value of up to six or seven significant digits of accuracy. Contrast with *double*.

floating-point—describes a number that contains decimal positions.

floating-point division—the operation in which two values are divided and either or both are floating-point values.

flowchart—a tool that helps programmers plan a program's logic by writing the steps in diagram form, as a series of shapes connected by arrows.

flow layout manager—a layout manager that places components in rows; when any row is filled, additional components automatically spill into the next row.

flushing—an operation to clear bytes that have been sent to a buffer for output but that have not yet been output to a hardware device.

folders—elements in a storage organization hierarchy. See also *directories*.

font—the size, weight, and style of a typeface.

for loop—a loop that can be used when a definite number of loop iterations is required.

foreach loop—the enhanced for loop.

formal parameters—the variables in a method declaration that accept the values from actual parameters. Contrast with *actual parameters*.

format specifier—in a `printf()` statement, a placeholder for a numeric value.

format string—in a `printf()` statement, a string of characters that includes optional text (that is displayed literally) and one or more format specifiers.

fragile—describes classes that are prone to errors.

frame—a GUI component that is similar to a window, but that has a title bar and border.

fully qualified identifier—describes a filename that includes the entire hierarchy in which a class is stored.

function—a method with no side effect, in some programming languages.

fundamental classes—basic classes contained in the `java.lang` package that are automatically imported into every program. Contrast with *optional classes*.

G

garbage value—the unknown value stored in an uninitialized variable.

generic programming—a feature of languages that allows methods to be used safely with multiple data types.

glass pane—a pane that resides above the content pane in a container. It can contain tool tips.

goes out of scope—describes what happens to a variable at the end of the block in which it is declared. Contrast with *comes into scope*.

gradient fill—a gradual shift from one color at one coordinate point to a different color at a second coordinate point.

graphical user interfaces (GUIs)—environments that allow users to interact with a program in a graphical environment.

GUI components—graphical user interface components, such as buttons and text fields, with which the user can interact.

H

hardware—the general term for computer equipment.

has-a relationship—a relationship based on composition.

hash code—a calculated number used to identify an object.

header—the first line of a method; its declaration.

heavyweight components—components that require interaction with the local operating system. Contrast with *lightweight components*.

height of a font—the sum of its leading, ascent, and descent.

hexadecimal numbering system—a numbering system based on 16 digits, 0 through F, in which each column represents a value 16 times higher than the column to its right.

high-level programming language—a language that uses a vocabulary of reasonable terms, such as *read*, *write*, or *add*, instead of referencing the sequences of on and off switches that perform these tasks. Contrast with *low-level programming language*.

HTML (Hypertext Markup Language)—a simple language used to create Web pages.

I

identifier—the name of a program component such as a class, object, or variable.

`if` clause—the part of an `if...else` statement that executes when the evaluated Boolean expression is true.

if...else statement—a statement that provides the mechanism to perform one action when a Boolean expression evaluates as true, and to perform a different action when a Boolean expression evaluates as false.

if statement—a single-alternative selection statement.

immutable—describes objects that cannot be changed.

implementation—the actions that execute within a method; the method body.

implementation hiding—a principle of object-oriented programming that describes the encapsulation of method details within a class.

implicit conversion—the automatic transformation of one data type to another. Also called *promotion*.

import statement—a Java statement that allows access to a built-in Java class that is contained in a package.

inclusion polymorphism—the situation in which a single method implementation can be used with a variety of related objects because they are objects of subclasses of the parameter type. See also *pure polymorphism*.

incrementing—the act of adding 1 to a variable.

indefinite loop—a loop in which the final number of iterations is unknown. Contrast with *definite loop*.

index—a subscript.

infinite loop—a loop that never ends.

information hiding—the object-oriented programming principle used when creating private access for data fields; a class's private data can be changed or manipulated only by a class's own methods, and not by methods that belong to other classes.

inheritance—a mechanism that enables one class to inherit, or assume, both the behavior and the attributes of another class.

initialization—the act of making an assignment at the time of variable declaration.

initialization list—a series of values provided for an array when it is declared.

inlining—an automatic process that optimizes performance by replacing calls to methods with implementations.

inner block—a block contained in an outer block.

inner classes—nested classes that require an instance. See also *nonstatic member classes*.

inner loop—a loop that is contained entirely within another loop.

input dialog box—a GUI object that asks a question and provides a text field in which the user can enter a response.

insertion sort—a sorting algorithm that operates by comparing each list element with earlier ones and, if the element is out of order, opening a spot for it by moving all subsequent elements down the list.

instance—an existing object of a class.

instance methods—methods used with object instantiations. See also *nonstatic methods*.

instance variables—the data components of a class.

instant access files—random access files.

instantiation—the process of creating an object.

int—the data type used to declare variables and constants that store integers in the range of −2,147,483,648 to +2,147,483,647.

integer—a whole number without decimal places.

integer division—the operation in which one integer value is divided by another; the result contains no fractional part.

interactive program—a program in which the user makes direct requests.

interface—a construct similar to a class, except that all of its methods must be abstract and all of its data (if any) must be `static final`; it declares method headers, but not the instructions within those methods. Also used to describe the part of a method that a client sees and uses—it includes the method's return type, name, and arguments.

interpreter—a program that translates language statements into machine code. An interpreter translates and executes one statement at a time. Contrast with *compiler*.

invoke—to call or execute a method.

is-a relationship—the relationship between an object and the class of which it is a member.

iteration—one loop execution.

J

Java—an object-oriented programming language used both for general-purpose business applications and for interactive, World Wide Web-based Internet applications.

Java API—the application programming interface, a collection of information about how to use every prewritten Java class.

Java applications—stand-alone Java programs.

Java ARchive (JAR) file—a file that compresses the stored data.

Java Enterprise Edition (EE)—a Java edition that includes all of the classes in the Java SE, plus a number of classes that are more useful to programs running on servers.

Java Foundation Classes (JFC)—selected classes from the `java.awt` package, including `Swing` component classes.

Java interpreter—the program that checks bytecode and communicates with the operating system, executing the bytecode instructions line by line within the Java Virtual Machine.

Java Micro Edition (ME)—a Java platform that is used for small devices such as cell phones.

Java SE 8—the most recent version of Java. The full, official name is Java Platform, Standard Edition 8.

Java Virtual Machine (JVM)—a hypothetical (software-based) computer on which Java runs.

`java.lang`—the package that is implicitly imported into every Java program and that contains the fundamental classes.

Javadoc—a documentation generator that creates Application Programming Interface (API) documentation in Hypertext Markup Language (HTML) format from Java source code.

Javadoc comment—a special form of block comment that provides a standard way to document Java code.

Javadoc tag—a keyword within a comment that the Javadoc tool can process.

JDK—the Java Standard Edition Development Kit.

jGRASP—a development environment and source code editor.

juncture styles—styles applied to lines that join; they include `JOIN_MITER`, `JOIN_ROUND`, and `JOIN_BEVEL`.

K

K & R style—the indent style in which the opening brace follows the header line; it is named for Kernighan and Ritchie, who wrote the first book on the C programming language. Contrast with *Allman style*.

key field—the field in a record that makes the record unique from all others.

keyboard buffer—a small area of memory where keystrokes are stored before they are retrieved into a program. Also called the *type-ahead buffer*.

keywords—the words that are part of a programming language.

L

label—an uneditable GUI component that is most often used to provide information for a user.

late method binding—the ability of an application to select the correct subclass method when the program executes. See also *dynamic method binding*.

layout manager—a class that controls component positioning in a UI environment.

leading—one of three measures of a Font's height; it is the amount of space between baselines. See also *ascent* and *descent*.

leaf menu item—a menu item that does not bring up another menu; in other words, it is at the end of a branch.

lexicographical comparison—a comparison based on the integer Unicode values of characters.

library of classes—a folder that provides a convenient grouping for classes.

lightweight components—components written completely in Java that do not have to rely on the code written to run in the local operating system. Contrast with *heavyweight components*.

line comments—comments that start with two forward slashes (//) and continue to the end of the current line. Line comments can appear on a line by themselves or at the end of a line following executable code. Contrast with *block comments*.

listener—an object that is interested in and reacts to an event.

literal constant—a value that is taken literally at each use. See also *unnamed constant*.

literal string—a series of characters that appear exactly as entered. Any literal string in Java appears between double quotation marks.

local classes—nested classes that are local to a block of code.

local variable—a variable known only within the boundaries of a method.

logic—describes the order of program statements that produce correct results.

logic error—a programming bug that allows a source program to be translated to an executable program successfully, but that produces incorrect results.

logical AND operator—an operator used between Boolean expressions to determine whether both are true. The AND operator is written as two ampersands (&&).

logical OR operator—an operator used between Boolean expressions to determine whether either expression is true. The OR operator is written as two pipes (||).

long—the data type that holds very large integers, from −9,223,372,036,854,775,808 to 9,223,372,036,854,775,807.

look and feel—the elements of design, style, and functionality in a user interface.

loop—a structure that allows repeated execution of a block of statements.

loop body—the block of statements that executes when the Boolean expression that controls the loop is true.

loop control variable—a variable whose value determines whether loop execution continues.

loop fusion—the technique of combining two loops into one.

lossless conversion—a data type conversion in which no data is lost.

lossy conversion—a data type conversion in which some data is lost.

low-level programming language—a language that corresponds closely to a computer processor's circuitry. Contrast with *high-level programming language*. Compare with *machine language*.

lvalue—an expression that can appear on the left side of an assignment statement. Contrast with *rvalue*.

M

machine code—machine language.

machine language—circuitry-level language; a series of on and off switches. Compare with *low-level programming language*.

magic number—a value that does not have immediate, intuitive meaning or a number that cannot be explained without additional knowledge. Unnamed constants are magic numbers.

matrix—a two-dimensional array.

member-level Javadoc comments— Javadoc comments that describe the fields, methods, and constructors of a class.

menu bar—a horizontal strip that is placed at the top of a container and that contains user options.

menus—lists of user options.

method—a program module that contains a series of statements that carry out a task.

method body—the set of statements between curly braces that follow the method header and carry out the method's actions.

method header—the declaration or first line of a method that contains information about how other methods interact with it.

method's type—the method's return type.

mission critical—a term that describes any crucial process in an organization.

mnemonic—a key that causes an already visible menu item to be chosen.

modulus operator—the percent sign; when it is used with two integers, the result is an integer with the value of the remainder after division takes place. Also called the *remainder operator*; sometimes called just *mod*.

multidimensional arrays—arrays that contain two or more dimensions.

multiple inheritance—the capability to inherit from more than one class; Java does not support multiple inheritance.

multiply and assign operator—an operator that alters the value of the operand on the left by multiplying the operand on the right by it; it is composed of an asterisk and an equal sign.

mutator methods—methods that set field values.

N

named constant—a named memory location whose value cannot change during program execution.

NaN—a three-letter abbreviation for *Not a Number*.

nanosecond—one-billionth of a second.

nested—describes the relationship of statements, blocks, or classes when one contains the other.

nested classes—classes contained in other classes.

nested if statements—describes if statements when one is contained within the other.

new operator—an operator that allocates the memory needed to hold an object.

nonabstract method—a method that is inherited.

nonstatic member classes—nested classes that require an instance. See also *inner classes*.

nonstatic methods—methods used with object instantiations. See also *instance methods*.

nonvolatile storage—storage that does not require power to retain information. Contrast with *volatile storage*.

NOT operator (!)—the operator that negates the result of any Boolean expression.

null String—an empty String created by typing a set of quotes with nothing between them.

numeric constant—a number whose value is taken literally at each use.

O

object—an instance of a class.

Object class—a class defined in the java.lang package that is imported automatically into every Java program; every Java class descends from the Object class.

object-oriented programs—programs that use a style of programming that involves creating classes, creating objects from those classes, and creating applications that use those objects. Contrast with *procedural programming*.

octothorpe—the pound sign.

one-dimensional array—an array that contains one column of values and whose elements are accessed using a single subscript. See also *single-dimensional array*.

open a file—the action that creates an object and associates a stream of bytes with it.

operand—a value used in an arithmetic statement.

operator precedence—the rules for the order in which parts of a mathematical expression are evaluated.

optional classes—classes that reside in packages that must be explicitly imported into programs. Contrast with *fundamental classes*.

out of bounds—describes a subscript that is not within the allowed range for an array.

outer block—a block that contains a nested block.

outer loop—a loop that contains another loop.

overloading—describes using one term to indicate diverse meanings, or writing multiple methods with the same name but with different arguments.

override—to use the child class's version of a field or method instead of the parent's.

override annotation—a directive that notifies the compiler of the programmer's intention to override a parent class method in a child class.

P

package—a named collection or library of classes. See also *library of classes*.

painting—the act of displaying or redisplaying a surface.

panel—a plain, borderless surface that can hold other GUI components.

parallel array—an array with the same number of elements as another, and for which the values in corresponding elements are related.

parameters—data items received by a method.

parent class—a base class.

parsing—the process of breaking something into its component parts.

Pascal casing—the style of using an uppercase letter to begin an identifier and to start each new word in an identifier. Contrast with *camel casing*. Compare to *upper camel casing*.

passed by reference—describes what happens when a reference (address) is passed to a method. Contrast with *passed by value*.

passed by value—describes what happens when a variable is passed to a method and a copy is made in the receiving method. Contrast with *passed by reference*.

passing arguments—the act of sending arguments to a method.

path—the complete list of the disk drive plus the hierarchy of directories in which a file resides.

path delimiter—the character used to separate path components.

pattern String—an argument composed of symbols that determine what a formatted number looks like.

permanent storage devices—hardware storage devices that retain data even when power is lost.

pixels—the picture elements, or tiny dots of light, that make up the image on a video monitor.

polygon—a geometric figure made of straight lines.

polymorphism—the feature of languages that allows the same word to be interpreted correctly in different situations based on the context; the act of using the same method name to indicate different implementations.

populating an array—the act of providing values for all of the elements in an array.

postfix ++ or the **postfix increment operator**—an operator that is composed by placing two plus signs to the right of a variable; it evaluates the variable, then adds 1 to it. Contrast with *prefix ++*.

posttest loop—a loop in which the loop control variable is tested after the loop body executes. Contrast with *pretest loop*.

preferred size—a Component's default size.

prefix ++ or the **prefix increment operator**—an operator that is composed by placing two plus signs to the left of a variable; it adds 1 to the variable, then evaluates it. Contrast with *postfix ++*.

prefix and postfix decrement operators—operators that subtract 1 from a variable before and after evaluating it, respectively.

pretest loop—a loop in which the loop control variable is tested before the loop body executes. Contrast with *posttest loop*.

primary key—a unique identifier for data within a database.

primary surface—the visible screen surface during double buffering.

priming read or **priming input**—the first input statement prior to a loop that will execute subsequent input statements for the same variable.

primitive type—a simple data type. Java's primitive types are byte, short, int, long, float, double, char, and boolean.

private access—describes a field or method that no other classes can access.

procedural programming—a style of programming in which sets of operations are executed one after another in sequence. Contrast with *object-oriented programming*.

procedures—sets of operations performed by a computer program.

program—a set of written computer instructions.

program comments—nonexecuting statements added to a Java file for the purpose of documentation.

program files—files that store software instructions.

program statements—similar to English sentences; they carry out the tasks that programs perform.

programmer-defined data type—a type that is created by a programmer and not built into the language; a class.

promotion—an implicit conversion.

prompt—a message that requests and describes user input.

property—an instance variable, field, or attribute of a class.

protected access—describes an intermediate level of security between public and private; a class's protected members can be used by a class and its descendants, but not by outside classes.

pseudocode—a tool that helps programmers plan a program's logic by writing plain English statements.

pseudorandom—describes numbers that appear to be random, but are the same set of numbers whenever the seed is the same.

public access—describes a field or method that outside classes can access.

pure polymorphism—the situation in which a single method implementation can be used with a variety of related objects because they are objects of subclasses of the parameter type. See also *inclusion polymorphism*.

R

ragged array—a two-dimensional array that has rows of different lengths.

random access files—files in which records can be located in any order.

random access memory (RAM)—temporary, volatile storage.

random number—a number whose value cannot be predicted.

range check—a series of statements that determine within which of a set of ranges a value falls.

range match—the process of comparing a value to the endpoints of numerical ranges to find a category in which the value belongs.

real-time—describes applications that require a record to be accessed immediately while a client is waiting.

record—a collection of fields that contain data about an entity.

redeclare a variable—to attempt to declare a variable twice—an illegal action.

reference—a variable that holds a memory address.

reference to an object—the name for a memory address where the object is held.

reference types—data types that hold memory addresses where values are stored.

register—to sign up an object as an event listener.

relational operator—an operator that compares two items; an expression that contains a relational operator has a Boolean value.

relative path—a path that depends on other path information to be complete.

remainder and assign operator—an operator that alters the value of the operand on the left by assigning the remainder when the left operand is divided by the right operand; it is composed of a percent sign and an equal sign (%=).

remainder operator—the percent sign; when it is used with two integers, the result is an integer with the value of the remainder after division takes place. Also called the *modulus operator*.

render—to paint or display a drawing.

rerender—to repaint or redisplay a drawing.

return a value—to send a data value from a called method back to the calling method.

return statement—a statement that ends a method, and frequently sends a value from a called method back to the calling method.

return type—the type of data that, upon completion of a method, is sent back to its calling method.

robustness—describes the degree to which a system is resilient to stress, maintaining correct functioning.

root directory—the main directory of a storage device, outside any folders.

runtime error—an error that occurs when a program compiles successfully but does not execute.

runtime exceptions—unplanned exceptions that occur during a program's execution. The term is also used more specifically to describe members of the RuntimeException class.

rvalue—an expression that can appear only on the right side of an assignment statement. Contrast with *lvalue*.

S

scalar—describes simple, primitive variables, such as int, double, or char.

scientific notation—a display format that more conveniently expresses large or small numeric values; a multidigit number is converted to a single-digit number and multiplied by 10 to a power.

scope—the part of a program in which a variable exists and can be accessed using its unqualified name.

scope level—in Java, a variable's block. See also *scope*.

scroll pane—a GUI object that provides scroll bars along the side or bottom of a pane, or both, so that the user can scroll initially invisible parts of the pane into view.

SDK—a software development kit, or a set of tools useful to programmers; the Java EE Development Kit.

searching an array—the process of comparing a value to a list of values in an array, looking for a match.

seed—a starting value.

seekable—describes a file channel in which operations can start at any specified position.

semantic errors—the type of errors that occur when a correct word is used in the wrong context in program code.

sentinel—a value that stops a loop.

sequence structure—a logical structure in which one step follows another unconditionally.

sequential access file—a data file that contains records that are accessed one after the other in the order in which they were stored.

shadowing—the action that occurs when a local variable hides a variable with the same name that is further away in scope.

short—the data type that holds small integers, from −32,768 to 32,767.

short-circuit evaluation—describes the feature of the AND and OR operators in which evaluation is performed only as far as necessary to make a final decision.

showInputDialog() method—a method that creates an input dialog box.

side effect—any action in a method other than returning a value.

signature—a method's name and the number, types, and order of arguments.

significant digits—refers to the mathematical accuracy of a value.

single-alternative selection—a decision structure that performs an action, or not, based on one alternative.

single-dimensional array—an array that contains one column of values and whose elements are accessed using a single subscript. See also *one-dimensional array*.

single-precision floating-point number—a type of value that is stored in a float.

software—the general term for computer programs.

sorting—the process of arranging a series of objects in some logical order.

source—a component on which an event is generated.

source code—programming statements written in a high-level programming language.

stack trace history list, or more simply **stack trace**—a list that displays all the methods that were called during program execution.

standard arithmetic operators—operators that are used to perform common calculations.

standard input device—normally the keyboard.

standard output device—normally the monitor.

state—the values of the attributes of an object.

static—a keyword that means a method is accessible and usable even though no objects of the class exist.

static import feature—a feature in Java that allows you to use static constants without their class name.

static member class—a type of nested class that has access to all static methods of its top-level class.

static method binding—the opposite of dynamic method binding; it occurs when a subclass method is selected while the program compiles rather than while it is running. See also *fixed method binding*.

stream—a pipeline or channel through which bytes flow into and out of an application.

String class—a class used to work with fixed-string data—that is, unchanging data composed of multiple characters.

String variable—a named object of the String class.

stroke—a line-drawing feature in Java 2D that represents a single movement using a drawing tool similar to a pen or pencil.

strongly typed language—a language in which all variables must be declared before they can be used.

stub—a method that contains no statements; programmers create stubs as temporary placeholders during the program development process.

subclass—a derived class.

subscript—an integer contained within square brackets that indicates one of an array's variables, or elements.

subtract and assign operator—an operator that alters the value of the operand on the left by subtracting the operand on the right from it; it is composed of a minus sign and an equal sign (–=).

subtype polymorphism—the ability of one method name to work appropriately for different subclasses of a parent class.

super—a Java keyword that always refers to a class's immediate superclass.

superclass—a base class.

Swing—a set of GUI elements such as dialog boxes and buttons that is newer and more portable than the set in the AWT; their names usually begin with *J*.

switch statement—a statement that uses up to four keywords to test a single variable against a series of exact integer or character values. The keywords are `switch`, `case`, `break`, and `default`.

symbolic constant—a named constant.

syntactic salt—describes a language feature designed to make it harder to write bad code.

syntactic sugar—describes aspects of a computer language that make it "sweeter," or easier, for programmers to use.

syntax—the rules that define how language elements are used together correctly to create usable statements.

syntax error—a programming error that occurs when a program contains typing errors or incorrect language use; a program containing syntax errors cannot be translated into an executable program.

system software—the set of programs that manage the computer. Contrast with *application software*.

system-triggered painting—describes a painting operation that occurs when the system asks a component to render its contents. Contrast with *application-triggered painting*.

T

table—a two-dimensional array; a matrix.

ternary operator—an operator that needs three operands.

text field—a GUI component into which the user can type a single line of text data.

text files—files that contain data that can be read in a text editor because the data has been encoded using a scheme such as ASCII or Unicode.

this reference—a reference to an object that is passed to any object's nonstatic class method.

threads of execution—units of processing that are scheduled by an operating system and that can be used to create multiple paths of control during program execution.

throw statement—a statement that sends an `Exception` out of a block or a method so it can be handled elsewhere.

throws clause—an exception specification in a method header.

TOCTTOU bug—an acronym that describes an error that occurs when changes take place from Time Of Check To Time Of Use.

token—a unit of data; the Scanner class separates input into tokens.

tool tips—popup windows that can help a user understand the purpose of components in an application; a tool tip appears when a user hovers a mouse pointer over the component.

top-level class—the containing class in nested classes.

top-level container—a container at the top of a containment hierarchy. The Java top-level containers are JFrame, JDialog, and JApplet.

try block—a block of code that a programmer acknowledges might generate an exception.

two-dimensional array—an array that contains two or more columns of values and whose elements are accessed using multiple subscripts. Contrast with *one-dimensional array*.

type-ahead buffer—the keyboard buffer.

type casting—an action that forces a value of one data type to be used as a value of another type.

type conversion—the process of converting one data type to another.

type-safe—describes a data type for which only appropriate behaviors are allowed.

type-wrapper classes—a method that can process primitive type values.

U

unary cast operator—a more complete name for the cast operator that performs explicit conversions.

unary operator—an operator that uses only one operand.

unchecked exceptions—exceptions that cannot reasonably be expected to be recovered from while a program is executing. Contrast with *checked exceptions*.

Unicode—an international system of character representation.

Unified Modeling Language (UML)—a graphical language used by programmers and analysts to describe classes and object-oriented processes.

unifying type—a single data type to which all operands in an expression are converted.

uninitialized variable—a variable that has been declared but that has not been assigned a value.

unnamed constant—a constant value that has no identifier associated with it. See also *literal constant*.

unreachable statements—statements that cannot be executed because the logical path can never encounter them; in some languages, including Java, an unreachable statement causes a compiler error. See also *dead code*.

upcast—to change an object to an object of a class higher in its inheritance hierarchy.

upper camel casing—Pascal casing.

V

validating data—the process of ensuring that a value falls within a specified range.

variable—a named memory location whose contents can be altered during program execution.

variable declaration—a statement that reserves a named memory location.

viewport—the viewable area in a JScrollPane.

virtual classes—the name given to abstract classes in some other programming languages, such as C++.

virtual key codes—codes that represent keyboard keys that have been pressed.

virtual keyboard—a computer keyboard that appears on the screen. A user operates it by using a mouse to point to and click keys; if the computer has a touch screen, the user touches keys with a finger or stylus.

virtual method calls—method calls in which the method used is determined when the program runs, because the type of the object used might not be known until the method executes.

void—a keyword that, when used in a method header, indicates that the method does not return any value when it is called.

volatile storage—memory that requires power to retain information. Contrast with *nonvolatile storage*.

W

while loop—a construct that executes a body of statements continually as long as the Boolean expression that controls entry into the loop continues to be true.

whitespace—any combination of nonprinting characters; for example, spaces, tabs, and carriage returns (blank lines).

wildcard symbol—a symbol used to indicate that it can be replaced by any set of characters. In a Java import statement, the wildcard symbol is an asterisk.

window—a rectangular container that can hold GUI components.

window decorations—the icons and buttons that are part of a window or frame.

windowed applications—programs that create a graphical user interface (GUI) with elements such as menus, toolbars, and dialog boxes.

wrapped—to be encompassed in another type.

wrapper—a class or object that is "wrapped around" a simpler element.

"write once, run anywhere" (WORA)—a slogan developed by Sun Microsystems to describe the ability of one Java program version to work correctly on multiple platforms.

X

x-axis—an imaginary horizontal line that indicates screen position.

x-coordinate—a position value that increases from left to right across a window.

Y

y-axis—an imaginary vertical line that indicates screen position.

y-coordinate—a position value that increases from top to bottom across a window.

Index

Note: Page numbers in **boldface** refer to definitions of key terms.